Z8000
Assembly Language
Programming

Z8000
Assembly Language
Programming

Lance A. Leventhal
Adam Osborne
Chuck Collins

OSBORNE/McGraw-Hill
Berkeley, California

Published by
OSBORNE/McGraw-Hill
630 Bancroft Way
Berkeley, California 94710
U. S. A

For information on translations and book distributors outside of the U. S. A. , please write OSBORNE/McGraw-Hill at the above address.

Z8000 Assembly Language Programming

1234567890 DODO 89876543210

ISBN 0-931988-36-5

Technical editors for this book were Joaquin Miller of Lovelace Computing, and Susanna Jacobson of OSBORNE/McGraw-Hill. Cover design by M. Borchers and T. Sullivan. Cover photography by A. Rosenberg.

Contents

Program Examples

1

Introduction to
Assembly Language Programming

This book describes assembly language programming. It assumes that you are familiar with *An Introduction to Microcomputers: Volume 1 — Basic Concepts* (Berkeley: Osborne/McGraw-Hill, 1980). Chapters 6 and 7 of that book are especially relevant. This book does not discuss the general features of computers, microcomputers, addressing methods, or instruction sets; you should refer to *An Introduction to Microcomputers: Volume 1* for that information.

HOW THIS BOOK HAS BEEN PRINTED

Notice that text in this book has been printed in boldface type and lightface type. This has been done to help you skip those parts of the book that cover subject matter with which you are familiar. You can be sure that lightface type only expands on information presented in the previous boldface type. Therefore, read only boldface type until you reach a subject about which you want to know more, at which point start reading the lightface type.

THE MEANING OF INSTRUCTIONS

The instruction set of a microprocessor is the set of binary inputs which produce defined actions during an instruction cycle. An instruction set is to a microprocessor what a function table is to a logic device such as a gate, adder, or shift register. Of course, the actions that the microprocessor performs in response to the instruction inputs are far more complex than the actions that combinatorial logic devices perform in response to their inputs.

An instruction is simply a binary bit pattern — it must be available at the data inputs to the microprocessor at the proper time in order to be interpreted as an instruction. For example, when the Z8000 microprocessor receives the 16-bit binary pattern 1000000000001000 as the input during an instruction fetch operation, the pattern means:

"Add the contents of Register RH0 to the contents of Register RL0."

Similarly, the pattern 1100100011111111 means:

"Load 11111111 into Register RL0."

The microprocessor (like any other computer) recognizes only binary patterns as instructions or data; it does not recognize words or octal, decimal, or hexadecimal numbers.

A COMPUTER PROGRAM

A program is a series of instructions that cause a computer to perform a particular task.

Actually, a computer program includes more than instructions; it also contains the data and the memory addresses that the microprocessor needs to accomplish the task defined by the instructions. Clearly, if the microprocessor is to perform an addition, it must have two numbers to add and a destination for the result. The computer program must determine the sources of the data and the destination of the result as well as specifying the operation to be performed.

All microprocessors execute instructions sequentially unless one of the instructions changes the execution sequence or halts the computer (i.e., the processor gets the next instruction from the next consecutive memory address unless the current instruction specifically directs it to do otherwise).

Ultimately every program becomes translated into a set of binary numbers. For example, this is the Z8000 program that adds the contents of memory locations 6000_{16} and 6002_{16} and places the result in memory location 6004_{16}:

```
0110000100000000
0110000000000000
0100000100000000
0110000000000010
0110011100000000
0110000000000100
```

This is a machine language, or object, program. If this program were entered into the memory of a Z8000-based microcomputer, the microcomputer would be able to execute it directly.

THE BINARY PROGRAMMING PROBLEM

There are many difficulties associated with creating programs as object, or binary machine language, programs. These are some of the problems:

1. The programs are difficult to understand or debug (binary numbers all look the same, particularly after you have looked at them for a few hours).
2. The programs are slow to enter since you must enter each bit individually using front panel switches.
3. The programs do not describe the task which you want the computer to perform in anything resembling a human readable format.
4. The programs are long and tiresome to write.
5. The programmer often makes careless errors that are very difficult to find.

For example, the **following version of the addition program shown above has two numbers transposed. Try to find the error:**

```
0110000100000000
0110000000000000
0010000100000000
0110000000000010
0110111100000000
0110000000000100
```

Although the computer handles binary numbers with ease, people do not. People find binary programs long, tiresome, confusing, and meaningless. Eventually, a programmer may start remembering some of the binary codes, but such effort should be spent more productively.

USING OCTAL OR HEXADECIMAL

We can improve the situation somewhat by writing instructions using octal or hexadecimal, rather than binary, numbers. We will use hexadecimal numbers in this book because they are shorter, and because they are the standard for the microprocessor industry. Table 1-1 shows the hexadecimal digits and their binary equivalents. **The Z8000 program to add two numbers now becomes:**

```
6100
6000
4100
6002
6F00
6004
```

At the very least, the hexadecimal version is shorter to write and not quite so tiring to examine.

Errors are somewhat easier to find in a sequence of hexadecimal digits. The erroneous version of the addition program, in hexadecimal form, becomes:

```
6100
6000
2100
6002
6F00
6004
```

The mistake is easier to spot.

What do we do with this hexadecimal program? The microprocessor understands only binary instruction codes. If your front panel has a hexadecimal keyboard instead of bit switches, you can key the hexadecimal program directly into memory — the keyboard logic translates the hexadecimal digits into binary numbers. But what if your front panel has only bit switches? You can convert the hexadecimal digits to binary by yourself, but this is a repetitive, tiresome task. People who attempt it make all sorts of petty mistakes, such as looking at the wrong line, dropping a bit, or transposing a bit or a digit. Besides, once we have converted our hexadecimal program we must still place the bits in memory through the switches on the front panel.

Hexadecimal Loader

These repetitive, grueling tasks are, however, perfect jobs for a computer. The computer never gets tired or bored and never makes mistakes. **The idea then is to write a program that accepts hexadecimal numbers, converts them into binary numbers, and places them in memory. This is a standard program provided with many microcomputers; it is called a hexadecimal loader.**

The hexadecimal loader is a program like any other. It occupies memory space: in some systems, only long enough to load another program; in others, it occupies a reserved, read-only section of memory. Your microcomputer may not have bit switches on its front panel; it may not even have a front panel. This reflects the machine designer's decision that binary programming is not only impossibly tedious but also wholly unnecessary. The hexadecimal loader in your system may be part of a larger program called a monitor, which also provides a number of tools for program debugging and analysis.

A hexadecimal loader certainly does not solve every programming problem. The hexadecimal version of the program is still difficult to read or understand; for example, it does not distinguish instructions from data or addresses, nor does the program listing provide any suggestion as to what the program does. What does 6100 or 6F00 mean? Memorizing a card full of codes is hardly an appetizing proposition. Furthermore, the codes will be entirely different for a different microprocessor, and the program will require a large amount of documentation.

Table 1-1. Hexadecimal Conversion Table

Hexadecimal Digit	Binary Equivalent	Decimal Equivalent
0	0000	0
1	0001	1
2	0010	2
3	0011	3
4	0100	4
5	0101	5
6	0110	6
7	0111	7
8	1000	8
9	1001	9
A	1010	10
B	1011	11
C	1100	12
D	1101	13
E	1110	14
F	1111	15

INSTRUCTION CODE MNEMONICS

An obvious programming improvement is to assign a name to each instruction code. The instruction code name is called a "mnemonic," or memory jogger. The instruction mnemonic should describe in some way what the instruction does.

Devising Mnemonics

In fact, every microprocessor manufacturer (they can't remember hexadecimal codes either) provides a set of mnemonics for the microprocessor instruction set. **You do not have to abide by the manufacturer's mnemonics;** there is nothing sacred about them. However, they are standard for a given microprocessor and therefore understood by all users. These are the instruction names that you will find in manuals, cards, books, articles, and programs. The problem with selecting instruction mnemonics is that not all instructions have "obvious" names. Some instructions do have obvious names (e.g., ADD, AND, OR), others have obvious contractions (e.g., SUB for subtraction, XOR for exclusive OR), while still others have neither. The result is such mnemonics as WMP, PCHL, and even SOB (try and guess what that means!). Most manufacturers come up with mostly reasonable names and a few hopeless ones. However, users who devise their own mnemonics rarely seem to do much better than the manufacturer.

Along with the instruction mnemonics, the manufacturer will usually assign names to the CPU registers. As with the instruction names, some register names are obvious (e.g., A for Accumulator) while others may have only historical significance. Again, we will use the manufacturer's suggestions simply to promote standardization.

An Assembly Language Program

If we use standard Z8000 instruction and register mnemonics, as defined by Zilog, our Z8000 addition program becomes:

```
LD      R0,%6000
ADD     R0,%6002
LD      %6004,R0
```

The program is still far from obvious, but at least some parts are comprehensible. ADD   R0,%6002 is a considerable improvement over 4100, and LD does suggest loading data into a register or memory location. **Such a program is an assembly language program.**

THE ASSEMBLER PROGRAM

How do we get the assembly language program into the computer? We have to translate it, either into hexadecimal or into binary numbers. **You can translate an assembly language program by hand,** instruction by instruction. This is called hand assembly.

Hand assembly of the addition program's instruction codes may be illustrated as follows:

Instruction Name		Hexadecimal Equivalent
LD	R0,%6000	61006000
ADD	R0,%6002	41006002
LD	%6004,R0	6F006004

As in the case of hexadecimal-to-binary conversion, hand assembly is a rote task which is uninteresting, repetitive, and subject to numerous minor errors. Picking the wrong line, transposing digits, omitting instructions, and misreading the codes are only a few of the mistakes that you may make. Most microprocessors complicate the task even further by having instructions with different word lengths. Some instructions are one word long while others are two or three words long. Some instructions require data in the second and third words; others require memory addresses, register numbers, or who knows what?

Assembly is another rote task that we can assign to the microcomputer. The microcomputer never makes any mistakes when translating codes; it always knows how many words and what format each instruction requires. The program that does this job is called an "assembler." The assembler program translates a user program, or "source" program written with mnemonics, into a machine language program, or "object" program, which the microcomputer can execute. The assembler's input is a source program and its output is an object program.

An assembler is a program, just as the hexadecimal loader is. However, assemblers are more expensive, occupy more memory, and require more peripherals and execution time than do hexadecimal loaders. While users may (and often do) write their own loaders, few care to write their own assemblers.

Assemblers have their own rules that you must learn to abide by. These include the use of certain markers (such as spaces, commas, semicolons, or colons) in appropriate places, correct spelling, the proper control information, and perhaps even the correct placement of names and numbers. These rules typically are a minor hindrance that can be quickly overcome.

ADDITIONAL FEATURES OF ASSEMBLERS

Early assembler programs did little more than translate the mnemonic names of instructions and registers into their binary equivalents. However, most assemblers now provide such additional features as:

1. Allowing the user to assign names to memory locations, input and output devices, and even sequences of instructions.
2. Converting data or addresses from various number systems (e.g., decimal or hexadecimal) to binary and converting characters into their ASCII or EBCDIC binary codes.
3. Performing some arithmetic as part of the assembly process.
4. Telling the loader program where in memory parts of the program or data should be placed.
5. Allowing the user to assign areas of memory as temporary data storage and to place fixed data in areas of program memory.
6. Providing the information required to include standard programs from program libraries, or programs written at some other time, in the current program.
7. Allowing the user to control the format of the program listing and the input and output devices employed.

Choosing an Assembler

All of these features, of course, involve additional cost and memory. Microcomputers generally have much simpler assemblers than do larger computers, but the tendency is always for the size of assemblers to increase. You will often have a choice of assemblers. The important criterion is not how many offbeat features the assembler has, but rather how convenient it is to work with in normal practice.

DISADVANTAGES OF ASSEMBLY LANGUAGE

The assembler, like the hexadecimal loader, does not solve all the problems of programming. One problem is the tremendous gap between the microcomputer instruction set and the tasks which the microcomputer is to perform. Computer instructions tend to do things like add the contents of two registers, shift the contents of the accumulator one bit, or place a new value into the program counter. On the other hand, a user generally wants a microcomputer to do something like check if an analog reading has exceeded a threshold, look for and react to a particular command from a teletypewriter, or activate a relay at the proper time. An assembly language programmer must translate such tasks into a sequence of simple computer instructions. The translation can be a difficult, time-consuming job.

Furthermore, **if you are programming in assembly language, you must have detailed knowledge of the particular microcomputer that you are using.** You must know what registers and instructions the microcomputer has, precisely how the instructions affect the various registers, what addressing methods the computer uses, and a myriad of other information. None of this information is relevant to the task which the microcomputer must ultimately perform.

Lack of Portability

In addition, assembly language programs are not portable. Each microcomputer has its own assembly language, which reflects its own architecture. An assembly language program written for the Z8000 will not run on the Motorola 6800, the Fairchild F8, or the National Semiconductor PACE. For example, the addition program written for the Motorola 6800 would be:

```
LDAA    $6000
ADDA    $6001
STAA    $6002
```

The lack of portability not only means that you won't be able to use your assembly language program on a different microcomputer, but it also means that you won't be able to use any programs that weren't specifically written for the microcomputer you are using. This is a particular drawback for microcomputers, since these devices are new and few assembly language programs exist for them. The result, too frequently, is that you are on your own. If you need a program to perform a particular task, you are not likely to find it in the small program libraries that most manufacturers provide. Nor are you likely to find it in an archive, journal article, or someone's old program file. You will probably have to write it yourself.

The Institute of Electrical and Electronic Engineers (IEEE) is in the process of defining a "universal" set of assembly language mnemonics,[1] capable of being used to describe every microprocessor's instruction set. But the IEEE does not have the power to enforce its mnemonics. Programmers, therefore, must use the IEEE mnemonics by choice if they are to become a universal standard.

HIGH-LEVEL LANGUAGES

The solution to many of the difficulties associated with assembly language programs is to use, instead, "high-level" or "procedure-oriented" languages. Such languages allow you to describe tasks in forms that are problem oriented rather than computer oriented. Each statement in a high-level language performs a recognizable function; it will generally correspond to many assembly language instructions. A program called a compiler translates the high-level language source program into object code or machine language instructions.

FORTRAN — A HIGH-LEVEL LANGUAGE

Many different high-level languages exist for different types of tasks. If, for example, you can express what you want the computer to do in algebraic notation, you can write your program in FORTRAN (Formula Translation Language), the oldest and one of the most widely used of the high-level languages. Now, if you want to add two numbers, you just tell the computer:

```
SUM = NUMB1+NUMB2
```

That is a lot simpler (and a lot shorter) than either the equivalent machine language program or the equivalent assembly language program. Other high-level languages include COBOL (for business applications), PASCAL (a language designed for structured programming), PL/I (a combination of FORTRAN, ALGOL, and COBOL), and APL and BASIC (languages that are popular for time-sharing systems).

ADVANTAGES OF HIGH-LEVEL LANGUAGES

Clearly, high-level languages make programs easier and faster to write. A common estimate is that a programmer can write a program about ten times as fast in a high-level language as compared to assembly language.[2-4] That is just writing the program; it does not include problem definition, program design, debugging, testing, or documentation, all of which become simpler and faster. The high-level language program is, for instance, partly self-documenting. Even if you do not know FORTRAN, you probably could tell what the statement illustrated above does.

Another advantage of high-level languages appears when you need to change an existing program. **Because a high-level language program expresses more directly the function it performs, it is easier to see what changes are necessary and where these changes should go.** Because there are fewer machine details to keep track of, it is easier to avoid introducing errors.

Machine Independence

High-level languages solve many other problems associated with assembly language programming. The high-level language has its own syntax (usually defined by a national or international standard). The language does not mention the instruction set, registers, or other features of a particular computer. The compiler takes care of all such details. Programmers can concentrate on their own tasks; they do not need a detailed understanding of the underlying CPU architecture — for that matter, they do not need to know anything about the computer they are programming.

Portability

Programs written in a high-level language are portable — at least, in theory. They will run on any computer or microcomputer that has a standard compiler for that language.

At the same time, all previous programs written in a high-level language for prior computers are available to you when programming a new computer. This can mean thousands of programs in the case of a common language like FORTRAN or BASIC.

DISADVANTAGES OF HIGH-LEVEL LANGUAGES

If all the good things we have said about high-level languages are true, if you can write programs faster and make them portable besides, why bother with assembly languages? Who wants to worry about registers, instruction codes, mnemonics, and all that garbage! As usual, there are disadvantages that balance the advantages.

Syntax

One obvious problem is that, as with assembly language, **you have to learn the "rules" or "syntax" of any high-level language** you want to use. A high-level language has a fairly complicated set of rules. You will find that it takes a lot of time just to get a program that is syntactically correct (and even then it probably will not do what you want). A high-level computer language is like a foreign language. If you have a little talent, you will get used to the rules and be able to turn out programs that the compiler will accept. Still, learning the rules and trying to get the program accepted by the compiler doesn't contribute directly to doing your job.

Cost of Compilers

Another obvious problem is that **you need a compiler to translate programs written in a high-level language.** Compilers are expensive and use a large amount of memory. While most assemblers occupy 2K to 16K bytes of memory (1K = 1024), compilers occupy 4K to 64K bytes. In addition, many compilers require external storage such as disks. So the amount of overhead involved in using the compiler is rather large.

Adapting Tasks to a Language

Furthermore, **only some compilers will make the implementation of your task simpler.** FORTRAN, for example, is well-suited to problems that can be expressed as algebraic formulas. If, however, your problem is controlling a printer, editing a string of characters, or monitoring an alarm system, your problem cannot be easily expressed in algebraic notation. In fact, formulating the solution in algebraic notation may be more awkward and more difficult than formulating it in assembly language. One answer is to use a more suitable high-level language. Languages specifically designed for tasks such as those mentioned above do exist — they are called system implementation languages. However, these languages are far less widely used and standardized than FORTRAN.

Inefficiency

High-level languages do not produce very efficient machine language programs. The basic reason for this is that compilation is an automatic process which is riddled with compromises to allow for many ranges of possibilities. The compiler works much like a computerized language translator — sometimes the words are right but the sounds and sentence structures are awkward. A simple compiler cannot know when a variable is no longer being used and can be discarded, or when a register should be used rather than a memory location, or when variables have simple relationships. The experienced programmer can take advantage of shortcuts to shorten execution time or reduce memory usage. A few compilers (known as optimizing compilers) can also do this, but such compilers are much larger than regular compilers.

SUMMARY OF ADVANTAGES AND DISADVANTAGES

The general advantages and disadvantages of high-level languages are:

Advantages:

- More convenient descriptions of tasks
- More efficient program coding
- Easier documentation
- Standard syntax
- Independence of the structure of a particular computer
- Portability
- Availability of library and other programs
- Easier to change programs

Disadvantages:

- Special rules
- Extensive hardware and software support required
- Orientation of common languages to algebraic or business problems
- Inefficient programs
- Difficulty of optimizing code to meet time and memory requirements
- Inability to use special features of a computer conveniently

HIGH-LEVEL LANGUAGES FOR MICROPROCESSORS

Microprocessor users will encounter several special difficulties when using high-level languages. Among these are:

- Few high-level languages exist for microprocessors
- No standard languages are widely available
- Few compilers actually run on microcomputers. Those that do often require very large amounts of memory
- Many microprocessor applications are not well-suited to high-level languages
- Memory costs are often critical in microprocessor applications

The lack of high-level languages is partly a result of the fact that microprocessors are quite new and are the products of semiconductor manufacturers rather than computer manufacturers.

Very few high-level languages exist for microprocessors. The most common are the PL/I type languages (such as Intel's PL/M, Motorola's MPL, Zilog's PLZ/SYS, and Signetics' PLμS), BASIC, and PASCAL.

Even the few high-level languages that exist do not conform to recognized standards, so the microprocessor user cannot expect to gain much program portability, access to program libraries, or use of previous experience or programs. The main advantages remaining are the reduction in programming effort and the smaller amount of detailed understanding of the computer architecture that is necessary.

Overhead

The overhead involved in using a high-level language with microprocessors is considerable. Many compilers for microprocessors will not run on a microprocessor-based system. Instead, they require a much larger computer; i.e., they are cross-compilers. A user must not only bear the expense of the larger computer but must also transfer the program from the larger computer to the micro. Compilers are available which run on the microcomputer for which they produce object code. Unfortunately, they require large amounts of memory, plus special supporting hardware and software.

Unsuitability

High-level languages also are not well-suited to certain microprocessor applications. Most of the common languages were devised either to help solve scientific problems or to handle business data processing. Many microprocessor applications involve sending data and control information to output devices and receiving data and status information from input devices. Often the control and status information consists of a few binary digits with very precise hardware-related meanings. If you try to write a typical control program in a high-level language, you often feel like someone who is trying to eat soup with chopsticks. For tasks in such areas as test equipment, terminals, navigation systems, signal processing, and business equipment, the high-level languages work much better than they do in instrumentation, communications, peripherals, and automotive applications.

Application Areas For Language Levels

Applications better suited to high-level languages are those which require large memories. If, as in a valve controller, electronic game, appliance controller, or small instrument, the cost of a single memory chip is important, then the inefficient memory use of high-level languages is intolerable. If, on the other hand, as in a terminal, test equipment, or word processing machine, the system has many thousands of bytes of memory anyway, this inefficiency is not as important. Clearly the size of the program and the volume of the product are important factors as well. A large program will greatly increase the advantages of high-level languages. On the other hand, a high-volume application will mean that fixed software development costs are not as important as memory costs that are part of each system.

WHICH LEVEL SHOULD YOU USE?

Which language level you use depends on your particular application. Let us briefly note some of the factors which may favor particular levels.

Machine Language:

- Virtually no one programs in machine language. Its use cannot be justified considering the low cost of an assembler and the increase in programming speed an assembler provides.

Assembly Language:

- Short to moderate sized programs
- Applications where memory cost is a factor
- Real-time control applications
- Limited data processing
- High-volume applications
- More input/output or control than computation

High-Level Languages:

- Long programs
- Low-volume applications requiring long programs
- Applications requiring large memories
- More computation than input/output or control
- Compatibility with similar applications using larger computers
- Availability of specific programs in a high-level language which can be used in the application
- Programs which are expected to undergo many changes

Other Considerations

Many other factors are also important, such as the availability of a larger computer for use in development, experience with particular languages, and compatibility with other applications.

If hardware will ultimately be the largest cost in your application, or if speed is critical, you should favor assembly language. But be prepared to spend extra time in software development in exchange for lower memory costs and higher execution speeds. If software will be the largest cost in your application, you should favor a high-level language. But be prepared to spend the extra money required for the supporting hardware and software.

Of course, no one except some theorists will object if you use both assembly and high-level languages. You can write the program originally in a high-level language and then patch some sections in assembly language.[5,6] However, most users prefer not to do this because it can create havoc in debugging, testing, and documentation.

FUTURE TRENDS IN LANGUAGE LEVELS

We expect that the future will tend to favor high-level languages for the following reasons:

- Programs always seem to add extra features and grow larger
- Hardware and memory are becoming less expensive
- Software and programmers are becoming more expensive
- Memory chips are becoming available in larger sizes, at lower "per bit" cost, so actual savings in chips are less likely
- More compilers are becoming available
- More suitable and more efficient high-level languages are being developed
- More standardization of high-level languages will occur

Assembly language programming of microprocessors will not be a dying art any more than it is now for large computers. But longer programs, cheaper memory, and more expensive programmers will make software costs a larger part of most applications. The edge in many applications will therefore go to high-level languages.

WHY THIS BOOK?

If the future would seem to favor high-level languages, why have a book on assembly language programming? The reasons are:

1. Most current microcomputer users program in assembly language (almost two-thirds, according to one recent survey).

2. Many microcomputer users will continue to program in assembly language since they need the detailed control that it provides.

3. No suitable high-level language has yet become widely available or standardized.

4. Many applications require the efficiency of assembly language.

5. An understanding of assembly language can help in evaluating high-level languages.

The rest of this book will deal exclusively with assemblers and assembly language programming. However, we do want readers to know that assembly language is not the only alternative. You should watch for new developments that may significantly reduce programming costs if such costs are a major factor in your application.

REFERENCES

1. W. P. Fischer, "Microprocessor Assembly Language Draft Standard," *Computer*, December 1979, pp. 96-109.

2. M. H. Halstead, *Elements of Software Science*, American Elsevier, New York, 1977.

3. L. H. Putman and A. Fitzsimmons, "Estimating Software Costs," *Datamation*, September 1979, pp. 189-98.

4. M. Phister, Jr., *Data Processing Technology and Economics*, Santa Monica Publishing Co., Santa Monica, Calif., 1976. Also available from Digital Press, Educational Services, Digital Equipment Corp., Bedford, Mass.

5. P. Caudill, "Using Assembly Coding to Optimize High-Level Language Programs," *Electronics*, February 1, 1979, pp. 121-24.

6. D. B. Wecker et al., "High Level Design Language Develops Low Level Microprocessor-Independent Software," *Computer Design*, June 1979, pp. 140-49.

2

Features of Assemblers

This chapter discusses the functions performed by assemblers, beginning with features common to most assemblers and proceeding through more elaborate capabilities such as macros and conditional assembly. **If you are a novice assembly language programmer, you should skim this chapter the first time you read it; stick to the boldface type** and skip the lightface type. A great deal of the information presented will not make any sense to you until you have read Chapter 3. Then return and reread this chapter.

As we mentioned previously, today's assemblers do much more than translate assembly language mnemonics into binary codes. But we will describe how an assembler handles the translation of mnemonics before describing additional assembler capabilities or how assemblers are used.

ASSEMBLY LANGUAGE FIELDS

Assembly language instructions (or "statements") are divided into a number of fields, as shown in Table 2-1.

The operation field is the only field that can never be empty; it always contains either an instruction mnemonic or a directive to the assembler, called a *pseudo-instruction, pseudo-operation, pseudo-op or assembler directive.*

The operand or address field may contain an address and/or data, or it may be blank.

The comment and label fields are optional. A programmer will assign a label to a statement or add a comment as a personal convenience, to make the program easier to read and use.

Table 2-1. The Fields of an Assembly Language Instruction

Label Field	Operation Field	Operand Field	Comment Field
START:	LD	R0,VAL1	! LOAD FIRST NUMBER INTO R0 !
	ADD	R0,VAL2	! ADD SECOND NUMBER TO R0 !
	LD	SUM,R0	! STORE SUM !
NEXT:	?	?	! NEXT INSTRUCTION !
.			
.			
.			
VAL1	WORD		
VAL2	WORD		
SUM	WORD		

FORMAT

Of course, the assembler must have some way of telling where one field ends and another begins. Assemblers that use punched card input often require that each field start in a specific card column. This is a *fixed format.* However, fixed formats are inconvenient when the input medium is paper tape; fixed formats are also a nuisance to programmers. The alternative is a *free format* where the fields may appear anywhere on the line.

DELIMITERS

If the assembler cannot use the position on the line to tell the fields apart, it must use something else. Most assemblers use a special symbol, or delimiter, at the beginning or end of each field. The most common delimiter is the space character. Commas, periods, semicolons, colons, slashes, question marks, and other characters that would not otherwise be used in assembly language programs may also serve as delimiters.

You will have to exercise a little care with delimiters. Some assemblers are fussy about extra spaces or the appearance of delimiters in comments or labels. A well-written assembler will handle these minor problems, but many assemblers are not well-written. Our recommendation is simple: avoid potential problems if you can.

The following rules will help:

1. Do not use extra spaces, particularly after commas that separate operands.

2. Do not use delimiter characters in names or labels.

3. Include standard delimiters even if your assembler does not require them. Your programs will run on any assembler.

SYNTAX

In addition to delimiting fields, special characters identify the way in which information must be interpreted, particularly in the operand and address fields. Taken together, these character interpretations constitute the syntax of the assembly language.

There are two initial suppliers of assemblers for the Z8000: Zilog and Advanced Micro Computers (AMC). Zilog is the inventor and primary source of the Z8000 chips; AMC is a wholly-owned subsidiary of Advanced Micro Devices (AMD), the second-source manufacturer of Z8000 components. These two companies have adopted different syntax for their respective assemblers. This book describes and uses both sets of syntax. A comparative summary of the more frequently used syntax is given later in this chapter, in Table 2-2.

LABEL FIELD

The label field is the first field in an assembly language instruction; it may be blank. If a label is present, the assembler defines the label as equivalent to the address of the first memory byte into which the instruction's object code gets loaded. You may subsequently use the label as an address, or as data in another instruction's operand field. The assembler will replace the label with the assigned address value when creating an object program.

Most assemblers require that labels start at the beginning of a line, with no preceding spaces; the first space on the line is treated as a delimiter, terminating the label field. A single space at the beginning of the line would cause the assembler to assume that the label field has nothing in it.

The Zilog and AMC assemblers use a colon (:) as the standard delimiter terminating label fields. For some assemblers a space will also terminate a label field. Some assemblers have rules regarding the number of spaces which must precede the mnemonic field if no label is present.

Labels In Jump Instructions

Labels are most frequently used in Jump, Call, or Branch instructions. These instructions place a new value in the program counter and thus alter the normal sequential execution of instructions. JUMP 150_{16} means "place the value 150_{16} in the program counter." The next instruction to be executed will be the one in memory location 150_{16}. The instruction JUMP START means "place the value assigned to the label START in the program counter." The next instruction to be executed will be the one at the address corresponding to the label START. This may be illustrated as follows:

```
START   LOAD REGISTER R1
        .
        .
        .
        .   (MAIN PROGRAM)
        .
        .
        .
        JUMP START
```

When the machine language version of this program is executed, the instruction JUMP START causes the address of the instruction labeled START to be placed in the program counter. This causes the instruction labeled START to be executed next.

Why use a label? Here are some reasons:

1. A label makes a program location easier to find and remember.

2. A label is easily moved to change or correct a program. The assembler will automatically change all instructions that use the label when the program is reassembled.

3. The assembler or loader can relocate the whole program by adding a constant (a *relocation constant*) to each address for which a label was used. Thus we can move the program to allow for the insertion of other programs or simply to rearrange memory.

4. The program is easier to use as a library program; i.e., it is easier for someone else to take your program and add it to some totally different program.

5. You do not have to figure out memory addresses. Figuring out memory addresses is particularly difficult with microprocessors which have instructions that vary in length.

You should assign a label to any instruction that you might want to refer to later.

Choosing Labels

The next question is how to choose a label. Some assemblers place restrictions on the number of characters a label may have (usually 5 or 6). The leading character must often be a letter, and the trailing characters must often be letters, numbers, or one of a few special characters. Beyond these restrictions, the choice is up to you.

Standard Zilog and AMC assemblers allow labels to have up to 127 characters — an absurdly large number. Selected special characters and reserved words are not allowed to appear in labels.

Our own preference is to **use labels that suggest their purpose,** i.e., mnemonic labels. Typical examples are ADDW in a routine that adds one word into a sum, SRETX in a routine that searches for the ASCII character ETX, or NKEYS for a location in data memory that contains the number of key entries. Meaningful labels are easier to remember and contribute to program documentation. Some programmers use a standard format for labels, such as starting with L0000. These labels are self-sequencing (you can skip a few numbers to permit insertions), but they do not help document the program.

A recent labeling convention supported by Zilog and AMC assemblers, and gaining in popularity, is the use of multi-word labels, where an underscore character (_) substitutes for the generally illegal space. Here are examples of such multi-word labels:

> FIRST_LABEL
> NO_GO

Zilog and AMC assemblers allow labels to use upper-case and/or lower-case letters. In the past, assemblers have usually recognized upper-case letters only, since teletype terminals and most other low-cost terminals could not handle lower-case letters. But the majority of modern terminals display upper-case and lower-case letters, which allows you to write programs that are much easier to read.

Recommendations for Labeling

Some label selection rules will keep you out of trouble. We recommend the following:

1. Do not use labels that are the same as operation codes or other assembler mnemonics. Most assemblers will not allow this usage; others will, but it is very confusing.

2. Do not use labels that are longer than the assembler permits. Assemblers have various rules for shortening labels that are too long.

3. Avoid special characters (non-alphabetic and non-numeric). Some assemblers will not permit them; others allow only certain ones.

4. Start each label with a letter. Such labels are always acceptable.

5. Do not use labels that could be confused with each other. Avoid the letters I, O, and Z, and the numbers 0, 1, and 2. Also avoid things like XXXX and XXXXX. There's no sense tempting fate and Murphy's Law.

6. When you are not sure if a label is legal, do not use it. You will not get any real benefit from discovering exactly what the assembler will accept.

These are recommendations, not rules. You do not have to follow them, but don't blame us if you waste time on silly problems.

OPERATION FIELD

An assembler's main task is to translate mnemonic operation codes into their binary equivalents. The assembler performs this task using a fixed table, much as you would if you were doing the assembly by hand.

The operation field does not require delimiter characters to mark its beginning or its end. The operation field begins with the first non-space character following the label field; or, if there is no label, the operation field begins with the first non-space character of the line. A space character marks the end of the operation field. Some assemblers require more than one space before the operation field if there is no label.

The operation field can contain an instruction mnemonic, a pseudo-operation or assembler directive mnemonic, or a specially defined macro mnemonic. Nothing else is allowed. Instruction mnemonics define individual instructions. For example, ADD, ADDB and ADDL are the instruction mnemonics for the word, byte and long word versions of the add instruction. Assembler directives and macros are introduced later in this chapter.

OPERAND FIELD

Assemblers allow parameters of the operand field to be specified in a variety of ways. Variations must, nevertheless, conform to strict rules of syntax that vary from one assembler to the next. Each parameter can be specified using a variety of data types, and can be interpreted by the assembler in a variety of ways.

Data Types

We will first describe six types of data that may appear in the operand field.

1. Decimal numbers.

A number appearing in the operand field is assumed to be a decimal number unless marked otherwise. For example, the instruction

```
ADD      R1,100
```

means to a Zilog assembler: "add the contents of memory location 100_{10} to CPU Register R1."

2. Other number systems.

Assemblers commonly allow numbers to be marked as binary, octal, or hexadecimal. Zilog and AMC favor hexadecimal numbers; they discourage the use of octal and binary numbers. Octal numbering is rarely used in the microcomputer industry. Binary numbers are long and prone to errors; this is particularly true when dealing with 16-bit microprocessors that frequently require 16-bit or 32-bit numbers in the operand field.

We recommend that you use hexadecimal numbers in Z8000 assembly language programs, since Zilog and AMC assemblers use hexadecimal numbers to list all addresses and object programs.

The following syntax is used by AMC and Zilog assemblers to identify different number bases. Common industry-wide syntax is also shown.

	Industry	AMC	Zilog
Binary	Preceding or trailing B or % e.g., 10010110%	Trailing B e.g., 10010110B	Preceding %(2) e.g., %(2)10010110
Octal	Preceding or trailing O, @, Q or C e.g., @ 173146	Trailing O or Q e.g., 173146Q	Preceding %(8) e.g., %(8)173146
Hexadecimal	Preceding or trailing H or $ e.g., 43A6H	Trailing H or preceding # e.g., 43A6H	Preceding % e.g., %43A6

3. Names.

Names can appear in the operand field; the name may represent either data or an address. **Remember, there is a difference between data and addresses.** A name representing data is frequently referred to as a "symbol." A name representing an address is frequently referred to as a "label." Consider the following example:

```
ADD     R6,#VAL         ! Zilog syntax !
ADD     R6,VAL;         % AMC syntax
```

VAL was defined as a constant somewhere in the program and is interpreted as a symbol representing a number. R6 is a label identifying a CPU register. The number represented by the symbol VAL is added to the location represented by the label R6, in this case a CPU register. For example, if VAL is equated to 5, then 5 will be added to CPU Register R6. Now consider a different example:

```
ADD     R6,VAL          ! Zilog syntax !
ADD     R6,VAL;         % AMC syntax
```

VAL was defined by use in the label field somewhere in the program and is now interpreted as a label, representing the address of a memory location. The contents of the memory location VAL are added to CPU Register R6.

4. The current value of the location counter (usually referred to as * or $).

This is useful mainly in Jump instructions; for example

```
JP      $+6             ! Zilog syntax !
JP      ^$+6;           % AMC syntax
```

causes a Jump to the memory location six bytes beyond the byte that contains the first byte of the JUMP instruction:

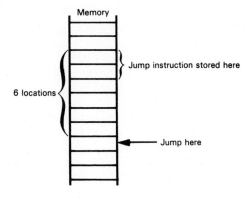

Most microprocessors have many two- and three-byte instructions. Thus, you will have difficulty determining exactly how far apart two assembly language statements are. Therefore, using offsets from the location counter frequently results in errors that you can avoid if you use labels.

5. Character codes (ASCII and EBCDIC).

Most assemblers allow text to be entered as ASCII strings. Such strings may be surrounded either with single or double quotation marks. A few assemblers also permit EBCDIC strings.

Zilog and AMC assemblers allow text to be entered as ASCII strings enclosed in single quotation marks.

We recommend that you use character strings for all text. It improves the clarity of the program and makes it easier to read.

6. Combinations of 1 through 5 above with arithmetic, logical, or special operators.

Arithmetic and Logical Expressions

Almost all assemblers allow simple arithmetic combinations such as START + 1. Some assemblers also permit multiplication, division, logical functions, shifts, etc. These combinations are referred to as *expressions*. Note that the assembler evaluates expressions at the time the program is being assembled (assembly time), not when it is being executed (execution or run time). The arithmetic evaluation done by the assembler is done with the values of labels, constants, etc., not with the run time data of the program.

Assemblers vary in the expressions they accept and how they interpret them. Complex expressions make a program difficult to read and understand.

We have made some recommendations in this chapter which we will now summarize and augment. In general, **you should strive for clarity and simplicity.** There is no payoff for being an expert in the intricacies of an assembler, or in having the most complex expression on the block. **We suggest the following approach:**

1. Use the clearest number system or character code for data. Masks and BCD numbers in decimal, ASCII characters in octal, or ordinary numerical constants in hexadecimal serve no purpose and therefore should not be used.

2. Remember to distinguish data and addresses.

3. Avoid using offsets from the location counter.

4. Keep expressions simple and obvious. Don't rely on obscure features of the assembler.

Operand Parameter Interpretation

If you look again at the description of names (data type 3) you will see that the name VAL can be interpreted by the assembler as a number or an address. There are many ways in which an assembler might interpret any parameter in the operand field. We will summarize the possibilities below, leaving detailed discussion to Chapter 3.

1. CPU registers.

A number of special labels identify Z8000 CPU registers. Table 3-8 lists labels used to identify the frequently used CPU registers. All register names are shown in Figure 3-3.

2. Condition codes.

A number of instructions execute in different ways depending on prevailing status conditions. Special labels designate these status conditions in the operand field, as summarized in Table 3-4.

3. Immediate data.

When a parameter is simply a number, subject to no special interpretation, it is referred to as immediate data. A special character usually precedes the number to identify it as immediate data. For example, Zilog syntax uses the # character to identify an immediate parameter. AMC syntax, on the other hand, assumes immediate data as the default case; that is to say, in the absence of any special identifying character, a number is assumed to be immediate data. This may be illustrated as follows:

```
ADD     R6,5;        % AMC syntax
ADD     R6,#5        ! Zilog syntax !
```

The instruction illustrated above adds 5 to the contents of CPU Register R6.

AMC syntax uses the ^ symbol preceding a label, and Zilog uses the # symbol preceding a label, to specify a form of immediate data. For example, the instruction

```
ADD     R6,#VAL      ! Zilog syntax !
ADD     R6,^VAL;      % AMC syntax
```

treats the value of the label VAL as an immediate operand. For example, suppose VAL is a label representing memory address $123A_{16}$; instead of adding the contents of memory location $123A_{16}$ to Register R6, the ADD instruction above would add the address itself, $123A_{16}$, to Register R6.

5. Addresses.

The Z8000 microprocessor has a variety of addressing modes which can be used to identify memory locations. A substantial portion of Chapter 3 is devoted to describing Z8000 addressing modes. Parameters representing memory address specifications occur very frequently in the operand field.

The following is a summary of AMC and Zilog syntax used to describe address parameters in the operand field:

a.   VAL is the address of the data (direct address):

```
LD        R0,VAL;              % AMC syntax
LD        R0,VAL               ! Zilog syntax !
```

b. $24A6_{16}$ is a direct address:

```
LD        R0,#24A6^;           % AMC syntax
LD        R0,%24A6             ! Zilog syntax !
```

c.   VAL is a direct address indexed by register R6:

```
LD        R0,VAL(R6);          % AMC syntax
LD        R0,VAL(R6)           ! Zilog syntax !
```

d.   Register R6 provides the memory address (register indirect, or implied memory addressing):

```
LD        R0,R6^;              % AMC syntax
LD        R0,@R6               ! Zilog syntax !
```

e.   Register R6 provides a base address to which the displacement VAL is added:

```
LD        R0,R6^(VAL);         % AMC syntax
LD        R0,R6(#VAL)          ! Zilog syntax !
```

f.   Register R6 provides a base address which is indexed by Register R8:

```
LD        R0,R6^(R8);          % AMC syntax
LD        R0,R6(R8)            ! Zilog syntax !
```

These addressing modes are described in detail in Chapter 3.

Z8001 addresses are segmented. 23-bit addresses are generated, but they are divided into two parts: a segment consisting of the 7 high-order address bits, and an offset that makes up the remaining 16 low-order bits. When a label is used to specify a Z8001 address, the label is assumed to represent a 23-bit segmented address. The actual segment number is implied, being set equal to the memory segment into which the label's instruction is actually loaded. Zilog syntax (but not AMC syntax) also gives you the option of specifying a segment number. If an exact segment number is specified, it must be enclosed within double magnitude symbols as follows:

<<3>> or <<SEGNO>>

COMMENT FIELD

All assemblers allow you to place comments in a source program. Comments have no effect on the object code, but they help you to read, understand, and document the program. Good commenting is an essential part of writing assembly language programs; programs without comments are very difficult to understand.

We will discuss commenting along with documentation in a later chapter, but here are some guidelines:

1. Use comments to tell what application task the program is performing, not how the microcomputer executes the instructions.

   Comments should say things like "IS TEMPERATURE ABOVE LIMIT?," "LINE FEED TO TTY," or "EXAMINE LOAD SWITCH."

   Comments should not say things like "ADD 1 TO ACCUMULATOR," "JUMP TO START," or "LOOK AT CARRY." You should describe how the program is affecting the system; internal effects on the CPU are seldom of any interest.

2. Keep comments brief and to the point. Details should be available elsewhere in the documentation.

3. Comment all key points.

4. Do not comment standard instructions or sequences that change counters or pointers; pay special attention to instructions that may not have an obvious meaning.

5. Do not use obscure abbreviations.

6. Make the comments neat and readable.

7. Comment all definitions, describing their purposes. Also mark all tables and data storage areas.

8. Comment sections of the program as well as individual instructions.

9. Be consistent in your terminology. You can and should be repetitive; you need not consult a thesaurus.

10. Leave yourself notes at points which you find confusing, e.g., "REMEMBER CARRY WAS SET BY LAST INSTRUCTION." You may drop these in final documentation.

A well-commented program is easy to use. You will recover the time spent in commenting many times over. We will try to show good commenting style in the programming examples, although we often over-comment for instructional purposes.

Zilog syntax requires comments to begin and end with an exclamation point (!). AMC syntax requires comments to begin with a percent sign (%); no ending character is required.

Table 2-2 summarizes the Zilog and AMC assembly language syntax rules which you will encounter most frequently.

Table 2-2. Standard AMC and Zilog Assembler Delimiters and Special Characters

Field	Function / Comment	Syntax	
		Zilog	AMC
Label	The optional label field, if present, must start with a character in the first character position of the line. With some assemblers, if the label is absent, the first one (or sometimes two) characters of the line must be blank. End of label field		
Operation	End of operation field	ƀ	ƀ
Operand or Address Field	Separator for more than one term in the operand field	, or ƀ	
	Hexadecimal number nnnn	%nnnn	#nnnn
	Symbolic immediate operand numeric immediate operand nnnn	#NAME	NAME
	Label used as an immediate address constant	#%nnnn	#nnnn
	Label used as a direct address	#LABEL	^LABEL
	Direct hexadecimal address nnnn	LABEL	LABEL
	Implied (Register Indirect) address	%nnnn	#nnnn^
	Index register	@Rn	Rn^
	Base address register	(Rn)	(Rn)
	Address displacement NAME	Rn	Rn^
	Hexadecimal address displacement nnnn	(#NAME)	(NAME)
	End of operand field	(#%nnnnn) ƀ	(#nnnn)
Comment	Start of optional comment field End of optional comment field	! !	%

nnnn	Represents four hexadecimal digits appearing in the operand field
LABEL	Represents a symbol defined as a label by use in the label field, or by declaration as an external symbol
NAME	Represents a symbol defined by giving it a numeric value using an assembler directive
Rn	Represents any 16-bit register except R0
ƀ	Represents a space character

ASSEMBLER DIRECTIVES

The function of an assembler, as we have already stated, is to convert a source program consisting of a sequence of assembly language statements into an object program consisting of numeric codes executable by the microprocessor. But the assembler is going to need additional information to perform this task. Where in memory is the object program going to reside? Every address label in the assembly language program will have a value that changes with the location of the object program in memory, yet no assembly language instruction can provide this information. Assembly language instructions identify operations which the CPU must perform; assembler directives provide the assembler with necessary additional information. **Directives generate no object code themselves, rather they provide the assembler with additional information it needs in order to perform its assigned task: to convert an assembly language source program into an executable object program.**

In addition to identifying the address in memory at which the object program will begin, we have encountered two other pieces of information which directives must provide:

1. Directives must set aside memory space to hold data that the program may need to operate on.

2. If you use names to identify data in the operand field of instructions (and we have encouraged you to do so), then at some point directives must assign values to these names.

The Z8000 is a very powerful microprocessor; frequently it will be used to execute very large programs. There is only one efficient way of generating very large programs: they must be generated as a large number of small programs. **A whole new class of directives provides the information an assembler needs to create a single large program out of many small parts.** Here are some of the types of information which assembler directives will have to provide:

1.   Entry Point.

Each small program's entry point must be identified. Knowing where in memory the program module resides is insufficient; the first instruction in the program module may not necessarily be the one which should be executed first. The address of the first instruction to be executed within the program is the program's entry point. This is specified as an address in the program.

2.   Global Names.

One program may assign a value to a name and declare the name to be global. This makes the value of the name available to other programs.

3.   External Names.

Another program may use a global name whose value has been specified in a different program. The program using the global name must declare it to be external.

4.   Internal Names.

In contrast, internal names are defined and used within a single program. If names are assigned a value within a program and not declared to be global or external, they are internal names. They have their value only in the program where they are defined. The Zilog assembler requires that these names be explicitly declared to be internal.

There is a third type of assembler directive: directives that help you write efficient programs. These directives are not necessary, in that they provide no information which the assembler could not obtain elsewhere; rather, they force you to write programs in a modular, structured fashion, which is generally considered the "right" way in the programming profession today.

In the discussion that follows, we will describe only those directives that an assembler must have in order to convert source programs to object code. We will describe directives conceptually, avoiding detailed descriptions of directive syntax.

To a programmer, a directive looks like an assembly language instruction; it has a mnemonic which must appear in the operation field and operands which must appear in the operand field. A directive can have a label and a comment field. But remember, despite its instruction-like appearance, a directive generates no object code. Numerous examples of directives are given in the paragraphs that follow.

ORIGIN DIRECTIVE

Every program must have an origin directive; it tells the assembler where in memory the program is to reside.

The assembler maintains a *location counter*, comparable to the microprocessor's program counter. **The location counter always contains the address of the memory location into which the instruction object code or data item currently being processed will be stored.** An origin directive causes the assembler to place a new value in its location counter, much as a jump instruction causes the microprocessor to place a new value in its program counter. The most common format for the origin directive is:

```
ORG     addr
```

ORG is the origin directive mnemonic. addr is the origin directive's operand.

The operand field of an origin directive provides the exact memory address for the first instruction object code or data item that follows. This address, illustrated above as addr, can be a numeric value or a name. If addr is a name, then it must be assigned a value using another directive. These two versions of the origin directive may be illustrated as follows:

```
ORG     %4000          ! Program starts at memory location 4000 !
ORG     START          ! Program origin is the value of START   !
```

Data can be contiguous with programs that use the data:

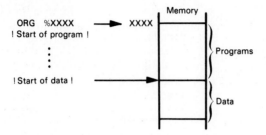

Or programs and data may reside in different areas of memory:

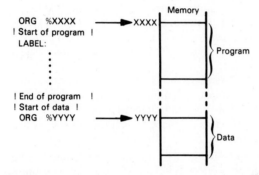

A program and/or data used by the program can be scattered around memory if for any reason such a memory organization is desirable. This may be illustrated as follows:

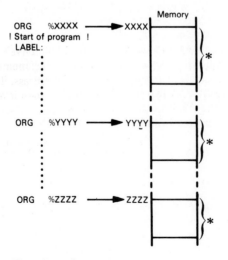

* Three pieces of one program

DATA DIRECTIVE

The next most common directives reserve space for data. In its simplest form **a data directive sets aside some number of memory locations to be used by a particular data item.** The data item is identified by the data directive's label. Here is a very simple illustration of a data directive:

```
              ORG  %0400
NUMB:         DATA 8
SNO:          DATA 3
```

The ORG directive assigns the value 0400_{16} to the location counter; the DATA directive appearing immediately afterwards sets aside eight memory locations from 0400_{16} through 0407_{16}, to be used by the data item labeled NUMB. Subsequently, every time the label NUMB appears as a name in an operand, the assembler will assign the value 0400_{16} to this name. Furthermore, the assembler will increment its location counter to 0408_{16} in order to bypass the space set aside for NUMB, so that the next entry is destined for memory location 0408_{16}. For example, the next entry illustrated is another DATA directive labeled SNO. Therefore the label SNO will be assigned the value 0408_{16} by the assembler. The illustration above shows three memory locations being set aside for SNO. Therefore the assembler will automatically increment the location counter to $040A_{16}$. An instruction following the two data directives would have its object code placed in memory beginning at location $040A_{16}$.

In addition to setting aside space for data, DATA directives can identify the **type of data and/or specify an initial data value.** Data may consist of character strings, unsigned binary data, signed binary data, binary coded decimal data, floating point numbers, etc. If you assign data types in this fashion, you are really doing so for your own convenience. The assembler might automatically assign a specific number of memory locations for a given data type, but there is no way in which the assembler can guarantee that your program logic uses data correctly. For example, if your program erroneously attempts to add two data items which have been specified as character strings, there is nothing the assembler can do to stop the operation. You will get whatever result happens to be generated by chance or mischance.

Zilog and AMC assemblers provide complex data typing as part of their various data directives. These additional complexities conform to the rules of structured programming; they make programs easier to read, but fundamentally they do nothing more than the simplest data directives, in that they assign an address to a data label and allocate space in memory for the labeled data item.

If **DATA directives assign initial values to data, then,** in addition to setting space aside in memory for the data item, **initial values are loaded into the assigned memory space.** Here is an example:

```
         ORG   %0480
MESSG:   DATA  'NOW IS THE TIME'
```

The data item with label MESSG is assumed to be fifteen bytes long, because fifteen characters are given. These fifteen bytes contain the characters "NOW IS THE TIME." The illustration above shows MESSG occupying memory locations 0480_{16} through $048E_{16}$. Note that you do not have to assign a number of data bytes in a separate data directive; the assembler is smart enough to count data bytes for itself in this instance.

You do not have to initialize data in the manner illustrated above. Your program logic could perform this initialization operation instead — and that way is usually preferable. If you initialize data using a data directive, then data is assigned these initial values only when the program is loaded into memory. If you restart the program without reloading it into memory, data is not reinitialized. If you wish to initialize data after a program has been loaded into memory, for example, without reloading the program, your program logic must contain appropriate instructions to perform this initialization. Of course, data which are never modified, such as messages, do not need to be reinitialized.

Reserve Directive

Data directives are also called reserve directives when they do not initialize data values.

Data/reserve directives are used most frequently to set aside RAM for data tables, stacks, address tables, etc.

You can use the data/reserve directive to reserve memory locations in program memory or in data memory; however, the RESERVE directive is more meaningful when applied to data memory.

Note the following features of DATA and RESERVE:

1. The label of the RESERVE directive is assigned the value of the first address reserved. For example, the directive:

        TEMP: RESERVE 20

   reserves 20 bytes of RAM and assigns the name TEMP to the address of the first byte.

2. You must specify the number of locations to be reserved. There is no default case.

3. Any data that happens to be in the reserved locations when your program is loaded will be left there.

CONSTANT DIRECTIVE

A name appearing in an instruction operand field must have a value assigned to it. If the name is also an instruction label elsewhere, then the address of the label becomes the value of the name. Consider the following example:

        ! Zilog syntax !

        HERE: LD   R1,#DATA
                 .
                 .
                 .
                 ADD   R2,#HERE

HERE is the label of the LD instruction; it is also a name in the operand field of the ADD instruction. Since it appears as a label, HERE automatically acquires a real value: the address of the first memory byte into which the LD instruction's object code gets loaded.

The name DATA, appearing in the operand field of the LD instruction, is not also shown as the label of any instruction. If a name does not appear elsewhere as the label of an instruction or data/reserve directive, then it must have its value assigned by a constant directive. **Constant directives must be used to assign values to all names whose values are not automatically assigned elsewhere.**

The constant directive may be illustrated as follows:

```
CONSTANT   label=data
```

The word CONSTANT or CONST appears in the operation field of the directive. The operand field contains the name and the value to be assigned to it, separated by an equal sign.

In the following example, the name VAL is assigned the value $327A_{16}$:

```
CONSTANT   VAL := %327A   ! Zilog syntax !
CONST      VAL  = #327A   % AMC syntax
```

Wherever VAL appears, the assembler will substitute the value $327A_{16}$.

Equate Directive

Most microprocessor assemblers call the constant directive *equate*, and use a slightly different format. The name whose value is being assigned appears in the label field of the directive. The operation field then contains a directive mnemonic, such as EQU, or an equal sign; the operation field contains the value to be assigned to the name. Thus the usual form of an equate directive is as follows:

```
label: EQU data
```

Placement of Definitions

Where do you place the equate (constant) directives? The best place is at the start of the program under appropriate comment headings such as I/O addresses, temporary storage, time constants, or program location. This makes the definitions easy to find if you want to change them; furthermore, another user will be able to look up all the definitions in one centralized place. Clearly this practice improves documentation, and makes the programs easier to use.

Definitions used only in a specific subroutine should appear at the start of the subroutine. Some assemblers differentiate between names that are local to a subroutine and names used throughout a program module; they use different terms, such as internal and local, to differentiate between the two. For example, internal names may be used throughout a program module, as compared to local names which are used within a single subroutine only.

INTERNAL, EXTERNAL AND GLOBAL NAMES

Assemblers allow you to specify names as internal, external or global.

Internal names are referenced only by the program module that contains the name definition. Unless otherwise specified, names are assumed to be internal.

Global names have their value specified in the program that declares the name to be global. The global specification tells the assembler that the name will be referenced by another program. The assembler holds the name and its assigned value in a special symbol table, for subsequent cross-reference.

An external name is one whose value has been assigned in another program. The other program must have specified the name as global when assigning it a value. Internal, external and global names might be defined at the beginning of a program as follows:

```
% Define global names to be referenced in other programs
% AMC Syntax
                GLOBAL    SUMA,PLACE
                CONST     SUMA=#217A;     % SUMA is a name
       PLACE:                            % PLACE is an instruction label
% Define internal names to be referenced only in their program
% AMC Syntax
                CONST     VAL=#327;       % VAL is a name
       LOC:                              % LOC is an instruction label
! Define internal names to be referenced only in this program !
! Zilog Syntax !
                CONSTANT VAL := %327A    ! VAL is a name !
       LOC:                              ! LOC is an instruction label !
```

AMC assemblers assume all names are internal unless they are declared to be external or global. Zilog assemblers provide an explicit internal declaration.

```
% Define external names whose values have been defined in a
% global declaration in another program

                EXTERNAL   NAMEA,NAMEB;
```

Notice that external names do not have values assigned to them since the value will be taken from a global name declaration given in another program. A global name will not have a value assigned to it via an equate directive if the name is an instruction label.

Use of Names

You could dispense completely with names and equate directives if you wrote the value of the name into every instruction where the name might otherwise have appeared. So why use names? The answer is: whenever you have a parameter that has some meaning besides its ordinary numeric value, **there is a possibility that the parameter will change.** If you have used names, you can accommodate such a change by modifying a single equate directive and then reassembling the program. You would otherwise have to comb through your program, changing the variable wherever it occurred — and hoping you had missed no change.

What names should you use? The best rules are much the same as we described for labels. Use TTY to describe a teletypewriter program, rather than X15. A bit time delay is best described by BTIME or BTDLY, rather than WW. The number of the GO key on the keyboard could be GOKEY, rather than HORSE. This advice seems straightforward, but a surprising number of programmers do not follow it.

PRINTOUT CONTROL DIRECTIVES

Every assembler provides a number of "housekeeping" directives which have no effect either on the program or the way it is stored in memory. These **housekeeping directives control the format of the listing** — that is, the way in which source and object programs are ultimately printed after an assembly has been completed. Here are some examples of housekeeping directives:

LIST

NAME

PAGE

SPACE

TITLE

LIST causes the assembler to generate a printout of the assembled program.

NAME and TITLE both specify information which will be printed at the top of every listing page.

PAGE causes the assembler to quit printing on the current page and continue printing at the top of the next page.

SPACE causes the assembler to skip printing a certain number of lines. Frequently you use the SPACE directive to leave a space between one program module and the beginning of the next; this makes the program easier to read.

END DIRECTIVE

END tells the assembler that there is no more program and it can complete the assembly. Assemblers often require an END directive as the last statement of a program.

LABELS WITH DIRECTIVES

Users often wonder if or when they can assign a label to a directive. These are our recommendations:

1. All EQUATE directives must have labels; they are useless otherwise, since the purpose of an EQUATE is to define its label.

2. DATA and RESERVE directives must have labels. The label identifies the first memory location used or assigned.

3. Other directives should not have labels. Some assemblers allow such labels, but we recommend against their use because there is no standard way to interpret them.

CONDITIONAL ASSEMBLY

Zilog and AMC assemblers allow you to include or exclude parts of the source program, depending on conditions existing at assembly time. This is called conditional assembly; it gives the assembler some of the flexibility of a compiler. A typical form is:

```
$IF CONDITION
.
.(CONDITIONAL PROGRAM)
.
.
$FI
```

If the expression CONDITION is true at assembly time, the instructions between $IF and $FI (two assembler directives) are included in the program. Typical uses of conditional assembly are:

- To include or exclude extra variables

- To place diagnostics or special conditions in test runs

- To allow data of various bit lengths

- To create specialized versions of a common program

Unfortunately, conditional assembly tends to clutter programs and make them difficult to read. Use conditional assembly only if it is necessary.

MACROS

You will often find that particular sequences of instructions occur many times in a source program. Repeated instruction sequences may reflect the needs of your program logic, or they may be compensating for deficiencies in your microprocessor's instruction set. You can avoid repeatedly writing out the same instruction sequence by using a macro.

Macros allow you to assign a name to an instruction sequence. You then use the macro name in your source program instead of the repeated instruction sequence. The assembler will replace the macro name with the appropriate sequence of instructions. This is shown in the following illustration.

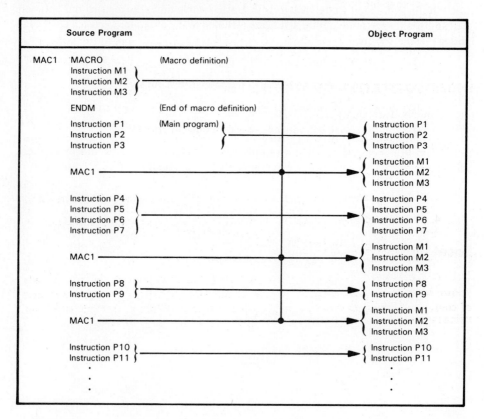

Macros are not the same as subroutines. A subroutine occurs once in a program, and program execution branches to the subroutine. A macro is expanded to an actual instruction sequence each time the macro occurs; thus a macro does not cause any branching.

ADVANTAGES OF MACROS

Macros have the following advantages:

1. Shorter source programs.

2. Better program documentation.

3. Use of debugged instruction sequences — once the macro has been debugged, you are sure of an error-free instruction sequence every time you use the macro.

4. Easier changes. Change the macro definition and the assembler makes the change for you every time the macro is used.

5. Inclusion of commands, keywords, or other computer instructions in the basic instruction set. You can use macros to extend or clarify the instruction set.

DISADVANTAGES OF MACROS

The disadvantages of macros are:

1. Repetition of the same instruction sequences since the macro is expanded every time it is used.

2. A single macro may create a lot of instructions.

3. Lack of standardization makes programs difficult to read and understand.

4. Possible effects on registers and flags that may not be clearly described.

Local or Global Variables

One problem is that, with some assemblers, variables used in a macro are only known within it (i.e., they are local rather than global). This can often create a great deal of confusion without any gain in return. You should be aware of this problem when using macros.[1]

TYPES OF ASSEMBLERS

Although all assemblers perform the same tasks, their implementations vary greatly. We will not try to describe all the existing types of assemblers; we will merely define the terms and indicate some of the choices.

CROSS-ASSEMBLER

A cross-assembler is an assembler that runs on a computer other than the one for which it assembles object programs.

The computer on which the cross-assembler runs is typically a large computer with extensive software support and fast peripherals — such as an IBM 360 or 370, a Univac 1108, or a Burroughs 6700. It may also be a microcomputer development system such as a Z-80 system. The computer for which the cross-assembler assembles programs is typically a micro like the Z8000 or 6502. Most cross-assemblers are written in FORTRAN or another high level language so that they are portable.

RESIDENT ASSEMBLER

A self-assembler or resident assembler is an assembler that runs on the computer for which it assembles programs. The self-assembler will require some memory and peripherals, and it may run quite slowly.

MACROASSEMBLER

A macroassembler is an assembler that allows you to define sequences of instructions as macros.

MICROASSEMBLER

A microassembler is an assembler used to write the microprograms that define the instruction set of a computer. Microprogramming has nothing specifically to do with microcomputers.[2,3]

META-ASSEMBLER

A meta-assembler is an assembler that can handle many different instruction sets. The user must define the particular instruction set being used.

ONE-PASS ASSEMBLER

A one-pass assembler is an assembler that goes through the assembly language program only once. Such an assembler must have some way of resolving forward references, e.g., Jump instructions which use labels that have not yet been defined.

TWO-PASS ASSEMBLER

A two-pass assembler is an assembler that goes through the assembly language source program twice. The first time the assembler simply collects and defines all the symbols; the second time it replaces the references with the actual definitions. A two-pass assembler has no problems with forward references but may be quite slow if no backup storage (like a floppy disk) is available; then the assembler must physically read the program twice from a slow input medium (like a teletypewriter paper tape reader). Most microprocessor-based assemblers require two passes.

ERRORS

Assemblers normally provide error messages, often consisting of a single coded letter. Some typical errors are:

- Undefined name (often a misspelling or an omitted definition)

- Illegal character (e.g., a 2 in a binary number)

- Illegal format (wrong delimiter or incorrect operands)

- Invalid expression (e.g., two operators in a row)

- Illegal value (usually too large)

- Missing operand

- Double definition (i.e., two different values assigned to one name)

- Illegal label (e.g., a label on a directive that cannot have one)

- Missing label

- Undefined operation code

- Syntax error (some rule of the assembler language has not been followed; e.g., a colon is missing after a label).

In interpreting assembler errors, you must remember that the assembler may get on the wrong track if it finds a stray letter, an extra space, or incorrect punctuation. Many assemblers will then proceed to misinterpret the succeeding instructions and produce meaningless error messages. Always look at the first error very carefully; subsequent ones may depend on it. Caution and consistent adherence to standard formats will eliminate many annoying mistakes.

LOADERS

The loader is the program which actually takes the output (object code) from the assembler and places it in memory. Loaders range from the very simple to the very complex. We will describe a few different types.

BOOTSTRAP LOADER

A bootstrap loader is a program that uses its own first few instructions to load the rest of itself or another loader program into memory. The bootstrap loader may be in ROM, or you may have to enter it into the computer memory using front panel switches. The assembler may place a bootstrap loader at the start of the object program that it produces.

RELOCATING LOADER

A relocating loader can load programs anywhere in memory. It typically loads each program into the memory space immediately following that used by the previous program. The relocating loader will change addresses assigned to labels in the program to reflect where the program is loaded. The programs, however, must themselves be capable of being moved around in this way; i.e., they must be relocatable. An absolute loader, in contrast, will always place a program in the same area of memory. Addresses are not changed.

LINKING LOADER

A linking loader loads programs and subroutines that have been assembled separately; it resolves cross references — that is, instructions in one program that refer to a label in another program. Object programs loaded by a linking loader must be created by an assembler that allows external references.

Link Editor

An alternative approach is to separate the linking and loading functions and have the linking performed by a program called a link editor. The linked programs are then loaded as a unit by a loader.

REFERENCES

1. A complete monograph on macros is M. Campbell-Kelly, *An Introduction to Macros* (New York: American Elsevier, 1973).

2. A. Osborne, *An Introduction to Microcomputers: Volume 1 — Basic Concepts*, second edition (Berkeley: Osborne/McGraw-Hill, 1980).

3. A. K. Agrawala and T.G. Rauscher, *Foundations of Microprogramming* (New York: Academic Press, 1976).

See also:

D. W. Barron, *Assemblers and Loaders* (New York: American Elsevier, 1972).

C. W. Gear, *Computer Organization and Programming* (New York: McGraw-Hill, 1974).

3

The Z8000 Assembly Language Instruction Set

We are now ready to start writing assembly language programs. We begin in this chapter by defining the individual instructions of the Z8000 assembly language instruction set, plus the syntax rules specified by Zilog and Advanced Micro Computers (AMC) Z8000 assemblers.

We do not discuss any aspects of microcomputer hardware, signals, or interfaces in this book. This information is described in detail in the Osborne 16-Bit Microprocessor Handbook.

In this book we look at programming techniques from the assembly language programmer's viewpoint, where pins and signals are irrelevant and there are no important differences between a minicomputer and a microcomputer.

Z8000 interrupts and direct memory access will be described in later chapters of this book, in conjunction with assembly language programming discussions of the same subjects.

Z8000 instructions may be divided into those which are frequently used (Table 3-1), occasionally used (Table 3-2), and seldom used (Table 3-3). If you are an experienced assembly language programmer, this categorization is not particularly important — and, depending on your own programming prejudices, it may not even be accurate. If you are a novice assembly language programmer, we recommend that you begin by writing programs using only instructions in the "frequently used" category. Once you have mastered the concepts of assembly language programming, you may examine other instructions and use them where appropriate.

Table 3-1. Frequently Used Instructions of the Z8000

Instruction Code	Meaning
ADC	Add with carry
ADD	Add
AND	Logical AND
CALL	Call subroutine
CALR	Call subroutine relative
CLR	Clear
CP	Compare
DEC	Decrement
DJNZ	Decrement and jump if not zero
IN	Input
INC	Increment
JP	Jump
JR	Jump relative
LD	Load (and move)
OR	Logical OR
OUT	Output
POP	Pop the stack
PUSH	Push stack
RET	Return
RL	Rotate left
RLC	Rotate left through carry
RR	Rotate right
RRC	Rotate right through carry
SBC	Subtract with carry
SLL	Shift left logical
SRL	Shift right logical
SUB	Subtract
XOR	Logical Exclusive OR

Only word versions of instructions are listed. Byte and long word versions, where available, have the same use frequency.

Table 3-2. Occasionally Used Instructions of the Z8000

Instruction Code	Meaning
BIT	Bit test
COM	Complement
CPD	Compare and decrement
CPDR	Compare, decrement and repeat
CPI	Compare and increment
CPIR	Compare, increment and repeat
DAB	Decimal adjust
DI	Disable interrupts
EI	Enable interrupts
EX	Exchange
HALT	Halt
IRET	Return from interrupt
LDD	Load and decrement
LDDR	Load, decrement and repeat
LDI	Load and increment
LDIR	Load, increment and repeat
LDK	Load constant
LDM	Load multiple
LDPS	Load program status
LDR	Load relative
MULT	Multiply
NEG	Negate
NOP	No operation
RES	Reset bit
RESFLG	Reset status
RLDB	Rotate left digit
RRDB	Rotate right digit
SDA	Shift dynamic arithmetic
SDL	Shift dynamic logical
SET	Set bit
SETFLG	Set status
SLA	Shift left arithmetic
SRA	Shift right arithmetic
TEST	Test
TRDB	Translate and decrement
TRIB	Translate and increment

Only word versions of instructions are listed. Byte and long word versions, where available, have the same use frequency.

Table 3-3. Seldom Used Instructions of the Z8000

Instruction Code	Meaning
COMFLG	Complement flags
CPSD	Compare strings and decrement
CPSDR	Compare strings, decrement and repeat
CPSI	Compare strings and increment
CPSIR	Compare strings, increment and repeat
DIV	Divide
EXTS	Extend sign
IND	Input and decrement
INDR	Input, decrement and repeat
INI	Input and increment
INIR	Input, increment and repeat
LDA	Load address
LDAR	Load address relative
LDCTL	Load control register
MBIT	Multi-micro bit test
MREQ	Multi-micro request
MRES	Multi-micro reset
MSET	Multi-micro set
OTDR	Output, decrement and repeat
OTIR	Output, increment and repeat
OUTD	Output and decrement
OUTI	Output and increment
SC	System call
SIN	Special input
SIND	Special input and decrement
SINDR	Special input, decrement and repeat
SINI	Special input and increment
SINIR	Special input, increment and repeat
SOTDR	Special output, decrement and repeat
SOTIR	Special output, increment and repeat
SOUT	Special output
SOUTD	Special output and decrement
SOUTI	Special output and increment
TCC	Test condition code
TRDRB	Translate, decrement and repeat
TRIRB	Translate, increment and repeat
TRTDB	Translate, test and decrement
TRTDRB	Translate, test, decrement and repeat
TRTIB	Translate, test and increment
TRTIRB	Translate, test, increment and repeat
TSET	Test and set

Only word versions of instructions are listed. Byte and long word versions, where available, have the same use frequency.

OPERATING MODES

There are two separate and unrelated sets of operating modes that shape the Z8000 assembly language instruction set and its memory addressing logic; they are:

1. system and normal modes, which affect the availability of instructions; and

2. segmented and non-segmented modes, which affect memory addressing logic.

SYSTEM AND NORMAL MODES

Both the Z8001 and the Z8002 can operate in either system mode or normal mode. A status flag setting determines the mode of operation.

Certain instructions, including all I/O instructions, can be executed only in system mode, not in normal mode. Also, separate stacks are maintained in memory for system and normal modes.

There are no other differences between system mode and normal mode.

If you are a novice assembly language programmer, keep the Z8000 in system mode and ignore normal mode; then you will be able to execute any Z8000 instruction. If you operate the Z8000 in normal mode, you may encounter instructions that execute in system mode only; and that will simply confuse you.

But there is a good reason for having separate system and normal modes. As any experienced assembly language programmer will tell you, assembly language programs can be divided into "system software" and "applications programs." System software includes those programs that tie the components of a computer system together; system software should be written in system mode. Applications programs cause the computer to perform a user's specific tasks, and should be written in normal mode.

SEGMENTED AND NON-SEGMENTED MODES

The major difference between segmented and non-segmented modes is that 16-bit memory addresses are computed in non-segmented mode, while 23-bit memory addresses are computed in segmented mode. The 23-bit segmented mode memory address is divided into a 16-bit offset and a 7-bit segment. The seven high-order bits of the address provide the segment; the 16 low- order bits of the address provide the offset.

The Z8002 can operate in non-segmented mode only; thus the Z8002 always generates a 16-bit memory address.

The Z8001 can operate in segmented or non-segmented mode, but in either case it generates a 23-bit memory address. In segmented mode the Z8001 computes all 23 address bits: the segment and the offset. In non-segmented mode the Z8001 computes the 16 offset address bits only, taking the 7 high-order segment bits from the Program Counter.

Segment Offset

A 23-bit memory address may be illustrated as follows:

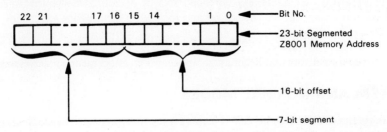

Z8000 memory is organized in bytes; therefore the 23-bit segmented memory address accesses 128 segments, with 65536 bytes per segment. The seven segment bits select a segment. The 16 offset bits address a byte within the selected segment.

Insofar as memory addressing logic is concerned, the Z8002 is equivalent to one segment of the Z8001 operating in non- segmented mode. This may be illustrated as follows:

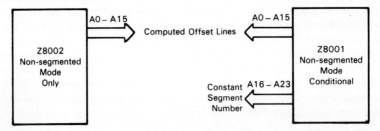

System/normal modes, and segmented/non-segmented modes have no impact on each other. Certain instructions can be executed in system mode, but not normal mode; also, different Stack Pointers are used in system and normal modes. Segmented and non-segmented modes, in contrast, calculate memory addresses in different ways. System and normal modes can each be selected with segmented or non-segmented mode.

Z8000 Mode Compatibility

The Z8002 operating in normal mode can directly replace a Z8001 operating in non-segmented, normal mode. The Z8002 operating in system mode is close, but not exactly equivalent to a Z8001 operating in non-segmented, system mode. This is because the Z8001 and the Z8002 have different interrupt handling logic, which does not affect normal mode, but does affect system mode — generating the incompatibility.

The Z8001 operating in segmented mode is completely incompatible with the Z8002.

CPU REGISTERS AND STATUS FLAGS

PROGRAMMABLE REGISTERS

Programmable registers of the Z8001 and Z8002 microprocessors are illustrated in Figures 3-1 and 3-2, respectively.

Registers R0 through R15 can be used as general purpose accumulators.

Index Registers

Registers R1 through R15 can function additionally as Index Registers for indexed memory addressing. Register R0 cannot be used as an Index Register; Register R0 can function only as an Accumulator or general purpose register.

Indirect Address Registers

Registers R1 through R15 can also function as indirect address registers for implied memory addressing in non-segmented mode. In segmented mode, 32-bit registers RR2 through RR14 can function as indirect address registers. Registers R0 and RR0 cannot function as indirect address registers for implied memory addressing.

Stack Pointer

Register R15 (in non-segmented mode) or Registers R14 and R15 (in segmented mode) function as the Stack Pointer in addition to serving as general purpose registers or as Index Registers. Thus R15 (and R14 in segmented mode) can be used in three different ways.

Register R15 (in non-segmented mode) or Registers R15 and R14 (RR14 in segmented mode) are duplicated. Different registers are used in system mode and normal mode. Therefore if you write into R15 in system mode, then switch to normal mode and read from R15, you will not read what you just wrote. In Figures 3-1 and 3-2 the duplicate registers are illustrated as R14N/R14S and R15N/R15S.

The Z8002 uses R15N in normal mode, and R15S in system mode.

The Z8001 uses R15N and R14N in normal mode; R15S and R14S are used in system mode.

These duplicate system and normal mode registers allow separate stacks to be maintained by system and normal modes.

Program Counter

The Program Counter is a simple 16-bit register for the Z8002. But for the Z8001, two 16-bit registers are used; one register holds the 16-bit Program Counter Offset, the other register holds the 7-bit Program Counter Segment Number.

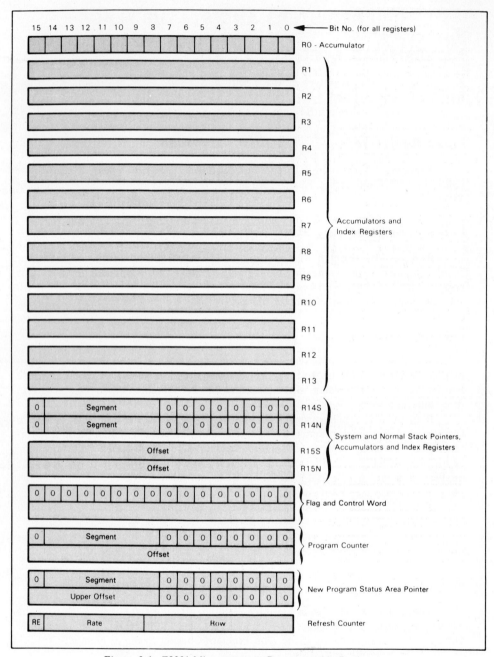

Figure 3-1. Z8001 Microprocessor Programmable Registers

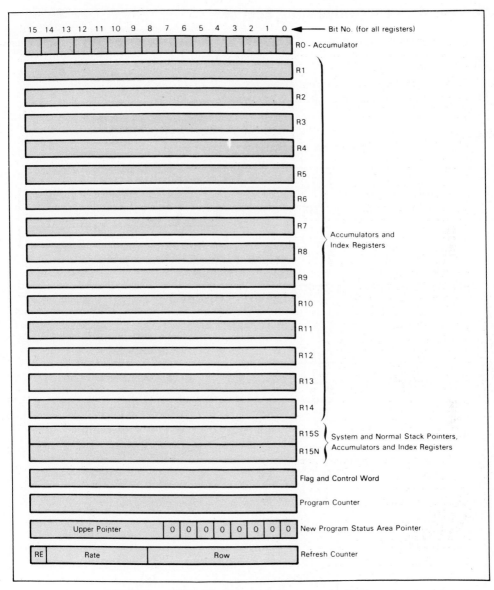

Figure 3-2. Z8002 Microprocessor Programmable Registers

New Program Status Area Pointer

The New Program Status Area Pointer is used by interrupt logic. It consists of one or two 16-bit words, as illustrated in Figures 3-1 and 3-2.

Following any interrupt acknowledgement, a vector address is created using the New Program Status Area Pointer, and a 10-bit or 11-bit displacement provided by interrupt acknowledgement logic, as follows:

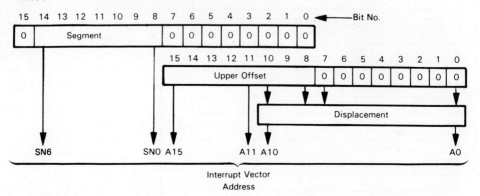

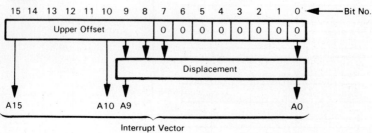

See Chapter 12 for a discussion of Z8000 interrupt logic and programming.

Refresh Counter

The Refresh Counter is a 16-bit register that is used to control refresh logic for external dynamic memory modules. This logic is important only if you are designing dynamic memory modules to operate in a Z8000 microcomputer system. **The Refresh Counter is of no interest to assembly language programmers.**

The Refresh Counter is enabled when 1 is written into its high-order bit; the Refresh Counter is disabled by writing 0 into the high-order bit. When enabled, Refresh Counter logic repeatedly decrements a six bit number whose initial value is stored in bits 9 through 14 of the Refresh Counter. Each time this value decrements to zero a special refresh machine cycle is executed. During the refresh machine cycle a "new address" is output on the Address/Data bus. This address is taken from bits 0-8 of the Refresh Counter. This 9-bit row address is then incremented by 2. **This description of the Refresh Counter is presented in the interests of completeness. You will rarely, if ever, use the Refresh Counter.**

STATUS

Flag and Control Word (FCW)

The Flag and Control Word provides the Z8001 and the Z8002 with Status and Control bits. These bits are interpreted as follows:

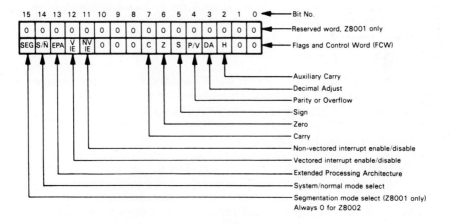

We use the abbreviation FCW to represent the Flag and Control Word Register.

The Parity, Overflow, Sign, Zero, and Carry status flags are absolutely standard.

Parity and Overflow share a status bit.

The Parity status is modified by logical instructions which test the parity of byte data. The status is set to 1 for even parity; it is reset to 0 for odd parity. Note that the parity of the data byte and the parity status taken together are always odd.

The Overflow status is usually set equal to the Exclusive OR of the carries out of the high-order bit and the next to high-order bit following arithmetic operations. This will occur when the result exceeds the capacity of the destination operand to represent a signed twos complement number. Some logical operations set the Overflow status to 1 if the high-order operand bit changes value, and reset the Overflow status to 0 if the high-order operand bit does not change value.

The Sign status is set to the value of the high-order result bit following all arithmetic operations and many logic operations.

The Zero status is set to 1 when the result of an operation (including the sign) is 0; it is reset to 0 otherwise.

The Carry status reports carries out of the high-order bit following arithmetic operations. This status is also used by some shift and rotate instructions. Subtract instructions reverse Carry status logic to report borrows. Thus the Carry status is set to 1 when there is no carry following a subtract operation; the Carry status resets to 0 if there is a carry following a subtract operation.

Most microprocessor instructions routinely modify status bits, whether or not such modifications are relevant to the operation performed. Z8000 status logic generally follows the PDP-11 minicomputer, but the Z8000 has a few anomalies. You should therefore consult Table 3-4, which summarizes the Z8000 instruction set, in order to determine how a particular status is affected by the execution of any specific instruction.

The Auxiliary Carry and Decimal Adjust status flags differ somewhat from normal use. These flags are modified by byte arithmetic instructions in order to make binary coded decimal arithmetic possible. Reading the value of these flags provides little useful information. The assembly language programmer should ignore these two flags unless doing decimal arithmetic.

Interrupt Enable

NVIE and VIE are used to enable and disable non-vectored and vectored interrupts, respectively. You enable interrupts by setting the appropriate status bit to 1, and you disable interrupts by resetting the appropriate status bit to 0.

Extended Processing Mode

The Z8000 architecture provides for extending the instruction set by reserving certain instruction codes for execution by devices external to the microprocessor chip. The EPA status flag is used to determine how the extended instruction codes are to be processed. When this bit is 1, extended instructions are processed by external devices. When this bit is 0, execution of an extended instruction causes an Extended Instruction trap.

System/Normal Modes

The S/N status flag is used to switch between system and normal modes. When this bit is 1, Z8000 microprocessors operate in system mode. When this bit is 0, Z8000 microprocessors operate in normal mode. Recall that system and normal modes have their own Stack Pointers; also, certain privileged instructions can only be executed in system mode.

Table 3-4. Condition Codes Used by the Z8000 Assembly
Language Instruction Set

AMC Code	Zilog Code	CC Value	Meaning	Status Conditions
TRUE (or blank)	(blank)	8	Always true	Any
CY LLT	C ULT	7	Carry Unsigned (logical) less than	C = 1
EQ ZR	EQ Z	6	Equal Zero	Z = 1
GE	GE	9	Signed greater than or equal	S ⊕ V = 0
GT	GT	A	Signed greater than	Z V (S ⊕ V) = 0
LE	LE	2	Signed less than or equal	Z V (S ⊕ V) = 1
LT	LT	1	Signed less than	S ⊕ V = 1
MI	MI	5	Minus	S = 1
NC LGE	NC UGE	F	No Carry Unsigned (logical) greater than or equal	C = 0
NE NZ	NE NZ	E	Not equal Not zero	Z = 0
NOV PO	NOV PO	C	No overflow Parity is odd	P/V = 0
PE OV	PE OV	4	Parity is even Overflow	P/V = 1
PL	PL	D	Plus	S = 0
LGT	UGT	B	Unsigned (logical) greater than	C V Z = 0
LLE	ULE	3	Unsigned (logical) less than or equal	C V Z = 1
FALSE	(No code)	0	Always false	None

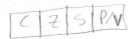

Segmented Non-Segmented Modes

The SEG status is used by the Z8001 microprocessor only. When this bit is set to 1, the Z8001 operates in segmented mode; when this bit is set to 0, the Z8001 operates in non-segmented mode. This bit is always 0 in the Z8002.

REGISTER DESIGNATIONS

Z8000 series microprocessor instructions use 8-bit, 16-bit, 32-bit or 69-bit registers, as illustrated in Figure 3-3. Register designations used by Zilog assembly language mnemonics are shown in Figure 3-3.

8-Bit Registers

Byte instructions use sixteen 8-bit registers, illustrated in Figure 3-3 by **RH0** through **RL7**.

16-Bit Registers

Word instructions use the sixteen 16-bit registers **R0 through R15.**

32-Bit Registers

Long-word instructions use general purpose registers in pairs. Eight 32-bit registers are available, shown in Figure 3-3 as **RR0 through RR14.**

Many Z8000 series instructions that use memory or registers have a word version and a byte version. A limited number of instructions have a long word version.

64-Bit Registers

Multiplication and division instructions sometimes use 64- bit registers, shown in Figure 3-3 as **RQ0 through RQ12.**

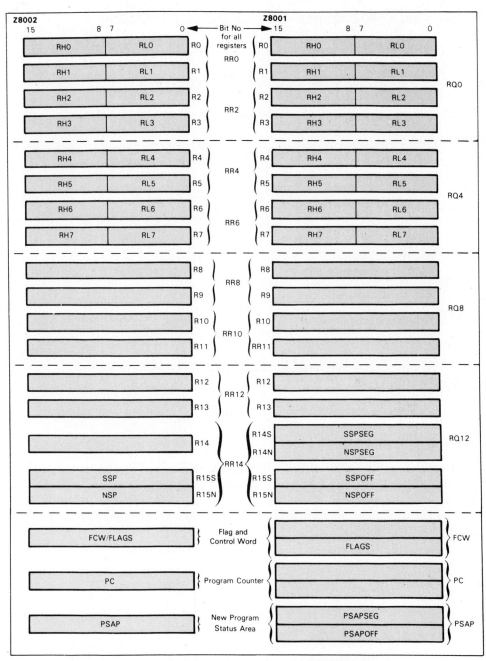

Figure 3-3. Register Designations for the Z8001 and Z8002 Microprocessors

MEMORY ADDRESSING MODES

All Z8000 memory is organized as bytes; nevertheless, memory can be accessed as bytes, 16-bit words or 32-bit long words.

Words and long words must start at bytes with even addresses. The following word and long word memory locations are legal:

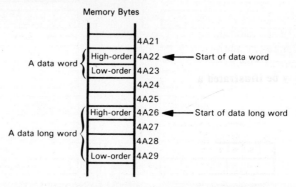

The following memory words and long words are illegal because they start at odd memory addresses:

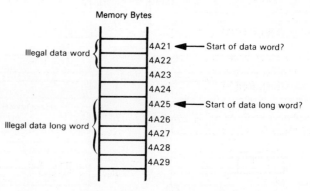

The illustrations in this book show memory as follows, with the address of a word shown on the right:

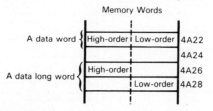

Note that the address on the right is the address of the word. It is also the address of the high-order byte, which is the byte on the left. The address of the low-order byte of the data word shown above is $4A23_{16}$.

SEGMENTED AND NON-SEGMENTED MODES

Most Z8001 memory addressing options have two forms, one for non-segmented mode, the other for segmented mode.

In non-segmented mode, all memory reference instructions compute 16-bit addresses. These 16-bit non-segmented memory addresses are held in a single 16-bit memory word, or a single 16-bit CPU Register.

In segmented mode, addresses are 23 bits wide. 23-bit segmented memory addresses are separated into a 7-bit segment number and a 16-bit offset. A 23-bit segmented memory address is held in two 16-bit memory words, or two CPU registers. The segment number is held in the first word; the offset is held in the second word. This may be illustrated as follows:

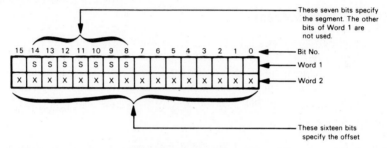

Address Segment and Address Offset

If you refer back to Figure 3-1, you will see that the Z8001 allocates two 16-bit words to the Program Counter and the Stack Pointer; they hold 23-bit addresses using the format illustrated above.

When a Z8001 is operating in non-segmented mode, memory reference instructions compute a 16-bit offset, while taking the segment number from the Program Counter Segment Register. This may be illustrated as follows:

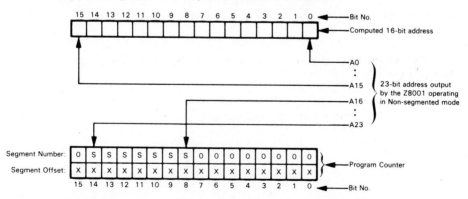

When the Z8001 is operating in segmented mode, memory reference instructions compute a segment number and an offset. The Program Counter segment number is not used in computing the memory address. Furthermore, the Program Counter segment number is not changed, or affected in any way, by the segment number which a memory reference instruction may compute as part of its memory addressing logic.

EFFECTIVE MEMORY ADDRESS

We use the term "effective memory address" to describe the memory address finally computed by any memory reference instruction, using any memory addressing option.

Memory addresses are computed using one or more of the following components:

1. A base address

2. An index

3. A displacement

Z8002 Base Address

The Z8002 specifies a base address as a 16-bit unsigned binary number, held in a single memory word, or one of the CPU registers R1 through R15.

The base address specified by a Z8001 takes different forms depending on whether the Z8001 is operating in segmented or non-segmented mode. In segmented mode further variations are possible, depending on whether the base address is held in CPU registers, or memory.

Z8001 Non-Segmented Base Address

In non-segmented mode, the Z8001 base address is specified as a 16-bit unsigned binary value, held in a single memory word, or in one of the CPU registers R1 through R15; the base address segment number is taken from the Program Counter.

Z8001 operating in segmented mode can specifiy a long-segmented base address or a short-segmented base address.

Z8001 Long-Segmented Base Address

A long-segmented base address can be held in general purpose registers or in memory. One of the seven 32-bit registers RR2 through RR14 can hold the long-segmented base address. RR0 cannot hold a long-segmented base address. If held in memory, any two contiguous memory words may be used. The first (lower address) 16-bit register or memory word specifies the segment, while the second (higher address) 16-bit register or memory word specifies the offset.

Z8001 Short-Segmented Base Address

The short-segmented base address occupies a single 16-bit word. Bits 7-0 specify an 8-bit offset. Bits 14-8 specify the 7-bit segment. A short-form segmented base address can occur only as part of an instruction. The Z8001 never specifies a short-segmented base address in a single CPU register.

Long- and short-segmented base addresses may be illustrated as follows:

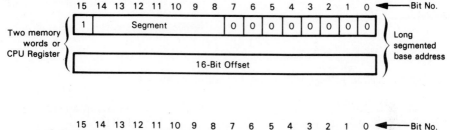

A short-segmented base address, on its own, can address only the first 256 bytes of any 65536 byte memory segment.

When a base address is held in program memory, the high-order bit of the first memory word is set to 1 to identify a two word, long-segmented base address. This bit is reset to 0 to identify a single word, short-segmented base address.

Index

An index is always a 16-bit unsigned binary value, held in one of the fifteen general purpose registers R1-R15. R0 cannot function as an Index Register.

In non-segmented mode there is no difference between an index and a base address.

Displacement

A displacement is always held in an instruction's object code. Displacements are never held in CPU registers. Displacements may be signed or unsigned binary numbers; they may be 7, 8, 12 or 16 bits wide.

OPERANDS IN MEMORY

The Z8000 offers nine basic memory addressing methods; some methods differ in segmented and non-segmented modes, others do not. We list memory addressing options below, with an asterisk identifying those methods that differ in segmented and non-segmented modes.

Memory Addressing options include:

1. Immediate

2.* Absolute or direct

3.* Implied or register indirect

4.* Implied with auto-increment or auto-decrement

5.* Direct indexed

6.* Base relative

7.* Base indexed

8. Program relative

9.* Indirect

The Z8000 instruction set uses its addressing options in a very regular way.

Immediate addressing is a special case wherein the instruction object code holds an operand.

Frequently used data memory reference instructions use immediate, direct, register indirect, and direct,indexed addressing modes.

Infrequently used data memory reference instructions use only implied (register indirect) memory addressing.

A very limited number of data reference instructions also use base relative addressing and base indexed addressing.

Input and output instructions use direct and register indirect addressing modes.

Program relative addressing is used by jump and subroutine call instructions. A few instructions use program relative addressing to access data memory, or to load memory addresses into registers.

Indirect addressing is used by a few jump and subroutine call instructions and the return instructions. The Z8000 has no data memory indirect addressing.

Implied memory addressing with auto-increment and auto-decrement is used only by string handling instructions. These instructions address source and destination strings using implied (register indirect) memory addressing. This address is either incremented or decremented each time the instruction is executed, so it points to the next string location, ready for the next execution of the string instruction.

IMMEDIATE MEMORY ADDRESSING

This memory addressing method stores one of the operands within the instruction's object code. The Z8000 has byte, word and long word immediate instructions.

Byte and word immediate instructions provide the immediate operand in the second word of the instruction's object code.

For a byte immediate instruction, the immediate data is repeated in both bytes of the second object code word. This may be illustrated as follows:

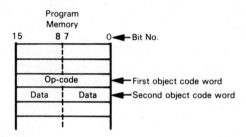

Consider the instruction:

```
ANDB     RH6,#4A;       % AMC syntax
ANDB     RH6,#%4A       ! Zilog syntax !
```

The contents of 8-bit register RH6 are ANDed with the immediate 8-bit data value $4A_{16}$. The result returns to RH6. This is illustrated in Figure 3-4.

The entire second object code word provides the immediate operand for an immediate word instruction. This may be illustrated as follows:

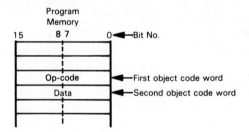

The immediate word version of the ANDB instruction previously illustrated is:

```
AND      R6,#4A3C;      % AMC syntax
AND      R6,#%4A3C      ! Zilog syntax !
```

The contents of 16-bit register R6 is ANDed with the immediate data value $4A3C_{16}$. The result is returned to R6. Figure 3-5 illustrates this instruction in non-segmented mode.

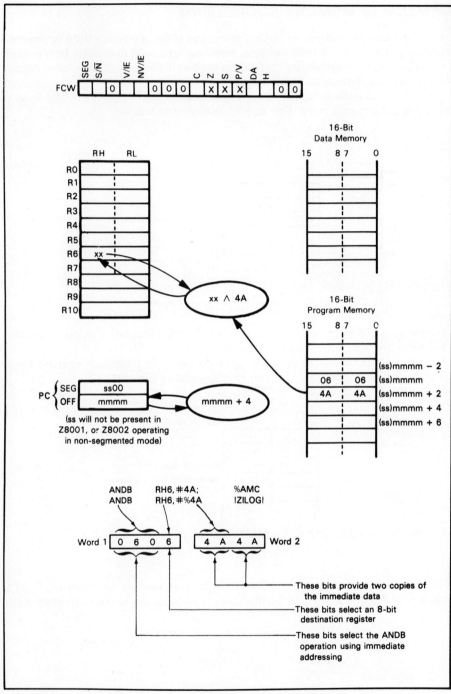

Figure 3-4. Immediate Addressing, Byte Instruction,
Illustrating Optional Segmentation Mode

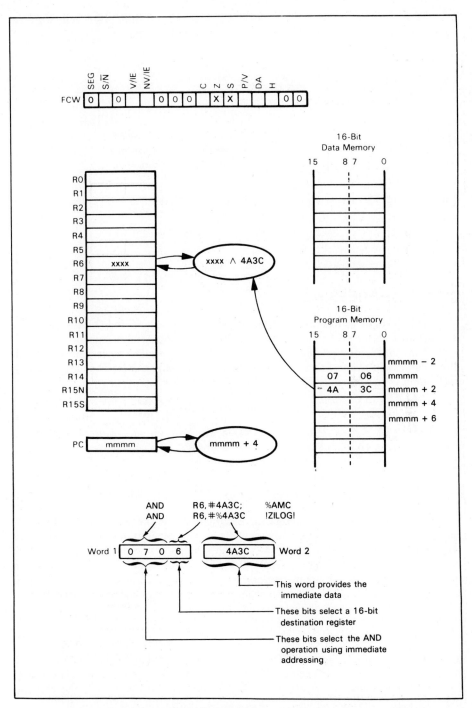

Figure 3-5. Immediate Addressing, Word Instruction in Non-Segmented Mode

Long word immediate instructions use the second and third object code words to provide an immediate operand. This may be illustrated as follows:

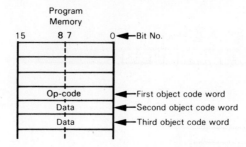

The following instruction adds a 32-bit immediate operand to the contents of 32-bit register RR4:

```
ADDL     RR4,#4A3C2D10;   % AMC syntax
ADDL     RR4,#%4A3C2D10   ! Zilog syntax !
```

32-bit immediate addressing is illustrated in Figure 3-6.

DIRECT ADDRESSING

This form of addressing uses the second, or the second and third words of an instruction's object code to identify the address of an operand in memory.

The Z8002, or the Z8001 operating in non-segmented mode stores a 16-bit direct address in the second word of the instruction's object code. The direct addressing version of the previously illustrated AND instruction is:

```
AND      R6,#4A3C^;       % AMC syntax
AND      R6,%4A3C         ! Zilog syntax !
```

The contents of 16-bit register R6 is ANDed with the contents of the memory word whose address is $4A3C_{16}$. The result is returned to R6. Non-segmented direct addressing is illustrated in Figure 3-7 for a word instruction.

When the Z8001 is operated in segmented mode, two variations of segmented direct addressing are available: long-segmented direct addressing and short-segmented direct addressing.

Long-segmented direct addressing instructions use the second and third object code words to specify a segmented direct address. The segment number is stored in the second object code word, while the 16-bit offset is stored in the third object code word.

Note that the data memory segment number provided by the direct address is in no way related to the program memory segment number provided by the Program Counter Segment Register. The two segment numbers can, and probably will differ. Consider the long-segmented direct addressing version of our AND instruction:

```
AND      R6,SEGLABEL;     % AMC syntax
AND      R6,<<%2A>>%4A3C  ! Zilog syntax !
```

The contents of 16-bit register R6 is ANDed with the contents of the memory word whose address is $4A3C_{16}$ in segment $2A_{16}$. The result is returned to 16-bit register R6. Figure 3-8 illustrates this instruction's addressing logic. In Figure 3-8, the program memory segment number, illustrated as ss, can have any value from 0 through $7F_{16}$.

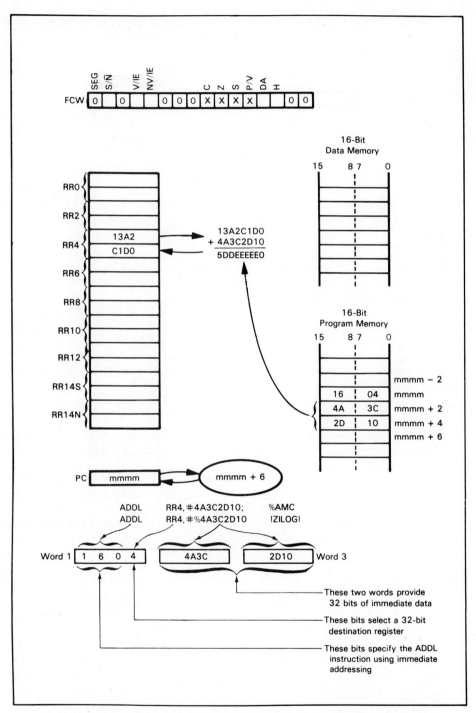

Figure 3-6. Immediate Addressing Long Word Instruction in Non-Segmented Mode

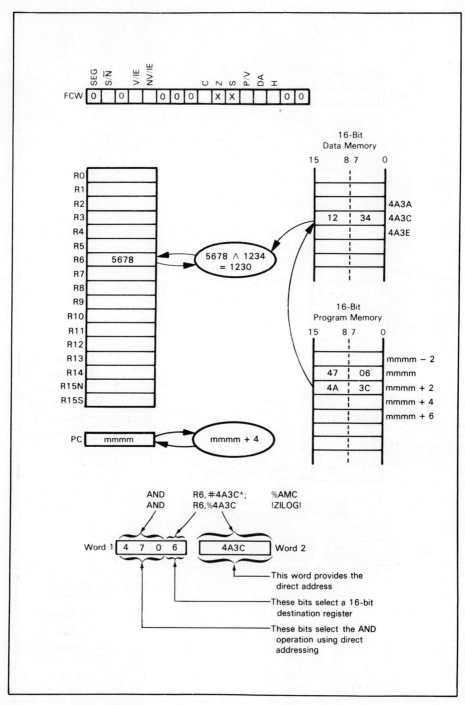

Figure 3-7. Direct Addressing Instruction in Non-Segmented Mode

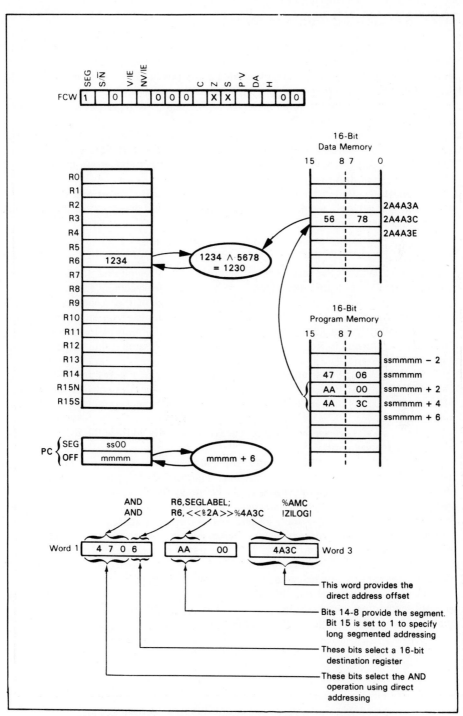

Figure 3-8. Direct Addressing Instruction in Segmented Mode,
Long Form

AMC Segmented Address Syntax

AMC syntax does not allow absolute segmented addresses to be specified; there is no AMC equivalent for the Zilog <<SEG>> segment specification. Instead, **AMC requires segmented addresses to be specified using labels.** Segment numbers are subsequently specifed via program origins and external labels, which allow the assembler to give the linking loader information necessary to complete segmented instructions' object codes while loading programs.

Note that the same three hexadecimal digits specify an AND operation using non-segmented direct addressing, or segmented direct address. The SEG bit of Flag and Control Word (FCW) differentiates between the two direct addressing modes. If the SEG bit is 0, then non-segmented addressing is assumed.

A short-segmented direct address packs the segment number and an 8-bit displacement into a single word. Here is the short-segmented direct addressing variation of our AND instruction:

```
AND     R6,SEGLABEL;      % AMC syntax
AND     R6, |<<%2A>>%3C|  ! Zilog syntax !
```

Zilog syntax uses the vertical bars to indicate a short-segmented address. AMC assemblers use a short-segmented address whenever the displacement fits in 8 bits.

The segment number and the offset are included in the second word of the instructions object code. In the illustration above, the contents of the data memory word with address $003C_{16}$ in segment $2A_{16}$ is ANDed with the contents of 16-bit register R6. The result is returned to R6. Short-segmented direct addressing is illustrated in Figure 3-9.

Observe that the first object code word is the same in Figures 3-9, 3-8 and 3-7. The SEG bit of the Flag and Control word specifies non-segmented or segmented addressing, while the high-order bit of word 2 differentiates between short and long segmentation.

Note that a short-segmented direct address can only address the first 256 bytes of any memory segment.

The three variations of direct memory addressing which we have illustrated are used by byte, word and long word instructions. Figures 3-7, 3-8, and 3-9 illustrate word instructions, but **direct addressing logic is identical for byte, word, and long word instructions. For a byte instruction, however, the contents of a single memory byte are accessed; this byte may have an odd address or even address. For a long word instruction the directly addressed data memory word, and the next sequential data memory word are accessed.** Figure 3-10 illustrates non-segmented direct memory addressing being used by a byte instruction; Figure 3-11 illustrates long-segmented direct memory addressing being used by a long word instruction.

Once again note that the SEG bit within the Flag and Control Word determines whether segmented or non-segmented direct memory addressing is used. The instruction object code does not make this specification.

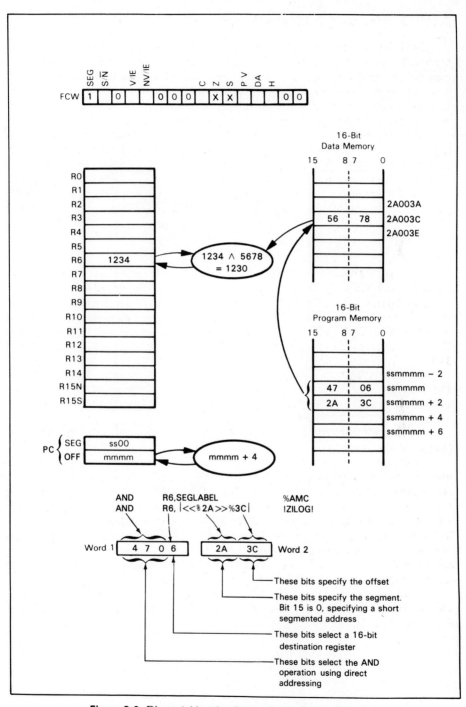

Figure 3-9. Direct Addressing Instruction in Segmented Mode,
Short Form

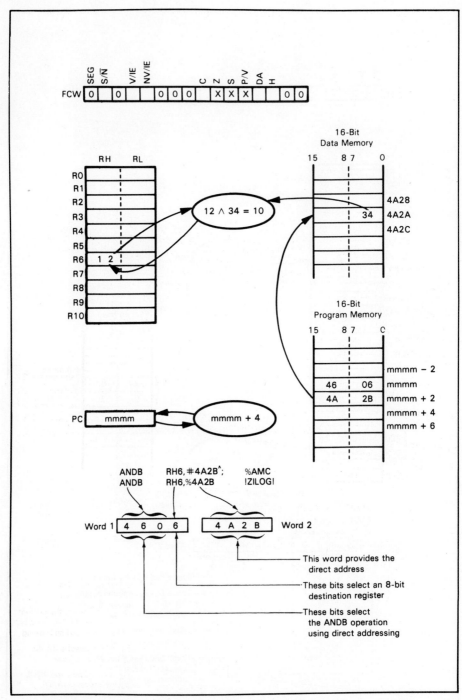

Figure 3-10. Direct Addressing for a Byte Instruction in Non-Segmented Mode

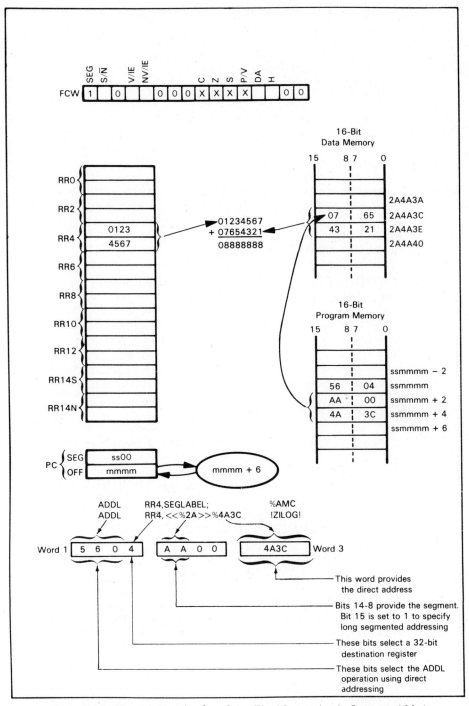

Figure 3-11. Direct Addressing for a Long Word Instruction in Segmented Mode

IMPLIED, OR REGISTER INDIRECT ADDRESSING

Fifteen of the sixteen 16-bit registers can hold a non- segmented data memory address. R0 is the only 16-bit register which cannot be used in this way. Consider the following implied memory addressing instruction:

```
AND        R6,R8^;          % AMC syntax
AND        R6,@R8           ! Zilog syntax !
```

The contents of the data memory location addressed by 16-bit register R8 is ANDed with the contents of 16-bit register R6. The result is returned to register R6.

Figure 3-12 illustrates non-segmented, register indirect (or implied) memory addressing.

In segmented mode one of the seven 32-bit registers RR2 through RR14 must provide the long-segmented address. Remember, the Z8001 does not allow short-segmented addresses to be held in a 16-bit register. Short-segmented addresses can only be stored in memory.

Figure 3-13 illustrates segmented, register indirect addressing; this instruction is the segmented version of the Figure 3-12 instruction.

IMPLIED ADDRESSING WITH AUTO INCREMENT OR AUTO DECREMENT

Some Z8000 string handling instructions automatically increment or decrement the implied memory address contained in a register. The address is incremented or decremented by 1 for a byte instruction or by 2 for a word instruction. There are no long word auto increment or auto-decrement instructions. Auto-increment/decrement logic leaves the implied memory address pointing to the next string element.

DIRECT INDEXED ADDRESSING

Direct indexed memory addressing is best visualized as the sum of direct and register indirect memory addressing. The direct address may be non-segmented, short-segmented, or long-segmented. A 16-bit index is added to this direct address. The index is taken from any one of the fifteen registers R1 through R15. R0 cannot serve as an Index Register.

The following are direct indexed variations of the direct addressing instructions which we illustrated earlier in this chapter:

1.   Non-segmented direct, indexed memory addressing:

```
AND        R6,#4A3C^(R8);    % AMC syntax
AND        R6,%4A3C(R8)      ! Zilog syntax !
```

The contents of register R6 is ANDed with the contents of the memory word addressed by summing $4A3C_{16}$ and the contents of Index Register R8. The result is returned to register R6. Figure 3-14 illustrates non-segmented direct, indexed memory addressing.

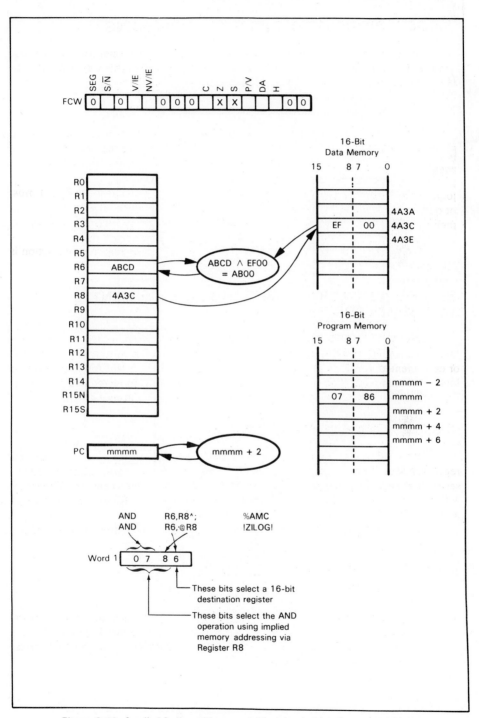

Figure 3-12. Implied Indirect Memory Addressing in Non-Segmented Mode

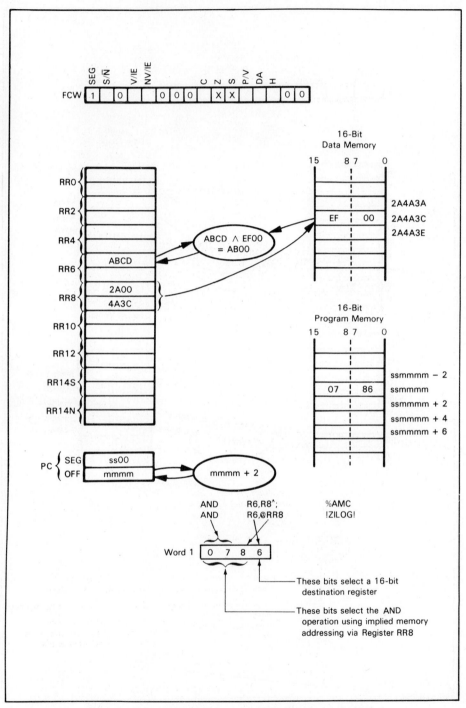

Figure 3-13. Implied Indirect Addressing in Segmented Mode

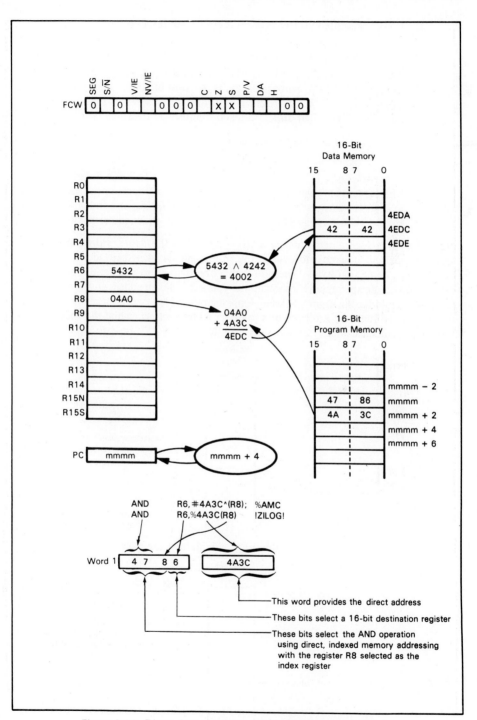

Figure 3-14. Direct, Indexed Addressing in Non-Segmented Mode

2. Long-segmented direct, indexed memory addressing:

```
AND     R6,SEGLABEL(R8);        % AMC syntax
AND     R6,<<%2A>>%4A3C(R8)     ! Zilog syntax !
```

The contents of register R6 is ANDed with the contents of the memory word in segmented $2A_{16}$, whose address is the sum of $4A3C_{16}$ and the contents of Index Register R8. The result is returned to register R6. Figure 3-15 illustrates long-segmented direct, indexed memory addressing.

3. Short-segmented direct, indexed memory addressing:

```
AND     R6,SEGLABEL(R6)%AMC syntax
AND     R6,|<<%2A>>%4A3C(R8)|            ! Zilog syntax !
```

The contents of register R6 is ANDed with the contents of the memory word in segment $2A_{16}$, whose address is the sum of 0036_{16} and Index Register R6. Figure 3-16 illustrates short-segmented direct, indexed memory addressing.

Note that long-segmented indexed addressing offers the same addressing range as short-segmented indexed addressing; the index, on its own, can address the entire offset space of 65,536 bytes. Therefore, the one-byte short-segmented base address offset is no handicap. Suppose, for example, you use indexed addressing to access a data table in the middle of a segment. Using long-segmented indexed addressing, the base of the data table might be provided by the direct address offset, while the Index register provides the displacement into the selected table:

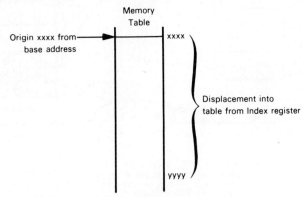

But you could just as easily have the index originate at the base of the segment:

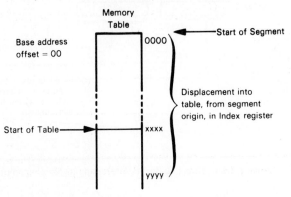

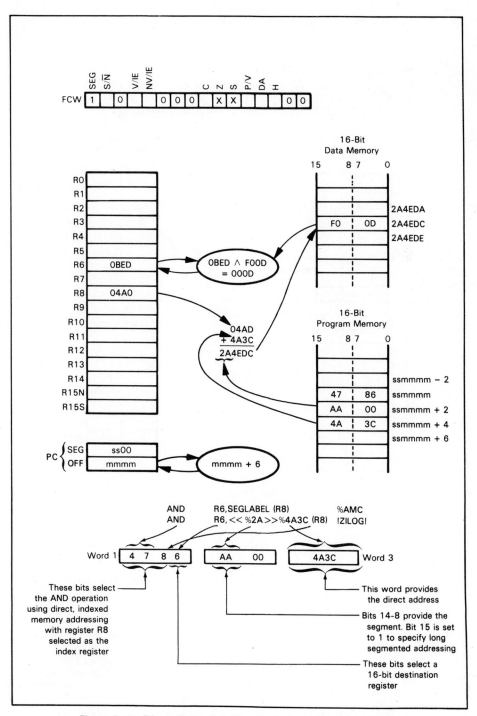

Figure 3-15. Direct, Indexed Addressing in Long-Segmented Mode

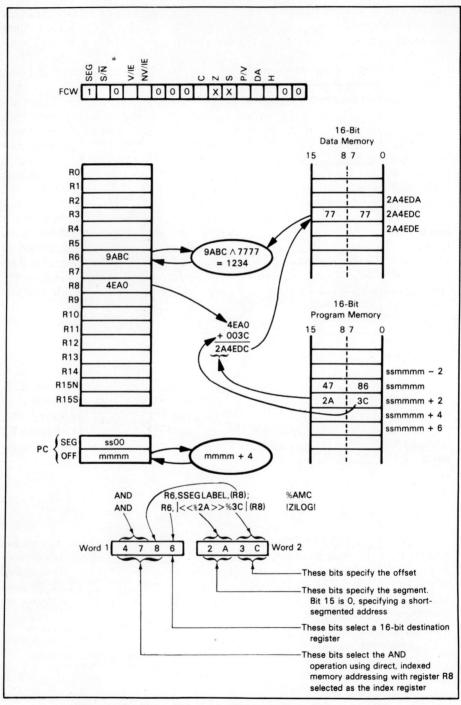

Figure 3-16. Direct, Indexed Addressing in Short-Segmented Mode

In Figure 3-14, register R8 contains the index $04A0_{16}$, which is added to the direct address $4A3C_{16}$ contained in the second word of the instruction's object code. Since non-segmented memory addressing is being used, the sum of $04A0_{16}$ and $4A3C_{16}$ provides the effective data memory address $4EDC_{16}$.

The contents of memory word $4EDC_{16}$ is ANDed with the contents of 16-bit register R6. The result is returned to 16-bit Register R6.

Figure 3-15 is a direct, indexed variation of Figure 3-8; if you compare the instruction object codes in these two figures, you will see that the only instruction object code change occurs in Word 1; the third hexadecimal digit, which was 0 for non-indexed direct memory addressing Figure 3-8, becomes 8 in Figure 3-15; this single object code change specifies direct, indexed memory addressing, with Register R8 functioning as Indexed Register. The SEG bit of the Flag and Control Word is set to 1 to specify segmented addressing. The high-order bit of Word 2 differentiates between long- and short-segmented direct addresses.

In Figure 3-15, the index taken from Register R8 is added to the direct address provided by the third word of the instruction object code; the segment number, taken from the second word of the instruction object code, is not modified by this addition. In Figure 3-15, the sum of the index and the base address do not generate a carry; but if R8 contained $F4A0_{16}$, rather than $04A0_{16}$, a carry would result. The carry would be discarded, since the index never modifies the segment number. This may be illustrated as follows:

$$\begin{array}{r} F4A0 \\ + \ 4A3C \\ \hline 3EDC \end{array}$$

carry discarded

The separation of segment number and offset during any address calculation is complete. For example, using short-segmented direct, indexed memory addressing, any carry resulting from the addition of the 8-bit direct address to the 16-bit index would be lost, rather than incrementing the segment number. If in Figure 3-16 Index Register R8 contained $FFF0_{16}$ rather $4EA0_{16}$, the following data memory address would be computed:

$$\begin{array}{r} FFF0 \\ + \ 003C \\ \hline 002C \end{array}$$

carry discarded

Direct index memory addressing, in all its variations, is used by byte, word and long word instructions. The fact that a byte or a long word of data memory is addressed has no effect whatsoever on the effective memory address computation. We discussed this subject in detail when describing direct memory addressing. To illustrate the point further, byte and long word instructions using direct, indexed memory addressing are illustrated in Figures 3-17 and 3-18.

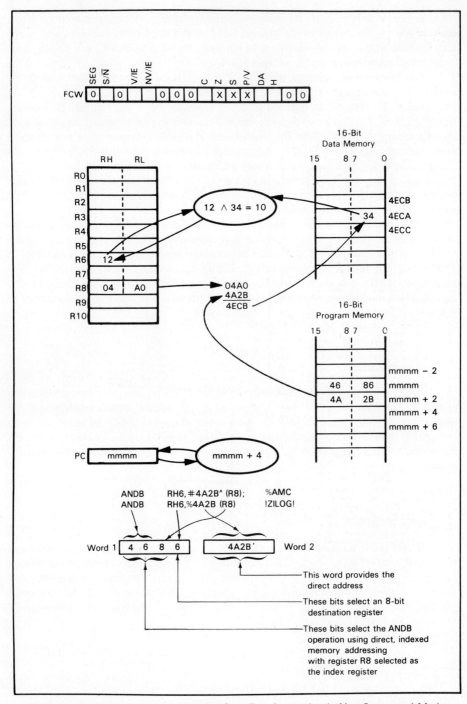

Figure 3-17. Direct, Indexed Addressing for a Byte Instruction in Non-Segmented Mode

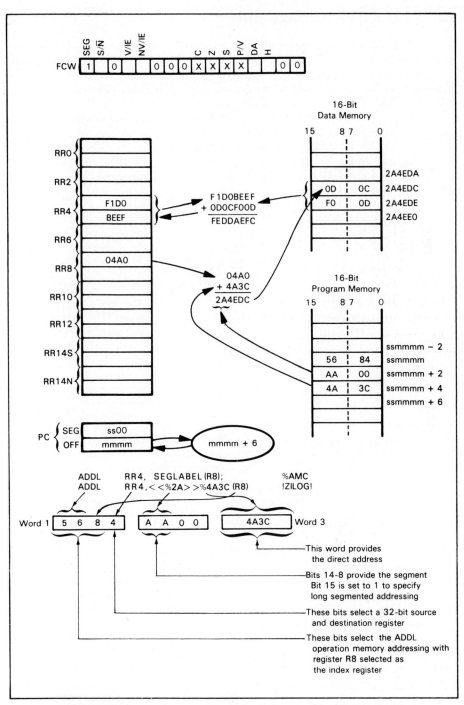

Figure 3-18. Direct, Indexed Addressing for a Long Word Instruction in Segmented Mode

BASE RELATIVE ADDRESSING

A few of the Z8000 primary memory reference instructions access data memory using base relative and base index addressing.

An instruction that specifies base relative addressing provides a 16-bit displacement in the second word of the instruction object code. This displacement is added to a base address held in general purpose registers.

In non-segmented mode there is no difference between base relative addressing and direct index addressing. Non-segmented base relative addressing adds a 16-bit value provided by the instruction object code to another 16-bit value taken from an Index Register. Although different words are used to describe the same components, direct indexed addressing in non-segmented mode does exactly the same thing. This may be illustrated as follows:

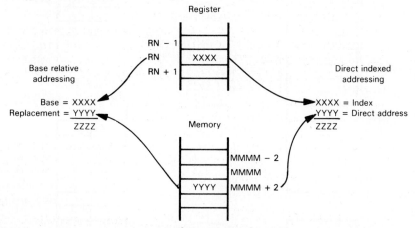

Different assembly language mnemonics are used to specify base relative addressing, as against index addressing, although in non-segmented mode the two are identical. The two sets of equivalent mnemonics may be illustrated as follows for an LD instruction in non-segmented mode:

```
LD      R4,#4A3C^(R8);    % AMC syntax
LD      R4,%4A3C(R8)      ! Zilog syntax !
LD      R4,R8^(#4A3C);    % AMC syntax
LD      R4,R8(#%4A3C)     ! Zilog syntax !
```

Both instructions will load into register R4 the contents of the memory word whose address is the sum of $4A3C_{16}$ and the contents of Register R8.

Although base relative addressing and direct indexed addressing are equivalent in non-segmented mode, it takes longer to compute a base relative address; you should therefore avoid using base relative addressing with the Z8002, or Z8001 executing in non-segmented mode.

When you use base relative addressing with the Z8001 in non-segmented mode, the segment number specified by the Program Counter continues to be used. Therefore base relative addressing in non-segmented mode allows the Z8001 microprocessor to address only the memory segment within which the base relative addressing instruction is located.

In segmented mode, base relative addressing and direct index addessing are not the same.

Segmented base relative addressing takes a base address from a thirty-two bit register pair. This base address specifies a data memory segment number. In contrast, long-segmented direct indexed addressing takes a thirty-two bit base address from the second and third work of the instruction object code. Consider these two variations of the same LD instruction:

```
LD      R4,SEGLABEL(R8)         % AMC syntax
LD      R4,<<%2A>>%4A3C(R8)     ! Zilog syntax !

LD      R4,RR8^(#04A0);         % AMC syntax
LD      R4,RR8(#%04A0)          ! Zilog syntax !
```

The first instruction uses long-segmented direct indexed addressing to access the same memory location as the second instruction, which specifies segmented base relative addressing. The first instruction, in fact, uses the exact same addressing logic as illustrated in Figure 3-15. The long-segmented base relative addressing instruction computes the same effective memory address, as illustrated in Figure 3-19.

Thus, long-segmented base relative addressing holds the data memory segment number in registers, where it can be modified under program control. Long-segmented direct indexed addressing holds the segment number in the instruction object code, which you should not modify if you are writing programs that conform to good programming practices.

There is no short-segmented version of base relative addressing, since a single 16-bit register cannot hold a short-segmented base address.

Although Figure 3-19 illustrates segmented base relative addressing accessing a single word of data memory, equivalent instructions can access a memory byte or long word. The effective memory address computation is identical for the three word sizes.

BASE INDEXED ADDRESSING

This is a minor variation of base relative addressing, which we have just described. An instruction that specifies base indexed addressing has a single 16-bit object-code word. The base address and the index are both held in registers.

We describe base indexed addressing as a companion of base relative addressing because the same few Z8000 instructions provide these two addressing options.

In non-segmented mode, base indexed addressing computes an effective data memory address by summing the contents of two 16- bit registers. Consider the following instruction:

```
LD      R2,R4^(R6);     % AMC syntax
LD      R2,R4(R6)       ! Zilog syntax !
```

An effective data memory address is computed by summing the contents of registers R6 and R8. Although one register is designated the base, while the other is designated the index, in non-segmented mode there is no difference between the two. The contents of the addressed data memory location are loaded into Register R2. This instruction is illustrated in Figure 3-20.

The Z8001, operating in non-segmented mode, continues to use the Program Counter segment with a base indexed address. Therefore non-segmented Z8001 base indexed addressing can only access locations within the current program segment.

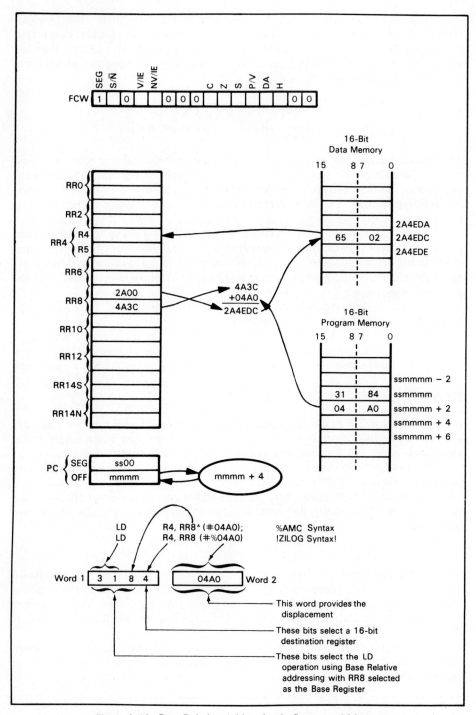

Figure 3-19. Base Relative Addressing in Segmented Mode

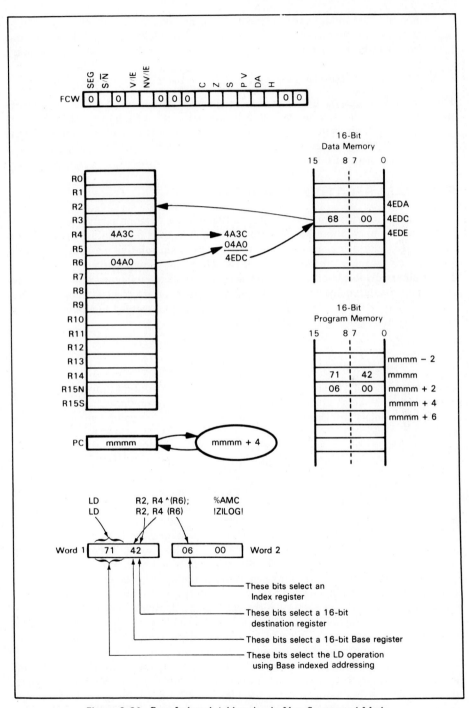

Figure 3-20. Base Indexed Addressing in Non-Segmented Mode

In segmented mode, base indexed addressing takes a base address, including a segment number, from one of the thirty-two bit registers RR2 through RR14; an index taken from a 16-bit register is added to the base. Consider the following instruction:

```
LD        R4,RR8^(R2)      % AMC
LD        R4,RR8(R2)       ! Zilog !
```

Figure 3-21 illustrates computation of this segmented base indexed address; it accesses the same memory location illustrated in Figure 3-19 for base relative addressing.

Note that there is no short-segmented version of a base indexed address, just as there is no short-segmented version of base relative addressing. In each case a thirty-two bit register pair must specify the base address.

PROGRAM RELATIVE ADDRESSING

A few primary memory reference instructions use program relative addressing to access data memory. Some Z8000 jump and branch instructions also use program relative memory addressing. **Instructions that use program relative memory addressing include a displacement in the instruction's object code. Some instructions provide a signed binary displacement; other instructions provide an unsigned binary displacement. This displacement will be added to, or subtracted from, the contents of the Program Counter, after the Program Counter has been incremented to address the next sequential instruction.**

Consider the following load relative instruction:

```
LDR       R2,^$-#0400;     % AMC syntax
LDR       R2,$-%0400       ! Zilog syntax !
```

This instruction will read 16 bits of data from a memory word that must be within the memory segment which holds the LDR instruction, and within the addressing range of a 16-bit signed binary displacement. Figure 3-22 illustrates the computation of this program relative address.

The Z8000 adds the displacement in the object code of the instruction ($FBFC_{16}$) to the value of the program counter after it has been incremented to address the next instruction.

However, the symbol $, for the assembler location counter, indicates the value of the location of the instruction in which the $ appears, *before* the program counter has been incremented, not the location of the next instruction.

In Figure 3-22, the memory word 400_{16} bytes before the beginning of the LDR instruction will be loaded. The LDR instruction occupies 4 bytes. Therefore, the object code displacement must be -404_{16} or $FBFC_{16}$ in twos complement notation.

When writing assembly language code, if you specify the displacement using the $ symbol, use the displacement from the beginning of the instruction. The assembler will automatically generate the correct object code displacement.

Although we have illustrated program relative addressing for a word instruction, there are equivalent long word and byte instructions. The same effective memory address computation is used for byte word or long word instructions.

Some instructions provide short displacements that are 7, 8 or 12 bits wide, and are part of a single instruction object code word. This short displacement is sometimes doubled, before being added to, or subtracted from, the Program Counter contents. In segmented mode the displacement is added to, or subtracted from, the offset word of the Program Counter.

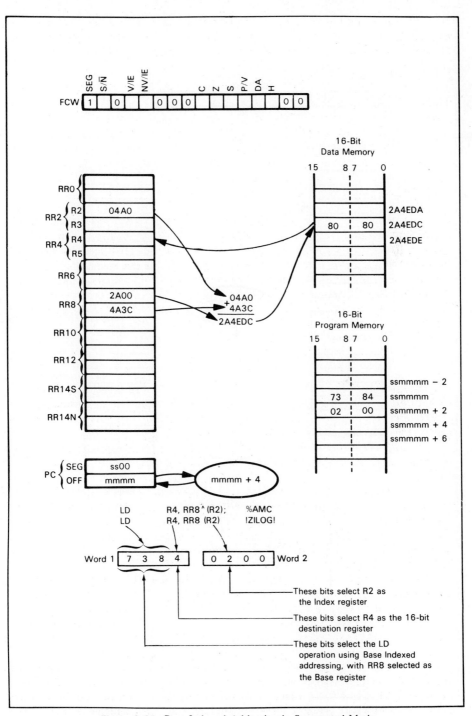

Figure 3-21. Base Indexed Addessing in Segmented Mode

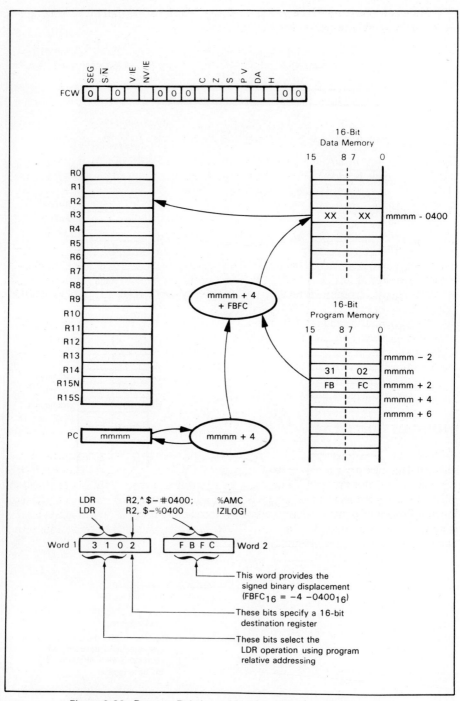

Figure 3-22. Program Relative Addressing with Long Displacement

Here is a summary of the program relative addressing variations to be found in the Z8000 assembly language instruction set:

CALR — A 12-bit signed binary displacement provided by the instruction object code is doubled, then subtracted from the incremented Program Counter.

DJNZ — A 7-bit unsigned binary displacement provided by the instruction object code is doubled, then subtracted from the incremented Program Counter.

JR — An 8-bit signed binary displacement provided by the instruction object code is doubled and added to the incremented Program Counter.

LDAR and LDR — A 16-bit signed binary displacement provided by the instruction object code is added to the incremented Program Counter. This displacement is not shifted before being added.

Consider the instruction:

```
JR      CY,^$+8;        % AMC syntax
JR      C,$+8           ! Zilog syntax !
```

If the carry status is true, the instruction above causes the displacement to be multiplied by two, then added to the Program Counter contents, after the Program Counter has been incremented to address the next sequential instruction. Figure 3-23 illustrates this jump relative instruction's address computation.

Program relative addressing does not have segmented and non-segmented versions. The displacement is always added to the Program Counter without modifying the segment number (if a segment number is present). Therefore in a segmented system, the branch will always occur within the current program segment.

Normally, program relative addressing is used with a label as the operand. The assembler automatically computes the displacement.

INDIRECT ADDRESSING

Certain variations of Z8000 jump, subroutine call and return instructions use selected data memory addressing modes to identify a memory location whose contents are loaded into the Program Counter, thus effecting a jump. These instructions, in effect, are using indirect addressing. In contrast, the standard jump instruction provides the new Program Counter contents within the instruction's object code or a register. To contrast these two addressing modes, Figure 3-24 illustrates an indirect addressing option, while Figure 3-25 illustrates a standard direct addressing jump.

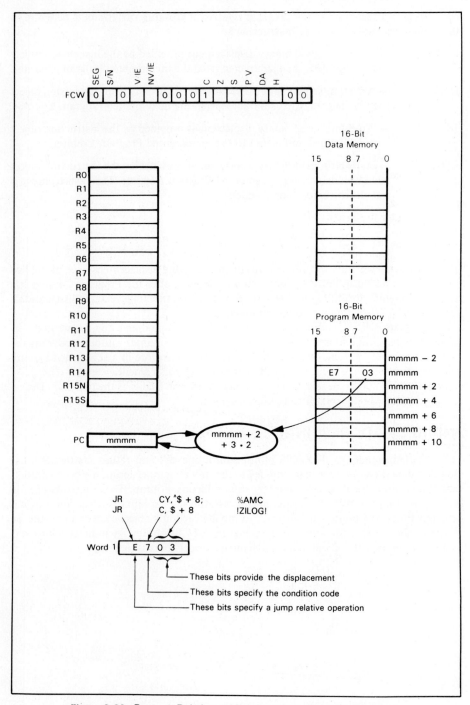

Figure 3-23. Program Relative Addressing with a Short Displacement

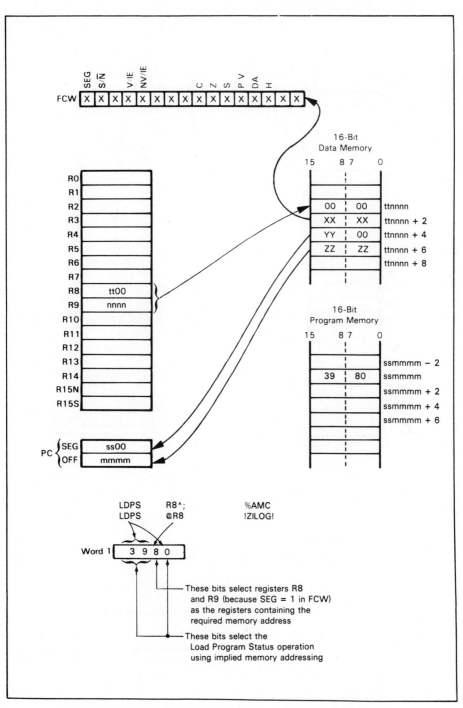

Figure 3-24. Equivalent to Indirect Addressing for a Jump Instruction

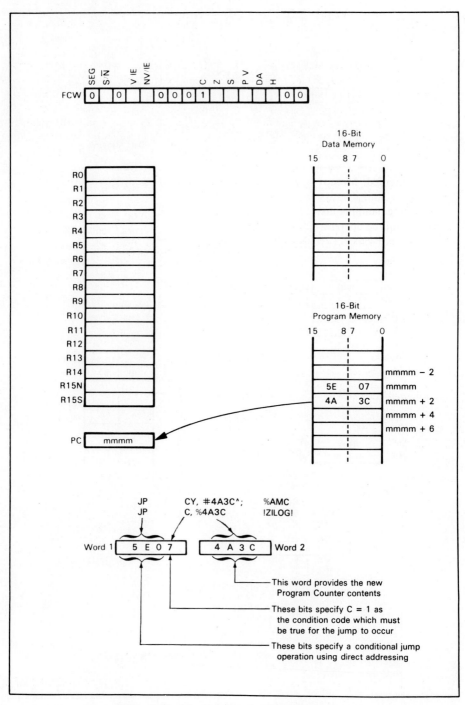

Figure 3-25. Direct Addressing Jump Instruction

STRING HANDLING INSTRUCTIONS

In the discussion which follows we define a "string" as any sequence of contiguous memory bytes, words, or long words that can be treated as a single unit of information, such that each element of the string can be operated on identically.

A characteristic of the Z8000 instruction set is that instructions which perform operations applicable to elements of a string have a set of standard variations designed to improve string handling efficiency. These variations use a Counter Register to define the length of a string remaining to be processed. The Counter Register, together with appropriate memory addresses, are automatically incremented or decremented. Moreover, within a single execution, an instruction may optionally process the entire string, or a single element of the string.

String handling instructions use register indirect (implied) memory addressing to specify a source operand and a destination operand. The string length is monitored by the Counter Register. This may be illustrated as follows:

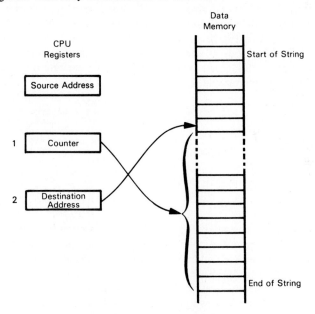

1   Initially specify entire string legth.
    Decrement each time a string element is processed.

2   Address current string element,
    then increment or decrement to
    address next string element

Standard variations of any string handling instruction offer the following options:

1. Perform the specified operation without any string handling options.

2. Perform the specified operation, decrement the Counter Register and the string address(es).

3. Perform the specified operation, decrement the Counter Register and increment the string address(es).

4. Perform the specified operation, decrement the Counter Register and string address(es), and repeat instruction execution until the Counter Register decrements to zero.

5. Perform the specified operation, decrement the Counter Register, increment the string address(es), and repeat instruction execution until the Counter Register decrements to zero.

The Counter Register always modifies the Overflow status. If the Counter Register does not contain zero after decrementing, P/V is reset to 0. When the Counter register has decremented to zero, however, P/V is set to 1.

Instruction variations 2) and 3) provide one step in an iterative loop which processes a string in some fashion. Variations 4) and 5) execute the entire loop within a single instruction. For example, the two-instruction loop:

```
                            ! Zilog syntax !
   LOOP:   LDD    @R2,@R3,R4   ! Move next word from source !
                            ! String to destination string !
                            ! Decrement string addresses !
                            ! and Counter Register !
           JR     NOV,LOOP     ! If Counter is not zero, return !
                            ! to LOOP !
```

is equivalent to this single instruction:

```
           LDDR   @R2,@R3,R4   ! Move source string to !
                            ! destination string !
```

There are occasions when additional operations must be performed on the string elements, over and above the operation performed by the string handling instruction. Options 2) and 3) allow such additional operations to be inserted between execution of the string instruction (LDD above), and subsequent test of Counter register contents to determine whether the entire string has been processed (JR above). Options 4) and 5) do not allow an additional steps to be inserted in this fashion.

Here is a summary of the Z8000 instructions that have the string handling variations described above:

Instruction	Decrement String Address(es)	Increment String Address(es)	Decrement Address(es) and repeat	Increment Address(es) and repeat
Compare				
CP	CPD	CPI	CPDR	CPIR
CPB	CPDB	CPIB	CPDRB	CPIRB
	CPSD	CPSI	CPSDR	CPSIR
	CPSDB	CPSIB	CPSDRB	CPSIRB
Input				
IN	IND	INI	INDR	INIR
INB	INDB	INIB	INDRB	INIRB
SIN	SIND	SINI	SINDR	SINIR
SINB	SINDB	SINIB	SINDRB	SINIRB
Load				
LD	LDD	LDI	LDDR	LDIR
LDB	LDDB	LDIB	LDDRB	LDIRB
Output				
OUT	OUTD	OUTI	OTDR	OTIR
OUTB	OUTDB	OUTIB	OTDRB	OTIRB
SOUT	OUTD	SOUTI	SOTDR	SOTIR
SOUTB	SOUTDB	SOUTIB	SOTDRB	SOTIRB
Translate				
	TRDB	TRIB	TRDRB	TRIRB
Translate and test				
	TRTDB	TRTIB	TRTDRB	TRTIRB

THE INSTRUCTION SET

Instructions often intimidate microcomputer users who are new to programming. Taken in isolation, the operations involved in the execution of a single instruction are usually easy to follow. We will isolate and explain these operations in the rest of this chapter.

Why are the instructions of a microcomputer referred to as an instruction "set"? Because the microcomputer designer selects (or at least should select) the instructions with great care; it must be easy to execute complex operations as a sequence of simple events, each of which is represented by one instruction from a well-designed instruction "set".

Table 3-5 summarizes the Z8000 microcomputer instruction set, with similar instructions grouped together. Individual instructions are listed numerically by object code in Table 3-6 and in alphabetic order by instruction mnemonic in Table 3-7.

You should use Table 3-5 once you understand the Z8000 instruction set. Refer to individual instruction descriptions when learning individual instructions, or when you are not sure how a particular instruction executes.

Abbreviations

The following abbreviations are used in Tables 3-5, 3-6, and 3-7:

addr	any 16-bit non-segmented address
addrls	any 32-bit long-segmented address
addrss	any 16-bit short-segmented address
adrsx	an address in the direct or direct indexed addressing modes
b8	immediate value in the range 0-7
b16	immediate value in the range 0-15
cc	condition codes, as summarized in Table 3-4
data8	8-bit immediate data value
data16	16-bit immediate data value
data32	32-bit immediate data value
disp	address displacement
epu	an Extended Processing Unit identifier: any of EPU0, EPU1, EPU2, or EPU3
FCW	the Flags and Control Word
FLAGS	low-order byte of FCW
flag	any or all of C, S, P, V, Z
int	either or both of NVI, VI
ioaddr	an I/O device 16-bit address
(I/O)	an identifier specifying that the prior address is an I/O address
MI	the MI signal input level
MO	the MO signal output level
MSB	the most significant (high-order) bit of any data value
n16	immediate value in the range 1-16
NSPOFF	Normal Stack Pointer offset
NSPSEG	Normal Stack Pointer segment
PC	Program Counter
PCOFF	Program Counter offset
PCSEG	Program Counter segment
PSAPOFF	Program Status Area Pointer offset
PSAPSEG	Program Status Area Pointer segment
rb	any byte register
rbd	any byte register serving as a destination
rbs	any byte register serving as a source
REFRESH	Refresh Counter
ri	any 16-bit index register
rid	any 16-bit register providing implied (register indirect) destination address
ris	any 16-bit register providing implied (register indirect) source address
rld	any 32-bit register serving as a destination
rls	any 32-bit register serving as a source
rqd	any 64-bit register serving as a destination
rw	any 16-bit register
rwd	any 16-bit register serving as a destination
rws	any 16-bit register serving as a source
SP	Stack Pointer (R15 or RR14)

Object Code:

aa	2-bit EPU identifier
b	immediate value corresponding to b8 or b16
c	condition code (see Table 3-4)
d	destination register
dddd	destination register
f	code for flags operated on: CZSP/V
h	high-order four bits of data 8
i	index or implied register. If i = 0 no register is specified
k	low-order four bits of data8
n	immediate value corresponding to n16, equal to n16-1
pppp	16-bit address word or most significant word of 32-bit address
qqqq	least significant word of 32-bit address

> Note: Where an address is shown as pppp qqqq, the qqqq word will be present for a long-segmented address; only the pppp word will be present for a non-segmented or short-segmented address.

r	register (see Table 3-8)
s	source register
ssss	source register
ttttttt	7-bit unsigned displacement
uu	any bit pattern
vv	code for interrupts (VI and/or NVI)
xx	8-bit address displacement
xxx	12-bit address displacement
xxxx	16-bit address displacement
yxyx	8-bit immediate data repeated in both bytes of a word
yy	8-bit immediate data
yyyy	16-bit immediate data or most significant word of 32-bit immediate data
zzzz	least significant word of 32-bit immediate data

Status flag

C	Carry status flag
Z	Zero status flag
S	Sign status flag
P	Parity status flag
V	Overflow status flag
D	Decimal-Adjust status flag
H	Half-Carry status flag
X	flag is affected by operation
(blank)	— flag is not affected by operation
1	flag is set by operation
0	flag is reset by operation
U	flag is undefined after operation

Operation Performed

[[]]	contents of the memory location or I/O port whose address is contained in the designated register
[]	contents of memory location, I/O port, or register
	data is transferred in the direct of the arrow
	data is exchanged between the designated locations on both sides of the arrows
OR	logical OR
	logical AND
+	logical Exclusive OR

Instruction Format

In Tables 3-5, 3-6, and 3-7 the instruction mnemonic and certain fixed parts of the operand field are shown in UPPER CASE: these parts are always used as shown. The variable parts of the operand field are shown in lower case, using the abbreviations listed above.

Instruction Object Codes

Instruction words are shown in Tables 3-6 and 3-7 as hexadecimal digits with 4-bit variable fields indicated by lower case letters (e.g., 67ib).

Instruction words with variable fields that are not multiples of 4 bits are shown as a pair of hexadecimal digits followed by 8 binary bits (e.g., 7C 000001vv).

Instruction Execution Times

Tables 3-5 and 3-6 list instructions execution times in clock periods. Real time is obtained by dividing the number of clock periods by the clock speed.

When several possible execution times are indicated (i.e., 15-19) the number of clock periods depends on addressing and segmentation modes. The relationship is as follows:

Addressing Mode	Clock Periods	
addr	x	The symbol x represents the minimum
addrss	y-3	clock periods of the range.
addrls	y-1	The symbol y represents the maximum
add(ri)	x + 1	clock periods of the range.
addrss(ri)	y-3	For example, if 15-19 clock periods are shown,
addrls(ri)	y	x = 15 and y = 19.

For two execution times (i.e., 10, 15) the first is for non-segmented mode, the second for segmented mode.

Instruction times which depend on condition flags are indicated with a slash (i.e., 13/7) with the first time(s) for condition met and the second for condition not met.

Table 3-5. A Summary of the Z8000 Instruction Set

Type	Mnemonic	Operand(s)	Op Code	Bytes	Clock Periods	H	D	V	P	S	Z	C	Operation Performed
O/I	IN*	rwd,@rw	3Dsd	2	10								[rwd] ← [[rw]](I/O)
	IN*	rwd,ioaddr	3Bd4 pppp	4	12								[rwd] ← [ioaddr](I/O) Input to 16-bit register rwd a data word from the I/O port addressed directly by ioaddr, or implied by rw.
	INB*	rbd,@rw	3Csd	2	10								[rbd] ← [[rw]](I/O)
	INB*	rbd,ioaddr	3Ad4 pppp	4	12								[rbd] ← [ioaddr](I/O) Input to 8-bit register rbd a data byte from the I/O port addressed directly by ioaddr, or implied by rw.
	IND*	@rid,@ris,rw	3Bs8 Ord8	4	21			X			U		[[rid]] ← [[ris]](I/O). [rid] ← [rid] − 2. [rw] ← [rw] − 1 If [rw] = 0 then V = 1. Otherwise V = 0.
	INDB*	@rid,@ris,rw	3As8 Ord8	4	21			X			U		[[rid]] ← [[ris]](I/O). [rid] ← [rid] − 1. [rw] ← [rw] − 1 If [rw] = 0 then V = 1. Otherwise V = 0. Input a 16-bit data word (for IND) or a data byte (for INDB) from the I/O port implied by ris to the memory word (for IND) or byte (for INDB) implied by rid. Decrement the implied memory address in rid by 2 (for IND) or by 1 (for INDB). Decrement the 16-bit counter rw by 1. If rw contains 0, set the Overflow status.
	INDR*	@rid,@ris,rw	3Bs8 Ord0	4	21/10**			X			U		[[rid]] ← [[ris]](I/O). [rid] ← [rid] − 2. [rw] ← [rw] − 1 If [rw] = 0 then V = 1. Otherwise reexecute.
	INDRB*	@rid,@ris,rw	3As8 Ord0	4	21/10**			X			U		[[rid]] ← [[ris]](I/O). [rid] ← [rid] − 1. [rw] ← [rw] − 1 If [rw] = 0 then V = 1. Otherwise reexecute. INDR and INDRB are identical to IND and INDB, respectively, except that INDR and INDRB are reexecuted until [rw] = 0.
	INI*	@rid,@ris,rw	3Bs0 Ord8	4	21			X			U		[[rid]] ← [[ris]](I/O). [rid] ← [rid] + 2. [rw] ← [rw] − 1 If [rw] = 0 then V = 1. Otherwise V = 0.
	INIB*	@rid,@ris,rw	3As0 Ord8	4	21			X			U		[[rid]] ← [[ris]](I/O). [rid] ← [rid] + 1. [rw] ← [rw] − 1 If [rw] = 0 then V = 1. Otherwise V = 0. INI and INIB are identical to IND and INDB, respectively, except that rid is incremented.
	INIR*	@rid,@ris,rw	3Bs0 Ord0	4	21/10**			X			U		[[rid]] ← [[ris]](I/O). [rid] ← [rid] + 2. [rw] ← [rw] − 1 If [rw] = 0 then V = 1. Otherwise reexecute.
	INIRB*	@rid,@ris,rw	3As0 Ord0	4	21/10**			X			U		[[rid]] ← [[ris]](I/O). [rid] ← [rid] + 1. [rw] ← [rw] − 1 If [rw] = 0 then V = 1. Otherwise reexecute INIR and INIRB are identical to INI and INIB, respectively, except that rid is incremented; also INIR and INIRB are reexecuted until [rw] = 0.
	OTDR*	@rid,@ris,rw	3BsA Ord0	4	21/10**			X			U		[[rid]](I/O) ← [[ris]]. [ris] ← [ris] − 2. [rw] ← [rw] − 1 If [rw] = 0 then V = 1. Otherwise reexecute.

* Privileged instruction — can be executed only in system mode.

** Number of clock periods depends on the number of repetitions for n/m**; n = minimum number of clock periods and m = number of clock periods added for each additional repetition of operation. The number of clock periods for an instruction which repeats k times is n + (k−1)•m.

Table 3-5. A Summary of the Z8000 Instruction Set (Continued)

Type	Mnemonic	Operand(s)	Op Code		Bytes	Clock Periods	Status								Operation Performed
							H	D	V	S	P	Z	C		
I/O (Continued)	OTDRB*	@rid,@ris,rw	3AsA	Ord0	4	21/10**			X			U		[[rid]](I/O) — [[ris]].[ris] − 1, [rw] — [rw] − 1. If [rw] = 0 then V = 1. Otherwise reexecute. Output a block of 16-bit words (for OTDR) or 8-bit bytes (for OTDRB) from memory to an I/O port. rw specifies the number of words or bytes. Memory is addressed, using implied memory addressing, by register ris, which is decremented after each output. 16-bit register rid specifies the I/O port.
	OTIR*	@rid,@ris,rw	3Bs2	Ord0	4	21/10**			X			U		[[rid]](I/O) — [[ris]].[ris] — [ris] + 2, [rw] — [rw] − 1. If [rw] = 0 then V = 1. Otherwise reexecute.
	OTIRB*	@rid,@ris,rw	3As2	Ord0	4	21/10**			X			U		[[rid]](I/O) — [[ris]].[ris] — [ris] + 1, [rw] — [rw] − 1. If [rw] = 0 then V = 1. Otherwise reexecute. OTIR and OTIRB are identical to OTDR and OTDRB, respectively, except that OTIR and OTIRB increment the memory address in ris.
	OUT*	@rw,rws	3Fds	pppp	2	10								[rw](I/O) — [rws]
	OUT*	ioaddr,rws	3Bs6	pppp	4	12								ioaddr(I/O) — [rws] Output the data word from 16-bit register rws to the I/O port addressed directly by ioaddr or implied by rw.
	OUTB*	@rw,rbs	3Eds	pppp	2	10								[rw](I/O) — [rbs]
	OUTB*	ioaddr,rbs	3As6	pppp	4	12								ioaddr(I/O) — [rbs] Output the data byte from 8-bit register rbs to the I/O port addressed directly by ioaddr or implied by rw.
	OUTD*	@rid,@ris,rw	3BsA	Ord8	4	21			X			U		[[rid]](I/O) — [[ris]].[ris] — [ris] − 2, [rw] — [rw] − 1 If [rw] = 0 then V = 1, otherwise V = 0.
	OUTDB*	@rid,@ris,rw	3AsA	Ord8	4	21			X			U		[[rid]](I/O) — [[ris]].[ris] — [ris] − 1, [rw] — [rw] − 1 If [rw] = 0 then V = 1; otherwise V = 0. Output a data word (for OUTD) or byte (for OUTDB) from the memory location addressed by register ris to the I/O port addressed by 16-bit register rid. Decrement ris by 2 (for OUTD) or 1 (for OUTDB). Decrement the counter 16-bit register rw.
	OUTI*	@rid,@ris,rw	3Bs2	Ord8	4	21			X			U		[[rid]](I/O) — [[ris]].[ris] — [ris] + 2, [rw] — [rw] − 1. If [rw] = 0 then V = 1; otherwise V = 0.
	OUTIB*	@rid,@ris,rw	3As2	Ord8	4	21			X			U		[[rid]](I/O) — [[ris]].[ris] — [ris] + 1, [rw] — [rw] − 1. If [rw] = 0 then V = 1; otherwise V = 0. OUTI and OUTIB are identical to OUTD and OUTDB, respectively, except that the memory address in ris is incremented.

*   Privileged instruction — can be executed only in system mode
** Number of clock periods depends on the number of repetitions for n/m**; n = minimum number of clock periods and m = number of clock periods added for each additional repetition of operation. The number of clock periods for an instruction which repeats k times is n + (k − 1)·m.

Table 3-5. A Summary of the Z8000 Instruction Set (Continued)

Type	Mnemonic	Operand(s)	Op Code	Bytes	Clock Periods	H	D	V	P	S	Z	C	Operation Performed
I/O (Continued)	SIN*	rwd,ioaddr	3Bd5 pppp	4	12								These instructions output "special I/O" status via ST0 - ST3: otherwise, they are identical to I/O instructions as follows:
	SINB*	rbd,ioaddr	3Ad5 ppp	4	12								SIN - IN(1) SINB - INB(1)
	SIND*	@rid,@ris,rw	3Bs9 0rd8	4	21			X			U		SIND - IND SINDB - INDB
	SINDB*	@rid,@ris,rw	3As9 0rd8	4	21/10**			X			U		SINDR - INDR SINDRB - INDRB
	SINDR*	@rid,@ris,rw	3Bs9 0rd0	4	21/10**			X			U		SINI - INI SINIB - INIB
	SINDRB*	@rid,@ris,rw	3As9 0rd0	4	21/10**			X			U		SINIR - INIR SINIRB - INIRB
	SINI*	@rid,@ris,rw	3Bs1 0rd8	4	21			X			U		DOTDR - OTDR DOTDRB - OTDRB
	SINIB*	@rid,@ris,rw	3As1 0rd8	4	21			X			U		SOTIR - OTIR SOTIRB - OTIRB
	SINIR*	@rid,@ris,rw	3Bs1 0rd0	4	21/10**			X			U		SOUT - OUT(1) SOUTB - OUTB(1)
	SINIRB*	@rid,@ris,rw	3As1 0rd0	4	21/10**			X			U		SOUTD - OUTD SOUTDB - OUTDB
	SOTDR*	@rid,@ris,rw	3BsB 0rd0	4	21/10**			X			U		SOUTI - OUTI SOUTIB - OUTIB
	SOTDRB*	@rid,@ris,rw	3AsB 0rd0	4	21/10**			X			U		(1)Only the direct addressing option exists for the special I/O version of this instruction.
	SOTIR*	@rid,@ris,rw	3Bs3 0rd0	4	21/10**			X			U		
	SOTIRB*	@rid,@ris,rw	3As3 0rd0	4	21/10**			X			U		
	SOUT*	ioaddr,rws	3Bs7 pppp	4	12								
	SOUTB*	ioaddr,rbs	3As7 pppp	4	12								
	SOUTD*	@rid,@ris,rw	3BsB 0rd8	4	21			X			U		
	SOUTDB*	@rid,@ris,rw	3AsB 0rd8	4	21			X			U		
	SOUTI	@rid,@ris,rw	3Bs3 0rd8	4	21			X			U		
	SOUTIB	@rid,@ris,rw	3As3 0rd8	4	21			X			U		
Primary Memory Reference	LD	rwd,adrsx	61id pppp qqqq	4/6	9-13								[rwd] ← [adrsx]
	LD	rwd,@ris	21id	2	7								[rwd] ← [[ris]] Load data from the 16-bit memory word addressed by adrsx or [ris] into 16-bit register rwd.
	LD	rwd,ris(disp)	31id xxxx	4	14								[rwd] ← [[ris] + disp] Load into 16-bit register rwd the contents of the 16-bit memory word addressed using base relative addressing.
	LD	rwd,ris(rw)	71id 0r00	4	14								[rwd] ← [[ris] + [rw]] Load into 16-bit register rwd the contents of the 16-bit memory word addressed using implied, indexed addressing.
	LDB	rbd,adrsx	60id pppp qqqq	4/6	9-13								[rbd] ← [adrsx]
	LDB	rbd,@ris	20id	2	7								[rbd] ← [[ris]] Load into 8-bit register rbd the contents of the memory byte addressed by adrsx or [ris].

* Privileged instruction — can be executed only in system mode.

** Number of clock periods depends on the operation. The number of repetitions for n/m**: n = minimum number of clock periods and m = number of clock periods added for each additional repetition of operation. The number of clock periods for an instruction which repeats k times is n + (k−1)·m.

Table 3-5. A Summary of the Z8000 Instruction Set (Continued)

Type	Mnemonic	Operand(s)	Op Code			Bytes	Clock Periods	Status							Operation Performed
								H	D	V	P	S	Z	C	
Primary Memory Reference (Continued)	LDB	rbd,ris(disp)	30id	xxxx		4	14								[rbd] ← [[ris] + disp] Load into 8-bit register rbd the contents of the memory byte addressed using base relative addressing.
	LDB	rbd,ris(rw)	70id	0r00		4	14								[rbd] ← [[ris] + [rw]] Load into 8-bit register rbd the contents of the memory byte addressed using implied, indexed addressing.
	LDL LDL	rld,adrsx rld,@ris	54id 14id	pppp	qqqq	4/6 2	12-16 11								[rld] ← [adrsx] [rld] ← [[ris]] Load into 32-bit register rld the contents of the 32-bit memory location addressed by adrsx or [ris].
	LDL	rld,ris(disp)	35id	xxxx		4	17								[rld] ← [[ris] + disp] Load into 32-bit register rld the contents of the 32-bit memory location addressed using base relative addressing.
	LDL	rld,ris(rw)	75id	0r00		4	17								[rld] ← [[ris] + [rid]] Load into 32-bit register rld the contents of the 32-bit memory location addressed using implied, indexed addressing.
	LD LD	adrsx,rws @rid,rws	6Fis 2Fds	pppp	qqqq	4/6 2	11-15 8								[adrsx] ← [rws] [[rid]] ← [rws] Store data from 16-bit register rws into memory word addressed by adrsx or [rid].
	LD	rid(disp),rws	33is	xxxx		4	14								[[rid] + disp] ← [rws] Store data from 16-bit register rws into memory word addressed using base relative addressing.
	LD	rid(rw),rws	73is	0r00		4	14								[[rid] + [rw]] ← [rws] Store data from 16-bit register rws into memory word addressed using implied, indexed addressing.
	LDB LDB	adrsx,rbs @rid,rbs	6Eis 2Eds	pppp	qqqq	4/6 2	11-15 8								[adrsx] ← [rbs] [[rid]] ← [rbs] Store data from 8-bit register rbs into memory byte addressed by adrsx or [rid].
	LDB	rid(disp),rbs	32is	xxxx		4	14								[[rid] + disp] ← [rbs] Store data from 8-bit register rbs into memory byte addressed using base relative addressing.

*   Privileged instruction — can be executed only in system mode.

** Number of clock periods depends on the number of repetitions for n/m**; n = minimum number of clock periods and m = number of clock periods added for each additional repetition of operation. The number of clock periods for an instruction which repeats k times is n + (k−1)·m.

Table 3-5. A Summary of the Z8000 Instruction Set (Continued)

Type	Mnemonic	Operand(s)	Op Code	Bytes	Clock Periods	H	D	V	P	S	Z	C	Operation Performed
Primary Memory Reference (Continued)	LDB	rid(rw),rbs	72is	4	14								[[rid] + [rw]] ← [rbs] Store data from 8-bit register rbs into memory byte addressed using implied, indexed addressing.
	LDL	adrsx,rls	5Dis pppp qqqq	4/6	14-18								[adrsx] ← [rls] Store data from 32-bit register rls into 32-bit memory long word addressed by adrsx or [rid].
	LDL	@rid,rls	1Dds	2	11								[[rid]] ← [rls]
	LDL	rid(disp),rls	37is	4	17								[[rid] + disp] ← [rls] Store data from 32-bit register rls into 32-bit memory long word addressed using base relative addressing.
	LDL	rid(rw),rls	77is	4	17								[[rid] + [rw]] ← [rls] Store data from 32-bit register rls into 32-bit memory long word addressed using implied, indexed addressing.
	LDA	rwd,adrsx	76id	4	12-13								[rwd] ← adrsx Load the non-segmented address into 16-bit register rwd.
	LDA	rid,adrsx	76id pppp qqqq	4/6	15-16								[rid] ← adrsx Load the segmented address, in segmented address format, into 32-bit register rid.
	LDA	rwd,ris(disp)	34id xxxx	4	15								[rwd] ← [ris] + disp
	LDA	rid,ris(disp)	34id xxxx	4	15								[rid] ← [ris] + disp Load the base relative address into 16-bit register rwd (nonsegmented mode) or 32-bit register rid (segmented mode).
	LDA	rwd,ris(rw)	74id 0r00	4	15								[rwd] ← [ris] + [rw]
	LDA	rid,ris(rw)	74id 0r00	4	15								[rid] ← [ris] + [rw] Load the implied, indexed memory address into 16-bit regiser rwd (nonsegmented mode) or 32-bit register rid (segmented mode).
	LDAR	rwd,disp16	340d xxxx	4	15								[rwd] ← [PC] + disp16 Load the program relative memory address into 16-bit register rwd.
	LDAR	rid,disp16	340d xxxx	4	15								[rid] ← [PC] + disp16 Load the program relative segmented memory address, in segmented format, into 32-bit register rid.
	LDR	rwd,disp16	310d xxxx	4	14								[rwd] ← [[PC] + disp16]
	LDRB	rbd,disp16	300d xxxx	4	14								[rbd] ← [[PC] + disp16]

* Privileged instruction — can be executed only in system mode.

** Number of clock periods depends on the number of repetitions for n/m**; n = minimum number of clock periods and m = number of clock periods added for each additional repetition of operation. The number of clock periods for an instruction which repeats k times is n + (k−1)·m.

Table 3-5. A Summary of the Z8000 Instruction set (Continued)

Type	Mnemonic	Operand(s)	Op Code	Bytes	Clock Periods	H	D	V	P	S	Z	C	Operation Performed
Primary Memory Reference (Continued)	LDRL	rld,disp16	350d xxxx	4	17								[rld] ← [[PC] + disp16] Load the memory word (for LDR), byte (for LDRB) or long word (for LDRL) addressed using program relative addressing into the 16-bit, 8-bit or 32-bit register.
	LDR	disp16,rws	330s xxxx	4	14								[[PC] + disp16] ← [rws]
	LDRB	disp16,rbs	320s xxxx	4	14								[[PC] + disp16] ← [rbs]
	LDRL	disp16,rls	370s xxxx	4	17								[[PC] + disp16] ← [rls] Load the register word (for LDR), byte (for LDRB) or long word (for LDRL) into the memory location addressed using program relative addressing.
Secondary Memory Reference	ADD	rwd,@ris	01id	2	7			×		×	×	×	[rwd] ← [rwd] + [[ris]]
	ADD	rwd,adrsx	41id pppp qqqq	4/6	9-13			×		×	×	×	[rwd] ← [rwd] + [adrsx] Add the contents of the addressed memory word to the 16-bit destination register.
	ADDB	rbd,@ris	00id	2	7	×	0	×		×	×	×	[rbd] ← [rbd] + [[ris]]
	ADDB	rbd,adrsx	40id pppp qqqq	4/6	9-13	×	0	×		×	×	×	[rbd] ← [rbd] + [adrsx] Add the contents of the addressed memory byte to the 8-bit destination register.
	ADDL	rld,@ris	16id	2	14			×		×	×	×	[rld] ← [rld] + [[ris]]
	ADDL	rld,adrsx	56id pppp qqqq	4/6	15-19			×		×	×	×	[rld] ← [rld] + [adrsx] Add the contents of the addressed memory long word to the 32-bit destination register.
	AND	rwd,@ris	07id	2	7				×	×	×		[rwd] ← [rwd] AND [[ris]]
	AND	rwd,adrsx	47id pppp qqqq	4/6	9-13				×	×	×		[rwd] ← [rwd] AND [adrsx] AND contents of destination 16-bit register with contents of memory word
	ANDB	rbd,@ris	06id	2	7				×	×	×		[rbd] ← [rbd] AND [[ris]]
	ANDB	rbd,adrsx	46id pppp qqqq	4/6	9-13				×	×	×		[rbd] ← [rbd] AND [adrsx] AND contents of destination 8-bit register with contents of memory byte.
	CLR	@rid	0Dd8	2	8								[[rid]] ← 0
	CLR	adrsx	4Di8 pppp	4/6	11-15								[adrsx] ← 0 Clear the memory word.
	CLRB	@rid	0Cd8	2	8								[[rid]] ← 0

*   Privileged instruction — can be executed only in system mode.

**   Number of clock periods depends on the number of repetitions for n/m**; n = minimum number of clock periods and m = number of clock periods added for each additional repetition of operation. The number of clock periods for an instruction which repeats k times is n + (k − 1)·m.

Table 3-5. A Summary of the Z8000 Instruction Set (Continued)

Type	Mnemonic	Operand(s)	Op Code	Bytes	Clock Periods	H	D	V	P	S	Z	C	Operation Performed
Secondary Memory Reference (Continued)	CLRB	adrsx	4Ci8 pppp qqqq	4/6	11-15								[adrsx] ← 0 / Clear the memory byte
	COM	@rid	0Dd0 pppp	2	12					×	×		[rid]] ← [[rid]]
	COM	adrsx	4DiO pppp qqqq	4/6	15-19					×	×		[adrsx] ← [[adrsx]] / Ones complement the memory word
	COMB	@rid	0Cd0 pppp	2	12				×	×	×		[rid]] ← [[rid]]
	COMB	adrsx	4CiO pppp qqqq	4/6	15-19				×	×	×		[adrsx] ← [[adrsx]] / Ones complement the memory byte
	CP	rwd,@ris	0Bid pppp	2	7			×		×	×	×	[rwd] ← [[ris]]
	CP	rwd,adrsx	4Bid pppp qqqq	4/6	9-13			×		×	×	×	[rwd] ← [adrsx]]
	CPB	rbd,@ris	0Aid pppp	2	7			×		×	×	×	[rbd] ← [[ris]]
	CPB	rbd,adrsx	4Aid pppp qqqq	4/6	9-13			×		×	×	×	[rbd] ← [adrsx]]
	CPL	rld,@ris	10id pppp	2	14			×		×	×	×	[rld] ← [[ris]]
	CPL	rld,adrsx	50id pppp qqqq	4/6	15-19			×		×	×	×	[rld] ← [adrsx]]
													Compare contents of register and memory location. Do not modify contents of register or memory location, but set status flags. Use 16-bit register/memory word for CP. 8-bit register/memory byte for CPB. 32-bit register/memory long word for CPL.
	CP	@rid,data16	0Dd1 yyyy pppp	4	11			×		×	×	×	[[rid]] – data16
	CP	adrsx,data16	4Di1 yyyy pppp qqqq	6/8	14-18			×		×	×	×	[adrsx] – data16
	CPB	@rid,data8	0Cd1 yxvx pppp	4	11			×	×	×	×	×	[[rid]] – data8
	CPB	adrsx,data8	4Ci1 yxvx pppp qqqq	6/8	14-18			×	×	×	×	×	[adrsx] – data8
													Compare contents of memory location with immediate data. Do not modify memory location, but set status flags. Use 16-bit memory word for CP. 8-bit memory byte for CPB.
	DEC	@rid,n16	2Bdn pppp	2	11			×		×	×		[rid]] ← [[rid]] – n16
	DEC	adrsx,n16	6Bin pppp qqqq	4/6	13-17			×		×	×		[adrsx] ← [adrsx]] – n16
	DECB	@rid,n16	2Adn pppp	2	11			×		×	×		[rid]] ← [[rid]] – n16
	DECB	adrsx,n16	6Ain pppp qqqq	4/6	13-17			×		×	×		[adrsx] ← [adrsx]] – n16
													Subtract the immediate value n16 from the memory word (for DEC) or memory byte (for DECB) addressed by adrsx or [rid]. Values in the range 1-16 are subtracted.

* Privileged instruction — can be executed only in system mode.

** Number of clock periods depends on the number of repetitions for n/m***: n = minimum number of clock periods and m = number of clock periods added for each additional repetition of operation. The number of clock periods for an instruction which repeats k times is n + (k−1)·m.

Table 3-5. A Summary of the Z8000 Instruction Set (Continued)

Type	Mnemonic	Operand(s)	Op Code	Bytes	Clock Periods	H	D	V	P	S	Z	C	Operation Performed
Secondary Memory Reference (Continued)	DIV	rld,@ris	1Bid	2	note 1			X		X	X	X	Divide
	DIV	rld,adrsx	5Bid pppp qqqq	4/6	note 1			X		X	X	X	Divide } see text for a discussion of these instructions
	DIVL	rqd,@ris	1Aid	2	note 1			X		X	X	X	Divide long
	DIVL	rqd,adrsx	5Aid pppp qqqq	4/6	15-19			X		X	X	X	Divide long
	EX	rwd,adrsx	6Did pppp qqqq	4/6	15-19								[rwd] — [adrsx]
	EX	rwd,@ris	2Dsd	2	12								[rwd] — [[ris]]
	EXB	rbd,adrsx	6Cid pppp qqqq	4/6	15-19								[rbd] — [adrsx]
	EXB	rbd,@ris	2Csd	2	12								[rbd] — [[ris]]
													Exchange contents of the addressed memory location with the selected register. Use 8-bit (for EXB) or 16-bit (for EX) registers and memory locations.
	INC	@rid,n16	29dn	2	11			X		X	X		[[rid]] — [[rid]] + n16
	INC	adrsx,n16	69dn pppp qqqq	4/6	13-17			X		X	X		[adrsx] — [adrsx] + n16
	INCB	@rid,n16	28dn	2	11			X		X	X		[[rid]] — [[rid]] + n16
	INCB	adrsx,n16	68dn pppp qqqq	4/6	13-17			X		X	X		[adrsx] — [adrsx] + n16
													Add the immediate value n16 to the memory word (for INC) or memory byte (for INCB) addressed by adrsx or [rid]. Values in the range 1 - 16 are added.
	MULT	rld,@ris	19id	2	note 2			O		X	X	X	Multiply
	MULT	rld,adrsx	59id pppp qqqq	4/6	note 2			O		X	X	X	Multiply } see text for a discussion of these instructions
	MULTL	rqd,@ris	18id	2	note 2			O		X	X	X	Multiply long
	MULTL	rqd,adrsx	58id pppp qqqq	4/6	12			O		X	X	X	Multiply long
	NEG	@rid	0Dd2	2	12			X		X	X	X	[[rid]] — − [[rid]]
	NEG	adrsx	4Di2 pppp qqqq	4/6	15-19			X		X	X	X	[adrsx] — − [adrsx]
	NEGB	@rid	0Cd2	2	12			X		X	X	X	[[rid]] — − [[rid]]
	NEGB	adrsx	4Ci2 pppp qqqq	4/6	15-19			X		X	X	X	[adrsx] — − [adrsx]
													Replace the contents of the memory word (for NEG) or byte (for NEGB) addressed by adrsx or [rid] with its twos complement.
	OR	rwd,@ris	05id	2	7				X	X	X		[rwd] — [rwd] OR [[ris]]
	OR	rwd,adrsx	45id pppp qqqq	4/6	9-13				X	X	X		[rwd] — [rwd] OR [adrsx]
													OR the contents of the specified 16-bit register and memory word. Place the result in the 16-bit register.
	ORB	rbd,@ris	04id	2	7				X	X	X		[rbd] — [rbd] OR [[ris]]

* Privileged instruction — can be executed only in system mode.

** Number of clock periods depends on the number of repetitions for n/m**. n = minimum number of clock periods and m = number of clock periods added for each additional repetition of operation. The number of clock periods for an instruction which repeats k times is n + (k − 1)·m.

Table 3-5. A Summary of the Z8000 Instruction Set (Continued)

Type	Mnemonic	Operand(s)	Op Code	Bytes	Clock Periods	H	D	V	P	S	Z	C	Operation Performed
Secondary Memory Reference (Continued)	ORB	rbd,adrsx	44id pppp	4/6	9-13				x	x	x		[rbd] ← [rbd] OR [adrsx]. OR the contents of the specified 8-bit register and memory byte. Place the result in the 8-bit register.
	SUB	rwd,@ris	03id	2	7			x		x	x	x	[rwd] ← [rwd] − [[ris]]
	SUB	rwd,adrsx	43id pppp qqqq	4/6	9-13			x		x	x	x	[rwd] ← [rwd] − [adrsx]
	SUBB	rbd,@ris	02id	2	7	x	1	x		x	x	x	[rbd] ← [rbd] − [[ris]]
	SUBB	rbd,adrsx	42id pppp qqqq	4/6	9-13	x	1	x		x	x	x	[rbf] ← [rbd] − [adrsx]
	SUBL	rld,@ris	12id	2	14			x		x	x	x	[rld] ← [rld] − [[ris]]
	SUBL	rld,adrsx	52id pppp qqqq	4/6	15-19			x		x	x	x	[rld] ← [rld] − [adrsx]. Subtract the contents of the addressed memory location from the selected destination register. Use 8-bit (for SUBB), 16-bit (for SUB) or 32-bit (for SUBL) memory locations and registers.
	TEST	@rid	0Dd4	2	8					x	x		[[rid]] OR 0
	TEST	adrsx	4Di4 pppp qqqq	4/6	11-15					x	x		[adrsx] OR 0
	TESTB	@rid	0Cd4	2	8				x	x	x		[[rid]] OR 0
	TESTB	adrsx	4Ci4 pppp qqqq	4/6	11-15				x	x	x		[adrsx] OR 0
	TESTL	@rid	1Cd0	2	13					x	x		[[rid]] OR 0
	TESTL	adrsx	5Ci0 pppp qqqq	4/6	16-20					x	x		[adrsx] OR 0. OR the specified memory contents with 0. Set status flags. Use a 16-bit location for TEST, an 8-bit location for TESTB, and a 32-bit location for TESTL.
	TSET	@rid	0Dd6	2	11					x			[s] ← [[rid]](MSB). [[rid]] ← FFFF
	TSET	adrsx	4Di6 pppp qqqq	4/6	14-18					x			[s] ← [adrsx](MSB). [adrsx] ← FFFF
	TSETB	@rid	0Cd6	2	11					x			[s] ← [[rid]](MSB). [[rid]] ← FF
	TSETB	adrsx	4Ci6 pppp qqqq	4/6	14-18					x			[s] ← [adrsx](MSB). [adrsx] ← FF. Move the most significant bit of the memory word (for TSET) or byte (for TSETB) to the sign status. Then fill the word or byte with 1 bits.
	XOR	rwd,@ris	09id	2	7					x	x		[rwd] ← [rwd] XOR [[ris]]
	XOR	rwd,adrsx	49id pppp qqqq	4/6	9-13					x	x		[rwd] ← [rwd] XOR [adrsx]
	XORB	rbd,@ris	08id	2	7				x	x	x		[rbd] ← [rbd] XOR [[ris]]
	XORB	rbd,adrsx	48id pppp qqqq	4/6	9-13				x	x	x		[rbd] ← [rbd] XOR [adrsx]. Exclusive OR the contents of the addressed memory location and register. Store the result in the register. Use 16-bit memory and registers for XOR. Use 8-bit memory and registers for XORB.

* Privileged instruction — can be executed only in system mode.

** Number of clock periods depends on the number of repetitions for n/m**; n = minimum number of clock periods and m = number of clock periods added for each additional repetition of operation. The number of clock periods for an instruction which repeats k times is n + (k−1)•m.

Table 3-5. A Summary of the Z8000 Instruction Set (Continued)

Type	Mnemonic	Operand(s)	Op Code	Bytes	Clock Periods	H	D	V	P	S	Z	C	Operation Performed
Immediate	LD	rwd,data16	210d yyyy	4	7								[rwd] ← data16; Load 16-bit immediate data into 16-bit register rwd.
	LD	@rid,data16	0Dd5 yyyy	4	11								[rid] ← data16; Load 16-bit immediate data into memory word addressed by rwd.
	LD	adrsx,data16	4Di5 yyyy pppp qqqq	6/8	14-18								[adrsx] ← data16; Load 16-bit immediate data into memory word addressed by adrsx or [rid].
	LDB	rbd,data8	Cdyy	2	5								[rbd] ← data8; Load immediate data byte into 8-bit register rbd.
	LDB	@rid,data8	0Cd5 yxyx	4	11								[rid] ← data8; Load immediate data byte into memory byte addressed by rid.
	LDB	adrsx,data8	4Ci5 yxyx pppp qqqq	6/8	14-18								[adrsx] ← data8; Load immediate data byte into memory byte addressed by adrsx or [rid].
	LDL	rld,data32	140d yyyy zzzz	6	11								[rld] ← data32; Load 32-bit immediate data into 32-bit register rld.
	LDK	rwd,b16	BDdb	2	5								[rwd] ← b16; Load the immediate 4-bit value b16 into the low-order four bits of rwd. Clear the remaining twelve bits of rwd.
	PUSH												(See Stack operations).
Jump	JP	@rid	1Ed8	2	10,15								[PC] ← [[rid]]
	JP	adrsx	5Ei8 pppp qqqq	4/6	7-11								[PC] ← [adrsx]; Jump to the specified memory location. This is the same as a conditional jump with cc = always true.
	JR	disp	E8xx	2	6								[PC] ← [PC] + (disp·2); Jump program relative. PC is incremented to the next sequential instruction before disp·2 is added as a signed binary number. This is the same as a conditional jump relative with cc = always true (blank).
	LDPS*	@ris	39s0	2	12 / 16	X	X	X	X	X	X	X	[FCW] ← [[ris]]. [PC] ← [[ris] + 2] (nonsegmented); [FCW] ← [[ris] + 2]. [PCSEG] ← [[ris] + 4]; [PCOFF] ← [[ris] + 6] (segmented)
	LDPS*	adrsx	79i0 pppp qqqq	4/6	16-17 / 20-23	X	X	X	X	X	X	X	[FCW] ← [adrsx]. [PC] ← [adrsx+2] (nonsegmented); [FCW] ← [adrsx+2]. [PCSEG] ← [adrsx+4]; [PCOFF] ← [adrsx+6] (segmented); Load program status and jump as described in accompanying text.

* Privileged instruction — can be executed only in system mode.

** Number of clock periods depends on the number of repetitions for n/m**; n = minimum number of clock periods and m = number of clock periods added for each additional repetition of operation. The number of clock periods for an instruction which repeats k times is n + (k−1)·m.

Table 3-5. A Summary of the Z8000 Instruction Set (Continued)

Type	Mnemonic	Operand(s)	Op Code	Bytes	Clock Periods	H	D	V	P	S	Z	C	Operation Performed
Subroutine Call and Return	CALL	@rid	1Fd0	2	10,15								(1) or (2), [PC] ← [[rid]]
	CALL	adrsx	5Fi0 pppp	4/6	12-21								(1) or (2), [PC] ← [adrsx]
	CALR	disp	Dxxx qqqq	2	10,15								(1) or (2), [PC] ← [PC] − disp·2 Program relative memory address. Call the addressed subroutine, saving information on the Stack as follows: (1) [SP] ← [SP] − 2, [[SP]] ← [PC] 16-bit PC (nonsegmented) (2) [SP] ← [SP] − 4, [[SP]] ← [PC] 32-bit PC (segmented)
	RET	cc	9E0c	2	10,13/7								If cc is "true" then [PC] ← [[SP]]. [SP] ← [SP] + 2 (for nonsegmented) or [SP] ← [SP] + 4 (for segmented). If the condition code specified by cc is "true", return from subroutine.
	SC	data8	7Fyy	2	33,39								System subroutine call. See accompanying text for a description of this instruction.
Immediate Operate	ADD	rwd,data16	010d yyyy	4	7			X		X	X	X	[rwd] ← [rwd] + data16
	ADDB	rbd,data8	000d yxyx	4	7	X	0	X		X	X	X	[rbd] ← [rbd] + data8
	ADDL	rrd,data32	160d yyyy zzzz	6	14			X		X	X	X	[rrd] ← [rrd] + data32 Add immediate data to the destination register. Use 32-bit data/register for ADDL, 16-bit data/register for ADD, 8-bit data/register for ADDB.
	AND	rwd,data16	070d yyyy	4	7					X	X		[rwd] ← [rwd] AND data16
	ANDB	rbd,data8	060d yxyx	4	7				X	X	X		[rbd] ← [rbd] AND data8 AND immediate data with destination register contents. Use 16-bit data/register for AND, 8-bit data/register for ANDB.
	CP	rwd,data16	0B0d yyyy	4	7			X		X	X	X	[rwd] − data16 Compare 16-bit register contents with immediate 16-bit data. Do not modify register contents, but save Status flags.
	CPB	rbd,data8	0A0d yxyx	4	7			X		X	X	X	[rbd] − data8 Compare 8-bit register contents with immediate 8-bit data. Do not modify register contents, but save Status flags.
	CPL	rld,data32	100d yyyy zzzz	6	14			X		X	X	X	[rld] − data32 Compare 32-bit register contents with immediate 32-bit data. Do not modify register contents, but save Status flags.
	CP												(See secondary memory reference for memory-immediate compare instructions.)
	DIV	rld,data16	1B0d yyyy	4	note 1			X		X	X	X	Divide ⎫ see accompanying text for a discussion of these
	DIVL	rqd,data32	1A0d yyyy zzzz	6	note 1			X		X	X	X	Divide long ⎭ instructions

* Privileged instruction — can be executed only in system mode.

** Number of clock periods depends on the number of repetitions for n/m**; n = minimum number of clock periods and m = number of clock periods added for each additional repetition of operation. The number of clock periods for an instruction which repeats k times is n + (k−1)·m.

Table 3-5. A Summary of the Z8000 Instruction Set (Continued)

Type	Mnemonic	Operand(s)	Op Code			Bytes	Clock Periods	H	D	V	P	S	Z	C	Operation Performed
Immediate Operate (Continued)	MULT	rld,data16	190d	yyyy		4	note 2			0		X	X	X	Multiply ⎰ see accompanying text for a discussion of these
	MULTL	rqd,data32	180d	yyyy	zzzz	6	note 2			0		X	X	X	Multiply long ⎱ instructions
	OR	rwd,data16	050d	yyyy		4	7					X	X		[rwd] — [rwd] OR data16 / OR the contents of the specified 16-bit register with the immediate data word.
	ORB	rbd,data8	040d	yxyx		4	7				X	X	X		[rbd] — [rbd] OR data8 / OR the contents of the specified 8-bit register with the immediate data byte.
	SUB	rwd,data16	030d	yyyy		4	7			X		X	X	X	[rwd] — [rwd] — data16
	SUBB	rbd,data8	020d	yxyx		4	7	X		X		X	X	X	[rbd] — [rbd] — data8
	SUBL	rld,data32	120d	yyyy	zzzz	6	14		1	X		X	X	X	[rld] — [rld] — data32 / Subtract immediate data from the destination register. Use 32-bit data/register for SUBL, 16-bit data/register for SUB, 8-bit data/register for SUBB.
	XOR	rwd,data16	090d	yyyy		4	7					X	X		[rwd] — [rwd] XOR data16
	XORB	rbd,data8	080d	yxyx		4	7				X	X	X		[rbd] — [rbd] XOR data8 / Exclusive-OR the contents of the register with immediate data. Store the result in the register. Use 16-bit register and data for XOR. Use 8-bit register and data for XORB.
Branch/Jump on Condition	DJNZ	rw,disp	Fr	1tttttt		2	11								[rw] — [rw] − 1. [PC] — [PC] + 2. If [rw] is not 0, then [PC] — [PC] − [disp·2]
	DBJNZ	rb,disp	Fr	0tttttt		2	11								[rb] — [rb] − 1. [PC] — [PC] + 2. If [rb] is not 0, then [PC] — [PC] − [disp·2] / Decrement a 16-bit register (for DJNZ) or an 8-bit register (for DBJNZ). Increment the Program Counter as per normal operation. If the decremented register contents is not 0, then subtract twice the displacement, as an unsigned binary number, from the incremented Program Counter, causing a branch back to a lower program memory address. If the decremented register contents is 0, continue execution with the next instruction.

* : Privileged instruction — can be executed only in system mode.
:: : Number of clock periods depends on the number of repetitions for n/m**. n = minimum number of clock periods for n/m**. m = number of clock periods added for each additional repetition of operation. The number of clock periods for an instruction which repeats k times is n + (k−1)·m.

Table 3-5. A Summary of the Z8000 Instruction Set (Continued)

Type	Mnemonic	Operand(s)	Op Code	Bytes	Clock Periods	H	D	V	P	S	Z	C	Operation Performed
Branch/Jump on Condition (Continued)	JP	cc,@rid	1Edc	2	10,15/7								If cc is true, [PC] ← [[rid]]
	JP	cc,adrsx	5Eic pppp qqqq	4/6	7-11								If cc is true, [PC] ← [adrsx]. Jump to the memory location specified by adrsx or [rid] if condition code cc is true.
	JR	cc,disp	Ecxx	2	6								If cc is true, [PC] ← [PC] + (disp·2). Jump program relative if condition code is true. PC is incremented to address the next sequential instruction before disp·2 is added as a signed binary number.
Register-Register Move	EX	rwd,rws	ADsd	2	6								[rwd] ← [rws]
	EXB	rbd,rbs	ACsd	2	6								[rbd] ← [rbs] Exchange registers' contents for 16-bit (EX) or 8-bit (EXB) registers.
	LD	rwd,rws	A1sd	2	3								[rwd] ← [rws]
	LDB	rbd,rbs	AOsd	2	3								[rbd] ← [rbs]
	LDL	rld,rls	94sd	2	5								[rld] ← [rls] Move data between any two 16-bit registers (for LD). 8-bit registers (for LDB) or 32-bit registers (for LDL).
Block Transfer and Search	CPD	rwd,@ris,rw,cc	BBs8 Ordc	4	20			×			×	U	[rwd] − [[ris]], Z = 1. If cc true, Z = 1. If [rw] − [rw] − 1. If [rw] = 0, V = 1; otherwise V = 0. If cc false, Z = 0.
	CPDB	rbd,@ris,rw,cc	BAs8 Ordc	4	20			×			×	U	[rbd] − [[ris]]. If cc true, Z = 1. If [rw] − [rw] − 1. If [rw] = 0, V = 1; otherwise V = 0. If cc false, Z = 0. Search a string for a condition. Compare a word in rwd (for CPD) or a byte in rbd (for CPDB) with the next word (for CPD) or byte (for CPDB) in a memory string, using implied memory addressing. Register and memory contents are not modified, nor are Status flags changed, but status conditions are compared with cc. If cc is true, Z is set to 1; otherwise Z is reset to 0. Decrement the implied memory address in ris by 2 for CPD, or by 1 for CPDB. Decrement 16-bit counter rw by 1. If rw is 0, set V to 1; otherwise reset V to 0.
	CPDR	rwd,@ris,rw,cc	BBsC Ordc	4	20/9**			×		U	×	U	See CPD.
	CPDRB	rbd,@ris,rw,cc	BAsC Ordc	4	20/9**			×		U	×	U	See CPDB. CPD and CPDB are identical to CPD and CPDB, respectively, except that instruction execution is repeated until either Z or V status is 1. Interrupts will be acknowledged between reexecutions.

* Privileged instruction — can be executed only in system mode.

** Number of clock periods depends on the number of repetitions for n/m**; n = minimum number of clock periods and m = number of clock periods added for each additional repetition of operation. The number of clock periods for an instruction which repeats k times is n + (k−1)·m.

Table 3-5. A Summary of the Z8000 Instruction Set (Continued)

Type	Mnemonic	Operand(s)	Op Code	Bytes	Clock Periods	H	D	V	P	S	Z	C	Operation Performed
Block Transfer and Search (Continued)	CPI	rwd,@ris,rw,cc	BBsO	4	20			X		U	X	U	[rwd] − [[ris]]. If cc true, Z = 1. If cc false, Z = 0. [ris] − [ris] + 2. [rw] − [rw] − 1. If [rw] = 0, V = 1; otherwise V = 0.
	CPIB	rbd,@ris,rw,cc	BAsO	4	20			X		U	X	U	[rbd] − [[ris]]. If cc true, Z = 1. If cc false, Z = 0. [ris] − [ris] + 1. [rw] − [rw] − 1. If [rw] = 0, V = 1; otherwise V = 0. CPI and CPIB are identical to CPD and CPDB, respectively, except that the implied memory address in ris is incremented by 2 for CPI, or by 1 for CPIB
	CPIR	rwd,@ris,rw,cc	BBs4	4	20/9**			X		U	X	U	See CPI.
	CPIRB	rbd,@ris,rw,cc	BAs4	4	20/9**			X		U	X	U	See CPIB. CPIR and CPIRB are identical to CPD and CPDB, respectively, except that the implied memory address in ris is incremented by 2 for CPI, or by 1 for CPIB, and instruction execution is repeated until either Z or V status is 1. Interrupts will be acknowleged between reexecutions.
	CPSD	@rid,@ris,rw,cc	BBsA	4	25			X		U	X	U	[ris] − [[rid]]. If cc true, Z = 1. If cc false, Z = 0. [rid] − [rid] − 2. [ris] − [ris] − 2. [rw] − [rw] − 1. If [rw] = 0, V = 1; otherwise V = 0.
	CPSDB	@rid,@ris,rw,cc	BAsA	4	25			X		U	X	U	[rid] − [[ris]]. If cc true, Z = 1. If cc false, Z = 0. [rid] − [rid] − 1. [ris] − [ris] − 1. [rw] − [rw] − 1. If [rw] = 0, V = 1; otherwise V = 0. Compare two strings for a condition. Compare the next word (for CPSD) or byte (for CPSDB) in a source string with the next word (for CPSD) or byte (for CPSDB) in a destination string. Both strings are addressed using implied memory addressing. No memory contents are modified, nor are any Status flags changed, but status conditions are compared with cc. If cc is true, Z is set to 1. Otherwise Z is reset to 0. Decrement the implied memory addresses in ris and rid by 2 for CPSD, or by 1 for CPSDB. Decrement 16-bit counter rw by 1. If rw is 0, set V to 1. Otherwise reset V to 0.
	CPSDR	@rid,@ris,rw,cc	BBsE	4	25/14**			X		U	X	U	See CPSD.
	CPSDRB	@rid,@ris,rw,cc	BAsE	4	25/14**			X		U	X	U	See CPSDB. CPSDR and CPSDRB are identical to CPSD and CPSDB, respectively, except that the instructions are reexecuted until either Z or V status is 1. Interrupts are acknowleged between reexecutions.

* Privileged instruction — can be executed only in system mode.

** Number of clock periods depends on the number of repetitions for n/m**. n = minimum number of clock periods and m = number of clock periods added for each additional repetition of operation. The number of clock periods for an instruction which repeats k times is $n + (k-1) \cdot m$.

Table 3-5. A Summary of the Z8000 Instruction Set (Continued)

Type	Mnemonic	Operand(s)	Op Code		Bytes	Clock Periods	Status								Operation Performed
							H	D	V	P	S	Z	C		
Block Transfer and Search (Continued)	CPSI	@rid,@ris,rw,cc	BBs2	Ordc	4	25			X		U	X	U	[[rid]] − [[ris]]. If cc is true Z = 1. If cc is false, Z = 0. [rid] ← [rid] + 2. [ris] ← [ris] + 2. [rw] ← [rw] − 1. If [rw] = 0, V = 1; otherwise V = 0.
	CPSIB	@rid,@ris,rw,cc	BAs2	Ordc	4	25			X		U	X	U	[[rid]] − [[ris]]. If cc is true, Z = 1. If cc is false, Z = 0. [rid] ← [rid] + 1. [ris] ← [ris] + 1. [rw] ← [rw] − 1. If [rw] = 0, V = 1; otherwise V = 0. CPSI and CPSIB are identical to CPSD and CPSDB, respectively, except that the implied memory addresses in rid and ris are incremented by 2 (for CPSI) or by 1 (for CPSIB).
	CPSIR	@rid,@ris,rw,cc	BBs6	Ordc	4	25/14**			X		U	X	U	See CPSI.
	CPSIRB	@rid,@ris,rw,cc	BAs6	Ordc	4	25/14**			X		U	X	U	See CPSIB. CPSIR and CPSIRB are identical to CPSD and CPSDB, respectively, except that the implied memory addresses in rid and ris are incremented by 2 (for CPSIR) or by 1 (for CPSIRB) and the instructions are reexecuted until either Z or V status is 1. Interrupts are acknowledged between reexecutions.
	LDD	@rid,@ris,rw	BBs9	Ord8	4	20			X			U		[[rid]] ← [[ris]]. [rid] ← [rid] − 2. [ris] ← [ris] − 2. [rw] ← [rw] − 1. If [rw] = 0, V = 1; otherwise V = 0.
	LDDB	@rid,@ris,rw	BAs9	Ord8	4	20			X			U		[[rid]] ← [[ris]]. [rid] ← [rid] − 1. [ris] ← [ris] − 1. [rw] ← [rw] − 1. If [rw] = 0, V = 1; otherwise V = 0. Transfer a word (for LDD) or a byte (for LDDB) from the memory location addressed by register ris to the memory location addressed by rid. Decrement addresses in rid and ris by 2 (for LDD) or 1 (for LDDB). Decrement the counter rw by 1. If rw contains 0, set the Overflow status to 1.
	LDDR	@rid,@ris,rw	BBs9	OrdO	4	20/9**			1			U		[[rid]] ← [[ris]]. [rid] ← [rid] − 2. [ris] ← [ris] − 2. [rw] ← [rw] − 1. If [rw] ≠ 0, reexecute. If [rw] = 0, V = 1 and end execution.
	LDDRB	@rid,@ris,rw	BAs9	OrdO	4	20/9**			1			U		[[rid]] ← [[ris]]. [rid] ← [rid] − 1. [ris] ← [ris] − 1. [rw] ← [rw] − 1. If [rw] ≠ 0, reexecute. If [rw] = 0, V = 1 and end execution. LDDR and LDDRB are identical to LDD and LDDB, respectively, except that LDDR and LDDRB reexecute until rw has decremented to 0.
	LDI	@rid,@ris,rw	BBs1	Ord8	4	20			X			U		[[rid]] ← [[ris]]. [rid] ← [rid] + 2. [ris] ← [ris] + 2. [rw] ← [rw] − 1. If [rw] = 0 then V = 1; otherwise V = 0.

* Privileged instruction — can be executed only in system mode.

** Number of clock periods depends on the number of repetitions for n/m**. n = minimum number of clock periods and m = number of clock periods added for each additional repetition of operation. The number of clock periods for an instruction which repeats k times is n + (k − 1)·m.

Table 3-5. A Summary of the Z8000 Instruction Set (Continued)

Type	Mnemonic	Operand(s)	Op Code		Bytes	Clock Periods	H	D	V	P	S	Z	C	Operation Performed
	LDIB	@rid, @ris, rw	BAs1	0rd8	4	20			×				U	[rid] ← [[ris]]. [rid] ← [rid] + 1. [ris] ← [ris] + 1. [rw] ← [rw] − 1. If [rw] = 0, then V = 1; otherwise V = 0. LDI and LDIB are identical to LDD and LDDB, respectively, except that the source and destination addresses ris and rid are incremented by 2 (for LDI) or 1 (for LDIB).
	LDIR	@rid, @ris, rw	BBs1	0rd0	4	20/9**			1				U	[rid] ← [[ris]]. [rid] ← [rid] + 2. [ris] ← [ris] + 2. [rw] ← [rw] − 1. If [rw] ≠ 0 then reexecute. [rw] = 0 then V = 1 and end execution.
	LDIRB	@rid, @ris, rw	BAs1	0rd0	4	20/9**			1				U	[rid] ← [[ris]]. [rid] ← [rid] + 1. [ris] ← [ris] + 1. [rw] ← [rw] − 1. If [rw] ≠ 0 then reexecute. If [rw] = 0 then V = 1 and end execution. LDIR and LDIRB are identical to LDD and LDDB, respectively, except that the source and destination addresses ris and rid are incremented; also, LDIR and LDIRB are reexecuted until rw decrements to 0.
	LDM	rwd, @ris, n16	1Cs1	0d0n	4	14/3**								[rwd] ← [[ris]] do n16 times incrementing register and memory addresses
	LDM	rwd, adrsx, n16	5Ci1	0d0n pppp qqqq	6/8	17-21/3**								[rwd] ← [adrsx] do n16 times incrementing register and memory addresses. Move a block of n16 memory words from memory to 16-bit registers. adrsx or @ris addresses the first, lowest addressed memory word. rwd addresses the first 16-bit register. n16 can have any value from 1 to 16. (See accompanying text for more details.)
	LDM	@ris, rws, n16	1Cd9	0s0n	4	14/3**								[[ris]] ← [rws] do n16 times incrementing register and memory addresses
	LDM	adrsx, rws, n16	5Ci9	0s0n pppp qqqq	6/8	17-21/3**								[adrsx] ← [rws] do n16 times incrementing register and memory addresses. This instruction is identical to the one above, except that data moves from registers to memory. Register contents are not affected.
	TRDB	@rid, @ris, rw	B8d8	0rs0	4	25			×				U	[rid] ← [[ris] + [[rid]]. [rw] ← [rw] − 1. [rid] ← [rid] − 1. Translate a memory byte, as described in the accompanying text. Decrement the destination address in rid and the byte counter in rw. If rw = 0, set V to 1. If rw ≠ 0, reset V to 0. Byte register RH1 contents is lost.

Type: Block Transfer and Search (Continued)

* Privileged instruction — can be executed only in system mode.
** Number of clock periods depends on the number of repetitions for n/m**; n = minimum number of clock periods and m = number of clock periods added for each additional repetition of operation. The number of clock periods for an instruction which repeats k times is n + (k−1)·m.

Table 3-5. A Summary of the Z8000 Instruction Set (Continued)

Type	Mnemonic	Operand(s)	Op Code	Bytes	Clock Periods	H	D	V	P	S	Z	C	Operation Performed
Block Transfer and Search (Continued)	TRDRB	@rid,@ris,rw	B8dC	0rs0	4	25/14**			1			U		[[rid]] ← [[ris] + [[rid]]. [rw] ← [rw] − 1. [rid] ← [rid] − 1. If [rw] = 0, V = 1 and end execution. If [rw] ≠ 0, reexecute. This instruction is identical to TRDB, except the instruction is reexecuted until [rw] = 0.
	TRIB	@rid,@ris,rw	B8d0	0rs0	4	25			x			U		[[rid]] ← [[ris] + [[rid]]. [rw] ← [rw] − 1. [rid] ← [rid] + 1. TRIB is identical to TRDB except that the destination address in rid is incremented.
	TRIRB	@rid,@ris,rw	B8d4	0rs0	4	25/14**			1			U		[[rid]] ← [[ris] + [[rid]]. [rw] ← [rw] − 1. [rid] ← [rid] + 1. If [rw] = 0, V = 1 and end execution. If [rw] ≠ 0, reexecute. TRIRB is identical to TRDB except that the destination address in rid is incremented; also, TRIRB is reexecuted until [rw] = 0.
	TRTDB	@rid,@ris,rw	B8dA	0rs0	4	25			x			x		[RH1] ← [[ris] + [[rid]]. [rw] ← [rw] − 1. [rid] ← [rid] − 1. Load a table byte into 8-bit register RH1, as described in the accompanying text. Reset Z status to 0 if [RH1] ≠ 0. Set Z status to 1 if [RH1] = 0. Decrement destination address rid and byte counter rw. If rw = 0, V = 1. If rw ≠ 0, V = 0.
	TRTDRB	@rid,@ris,rw	B8dE	0rsE	4	25/14**			x			x		[RH1] ← [[ris] + [[rid]]. [rw] ← [rw] − 1. [rid] ← [rid] − 1. If [rw] = 0, V = 1. If [rw] ≠ 0, V = 0. If [RH1] = 0, Z = 1; otherwise Z = 0. TRTDRB is identical to TRTDB except that TRTDRB is reexecuted until V = 1 or Z = 0.
	TRTIB	@rid,@ris,rw	B8d2	0rs0	4	25			x			x		[RH1] ← [[ris] + [[rid]]. [rw] ← [rw] − 1. [rid] ← [rid] + 1. TRTIB is identical to TRTDB except that TRTIB increments the destination address in rid.
	TRTIRB	@rid,@ris,rw	B8d6	0rsE	4	25/14**			x			x		[RH1] ← [[ris] + [[rid]]. [rw] ← [rw] − 1. [rid] ← [rid] + 1. If [rw] = 0, V = 1. If [rw] ≠ 0, V = 0. If [RH1] = 0, Z = 1; otherwise Z = 0. TRTIRB is identical to TRTIRB except that TRTIRB increments the destination address in rid and reexecutes until V = 1 or Z = 0.

* Privileged instruction — can be executed only in system mode.

** Number of clock periods depends on the number of repetitions for n/m**, n = minimum number of clock periods and m = number of clock periods added for each additional repetition of operation. The number of clock periods for an instruction which repeats k times is n + (k−1)•m.

Table 3-5. A Summary of the Z8000 Instruction Set (Continued)

Type	Mnemonic	Operand(s)	Op Code	Bytes	Clock Periods	H	D	V	P	S	Z	C	Operation Performed
	ADC	rwd,rws	B5sd	2	5	X		X		X	X	X	[rwd] ← [rwd] + [rws] + C
	ADCB	rbd,rbs	B4sd	2	5	X	0	X		X	X	X	[rbd] ← [rbd] + [rbs] + C. Add the source register contents plus the initial Carry to the destination register. Use 16-bit registers for ADC. Use 8-bit registers for ADCB.
	ADD	rwd,rws	81sd	2	4	X		X		X	X	X	[rwd] ← [rwd] + [rws]
	ADDB	rbd,rbs	80sd	2	4	X	0	X		X	X	X	[rbd] ← [rbd] + [rbs]
	ADDL	rld,rls	96sd	2	8			X		X	X	X	[rld] ← [rld] + [rls]. Add the Source register contents to the Destination register. Use 32-bit registers for ADDL, 16-bit registers for ADD and 8-bit registers for ADDB.
	AND	rwd,rws	87sd	2	4					X	X		[rwd] ← [rwd] AND [rws]
	ANDB	rbd,rbs	86sd	2	4				X	X	X		[rbd] ← [rbd] AND [rbs]. AND the Source register contents with the Destination register contents. Use 16-bit registers for AND and 8-bit registers for ANDB
	CP	rwd,rws	8Bsd	2	4			X		X	X	X	[rwd] − [rws]. Compare 16-bit register contents by subtracting the Source register from the Destination register values. Do not modify any register contents, but set Status flags.
	CPB	rbd,rbs	8Asd	2	4			X		X	X	X	[rbd] − [rbs]. Compare 8-bit register contents by subtracting the Source register from the Destination register values. Do not modify any register contents, but set Status flags.
	CPL	rld,rls	90sd	2	8			X		X	X	X	[rld] − [rls]. Compare 32-bit register contents by subtracting the Source register from the Destination register values. Do not modify any register contents, but set Status flags.

Type: Register-Register Operate

* Privileged instruction — can be executed only in system mode.
** Number of clock periods depends on the number of repetitions for n/m**: n = minimum number of clock periods and m = number of clock periods added for each additional repetition of operation. The number of clock periods for an instruction which repeats k times is n + (k−1)•m.

Table 3-5. A Summary of the Z8000 Instruction Set (Continued)

Type	Mnemonic	Operand(s)	Op Code	Bytes	Clock Periods	H	D	V	P	S	Z	C	Operation Performed
Register-Register Operate	DIV	rld,rws	9Bsd	2	note 1			X		X	X	X	Divide 32-bit destination register contents by 16-bit source operand. Remainder goes to the first 16 bits of the destination register; quotient to second 16 bits of destination register.
	DIVL	rqd,rls	9Asd	2	note 1			X		X	X	X	Divide 64-bit destination register contents by 32-bit source operand. Remainder goes to the first 32 bits of the destination register; quotient to second 32 bits of destination register.
	MULT	rld,rws	99sd	2	note 2			0		X	X	X	Multiply contents of second 16 bits of 32-bit destination register by 16-bit source operand. Result to 32-bit destination register.
	MULTL	rqd,rls	98sd	2	note 2			0		X	X	X	Multiply contents of second 32 bits of 64-bit destination register by 32-bit source operand. Result goes to 64-bit destination register.

* Privileged instruction — can be executed only in system mode.
** Number of clock periods depends on the number of repetitions for n/m**: n = minimum number of clock periods and m = number of clock periods added for each additional repetition of operation. The number of clock periods for an instruction which repeats k times is n + (k−1)·m.

Table 3-5. A Summary of the Z8000 Instruction Set (Continued)

Type	Mnemonic	Operand(s)	Op Code	Bytes	Clock Periods	H	D	V	P	S	Z	C	Operation Performed
Register-Register Operate (Continued)	OR	rwd,rws	85sd	2	4					X	X		[rwd] ← [rwd] OR [rws]
	ORB	rbd,rbs	84sd	2	4				X	X	X		[rbd] ← [rbd] OR [rbs] OR the contents of the Source register with the Destination register contents. Use 16-bit registers for OR and 8-bit register for ORB
	RLDB	rbd,rbs	BEsd	2	9					X	X		Left rotate BCD digits in two 8-bit registers specified by rbd and rbs. The same register cannot be specified for rbd and rbs. Digits are rotated as follows:
	RRDB	rbd,rbs	BCsd	2	9					X	X		Right rotate BCD digits in two 8-bit registers specified by rbd and rbs. The same register cannot be specified for rbd and rbs. Digits are rotated as follows:
	SBC	rwd,rws	B7sd	2	5			X		X	X	X	[rwd] ← [rwd] − [rws] − C
	SBCB	rbd,rbs	B6sd	2	5	X	1	X		X	X	X	[rbd] ← [rbd] − [rbs] − C Subtract the Source register contents, plus the initial Carry, from the Destination register contents using twos complement arithmetic. Use 16-bit registers for SBC. Use 8-bit registers for SBCB.

* Privileged instruction — can be executed only in system mode.

** Number of clock periods depends on the number of repetitions for n/m**; n = minimum number of clock periods and m = number of clock periods added for each additional repetition of operation. The number of clock periods for an instruction which repeats k times is n + (k−1)·m.

Table 3-5. A Summary of the Z8000 Instruction Set (Continued)

Type	Mnemonic	Operand(s)	Op Code	Bytes	Clock Periods	H	D	V	P	S	Z	C	Operation Performed
Register-Register Operate (Continued)	SUB	rwd,rws	83sd	2	4	X		X		X	X	X	[rwd] ← [rwd] − [rws]
	SUBB	rbd,rbs	82sd	2	4	X	1	X		X	X	X	[rbd] ← [rbd] − [rbs] Subtract the Source register contents from the Destination register. Use 32-bit registers for SUBL. 16-bit registers for SUB. 8-bit registers for SUBB.
	SUBL	rld,rls	92sd	2	8								[rld] ← [rld] − [rls]
	XOR	rwd,rws	89sd	2	4					X	X		[rwd] ← [rwd] XOR [rws] Exclusive-OR the contents of Source and Destination registers. Store the result in the Destination register. Use 16-bit registers for XOR. Use 8-bit registers for XORB.
	XORB	rbd,rbs	88sd	2	4				X	X	X		[rbd] ← [rbd] XOR [rbs]
Register Operate	CLR	rwd	8Dd8	2	7								[rwd] ← 0 Clear the Selected Word register.
	CLRB	rbd	8Cd8	2	7								[rbd] ← 0 Clear the Selected Byte register.
	COM	rwd	8Dd0	2	7								[rwd] ← $\overline{[rwd]}$ Complement the Selected Word register.
	COMB	rbd	8Cd0	2	7								[rbd] ← $\overline{[rbd]}$ Complement the Selected Byte register.
	DAB	rbd	B0d0	2	5				U	X	X	X	Decimal adjust contents of 8-bit register rbd.
	DEC	rwd,n16	ABdn	2	4			X		X	X		[rwd] ← [rwd] − n16
	DECB	rbd,n16	AAdn	2	4			X		X	X		[rbd] ← [rbd] − n16 Subtract the immediate value n16 from a 16-bit register (for DEC) or an 8-bit register (for DECB).
	EXTS	rld	B1dA	2	11								Bits 16 to 31 of [rld] ← bit 15 of [rld]. The sign bit of the low-order word of the register pair is copied into all bits of the high-order word of the register pair.
	EXTSB	rwd	B1d0	2	11								Bits 8 to 15 of [rwd] ← bit 7 of [rwd]. The sign bit of the low-order byte of the register is copied into all bits of the high-order byte of the register.
	EXTSL	rqd	B1d7	2	11								Bits 32 to 63 of [rqd] ← bit 31 of [rqd]. The sign bit of the low-order register pair of the Quadruple register is copied into all bits of the high-order register pair.

* Privileged instruction — can be executed only in system mode.
** Number of clock periods depends on the number of repetitions for n/m**; n = minimum number of clock periods and m = number of clock periods added for each additional repetition of operation. The number of clock periods for an instruction which repeats k times is n + (k−1)·m.

Table 3-5. A Summary of the Z8000 Instruction Set (Continued)

Type	Mnemonic	Operand(s)	Op Code	Bytes	Clock Periods	H	D	V	P	S	Z	C	Operation Performed
	INC	rwd,n16	A9dn	2	4			x		x	x		[rwd] ← [rwd] + n16
	INCB	rbd,n16	A8dn	2	4			x		x	x		[rbd] ← [rbd] + n16 — Add the immediate value n16 to a 16-bit register (for INC) or an 8-bit register (for INCB).
	NEG	rwd	8Dd2	2	7			x		x	x	x	[rwd] ← −[rwd]
	NEGB	rbd	8Cd2	2	7			x		x	x	x	[rbd] ← −[rbd] — Replace the contents of the 16-bit register (for NEG) or 8-bit register (for NEGB) with its twos complement.
	RL	rwd,1	B3d0	2	6			x		x	x	x	Left rotate contents of word (for RL) or byte (for RLB) register, n bits (n = 1 or 2), as follows:
	RL	rwd,2	B3d2	2	7			x		x	x	x	
	RLB	rbd,1	B2d0	2	6			x		x	x	x	
	RLB	rbd,2	B2d2	2	7			x		x	x	x	
	RLC	rwd,1	B3d8	2	6			x		x	x	x	See accompanying text for a discussion of the Overflow status for all Register Operate shift and rotate instructions. Left rotate through Carry contents of word (for RLC) or byte (for RLCB) register, n bits (n = 1 or 2), as follows:
	RLC	rwd,2	B3dA	2	7			x		x	x	x	
	RLCB	rbd,1	B2d8	2	6			x		x	x	x	
	RLCB	rbd,2	B2dA	2	7			x		x	x	x	

Type: Register Operate (Continued)

* Privileged instruction — can be executed only in system mode.
** Number of clock periods depends on the number of repetitions for n/m**; n = minimum number of clock periods and m = number of clock periods added for each additional repetition of operation. The number of clock periods for an instruction which repeats k times is n + (k−1)·m.

Table 3-5. A Summary of the Z8000 Instruction Set (Continued)

Type	Mnemonic	Operand(s)	Op Code	Bytes	Clock Periods	Status H	D	V	P	S	Z	C	Operation Performed
Register Operate (Continued)	RR	rwd,1	B3d4	2	6			X		X	X	X	Right rotate contents of word (for RR) or byte (for RRB) register, n bits (n = 1 or 2), as follows:
	RR	rwd,2	B3d6	2	7			X		X	X	X	
	RRB	rbd,1	B2d4	2	6			X		X	X	X	
	RRB	rbd,2	B2d6	2	7			X		X	X	X	
	RRC	rwd,1	B3dC	2	6			X		X	X	X	Right rotate through Carry contents of word (for RRC) or byte (for RRCB) register, n bits (n = 1 or 2), as follows:
	RRC	rwd,2	B3dE	2	7			X		X	X	X	
	RRCB	rbd,1	B2dC	2	6			X		X	X	X	
	RRCB	rbd,2	B2dE	2	7			X		X	X	X	
	SDA	rwd,rw	B3dB 0r00	4	18/3**			X		X	X	X	Shift arithmetic the contents of a byte (for SDAB) word (for SDA) or long word (for SDAL) register. [rw] specifies the number of shift bit positions, and the direction (+ for left shift, − for right shift). 0 shift is allowed; it causes no shift, but sets status. [rw] value range is −8 to +8 for SDAB. −16 to +16 for SDA −32 to +32 for SDAL. Bits 0 to 4 of [rw] are active, with bit 15 used for sign. Shifts occur as follows:
	SDAB	rbd,rw	B2dB 0r00	4	18/3**			X		X	X	X	
	SDAL	rld,rw	B3dF 0r00	4	18/3**			X		X	X	X	

* Privileged instruction — can be executed only in system mode.
** Number of clock periods depends on the number of repetitions for n/m**; n = minimum number of clock periods and m = number of clock periods added for each additional repetition of operation. The number of clock periods for an instruction which repeats k times is n + (k−1)·m.

Table 3-5. A Summary of the Z8000 Instruction Set (Continued)

Type	Mnemonic	Operand(s)	Op Code	Bytes	Clock Periods	H	D	V	P	S	Z	C	Operation Performed
Register Operate (Continued)	SDL	rwd,rw	B3d3 0r00	4	18/3**							x	SDL, SDLB and SDLL are equivalent to SDA, SDAB and SDAL, respectively, but they perform logical right shifts. Left shifts are identical. Shifts may be illustrated as follows:
	SDLB	rbd,rw	B2d3 0r00	4	18/3**							x	
	SDLL	rld,rw	B3d7 0r00	4	18/3**							x	
	SLA	rwd,data16	B3d9 yyyy	4	16/3**			U		x	x	x	SLA, SLAB and SLAL are identical to SDA, SDAB and SDAL, respectively, when these instructions are performing left shifts, except that SLA, SLAB and SLAL specify the shift bit count immediately.
	SLAB	rbd,data16	B2d9 yyyy	4	16/3**			U		x	x	x	
	SLAL	rld,data16	B3dD yyyy	4	16/3**			U		x	x	x	
	SLL	rwd,data16	B3d1 yyyy	4	16/3**			U		x	x	x	SLL, SLLB and SLLL are identical to SDL, SDLB and SDLL, respectively, when these instructions are performing left shifts, except that SLL, SLLB and SLLL specify the shift bit count immediately.
	SLLB	rbd,data16	B2d1 yyyy	4	16/3**			U		x	x	x	
	SLLL	rld,data16	B3d5 yyyy	4	16/3**			U		x	x	x	
	SRA	rwd,data16	-B3d9 yyyy	4	16/3**			0		x	x	x	SRA, SRAB and SRAL are identical to SDA, SDAB and SDAL, respectively, when these instructions are performing right shifts, except that SRA, SRAB, and SRAL specify the shift bit count immediately.
	SRAB	rbd,data16	B2d9 yyyy	4	16/3**			0		x	x	x	
	SRAL	rld,data16	B3dD yyyy	4	16/3**			0		x	x	x	
	SRL	rwd,data16	B3d1 yyyy	4	16/3**			U		x	x	x	SRL, SRLB and SRLL are identical to SDL, SDLB and SDLL, respectively, when these instructions are performing right shifts, except that SRL, SRLB and SRLL specify the shift bit count immediately.
	SRLB	rbd,data16	B2d1 yyyy	4	16/3**			U		x	x	x	
	SRLL	rld,data16	B3d5 yyyy	4	16/3**			U		x	x	x	
	TSET	rwd	8Dd6	2	7					x			$[s] \leftarrow [rwd](MSB). [rwd] \leftarrow FFFF$
	TSETB	rbd	8Cd6	2	7					x			$[s] \leftarrow [rbd](MSB). [rbd] \leftarrow FF$ Move the most significant bit of the 16-bit register (for TSET) or 8-bit register (TSETB) to the Sign status. Then fill the register with 1 bits.
	TEST	rwd	8Dd4	2	7					x	x	x	$[rwd]$ OR 0
	TESTB	rbd	8Cd4	2	7					x	x	x	$[rbd]$ OR 0
	TESTL	rld	9Cd0	2	13				x	x	x	x	$[rld]$ OR 0 OR the specified register contents with 0. Set Status flags based on the result. Test a 32-bit register for TESTL, a 16-bit register for TEST and an 8-bit register for TESTB.

Diagram (Operation Performed, SDL group):

Right: 7 6 ... 2 1 0 / 15 14 ... 2 1 0 / 31 30 ... 2 1 0

Left: 7 6 ... 2 1 0 / 15 14 ... 2 1 0 / 31 30 ... 2 1 0

* Privileged instruction — can be executed only in system mode.

** Number of clock periods depends on the number of repetitions for n/m**: n = minimum number of clock periods and m = number of clock periods added for each additional repetition of operation. The number of clock periods for an instruction which repeats k times is n + (k–1)·m.

Table 3-5. A Summary of the Z8000 Instruction Set (Continued)

Type	Mnemonic	Operand(s)	Op Code	Bytes	Clock Periods	H	D	V	P	S	Z	C	Operation Performed
Stack	LDCTL*	NSPSEG,rws	7DsE	2	7								[NSPSEG] ← [rws]
	LDCTL*	rwd,NSPSEG	7Dd6	2	7								[rwd] ← [NSPSEG] Transfer data between a 16-bit register and the Z8001 normal Stack Pointer Segment Address register (R14N).
	LDCTL*	NSPOFF,rws	7DsF	2	7								[NSPOFF] ← [rws]
	LDCTL*	rwd,NSPOFF	7Dd7	2	7								[rwd] ← [NSPOFF] Transfer data between a 16-bit register and the normal Stack Pointer Address register (R15N).
	POP	rwd,@ris	97sd	2	8								[rwd] ← [[ris]], [ris] ← [ris] + 2
	POP	@rid,@ris	17sd	2	12								[rid]] ← [[ris]], [ris] ← [ris] + 2
	POP	adrsx,@ris	57si pppp qqqq	4/6	15-19								[adrsx] ← [[ris]], [ris] ← [ris] + 2 Pop the memory word addressed by ris, the designated Stack Pointer. Any register with the exception of R0 (for non-segmented) or RR0 (for segmented) can be designated as the Stack Pointer. The popped word is loaded into a 16-bit register, or the memory location addressed by adrsx or [rid]. The Stack Pointer is then incremented by 2.
	POPL	rid,@ris	95id	2	12								[rid] ← [[ris]], [ris] ← [ris] + 4
	POPL	@rid,@ris	15id	2	19								[[rid]] ← [[ris]], [ris] ← [ris] + 4
	POPL	adrsx,@ris	55si pppp qqqq	4/6	22-26								[adrsx] ← [[ris]], [ris] ← [ris] + 4 POPL is identical to POP, except that a 32-bit long word is popped, and the Stack Pointer is incremented by 4.
	PUSH	@rid,rws	93is	2	9								[rid] ← [rid] - 2, [[rid]] ← [rws]
	PUSH	@rid,@ris	13is	2	13								[rid] ← [rid] - 2, [[rid]] ← [[ris]]
	PUSH	@rid,adrsx	53di pppp qqqq	4/6	13-17								[rid] ← [rid] - 2, [[rid]] ← [adrsx]
	PUSH	@rid,data16	0Dd9 yyyy	4	12								[rid] ← [rid] - 2, [[rid]] ← data16 Decrement rid, the designated Stack Pointer, and push a 16-bit word onto the memory stack addressed by rid. Any register with the exception of R0 (for non-segmented) or RR0 (for segmented) can be designated as the Stack Pointer. The pushed word can come from a register, the memory word addressed by adrsx or [ris], or it may be immediate data.

* Privileged instruction — can be executed only in system mode.

** Number of clock periods depends on the number of repetitions for n/m**; n = minimum number of clock periods and m = number of clock periods added for each additional repetition of operation. The number of clock periods for an instruction which repeats k times is n + (k-1)·m.

Table 3-5. A Summary of the Z8000 Instruction Set (Continued)

Type	Mnemonic	Operand(s)	Op Code	Bytes	Clock Periods	H	D	V	P	S	Z	C	Operation Performed
Stack (Continued)	PUSHL	@rid,rls	91is	2	12								$[rid] \leftarrow [rid] - 4, [[rid]] \leftarrow [rls]$
	PUSHL	@rid,@ris	11is	2	20								$[rid] \leftarrow [rid] - 4, [[rid]] \leftarrow [[ris]]$
	PUSHL	@rid,adrsx	51di pppp qqqq	4/6	20-24								$[rid] \leftarrow [rid] - 4, [[rid]] \leftarrow [adrsx]$
													PUSHL is identical to PUSH except that the Stack Pointer is decremented by 4, and a 32-bit long word is pushed. There is no immediate version of PUSHL.
Bit Operations	BIT	rwd,b16	A7db	2	4						X		$Z \leftarrow$ NOT bit b16 of [rwd]
	BIT	@rid,b16	27ib	2	8						X		$Z \leftarrow$ NOT bit b16 of [[rid]]
	BIT	adrsx,b16	67ib pppp qqqq	4/6	10-14						X		$Z \leftarrow$ NOT bit b16 of [adrsx]
	BIT	rwd,rws	270s 0d00	4	10								$Z \leftarrow$ NOT bit [rws] of [rwd]
													Set the Z status to the complement of the specified bit, which may be in a 16-bit register or memory word. The bit may be specified immediately, or for a register it may be specified by the low-order four bits of a 16-bit register.
	BITB	rbd,b8	A6db	2	4						X		$Z \leftarrow$ NOT bit b8 of [rbd]
	BITB	@rid,b8	26ib	2	8						X		$Z \leftarrow$ NOT bit b8 of [[rid]]
	BITB	adrsx,b8	66ib pppp qqqq	4/6	10-14						X		$Z \leftarrow$ NOT bit b8 of [adrsx]
	BITB	rbd,rws	260s 0d00	4	10								$Z \leftarrow$ NOT bit [rws] of [rbd]
													Set the Z status to the complement of the specified bit, which may be in an 8-bit register or memory byte. The bit may be specified immediately, or for a register it may be specified by the low-order three bits of one of the registers R0 - R7.
	RES	rwd,b16	A3db	2	4								Bit b16 of [rwd] $\leftarrow 0$
	RES	@rid,b16	23ib	2	11								Bit b16 of [[rid]] $\leftarrow 0$
	RES	adrsx,b16	63ib pppp qqqq	4/6	13-17								Bit b16 of [adrsx] $\leftarrow 0$
	RES	rwd,rws	230s 0d00	4	10								Bit [rws] of [rwd] $\leftarrow 0$
													Clear the specified bit, which may be in a 16-bit register or memory word. The bit may be specified immediately, or for a register it may be specified by the low-order four bits of a 16-bit register.
	RESB	rbd,b8	A2db	2	4								Bit b8 of [rbd] $\leftarrow 0$
	RESB	@rid,b8	22ib	2	11								Bit b8 of [[rid]] $\leftarrow 0$
	RESB	adrsx,b8	62ib pppp qqqq	4/6	13-17								Bit b8 of [adrsx] $\leftarrow 0$
	RESB	rbd,rws	220s 0d00	4	10								Bit [rws] of [rbd] $\leftarrow 0$
													Clear the specified bit, which may be in an 8-bit register or memory byte. The bit may be specified immediately, or for a register it may be specified by the low-order three bits of one of the registers R0 - R7.

* Privileged instruction — can be executed only in system mode.

** Number of clock periods depends on the number of repetitions for n/m**; n = minimum number of clock periods and m = number of clock periods added for each additional repetition of operation. The number of clock periods for an instruction which repeats k times is $n + (k-1) \cdot m$.

Table 3-5. A Summary of the Z8000 Instruction Set (Continued)

Type	Mnemonic	Operand(s)	Op Code	Bytes	Clock Periods	H	D	V	P	S	Z	C	Operation Performed
Bit Operations (Continued)	SET	rwd,b16	A5db	2	4								Bit b16 of [rwd] ← 1
	SET	@rid,b16	25ib	2	11								Bit b16 of [[rid]] ← 1
	SET	adrsx,b16	65ib pppp qqqq	4/6	13-17								Bit b16 of [adrsx] ← 1
	SET	rwd,rws	250s 0d00	4	10								Bit [rws] of [rwd] ← 1
	SETB	rbd,b8	A4db	2	4								Bit b8 of [rbd]
	SETB	@rid,b8	24ib	2	11								Bit b8 of [[rid]]
	SETB	adrsx,b8	64ib pppp qqqq	4/6	13-17								Bit b8 of [adrsx]
	SETB	rbd,rws	240s 0d00	4	10								Bit [rws] of [rbd]
													SET and SETB instructions are equivalent to RES and RESB instructions, respectively, except that the selected bit is set.
Interrupt	DI*	int	7C 000000vv	2	7								Disable the indicated interrupt(s). Either or both of VI and NVI may be indicated
	EI*	int	7C 000001vv	2	7								Enable the indicated interrupt(s) Either or both of VI and NVI may be indicated
	IRET*		7B00	2	13,16	X	X	X	X	X	X	X	[SP] ← [SP] + 2 [FCW]: [SP] ← [SP] - [[SP]] (Nonsegmented) [SP] ← [SP] + 2. [PC] ← [[SP]] [SP] ← [SP] + 2 [FCW]: [SP] ← [SP] - [[SP]] (Segmented) [SP] ← [SP] + 4. Return from interrupt. Pop and discard identifier word. Pop flag and control word. Pop Program Counter.
	LDCTL*	PSAPSEG,rws	7DsC	2	7								[PSAPSEG] ← [rws]
	LDCTL*	rwd,PSAPSEG	7Dd4	2	7								[rwd] ← [PSAPSEG] These two instructions transfer data between the Z8001 Program Status Area Pointer Segment register, and a 16-bit general purpose register.
	LDCTL*	PSAPOFF,rws	7DsD	2	7								[PSAPOFF] ← [rws]
	LDCTL*	rwd,PSAPOFF	7Dd5	2	7								[rwd] ← [PSAPOFF] These two instructions transfer data between the Program Status Area Pointer and a 16-bit general purpose register.

* Privileged instruction — can be executed only in system mode.

** Number of clock periods depends on the number of repetitions for n/m**: n = minimum number of clock periods and m = number of clock periods added for each additional repetition of operation. The number of clock periods for an instruction which repeats k times is n + (k-1)•m.

Table 3-5. A Summary of the Z8000 Instruction Set (Continued)

Type	Mnemonic	Operand(s)	Op Code	Bytes	Clock Periods	H	D	V	P	S	Z	C	Operation Performed
Status	COMFLG	flag	8Df5	2	7			x	x	x	x	x	Complement each status named in the operand. Any or all of C, Z, S, P, or O may be named in any order.
	LDCTL*	FCW,rws	7DsA	2	7	x	x	x	x	x	x	x	[FCW] ← [rws] Load register contents into FCW. Unassigned bits of FCW are not affected.
	LDCTL*	rwd,FCW	7Dd2	2	7								[rwd] ← [FCW] Load FCW contents into selected register. Unassigned bits of FCW are reset to 0 in rwd.
	LDCTLB	FLAGS,rbs	8Cc9	2	7			x	x	x	x	x	[FLAGS] ← [rbs] Load byte register contents into low-order byte of FCW. Bits 0 and 1, which are unassigned, are not affected.
	LDCTLB	rbd,FLAGS	8Cd1	2	7								[rbd] ← [FLAGS] Load the low-order byte of FCW into byte register rbd. Bits 0 and 1 of rbd are reset to 0.
	RESFLG	flag	8Df3	2	7			x	x	x	x	x	Reset to 0 each status named in the operand.
	SETFLG	flag	8Df1	2	7			x	x	x	x	x	Set to 1 each status named in the operand.
	TCC	cc,rwd	AFdc	2	5								If cc is "true" then set bit 0 of Register rwd. Otherwise reset bit 0 of Register rwd.
	TCCB	cc,rbd	AEdc	2	5								If cc is "true" then set bit 0 of Register rbd. Otherwise reset bit 0 of Register rbd.

* Privileged instruction — can be executed only in system mode.
** Number of clock periods depends on the number of repetitions for n/m**: n = minimum number of clock periods and m = number of clock periods added for each additional repetition of operation. The number of clock periods for an instruction which repeats k times is n + (k−1)·m.

Table 3-5. A Summary of the Z8000 Instruction Set (Continued)

Type	Mnemonic	Operand(s)	Op Code	Bytes	Clock Periods	H	D	V	P	S	Z	C	Operation Performed
Other (CPU and Bus Control)	HALT		7A00	2	8/3**								Halt CPU until reset or interrupt
	LDCTL*	REFRESH,rws	7DsB	2	7								[REFRESH] ← [rws] Transfer the contents of the specified 16-bit register into the Dynamic Memory Refresh Control register.
	LDCTL*	rwd,REFRESH	7Dd3	2	7								[rwd] ← [REFRESH] Transfer the contents of the Dynamic Memory Refresh Control register to the specified 16-bit register.
	MBIT*		7B0A	2	7					X			[S] ← MI Set Sign status to 1 if MI is input active(1). Reset Sign status to 0 if MI is input inactive (0).
	MREQ*	rwd	7BdD	2	12/7**					X	X		[Z] ← 0. If MI = 1 then [S] ← 0 and [MO] ← 0. If MI = 0 then [MO] ← 1 Decrement [rwd] to 0. If MI is still 0 then [S] ← 0. [MO] ← 0. If MI is now 1 then [S] ← 1. [Z] ← 1. Execute a multi-micro bus request, as described in accompanying text.
	MRES*		7B09	2	5								[MO] ← 0 Output MO inactive (0).
	MSET*		7B08	2	5								[MO] ← 1 Output MO active (1).
	NOP		8D07	2	7								No operation.
Extended Instructions	XCTL	epu,data8	8E 000001aa hO kO	4	10	X	X	X		X	X	X	CPU: no operation EPU: internal operation
	XLDCTL	epu,FLAGS, data8	8E 000010 aa hO kO	4	13	X	X	X		X	X	X	EPU ← [FLAGS]
	XLDCTL	FLAGS,epu, data8	8E 000000aa hO kO	4	13	X	X	X		X	X	X	[FLAGS] ← EPU These two instructions transfer data between an Extended Processing Unit and the flags byte of the Flag and Control Word.

* Privileged instruction — can be executed only in system mode.

** Number of clock periods depends on the number of repetitions for n/m**: n = minimum number of clock periods and m = number of clock periods added for each additional repetition of operation. The number of clock periods for an instruction which repeats k times is n + (k−1)·m.

Table 3-5. A Summary of the Z8000 Instruction Set (Continued)

Type	Mnemonic	Operand(s)	Object Code	Bytes	Clock Periods	H	D	V	P	S	Z	C	Operation Performed
Extended Instructions (Continued)	XLDM	rwd,epu,n16, data8	8F 000000aa hd kn	4	10/3**								[rwd] ← EPU do n16 times incrementing register address (r0 follows r15)
	XLDM	@rid,epu,n16, data8	0F dddd11aa h0 kn	4	10-15/3**								[[rid]] ←EPU do n16 times incrementing memory address
	XLDM	adrsx,epu,n16, data8	4F dddd11aa h0 kn	6/8	10-15/3**								[adrsx] ← EPU do n16 times incrementing memory address

These three instructions move a block of n16 data words from an Extended Processing Unit to 16-bit registers or to memory. rwd addresses the first 16-bit register; adrsx or @rid addresses the first, lowest addressed memory word. n16 can have any value from 1 to 16. |
| | XLDM | epu,rws,n16, data8 | 8F 000010aa hs kn | 4 | 10/3** | | | | | | | | EPU ← [rws] do n16 times incrementing register address (r0 follows r15) |
| | XLDM | epu,@ris,n16, data8 | 0F ssss01aa h0 kn | 4 | 10-15/3** | | | | | | | | EPU ← [[ris]] do n16 times incrementing memory address |
| | XLDM | epu,adrsx,n16, data8 | 4F ssss01aa h0 kn | 6/8 | 10-15/3** | | | | | | | | EPU ← [adrsx] do n16 times incrementing memory address

These three instructions move a block of n16 data words from 16-bit registers or memory to an Extended Processing Unit. They correspond to the XLDM instructions above in all other respects. |

* Privileged instruction — can be executed only in system mode.
** Number of clock periods depends on the number of repetitions for n/m**; n = minimum number of clock periods and m = number of clock periods added for each additional repetition of operation. The number of clock periods for an instruction which repeats k times is n + (k−1)·m.

Table 3-6. Z8000 Instruction Set Object Codes - Alphabetic Listing

Mnemonic		Object Code	Bytes	Clock Periods	Mnemonic		Object Code	Bytes	Clock Periods
ADC	rwd,rws	B5sd	2	5	CALR	disp	Dxxx	2	10/15
ADCB	rbd,rbs	B4sd	2	5	CLR	adrsx	4Di8	4/6	11-15
ADD	rwd,adrsx	41id	4/6	9-13			pppp		
		pppp					qqqq		
		qqqq				rwd	8Dd8	2	7
	rwd,data16	010d	4	7		@rid	0Dd8	2	8
		yyyy			CLRB	adrsx	4Ci8	4/6	11-15
	rwd,rws	81sd	2	4			pppp		
	rwd,@ris	01id	2	7			qqqq		
ADDB	rbd,adrsx	40id	4/6	9-13		rbd	8Cd8	2	7
		pppp				@rid	0Cd8	2	8
		qqqq			COM	adrsx	4Di0	4/6	15-19
	rbd,data8	000d	4	7			pppp		
		yxyx					qqqq		
	rbd,rbs	80sd	2	4		rwd	8Dd0	2	7
	rbd,@ris	00id	2	7		@rid	0Dd0	2	12
ADDL	rld,adrsx	56id	4/6	15-19	COMB	adrsx	4Ci0	4/6	15-19
		pppp					pppp		
		qqqq					qqqq		
	rld,data32	160d	6	14		rbd	8Cd0	2	7
		yyyy				@rid	0Cd0	2	12
		zzzz			COMFLG	flag	8Df5	2	7
	rld,rls	96sd	2	8	CP	adrsx,data16	4Di1	6/8	14-18
	rld,@ris	16id	2	14			yyyy		
AND	rwd,adrsx	47id	4/6	9-13			pppp		
		pppp					qqqq		
		qqqq				rwd,adrsx	4Bid	4/6	9-13
	rwd,data16	070d	4	7			pppp		
		yyyy					qqqq		
	rwd,rws	87sd	2	4		rwd,data16	0B0d	4	7
	rwd,@ris	07id	2	7			yyyy		
ANDB	rbd,adrsx	46id	4/6	9-13		rwd,rws	8Bsd	2	4
		pppp				rwd,@ris	0Bid	2	7
		qqqq				@rid,data16	0Dd1	4	11
	rbd,data8	060d	4	7			yyyy		
		yxyx			CPB	adrsx,data8	4Ci1	6/8	14-18
	rbd,rbs	86sd	2	4			yxyx		
	rbd,@ris	06id	2	7			pppp		
BIT	adrsx,b16	67ib	4/6	10-14			qqqq		
		pppp				rbd,adrsx	4Aid	4/6	9-13
		qqqq					pppp		
	rwd,b16	A7db	2	4			qqqq		
	@rid,b16	27ib	2	8		rbd,data8	0A0d	4	7
	rwd,rws	270s	4	10			yxyx		
		0d00				rbd,rbs	8Asd	2	4
BITB	adrsx,b8	66ib	4/6	10-14		rbd,@ris	0Aid	2	7
		pppp				@rid,data8	0Cd1	4	11
		qqqq					yxyx		
	rbd,b8	A6db	2	4	CPL	rld,adrsx	50id	4/6	15-19
	@rid,b8	26ib	2	8			pppp		
	rbd,rws	260s	4	10			qqqq		
		0d00				rld,data32	100d	6	14
CALL	adrsx	5Fi0	4/6	12-21			yyyy		
		pppp					zzzz		
		qqqq				rld,rls	90sd	2	8
	@rid	1Fd0	2	10/15		rld,@ris	10id	2	14

Table 3-6. Z8000 Instruction Set Object Codes - Alphabetic Listing (Continued)

Mnemonic		Object Code	Bytes	Clock Periods		Mnemonic		Object Code	Bytes	Clock Periods
CPD	rwd,@ris,rw,cc	BBs8 Ordc	4	20		DIVL	rqd,adrsx	5Aid pppp qqqq	4/6	note 1
CPDB	rbd,@ris,rw,cc	BAs8 Ordc	4	20			rqd,data32	1A0d yyyy zzzz	6	note 1
CPDR	rwd,@ris,rw,cc	BBsC Ordc	4	20/9**			rqd,rls	9Asd	2	note 1
CPDRB	rbd,@ris,rw,cc	BAsC Ordc	4	20/9**			rqd,@ris	1Aid	2	note 1
CPI	rwd,@ris,rw,cc	BBs0 Ordc	4	20		DJNZ	rw,disp	Fr 0ttttttt	2	11
						DBJNZ	rb,disp	Fr 1ttttttt	2	11
CPIB	rbd,@ris,rw,cc	BAs0 Ordc	4	20		*EI	int	7C 000001vv	2	7
CPIR	rwd,@ris,rw,cc	BBs4 Ordc	4	20/9**		EX	rwd,adrsx	6Did pppp qqqq	4/6	15-19
CPIRB	rbd,@ris,rw,cc	BAs4 Ordc	4	20/9**			rwd,rws	ADsd	2	6
							rwd,@ris	2Dsd	2	12
CPSD	@rid,@ris,rw,cc	BBsA Ordc	4	25		EXB	rbd,adrsx	6Cid pppp qqqq	4/6	15-19
CPSDB	@rid,@ris,rw,cc	BAsA Ordc	4	25			rbd,rbs	ACsd	2	6
CPSDR	@rid,@ris,rw,cc	BBsE Ordc	4	25/14**			rbd,@ris	2Csd	2	12
CPSDRB	@rid,@ris,rw,cc	BAsE Ordc	4	25/14**		Extended Instructions		8E eeee01aa eeee	4	10
CPSI	@rid,@ris,rw,cc	BBs2 Ordc	4	25				8E eeee11aa eeee	4	10
CPSIB	@rid,@ris,rw,cc	BAs2 Ordc	4	25				8F 0eee00aa eden	4	10/3**
CPSIR	@rid,@ris,rw,cc	BBs6 Ordc	4	25/14**				8F 0eee10aa esen	4	10/3**
CPSIRB	@rid,@ris,rw,cc	BAs6 Ordc	4	25/14**				8E eeee10aa e0e0	4	13
DAB	rbd	B0d0	2	5				8E eeee00aa e0e0	4	13
DEC	adrsx,n16	6Bin pppp qqqq	4/6	13-17				0F ssss01aa eeen	4	10-15/3**
	rwd,n16	ABdn	2	4				4F ssss01aa eeen ppppqqqq	6/8	10-15/3**
	@rid,n16	2Bdn	2	11				0F dddd11aa eeen	4	10-15/3**
DECB	adrsx,n16	6Ain pppp qqqq	4/6	13-17				4Fdddd11aa eeen ppppqqqq	6/8	10-15/3**
	rbd,n16	AAdn	2	4		EXTS	rld	B1dA	2	11
	@rid,n16	2Adn	2	11		EXTSB	rwd	B1d0	2	11
*DI	int	7C 000000vv	2	7		EXTSL	rqd	B1d7	2	11
DIV	rld,adrsx	5Bid pppp qqqq	4/6	note 1		*HALT		7A00	2	8/3**
	rld,data16	1B0d yyyy	4	note 1		*IN	rwd,ioaddr	3Bd4 pppp	4	12
	rld,rws	9Bsd	2	note 1			rwd,@rw	3Dsd	2	10
	rld,@ris	1Bid	2	note 1						

*   Privileged instruction — can be executed only in system mode.

** Number of clock periods depends on the number of repetitions for n/m**; n = minimum number of clock periods and m = number of clock periods added for each additional repetition of operation. The number of clock periods for an instruction which repeats k times is n + (k−1)·m.

Table 3-6. Z8000 Instruction Set Object Codes - Alphabetic Listing (Continued)

Mnemonic		Object Code	Bytes	Clock Periods	Mnemonic		Object Code	Bytes	Clock Periods
*INB	rbd,ioaddr	3Ad4 pppp	4	12	LD (Cont.)	rwd,ris(rw)	71id 0r00	4	14
	rbd,@rw	3Csd	2	10		rwd,@ris	21id	2	7
INC	adrsx,n16	69in pppp qqqq	4/6	13-17		rid(disp),rws	33is xxxx	4	14
	rwd,n16	A9dn	2	4		rid(rw),rws	73is 0r00	4	14
	@rid,n16	29dn	2	11		@rid,data16	0Dd5 yyyy	4	11
INCB	adrsx,n16	68in pppp qqqq	4/6	13-17		@rid,rws	2Fds	2	8
	rbd,n16	A8dn	2	4	LDB	adrsx,data8	4Ci5 yxyx pppp qqqq	6/8	14-18
	@rid,n16	28dn	2	11		adrsx,rbs	6Eis pppp qqqq	4/6	11-15
*IND	@rid,@ris,rw	3Bs8 0rd8	4	21		rbd,adrsx	60id pppp qqqq	4/6	9-13
*INDB	@rid,@ris,rw	3As8 0rd8	4	21		rbd,data8	Cdyy	2	5
*INDR	@rid,@ris,rw	3Bs8 0rd0	4	21/10**		rbd,rbs	A0sd	2	3
*INDRB	@rid,@ris,rw	3As8 0rd0	4	21/10**		rbd,ris(disp)	30id xxxx	4	14
*INI	@rid,@ris,rw	3Bs0 0rd8	4	21		rbd,ris(rw)	70id 0r00	4	14
*INIB	@rid,@ris,rw	3As0 0rd8	4	21		rbd,@ris	20id	2	7
*INIR	@rid,@ris,rw	3Bs0 0rd0	4	21/10**		rid(disp),rbs	32is xxxx	4	14
*INIRB	@rid,@ris,rw	3As0 0rd0	4	21/10**		rid(rw),rbs	72is 0r00	4	14
*IRET		7B00	2	13,16		@rid,data8	0Cd5 yxyx	4	11
JP	cc,adrsx	5Eic pppp qqqq	4/6	7-11		@rid,rbs	2Eds	2	8
	cc,@rid	1Edc	2	10,15/7					
JR	cc,disp	Ecxx	2	6					
LD	adrsx,data16	4Di5 yyyy pppp qqqq	6/8	14-18					
	adrsx,rws	6Fis pppp qqqq	4/6	11-15					
	rwd,adrsx	61id pppp qqqq	4/6	9-13					
	rwd,data16	210d yyyy	4	7					
	rwd,rws	A1sd	2	3					
	rwd,ris(disp)	31id xxxx	4	14					

*   Privileged instruction — can be executed only in system mode.
**   Number of clock periods depends on the number of repetitions for n/m**; n = minimum number of clock periods and
     m = number of clock periods added for each additional repetition of operand.
     The number of clock periods for an instruction which repeats k times is n + (k − 1) · m.

Table 3-6. Z8000 Instruction Set Object Codes - Alphabetic Listing (Continued)

Mnemonic		Object Code	Bytes	Clock Periods	Mnemonic		Object Code	Bytes	Clock Periods
LDL	adrsx,rls	5Dis pppp qqqq	4/6	14-18	LDD	@rid,@ris,rw	BBs9 0rd8	4	20
	rld,adrsx	54id pppp qqqq	4/6	12-16	LDDB	@rid,@ris,rw	BAs9 0rd8	4	20
					LDDR	@rid,@ris,rw	BBs9 0rd0	4	20/9**
	rld,data32	140d yyyy zzzz	6	11	LDDRB	@rid,@ris,rw	BAs9 0rd0	4	20/9**
	rld,rls	94sd	2	5	LDI	@rid,@ris,rw	BBs1 0rd8	4	20
	rld,ris(disp)	35id xxxx	4	17	LDIB	@rid,@ris,rw	BAs1 0rd8	4	20
	rld,ris(rw)	75id 0r00	4	17	LDIR	@rid,@ris,rw	BBs1 0rd0	4	20/9**
	rld, @ris	14id	2	11	LDIRB	@rid,@ris,rw	BAs1 0rd0	4	20/9**
	rid(disp),rls	37is xxxx	4	17	LDK	rwd,b16	BDdb	2	5
	rid(rw),rls	77is 0r00	4	17	LDM	adrsx,rws,n16	5Ci9 0sOn pppp qqqq	6/8	17-21/3**
	@rid,rls	1Dds	2	11		rwd,adrsx,n16	5Ci1 0dOn pppp qqqq	6/8	17-21/3**
LDA	rld,adrsx	76id pppp qqqq	4/6	13-16		rwd,@ris,n16	1Cs1 0dOn	4	14/3**
	rld,ris(disp)	34id xxxx	4	15		@rid,rws,n16	1Cd9 0sOn	4	14/3**
	rld,ris(rw)	74id 0r00	4	15	*LDPS	adrsx	79i0 pppp qqqq	4/6	16-23
	rwd,adrsx	76id pppp	4	12-13		@ris	39s0	2	12,16
	rwd,ris(disp)	34id xxxx	4	15	LDR	disp,rws	330s xxxx	4	14
	rwd,ris(rw)	74id 0r00	4	15		rwd,disp	310d xxxx	4	14
LDAR	rld,disp	340d xxxx	4	15	LDRB	disp,rbs	320d xxxx	4	14
	rwd,disp	340d xxxx	4	15		rbd,disp	300d xxxx	4	14
*LDCTL	FCW,rws	7DsA	2	7	LDRL	disp,rls	370s xxxx	4	17
	NSPOFF,rws	7DsF	2	7		rld,disp	350d xxxx	4	17
	NSPSEG,rws	7DsE	2	7	*MBIT		7B0A	2	7
	PSAPOFF,rws	7DsD	2	7	*MREQ	rwd	7BdD	2	12/7**
	PSAPSEG,rws	7DsC	2	7	*MRES		7B09	2	5
	REFRESH,rws	7DsB	2	7	*MSET		7B08	2	5
	rwd,FCW	7Dd2	2	7					
	rwd,NSPOFF	7Dd7	2	7					
	rwd,NSPSEG	7Dd6	2	7					
	rwd,PSAPOFF	7Dd5	2	7					
	rwd,PSAPSEG	7Dd4	2	7					
	rwd,REFRESH	7Dd3	2	7					
LDCTLB	FLAGS,rbs	8Cs9	2	7					
	rbs,FLAGS	8Cd1	2	7					

*   Priviledged instruction — can be executed only in system mode.

**   Number of clock periods depends on the number of repetitions for n/m**; n = minimum number of clock periods and m = number of clock periods added for each additional repetition of operation. The number of clock periods for an instruction which repeats k times is n + (k−1)•m.

Table 3-6. Z8000 Instruction Set Object Codes - Alphabetic Listing (Continued)

Mnemonic		Object Code	Bytes	Clock Periods
MULT	rld,adrsx	59id	4/6	note 2
		pppp		
		qqqq		
	rld,data16	190d	4	note 2
		yyyy		
	rld,rws	99sd	2	note 2
	rld,@ris	19id	2	note 2
MULTL	rqd,adrsx	58id	4/6	note 2
		pppp		
		qqqq		
	rqd,data32	180d	6	note 2
		yyyy		
		zzzz		
	rqd,rls	98sd	2	note 2
	rqd,@ris	18id	2	note 2
NEG	adrsx	4Di2	4/6	15-19
		pppp		
		qqqq		
	rwd	8Dd2	2	7
	@rid	0Dd2	2	12
NEGB	adrsx	4Ci2	4/6	15-19
		pppp		
		qqqq		
	rbd	8Cd2	2	7
	@rid	0Cd2	2	12
NOP		8D07	2	7
OR	rwd,adrsx	45id	4/6	9-13
		pppp		
		qqqq		
	rwd,data16	050d	4	7
		yyyy		
	rwd,rws	85sd	2	4
	rwd,@ris	05id	2	7
*LDCTL	FCW,rws	7DsA	2	7
	NSPOFF,rws	7DsF	2	7
	NSPSEG,rws	7DsE	2	7
	PSAPOFF,rws	7DsD	2	7
	PSAPSEG,rws	7DsC	2	7
	REFRESH,rws	7DsB	2	7
	rwd,FCW	7Dd2	2	7
	rwd,NSPOFF	7Dd7	2	7
	rwd,NSPSEG	7Dd6	2	7
	rwd,PSAPOFF	7Dd5	2	7
	rwd,PSAPSEG	7Dd4	2	7
	rwd,REFRESH	7Dd3	2	7
LDCTLB	FLAGS,rbs	8Cs9	2	7
	rbs,FLAGS	8Cd1	2	7
LDD	@rid,@ris,rw	BBs9	4	20
		Ord8		
LDDB	@rid,@ris,rw	BAs9	4	20
		Ord8		

Mnemonic		Object Code	Bytes	Clock Periods
LDDR	@rid,@ris,rw	BBs9	4	20/9**
		Ord0		
LDDRB	@rid,@ris,rw	BAs9	4	20/9**
		Ord0		
LDI	@rid,@ris,rw	BBs1	4	20
		Ord8		
LDIB	@rid,@ris,rw	BAs1	4	20
		Ord8		
LDIR	@rid,@ris,rw	BBs1	4	20/9**
		Ord0		
LDIRB	@rid,@ris,rw	BAs1	4	20/9**
		Ord0		
LDK	rwd,b16	BDdb	2	5
LDM	adrsx,rws,n16	5Ci9	6/8	17-21/3**
		OsOn		
		pppp		
		qqqq		
	rwd,adrsx,n16	5Ci1	6/8	17-21/3**
		OdOn		
		pppp		
		qqqq		
	rwd,@ris,n16	1Cs1	4	14/3**
		OdOn		
	@rid,rws,n16	1Cd9	4	14/3**
		OsOn		
*LDPS	adrsx	79i0	4/6	16-23
		pppp		
		qqqq		
	@ris	39s0	2	12,16
LDR	disp,rws	330s	4	14
		xxxx		
	rwd,disp	310d	4	14
		xxxx		
LDRB	disp,rbs	320d	4	14
		xxxx		
	rbd,disp	300d	4	14
		xxxx		
LDRL	disp,rls	370s	4	17
		xxxx		
	rld,disp	350d	4	17
		xxxx		
*MBIT		7B0A	2	7
*MREQ	rwd	7BdD	2	12/7**
*MRES		7B09	2	5
*MSET		7B08	2	5
MULT	rld,adrsx	59id	4/6	note 2
		pppp		
		qqqq		
	rld,data16	190d	4	note 2
		yyyy		
	rld,rws	99sd	2	note 2
	rld,@ris	19id	2	note 2

*   Priviledged instruction — can be executed only in system mode.

** Number of clock periods depends on the number of repetitions for n/m**; n = minimum number of clock periods and m = number of clock periods added for each additional repetition of operation.
The number of clock periods for an instruction which repeats k times is n + (k−1)•m.

Table 3-6. Z8000 Instruction Set Object Codes - Alphabetic Listing (Continued)

Mnemonic		Object Code	Bytes	Clock Periods	Mnemonic		Object Code	Bytes	Clock Periods
MULTL	rqd,adrsx	58id	4/6	note 2	*OUTI	@rid,@ris,rw	3Bs2	4	21
		pppp					Ord8		
		qqqq			*OUTIB	@rid,@ris,rw	3As2	4	21
	rqd,data32	180d	6	note 2			Ord8		
		yyyy			POP	adrsx,@ris	57si	4/6	16-19
		zzzz					pppp		
	rqd,rls	98sd	2	note 2			qqqq		
	rqd,@ris	18id	2	note 2		rwd,@ris	97sd	2	8
NEG	adrsx	4Di2	4/6	15-19		@rid,@ris	17sd	2	12
		pppp			POPL	adrsx,@ris	55si	4/6	23-26
		qqqq					pppp		
	rwd	8Dd2	2	7			qqqq		
	@rid	0Dd2	2	12		rld,@ris	95id	2	12
NEGB	adrsx	4Ci2	4/6	15-19		@rid,@ris	15id	2	19
		pppp			PUSH	@rid,adrsx	53di	4/6	14-7
		qqqq					pppp		
	rbd	8Cd2	2	7			qqqq		
	@rid	0Cd2	2	12		@rid,data16	0Dd9	4	12
NOP		8D07	2	7			yyyy		
OR	rwd,adrsx	45id	4/6	9-13		@rid,rws	93is	2	9
		pppp				@rid,@ris	13is	2	13
		qqqq			PUSHL	@rid,adrsx	51di	4/6	21-24
	rwd,data16	050d	4	7			pppp		
		yyyy					qqqq		
	rwd,rws	85sd	2	4		@rid,rls	91is	2	12
	rwd,@ris	05id	2	7		@rid,@ris	11is	2	20
ORB	rbd,adrsx	44id	4/6	9-13	RES	adrsx,b16	63ib	4/6	13-17
		pppp					pppp		
		qqqq					qqqq		
	rbd,data8	040d	4	7		rwd,b16	A3db	2	4
		yxyx				rwd,rws	230s	4	10
	rbd,rbs	84sd	2	4			0d00		
	rbd,@ris	04id	2	7		@rid,b16	23ib	2	11
*OTDR	@rid,@ris,rw	3BsA	4	21/10**	RESB	adrsx,b8	62ib	4/6	13-17
		Ord0					pppp		
*OTDRB	@rid,@ris,rw	3AsA	4	21/10**			qqqq		
		Ord0				rbd,b8	A2db	2	4
*OTIR	@rid,@ris,rw	3Bs2	4	21/10**		rbd,rws	220s	4	10
		Ord0					0d00		
*OTIRB	@rid,@ris,rw	3As2	4	21/10**		@rid,b8	22ib	2	11
		Ord0			RESFLG	flag	8Df3	2	7
*OUT	ioaddr,rws	3Bs6	4	12	RET	cc	9E0c	2	10,13/7
		pppp			RL	rwd,1	B3d0	2	6
	@rw,rws	3Fds	2	10		rwd,2	B3d2	2	7
*OUTB	ioaddr,rbs	3As6	4	12	RLB	rbd,1	B2d0	2	6
		pppp				rbd,2	B2d2	2	7
	@rw,rbs	3Eds	2	10	RLC	rwd,1	B3d8	2	6
*OUTD	@rid,@ris,rw	3BsA	4	21		rwd,2	B3dA	2	7
		Ord8			RLCB	rbd,1	B2d8	2	6
*OUTDB	@rid,@ris,rw	3AsA	4	21		rbd,2	B2dA	2	7
		Ord8			RLDB	rbd,rbs	BEsd	2	9

*   Priviledged instruction — can be executed only in system mode.

**   Number of clock periods depends on the number of repetitions for n/m**; n = minimum number of clock periods and m = number of clock periods added for each additional repetition of operation.
The number of clock periods for an instruction which repeats k times is n + (k−1)•m.

Table 3-6. Z8000 Instruction Set Object Codes - Alphabetic Listing (Continued)

Mnemonic		Object Code	Bytes	Clock Periods	Mnemonic		Object Code	Bytes	Clock Periods
RR	rwd,1	B3d4	2	6	*SINI	@rid, @ris,rw	3Bs1	4	21
	rwd,2	B3d6	2	7			Ord8		
RRB	rbd,1	B2d4	2	6	*SINIB	@rid, @ris,rw	3As1	4	21
	rbd,2	B2d6	2	7			Ord8		
RRC	rwd,1	B3dC	2	6	*SINIR	@rid, @ris,rw	3Bs1	4	21/10**
	rwd,2	B3dE	2	7			Ord0		
RRCB	rbd,1	B2dC	2	6	*SINIRB	@rid, @ris,rw	3As1	4	21/10**
	rbd,2	B2dE	2	7			Ord0		
RRDB	rbd,rbs	BCsd	2	9	SLA	rwd,data16	B3d9	4	16/3**
SBC	rwd,rws	B7sd	2	5			yyyy		
SBCB	rbd,rbs	B6sd	2	5	SLAB	rbd,data16	B2d9	4	16/3**
SC	data8	7Fyy	2	33,39			yyyy		
SDA	rwd,rw	B3dB	4	18/3**	SLAL	rld,data16	B3dC	4	16/3**
		Or00					yyyy		
SDAB	rbd,rw	B2dB	4	18/3**	SLL	rwd,data16	B3d1	4	16/3**
		Or00					yyyy		
SDAL	rld,rw	B3dF	4	18/3**	SLLB	rbd,data16	B2d1	4	16/3**
		Or00					yyyy		
SDL	rwd,rw	B3d3	4	18/3**	SLLL	rld,data16	B3d5	4	16/3**
		Or00					yyyy		
SDLB	rbd,rw	B2d3	4	18/3**	*SOTDR	@rid, @ris,rw	3BsB	4	21/10**
		Or00					Ord0		
SDLL	rld,rw	B3d7	4	18/3**	*SOTDRB	@rid, @ris,rw	3AsB	4	21/10**
		Or00					Ord0		
SET	adrsx,b16	65ib	4/6	13-17	*SOTIR	@rid, @ris,rw	3Bs3	4	21/10**
		pppp					Ord0		
		qqqq			*SOTIRB	@rid, @ris,rw	3As3	4	21/10**
	rwd,b16	A5db	2	4			Ord0		
	rwd,rws	2505	4	10	*SOUT	ioaddr,rws	3Bs7	4	12
		0d00					pppp		
	@rid,b16	25ib	2	11	*SOUTB	ioaddr,rbs	3As7	4	12
SETB	adrsx,b8	64ib	4/6	13-17			pppp		
		pppp			*SOUTD	@rid, @ris,rw	3BsB	4	21
		qqqq					Ord8		
	rbd,b8	A4db	2	4	*SOUTDB	@rid, @ris,rw	3AsB	4	21
	rbd,rws	240s	4	10			Ord8		
		0d00			*SOUTI	@rid, @ris,rw	3Bs3	4	21
	@rid,b8	24ib	2	11			Ord8		
SETFLG	flag	8Df1	2	7	*SOUTIB	@rid, @ris,rw	3As3	4	21
*SIN	rwd,ioaddr	3Bd5	4	12			Ord8		
		pppp			SRA	rwd,data16	B3d9	4	16/3**
*SINB	rbd,ioaddr	3Ad5	4	12			yyyy		
		pppp			SRAB	rbd,data16	B2d9	4	16/3**
*SIND	@rid, @ris,rw	3Bs9	4	21			yyyy		
		Ord8			SRAL	rld,data16	B3dD	4	16/3**
*SINDB	@rid, @ris,rw	3As9	4	21			yyyy		
		Ord8			SRL	rwd,data16	B3d1	4	16/3**
*SINDR	@rid, @ris,rw	3Bs9	4	21/10**			yyyy		
		Ord0			SRLB	rbd,data16	B2d1	4	16/3**
*SINDRB	@rid, @ris,rw	3As9	4	21/10**			yyyy		
		Ord0			SRLL	rld,data16	B3d5	4	16/3**
							yyyy		

* Priviledged instruction — can be executed only in system mode.

** Number of clock periods depends on the number of repetitions for n/m**; n = minimum number of clock periods and m = number of clock periods added for each additional repetition of operation.
The number of clock periods for an instruction which repeats k times is n + (k−1)•m.

Table 3-6. Z8000 Instruction Set Object Codes - Alphabetic Listing (Continued)

Mnemonic		Object Code	Bytes	Clock Periods	Mnemonic		Object Code	Bytes	Clock Periods
SUB	rwd,adrsx	43id	4/6	9-13	TRDRB	@rid,@ris,rw	B8dC	4	25/14**
		pppp					OrsO		
		qqqq			TRIB	@rid,@ris,rw	B8d0	4	25
	rwd,data16	030d	4	7			OrsO		
		yyyy			TRIRB	@rid,@ris,rw	B8d4	4	25/14**
	rwd,rws	83sd	2	4			OrsO		
	rwd,@ris	03id	2	7	TRTDB	@rid,@ris,rw	B8dA	4	25
SUBB	rbd,adrsx	42id	4/6	9-13			OrsO		
		pppp			TRTDRB	@rid,@ris,rw	B8dE	4	25/14**
		qqqq					OrsE		
	rbd,data8	020d	4	7	TRTIB	@rid,@ris,rw	B8d2	4	25
		yxyx					OrsO		
	rbd,rbs	82sd	2	4	TRTIRB	@rid,@ris,rw	B8d6	4	25/14**
	rbd,@ris	02id	2	7			OrsE		
SUBL	rld,adrsx	52id	4/6	15-19	TSET	adrsx	4Di6	4/6	14-18
		pppp					pppp		
		qqqq					qqqq		
	rld,data32	120d	6	14		rwd	8Dd6	2	7
		yyyy				@rid	0Dd6	2	11
		zzzz			TSETB	adrsx	4Ci6	4/6	14-18
	rld,rls	92sd	2	8			pppp		
	rld,@ris	12id	2	14			qqqq		
TCC	cc,rwd	AFdc	2	5		rbd	8Cd6	2	7
TCCB	cc,rbd	AEdc	2	5		@rid	0Cd6	2	11
TEST	adrsx	4Di4	4/6	11-15	XOR	rwd,adrsx	49id	4/6	9-13
		pppp					pppp		
		qqqq					qqqq		
	rwd	8Dd4	2	7		rwd,data16	090d	4	7
	@rid	0Dd4	2	8			yyyy		
TESTB	adrsx	4Ci4	4/6	11-15		rwd,rws	89sd	2	4
		pppp				rwd,@ris	09id	2	7
		qqqq			XORB	rbd,adrsx	48id	4/6	9-13
	rbd	8Cd4	2	7			pppp		
	@rid	0Cd4	2	8			qqqq		
TESTL	adrsx	5Ci0	4/6	16-20		rbd,data8	080d	4	7
		pppp					yxyx		
		qqqq				rbd,rbs	88sd	2	4
	rld	9Cd0	2	13		rbd,@ris	08id	2	7
	@rid	1Cd0	2	13					
TRDB	@rid,@ris,rw	B8d8	4	25					
		OrsO							

* Priviledged instruction — can be executed only in system mode.

** Number of clock periods depends on the number of repetitions for n/m**; n = minimum number of clock periods and m = number of clock periods added for each additional repetition of operation. The number of clock periods for an instruction which repeats k times is n + (k−1)•m.

Table 3-6. Z8000 Instruction Set Object Codes - Alphabetic Listing (Continued)

Note 1

Divisor	DIV			DIVL		
	Not Aborted	Divisor is Zero	Dividend Too Large	Not Aborted	Divisor is Zero	Dividend Too Large
adrsx	96-100	14-18	26-29	724-728	31-35	52-56
All Others	95	13	25	723	30	51

Note 2

Multiplier	MULT		MULTL	
	Normal	Multiplier is Zero	Normal	Multiplier is Zero
adrsx	71-75	19-22	$283 + 7 \cdot m - 287 + 7 \cdot m$	31-35
All Others	70	18	$282 + 7 \cdot m$	30

Table 3-7. Z8000 Object Codes - Numeric Listing

Object Code	Instruction		Object Code	Instruction	
000d yy00	ADDB	rbd,data8	19id	MULT	rld,@ris
00id	ADDB	rbd,@ris	1A0d yyyy zzzz	DIVL	rqd,data32
010d yyyy	ADD	rwd,data16	1Aid	DIVL	rqd,@ris
01id	ADD	rwd,@ris	1B0d yyyy	DIV	rld,data16
020d yy00	SUBB	rbd,data8	1Bid	DIV	rld,@ris
02id	SUBB	rbd,@ris	1Cd0	TESTL	@rid
030d yyyy	SUB	rwd,data16	1Cs1 0d0n	LDM	rwd,@ris,n16
03id	SUB	rwd,@ris	1Cd9 0s0n	LDM	@rid,rws,n16
040d yy00	ORB	rbd,data8	1Dds	LDL	@rid,rls
04id	ORB	rbd,@ris	1Edc	JP	cc,@rid
050d yyyy	OR	rwd,data16	1Fd0	CALL	@rid
05id	OR	rwd,@ris	20id	LDB	rbd,@ris
060d yy00	ANDB	rbd,data8	210d yyyy	LD	rwd,data16
06id	ANDB	rbd,@ris	21id	LD	rwd,@ris
070d yyyy	AND	rwd,data16	220s 0d00	RESB	rbd,rws
07id	AND	rwd,@ris	22ib	RESB	@rid,b8
080d yy00	XORB	rbd,data8	230s 0d00	RES	rwd,rws
08id	XORB	rbd,@ris	23ib	RES	@rid,b16
090d yyyy	XOR	rwd,data16	240s 0d00	SETB	rbd,rws
09id	XOR	rwd,@ris	24ib	SETB	@rid,b8
0A0d yy00	CPB	rbd,data8	250s 0d00	SET	rwd,rws
0Aid	CPB	rbd,@ris	25ib	SET	@rid,b16
0B0d yyyy	CP	rwd,data16	260s 0d00	BITB	rbd,rws
0Bid	CP	rwd,@ris	26ib	BITB	@rid,b8
0Cd0	COMB	@rid	270s 0d00	BIT	rwd,rws
0Cd1 yy00	CPB	@rid,data8	27ib	BIT	@rid,b16
0Cd2	NEGB	@rid	28dn	INCB	@rid,n16
0Cd4	TESTB	@rid	29dn	INC	@rid,n16
0Cd5 yy00	LDB	@rid,data8	2Adn	DECB	@rid,n16
0Cd6	TSETB	@rid	2Bdn	DEC	@rid,n16
0Cd8	CLRB	@rid	2Csd	EXB	rbd,@ris
0Dd0	COM	@rid	2Dsd	EX	rwd,@ris
0Dd1 yyyy	CP	@rid,data16	2Eds	LDB	@rid,rbs
0Dd2	NEG	@rid	2Fds	LD	@rid,rws
0Dd4	TEST	@rid	300d xxxx	LDRB	rbd,disp
0Dd5 yyyy	LD	@rid,data16	30id xxxx	LDB	rbd,ris(disp)
0Dd6	TSET	@rid	310d xxxx	LDR	rwd,disp
0Dd8	CLR	@rid	31id xxxx	LD	rwd,ris(disp)
0Dd9 yyyy	PUSH	@rid,data16	320s xxxx	LDRB	disp,rbs
0E uu	Unimplemented; traps if EPA bit of FCW is zero		32is xxxx	LDB	rid(disp),rbs
			330s xxxx	LDR	disp,rws
0F ssss 01aa h0kn	XLDM	epu,ris,n16,data8	33is xxxx	LD	rid(disp),rws
0F dddd 11aa h0kn	XLDM	rid,epu,n16,data8	340d xxxx	LDAR	rld,disp
100d yyyy zzzz	CPL	rld,data32			rwd,disp
10id	CPL	rld,@ris	34id xxxx	LDA	rld,ris(disp)
11is	PUSHL	@rid,@ris			rwd,ris(disp)
120d yyyy zzzz	SUBL	rld,data32	350d xxxx	LDRL	rld,disp
12id	SUBL	rld,@ris	35id xxxx	LDL	rld,ris(disp)
13is	PUSH	@rid,@ris	370s xxxx	LDRL	disp,rls
140d yyyy zzzz	LDL	rld,data32	37is xxxx	LDL	rid(disp),rls
14id	LDL	rld,@ris	39s0	LDPS	@ris
15id	POPL	@rid,@ris	3As0 0rd0	INIRB	@rid,@ris,rw
160d yyyy zzzz	ADDL	rld,data32	3As0 0rd8	INIB	@rid,@ris,rw
16id	ADDL	rld,@ris	3As1 0rd0	SINIRB	@rid,@ris,rw
17sd	POP	@rid,@ris	3As1 0rd8	SINIB	@rid,@ris,rw
180d yyyy zzzz	MULTL	rqd,data32	3As2 0rd0	OTIRB	@rid,@ris,rw
18id	MULTL	rqd,@ris	3As2 0rd8	OUTIB	@rid,@ris,rw
190d yyyy	MULT	rld,data16			

Table 3-7. Z8000 Object Codes - Numeric Listing (Continued)

Object Code	Instruction	
3As3 Ord0	SOTIRB	@rid,@ris,rw
3As3 Ord8	SOUTIB	@rid,@ris,rw
3Ad4 pppp	INB	rbd,ioaddr
3Ad5 pppp	SINB	rbd,ioaddr
3As6 pppp	OUTB	ioaddr,rbs
3As7 pppp	SOUTB	ioaddr,rbs
3As8 Ord0	INDRB	@rid,@ris,rw
3As8 Ord8	INDB	@rid,@ris,rw
3As9 Ord0	SINDRB	@rid,@ris,rw
3As9 Ord8	SINDB	@rid,@ris,rw
3AsA Ord0	OTDRB	@rid,@ris,rw
3AsA Ord8	OUTDB	@rid,@ris,rw
3AsB Ord0	SOTDRB	@rid,@ris,rw
3AsB Ord8	SOUTDB	@rid,@ris,rw
3Bs0 Ord0	INIR	@rid,@ris,rw
3Bs0 Ord8	INI	@rid,@ris,rw
3Bs1 Ord0	SINIR	@rid,@ris,rw
3Bs1 Ord8	SINI	@rid,@ris,rw
3Bs2 Ord0	OTIR	@rid,@ris,rw
3Bs2 Ord8	OUTI	@rid,@ris,rw
3Bs3 Ord0	SOTIR	@rid,@ris,rw
3Bs3 Ord8	SOUTI	@rid,@ris,rw
3Bd4 pppp	IN	rwd,ioaddr
3Bd5 pppp	SIN	rwd,ioaddr
3Bs6 pppp	OUT	ioaddr,rws
3Bs7 pppp	SOUT	ioaddr,rws
3Bs8 Ord0	INDR	@rid,@ris,rw
3Bs8 Ord8	IND	@rid,@ris,rw
3Bs9 Ord0	SINDR	@rid,@ris,rw
3Bs9 Ord8	SIND	@rid,@ris,rw
3BsA Ord0	OTDR	@rid,@ris,rw
3BsA Ord8	OUTD	@rid,@ris,rw
3BsB Ord0	SOTDR	@rid,@ris,rw
3BsB Ord8	SOUTD	@rid,@ris,rw
3Csd	INB	rbd,@rw
3Dsd	IN	rwd,@rw
3Eds	OUTB	@rw,rbs
3Fds	OUT	@rw,rws
40id pppp qqqq	ADDB	rbd,adrsx
41id pppp qqqq	ADD	rwd,adrsx
42id pppp qqqq	SUBB	rbd,adrsx
43id pppp qqqq	SUB	rwd,adrsx
44id pppp qqqq	ORB	rbd,adrsx
45id pppp qqqq	OR	rwd,adrsx
46id pppp qqqq	ANDB	rbd,adrsx
47id pppp qqqq	AND	rwd,adrsx
48id pppp qqqq	XORB	rbd,adrsx
49id pppp qqqq	XOR	rwd,adrsx
4Aid pppp qqqq	CPB	rbd,adrsx
4Bid pppp qqqq	CP	rwd,adrsx
4CiO pppp qqqq	COMB	adrsx
4Ci1 yy00 pppp qqqq	CPB	adrsx,data8
4Ci2 pppp qqqq	NEGB	adrsx
4Ci4 pppp qqqq	TESTB	adrsx
4Ci5 yy00 pppp qqqq	LDB	adrsx,data8

Object Code	Instruction	
4Ci6 pppp qqqq	TSETB	adrsx
4Ci8 pppp qqqq	CLRB	adrsx
4Di0 pppp qqqq	COM	adrsx
4Di1 yyyy pppp qqqq	CP	adrsx,data16
4Di2 pppp qqqq	NEG	adrsx
4Di4 pppp qqqq	TEST	adrsx
4Di5 yyyy pppp qqqq	LD	adrsx,data16
4Di6 pppp qqqq	TSET	adrsx
4Di8 pppp qqqq	CLR	adrsx
4Euu	Unimplemented; bit of FCW is zero.	
4F ssss 01aa h0kn	XLDM	epu,adrsx,n16,data8
4F dddd 11aa h0kn	XLDM	adrsx,epu,n16,data8
50id pppp qqqq	CPL	rld,adrsx
51di pppp qqqq	PUSHL	@rid,adrsx
52id pppp qqqq	SUBL	rld,adrsx
53di pppp qqqq	PUSH	@rid,adrsx
54id pppp qqqq	LDL	rld,adrsx
55si pppp qqqq	POPL	adrsx,@ris
56id pppp qqqq	ADDL	rld,adrsx
57si pppp qqqq	POP	adrsx,@ris
58id pppp qqqq	MULTL	rqd,adrsx
59id pppp qqqq	MULT	rld,adrsx
5Aid pppp qqqq	DIVL	rqd,adrsx
5Bid pppp qqqq	DIV	rld,adrsx
5CiO pppp qqqq	TESTL	adrsx
5Ci1 0d0n pppp qqqq	LDM	rwd,adrsx,n16
5Ci9 0s0n pppp qqqq	LDM	adrsx,rws,n16
5Dis pppp qqqq	LDL	adrsx,rls
5Eic pppp qqqq	JP	cc,adrsx
5FiO pppp qqqq	CALL	adrsx
60id pppp qqqq	LDB	rbd,adrsx
61id pppp qqqq	LD	rwd,adrsx
62ib pppp qqqq	RESB	adrsx,b8
63ib pppp qqqq	RES	adrsx,b16
64ib pppp qqqq	SETB	adrsx,b8
65ib pppp qqqq	SET	adrsx,b16
66ib pppp qqqq	BITB	adrsx,b8
67ib pppp qqqq	BIT	adrsx,b16
68in pppp qqqq	INCB	adrsx,n16
69in pppp qqqq	INC	adrsx,n16
6Ain pppp qqqq	DECB	adrsx,n16
6Bin pppp qqqq	DEC	adrsx,n16
6Cid pppp qqqq	EXB	rbd,adrsx
6Did pppp qqqq	EX	rwd,adrsx
6Eis pppp qqqq	LDB	adrsx,rbs
6Fis pppp qqqq	LD	adrsx,rws
70id Or00	LDB	rbd,ris(rw)
71id Or00	LD	rwd,ris(rw)
72is Or00	LDB	rid(rw),rbs
73is Or00	LD	rid(rw),rws

Table 3-7. Z8000 Object Codes - Numeric Listing (Continued)

Object Code	Instruction	
74id 0r00	LDA	rld,ris(rw)
		rwd,ris(rw)
75id 0r00	LDL	rld,ris(rw)
76id pppp qqqq	LDA	rld,adrsx
		rwd,adrsx
77is 0r00	LDL	rid(rw),rls
79i0 pppp qqqq	LDPS	adrsx
7A00	HALT	
7B00	IRET	
7B08	MSET	
7B09	MRES	
7B0A	MBIT	
7BdD	MREQ	rwd
7C 000000vv	DI	int
7C 000001vv	EI	int
7Dd2	LDCTL	rwd,FCW
7Dd3	LDCTL	rwd,REFRESH
7Dd4	LDCTL	rwd,PSAPSEG
7Dd5	LDCTL	rwd,PSAPOFF
7Dd6	LDCTL	rwd,NSPSEG
7Dd7	LDCTL	rwd,NSPOFF
7DsA	LDCTL	FCW,rws
7DsB	LDCTL	REFRESH,rws
7DsC	LDCTL	PSAPSEG,rws
7DsD	LDCTL	PSAPOFF,rws
7DsE	LDCTL	NSPSEG,rws
7DsF	LDCTL	NSPOFF,rws
7Fyy	SC	data8
80sd	ADDB	rbd,rbs
81sd	ADD	rwd,rws
82sd	SUBB	rbd,rbs
83sd	SUB	rwd,rws
84sd	ORB	rbd,rbs
85sd	OR	rwd,rws
86sd	ANDB	rbd,rbs
87sd	AND	rwd,rws
88sd	XORB	rbd,rbs
89sd	XOR	rwd,rws
8Asd	CPB	rbd,rbs
8Bsd	CP	rwd,rws
8Cd0	COMB	rbd
8Cd1	LDCTLB	rbd,FLAGS
8Cd2	NEGB	rbd
8Cd4	TESTB	rbd
8Cd6	TSETB	rbd
8Cd8	CLRB	rbd
8Cs9	LDCTLB	FLAGS,rbs
8D07	NOP	
8Dd0	COM	rwd
8Df1	SETFLG	flag
8Dd2	NEG	rwd
8Df3	RESFLG	flag
8Dd4	TEST	rwd
8Df5	COMFLG	flag
8Dd6	TSET	rwd
8Dd8	CLR	rwd

Object Code	Instruction	
8E 000000aa h0k0	XLDCTL	FLAGS,epu,data8
8E 000001aa h0k0	XCTL	epu,data8
8E 000010aa h0k0	XLDCTL	epu,FLAGS,data8
8F 000000aa hdkn	XLDM	rwd,epu,n16,data8
8F 000010aa hskn	XLDM	epu,rws,n16,data8
90sd	CPL	rld,rls
91is	PUSHL	@rid,rls
92sd	SUBL	rld,rls
93is	PUSH	@rid,rws
94sd	LDL	rld,rls
95id	POPL	rld,@ris
96sd	ADDL	rld,rls
97sd	POP	rwd,@ris
98sd	MULTL	rqd,rls
99sd	MULT	rld,rws
9Asd	DIVL	rqd,rls
9Bsd	DIV	rld,rws
9Cd0	TESTL	rld
9E0c	RET	cc
A0sd	LDB	rbd,rbs
A1sd	LD	rwd,rws
A2db	RESB	rbd,b8
A3db	RES	rwd,b16
A4db	SETB	rwd,b8
A5db	SET	rwd,b16
A6db	BITB	rbd,b8
A7db	BIT	rwd,b16
A8dn	INCB	rbd,n16
A9dn	INC	rwd,n16
AAdn	DECB	rbd,n16
ABdn	DEC	rwd,n16
ACsd	EXB	rbd,rbs
ADsd	EX	rwd,rws
AEdc	TCCB	cc,rbd
AFdc	TCC	cc,rwd
B0d0	DAB	rbd
B1d0	EXTSB	rwd
B1d7	EXTSL	rqd
B1dA	EXTS	rld
B2d0	RLB	rbd,1
B2d1 yyyy	SLLB	rbd,data16
B2d1 yyyy	SRLB	rbd,data16
B2d2	RLB	rbd,2
B2d3 0r00	SDLB	rbd,rw
B2d4	RRB	rbd,1
B2d6	RRB	rbd,2
B2d8	RLCB	rbd,1
B2d9 yyyy	SLAB	rbd,data16
B2d9 yyyy	SRAB	rbd,data16
B2dA	RLCB	rbd,2
B2dB 0r00	SDAB	rbd,rw
B2dC	RRCB	rbd,1
B2dE	RRCB	rbd,2
B3d0	RL	rwd,1
B3d1 yyyy	SLL	rwd,data16
B3d1 yyyy	SRL	rwd,data16

Table 3-7. Z8000 Object Codes - Numeric Listing (Continued)

Object Code	Instruction		Object Code	Instruction	
B3d2	RL	rwd,2	BAs1 0rd8	LDIB	@rid,@ris,rw
B3d3 0r00	SDL	rwd,rw	BAs2 0rdc	CPSIB	@rid,@ris,rw,cc
B3d4	RR	rwd,1	BAs4 0rdc	CPIRB	rbd,@ris,rw,cc
B3d5 yyyy	SLLL	rld,data16	BAs6 0rdc	CPSIRB	@rid,@ris,rw,cc
B3d5 yyyy	SRLL	rld,data16	BAs8 0rdc	CPDB	rbd,@ris,rw,cc
B3d6	RR	rwd,2	BAs9 0rd0	LDDRB	@rid,@ris,rw
B3d7 0r00	SDLL	rld,rw	BAs9 0rd8	LDDB	@rid,@ris,rw
B3d8	RLC	rwd,1	BAsA 0rdc	CPSDB	@rid,@ris,rw,cc
B3d9 yyyy	SLA	rwd,data16	BAsC 0rdc	CPDRB	rbd,@ris,rw,cc
B3d9 yyyy	SRA	rwd,data16	BAsE 0rdc	CPSDRB	@rid,@ris,rw,cc
B3dA	RLC	rwd,2	BBs0 0rdc	CPI	rwd,@ris,rw,cc
B3dB 0r00	SDA	rwd,rw	BBs1 0rd0	LDIR	@rid,@ris,rw
B3dC	RRC	rwd,1	BBs1 0rd8	LDI	@rid,@ris,rw
B3dD yyyy	SLAL	rld,data16	BBs2 0rdc	CPSI	@rid,@ris,rw,cc
B3dD yyyy	SRAL	rld,data16	BBs4 0rdc	CPIR	rwd,@ris,rw,cc
B3dE	RRC	rwd,2	BBs6 0rdc	CPSIR	@rid,@ris,rw,cc
B3dF 0r00	SDAL	rld,rw	BBs8 0rdc	CPD	rwd,@ris,rw,cc
B4sd	ADCB	rbd,rbs	BBs9 0rd0	LDDR	@rid,@ris,rw
B5sd	ADC	rwd,rws	BBs9 0rd8	LDD	@rid,@ris,rw
B6sd	SBCB	rbd,rbs	BBsA 0rdc	CPSD	@rid,@ris,rw,cc
B7sd	SBC	rwd,rws	BBsC 0rdc	CPDR	rwd,@ris,rw,cc
B8d0 0rs0	TRIB	@rd,@ris,rw	BBsE 0rdc	CPSDR	@rid,@ris,rw,cc
B8d2 0rs0	TRTIB	@rid,@ris,rw	BCsd	RRDB	rbd,rbs
B8d4 0rs0	TRIRB	@rid,@ris,rw	BDdb	LDK	rwd,b16
B8d6 0rsE	TRTIRB	@rid,@ris,rw	BEsd	RLDB	rbd,rbs
B8d8 0rs0	TRDB	@rid,@ris,rw	Cdyy	LDB	rbd,data8
B8dA 0rs0	TRTDB	@rid,@ris,rw	Dxxx	CALR	disp
B8dC 0rs0	TRDRB	@rid,@ris,rw	Ecxx	JR	cc,disp
B8dE 0rsE	TRTDRB	@rid,@ris,rw	Fr 0ttttttt	DBJNZ	rb,disp
BAs0 0rdc	CPIB	rbd,@ris,rw,cc	Fr 1ttttttt	DJNZ	rw,disp
BAs1 0rd0	LDIRB	@rid,@ris,rw			

STANDARD OPERAND ADDRESSING METHODS

When discussing Z8000 addressing modes, we stated that the Z8000 instruction set uses available addressing methods in a very orderly fashion. A majority of instructions identify a source and/or destination operand using one of the following five operand identification methods:

1. A CPU register is specified

2. Immediate addressing

3. Register indirect (or implied) memory addressing.

4. Direct memory addressing

5. Direct indexed memory addressing.

Whatever combination of operand identification methods you might use, remember that the destination operand always precedes the source operand, with a comma separating the two, when an assembly language instruction requires both operands to be specified.

In the discussion of individual instructions which follows, we use the term "standard operand addressing" to specify the five operand identification methods described above. As you will see, many instructions use these standard operand addressing methods.

Six of the bits of the first instruction object code word specify the selected operand identification method. The exact bit locations differ depending on whether a source or a destination operand is being identified, as illustrated in Figure 3-26.

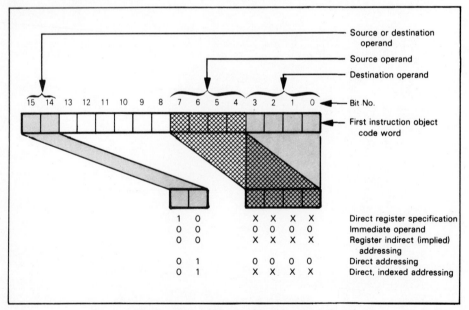

Figure 3-26. Standard Addressing Modes, as Identified in the
First Word of an Instruction's Object Code

The immediate operand will be in the second object code word for a byte or word instruction; the immediate operand will be in the second and third object code words for a long word instruction.

The direct address will be in the second object code word for a non-segmented or a short-segmented memory address; the direct address will be in the second and third object code words for a long segmented memory address.

XXXX is a 4-bit code that identifies a register, as summarized in Table 3-8.

The abbreviations used to specify addressing mode options are listed in Table 3-9.

Table 3-8. CPU Register Identification in Instruction Object Codes

Code	Byte Instruction	Word Instruction	Multiply/Divide and Long Word Instruction	Long Multiply/Divide Instruction
0000	RH0	R0	RR0	RQ0
0001	RH1	R1		
0010	RH2	R2	RR2	
0011	RH3	R3		
0100	RH4	R4	RR4	RQ4
0101	RH5	R5		
0110	RH6	R6	RR6	
0111	RH7	R7		
1000	RL0	R8	RR8	RQ8
1001	RL1	R9		
1010	RL2	R10	RR10	
1011	RL3	R11		
1100	RL4	R12	RR12	RQ12
1101	RL5	R13		
1110	RL6	R14	RR14	
1111	RL7	R15		

Table 3-9. Addressing Modes

R	-	Direct register specification
IM	-	Immediate addressing
DA	-	Direct memory addressing
IR	-	Register indirect (implied) memory addressing
X	-	Direct indexed memory addressing
BR	-	Base relative memory addressing
BX	-	Base indexed memory addressing
PR	-	Program relative memory addressing
I	-	Indirect memory addressing
S	-	Stack memory addressing
IRI	-	Register indirect memory addressing with auto increment
IRD	-	Register indirect memory addressing with auto decrement

ASSEMBLY LANGUAGE SYNTAX

All examples in this chapter illustrate AMC syntax and Zilog syntax: Syntax rules are defined in Chapter 2. A syntax summary is given in the following paragraphs. Tables 3-10 and 3-11 summarize addressing mode syntax and the differences between AMC and Zilog syntax.

1. When a source and a destination are specified in the operand field, the destination always precedes the source. Here is an example from Figure 3-7:

```
AND     R6,#4A3C^;        % AMC syntax
AND     R6,%4A3C          ! Zilog syntax !
```

The memory word with direct address $4A3C_{16}$ is the source.

2. Hexadecimal data are identified in Zilog syntax by an initial %. AMC syntax uses an initial # to identify hexadecimal data. The example above shows both of these notations.

3. Zilog syntax uses an initial # to identify an immediate operand. AMC syntax assumes an immediate operand as the default case for numeric operands and for symbolic constants. Here is the example from Figure 3 - 5 :

```
AND     R6,#4A3C;         % AMC syntax
AND     R6,#%4A3C         ! Zilog syntax !
```

The immediate operand $4A3C_{16}$ is the source.

4. AMC syntax makes special use of a character preceding a label to specify the value of the label, treated as an immediate data address constant. Here are some examples for the various addressing modes:

```
LD      R6,^LABEL;        % Immediate direct address
LD      R6,^LABEL(R2);    % Immediate direct indexed address
LD      R6,^(R2^(#400));  % Immediate base relative address
LD      R6,^(R2^(R1));    % Immediate base indexed address
```

In each instance, the source operand is the value of the address, not the contents of the addressed memory word.

Whether or not the AMC assembler considers a symbol to be a label depends on how it was defined. If a symbol is defined by use in a label field, the assembler considers it to be a label. An external symbol is also considered to be a label. The location counter symbol, $, is a label. All of these symbols must be preceded by a character, if their value is to be used as immediate data.

On the other hand, if the symbol was defined in a constant assembler directive, it is always assumed to be an immediate data value. Then, if you want to use it as a direct address, it must be followed by a character. See the next rule.

Table 3-10. Z8000 Assembler Addressing Mode Syntax

Addressing Mode	AMC Syntax	Zilog Syntax
Register	R8	R8
Immediate	CONSTANT 8 ^LABEL	#CONSTANT #8 #LABEL
Register Indirect	R8 ^	@ R8
Direct	LABEL #6000^ LABEL + OFFSET	LABEL %6000 LABEL + OFFSET
Direct Indexed	LABEL (R8) #6000 ^ (R8)	LABEL (R8) %6000 (R8)
Base Relative	R8 ^ (OFFSET) R8 ^ (#100)	R8 (#OFFSET) R8 (#%100)
Base Indexed	R8 ^ (R1)	R8 (R1)
Program Relative	LABEL ^ $+#100	LABEL $+%100
I/O Port	CONSTANT 8 R8	CONSTANT 8 @R8

Table 3-11. Z8000 AMC/Zilog Assembler Syntax Differences

	AMC	Zilog
Immediate Data	Numbers and symbolic constants are assumed to be immediate data. Labels must be preceded by ^ .	All immediate operands must be preceded by #
Indirect Register	Register name followed by ^	Register name preceded by @
Base Relative	Register name followed by ^	Register name
Numeric Direct Address	Number or symbolic constant followed by ^	Number
Direct Address Offset	Offset following + or −	Offset following + or −
Hexadecimal	Number preceded by #	Number preceded by %
Segmented Addresses	Segmented addresses must be labels. Assembler uses short segmented address wherever possible	Segment number enclosed in < < > >. Short segmented address enclosed in | |
I/O Ports	Port Address or Register Name	Port Address or Register Name preceded by @

5. Zilog syntax assumes a direct address as the default case for any operand. AMC syntax uses a trailing ^ to specify a numeric direct address. Here is the example from Figure 3-7:

```
AND     R6,#4A3C^;                  % AMC syntax
AND     R6,%4A3C                    ! Zilog syntax !
```

The source is identified using direct address $4A3C_{16}$.

For %4A3C (or #4A3C) we could substitute a label:

```
AND     R6,MEMLOC;                  % AMC syntax
AND     R6,MEMLOC                   ! Zilog syntax !
```

AMC syntax does not use a trailing ^ to identify a label as a direct address; for labels AMC syntax assumes direct addressing as the default case.

6. Using Zilog syntax a segment number is enclosed in double cornered brackets <<SS>>. AMC syntax requires that all segmented direct addresses be specified using labels. Here is the example from Figure 3-8:

```
AND     R6,SEGLABEL;                % AMC syntax
AND     R6,<<%2A>>%4A3C             ! Zilog syntax !
```

The source is specified by the long segmented direct address $4A3C_{16}$ within segment $2A_{16}$.

7. Using Zilog syntax a short segmented address is enclosed by vertical bars. The AMC assemblers automatically use a short segmented address whenever possible. Here is the example from Figure 3-9:

```
AND     R6,SEGLABEL;                % AMC syntax
AND     R6,|<<%2A>>%3C|             ! Zilog syntax
```

The source is specified by the short segmented direct address $003C_{16}$ within segment $2A_{16}$.

8. Zilog uses a preceding @ and AMC uses a trailing ^ to specify a register indirect (implied) memory address

Here is the example from Figure 3-12:

```
AND     R6,R8^;                     % AMC syntax
AND     R6,@R8                      ! Zilog syntax !
```

The source is specified using register indirect addressing, via 16-bit register R8.

9. An Index Register is enclosed by simple parentheses: (R8). Here is the example from Figure 3-14:

```
AND     R6,#4A3C^(R8);              % AMC syntax
AND     R6,%4A3C(R8)                ! Zilog syntax !
```

The source is identified using direct, indexed addressing; 16-bit register R8 is the Index Register.

10. A name or an immediate hexadecimal value appearing between simple brackets identifies a displacement or offset for base relative addressing. Here is the example from Figure 3-19:

```
LD      R4,RR8^(#04A0);             % AMC syntax
LD      R4,RR8(#%04A0)              ! Zilog syntax !
```

The source is identified using base relative addressing. 32-bit register RR8 holds the long-segmented base address. The displacement $04A0_{16}$ is added to this base address.

11. The $+$ or $-$ operators are used to indicate a displacement or offset used in direct addressing. This may be illustrated as follows:

```
LD      R4,MEMLOC+20        % AMC syntax
LD      R4,MEMLOC+20        ! Zilog syntax !
```

The source is identified using direct addressing. The address of the source
is the sum of 20_{10} and the value of the symbol MEMLOC.

12. An I/O Port address can be specified using direct addressing or register indirect addressing. Zilog uses standard direct or register indirect addressing syntax for I/O ports. AMC uses immediate syntax for a direct I/O port address and direct register syntax for a register indirect I/O port address. This may be illustrated as follows:

```
IN      R0,#0400;           % AMC syntax
IN      R0,%0400            ! Zilog syntax !
```

The source is identified as I/O Port 400_{16}.

```
IN      R0,R6;              % AMC syntax
IN      R0,@R6              ! Zilog syntax !
```

The source is an I/O port whose address is in Register R6.

Z8000 INSTRUCTION DESCRIPTIONS

In this section, we present the instructions in alphabetical order and describe them in great detail. This is the primary reference section for the instruction set. Note, however, that the information contained here was also summarized for convenience and presented in Table 3-5. We will discuss the syntax used by both AMC and Zilog assemblers. In the remaining chapters we arbitrarily use Zilog syntax.

Early production Z8000 chips do not execute all instructions correctly. This is mentioned in the descriptions of the instructions. Table 3-18 at the end of this chapter summarizes this information.

ADC — Add Words with Carry Register to Register

ADCB — Add Bytes with Carry Register to Register

Addressing Options		ADC	dst,src
dst	**src**	ADCB	dst,src
R	R		

The symbols dst and src are the destination and source operands, respectively; they must both be specified as CPU registers using direct register addressing. 16-bit CPU registers must be specified for ADC; 8-bit CPU registers must be specified for ADCB. The contents of the destination and source operand registers are treated as twos complement binary numbers and, together with the value of the Carry status, are added. The sum is returned in the destination register, whose prior contents are lost.

An anomaly of the Z8000 instructions set is the fact that ADC and ADCB are its only add-with-carry instructions. These two instructions can add only the contents of CPU registers; they do not allow either the source or the destination operand to be specified as a memory location.

The ADC and ADCB instructions' object codes may be illustrated as follows:

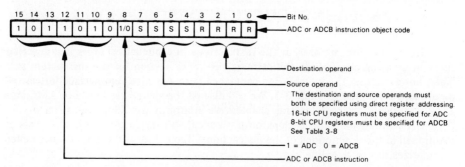

The C, Z, S, and V status flags are modified by the ADC and the ADCB instructions. In addition, the ADCB instruction modifies the H Status and resets DA to 0.

Figure 3-27 illustrates execution of the ADC instruction:

```
ADC      R4,R7;          % AMC syntax
ADC      R4,R7           ! Zilog syntax !
```

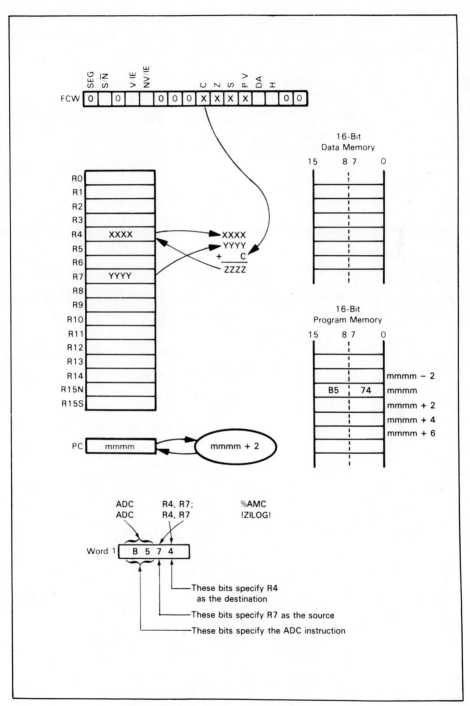

Figure 3-27. Execution of the ADC Instruction

Suppose register R4 initially contains $276A_{16}$, while register R7 contains $A3B0_{16}$, and the Carry status is 1, indicating a carry during the previous operation. This is what happens when the ADC instruction illustrated above is executed:

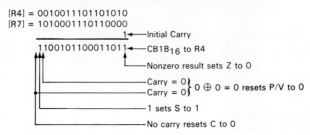

Figure 3-28 illustrates execution of the ADCB instruction:

```
ADCB    RL2,RH5;        % AMC syntax
ADCB    RL2,RH5         ! Zilog syntax !
```

Suppose register RL2 initially contains $2A_{16}$, RH5 initially contains 30_{16}, and the Carry status is 0. This is what happens when the ADCB instruction illustrated above is executed.

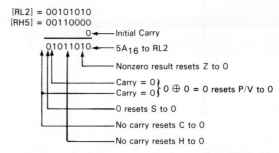

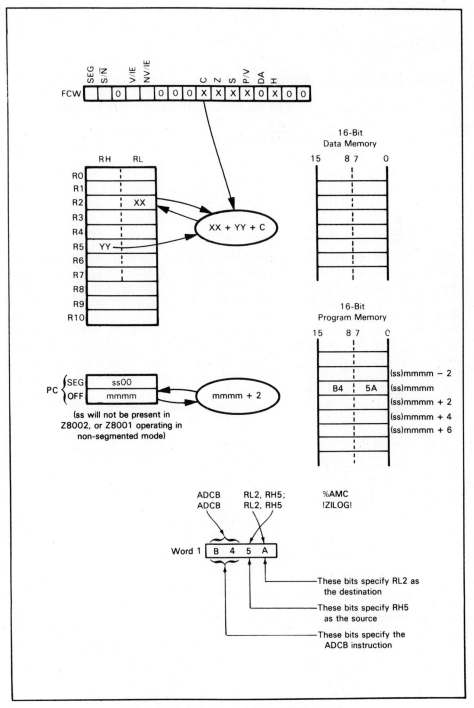

Figure 3-28. Execution of the ADCB Instruction

ADD — Add Words

ADDB — Add Bytes

ADDL — Add Long Words

This is the general format for the ADD, ADDB and ADDL instructions:

Addressing Options	
dst	src
R	R
R	IM
R	IR
R	DA
R	X

ADD   dst,src
ADDB   dst,src
ADDL   dst,src

The symbol dst is a destination operand which must be specified using direct register addressing. A 16-bit CPU register must be specified for ADD; an 8-bit CPU register must be specified for ADDB; a 32-bit CPU register must be specified for ADDL.

The symbol src is a source operand which can be specified using any standard operand addressing method (see Figure 3-26).

The source and destination operands are both assumed to be twos complement binary numbers. When the ADD, ADDB or ADDL instruction is executed, the source and destination operands are added using twos complement signed binary arithmetic. The sum is returned in the destination operand CPU register, whose prior contents are lost. The source operand is not modified.

The ADD, ADDB and ADDL instructions' object code may be illustrated as follows:

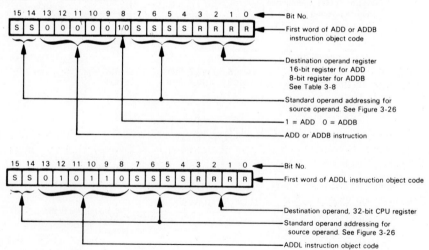

The C, Z, S, and V statuses are modified by the ADD, ADDL and ADDB instructions. In addition, the ADDB instruction modifies the H status and resets the DA status to 0.

Figure 3-29 illustrates execution of the ADD instruction:

In some instances, you can use the LDA instruction to add the contents of two registers, or to add an immediate operand and the contents of a register. See the discussion of the LDA instruction.

```
ADD     R7,#423A^;      % AMC syntax
ADD     R7,%423A        ! Zilog syntax !
```

Using the operands illustrated in Figure 3-29, this is what happens:

```
        [R7] = 1010001110110000
   [476A16] = 0010011101101010
              1100101100011010 ◄── CBIA16 to R7
                                └── Nonzero result resets Z to 0
                                    Carry = 0 }
                                    Carry = 0 } 0 ⊕ 0 = 0 resets P/V to 0
                                    1 sets S to 1
                                    Carry = 0 resets C to 0
```

Figure 3-30 illustrates execution of the ADDB instruction:

```
ADDB    RH7,#423A^;     % AMC syntax
ADDB    RH7,%423A       ! Zilog syntax !
```

Using the operand values illustrated in Figure 3-30, this is what happens:

```
       [RH7] = 00101010
   [423A16] = 00110000
               01011010 ◄── 5A16 to RH7
                         └── Nonzero result resets Z to 0
                             No carry resets H to 0
                             Carry = 0 }
                             Carry = 0 } 0 ⊕ 0 = 0 resets P/V to 0
                             0 resets S to 0
                             No carry resets C to 0
```

Figure 3-11, which illustrated direct addressing earlier in this chapter, also illustrates execution of the following ADDL instruction:

```
ADDL    RR4,SEGLABEL;       % AMC syntax
ADDL    RR4,<<%2A>>%4A3C    ! Zilog syntax !
```

Suppose 32-bit register RR4 initially contains $2A364217_{16}$, while the 32-bit memory word selected by the long-segmented direct memory address contains $42C31A25_{16}$. This is what happens when the ADDL instruction is executed:

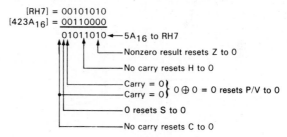

```
      [RR4] = 00101010001101100100001000010111
  [2A4A3C16] = 01000010110000110001101000100101
               01101100111110010101110000111100 ◄── 6CF95C3C16 to RR4
                                                 └── Nonzero result resets Z to 0
                                                     Carry = 0 }
                                                     Carry = 0 } 0 ⊕ 0 = 0 resets P/V to 0
                                                     0 resets S to 0
                                                     0 resets C to 0
```

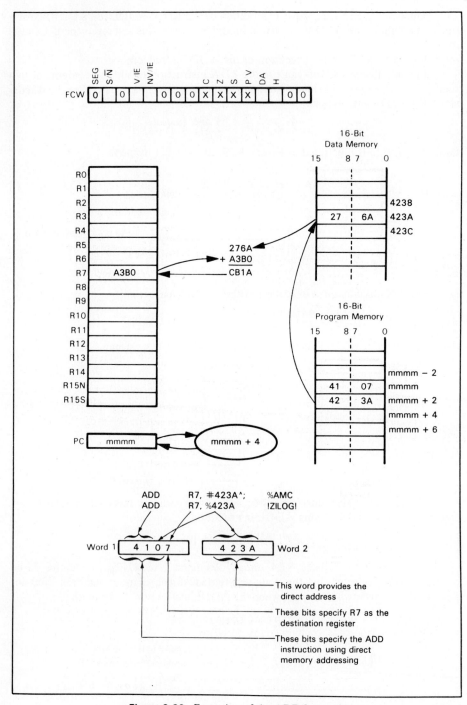

Figure 3-29. Execution of the ADD Instruction

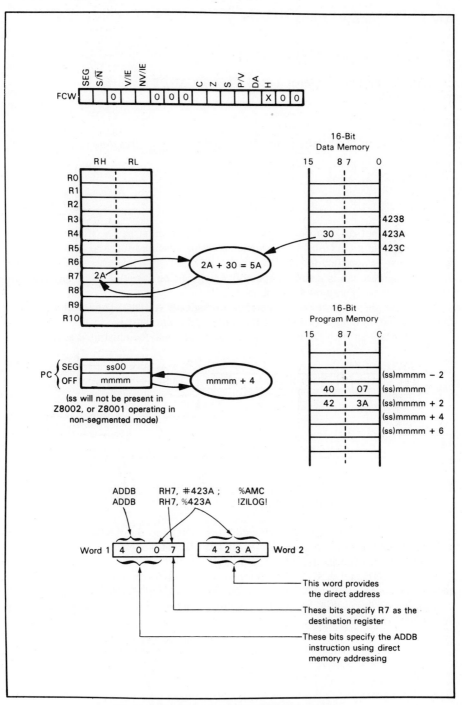

Figure 3-30. Execution of the ADDB Instruction

AND — Logically AND Words

ANDB — Logically AND Bytes

This is the general format for the AND and ANDB instructions:

Addressing Options	
dst	**src**
R	R
R	IM
R	IR
R	DA
R	X

ADN   dst,src
ANDB   dst,src

The symbol dst is a destination operand which must be specified using direct register addressing. A 16-bit CPU register must be specified for AND; an 8-bit CPU register must be specified for ANDB.

The symbol src is a source operand which can be specified using any standard operand addressing method (see Figure 3- 26).

The source and destination operands are logically ANDed. The result is returned in the destination operand CPU register, whose prior contents are lost.

The AND and ANDB instructions' object code may be illustrated as follows:

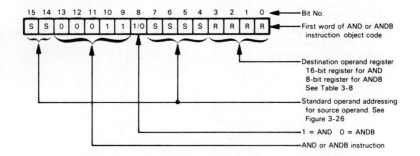

The Z and S statuses are modified by the AND and the ANDB instructions. In addition, the ANDB instruction modifies the P/V status to reflect the parity of the result byte. (P = 1 for even parity, 0 for odd parity).

Since AND and ANDB were the instructions most commonly used to illustrate addressing modes, you will find numerous examples illustrating execution of both instructions earlier in this chapter. For example, Figure 3-5 illustrates execution of the immediate AND instruction:

```
AND     R6,#4A3C;       % AMC syntax
AND     R6,%4A3C        ! Zilog syntax !
```

Suppose register R6 initially contained 2376_{16}; this is what happens when the AND instruction illustrated above is executed:

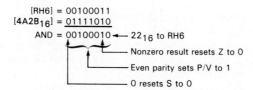

```
     [R6] = 0010001101110110
[4A3C₁₆] = 0100101000111100
     AND = 0000001000110100 ◄──── 0234₁₆ to R6
                │        │
                │        └──── Nonzero result resets Z to 0
                └──────────── 0 resets S to 0
```

Figure 3-10, for example, illustrates execution of the direct addressing AND instruction:

```
ANDB     RH6,#4A2B^;     % AMC syntax
ANDB     RH6,%4A2B       ! Zilog syntax !
```

Suppose register RH6 initially contains 23_{16} while the memory byte with address $4A2B_{16}$ contains $7A_{16}$; this is what happens when the instruction illustrated above is executed:

```
    [RH6] = 00100011
[4A2B₁₆] = 01111010
     AND = 00100010 ◄──── 22₁₆ to RH6
             │   │
             │   └──── Nonzero result resets Z to 0
             │
             └──────── Even parity sets P/V to 1
             │
             └──────── 0 resets S to 0
```

BIT — Test The Value Of Any Bit In A 16-Bit Word

BITB — Test The Value Of Any Bit In A Byte

This is the general format for the BIT and BITB assembly language instructions:

Addressing Options	
dst	src
R	IM
IR	IM
DA	IM
X	IM
R	R

BIT   dst,src
BITB   dst,src

The symbol dst is a destination operand which can be specified using any standard operand addressing method, with the exception of immediate addressing.

The symbol src is a source operand which must be specified as a 16-bit CPU register, using direct register addressing, or as immediate data. For BITB, the source register must be one of the registers R0-R7.

The source operand specifies the bit position within the destination operand which is to be tested. Neither the source nor the destination operands are modified. The complement of the value of the selected bit is returned in the Z status.

There are two versions of the BIT and BITB instructions. The first version uses one of the standard operand addressing methods, but not immediate addressing, to identify a destination word or byte. The four low order instruction object code bits specify the bit within the data word that is to be tested. The object code for this version of the BIT and BITB instructions may be illustrated as follows:

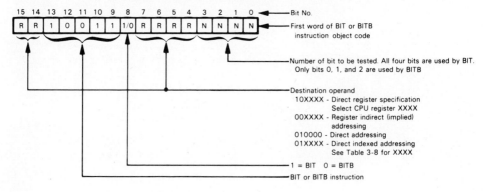

The second version of the BIT and BITB instructions requires the source and destination operands to be specified as CPU registers. The destination operand must be specified using direct register addressing. A 16-bit CPU register must be specified as the BIT destination operand; an 8-bit CPU register must be specified as the BITB destination operand. A 16-bit CPU register must be specified as the source operand for BIT or BITB. Any 16-bit register can be specified as the BIT source operand; however, one of the registers R0 - R7 must be specified as the source operand for BITB. The four low order bits of the source operand register are significant for BITB. Only the low order three bits of the source operand register are significant for BITB. The significant bits of the source operand register specify the bit position within the destination operand that is to be tested. As with the first version of BIT and BITB, the complement of the value of the tested bit is returned in the Z status. The object code for the second version of the BIT and BITB instructions may be illustrated as follows:

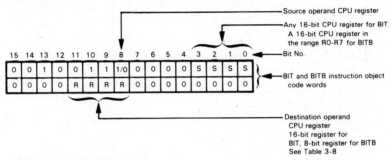

Table 3-8 defines SSSS and RRRR register designations.
Only the Z status is modified by BIT and BITB instructions.
Figure 3-31 illustrates execution of the BIT instruction:

```
BIT      #423A^(R10),5;   % AMC Syntax
BIT      %423A(R10),#5    ! Zilog Syntax !
```

This is the first version of the BIT instruction; it illustrates non-segmented, direct indexed addressing, selecting bit 5 of a 16-bit data memory word with address $463A_{16}$. Since bit 5 of the data word is 1, the Z status will be reset to 0. No other data modifications occur.

Figure 3-32 illustrates execution of the BITB instruction:

```
BITB     RH2,R4;          % AMC syntax
BITB     RH2,R4           ! Zilog syntax !
```

As illustrated in Figure 3-32, the low order three bits of register R4 select bit 3 of register RH2; bit 3 of register RH2 is 1, therefore the Z status is reset to 0.

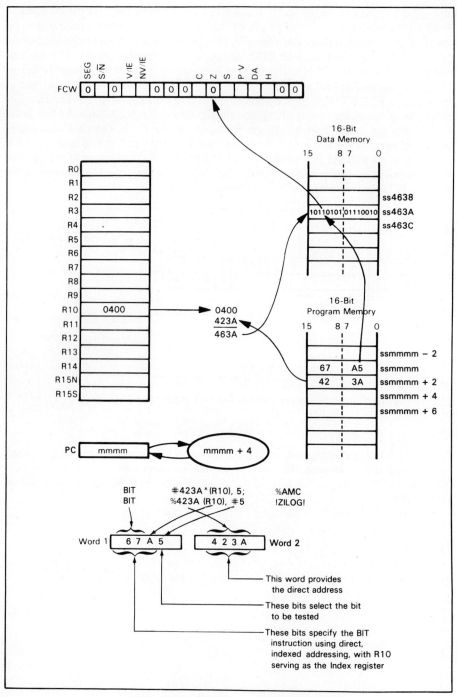

Figure 3-31. Execution of the BIT Instruction

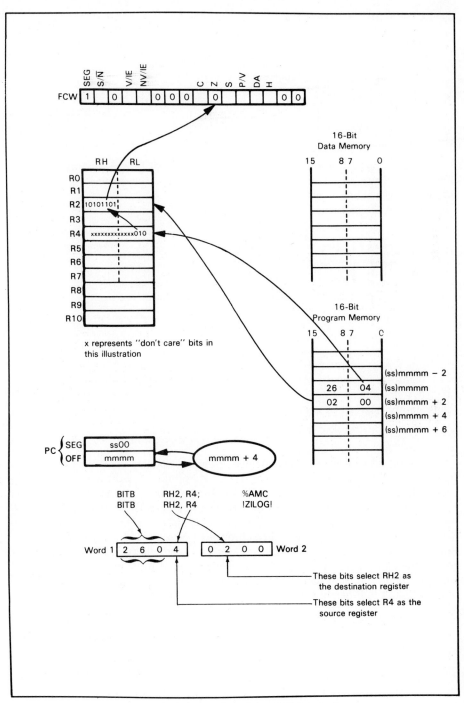

Figure 3-32. Execution of the BITB Instruction

CALL — Call Subroutine

This is the general format for the CALL assembly language instruction:

Addressing Options
dst
IR
DA
X

CALL   dst

The symbol dst is a destination operand which can be specified using register indirect (implied), direct or direct indexed addressing. The destination operand is interpreted as a subroutine's execution address.

The CALL instruction's object code may be illustrated as follows:

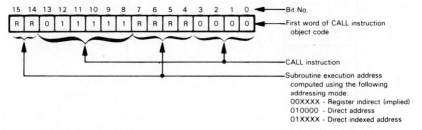

The CALL instruction does not modify any status flags.

Figures 3-33 and 3-34 illustrate execution of the CALL instruction in non-segmented and segmented modes, respectively. Figure 3-33 illustrates execution of the following non-segmented instruction:

```
CALL     #2000^(R8);     % AMC syntax
CALL     %2000(R8)       ! Zilog syntax !
```

Figure 3-33 shows the incremented Program Counter contents (in this case mmmm + 4) being pushed onto the stack. Assuming that the program is being executed in normal mode, register R15N is functioning as the Stack Pointer. This register contains $C084_{16}$, Its contents are decremented by 2. Then mmmm + 4 is written into memory location $C082_{16}$. After the incremented Program Counter contents have been pushed onto the stack, the subroutine execution address is loaded into the Program Counter. The call instruction in Figure 3-33 uses direct, indexed addressing to specify the subroutine execution address. 0800_{16}, taken from Index Register R8, is added to 2000_{16}, the base address provided by the CALL instruction; the sum (2800_{16}) is loaded into the Program Counter.

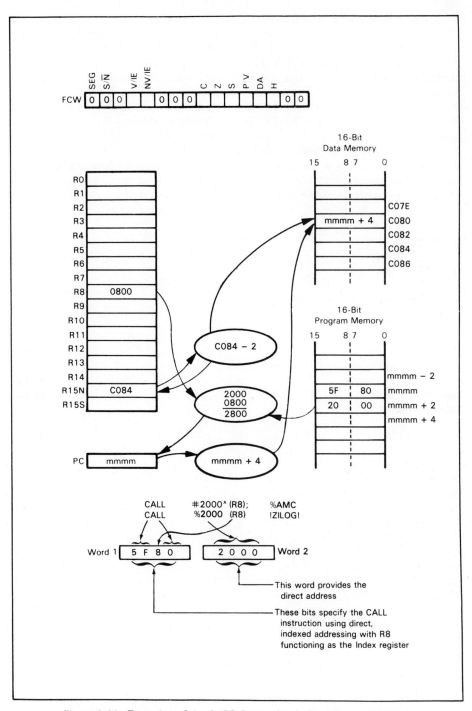

Figure 3-33. Execution of the CALL Instruction in Non-Segmented Mode

Figure 3-34 illustrates the same CALL instruction as Figure 3-33, however, the CALL instruction is executed in segmented mode. Three different segment numbers are illustrated. Program memory initially is in segment SS, which may have any value between 0 and $7F_{16}$. The stack is in segment 02_{16}. The incremented Program Counter contents are pushed onto the stack. The stack pointer is decremented by 2. The Program Counter offset, after being incremented, goes into the first stack word at $02C082_{16}$. The stack pointer is decremented by 2 again. The Program Counter segment is pushed onto the second stack word at $02C080_{16}$. The final stack pointer address will be $C080_{16}$, in segment 02. The subroutine execution address is computed by adding the offset 2000_{16} to the index provided by R8, which is 0800_{16}. This yields the address 2800_{16} in segment 30_{16}. Remember that long-segmented addresses in an instructions object code have the high order bit of the segment byte set to 1 to specify a long-segmented address. That is why $B0_{16}$ in the second word of the CALL instructions object code selects segment 30_{16}.

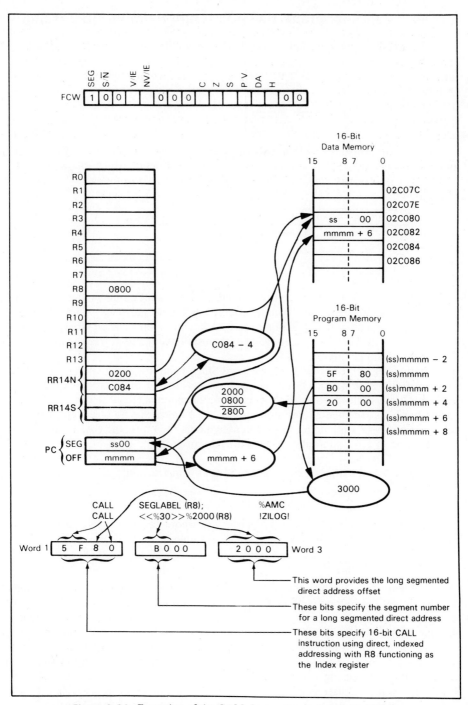

Figure 3-34. Execution of the CALL Instruction in Segmented Mode

CALR — Call Subroutine Using Program Relative Addressing

This is the general format for the CALR assembly language instruction:

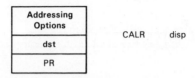

The symbol disp is an address displacement; it is the distance between the execution address of a subroutine and the address of the instruction which follows CALR. The CALR instruction's object code may be illustrated as follows:

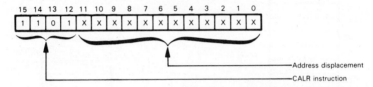

When the CALR instruction is executed, the Program Counter is incremented to address the next sequential instruction, then pushed onto the stack. A new Program Counter value is computed by shifting the CALR instruction's signed binary displacement one bit to the left, in effect doubling it, then subtracting this doubled displacement from the program counter.

In non-segmented mode, a single word Stack Pointer is used, and a single word Program Counter is pushed onto the stack. In segmented mode, a two word Stack Pointer is used, and two words of Program Counter contents are pushed onto the stack (offset first). But segmented and non-segmented modes have no direct effect on the subroutine address computation. In segmented mode, therefore, the CALR instruction must be used to call a subroutine within the current program segment, as specified by the Program Counter.

Figure 3-35 illustrates execution of the CALR instruction:

```
CALR    ^$-#400;        % AMC syntax
CALR    $-%400          ! Zilog syntax !
```

In a real assembly language program, you would be more likely to identify a subroutine using a label. Here is one possible example:

```
CALR    SUBA;           % AMC syntax
CALR    SUBA            ! Zilog syntax !
```

In Figure 3-35, the operand is shown as a displacement from the current program counter so that the address computation is easier to follow. As illustrated, the required subroutine execution address is 400_{16} less than the current Program Counter contents. But the displacement will be subtracted from the Program Counter after it has been incremented to address the next sequential instruction. Therefore, it will be necessary to subtract 402_{16} from the incremented Program Counter contents in order to yield the same result as subtracting 400_{16} from the current Program Counter contents. Hence, 402 is the required diplacement. The displacement, as stored in the instruction object code, is half of the required displacement, which is why 201_{16} is shown in Figure 3-35.

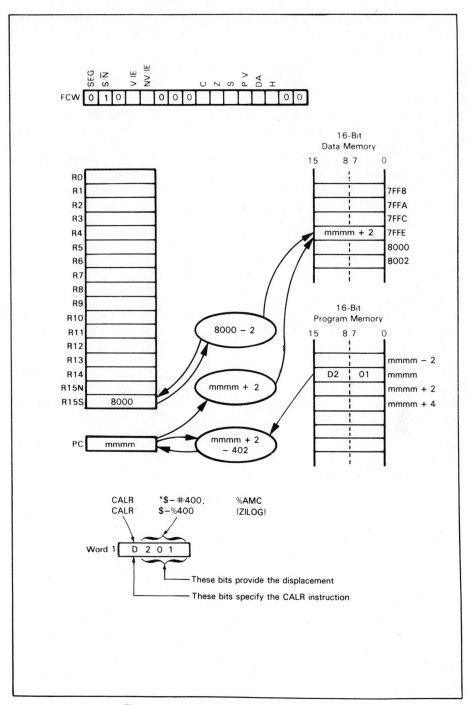

Figure 3-35. Execution of the CALR Instruction

If mmmm were in fact 1000_{16}, the required subroutine execution address would be $0C00_{16}$. The required subroutine execution address is computed correctly in Figure 3-35. This may be illustrated as follows:

1000 + 2 = 1002	Increment program counter
201 · 2 = 402	Shift displacement
1002 – 402 = 0C00	Subtract

Since a 12-bit displacement is shifted one position to the left before being subtracted, the CALR instruction, in effect, uses a 13-bit signed binary displacement. Therefore the displacement can have effective values ranging between -4096_{10} and $+4094_{10}$. Since this displacement is subtracted from the Program Counter after it has been incremented by two, the actual subroutine execution address can lie anywhere in the range -4092_{10} through $+4098_{10}$ from the program memory location which holds the actual CALR instruction object code.

CLR — Clear a 16 Bit Word

CLRB — Clear a Byte

This is the general format for the CLR and CLRB assembly language instructions:

Addressing Options
dst
R IR DA X

```
CLR     dst
CLRB    dst
```

The symbol dst is a destination operand which can be specified using any standard operand addressing method, with the exception of immediate addressing. The destination operand contents are reset to 0. The CLR and CLRB instructions' object code may be illustrated as follows:

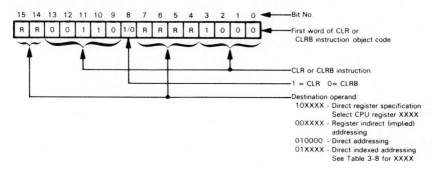

The instruction:

```
CLR     R4^;            % AMC syntax
CLR     @R4             ! Zilog syntax !
```

will clear the memory word whose address is contained in 16-bit register R4. The instruction:

```
CLR     R4;             % AMC syntax
CLR     R4              ! Zilog syntax !
```

will load zero into 16-bit register R4.

The CLRB instruction:

```
CLRB    R4^;            % AMC syntax
CLRB    @R4             ! Zilog syntax !
```

will reset to zero the contents of the memory byte addressed by 16-bit register R4. In order to clear 16-bit register R4 itself, instead of using a single CLR instruction you could use the following two CLRB instructions:

```
CLRB    RH4;            % AMC syntax
CLRB    RL4;

CLRB    RH4             ! Zilog syntax !
CLRB    RL4
```

COM — Complement a 16 Bit Word

COMB — Complement a Byte

This is the general format for the COM and COMB assembly language instructions:

Addressing Options
dst
R
IR
DA
X

```
COM    dst
COMB   dst
```

The symbol dst is a destination operand that can be specified using any of the standard operand identification methods with the exception of immediate addressing. The contents of the identified destination operand is ones complemented. The COM and COMB instructions' object code may be illustrated as follows:

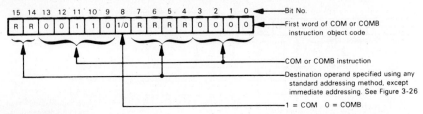

The Z and S statuses are modified by the COM instruction. The COMB instruction also modifies the P/V status to reflect the parity of the result (even parity = 1, odd parity = 0). When the instruction:

```
COM    R3;            % AMC syntax
COM    R3             ! Zilog syntax !
```

is executed, the contents of 16-bit register R3 is complemented. If R3 originally contains $423A_{16}$, this is what happens:

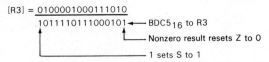

The COMB instruction:

```
COMB   #423A^;        % AMC syntax
COMB   %423A          ! Zilog syntax !
```

will complement the contents of the memory byte with address $423A_{16}$. If this memory byte initially contains $3A_{16}$, this is what happens when the COMB instruction is executed:

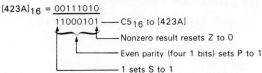

COMFLG — Complement Status Flags

This is the general format for the COMFLG instruction:

```
COMFLG        flags
```

The symbol "flags" may be the designation for one or more of the status flags: Carry, Zero, Sign, Parity, and Overflow. The Zilog and AMC assemblers use different abbreviations for the statuses:

Status	Zilog Syntax	AMC Syntax
Carry	C	CY
Zero	Z	ZR
Sign	S	SGN
Parity*	P	PY
Overflow*	V	OV

*Parity and Overflow are the same flag.

COMFLG complements the contents of the identified status bits of the Flag and Control Word. You can list the status bits in any sequence.

The COMFLG instruction's object code may be illustrated as follows:

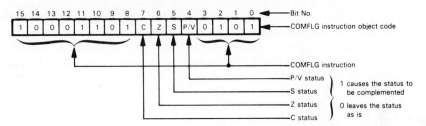

The status flags modified by the COMFLG instruction will depend on the flags specified in the operand field. No flags other than those specifically identified are modified.

The instruction:

```
COMFLG   CY;              % AMC syntax
COMFLG   C                ! Zilog syntax !
```

will complement just the Carry status. Other statuses are not modified. On the other hand, the instruction:

```
COMFLG   PY,SGN,ZR,CY;    % AMC syntax
COMFLG   P,S,Z,C          ! Zilog syntax !
```

will complement all four statuses.

CP — Compare Words

CPB — Compare Bytes

This is the general format for the CP and CPB assembly language instructions:

Addressing Options		CP	dst,src
		CPB	dst,src

dst	src
R	R
R	IM
R	IR
R	DA
R	X
IR	IM
DA	IM
X	IM

The symbols dst and src are destination and source operands, respectively. If dst is specified as a CPU register, then src is specified using any standard operand addressing method. If dst is specified using register indirect (implied), direct or direct indexed addressing, however, src must be specified as an immediate operand.

The two operands are compared by subtracting the source operand from the destination operand using twos complement addition. The result is discarded. Neither the source nor the destination operands change, but status flags are modified to reflect the result of the subtraction; therefore, they can be used by subsequent conditional instructions.

When using condition codes from Table 3-4 to test status bits after a compare instruction, remember that the relation is:

destination condition source

For example, "greater than" means that the destination operand is greater than the source operand.

Remember that the Carry status is set to 1 for no carry and it is reset to 0 for a carry since the Carry status reports borrows following subtraction.

There are two versions of the CP and CPB instructions; the first version uses the standard operand addressing methods to specify a source operand, while the destination operand is held in a CPU register. The object code for this first form of the CP and CPB instructions may be illustrated as follows:

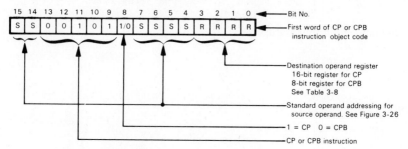

The C, Z, S, and V status flags are modified when the CP or CPB instruction is executed.

Figure 3-36 illustrates execution of the instruction:

```
CP      R6,#2800^;      % AMC syntax
CP      R6,%2800        ! Zilog syntax !
```

If register R6 contains $230F_{16}$, while memory word 2800_{16} contains $362A_{16}$, then when the instruction illustrated in Figure 3-36 is executed, this is what happens:

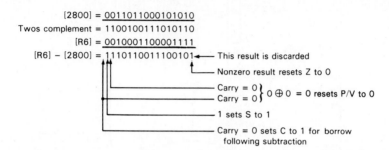

The second form of the CP and CPB instructions provides an immediate source operand, while the destination operand is specified using register indirect, direct, or direct indexed addressing. This object code may be illustrated as follows:

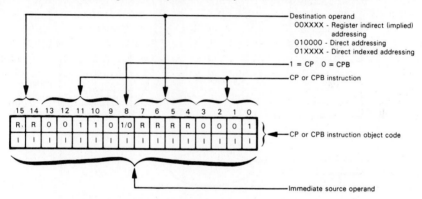

The C, Z, S, and V status flags are modified when the CP or the CPB instruction is executed.

Figure 3-37 illustrates the CPB instruction using the second instruction format. This is the CPB instruction illustrated:

```
CPB     RR4^,BYTE;      % AMC syntax
CPB     @RR4,#BYTE      ! Zilog syntax !
```

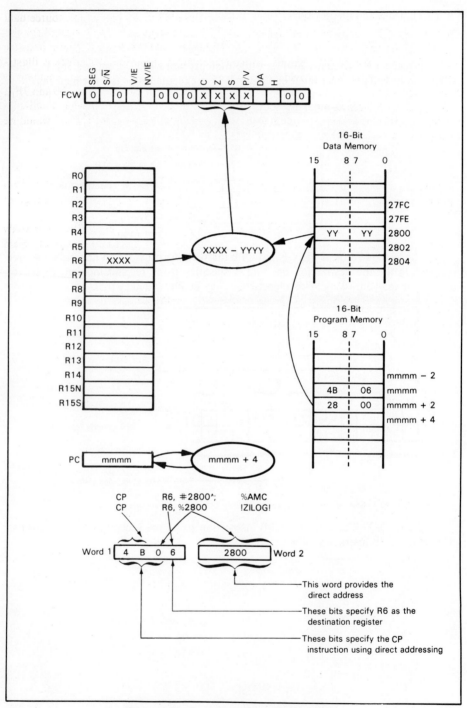

Figure 3-36. Execution of the CP Instruction

Notice that the label BYTE has been used to identify an immediate source data byte in the CPB instructions operand field. This immediate data is illustrated for the general case using YY in both bytes of the second instruction object code word. Register indirect addressing specifies the destination operand; since segmented mode is illustrated, 32-bit register RR4 provides the implied memory address. The data segment is illustrated for the general case using TT, which can have any value between 00 and $7F_{16}$. The same CPB instruction executed in non-segmented mode might provide a non-segmented implied memory address in register R5, in which case the instruction would be rewritten as follows:

```
CPB     R5^,BYTE;      % AMC syntax
CPB     @R5,#BYTE      ! Zilog syntax !
```

In this form the instruction would execute exactly as illustrated in Figure 3-37. The program and data memory addresses would lose their segment numbers, and the Program Counter would have no segment register. No other changes would occur.

If the CPB instruction illustrated in Figure 3-37 were executed with YY initially having the value $3C_{16}$, while XX initially has the value $2A_{16}$, then this is what would occur:

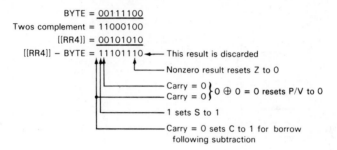

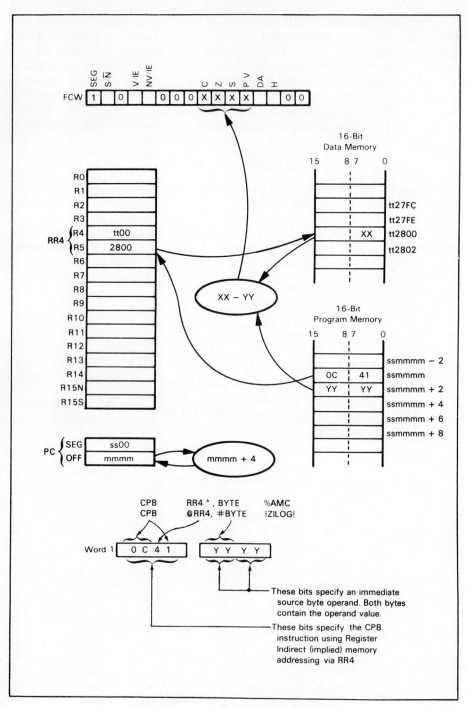

Figure 3-37. Execution of the CPB Instruction

CPD — Compare Words and Decrement

CPDB — Compare Bytes and Decrement

This is the general format for the CPD and the CPDB instructions:

Addressing Options		
dst	**src**	**cnt**
R	IR	R

CPD   dst,src,cnt,cc
CPDB   dst,src,cnt,cc

The symbol dst is a destination operand which must be specified using direct register addressing, as a 16-bit CPU register for CPD, or an 8-bit CPU register for CPDB.

The symbol src is a source operand which must be specified using register indirect (implied) addressing.

The symbol cnt is a counter which must be specified as a 16-bit CPU register for both CPD and CPDB.

The symbol cc is a condition code which must be specified using one of the labels shown in the "code" column of Table 3- 4.

CPD and CPDB are string search instructions. They are designed to serve as one step of an instruction loop that searches a string, beginning with the highest string address, and ending at the lowest string address. For each step of the search, the destination operand is compared to the source operand. The comparison is performed by subtracting the source operand from the destination operand using two's complement addition. The result of the subtraction is discarded; neither the source operand nor the destination operand is modified to reflect the result of the subtraction. However, status flags are compared with the condition specified by CC. If there is a condition match, then the Zero status is set to 1; otherwise the Zero status is cleared.

When using comparison condition codes from Table 3-4, the relation is:

destination condition source

For example, the "greater than" condition is matched if the destination operand is greater than the source operand.

At the end of each CPD or CPDB instruction's execution, the source operand address is decremented by 1 for CPDB, or by 2 for CPD, so as to address the next byte or word in the string.

16-bit Counter Register contents are decremented by 1 for CPD or CPDB. If the Counter Register decrements to zero, then the Overflow status is set to 1; the Overflow status is cleared otherwise.

The CPD and CPDB instruction object codes may be illustrated as follows:

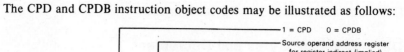

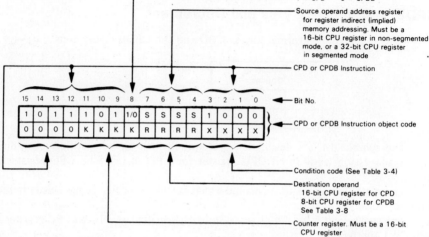

The Zero status is set to 1 when a match is detected between the specified condition code and the status flag settings generated by the compare. The overflow status is set to 1 if the counter register decrements to zero, indicating the end of the search. The Zero and Overflow statuses are reset to 0 otherwise. The values of Carry and Sign status flags are undefined after CPD or CPDB.

Figure 3-38 illustrates execution of the following CPDB instruction:

```
CPDB:    RL0,R9^,R10,LLT,    % AMC syntax
CPDB:    RL0,@R9,R10,ULT     ! Zilog syntax !
```

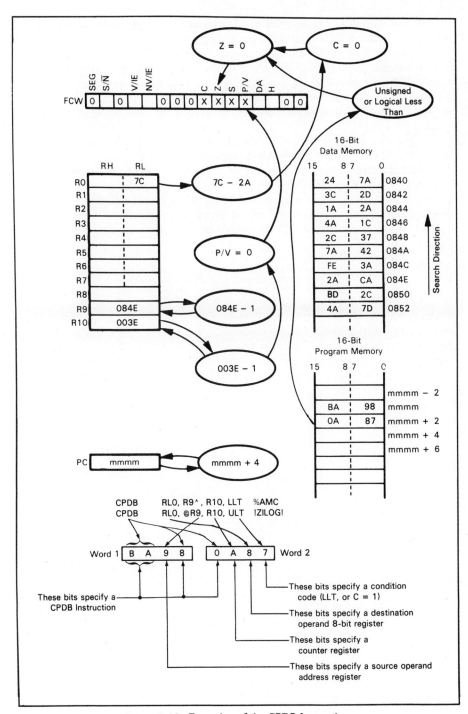

Figure 3-38. Execution of the CPDB Instruction

Figure 3-38 shows a data string in data memory being compared with the data byte held in 8-bit register RL0. RL0 is the destination operand. 16-bit register R9 addresses the byte within the data string that is currently being compared. Thus R9 addresses the source operand. 16-bit register R10 identifies the number of bytes within the string that remain to be compared. Since the logical or unsigned less than condition has been specified in the operand field, the Z status will be set to 1 whenever the contents of register RL0 are less than the contents of the byte of the data string that is currently being compared.

After each execution of the CPD or CPDB instruction, you will have to use conditional instructions that test the Zero and Overflow statuses. If the Zero status is 1, then the specified condition has been encountered. If the Overflow status is 1, then the end of the string has been encountered and the string search is complete. Remember, the Carry and Sign status flags are also modified by the CPD and CPDB instructions, but they are left undefined at the end of the instruction's execution. Here is a simple instruction loop containing the CPDB instruction illustrated above:

```
LOOP:   CPDB    RL0,@R9,R10,ULT      ! Zilog syntax !
        JP      NZ,NEXT
        .               These instructions process a string byte
        .               when the contents of RL0 are less than the
        .               contents of the string byte. These instructions
        .               must not modify the P/V status.
NEXT:   JP      NOV,LOOP
```

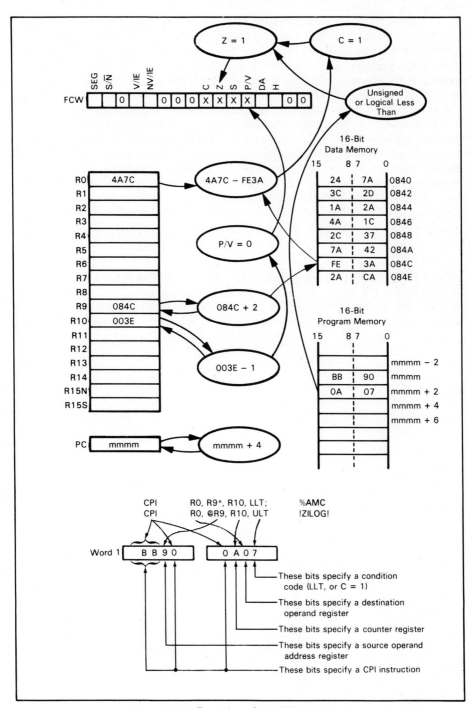

Figure 3-39. Execution of the CPI Instruction

The instruction sequence illustrated above first executes the CPDB instruction described in Figure 3-39; then a JP instruction is executed to test whether the contents of RL0 are less than the string byte. If the Z status is 0, then the contents of RL0 were not less than the contents of the string byte; the JP NZ, NEXT instruction causes a branch to the second JP instruction, labeled NEXT. But if the Z status is 1, then some unspecified sequence of instructions is executed to process the identified string byte. These unspecified instructions must not modify the P/V status, because the JP NOV, LOOP instruction at NEXT tests the Overflow status to determine whether the end of the loop has been reached. As long as the Overflow status is 0, this JP instruction will cause a branch back to LOOP. But when the Overflow status is 1, which will occur when register R10 decrements to zero, then the next sequential instruction will be executed, terminating the loop.

We do not separately illustrate execution of the CPD instruction since the illustration would be almost identical to Figure 3-38. Moreover, the very similar CPI instruction is illustrated in Figure 3-39. The CPD instruction:

```
CPD     R0,R9^,R10,ULT   % AMC syntax
CPD     R0,@R9,R10,LLT   ! Zilog syntax !
```

might be considered the CPD equivalent of Figure 3-38. This instruction will compare the contents of R0, rather than RL0, with the data string. Since R0 is a 16-bit register, the data string will be compared in 16-bit increments, which means that the string address held in register R9 must always be even, and will be incremented by 2 at the conclusion of each CPD instruction execution.

CPDR — Compare Words, Decrement and Repeat

CPDRB — Compare Bytes, Decrement and Repeat

The CPDR/CPDRB instructions are identical to CPD and CPDB, respectively, except that the instructions are re-executed until either the Z status or the P/V status is 1.

This is the general format for the CPDR and the CPDRB instructions:

Addressing Options		
dst	src	cnt
R	IR	R

CPDR   dst,src,cnt,cc
CPDRB   dst,src,cnt,cc

The symbol dst is a destination operand which must be specified using direct register addressing as a 16-bit CPU register for CPDR, or an 8-bit CPU register for CPDRB.

The symbol src is a source operand which must be specified using register indirect (implied) addressing.

The symbol cnt is a counter which must be specified as a 16- bit CPU register for both CPDR and CPDRB.

The symbol cc is a condition code which must be specified using one of the labels shown in the "code" column of Table 3-4.

CPDR and CPDRB are string search instructions. They are designed to function as a single instruction loop that searches a string, beginning with the highest string address, and ending at the lowest string address. For each step of the search, the destination operand is compared to the source operand. The comparison is performed by subtracting the source operand from the destination operand using twos complement addition. The result of the subtraction is discarded; neither the source operand nor the destination operand is modified to reflect the result of the subtraction. However, status flags are compared with the condition specified by cc. If there is a condition match, then the Zero status is set to 1; the Zero status is cleared otherwise.

When using comparison conditions codes from Table 3-4, the relation is:

destination condition source

For example, the "greater than" condition is matched if the destination operand is greater than the source operand.

After each iterative execution of the CPDR or CPDRB instruction, the source operand address is decremented by 1 for CPDRB, or by 2 for CPDR, so as to address the next byte or word in the string.

The 16-bit Counter Register contents are decremented by 1 after each iterative execution of CPDR or CPDRB. If the Counter Register decrements to 0, then the Overflow status is set to 1; the Overflow status is cleared otherwise.

Execution of CPIR or CPIRB continues until either the Zero status or Overflow status is set to one.

The CPDR and CPDRB instruction object codes may be illustrated as follows:

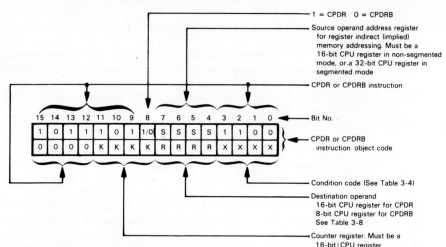

The Zero status is set to 1 when a match is detected between the specified condition code and the status flag settings generated by the compare. The Overflow status is set to 1 if the counter register decrements to zero, indicating the end of the search. The Zero and Overflow statuses are reset to 0 otherwise. The values of the Carry and Sign status flags are left undefined after the CPDR and the CPDRB instructions.

In order to best compare and contrast the CPDR/CPDRB instructions with the CPD/CPDB instructions, let us look again at the simple instruction loop which we used to illustrate the CPDB instruction. This is the CPDRB version:

```
LOOP:    CPDRB   RL0,@R9,R10,ULT    ! Zilog syntax !
         JP      NZ,NEXT
         .              These instructions process a string byte when
         .              the contents of RL0 are less than the string
         .              byte. These instructions must not modify the
         .              P/V status.
NEXT:    JP      NOV,LOOP
```

The CPDB and CPDRB instruction sequences are essentially identical; but the execution sequence changes. For CPDB, one byte is compared each time the CPDB instruction is executed. Therefore the two JP instructions will be executed once for each byte of the source data string that is compared. Using CPDRB, however, execution of the CPDRB instruction will continue until either the Z or P/V status is 1. Therefore, the two JP instructions will be executed only when a "match" byte is found in the source data string (in this case when the contents of RL0 are less than the contents of the string byte) or when the end of the loop is detected. The CPDRB instruction will therefore save a lot of execution time.

Once a CPDR or CPDRB instruction starts to execute, it could conceivably continue executing for a long time if it were searching a long string with few bytes matched. This would present interrupt logic with problems. In order to prevent any such problems, the Z8000 allows interrupts to be acknowledged between each iterative execution of the CPDR or CPDRB instruction. Furthermore, the Program Counter value saved during the interrupt acknowledge process is the address of the CPDR or CPDRB instruction, so that execution of this instruction will continue from the point of interrupt, after the interrupt has been serviced. Seven clock periods must be added to the CPDR or CPDRB instruction's execution time to account for each interrupt acknowledged during the instruction's execution.

CPI — Compare Words and Increment

CPIB — Compare Bytes and Increment

The CPI and CPIB instructions are almost identical to the CPD and CPDB instructions. The only difference is that CPI/CPIB increment the source operand memory address register; this register is decremented by CPD/CPDB.

This is the general format for the CPI and the CPIB instructions:

Addressing Options			
dst	src	cnt	
R	IR	R	

CPI dst,src,cnt,cc
CPIB dst,src,cnt,cc

The symbol dst is a destination operand which must be specified using direct register addressing as a 16-bit CPU register for CPI, or an 8-bit CPU register for CPIB.

The symbol src is a source operand which must be specified using register indirect (implied) addressing.

The symbol cnt is a counter which must be specified as a 16- bit CPU register for both CPI and CPIB.

The symbol cc is a condition code which must be specified using one of the labels shown in the "code" column of Table 3- 4.

CPI and CPIB are string search instructions. They are designed to serve as one step of an instruction loop that searches a string, beginning with the lowest string address, and ending at the highest string address. For each step of the search, the destination operand is compared to the source operand. The comparison is performed by subtracting the source operand from the destination operand using two's complement addition. The result of the subtraction is discarded; neither the source operand nor the destination operand is modified to reflect the result of the subtraction. However, status flags are compared with the condition specified by cc. If there is a condition match, then the Zero status is set to 1; the Zero status is cleared otherwise.

When using comparison conditions codes from Table 3-4, the relation is:

destination condition source

For example, the "greater than" condition is matched if the destination operand is greater than the source operand.

After each iterative execution of the CPI or CPIB instruction, the source operand address is incremented by 1 for CPIB, or by 2 for CPI, so as to address the next byte or word in the string.

The 16-bit Counter Register contents are decremented by 1 for CPI or CPIB. If the Counter Register decrements to 0, then the Overflow status is set to 1; the Overflow status is cleared otherwise.

The CPI and CPIB instruction object codes may be illustrated as follows:

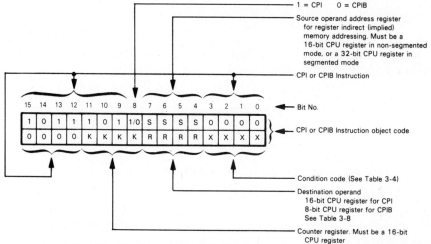

The Zero status is set to 1 when a match is detected between the specified condition code and the status flag settings generated by the compare. The Overflow status is set to 1 if the Counter Register decrements to zero, indicating the end of the search. The Zero and Overflow statuses are reset to 0 otherwise. The values of the Carry and Sign status flags are undefined after the CPI and CPIR instructions.

Figure 3-39 illustrates execution of the following CPI instruction:

```
CPI     R0,R9^R10,LLT;   % AMC syntax
CPI     R0,@R9,R10,ULT   ! Zilog syntax !
```

This instruction has deliberately been chosen to be as close as possible to the CPDB instruction illustrated in Figure 3-39; this makes direct comparison easier.

Figure 3-39 shows a data string in data memory being compared with the data word held in 16-bit register R0. R0 is the destination operand. 16-bit register R9 addresses the word within the data string that is currently being compared. Thus R9 addresses the source operand. 16-bit register R10 identifies the number of words within the string that remain to be compared. Since the logical or unsigned less than condition has been specified in the operand field, the Z status will be set to 1 whenever the contents of R0 are less than the contents of the word currently being compared. Both operands are treated as unsigned numbers.

After each execution of the CPI or CPIB instruction, you will have to use conditional instructions that test the Zero and Overflow statuses. If the Zero status is 1, then the specified condition has been encountered. If the Overflow status is 1, then the end of the string has been encountered and the string search is complete. Remember, the Carry and Sign status flags are also modified by the CPI and CPIB instructions, but they are left undefined at the end of the instruction's execution. Here is a simple instruction loop containing the CPIB instruction:

```
LOOP:    CPIB    RL0,@R9,R10,ULT  ! Zilog syntax !
         JP      NZ,NEXT
           .            These instructions process a string byte
           .            when the contents of RL0 are less than the
           .            contents of the string byte. These instructions
                        must not modify the P/V status.
NEXT:    JP      NOV,LOOP
```

See CPD/CPDB for a description of a similar instruction loop. This loop will search the string in the opposite direction.

CPIR — Compare Words, Increment and Repeat

CPIRB — Compare Bytes, Increment and Repeat

The CPIR and CPIRB instructions are identical to CPI and CPIB except that CPIR and CPIRB are re-executed until either the Z status or the P/V status is 1.
This is the general format for the CPIR and the CPIRB instructions:

Addressing Options				
dst	src	cnt	CPIR	dst,src,cnt,cc
R	IR	R	CPIRB	dst,src,cnt,cc

The symbol dst is a destination operand which must be specified using direct register addressing as a 16-bit CPU register for CPIR, or an 8-bit CPU register for CPIRB.

The symbol src is a source operand which must be specified using register indirect (implied) addressing.

The symbol cnt is a counter which must be specified as a 16-bit CPU register for both CPIR and CPIRB.

The symbol cc is a condition code which must be specified using one of the labels shown in the "code" column of Table 3- 4.

CPIR and CPIRB are string search instructions. They are designed to function as a single instruction loop that searches a string, beginning with the lowest string address, and ending at the highest string address. For each step of the search, the destination operand is compared to the source operand. The comparison is performed by subtracting the source operand from the destination operand using two's complement addition. The result of the subtraction is discarded; neither the source operand nor the destination operand is modified to reflect the result of the subtraction. However, status flags are compared with the condition specified by cc. If there is a condition match, then the Zero status is set to 1; the Zero status is cleared otherwise.

When using comparison conditions codes from Table 3-4, the relation is:

destination condition source

For example, the "greater than" condition is matched if the destination operand is greater than the source operand.

After each iterative execution of the CPIR or CPIRB instruction, the source operand address is incremented by 1 for CPIRB, or by 2 for CPIR, so as to address the next byte or word in the string.

16-bit Counter Register contents are decremented by 1 for CPIR or CPIRB. If the Counter Register decrements to 0, then the Overflow status is set to 1; the Overflow status is cleared otherwise.

Execution of CPIR or CPIRB continues until either the zero status or Overflow status is set to one.

The CPIR and CPIRB instruction object codes may be illustrated as follows:

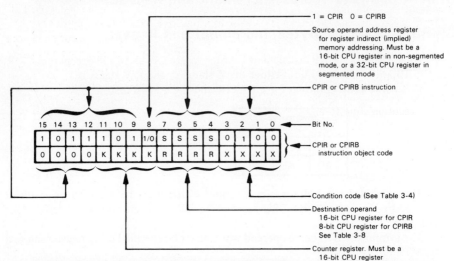

The Zero status is set to 1 when a match is detected between the specified condition code and the status flag settings generated by the compare. The Overflow status is set to 1 if the Counter Register decrements to zero, indicating the end of the search. The Zero and Overflow statuses are reset to 0 otherwise. The values of the Carry and Sign status flags are undefined after the CPIR and CPIRB instructions.

CPIR and CPIRB have the same relationship with CPI/CPIB as described earlier for CPDR/CPDRB and CPD/CPDB.

Here is the CPIRB version of the simple instruction loop which we used to illustrate the CPIB instruction:

```
LOOP      CPIRB   RL0,@R9,R10,ULT   ! Zilog syntax !
          JP      NZ,NEXT
          .               These instructions process a string byte
          .               whenever the contents of RL0 are less than
          .               the contents of the string byte. These
          .               instructions must not modify the P/V status.
NEXT      JP      NOV,LOOP
```

For the CPI loop, the two JP instructions will be executed once for each byte of the source data string that is compared. Using CPIRB, however, execution of the CPIRB instruction will continue until the Z or P/V status is 1. Therefore, the two JP instructions will be executed only when a "match" byte is found in the source data string (in this case when the contents of RL0 are less than the contents of the string byte) or when the end of the loop is detected. Using the CPIRB instruction will therefore save a lot of execution time.

Once a CPIR or CPIRB instruction starts to execute, it could conceivably continue executing for a long time if it were searching a long string with few bytes matched. This would present interrupt logic with problems. In order to prevent any such problems, the Z8000 allows interrupts to be acknowledgd between each iterative execution of the CPIR or CPIRB instruction. Furthermore, the Program Counter value saved during the interrupt acknowledge process is the address of the CPIR or CPIRB instruction, so that execution of this instruction will continue from the point of interrupt, after the interrupt has been serviced. Seven clock periods must be added to the CPIR or CPIRB instruction's execution time to account for each interrupt acknowledged during the instruction's execution.

CPL — Compare Long Words

CPL is the long word version of the CP and CPB instruction which we just described. This is the general format for the CPL assembly language instruction:

Addressing Options	
dst	src
R	R
R	IM
R	IR
R	DA
R	X

CPL   dst,src

There is only one version of the CPL instruction; it requires that dst be specified using register direct addressing, as a 32- bit CPU register, while src is specified using any standard operand addressing method. (See Figure 3-26.)

The CPL instruction compares two 32-bit operands by subtracting the source operand from the destination operand using twos complement addition. The result is discarded. Neither the source nor the destination operands change, but status flags are modified to reflect the result of the subtraction; therefore status flags can be used by subsequent conditional instructions.

When using condition codes from Table 3-4 to test status bits after a compare instruction, remember that the relation is:

destination condition source

For example, "greater than" means that the destination operand is greater than the source operand.

Remember that the Carry status is set to 1 for no Carry and to 0 for a carry since the Carry status reports borrows following subtraction.

The CPL instruction's object code may be illustrated as follows:

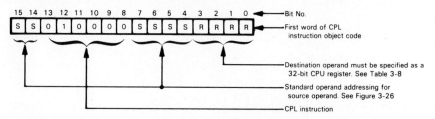

The C,Z,S, and V status flags are modified when the CPL instruction is executed. Figure 3-40 illustrates execution of the CPL instruction:

```
CPL        RR6,DATA32;      % AMC syntax
CPL        RR6,#DATA32      ! Zilog syntax !
```

DATA32 is a label representing 32-bit immediate data; this data is shown in Figure 3-40 as JJJJKKKK in the second and third instruction object code words. In order to represent some arbitrary, exact immediate data, we could rewrite the CPL instruction as follows:

```
CPL        RR6,#4A10012C;   % AMC syntax
CPL        RR6,#%4A10012C   ! Zilog syntax !
```

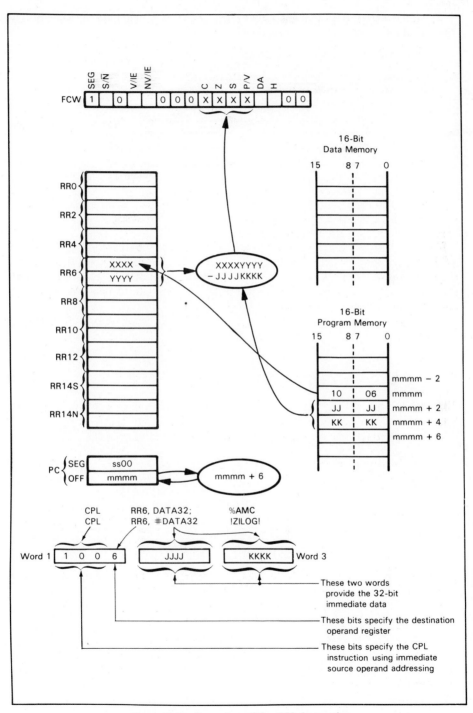

Figure 3-40. Execution of the CPL Instruction

If the register RR6 contains $326A427C_{16}$, then this is what happens when the CPL instruction illustrated above is executed:

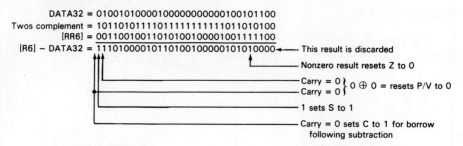

```
        DATA32 = 01001010000100000000000100101100
Twos complement = 10110101111011111111111011010100
         [RR6] = 00110010011010100100001001111100
  [R6] − DATA32 = 11101000010110100100000101010000 ◄──── This result is discarded
```
Nonzero result resets Z to 0

Carry = 0 ⎱ 0 ⊕ 0 = resets P/V to 0
Carry = 0 ⎰

1 sets S to 1

Carry = 0 sets C to 1 for borrow
following subtraction

CPSD — Compare Word Strings and Decrement

CPSDB — Compare Byte Strings and Decrement

The CPSD and CPSDB instructions are identical to CPD and CPDB respectively, except that register indirect (implied) memory addressing is used by CPSD and CPSDB to identify both the source and the destination operands, both of which are data memory strings.

This is the general format for the CPSD and CPSDB instructions:

Address Options		
dst	src	cnt
IR	IR	R

CPSD   dst,src,cnt,cc
CPSDB   dst,src,cnt,cc

The symbol dst is a destination operand which must be specified using register indirect (implied) addressing.

The symbol src is a source operand which is also specified using register indirect (implied) addressing.

The symbol cnt is a counter which must be specified as a 16-bit CPU register for both CPSD and CPSDB.

The symbol cc is a condition code which must be specified using one of the labels shown in the "code" column of Table 3-4.

CPSD and CPSDB are string search instructions. They are designed to serve as one step of an instruction loop that compares two strings, beginning with the highest string address, and ending at the lowest string address. For each step of the search, the destination operand is compared to the source operand. The comparison is performed by subtracting the source operand from the destination operand using twos complement addition. The result of the subtraction is discarded; neither the source operand nor the destination operand is modified to reflect the result of the subtraction. However, status flags are compared with the condition specified by cc. If there is a condition match, then the Zero status is set to 1; the Zero status is cleared otherwise.

When using comparison condition codes from Table 3-4, the relation is:

destination condition source

For example, the "greater than" condition is matched if the destination operand is greater than the source operand.

At the end of each CPSD or CPSDB instructions execution, the source and destination addresses are both decremented by 1 for CPSDB, or by 2 for CPSD, so as to address the next byte or word in each string.

The 16-bit Counter Register contents are decremented by 1 for CPSD or CPSDB. If the Counter Register decrements to 0, then the Overflow status is set to 1; the Overflow status is cleared otherwise.

The CPSD and CPSDB instruction object codes may be illustrated as follows:

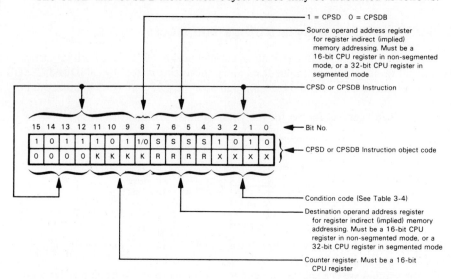

The Zero status is set to 1 when a match is detected between the specified condition code and the status flag settings generated by the compare. The Overflow status is set to 1 if the Counter Register decrements to zero, indicating the end of the search. The Zero and Overflow statuses are reset to 0 otherwise. The values of the Carry and Sign status flags are undefined after the CPSD and CPSDB instructions.

Figure 3-41 illustrates execution of the following CPSDB instruction:

```
CPSDB    R3^,R8^,R10,NE;    % AMC syntax
CPSDB    @R3,@R8,R10,NE     ! Zilog syntax !
```

Figure 3-41 shows two data strings in data memory being compared. 16-bit register R3 addresses the destination operand byte. 16-bit register R8 addresses the source operand byte. 16- bit register R10 identifies the number of bytes within the two strings that remain to be compared. Since the NE condition has been specified in the operand field, the Z status will be set to 1 whenever dissimilar bytes are encountered in the data strings. In other words, program logic is looking for unequal bytes in two supposedly identical strings.

After each execution of the CPSD and CPSDB instruction, you will have to use conditional instructions that test the Zero and Overflow statuses. If the Zero status is 1, then the specified condition has been encountered. If the Overflow status is 1, then the end of the string has been encountered and the string search is complete. Remember, the Carry and Sign status flags are also modified by the CPSD and CPSDB instructions, but they are left undefined at the end of the instruction's execution. Here is a simple instruction loop containing the CPSDB instruction illustrated above:

```
LOOP:    CPSDB    @R3,@R8,R10,NE    ! Zilog syntax !
         JP       NZ,NEXT
         .
         .       These instructions process dissimilar
         .       bytes, when detected
         .
NEXT:    JP       NOV,LOOP
```

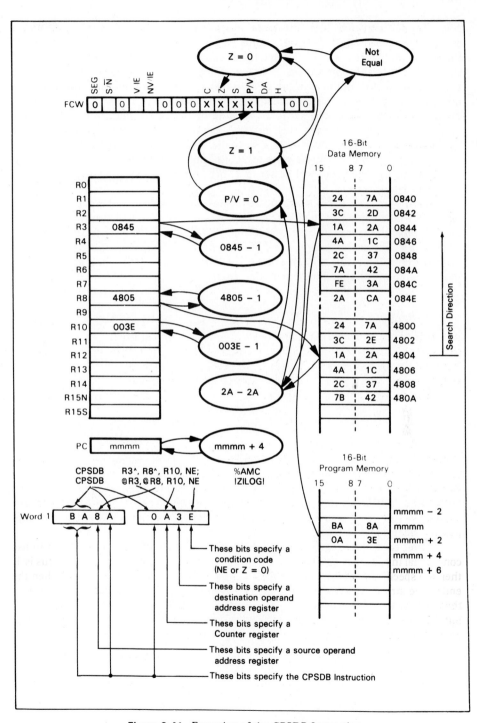

Figure 3-41. Execution of the CPSDB Instruction

As the instruction loop illustrated above is re-executed, bytes from the source string (at the top of Figure 3-41) are compared with bytes from the destination string (at the bottom of Figure 3-41). Notice that the Z status is used twice; the condition of the Z status following the comparison is tested, since the NE condition code has been specified in the operand field of the CPSDB instruction. Based on the Z status level at this tme, a final Z status level is loaded into the Flag and Control word. In Figure 3-41, the Z status will normally be set to 1 following the compare, since most bytes of the source and destinations strings will b identical. But this will cause the Z status within the Flag and Control Word to be reset to 0, since the NE condition has been specified. Conversely, any time the Z status is reset to 0 following a comparison, the Z status within the Flag and Control Word will be set to 1, because the specified condition has been matched.

Each time the CPSDB instruction executes, program logic will move on to the JP NZ,NEXT instruction, which either passes program control on to instructions that handle dissimilar bytes, or branches to the second JP instruction. The second JP instruction, JP NOV,LOOP branches back to the CPSDB instruction if the Overflow status is 0. But when the Overflow status is 1 at the end of the loop, program logic continues to the next sequential instruction, and loop execution ceases.

CPSDR — Compare Word String, Decrement and Repeat

CPSDRB — Compare Byte Strings, Decrement and Repeat

The CPSDR and CPSDRB instructions are identical to the CPSD and CPSDB instructions, respectively, except that CPSDR and CPSDRB are re-executed until either the Z status or the P/V status is 1.

This is the general format for the CPSDR and CPSDRB instructions:

Addressing Options		
dst	**src**	**cnt**
IR	IR	R

CPSDR   dst,src,cnt,cc
CPSDRB   dst,src,cnt,cc

The symbol dst is a destination operand which must be specified using register indirect (implied) addressing.

The symbol src is a source operand which is also specified using register indirect (implied) addressing.

The symbol cnt is a counter which must be specified as a 16-bit CPU register for both CPSDR and CPSDRB.

The symbol cc is a condition code which must be specified using one of the labels shown in the "code" column of Table 3-4.

CPSDR and CPSDRB are string search instructions. They are designed to function as single instruction loops that compare two strings, beginning with the highest string address, and ending at the lowest string address. For each step of the search, the destination operand is compared to the source operand. The comparison is performed by subtracting the source operand from the destination operand using twos complement addition. The result of the subtraction is discarded; neither the source operand nor the destination operand is modified to reflect the result of the subtraction. However, status flags are compared with the condition specified by cc. If there is a condition match, then the Zero status is set to 1; the Zero status is cleared otherwise.

When using comparison condition codes from Table 3-4, the relation is:

destination condition source

For example, the "greater than" condition is matched if the destination operand is greater than the source operand.

After each iterative execution of the CPSDR or CPSDRB instruction, the source and destination addresses are both decremented by 1 for CPSDRB, or by 2 for CPSDR, so as to address the next byte or word in each string.

The 16-bit Counter Register contents are decremented by 1 for CPSDR or CPSDRB. If the Counter Register decrements to 0, then the Overflow status is set to 1; the Overflow status is cleared otherwise.

Execution of CPSDR or CPSDRB is repeated until either Zero status or Overflow status is set to 1.

The CPSDR and CPSDRB instruction object codes may be illustrated as follows:

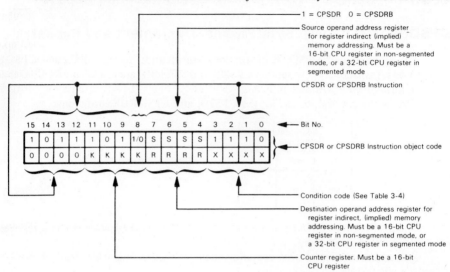

The Zero status is set to 1 when a match is detected between the specified condition code, and the status flag settings generated by the compare. The Overflow status is set to 1 if the Counter Register decrements to zero, indicating the end of the search. The Zero and Overflow statuses are reset to 0 otherwise. The values of the Carry and Sign status bits are undefined after the CPSDR and CPSDRB instructions.

CPSDR/CPSDRB have the same relationship with CPSD/CPSDR as CPIR/CPIRB has with CPI/CPIB, or CPDR/CPDRB has with CPD/CPDB.

Here is the CPSDRB version of the simple instruction loop which we used to illustrate the CPSDB instruction:

```
LOOP        CPSDRB      @R3,@R8,R10,NE   ! Zilog syntax !
            JP          NZ,NEXT
            .
            .           These instructions process dissimilar
            .           bytes, when detected.
            .
NEXT        JP          NOV,LOOP
```

For the CPSDB loop, the two JP instructions will be executed once for each byte of the two data strings that is compared. Using CPSDRB, however, execution of the CPSDRB instruction will continue until the Z or P/V status is 1. Therefore, the two JP instuctions will be executed only when dissimilar bytes are found in the source and destination data strings, or when the end of the loop is detected. Using the CPSDRB instruction will therefore save a lot of execution time.

Once a CPSDR or CPSDRB instruction starts to execute, it could conceivably continue executing for a long time if it were searching long strings with few dissimilar bytes. This would present interrupt logic with problems. In order to prevent any such problems, the Z8000 allows interrupts to be acknowledged between each iterative execution of the CPSDR or CPSDRB instruction. Furthermore, the Program Counter value saved during the interrupt acknowledge process is the address of the CPSDR or CPSDRB instruction, so that execution of this instruction will continue from the point of interrupt, after the interrupt has been serviced. Seven clock periods must be added to the CPSDR or CPSDRB instruction's execution time to account for each interrupt acknowledged during the instruction's execution.

CPSI — Compare Word Strings and Increment

CPSIB — Compare Byte Strings and Increment

The CPSI and CPSIB instructions are identical to CPI and CPIB, respectively, except that register indirect (implied) memory addressing is used by CPSI and CPSIB to identify the source and the destination operands, both of which are data memory strings.

This is the general format for the CPSI and CPSIB instructions:

Addressing Options		
dst	src	cnt
IR	IR	R

CPSI   dst,src,cnt,cc
CPSIB   dst,src,cnt,cc

The symbol dst is a destination operand which must be specified using register indirect (implied) addressing.

The symbol src is a source operand which is also specified using register indirect (implied) addressing.

The symbol cnt is a counter which must be specified as a 16-bit CPU register for both CPSI and CPSIB.

The symbol cc is a condition code which must be specified using one of the labels shown in the "code" column of Table 3-4.

CPSI and CPSIB are string search instructions. They are designed to serve as one step of an instruction loop that compares two strings, beginning with the lowest string address, and ending at the highest string address. For each step of the search, the destination operand is compared to the source operand. The comparison is performed by subtracting the source operand from the destination operand using twos complement addition. The result of the subtraction is discarded; neither the source operand nor the destination operand is modified to reflect the result of the subtraction. However, status flags are compared with the condition specified by cc. If there is a condition match, then the Zero status is set to 1; the Zero status is cleared otherwise.

When using comparison condition codes from Table 3-4, the relation is:

destination condition source

For example, the "greater than" condition is matched if the destination operand is greater than the source operand.

At the end of each CPSI or CPSIB instructions execution, the source and destination addresses are both incremented by 1 for CPSIB, or by 2 for CPSI, so as to address the next byte or word in each string.

The 16-bit Counter Register contents decrement by 1 for CPSI or CPSIB. If the Counter Register decrements to 0, then the Overflow status is set to 1; the Overflow status is cleared otherwise.

The CPSI and CPSIB instruction object codes may be illustrated as follows:

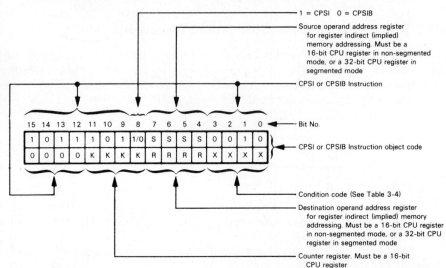

The Zero status is set to 1 when a match is detected between the specified condition code and the status flag settings generated by the compare. The Overflow status is set to 1 if the Counter register decrements to zero, indicating the end of the search. The Zero and Overflow status flags are reset to 0 otherwise. The values of the Carry and Sign status flags are undefined after the CPSI and CPSIB instructions.

Figure 3-42 illustrates execution of the following CPSIB instruction:

```
CPSIB    R3^,R8^,R10,NE;    % AMC syntax
CPSIB    @R3,@R8,R10,NE     ! Zilog syntax !
```

To make instruction comparisons as simple as possible, this instruction is almost identical to the CPSDB instruction illustrated in Figure 3-41.

Figure 3-42 shows two data strings in data memory being compared. 16-bit register R3 addresses the destination operand byte. 16-bit register R8 addresses the source operand byte. 16- bit register R10 identifies the number of bytes within the two strings that remain to be compared. Since the NE condition has been specified in the operand field, the Z status will be set to 1 whenever dissimilar bytes are encountered in the data strings. In other words, program logic is looking for unequal bytes in two supposedly identical strings.

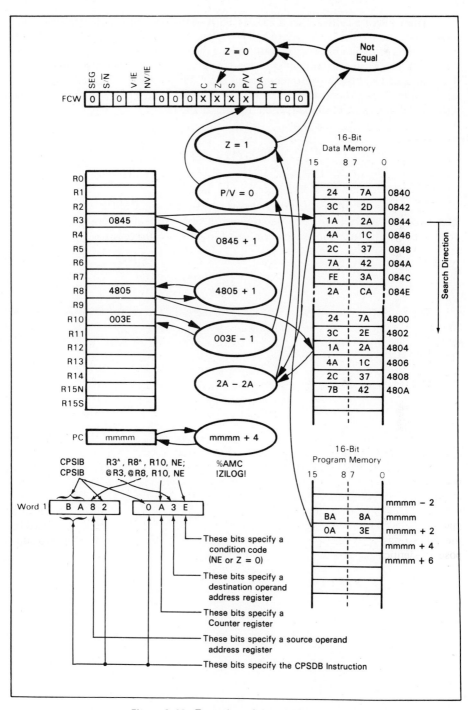

Figure 3-42. Execution of the CPSIB Instruction

After each execution of the CPSI or CPSIB instruction, you will have to use conditional instructions that test the Zero and Overflow statuses. If the Zero status is 1, then the specified condition has been encountered. If the Overflow status is 1, then the end of the string has been encountered and the string search is complete. Remember, the Carry and Sign statuses are also modified by the CPSI and CPSIB instructions, but they are left undefined at the end of the instruction's execution. Here is a simple instruction loop containing the CPSIB instruction illustrated above:

```
LOOP:     CPSIB    @R3,@R8,R10,NE  ! Zilog syntax !
          JP       NZ,NEXT
          .
          .        These instructions process dissimilar bytes,
          .        when detected.
          .
NEXT:     JR       NOV,LOOP
```

Since this CPSIB instruction is almost identical to the CPSDB example instruction, see the CPSDB instruction description for discussion of the program loop illustrated above. The two loops search the string in opposite directions.

CPSIR — Compare Word Strings, Increment and Repeat

CPSIRB — Compare Byte Strings, Increment and Repeat

The CPSIR and CPSIRB instructions are identical to the CPSI and CPSIB instructions, respectively, except that CPSIR and CPSIRB are re-executed until either the Z status or the P/V status is 1.

This is the general format for the CPSIR and CPSIRB instructions:

Addressing Options		
dst	src	cnt
IR	IR	R

CPSIR   dst,src,cnt,cc
CPSIRB   dst,src,cnt,cc

The symbol dst is a destination operand which must be specified using register indirect (implied) addressing.

The symbol src is a source operand which is also specified using register indirect (implied) addressing.

The symbol cnt is a counter which must be specified as a 16- bit CPU register for both CPSIR and CPSIRB.

The symbol cc is a condition code which must be specified using one of the labels shown in the "code" column of Table 3-4.

CPSIR and CPSIRB are string search instructions. They are designed to function as a single instruction loop that compares two strings, beginning with the lowest string address, and ending at the highest string address. For each step of the search, the destination operand is compared to the source operand. The comparison is performed by subtracting the source operand from the destination operand using twos complement addition. The result of the subtraction is discarded; neither the source operand nor the destination operand is modified to reflect the result of the subtraction. However, status flags are compared with the condition specified by cc. If there is a condition match, then the Zero status is set to 1; the Zero status is cleared otherwise.

When using comparison condition codes from Table 3-4, the relation is:

destination condition source

For example, the "greater than" condition is matched if the destination operand is greater than the source operand.

After each iterative execution of the CPIR or CPIRB instruction, the source and destination addresses are both incremented by 1 for CPSIRB, or by 2 for CPSIR, so as to address the next byte or word in each string.

The 16-bit Counter Register contents are decremented by 1 for CPSIR or CPSIRB. If the Counter Register decrements to 0, then the Overflow status is set to 1; the Overflow status is cleared otherwise.

Execution of the CPSIR or CPSIRB instruction is repeated until either status or Overflow status is set to 1.

The CPSIR and CPSIRB instruction object codes may be illustrated as follows:

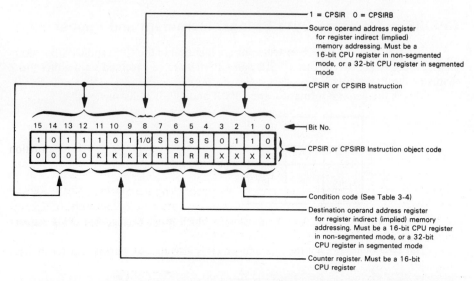

The Zero status is set to 1 when a match is detected between the specified condition code and the status flag settings generated by the compare. The Overflow status is set to 1 at the end of the search. The Zero and Overflow status flags are reset to 0 otherwise. The values of the Carry and Sign status flags are undefined after the CPSIR and CPSIRB instructions.

Here is the CPSIRB version of the simple instruction loop which we used to illustrate the CPDB instruction. The CPDRB version would be as follows:

```
LOOP:    CPSIRB   @R3,@R8,R10,NE      ! Zilog syntax !
         JP       NZ,NEXT
         .
         .        These instructions process dissimilar bytes,
         .        when detected.
NEXT:    JP       NOV,LOOP
```

For the CPSIB loop, the two JP instructions will be executed once for each byte of the two data strings that are compared. Using CPSIRB, however, execution of the CPSIRB instruction will continue until the Z or P/V status is 1. Therefore, the two JP instructions will be executed only when dissimilar bytes are found in the source and destination data strings, or when the end of the loop is detected. Using the CPSIRB instruction will therefore save a lot of execution time.

Once a CPSIR or CPSIRB instruction starts to execute, it could conceivably continue executing for a long time if it were searching long strings with few dissimilar bytes. This would present interrupt logic with problems. In order to prevent any such problems, the Z8000 allows interrupts to be acknowledged between each iterative execution of the CPSIR or CPSIRB instruction. Furthermore, the Program Counter value saved during the interrupt acknowledge process is the address of the CPSIR or CPSIRB instruction, so that execution of this instruction will continue from the point of interrupt, after the interrupt has been serviced. Seven clock periods must be added to the CPSIR or CPSIRB instruction's execution time to account for each interrupt acknowledged during the instruction's execution.

DAB — Decimal Adjust

This is the general format for the DAB instruction:

Addressing Options
dst
R

DAB   dst

The symbol dst must be specified as an 8-bit CPU register. The DAB instruction assumes that this register contains the result of adding two 8-bit binary coded decimal numbers using the ADDB or ADCB instruction, or that it contains the result of subtracting two 8-bit binary coded decimal numbers using the SUBB or SBCB instruction. The DAB instruction adjusts this result to generate a valid binary coded decimal answer. Table 3-12 summarizes the actual operations performed by the DAB instruction.

The DAB instruction's object code may be illustrated as follows:

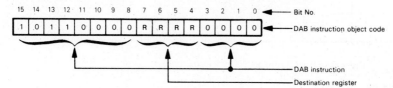

The Carry status is modified by the DAB instruction as specified in Table 3-12. The Zero status is modified in the standard way, being set to 1 if the DAB instruction generates a zero result. The Sign status is also modified by the DAB instruction in the standard way, but it is meaningless for a binary coded decimal number; the Sign status is set equal to the high-order bit of the DAB result, but in a binary coded decimal number this bit does not represent the sign of the number.

Some early production chips leave the Sign status unaffected. Some early production chips modify the parity status, indicating the parity of the result. See Table 3-18 at the end of this chapter for more information.

If the destination register does not contain the result of an addition or subtraction of valid binary coded decimal numbers, or if the flags have been disturbed since the addition or subtraction, the result of the DAB instruction is undefined.

```
ADDB    RH3,RH2;        % AMC syntax
DAB     RH3;

ADDB    RH3,RH2         ! Zilog syntax !
DAB     RH3
```

Table 3-12. Operations Performed by the DAB Instruction

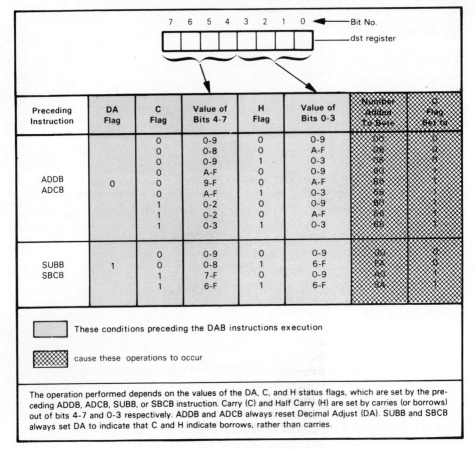

Preceding Instruction	DA Flag	C Flag	Value of Bits 4-7	H Flag	Value of Bits 0-3	Number Added To Byte	C Flag Set to
ADDB ADCB	0	0	0-9	0	0-9	00	0
		0	0-8	0	A-F	06	0
		0	0-9	1	0-3	06	0
		0	A-F	0	0-9	60	1
		0	9-F	0	A-F	66	1
		0	A-F	1	0-3	66	1
		1	0-2	0	0-9	60	1
		1	0-2	0	A-F	66	1
		1	0-3	1	0-3	66	1
SUBB SBCB	1	0	0-9	0	0-9	00	0
		0	0-8	1	6-F	FA	0
		1	7-F	0	0-9	A0	1
		1	6-F	1	6-F	9A	1

☐ These conditions preceding the DAB instructions execution

▨ cause these operations to occur

The operation performed depends on the values of the DA, C, and H status flags, which are set by the preceding ADDB, ADCB, SUBB, or SBCB instruction. Carry (C) and Half Carry (H) are set by carries (or borrows) out of bits 4-7 and 0-3 respectively. ADDB and ADCB always reset Decimal Adjust (DA). SUBB and SBCB always set DA to indicate that C and H indicate borrows, rather than carries.

The contents of Register RH2 are added to Register RH3; both registers are assumed to initially contain valid binary coded decimal numbers. After the ADDB instruction has been executed RH3 will not contain a binary coded decimal number, but the DAB instruction will suitably adjust the contents of RH3. If RH3 initially contains 32, and RL3 initially contains 58, this is what happens:

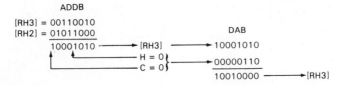

The correct binary coded decimal result (90) is generated by DAB in 8-bit register RH3. The Z status will be 0 for a nonzero result. S will be 1, reflecting the high order result bit. There is no carry so C = 0.

DEC — Decrement Word

DECB — Decrement Byte

This is the general format for the DEC and DECB instructions:

Addressing Options	
dst	**src**
R	IM
IR	IM
DA	IM
X	IM

DEC   dst,data
DECB   dst,data

The symbol dst is a 16-bit register or memory location for DEC; it is an 8-bit register or memory location for DECB. The symbol dst is specified using any standard operand addressing method with the exception of immediate addressing. (see Figure 3-26).

A 4-bit unsigned binary immediate operand, specified by data, is subtracted from the destination location using twos complement arithmetic. The word data may be omitted from the operand field, in which case a default value of 1 is assumed. The word data can have values ranging from 1 to 16; values are encoded as (data − 1) in the instruction object code, with values ranging from 0 for 1, to F_{16} for 16.

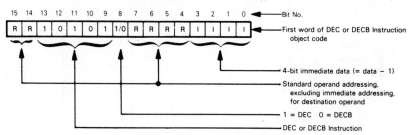

The Z, S, and V statuses are modified by the DEC and DECB instructions. Figure 3-43 illustrates execution of the DEC instruction:

```
DEC    RR2^,8;       % AMC syntax
DEC    @RR2,#8       ! Zilog syntax !
```

Register indirect (implied) memory addressing is used to specify a long-segmented memory address: word 8000_{16} in segment TT. 8 is subtracted from the contents of this memory word. Since the memory word contains 0768_{16}, it will contain 0760_{16} after the DEC instruction has executed.

In non-segmented mode, the DEC instruction, would specify 16-bit Register R2, which contains the address 8000_{16}; in 16-bit Register R3 would be unused.

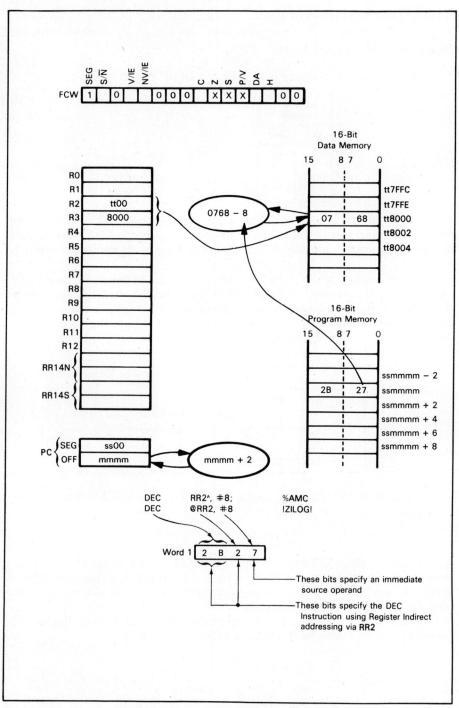

Figure 3-43. Execution of the DEC Instruction

The DECB instruction executes as illustrated in Figure 3-43, except that the contents of a single memory byte is decremented. For example, the following instruction would leave the value 60_{16} in memory byte 8000_{16} within segment TT.

```
DECB    RR2^,8;         % AMC syntax
DECB    @RR2,#8         ! Zilog syntax !
```

Remember, you do not have to include a source operand if you are decrementing by 1 since 1 is the default value. For example, the instruction:

```
DEC     RR2^            % AMC syntax
DEC     @RR2            ! Zilog syntax !
```

would reduce the contents of memory location $TT8000_{16}$ from 0768_{16} to 0767_{16}, in Figure 3-43. When the instruction is executed, this is what happens:

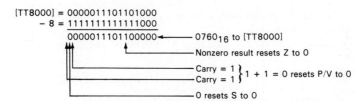

DI — Disable Interrupt

DI is a privileged instruction.

This is the general format for the DI instruction:

DI   int

The DI instruction disables vectored and/or non-vectored interrupts by resetting the appropriate bits to 0 in the Flag and Control Word. The symbol int in the operand field specifies the interrupts to be disabled as follows:

DI	VI	Disable vectored interrupt
DI	NVI	Disable non-vectored interrupt
DI	VI,NVI	Disable vectored and non-vectored interrupts
	NVI,VI	

Thus, you can disable vectored interrupts only, non-vectored interrupts only, or both vectored and non-vectored interrupts.

The DI instruction's object code may be illustrated as follows:

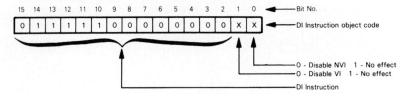

Only the VI and NVI bits of the flag and control word are modified by the DI instruction.

The instruction:

```
DI      VI;            % AMC syntax
DI      VI             ! Zilog syntax !
```

would disable vectored interrupts, while not affecting the status of non-vectored interrupts. In other words, the VI bit of the Flag and Control Word would be reset to 0, while the NVI bit keeps its prior contents.

DIV — Divide Words

DIVL — Divide Long Words

This is the general format for the DIV and DIVL instructions:

Addressing Options	
dst	src
R	R
R	IM
R	IR
R	DA
R	X

DIV   dst,src
DIVL   dst,src

The symbol dst is destination operand which must be specified using direct register addressing. A 32-bit CPU register must be specified for DIV; a 64-bit CPU register must be specified for DIVL.

The symbol src is a source operand which can be specified using any standard operand addressing method (see Figure 3-26). A 16-bit operand is specified for DIV; a 32-bit operand is specified for DIVL.

The source and destination operands are treated as twos complement binary numbers. The destination operand contains the dividend. The source operand contains the divisor. The destination operand (dividend) is divided by the source operand (divisor). The quotient is returned in the low order half of the destination operand, while the remainder is returned in the high order half of the destination operand. The low order half of the destination operand is the half with the highest register number. For example, if RR4 is specified as the destination operand for a DIV instruction, then R4 is the high order half of RR4, while R5 is the low order half of RR4. Thus, the quotient will be returned in R5, while the remainder is returned in R4. If RQ4 is specified as the destination operand for the DIVL instruction, then RR4 is the high order half of RQ4, while RR6 is the low order half of RQ4. Thus the quotient would be returned in RR6, while the remainder is returned in RR4.

When the divisor and/or the dividend is a negative number, then the remainder is always computed with the same sign as the dividend. This sign logic may be illustrated as follows:

$$\frac{+\ 105}{+\ 10} = +\ 10, \text{ remainder} = +\ 5$$

$$\frac{-\ 105}{+\ 10} = -\ 10, \text{ remainder} = -\ 5$$

$$\frac{-\ 105}{-\ 10} = +\ 10, \text{ remainder} = -\ 5$$

$$\frac{+\ 105}{-\ 10} = -\ 10, \text{ remainder} = +\ 5$$

The DIV and DIVL instruction object code may be illustrated as follows:

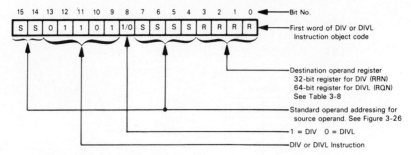

The DIV and DIVL instructions modify the C, Z, S, and V statuses in very logical, but not exactly standard ways. We will therefore describe in detail how each status is modified.

The Carry status (C) is set if the quotient does not fall within the bounds of the smallest and largest numbers that can be returned in half of the destination operand. For DIV, the Carry status is set to 1 if the quotient is outside the range -2^{15} to $+2^{15}-1$. For DIVL, the Carry status is set to 1 if the quotient is outside the range -2^{31} to $+2^{31}-1$. The Carry status is reset to 0 otherwise.

The Z status is set to 1 if the quotient or the divisor is 0. The Z status is reset to 0 otherwise.

The Sign status (S) is modified in different ways depending on whether the DIV/DIVL instruction is or is not successfully executed. If the DIV/DIVL instruction is successfully executed, then the Sign status is set to 1 when the quotient is negative, and it is reset to 0 when the quotient is positive. But if the DIV/DIVL instruction is aborted, then the sign status reflects the sign of the divisor.

The Overflow status (V) is set to 1 if the divisor is zero, or if the quotient is too large to fit in the low order half of the destination operand. The Overflow status is reset to 0 otherwise.

The DIV instruction is aborted if the divisor is zero, or if the absolute value for the high order half of the dividend is larger than the absolute value of the entire divisor.

Execution of the DIV and DIVL instructions is illustrated in Figures 3-44 and 3-45, respectively.

Figure 3-44 illustrates executions of the following DIV instructions:

```
DIV     RR4,#4080;      % AMC syntax
DIV     RR4,#%4080      ! Zilog syntax !
```

Using the operands illustrated in Figure 3-44, status flags will be modified as follows:

    C = 0 since quotient fits within R5
    Z = 0 since quotient is not zero
    S = 0 since quotient is positive
   P/V = 0 since the divisor was not zero and the quotient fits within R5

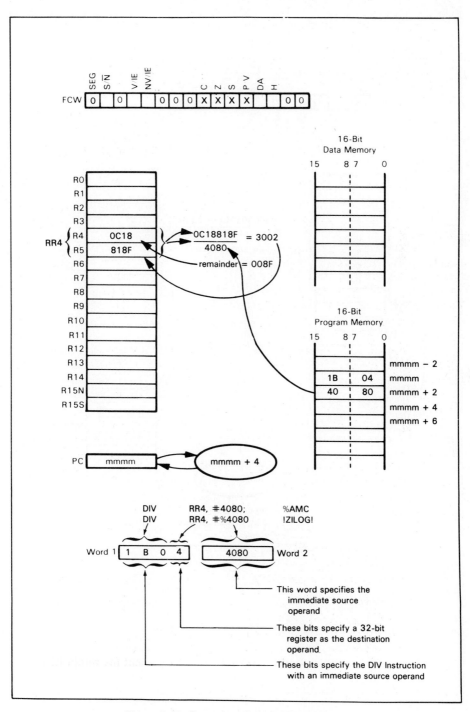

Figure 3-44. Execution of the DIV Instruction

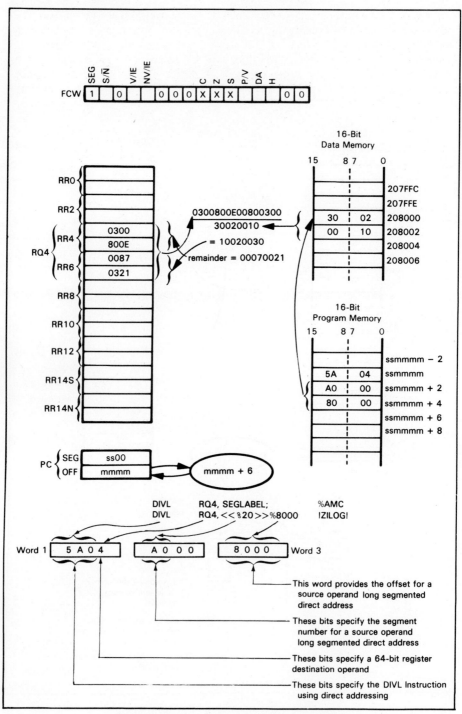

Figure 3-45. Execution of the DIVL Instruction

Figure 3-44 illustrates one of the simplest forms that the DIV instruction can take. The divisor is specified within the operand field of the DIV instruction as an immediate data value. The instruction itself is executed in non-segmented mode. Figure 3-45 illustrates a slightly more complex variation. A 64-bit divisor is divided by a 32-bit dividend. The divisor is stored in two memory words which are identified using long-segmented direct memory addressing. The event sequences illustrated in Figure 3-45 are identical to those illustrated in Figure 3-44, notwithstanding the larger numbers and the more complex addressing mode.

Some early production chips do not set V correctly. With some early production chips, division by zero can cause the next instruction to execute incorrectly. See Table 3-18 at the end of this chapter for more information.

DJNZ — Decrement Word Register and Jump if not Zero

DBJNZ — Decrement Byte Register and Jump if not Zero

The DJNZ instruction has been reported as not working properly on some Z8000 microprocessors; however, the instruction did work on the microprocessor used to test programs in this book.

This is the general format for the DJNZ and DBJNZ instructions:

Addressing Options		DJNZ	r,disp
r	disp	DBJNZ	r,disp
R	PR		

The symbol r is the Counter Register. A 16-bit register must be specified for DJNZ; an 8-bit register must be specified for DBJNZ.

The symbol disp is a 7-bit, unsigned binary displacement, which is used to compute a backward branch address.

When the DJNZ or DBJNZ instruction is executed, the contents of the Counter Register are decremented by one. If after being decremented, the Counter Register contents are zero, the next sequential instruction is executed. If after being decremented, the Counter Register contains a nonzero value, a branch address is computed using disp. The disp value is doubled, then subtracted from the Program Counter, after the Program Counter has been incremented to address the next sequential instruction. Thus, the DJNZ and DBJNZ instructions can branch back to any memory location up 252 bytes preceding their own locations. This may be illustrated as follows:

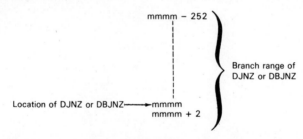

The DJNZ and DBJNZ instructions object code may be illustrated as follows:

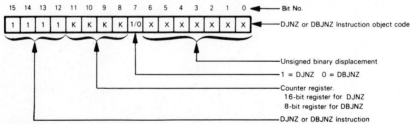

No status flags are modified when the DJNZ or DBJNZ instruction is executed.

Consider the following instruction sequence:

```
            LDB     RL0,#10         ! Zilog syntax !
  LOOP:      :                      ! Start of iterative instruction !
             :                      ! loop !
             :      Any instruction sequence occupying less than
             :      252 bytes of object code may occur here. The
             :      sequence will be repeated ten times.
            DBJNZ   RL0,LOOP        ! End of iterative instruction !
                                    ! loop !
  NEXT:
```

Execution of this DBJNZ instruction is illustrated in Figure 3-46.

8-bit Register RL0 is initially loaded with a counter, representing the number of times an instruction sequence is to be executed. The instruction sequence begins with the instruction labelled LOOP and ends with DBJNZ instruction. Each time the DBJNZ instruction is executed, 8-bit Register RL0 contents are decremented by 1. So long as RL0 does not contain 0 after being decremented, the instruction labelled LOOP is executed following the DBJNZ instruction. But the instruction labelled NEXT is executed following the DBJNZ instruction when the RL0 register's contents are 0 after being decremented. In Figure 3-46 the actual displacement 60_{16} has arbitrarily been selected to represent LOOP in the instruction object code. Remember, the assembler would compute this displacement for you, knowing the address of LOOP and the address of the DBJNZ instruction.

Note that the DJNZ and DBJNZ instructions are designed for small program loops. They can only branch backwards, to instructions whose memory addresses are smaller than their own. Moreover, the branch address must be within 252 bytes of the DJNZ or DBJNZ instruction's own address.

Some early production chips do not execute DJNZ correctly. See Table 3-18 at the end of this chapter for more information.

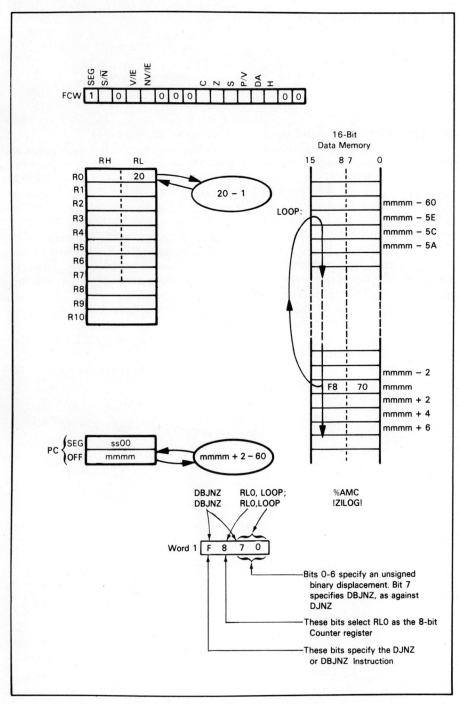

Figure 3-46. Execution of the DBJNZ Instruction

EI — Enable Interrupts

EI is a privileged instruction.
This is the general format for the EI instruction:

EI int

The EI instruction enables vectored and/or non-vectored interupts by setting the appropriate bits to 1 in the Flag and Control Word. The operand field specifies the interrupts to be disabled as follows:

VI — vectored interrupts
NVI — non-vectored interrupts

Thus, you can enable vectored interrupts only, non-vectored interrupts only, or both vectored and non-vectored interrupts.
The EI instructions' object code may be illustrated as follows:

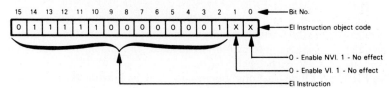

Only the VI and NVI bits of the Flag and Control word are modified by the EI instruction.
The instruction:

```
EI      VI;             % AMC syntax
EI      VI              ! Zilog syntax !
```

would enable vectored interrupts, while not affecting the status of non-vectored interrupts. In other words, the VI bit of the Flag and Control Word would be set to 1, while the NVI bit keeps its prior content.

EX — Exchange Words

EXB — Exchange Bytes

This is the general format for the EX and EXB instructions:

Addressing Options	
dst	src
R	R
R	IR
R	DA
R	X

EX   dst,src
EXB dst,src

The symbol dst is a destination operand which must be specified using direct register addressing. A 16-bit CPU register must be specified for EX; an 8-bit CPU register must be specified for EXB.

The symbol src is a source operand which can be specified using any standard operand addressing method, with the exception of immediate addressing. (See Figure 3-26.) When the EX or EXB instruction is executed, the contents of the source and destination operands are exchanged.

The EX and EXB instructions' object code may be illustrated as follows:

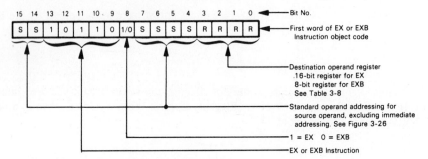

No status flags are modified by the EX or EXB instructions.

Execution of EX and EXB instructions are illustrated in Figures 3-47 and 3-48 respectively. In Figure 3-47 the following EX instructions' execution is illustrated:

```
EX      R3,R8^;         % AMC
EX      R3,@R8          ! ZILOG !
```

This instruction represents a straightforward swap of 16-bit data between CPU register R3 and a memory addressed by CPU Register R8.

The following EXB instruction is illustrated in Figure 3-48:

```
EXB     RH3,R8^;        % AMC
EXB     RH3,@R8         ! ZILOG !
```

This instruction is equivalent to half of the word exchange illustrated in Figure 3-46. Contents of 8-bit Register RH3, which is the high order byte of 16-bit Register R3, is exchanged with the contents of the memory byte addressed by 16-bit Register R8.

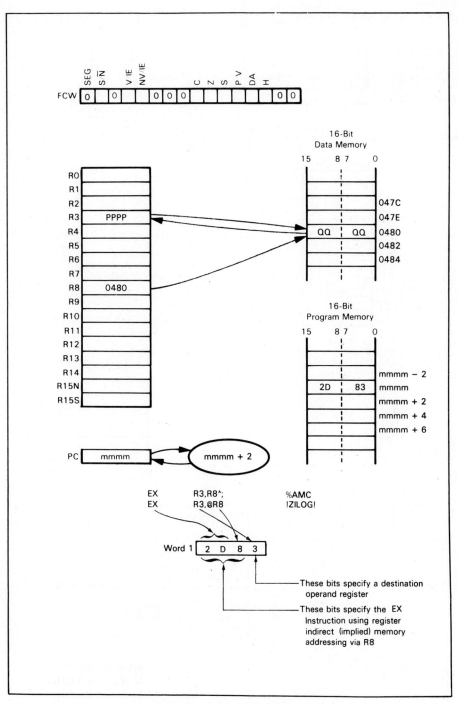

Figure 3-47. Execution of the EX Instruction

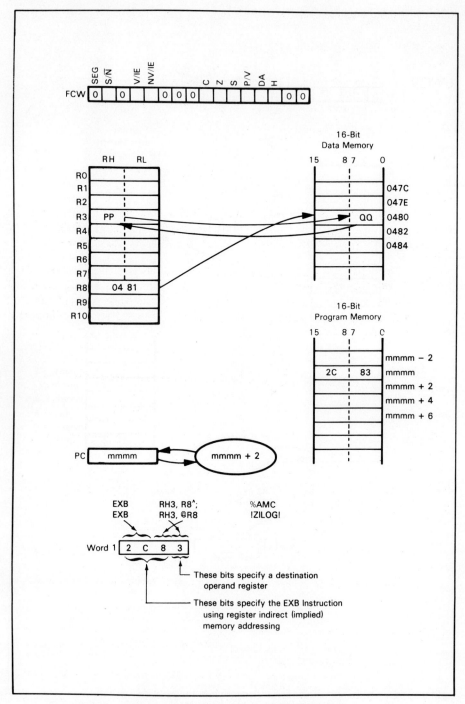

Figure 3-48. Execution of the EXB Instruction

EXTS — Extend Word Sign Bit

EXTSB — Extend Byte Sign Bit

EXTSL — Extend Long Word Sign Bit

This is the general format for the EXTS, EXTSB, and EXTSL instructions:

Addressing Options
dst
R

```
EXTS    dst
EXTSB   dst
EXTSL   dst
```

The symbol dst is the destination operand, which must be specified using direct register addressing. A 16-bit CPU register must be specified for EXTSB. A 32-bit CPU register must be specified for EXTS. A 64-bit CPU register must be specified for EXTSL.

When any one of these three instructions is executed, the high-order bit of the low order half of the destination CPU register is propagated through the high order half of the register. Thus the operand doubles in size while retaining its sign and value.

The EXTS, the EXTSB, and EXTSL instructions' object code may be illustrated as follows:

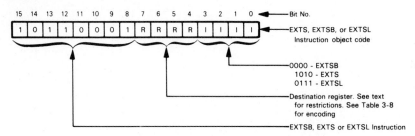

No status flags are modified by the EXTS, EXTSB, or EXTSL instruction.

Consider the following EXTSB instructions:

```
EXTSB   R3;             % AMC syntax
EXTSB   R3              ! Zilog syntax !
```

If RL3 initially contains $2A_{16}$, then when the instruction illustrated above is executed, RH3 is cleared, since the high order bit of RL3 is 0.

Similarly, if R5 contains $A52A_{16}$, then execution of the instruction:

```
EXTS    RR4;            % AMC syntax
EXTS    RR4             ! Zilog syntax !
```

will load $FFFF_{16}$ into R4, since the high-order bit of R5 is 1.

If RR6 contains $A52A3041_{16}$, then execution of the instruction:

```
EXTSL   RQ4;            % AMC syntax
EXTSL   RQ4             ! Zilog syntax !
```

will load $FFFFFFFF_{16}$ into RR4, since the high order bit of RR6 is 1.

HALT — Halt Program Execution

HALT is a privileged instruction.
This is the format for the HALT instruction:

HALT

The HALT instruction has no operands.

When the HALT Instruction is executed, program execution ceases, but register and status contents are preserved. The Refresh Counter continues to operate. Program execution can be re-started by an external Reset signal, or by an interrupt request. Both the Reset and the interrupt request are processed as they would be under any other circumstances.

This is the Halt Instructions' object code:

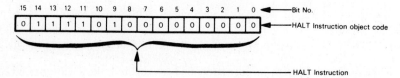

IN — Input a Word

INB — Input a Byte

IN and INB are privileged instructions.
This is the general format for the IN and INB instructions:

Addressing Options	
dst	src
R	IR
R	DA

IN   dst,src
INB   dst,src

The symbol dst is a destination operand, which must be specified using direct register addressing. A 16-bit CPU register must be specified for IN; an 8-bit CPU register must be specified for INB.

The symbol src is a source operand identifying an I/O Port. The 16-bit I/O Port address is generated using direct addressing, or register indirect (implied) addressing. INB must address an odd numbered port.

When IN or INB is executed, data is transferred from the I/O Port addressed by the source operand to the CPU register selected by the destination operand. IN transfers a word of data from an I/O Port to a 16-bit CPU register. INB transfers a byte of data (Bits 0-7) from an I/O Port to an 8-bit CPU register.

The IN and INB instructions have two object code formats, which may be illustrated as follows:

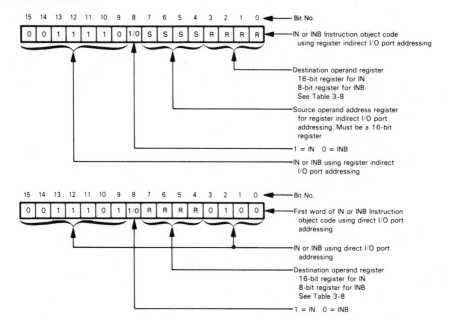

No status flags are modified by the IN or INB instructions.

Figure 3-49 illustrates execution of the following IN instruction:

```
IN      R0,R3;          % AMC syntax
IN      R0,@R3          ! Zilog syntax !
```

This instruction causes 16 bits of data, illustrated generally in Figure 3-49 as PPPP, to be transferred from an I/O Port selected by the address 0400_{16}, to 16-bit register R0.

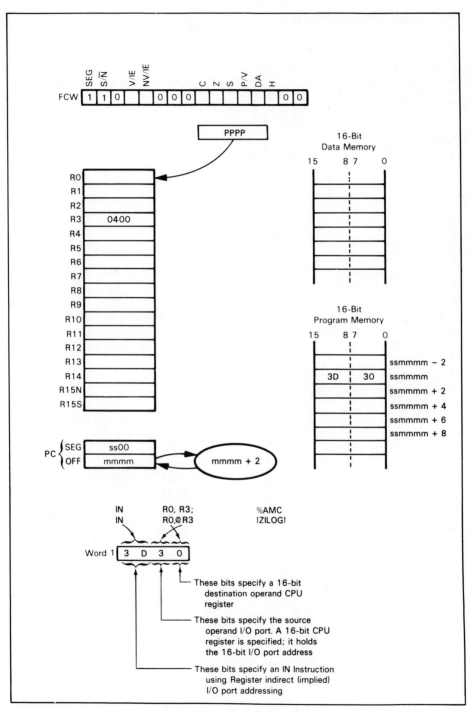

Figure 3-49. Execution of the IN Instruction

INC — Increment Word

INCB — Increment Byte

This is the general format for the INC and INCB instructions:

Addressing Options	
dst	src
R	IM
IR	IM
DA	IM
X	IM

INC   dst,data
INCB   dst,data

The symbol dst is a 16-bit register or memory location for INC; it is an 8-bit register or memory location for INCB. The symbol dst is specified using any standard operand addressing method with the exception of immediate addressing. (See Figure 3-26).

A 4-bit unsigned binary immediate operand, specified by data, is added to the destination location using twos complement arithmetic. The symbol data may be omitted from the operand field, in which case a default value of 1 is assumed. The symbol data can have values ranging from 1 to 16; values are encoded as (data − 1) in the instruction object code, with values ranging from 0 for 1, to F_{16} for 16.

The INC and INCB instructions' object code may be illustrated as follows:

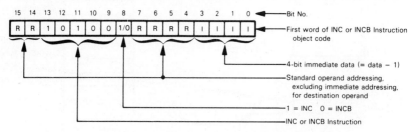

The Z, S, and V statuses are modified by the INC and INCB instructions.

Figure 3-50 illustrates execution of the INC instruction:

```
INC     RR2^,8;        % AMC syntax
INC     @RR2,#8        ! Zilog syntax !
```

This is the INC version of the DEC instruction illustrated in Figure 3-43.

In Figure 3-50, register indirect (implied) memory addressing is used to specify a long segmented memory address: word 8000_{16} in segment TT. 8 is added to the contents of this memory word. Since the memory word contains 0768_{16}, it will contain 0770_{16} after the INC instruction has executed.

In non-segmented mode, the INC instruction illustrated in Figure 3-50, would contain the address 8000_{16} in 16-bit Register R2; Register R3 would be unused.

The INCB instruction executes as illustrated in Figure 3-50, except that the contents of a single memory byte are incremented. For example, the instruction:

```
INCB    RR2^,8;        % AMC syntax
INCB    @RR2,#8        ! Zilog syntax !
```

would leave the value 70_{16} in memory byte 8000_{16} within segment TT.

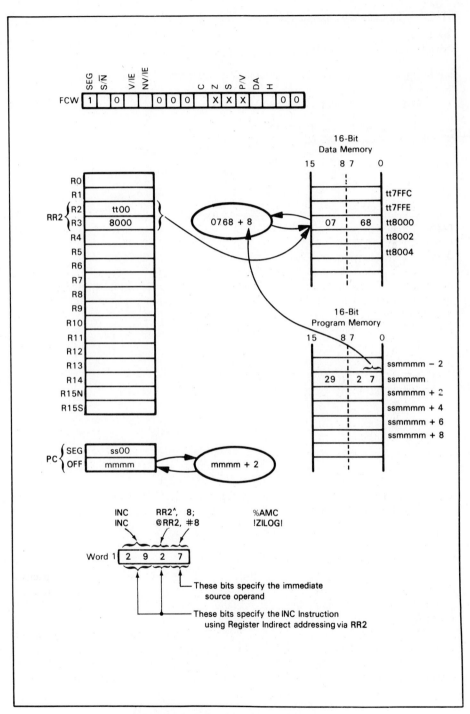

Figure 3-50. Execution of the INC Instruction

Remember, you do not have to include a source operand if you are incrementing by 1, since 1 is the default value. For example, the instruction

```
INC     @RR2
```

would increase the contents of memory location $TT8000_{16}$ from 0768_{16} to 0769_{16}, in Figure 3-50.

When the instruction illustrated in Figure 3-50 is executed, this is what happens:

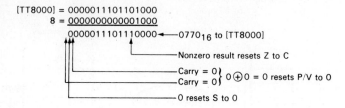

IND — Input Word and Decrement

INDB — Input Byte and Decrement

The IND and INDB instructions are privileged. This is the general format for the IND and INDB instructions:

Addressing Options		
dst	src	r
IR	IR	R

IND   dst,src,r
INDB   dst,src,r

The symbol dst is a destination operand which is specified using register indirect (implied) addressing. The symbol dst selects a memory location.

The symbol src is a source operand which uses register indirect (implied) addressing to specify an I/O Port address. A 16-bit register must be specified for src. Therefore 65536 I/O Ports can be addressed. INDB must address an odd numbered port.

The symbol r is a Counter Register which must be specified as a 16-bit CPU register.

When the IND or INDB instruction is executed, data is transferred from the I/O Port identified by the source operand to the memory location addressed by the destination operand. A data word is transferred for IND; a data byte is transferred for INDB. The destination operand address is then decremented by 1 for INDB, or by 2 for IND. The Counter Register is always decremented by 1. If the Counter Register contains 0 after being decremented, then the Overflow status is set to 1; the Overflow status is reset to 0 otherwise.

The IND/INDB instructions provide one iteration in an instruction sequence that moves a string of data from an I/O Port to a block of contiguous memory locations. Because the memory address is decremented, data will be stored first in the memory location with the highest address and last in the memory location with the lowest address. This may be illustrated as follows:

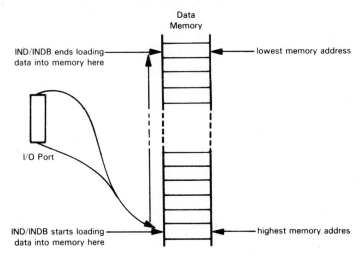

The IND and INDB instructions' object code may be illustrated as follows:

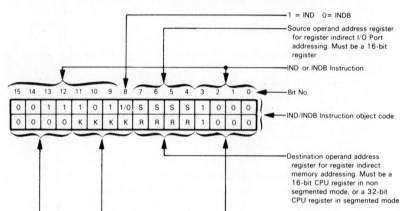

Only the Overflow status is modified by the IND or INDB instruction. As explained previously, the Overflow status is set to 1 when the Counter Register decrements to 0. The Overflow status is cleared otherwise.

Figure 3-51 illustrates execution of the IND instruction:

```
IND     R4^,R3,R5;      % AMC syntax
IND     @R4,@R3,R5      ! Zilog syntax !
```

Using the operands illustrated in Figure 3-51, one word of data will be loaded from I/O Port 0400_{16} into a word of memory at address 0800_{16}.

By examining Figures 3-51, it is impossible to say whether the beginning of a data transfer is being illustrated, or whether the data transfer is partially completed. For example, it is conceivable that R5 initially contained a much larger number, in which case R4 would initially have held a much larger address; a large block of data may already have been transferred from I/O Port 0400_{16} into memory words with addresses 0802_{16} and higher.

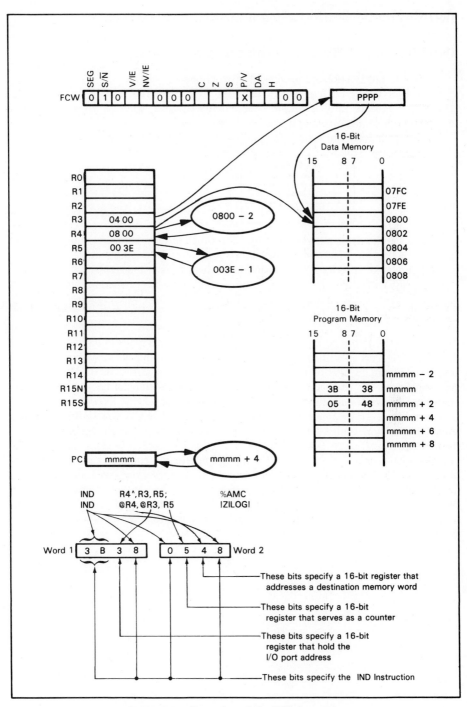

Figure 3-51. Execution of the IND Instruction

INDR — Input Word, Decrement and Repeat

INDRB — Input Byte, Decrement and Repeat

INDR and INDRB are privileged instructions.

The INDR/INDRB instructions differ from IND/INDB only in that INDR/INDRB re-execute until a counter decrements to zero, whereas IND/INDB cease execution after transferring one word or byte of data.

This is the general format for the INDR and INDRB instructions:

Addressing Options		
dst	src	r
IR	IR	R

INDR   dst,src,r
INDRB   dst,src,r

The symbol dst is a destination operand which is specified using register indirect (implied) addressing. The symbol dst selects a memory location.

The symbol src is a source operand which uses register indirect (implied) addressing to specify an I/O Port address. A 16-bit register must be specified for src. Therefore 65536 I/O Ports can be addressed. INDRB must address an odd numbered port.

The symbol r is a Counter Register which must be specified as a 16-bit CPU register.

When the INDR or INDRB instruction is executed, a block of data is transferred from the I/O Port identified by the source operand to a block of memory locations addressed by the destination operand. Data words are transferred for INDR; data bytes are transferred for INDRB. After each word or byte is transferred, the destination operand address is decremented by 1 for INDRB, or by 2 for INDR. The Counter Register is always decremented by 1 after each transfer. The INDR/INDRB instruction keeps re-executing until the Counter Register contents are 0. INDR/INDRB execution then ceases.

The Overflow status is set to 1 when the instruction completes execution.

The INDR/INDRB instructions provide the entire event sequence needed to move a string of data from an I/O Port to a block of contiguous memory locations. Because the memory address is decremented, data will be stored first in the memory location with the highest address and last in the memory location with the lowest address for the IND/INDB instructions.

The INDR and INDRB instructions object code may be illustrated as follows:

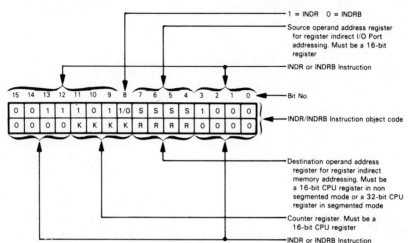

Only the Overflow status is modified by the INDR or INDRB instruction. As explained previously, the Overflow status is always set to 1.

The INDR version of the instruction illustrated in Figure 3-51 is:

```
INDR    R4^,R3,R5;      % AMC syntax
INDR    @R4,@R3,R5      ! Zilog syntax !
```

Using the operand illustrated in Figure 3-51, $3E_{16}$ (62_{10}) words of data will be loaded from I/O Port 0400_{16} into a block of memory beginning with the memory word at address 0800_{16}, and ending at the memory word at address 0786_{16}.

An illustration of the INDR instruction's execution would not differ from Figure 3-51 except that the two instructions have different object codes. This is because Figure 3-51 does not illustrate the fact that the IND (or INDB) instruction ceases executing after transferring one word (or one byte) of data from an I/O port to a memory location, whereas the equivalent INDR (or INDRB) instruction will continue executing until the Counter Register has decremented to zero.

In order to achieve the same total data transfer, therefore, the INDR instruction:

```
INDR    R4^,R3,R5;      % AMC syntax
INDR    @R4,@R3,R5      ! Zilog syntax !
```

would have to be duplicated by the instruction pair:

```
LOOP:   IND     R4^,R3,R5;      % AMC syntax
        JR      NOV,LOOP

LOOP    IND     @R4,@R3,R5      ! Zilog syntax !
        JR      NOV,LOOP
```

If you simply wish to move a block of data from an I/O port to memory, then clearly the INDR instruction is preferable to the IND/JP instruction pair; the instruction pair requires more memory for its object code and takes longer to execute. However, you cannot execute the INDR instruction unless you are sure that the I/O port will have data available when needed, or that external logic will appropriately extend INDR execution machine cycles to accommodate input data that would otherwise not be available on time.

If the data being input must be processed byte by byte, or word by word, then you cannot use the INDR instruction; instead, you must use an IND instruction loop which might be illustrated for the general case as follows:

```
LOOP:   IND     @RP,@RA,RC      ! Zilog syntax !
        .
        .       Instructions here process the data input
        .       by IND, but must preserve the P/V status
        .
        JP      NOV,LOOP
```

Once an INDR or INDRB instruction starts to execute, it could conceivably continue executing for a long time if it were inputting a large block of data. This would present interrupt logic with problems. In order to prevent any such problems, the Z8000 allows interrupts to be acknowledged between each iterative execution of the INDR or INDRB instruction. Furthermore, the Program Counter value saved during the interrupt acknowledgement process is the address of the INDR or INDRB instruction, so that execution of this instruction will continue from the point of interrupt, after the interrupt has been serviced. Seven clock periods must be added to the INDR or INDRB instruction's execution time to account for each interrupt acknowledged during the instruction's execution.

INI - Input Word and Increment

INIB - Input Byte and Increment

The INI and INIB instructions are privileged.

The INI/INIB instructions are almost identical to IND/INDB; the only difference is that INI/INIB increment memory addresses which IND/INDB decrement.

Addressing Options				
dst	**src**	**r**	INI	dst,src,r
IR	IR	R	INIB	dst,src,r

The symbol dst is a destination operand which is specified using register indirect (implied) addressing. The symbol dst selects a memory location.

The symbol src is a source operand which uses register indirect (implied) addressing to specify an I/O Port address. A 16-bit register must be specified for src. Therefore 65536 I/O Ports can be addressed. INIB must address an odd numbered port.

The symbol r is a Counter Register which must be specified as a 16-bit CPU register.

When the INI or INIB instruction is executed, data is transferred from the I/O Port identified by the source operand to the memory location addressed by the destination operand. A data word is transferred for INI; a data byte is transferred for INIB. The destination operand address is then incremented by 1 for INIB, or by 2 for INI. The Counter Register is always decremented by 1. If the Counter Register contains 0 after being decremented, then the Overflow status is set to 1; the Overflow status is reset to 0 otherwise.

The INI/INIB instructions provide one iteration in an instruction sequence that moves a string of data from an I/O Port to a block of contiguous memory locations. Because the memory address is incremented, data will be stored first in the memory location with the lowest address and last in the memory location with the highest address. This may be illustrated as follows:

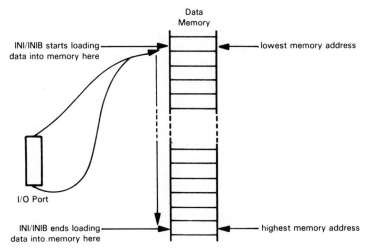

The INI and INIB instructions object code may be illustrated as follows:

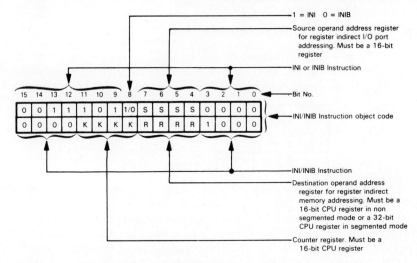

Only the Overflow status is modified by the INI or INIB instruction. As explained previously, the Overflow status is set to 1 when the Counter Register decrements to 0. The Overflow status is cleared otherwise.

Figure 3-52 illustrates execution of the INI instruction:

```
INI     R4^,R3,R5;      % AMC syntax
INI     @R4,@R3,R5      ! Zilog syntax !
```

Using the operands illustrated in Figure 3-51, word of data will be loaded from I/O Port 0400_{16} into the memory word at address 0800_{16}. By examining Figures 3-51, it is impossible to say whether the beginning of a data transfer is being illustrated, or whether the data transfer is partially completed. For example, it is conceivable that R5 initially contained a much larger number, in which case R4 would initially have held a much larger address; a large block of data may already have been transferred from I/O Port 0400_{16} into memory words with addresses 0802_{16} and higher.

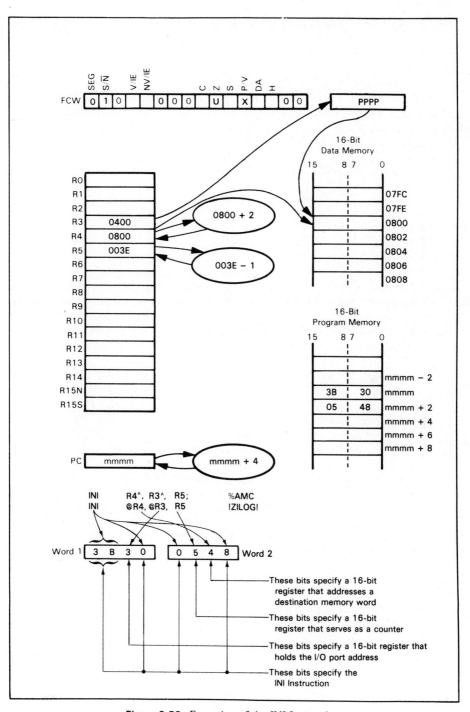

Figure 3-52. Execution of the INI Instruction

INIR - Input Word, Decrement and Repeat

INIRB - Input Byte, Decrement and Repeat

The INIR and INIRB instructions are privileged.

The INIR/INIRB instructions differ from INI/INIB only in that INIR/INIRB re-execute until a counter decrements to zero, whereas INI/INIB cease execution after transferring one word or byte of data. INIR/INIRB are also almost identical to INDR/INDRB; the only difference is that INIR/INIRB increment memory addresses which INDR/INDRB decrement.

This is the general format for the INIR and INIRB instructions:

Addressing Options					
dst	src	r		INIR	dst,src,r
IR	IR	R		INIRB	dst,src,r

The symbol dst is a destination operand which is specified using register indirect (implied) addressing. The symbol dst selects a memory location.

The symbol src is a source operand which uses register indirect (implied) addressing to specify an I/O Port address. A 16-bit register must be specified for src. Therefore 65536 I/O Ports can be addressed. INIRB must address an odd numbered port.

The symbol r is a Counter Register which must be specified as a 16-bit CPU register.

When the INIR or INIRB instruction is executed, a block of data is transferred from the I/O Port identified by the source operand to a block of memory locations addressed by the destination operand. Data words are transferred for INIR; data bytes are transferred for INIRB. After each word or byte is transferred, the destination operand address is incremented by 1 for INIRB, or by 2 for INIR. The Counter Register is always decremented by 1. The INIR/INIRB instruction keeps re-executing until the Counter Register contents are 0. INIR/INIRB execution then ceases.

The Overflow status is set to 1 when the instruction completes execution.

The INIR/INIRB instructions provide the entire event sequence needed to move a string of data from an I/O Port to a block of contiguous memory locations. Because the memory address is incremented, data will be stored first in the memory location with the lowest address and last in the memory location with the highest address, illustrated for the INI/INIB instructions.

The INIR and INIRB instructions' object code may be illustrated as follows:

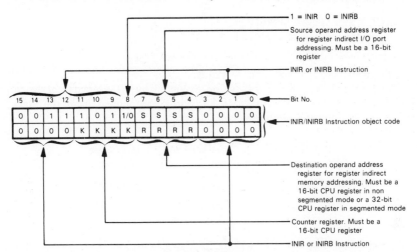

Only the Overflow status is modified by the INIR or INIRB instruction. As explained previously, the Overflow status is always set to 1.

The INIR version of the instruction illustrated in Figure 3- 52 is:

```
INIR    R4^,R3,R5;      % AMC syntax
INIR    @R4,@R3,R5      ! Zilog syntax !
```

An illustration of the INIR instruction's execution would not differ from Figure 3-52, except that the two instructions have different object codes. This is because Figure 3-52 does not illustrate the fact that the INI (or INIB) instruction ceases executing after transferring one word (or one byte) of data from an I/O port to a memory location, whereas the equivalent INIR (or INIRB) instruction will continue executing until the Counter Register has decremented to zero.

In order to achieve the same total data transfer, therefore, the INIR instruction:

```
INIR    R4^,R3,R5;      % AMC syntax
INIR    @R4,@R3,R5      ! Zilog syntax !
```

would have to be duplicated by the instruction pair:

```
LOOP:   INI     R4^,R3,R5;      % AMC syntax
        JR      NOV,LOOP;

LOOP:   INI     @R4,@R3,R5      ! Zilog syntax !
        JR      NOV,LOOP
```

See the INDR/INDRB description for a discussion of these alternate execution loops.

Once an INIR or INIRB instruction starts to execute, it could conceivably continue executing for a long time if it were inputting a large block of data. This would present interrupt logic with problems. In order to prevent any such problems, the Z8000 allows interrupts to be acknowledged between each iterative execution of the INIR or INIRB instruction. Furthermore, the Program Counter value saved during the interrupt acknowledge process is the address of the INIR or INIRB instruction, so that execution of this instruction will continue from the point of interrupt, after the interrupt has been serviced. Seven clock periods must be added to the INIR or INIRB instruction's execution time to account for each interrupt acknowledged during the instruction's execution.

IRET - Return from Interrupt

IRET is a privileged instruction.
This is the format for the IRET instruction:

IRET

The IRET instruction has no operands.

IRET should be the last instruction executed by an interrupt service routine. When this instruction is executed, 16-bit words are popped from the stack, into registers, in the following sequence:

Non-Segmented Mode Stack	Word Destination	Segmented Mode Stack
Identifier word	Popped and discarded	Identifier word
Status word	To Flag and Control Word	Status word
(Not present)	To Program Counter Segment Register	Program Counter
Program Counter	To Program Counter (or PC Offset Register)	Program Counter

The identifier is an undefined 16-bit word that is pushed onto the stack during the interrupt acknowledge sequence; it is popped and discarded by IRET.

The new Flag and Control Word contents popped from the stack do not become effective until the beginning of the next instruction's execution. The Flag and Control word bits, including the status flags, are set according to the status word popped from the stack.

The IRET instructions' object code may be illustrated as follows:

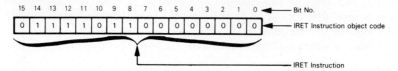

Figures 3-53 and 3-54 illustrate execution of the IRET instruction in non-segmented and segmented modes, respectively.

For a discussion of interrupt service routines, see Chapter 12.

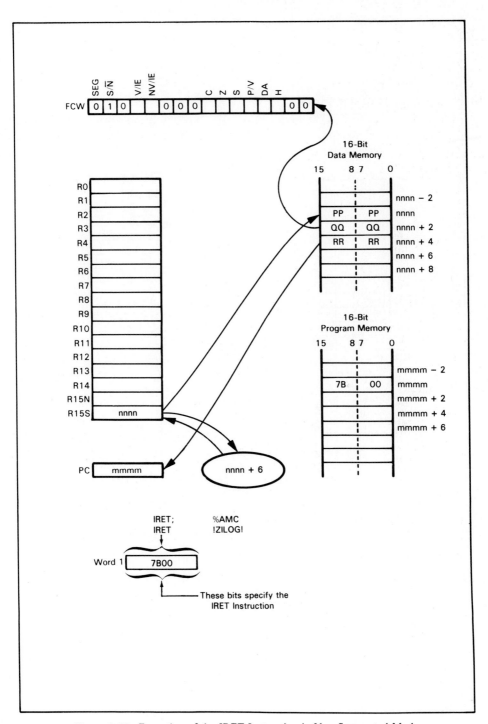

Figure 3-53. Execution of the IRET Instruction in Non-Segmented Mode

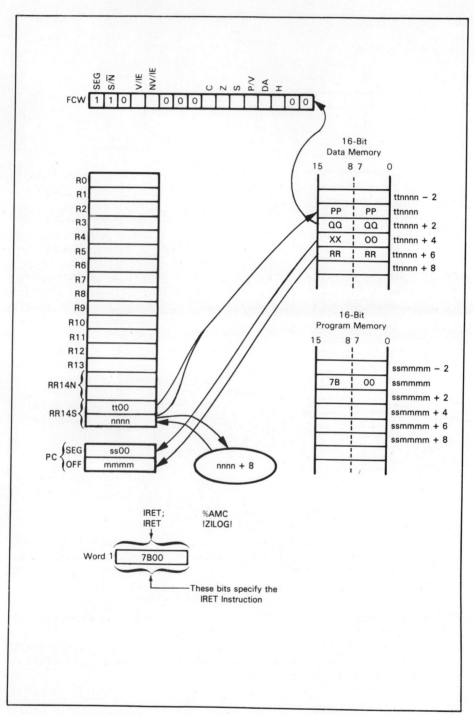

Figure 3-54. Execution of the IRET Instruction in Segmented Mode

JP - Jump Conditional

This is the general format for the JP instruction:

Addressing Options
dst
IR DA X

JP   cc,dst

The symbol dst is a destination operand which is used to compute a new Program Counter value. The destination address can be specified as a register indirect (implied), direct or direct indexed address.

The symbol cc is a condition code which must be specified using one of the mnemonics illustrated in the code column of Table 3-4, or can be omitted.

When the JP instruction is executed, the status condition identified by cc is compared with status settings in the Flag and Control word. If there is not a match, the next sequential instruction is executed. If there is a match, a new Program Counter value is computed using the addressing method specified for the destination operand. Note that the address computed for the destination operand is loaded into the Program Counter. The new Program Counter value is not read from the data memory location addressed by the destination operand.

In non-segmented mode, a 16-bit address is computed. In segmented mode, a 32-bit address is computed.

The JP instruction's object code may be illustrated as follows:

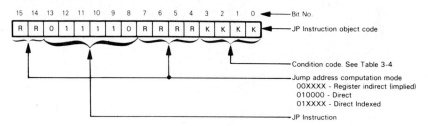

No status flags are modified by the JP instruction.

JP instruction execution is illustrated for non-segmented and segmented modes in Figures 3-55 and 3-56 respectively. These two figures illustrate execution of the instruction:

```
JP        ZR,LABEL(R8);    % AMC syntax
JP        Z,LABEL(R8)      ! Zilog syntax !
```

The two instructions illustrated are identical, apart from allowances made for segmented or non-segmented modes.

In Figure 3-55 direct indexed addressing is specified. LABEL is shown with the actual value 4000_{16}. At some point in the program LABEL will have to be equated to this value using an Equate assembler directive.

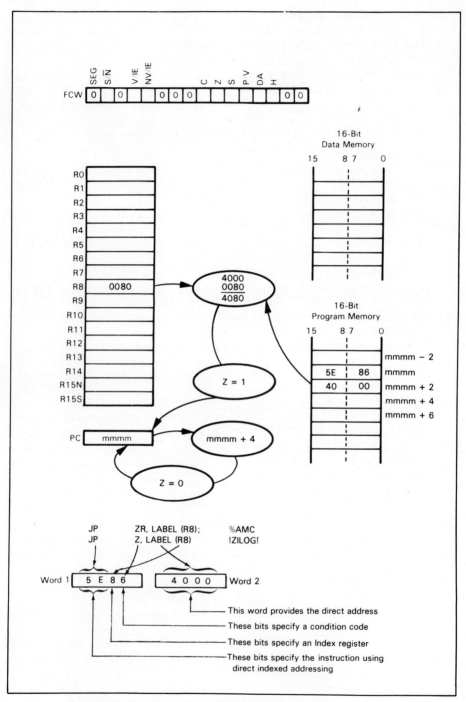

Figure 3-55. Execution of the JP Instruction in Non-Segmented Mode

If jump conditions are satisfied, then the new address loaded into the Program Counter will be 4080_{16}, the direct address provided by the second word of the JP instructions, plus 0080_{16}, the contents of Index Register R8. This new value is loaded into the Program Counter if the Zero status is 1, since Z is the condition code specified in the JP operand field. If the Zero status is 0, then the Program Counter is incremented by four to address the next sequential instruction.

In Figure 3-56 a segment number is also specified, but otherwise the instruction is identical to Figure 3-55. The label SEG is used to specify a segment, which is illustrated as 03_{16} in Figure 3-56. Remember, 83_{16} is stored in the second word of the instruction code, since the high-order bit of the second word is set to one to identify a long-segmented direct address. At some point in the program, the label SEG will have had to be equated to the value 03_{16}. SEGLABEL would have to be defined if you are using an AMC assembler. Again Z is the condition code specified in the operand field of the JP instruction. Therefore, if the Zero status is 1, 03_{16} is loaded into the high-order byte of the SEG Program Counter Register, while 4080_{16} is loaded into the Offset Register of the Program Counter. But if the Zero status is 0, the Program Counter is incremented by six to address the next sequential instruction.

The new Program Counter address must be even, since all instruction object codes are at least 16 bits wide, and must begin on even byte address boundaries.

The JP instruction illustrated in Figure 3-56 could be encoded more economically by loading 4000_{16} into Index Register R8, and using a short-segmented direct address, as follows:

```
JP      ZP,SEGLABEL(R8);    % AMC syntax
JP      Z,<<SEG>>LABEL(R8)  ! Zilog syntax !
```

If you are using a Zilog assembler, SEG would have to be equated to 03_{16} and LABEL would have to be equated to 80_{16}. If you are using an AMC assembler, SEGLABEL would have to be defined.

With some early production chips, if a jump is executed in non-segmented mode, the internally stored PC segment may be affected. The PC segment will be incorrect if the SEG flag is set to return to segmented mode. This problem can be avoided by always using a system Call trap to return to segmented mode. See Table 3-18 at the end of this chapter for more information.

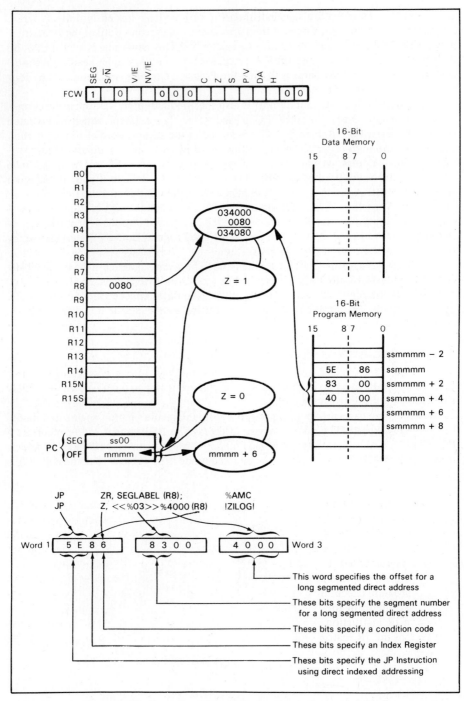

Figure 3-56. Execution of the JP Instruction in Segmented Mode

JR - Jump Relative on Condition

This is the general format for the JR instruction:

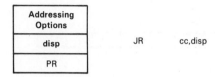

The symbol cc is a condition code which must be specified using one of the mnemonics illustrated in the code column of Table 3-4, or may be omitted.

The symbol disp is an 8-bit, signed binary displacement, which is used to compute a branch program memory address when branch conditions are met.

When the JR instruction is executed, the condition code specified by cc is compared with Status Register bit settings in the Flag and Control Word. If there is no match, the next sequential instruction is executed. If there is a match, disp is used to compute the new program address; disp is shifted left one bit position, then added, as a signed binary number, to the Program Counter value, after the Program Counter has been incremented to address the next sequential instruction. This form of program relative addressing is illustrated in Figure 3- 23.

The JR instruction object code may be illustrated as follows:

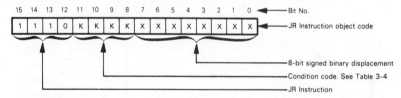

No status flags are modified by the JR instruction. Execution of the JR instruction is illustrated in Figure 3-23 and in Figure 3-57. In Figure 3-57, the following JR instruction is illustrated:

```
JR      ZR,LABEL;      % AMC syntax
JR      Z,LABEL        ! Zilog syntax !
```

Since the condition code specified in the operand field of the JR instruction is Z, a branch will occur when the Zero status is 1. A new Program Counter value is then computed by doubling the 8-bit signed binary displacement provided in the instruction object code, and adding it to the Program Counter contents, after the Program Counter has been incremented to address the next sequential instruction.

Using the displacement actually illustrated in Figure 3-57, a branch, if taken, will advance program execution to memory word mmmm $+ 130_{16}$. The assembler computes this displacement for the object code.

The JR instruction can be used if the label is within -254 to $+256$ bytes of the first byte of the JR instruction. This is shown by the following calculations:

-128	$+127$	range of displacement
*2	*2	left shift one bit
-256	$+254$	
$+ \ 2$	$+ \ 2$	program counter increment
-254	$+256$	range of the jump

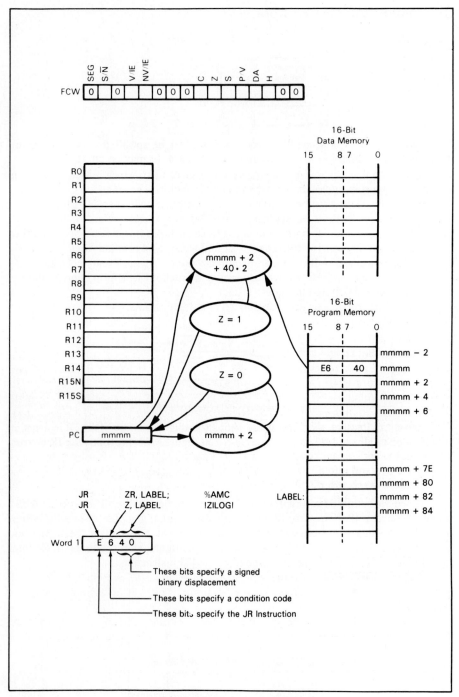

Figure 3-57. Execution of the JR Instruction

LD - Move a Data Word

LDB - Move a Data Byte

This is the general format for the LD and LDB instructions:

Addressing Options	
dst	**src**
R	R
R	IM
R	IR
R	DA
R	X
R	BR
R	BX
BR	R
BX	R
IR	R
DA	R
X	R
IR	IM
DA	IM
X	IM

LD   dst,src
LD   dst,src

The symbol dst is a destination operand which can be specified using any addressing method with the exception of immediate addressing.

The symbol src is a source operand which can be specified using any addressing method, including immediate addressing.

A data word (for LD) or a data byte (for LDB) is moved from the source to the destination. Although a wide variety of addressing methods can be used to specify the source and destination operands, there are restrictions imposed on the allowed combinations of addressing methods, which are summarized in Table 3-13.

As you will see from Table 3-13 most LD and LDB instructions move data between a CPU register and a memory location. A few LD and LDB instructions load an immediate operand into a memory location. There are no LD or LDB instructions that move data between two memory locations.

A number of different instructions object codes are used by LD and LDB instructions. For standard source operand addressing, object codes may be illustrated as follows:

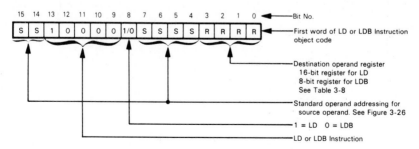

Table 3-13. LD and LDB Instruction Allowed Operand Addressing Combinations

		Source Operand						
		Register Rn, RLn or RHn	Immediate Data	Register Indirect Rn or RRn	Direct Label	Direct Indexed Label (Rn)	Base Relative RRn (DISP) or Rn (DISP)	Base Indexed RRn (Rm) or Rn (Rm)
Destination Operand	Register RLn Rn, or RHn	X	X	X	X	X	X	X
	Immediate Data							
	Register Indirect Rn or RRn	X	X					
	Direct Label	X	X					
	Direct Indexed Label (Rn)	X	X					
	Base Relative RRn (DISP) or Rn (DISP)	X						
	Base Indexed RRn (Rm) or Rn (Rm)	X						

X represents allowed combinations

The LDB instruction has a one word object code version when an immediate byte of data is to be loaded into an 8-bit CPU register. This object code may be illustrated as follows:

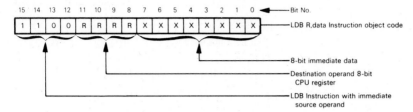

When base relative addressing is used to specify the source operand, the following instruction object code is used:

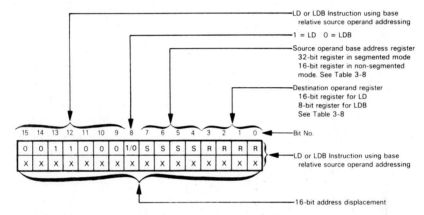

When base relative addressing is used to specify the destination operand, the instruction object code changes as follows:

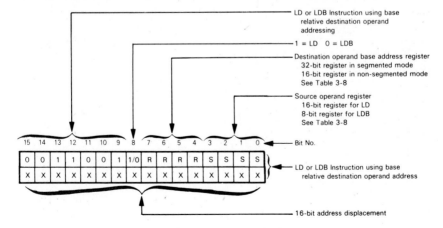

For base indexed source and destination operand addressing, these totally different object codes are used:

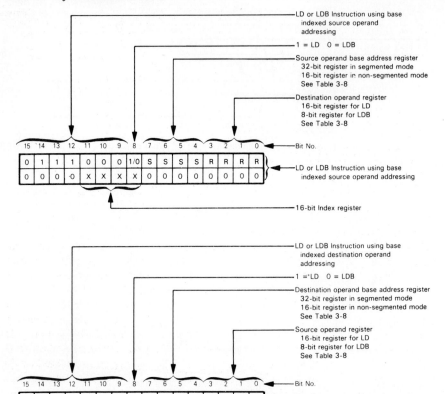

When data is moved from a CPU register to a memory location, the following instruction object code is used:

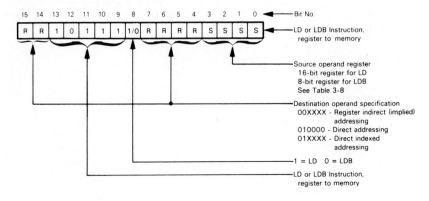

When immediate data is moved to a memory word or byte, the following instruction object code is used:

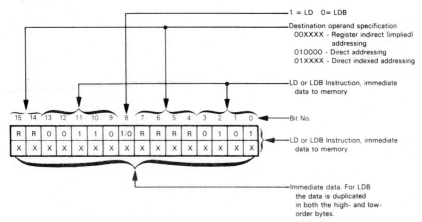

None of the LD or LDB instructions modify any statuses.

Table 3-14 illustrates the syntax of the allowed forms of the LD instruction. The same syntax is used for LDB instructions, except that the source or destination data register must be an 8- bit CPU register RH0-RH7 or RL0-RL7. Except as noted, the same syntax is used for the LDL instruction to be described next.

A few specific LD and LDB instructions were illustrated earlier in this chapter when we described memory addressing methods. In particular, Figure 3-19 illustrates an LD instruction using base relative addressing. Figure 3-20 and 3-21 illustrate LD instructions using base indexed addressing. There is nothing noteworthy about the simple movement of data from a source location to a destination location; therefore we do not include further illustrations of LD instructions. Any of the addressing methods illustrations can be converted into an LD instruction illustration simply by moving the contents of the source location to the destination location, ignoring all other operations.

NOTE: Beware of interrupts when executing LD instructions in Normal mode, with R15N or as the destination register. With some early production Z8000 chips, if an interrupt is acknowledged as soon as the instruction completes execution, R15S will receive the data that was intended for R15N. Since the programmer generally cannot know if an interrupt will occur, it is best not to use these instructions to load R15N when using a microcomputer containing one of these early production chips. See Table 3-18 at the end of this chapter for more information. Usually the system will load the stack pointer for you, and you will manipulate it with PUSH and POP, so this problem will not arise.

Table 3-14. Syntax of Load Instructions

	AMC	Zilog	Addressing Modes	Meaning
Load Register	LD R8,8; LD R8,DATA;	LD R8,#8 LD R8,#DATA	R,IM	Load R8 from immediate data
	LD R8,R1;	LD R8,R1	R,R	Load R8 from R1
	LD R8,R1^;	LD R8,@R1	R,IR	Load R8 from memory at address in R1
	LD R8,LABEL; LD R8,#6000^;	LD R8,LABEL LD R8,%6000	R,DA	Load R8 from memory at address LABEL (or 6000_{16})
	LD R8,LABEL(R1); LD R8,#6000^(R1);	LD R8,LABEL(R1) LD R8,%6000(R1)	R,X	Load R8 from memory at address LABEL (or 6000_{16}) plus index in R1
	LD R8,R2^(DATA); LD R8,R2^(10);	LD R8,R2(#DATA) LD R8,R2(#10)	BR	Load R8 from memory at base address in R2 plus offset DATA (or10_{10})
	LD R8,R2^(R1);	LD R8,R2(R1)	BX	Load R8 from memory at base address in R2 plus offset in R1
Load Memory	LD R1^,R8;	LD @R1,R8	IR,R	Load memory at address in R1 from R8
	LD LABEL,R8; LD #6000^,R8;	LD LABEL,R8 LD %6000,R8	DA,R	Load memory at address (or 6000_{16}) from R8
	LD LABEL(R1),R8; LD #6000^(R1),R8;	LD LABEL(R1),R8 LD %6000(R1),R8	X,R	Load memory at address LABEL (or 6000_{16}) plus index in R1, from R8
	LD R2^(DATA),R8; LD R2^(10);R8;	LD R1(#DATA),R8 LD R1(#10),R8	BR,R	Load memory at base address in R2 plus offset DATA (or 10_{10}), from R8
	LD R2^(R1),R8;	LD R2(R1),R8	BX,R	Load memory at base address in R2, plus offset in R1, from R8
	• LD R1^,10; LD R1^,DATA;	LD @R1,#10 LD @R1,#DATA	IR,IM	Load memory at address in R1 from immediate data

	• LD LABEL,10;
	LD #6000^,10;
	LD LABEL,DATA;
	LD #6000^,DATA;
		LD LABEL,#10
		LD %6000,#10
		LD LABEL,#DATA
		LD %6000,#DATA
			DA,IM	Load memory at address LABEL (or 6000_{16}) from immediate data

	• LD LABEL(R1),10;
	LD #6000^(R1),10;
	LD LABEL(R1),DATA;
	LD #6000^(R1),DATA;
		LD LABEL(R1),#10
		LD %6000(R1),#10
		LD LABEL(R1),#DATA
		LD %6000(R1),#DATA
			X,IM	Load memory at address LABEL (or 6000_{16}), plus index in R1, from immediate data

• LD and LDB only, not available for LDL

LDA - Load Address

This is the general format for the LDA instruction:

Addressing Options	
dst	**src**
R	DA
R	X
R	BR
R	BX

LDA   dst,addr

The symbol dst is the destination operand which must be specified using direct register addressing. A 16-bit CPU register is loaded in non-segmented mode; a 32-bit CPU register is loaded in segmented mode.

The addr is a source operand address; it can be specified as a direct, direct indexed, base relative or base indexed address.

AMC assemblers do not use the LDA mnemonic; instead they use the LD mnemonic with the address specified as an immediate operand address constant. This may generate either an LD or an LDA instruction object code, depending on the addressing mode and the version of the AMC assembler being used. To specify an address constant to be used as an immediate operand, place a ^ character in front of the operand. See Table 3-15 for the AMC syntax.

When the LDA instruction is executed, the computed source operand address is loaded into th destination CPU register. That is to say, the memory address rather than the contents of the addressed memory word is loaded into the destination register.

Different instruction object codes are used by the LDA instruction with its various addressing options; they may be illustrated as follows:

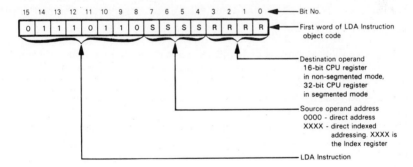

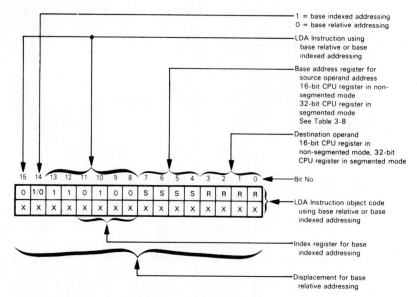

No status flags are modified by the LDA instruction.

LDA instruction execution is illustrated in Figure 3-58 for non-segmented mode, and in Figure 3-59 for segmented mode. Essentially the same instruction is illustrated in both of these figures. These are the instructions illustrated:

```
LD     R2,^LABEL(R4);          % AMC syntax
LDA    R2,LABEL(R4)            ! Zilog syntax !

LD     R2,^SEGLABEL(R4);       % AMC syntax
LDA    RR2,<<SEG>>LABEL(R4)    ! Zilog syntax !
```

LABEL is a label which has the value 4800_{16}. An appropriate assembler directive must equate LABEL to this value, or it must be defined by being used elsewhere as a label. In Figure 3-60 the label SEG is used to specify the segment. Segment 08_{16} is used. If you are using a Zilog assembler SEG will also have to be equated to 08_{16} at some point in the program. If you are using an AMC assembler, you will have to define SEGLABEL somewhere in the program. Note that 88_{16} appears in the second word of the LDA instruction object code for the long segmented mode; the higher order bit of the second word is set to 1, indicating a long-segmented address.

Direct, indexed addressing has been specified in Figures 3-58 and Figure 3-59. In Figure 3-58, the effective memory address is simply the sum of the second instruction object code word, and the contents of CPU register R4. This effective memory address is loaded into register R2.

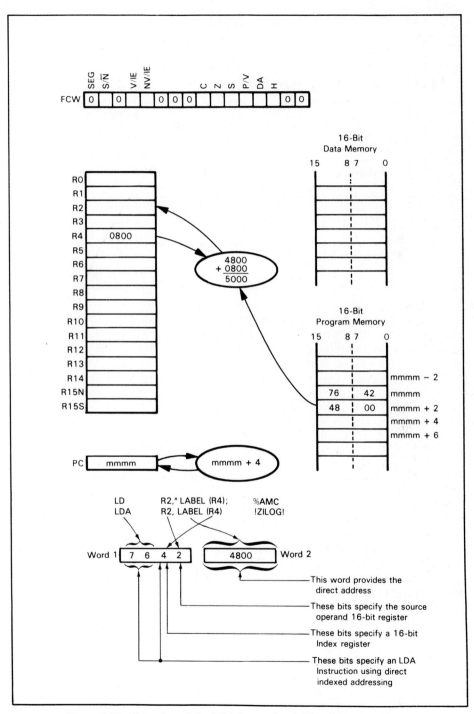

Figure 3-58. Execution of the LDA Instruction in Non-Segmented Mode

Table 3-15. Syntax of Load Address Instructions

	AMC	Zilog	Addressing Mode	Meaning
Load Register	LD R8,^ LABEL;	LDA R8,LABEL	DA	Load R8 with value of LABEL
	LD R8,^ $;	LDA R8,$	DA	Load R8 with value of location counter
	LD R8,^ LABEL(R1);	LDA R8,LABEL(R1)	X	Load R8 with value of LABEL plus index in R1
	LD R8,^ (R2 (DATA)); LD R8,^ (R2 ^ (10));	LDA R8,R2(#DATA) LDA R8,R2(#10)	BR	Load R8 with base address in R2 plus offset DATA (or 10_{10})
	LD R8,^(R2^(R1));	LDA R8,R2(R1)	BX	Load R8 with base address in R2 plus offset in R1

In Figure 3-59, the offset portion of the effective memory address is computed exactly described for the non-segmented version in Figure 3-58. The offset is loaded into the low-order half of RR2. The segment number is loaded into the high-order half of RR2. The low-order byte of the segment number register is unused.

Note that AMC syntax specifies R2 for both segmented and non-segmented mode. However, RR2 is loaded as described in this paragraph when operating in segmented mode. Zilog syntax specifies R2 when assembling for non-segmented mode and RR2 when assembling for segmented mode.

Note that the LDA instruction executed in non-segmented mode is equivalent to a variety of other instructions - depending on the LDA addressing options selected.

A non-segmented LDA instruction that specifies direct addressing is equivalent to an LD instruction that loads immediate data to a CPU register. These two instructions are comparable:

```
        LDA     R3,DATA         ! Zilog syntax !
                                ! Load direct address DATA !
                                ! into R3 !
        LD      R3,#DATA        ! Load immediate data into R3 !
```

which is why AMD syntax uses the LD instruction instead of the LDA equivalent.

If a non-segmented LDA instruction specifies direct, indexed addressing, it adds an immediate operand and the contents of a 16-bit CPU register, storing the sum in another 16-bit CPU register. With the exception of status flag settings, the following instructions are equivalent:

```
        LDA     R2,LABEL(R2)    ! Zilog syntax !
                                ! Load direct indexed address !
                                ! into register !
        ADD     R2,#LABEL       ! Add immediate data to R2 !
```

Here are equivalent instructions using AMC syntax:

```
        LD      R2,^LABEL(R2);  % AMC syntax
        ADD     R2,^LABEL;
```

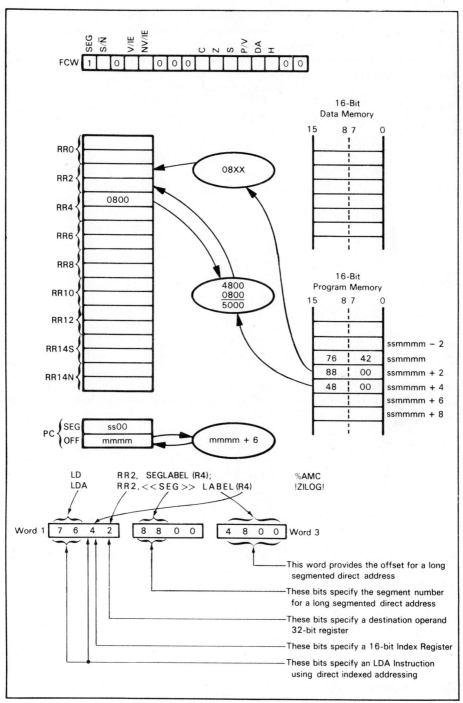

Figure 3-59. Execution of the LDA Instruction in Segmented Mode with a Long Segmented Address

Remember, the LDA instruction modifies no status flags.

An LDA instruction that specifies direct indexed addressing has no ADD equivalent when the Index and destination registers differ.

In non-segmented mode, base relative addressing and direct indexed addressing are functionally identical.

If a non-segmented LDA instruction specifies base indexed addressing, it stores the sum of two CPU registers in any CPU register. If the destination register is the same as the Base or Index register, then the LDA has an equivalent ADD instruction. For example, these two instructions are equivalent, apart from status flag settings:

```
                           % AMC syntax
    LD      R4,^(R6^(R4));  % Load base indexed address
                           % into Register

    ADD     R4,R6;         % Add R6 contents to R4


                           ! Zilog syntax !
    LDA     R4,@R6(R4)     ! Load base indexed address !
                           ! into Register !

    ADD     R4,R6          ! Add R6 contents to R4 !
```

Note that the instruction:

```
    LD      R4,^(R4^(R6));  % AMC syntax
    LDA     R4,R4(R6)       ! Zilog syntax !
```

is functionally equivalent to:

```
    LD      R4,^(R6^(R4));  % AMC syntax
    LDA     R4,R6(R4)       ! Zilog syntax !
```

If the destination register is not the same as either the Base or the Index register, then the LDA instruction becomes a new variation of the ADD instruction. For example,

```
    LD      R5,^(R6^(R4));  % AMC syntax
    LDA     R5,R6(R4)       ! Zilog syntax !
```

stores the sum of R6 and R4 in R5.

Table 3-15 summarizes the syntax of the LDA instruction.

LDAR - Load Program Relative Address

This is the general format for the LDAR instruction:

Addressing Options	
dst	**disp**
R	PR

LDAR   dst,disp

The symbol dst is a destination operand which must be specified using direct register addressing. A 16-bit CPU register must be specified in non-segmented mode; a 32-bit CPU register must be specified in segmented mode.

The symbol disp is a 16-bit signed binary displacement; it is used to compute a program relative memory address.

AMC assemblers do not use the LDAR mnemonic; instead they use the LDR mnemonic with the address specified as an immediate operand address constant. LDAR object code is generated.

When the LDAR instruction is executed, a memory address is computed by adding the displacement from the instruction and the address held in the Program Counter after the Program Counter has been incremented to address the next sequential instruction. This address is loaded into the destination operand CPU register. The symbol disp is not added to the Program Counter itself. In segmented mode, disp and the PC Offset are added. If there is a carry, it is discarded. The PC Segment Register contents are copied to the destination operand CPU register.

The LDAR instruction object code may be illustrated as follows:

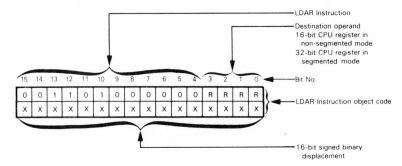

No status flags are modified by the LDAR instruction.

LDAR instruction execution is illustrated in Figure 3-60 for non-segmented mode, and in Figure 3-61 for segmented mode. Essentially the same instruction is illustrated in both of these figures. These are the instructions illustrated.

```
                              ! Zilog syntax !
     LDAR    R6,LABEL         ! non-segmented mode !
     LDAR    RR6,LABEL        ! segmented mode !

                              % AMC syntax
     LDR     R6,^LABEL        % non-segmented mode
     LDR     R6,^LABEL;       % segmented mode
```

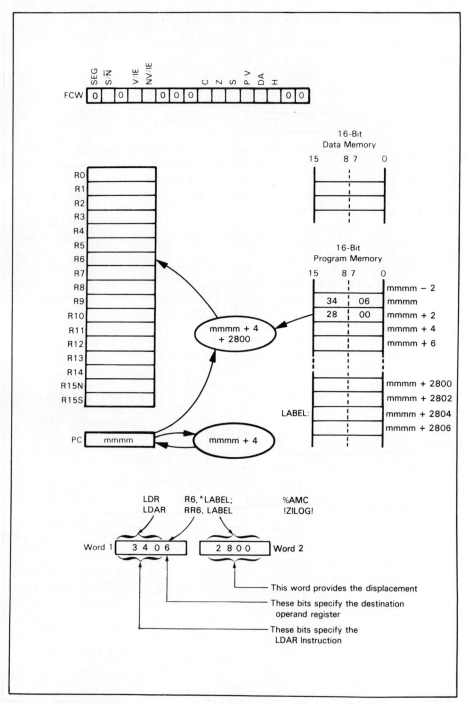

Figure 3-60. Execution of the LDAR Instruction in Non-Segmented Mode

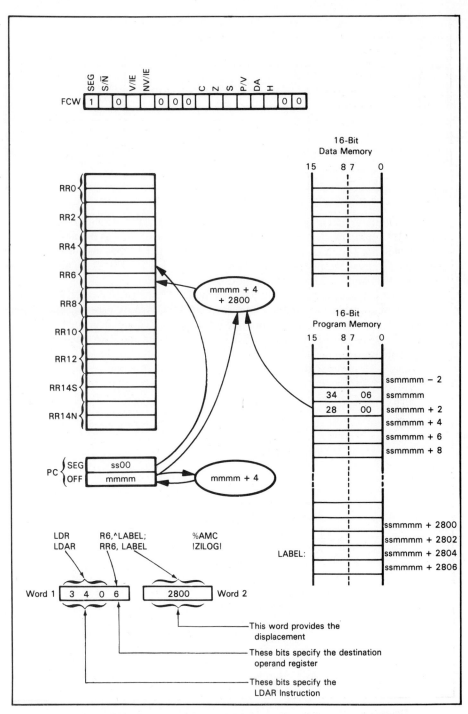

Figure 3-61. Execution of the LDAR Instruction in Segmented Mode

Table 3-16. Syntax of Load Address Relative Instruction

	AMC	Zilog	Addressing	Meaning
Load Register	LDR R8,^ LABEL;	LDAR R8,LABEL	R,PR	Load R8 with address of LABEL using program relative addressing
	LDR R8,^ $-#250;	LDAR R8,$-%250	R,PR	Load R8 with address of memory location 250_{16} bytes before this instruction

The displacement is shown in Figures 5-60 and 5-61 with the value 2800_{16}. The assembler will automatically compute the value of the displacement as the difference between the memory address of the instruction following the LDAR instruction and the memory address of the instruction or data whose label is LABEL. The label must be within $+32771$ and -32764 bytes of the LDAR instruction.

Note that there is no difference between the LDAR instruction object code in segmented or non-segmented modes. Note also that AMC syntax uses R6 in both segmented and non-segmented mode. In segmented mode RR6 will be loaded. Zilog syntax specifies R6 when assembling for non-segmented mode and RR6 when assembling for segmented mode.

Table 3-16 summarizes the syntax of the LDAR instruction.

LDCTL - Load Control Register (Word)

LDCTLB - Load Control Register (Byte)

The LDCTL instruction is privileged.
This is the general format for the LDCTL and LDCTLB instructions:

Addressing Options		LDCTL dst,src
dst	src	LDCTLB dst,src
R	*	
*	R	

* one of the special
CPU registers

Symbols dst and src are destination and source operands respectively. One of the two operands must be specified using direct register addressing as a CPU register. The other operand must be one of the CPU system registers.

The mnemonics FLAGS, FCW, REFRESH, PSAPSEG, PSAOFF, NSPSEG, or NSPOFF must be used to identify the system CPU register being accessed.

When the LDCTLB instruction is executed, a byte of data is transferred from the Flags byte of the Flag and Control Word to a CPU register or from a CPU register to the Flags byte of the Flag and Control Word. When the LDCTL instruction is executed, a word of data is transferred from the system register to a CPU register, or from a CPU register to a system register.

LDCTL/LDCTLB instruction object codes may be illustrated as follows:

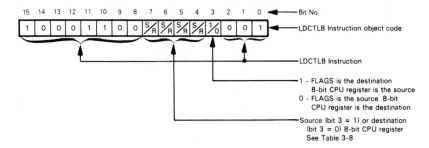

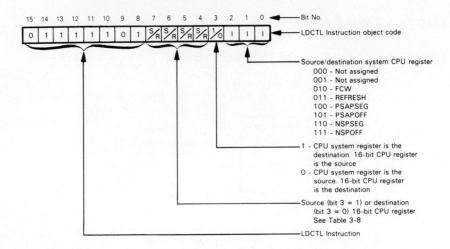

We will describe the LDCTL/LDCTLB instruction separately for the different CPU system registers which can be specified in the operand field.

LDCTL FCW - Load/Store Flag And Control Word

This version of the LDCTL instruction is privileged.
The format for this version of the LDCTL instruction is:

```
                              % AMC syntax
    LDCTL   R,FCW;            % FCW is the source
    LDCTL   FCW,R;            % FCW is the destination

                              ! Zilog syntax !
    LDCTL   R,FCW             ! FCW is the source !
    LDCTL   FCW,R             ! FCW is the destination !
```

R must be a 16-bit CPU register.
FCW selects the entire Flag and Control Word.

Data is transferred between the selected 16-bit CPU register, and the Flag and Control Word. When data is transferred from the Flag and Control Word to the 16-bit CPU register, unassigned flag and control word bits generate 0's in corresponding CPU register bit positions. For the instruction:

```
    LDCTL   FCW,R8;           % AMC syntax
    LDCTL   FCW,R8            ! Zilog syntax !
```

this may be illustrated as follows:

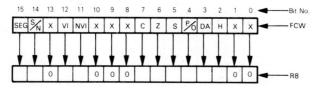

Within register R8, bits 15, 14, 12, 11, 7, 6, 5, 4, 3 and 2 acquire the status levels reported in the Flag and Control Word. Bits 13, 10, 9, 8, 1 and 0 are always reset to 0.

No flags are affected by this instruction.

When data is transferred from a 16-bit CPU register to the Flag and Control Word, unassigned Flag and Control Word bit positions are ignored and bypassed. For the instruction:

```
    LDCTL   R8,FCW;           % AMC syntax
    LDCTL   R8,FCW            ! Zilog syntax !
```

this may be illustrated as follows:

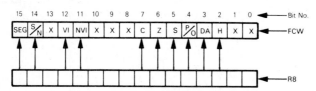

Technically speaking, there is nowhere for data from R8 bits 0, 1, 8, 9 or 10 to go; these bit positions do not exist within the Flag and Control Word. Bit position 13 does exist, but FCW logic keeps this bit at 0. To a programmer, therefore, bit 13 of FCW appears not to exist.

LDCTL NSPSEG - Load/Store Normal Stack Pointer Segment Register

LDCTL NSPOFF - Load/Store Normal Stack Pointer Offset Register

These versions of the LDCTL instruction are privileged.

This is the format for these versions of the LDCTL instruction:

```
                        % AMC syntax
      LDCTL   R,NSPSEG;   % NSPSEG is the source
      LDCTL   NSPSEG,R;   % NSPSEG is the destination
      LDCTL   R,NSPOFF;   % NSPOFF is the source
      LDCTL   NSPOFF,R;   % NSPOFF is the destination


                        ! Zilog syntax !
      LDCTL   R,NSPSEG    ! NSPSEG is the source !
      LDCTL   NSPSEG,R    ! NSPSEG is the destination !
      LDCTL   R,NSPOFF    ! NSPOFF is the source !
      LDCTL   NSPOFF,R    ! NSPOFF is the destination !
```

R must be a 16-bit CPU register.

NSPSEG selects the Normal Stack Pointer Segment Register, which is normal mode register R14N. This register is only used by the Z8001 operating in segmented mode.

NSPOFF selects the Normal Stack Pointer Offset Register, which is register R15N in normal mode for the Z8001 or the Z8001.

These two versions of the LDCTL instruction perform a simple word data swap between the specified 16-bit CPU register and R14N or R15N. No bits are unassigned, nor are any bits treated in a special way, as they were by other versions of the LDCTL instruction.

Since the LDCTL instruction is privileged, it is being executed in system mode. The instruction moves data into two Normal mode registers, which would otherwise be inaccessible to instructions executing in System mode. Thus, a program executing in system mode is able to initialize the Stack Pointer for normal mode operations.

You do not need LDCTL instructions that load the System mode Stack Pointer Segment or Offset Registers. In System mode these two registers can be accessed as R14 and R15. Normal mode programs must not be allowed access to any System Mode facilities.

Since the LDCTL instruction is executing in System mode, interrupts will use the system stack and no special care is required to keep the normal stack pointer valid.

Thus the instruction:

```
      LDCTL   NSPOFF,R5;   % AMC syntax
      LDCTL   NSPOFF,R5    ! Zilog syntax !
```

initializes the non-segmented Normal Mode Stack Pointer of a program executed in system mode. R5 holds the Stack Pointer origin address.

LDCTL Refresh - Load/Store Refresh Register

This version of the LDCTL instruction is privileged.

The format for this version of the LDCTL instruction is:

```
                        % AMC syntax
    LDCTL   R,REFRESH;   % REFRESH is the source
    LDCTL   REFRESH,R;   % REFRESH is the destination

                        ! Zilog syntax !
    LDCTL   R,REFRESH    ! REFRESH is the source !
    LDCTL   REFRESH,R    ! REFRESH is the destination !
```

R must be a 16-bit CPU register.

REFRESH selects the System Refresh Register. This register is used only by Z8000 dynamic memory refresh logic.

When the instruction:

```
    LDCTL   REFRESH,R4;   % AMC syntax
    LDCTL   REFRESH,R4    ! Zilog syntax !
```

is executed, data is transferred from bits 1 through 15 of 16-bit CPU register R4, to the REFRESH register. Bit 0 of the REFRESH register is unassigned; therefore no transfer from bit 0 of the 16-bit CPU register occurs.

When the instruction:

```
    LDCTL   R4,REFRESH;   % AMC syntax
    LDCTL   R4,REFRESH    ! Zilog syntax !
```

is executed only bits 1 through 8 of the REFRESH counter are loaded into CPU register R4. These bits identify the portion of dynamic memory about to be refreshed.

LDCTL PSAPSEG - Load/Store Program Status Area Pointer Segment Register

This version of the LDCTL is privileged.

The format for this version of the LDCTL instruction is:

```
                        % AMC syntax
    LDCTL   R,PSAPSEG;      % PSAPSEG is the source
    LDCTL   PSAPSEG,R;      % PSAPSEG is the destination

                        ! Zilog syntax !
    LDCTL   R,PSAPSEG       ! PSAPSEG is the source !
    LDCTL   PSAPSEG,R       ! PSAPSEG is the destination !
```

R must be a 16-bit CPU register.

PSAPSEG selects the Program Status Area Pointer Segment Register. This register is available only in the Z8001; it is used by Z8000 interrupt logic to identify the beginning of an interrupt vector memory block. For details see Chapter 12.

As its name would imply, the Program Status Area Pointer Segment Register is the segment half of an address register; as is the case with all segment registers, bits 8 through 14 provide a segment number, while bits 0 through 7 and bit 15 are unassigned. In consequence, when the instruction:

```
    LDCTL   R3,PSAPSEG;     % AMC syntax
    LDCTL   R3,PSAPSEG      ! Zilog syntax !
```

is executed, unassigned bits of PSAPSEG generate 0's in corresponding bit positions of R3, while the segment number for the Program Status Area Pointer is loaded into bits 8 through 14 of R3. This may be illustrated as follows:

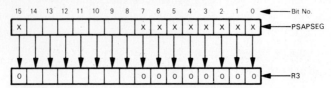

When a reverse data transfer is executed via the instruction:

```
    LDCTL   PSAPSEG,R3      % AMC syntax
    LDCTL   PSAPSEG,R3      ! Zilog syntax !
```

bits 8 through 14 of register R3 generate a new segment number within PSAPSEG. Other bit settings of R3 are ignored.

An interrupt can occur between loading PSAPSEG and PSAPOFF. Special care must be taken to be sure the combination of PSAPSEG and PSAPOFF always points to a valid Program Status Area, even if an interrupt occurs between changing PSAPSEG and changing PSAPOFF.

LDCTL PSAPOFF - Load/Store Program Status Area Pointer Offset Register

This version of the LDCTL instruction is privileged.
The format for this version of the LDCTL instruction is:

```
                    % AMC syntax
    LDCTL   R,PSAPOFF;     % PSAPOFF is the source
    LDCTL   PSAPOFF,R;     % PSAPOFF is the destination

                    ! Zilog syntax !
    LDCTL   R,PSAPOFF      ! PSAPOFF is the source !
    LDCTL   PSAPOFF,R      ! PSAPOFF is the destination !
```

R must be a 16-bit CPU register.

PSAPOFF selects the Program Status Area Pointer Offset Register. This register identifies the beginning memory address for an interrupt vector in a Z8001 or a Z8002. For details see Chapter 12.

Only the high-order byte of PSAPOFF is assigned. Nevertheless, a 16-bit CPU register must be specified with PSAPOFF in the operand field of the LDCTL instruction. When the instruction:

```
    LDCTL   R9,PSAPOFF;    % AMC syntax
    LDCTL   R9,PSAPOFF     ! Zilog syntax !
```

is executed, the high-order byte of PSAPOFF is loaded into the high order byte of register R9; the low order byte of register R9 is reset to 0. When the reverse instruction:

```
    LDCTL   PSAPOFF,R9     % AMC syntax
    LDCTL   PSAPOFF,R9     ! Zilog syntax !
```

is executed, the high-order byte of register R9 is transferred to the high-order byte of PSAPOFF. The low-order byte of register R9 is ignored.

When operating in segmented mode you may also want to change PSAPSEG. An interrupt can occur between loading PSAPOFF and PSAPSEG. Special programming care must be taken to be sure the combination of PSAPSEG and PSAPOFF always points to a valid Program Status Area, even if an interrupt occurs between changing PSAPOFF and changing PSAPSEG.

LDCTLB FLAGS - Load/Store Status Flags

This is the only version of the LDCTL instruction which is not privileged. The format for this version of the LDCTL instruction is:

```
                        % AMC syntax
LDCTLB  R,FLAGS;        % R is the destination
LDCTLB  FLAGS,R;        % FLAGS is the destination

                        ! Zilog syntax !
LDCTLB  R,FLAGS         ! R is the destination !
LDCTLB  FLAGS,R         ! FLAGS is the destination !
```

R must be an 8-bit CPU register.

FLAGS selects the C, Z, S, P/V, DA and H status bits from the Flag and Control Word, with the following bit positions, as compared to an 8-bit CPU register:

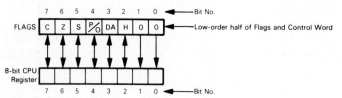

When the instruction:

```
LDCTLB  R,FLAGS;        % AMC syntax
LDCTLB  R,FLAGS         ! Zilog syntax !
```

is executed, status settings are read from the Flag and Control Word, into an 8-bit CPU register, as follows:

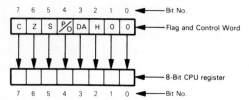

No flags are affected by this instruction.

When the instruction:

```
LDCTLB  R,FLAGS;        % AMC syntax
LDCTLB  FLAGS,R         ! Zilog syntax !
```

is executed, bits 2 through 7 of the selected 8-bit CPU register are loaded into bits 2 through 7 of the Flag and Control Word as follows:

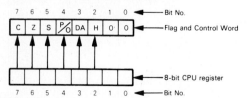

This version of the LDCTL instruction is used to read or set arithmetic and logic statuses within the Flag and Control word. But this version of the LDCTL instruction cannot access system status bits such as the segmentation, system/normal mode, or interrupt/disable bits.

LDD - Move Word and Decrement

LDDB - Move Byte and Decrement

This is the general format for the LDD and LDDB instructions:

Addressing Options		
dst	src	r
IR	IR	R

LDD   dst,src,r
LDDB   dst,src,r

The symbols dst and src are destination and source operands, respectively, which must both be specified using register indirect (implied) memory addressing. As is standard for register indirect addressing, 16-bit CPU registers must be specified in non-segmented mode and 32-bit CPU registers must be specified in segmented mode.

The symbol r is a Counter Register which is always specified as a 16-bit CPU register.

When the LDD or LDDB instruction is executed, data is transferred from the source memory location to the destination memory location. A data word is transferred for LDD; a data byte is transferred for LDDB. The source and destination addresses are both decremented by 1 for LDDB, or by 2 for LDD. The Counter Register is always decremented by 1. If the Counter Register contains 0 after being decremented, then the Overflow status is set to 1; the Overflow status is reset to 0 otherwise.

The LDD/LDDB instructions provide one interaction in an instruction sequence that moves a block of data from one place in memory to another. Because the source and destination memory addresses are both decremented, data will be transferred first between memory locations having the highest memory addresses, and last between memory locations having the lowest memory addresses.

The LDD and LDDB instructions' object code may be illustrated as follows:

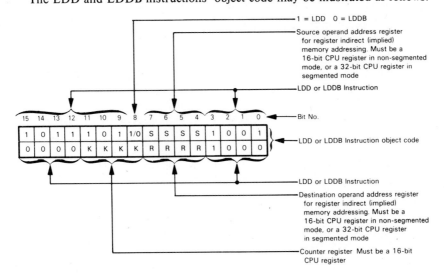

The Overflow status is modified by the LDD or LDDB instruction. As explained previously, the Overflow status is set to 1 when the Counter Register decrements to 0; the Overflow status is cleared otherwise. The Zero status is undefined.

Figure 3-62 illustrates execution of the LDD instruction:

```
LDD     R4^,R12^,R1;    % AMC syntax
LDD     @R4,@R12,R1     ! Zilog syntax !
```

This instruction is executed in non-segmented mode. The very similar LDI instruction is illustrated in Figure 3-62, executing in segmented mode.

Figure 3-62 shows a data word, illustrated generally as PPPP, being moved from memory location $86C0_{16}$ to memory location 4820_{16}. The operation illustrated is part of a block move. Earlier transfers will have occurred from memory words with addresses $86CEL2_{16}$ and higher, to memory words with addresses 4822_{16} and higher. $3D_{16}$ words remain to be moved; they will be moved from memory words with addresses $86BE_{16}$ and lower to memory words with addresses $481E_{16}$ and lower. But the LDD instruction will have to be re-executed to enable each word to be moved. Here is an appropriate instruction pair that will perform the required block data move:

```
                        ! Zilog syntax !
LOOP:   LDD     @R4,@R12,R1     ! move next data word !
        JR      NOV,LOOP        ! Re-execute on no overflow !

                        % AMC syntax
LOOP:   LDD     R4^,R12^,R1;    % Move next data word
        JR      NOV,LOOP;       % Re-execute on no overflow
```

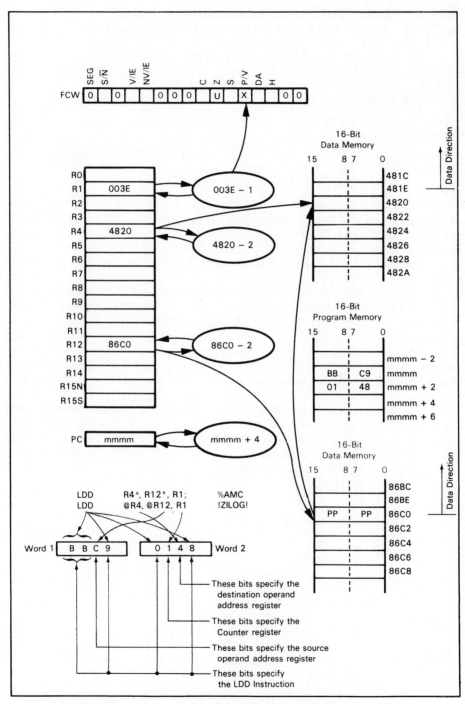

Figure 3-62. Execution of the LDD Instruction in Non-Segmented Mode

LDDR - Move Word and Decrement and Repeat
LDDRB - Move Byte and Decrement and Repeat

The LDDR and LDDRB instructions are identical to LDD and LDDR, respectively, except that LDDR and LDDRB re-execute until an entire block of data has been moved.

This is the general format for the LDDR and LDDRB instructions:

Addressing Options		
dst	src	r
IR	IR	R

LDDR   dst,src,r
LDDRB   dst,src,r

The symbols dst and src are destination and source operands, respectively, which must both be specified using register indirect (implied) memory addressing. As is standard for register indirect addressing, 16-bit CPU registers must be specified in non-segmented mode and 32-bit CPU registers must be specified in segmented mode.

The symbol r is a Counter Register which is always specified as a 16-bit CPU register.

When the LDDR or LDDRB instruction is executed, a block of data is transferred from sequential source memory locations to sequential destination memory locations. Data words are transferred for LDDR; data bytes are transferred for LDDRB. The source and destination addresses are both decremented by 1 for LDDRB, or by 2 for LDDR. The Counter Register is always decremented by 1. If the Counter Register contains 0 after being decremented, then the Overflow status is set 1 and instruction execution ceases; the Overflow status is reset to 0 otherwise, and instruction execution continues.

The LDDR/LDDRB instructions provide the entire instruction sequence needed to move a block of data between two memory buffers. Because the source and destination memory addresses are both decremented, data will be transferred first between memory locations having the highest memory addresses, and last between memory locations having the lowest memory addresses.

The LDDR and LDDRB instructions' object code may be illustrated as follows:

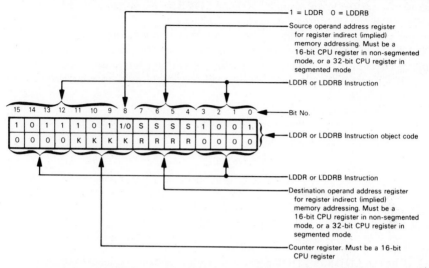

The Overflow status is modified by the LDDR or LDDRB instruction. As explained previously, the Overflow status is set to 1 when the Counter Register decrements to 0 at the end of the instruction's execution. The Zero status is undefined.

LDDR and LDDRB instructions' execution is not illustrated; illustrations would be the same for LDDR/LDDRB, or LDD/LDDB. Figure 3-62, for example, also illustrates execution of the LDDR instruction:

```
LDDR     R4^,R12^,R1;     % AMC syntax
LDDR     @R4,@R12,R1      ! Zilog syntax !
```

The only difference between the LDD/LDDB and LDDR/LDDRB instructions is that LDD/LDDB transfer one word (or byte) of data on each execution, whereas LDDR/LDDRB, on each execution, transfer the number of words (or bytes) specified in the Counter Register. Thus, the single instruction:

```
LDDR     R4^,R12^,R1;     % AMC syntax
LDDR     @R4,@R12,R1      ! Zilog syntax !
```

will replace the instruction pair:

```
LOOP:    LDD     @R4,@R12,R1      ! Zilog syntax !
         JR      NOV,LOOP

LOOP:    LDD     R4^,R12^,R1;     % AMC syntax
         JR      NOV,LOOP;
```

If you simply wish to move a block of data from a source to a destination, then clearly you are better off using LDDR or LDDRB, as compared to LDD or LDDB. LDD/LDDB require more object code and will take longer to execute. But if you need to perform any operations on the data in transit, then you must use LDD or LDDB. Suppose, for example, data being transferred from a source block to a destination block must be checked, byte by byte, for specific ASCII character values. You could not use the LDDRB instruction in this case. Instead you would have to use some instruction sequence such as:

```
                                 ! Zilog syntax !
     LOOP:   CPB     @R12,#CHR    ! Compare next source byte with !
                                  ! special character !
             JR      NE,NEXT      ! If not equal go directly to !
                                  ! byte move !
             -
             -
             -            Instructions that process a special
             -            character must be here
             -
             -
     NEXT:   LDDR    @R4,@R12,R1  ! Move next byte !
             JR      NOV,LOOP     ! Return for next byte if !
                                  ! counter is not zero !
```

Once an LDDR or LDDRB instruction starts to execute, it could conceivably continue executing for a long time if it were moving a large block of data. This would present interrupt logic with problems. In order to prevent any such problems, the Z8000 allows interrupts to be acknowledged between each iterative execution of the LDDR or LDDRB instruction. Furthermore, the Program Counter value saved during the interrupt acknowledgement process is the address of the LDDR or LDDRB instruction, so that execution of this instruction will continue from the point of interrupt, after the interrupt has been serviced. Seven clock periods must be added to the LDDR or LDDRB instruction's execution time to account for each interrupt acknowledged during the instruction's execution.

LDI - Move Word and Increment
LDIB - Move Byte and Increment

The LDI and LDIB instructions are identical to LDD and LDDB, respectively, except that LDI and LDIB increment memory addresses which are decremented by LDD and LDDB.

This is the general format for the LDI and LDIB instructions:

Addressing Options		
dst	src	r
IR	IR	R

LDI   dst,src,r
LDIB   dst,src,r

The symbols dst and src are destination and source operands, respectively, which must both be specified using register indirect (implied) memory addressing. As is standard for register indirect addressing, 16-bit CPU registers must be specified in non-segmented mode and 32-bit CPU registers must be specified in segmented mode.

The symbol r is a Counter Register which is always specified as a 16-bit CPU register.

When the LDI or LDIB instruction is executed, data is transferred from the source memory location to the destination memory location. A data word is transferred for LDD; a data byte is transferred for LDDB. The source and destination addresses are both incremented by 1 for LDDB, or by 2 for LDD. The Counter Register is always decremented by 1. If the Counter Register contains 0 after being decremented, then the Overflow status is set 1; the Overflow status is reset to 0 otherwise.

The LDI/LDIB instructions provide one iteration in an instruction sequence that moves a block of data from one place in memory to another. Because the source and destination memory addresses are both incremented, data will be transferred first between memory locations having the lowest memory addresses, and last between memory locations having the highest memory addresses.

The LDI and LDIB instructions' object code may be illustrated as follows:

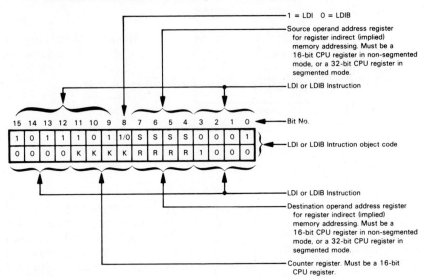

The Overflow status is modified by the LDDR or LDDRB instruction. As explained previously, the Overflow status is set to 1 when the Counter Register decrements to 0 at the end of the instruction's execution. The Zero status is undefined.

Figure 5-63 illustrates execution of the LDI instruction:

```
LDI     RR4^,RR12^,R1;   % AMC syntax
LDI     @RR4,@RR12,R1    ! Zilog syntax !
```

This instruction is executed in segmented mode. A very similar LDD instruction is illustrated in Figure 3-62, executing in segmented mode.

Figure 3-63 shows a data word, illustrated generally as PPPP, being moved from memory location $3086C0_{16}$ to memory location 064820_{16}. The operation illustrated is part of a block move. Earlier transfers will have occurred from memory words with addresses $3086C2_{16}$ and lower, to memory words with addresses 064822_{16} and lower. $3D_{16}$ words remain to be moved; they will be moved from memory words with addresses $3086BE_{16}$ and higher, to memory words with addresses $06481E_{16}$ and higher. But the LDI instruction will have to be re-executed to enable each word to be moved. Here is an appropriate instruction pair that will perform the required block data move:

```
                              ! Zilog syntax !
        LOOP:   LDI     @RR4,@RR12,R1    ! Move next data word !
                JR      NOV,LOOP         ! Re-execute on no overflow !

                              % AMC syntax
        LOOP:   LDI     RR4^,RR12^,R1:   % Move next data word
                JR      NOV,LOOP;        % Re-execute on no overflow
```

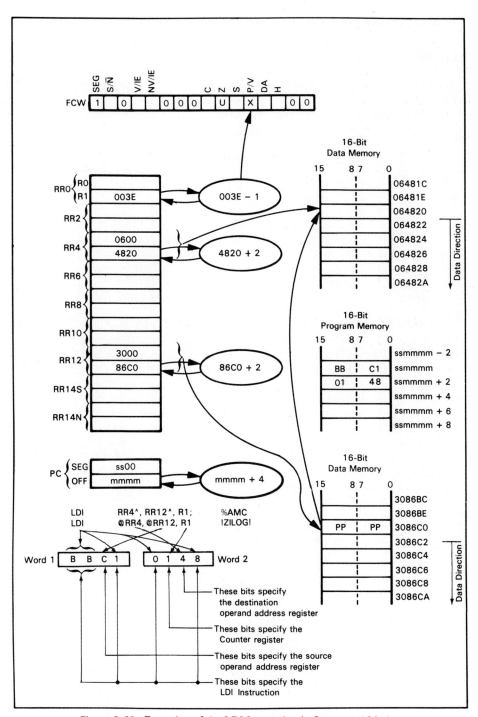

Figure 3-63. Execution of the LDI Instruction in Segmented Mode

LDIR - Move Word Increment and Repeat

LDIRB - Move Byte Increment and Repeat

The LDIR and LDIRB instructions are identical to LDI and LDIB, respectively, except that LDIR and LDIRB re-execute until an entire block of data has been moved. This is the general format for the LDIR and LDIRB instructions:

Addressing Options				
dst	src	r	LDIR	dst,src,r
IR	IR	R	LDIRB	dst,src,r

The symbols dst and src are destination and source operands, respectively, which must both be specified using register indirect (implied) memory addressing. As is standard for register indirect addressing, 16-bit CPU registers must be specified in non-segmented mode and 32-bit CPU registers must be specified in segmented mode.

The symbol r is a Counter Register which is always specified as a 16-bit CPU register.

When the LDIR or LDIRB instruction is executed, a block of data is transferred from sequential source memory locations to sequential destination memory locations. Data words are transferred for LDIR; data bytes are transferred for LDIRB. The source and destination addresses are both incremented by 1 for LDIRB, or by 2 for LDIR. The Counter Register is always decremented by 1. If the Counter Register contains 0 after being decremented, the Overflow status is set 1 and instruction execution ceases; the Overflow status is reset to 0 otherwise, and instruction execution continues.

The LDIR/LDIRB instructions provide the entire instruction sequence needed to move a block of data between two memory buffers. Because the source and destination memory addresses are both incremented, data will be transferred first between memory locations having the lowest memory addresses, and last between memory locations having the highest memory addresses.

The LDIR and LDIRB instructions' object code may be illustrated as follows:

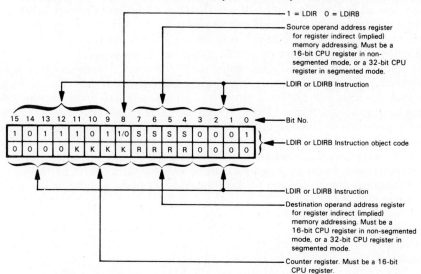

Only the Overflow status is modified by the LDIR or LDIRB instruction. As explained previously, the Overflow status is set to 1 when the counter Register decrements to 0, at the end of the instruction's execution.

LDIR and LDIRB instructions' execution is not illustrated; illustrations would be the same for LDIR/LDIRB, or LDI/LDIB. Figure 3-63, for example, also illustrates execution of the LDDR instruction:

```
LDIR      RR4^,R12^,R1;   % AMC syntax
LDIR      @RR4,@RR12,R1   ! Zilog syntax !
```

The only difference between the LDI/LDIB and LDIR/LDIRB instructions is that LDI/LDIB transfer one word (or byte) of data on each execution, whereas LDIR/LDIRB, on each execution, transfer the number of words (or bytes) specified in the Counter Register. Thus, the single instruction:

```
LDIR      RR4^,RR12^,R1;  % AMC syntax
LDIR      @RR4,@RR12,R1   ! Zilog syntax !
```

will replace the instruction pair:

```
LOOP:     LDI       @RR4,@RR12,R1    ! Zilog syntax !
          JR        NOV,LOOP

LOOP:     LDI       RR4^,RR12^,R1;   % AMC syntax
          JR        NOV,LOOP
```

If you simply wish to move a block of data from a source to a destination, then clearly you are better off using LDIR or LDIRB, as compared to LDI or LDIB. LDI/ LDIB require more object code and will take longer to execute. But if you need to perform any operations on the data in transit, then you must use LDI or LDIB. See the description of LDDR/LDDRB for further discussion of this subject.

Once an LDIR or LDIRB instruction starts to execute, it could conceivably continue executing for a long time if it were moving a large block of data. This would present interrupt logic with problems. In order to prevent any such problems, the Z8000 allows interrupts to be acknowledged between each iterative execution of the LDIR or LDIRB instruction. Furthermore, the Program counter value saved during the interrupt acknowledgement process is the address of the LDIR or LDIRB instruction, so that execution of this instruction will continue from the point of interrupt, after the interrupt has been serviced. Seven clock periods must be added to the LDIR or LDIRB instruction's execution time to account for each interrupt acknowledged during the instruction's execution.

LDK - Load Constant

This is the general format for the LDK instruction:

Addressing Options	
dst	data
R	IM

LDK   dst,data

The symbol dst is the destination operand which must be specified using direct register addressing. A 16-bit CPU register must be specified.

The symbol data is a 4-bit immediate source operand.

When the LDK instruction is executed, the 4-bit immediate value specified for the source operand is loaded into the low order 4 bits of the destination CPU register; the remaining 12 bits of the destination CPU register are reset to 0.

The LDK instruction object code may be illustrated as follows

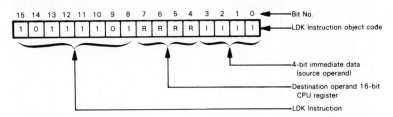

No status flags are modified by the LDK instruction.

The LDK instruction is used to load small immediate values into registers via an economical 16-bit object code.

Figure 3-64 illustrates execution of the LDK instruction:

```
LDK     R2,#A;          % AMC syntax
LDK     R2,#%A          ! Zilog syntax !
```

As illustrated, this instruction loads $000A_{16}$ into 16-bit register R2.

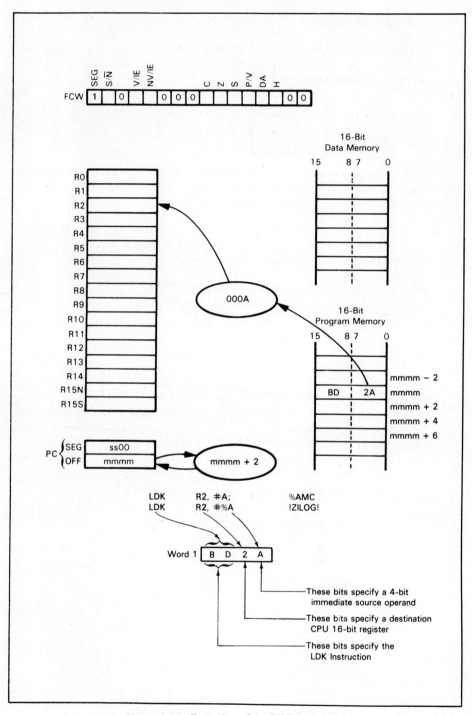

Figure 3-64. Execution of the LDK Instruction

LDL - Load Long Word

The LDL instruction is the long word version of the LD instruction, described earlier. There are LDL versions of all LD instructions with the exception of versions that would load immediate data into memory.

This is the general format for the LDL instruction:

Addressing Options			
dst	src		
R	R	LDL	dst,src
R	IM		
R	IR		
R	DA		
R	X		
R	BR		
R	BX		
BR	R		
BX	R		
IR	R		
DA	R		
X	R		

The symbol dst is the destination operand which may be specified using any addressing method with the exception of immediate addressing.

The symbol src is a source operand which can be specified using any allowed addressing method.

Although a wide variety of source and destination operand addressing methods are allowed, the combinations in which they can be used are restricted. The allowed combinations are the same as those in Table 3-14, except that the only combination allowed with an immediate source operand is a register destination operand. The LDL instruction requires either the source or destination operand to be a 32-bit CPU register.

For standard source and destination operand addressing, object codes may be illustrated as follows:

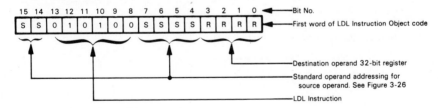

When base relative addressing is used to specify the source operand, the following instruction object code is used:

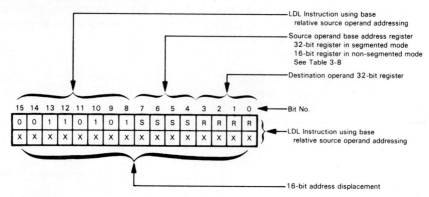

When base relative addressing is used to specify the destination operand, the instruction object code changes as follows:

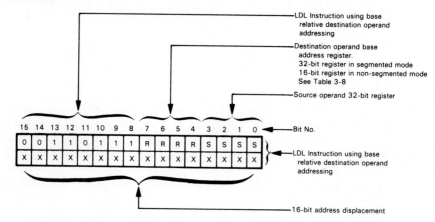

For base indexed source and destination operand addressing, these totally different object codes are used:

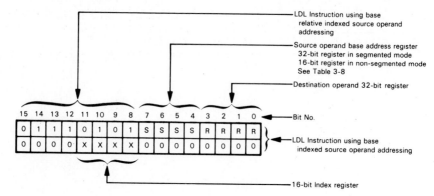

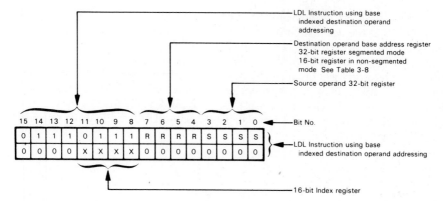

When data is moved from a CPU register to a memory location using standard addressing, the following instruction object code is used:

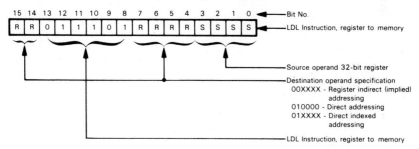

No LDL instruction modifies any status flag.

Table 3-14 in the description of the LD and LDB instructions illustrates the allowed source and destination operand addressing options for LDL instructions. As noted there, the LDL instruction cannot be used to load immediate data into memory. The source or destination data register must be one of the 32-bit CPU registers RR0-RR14.

Figure 3-65 illustrates the LDL instruction:

```
LDL      SEGLABEL(R4),RR8;       % AMC syntax
LDL      <<SEG>>LABEL(R4),RR8    ! Zilog syntax !
```

Actual values for SEG and LABEL appear in the illustration. If you use a Zilog assembler, you will use equate directives to assign values to SEG and LABEL. If yours is an AMC assembler, you will define SEGLABEL by using it as a label.

Figure 3-66 illustrates the non-segmented version of the same instruction:

```
LDL      LABEL(R4),RR8;       % AMC syntax
LDL      LABEL(R4),RR8        ! Zilog syntax !
```

NOTE: Beware of interrupts when executing LDL instructions in Normal mode, with RR14N as the destination register. With some early production Z8000 chips, if an interrupt is acknowledged as soon as the instruction completes execution, RR14S will receive the data that was intended for RR14N. Since the programmer generally cannot know if an interrupt will occur, it is best not to use these instructions to load RR14N when using a microcomputer containing one of these early production chips. See Table 3-18 at the end of this chapter for more information. Usually the system will load the stack pointer for you, and you will manipulate it with PUSH and POP, so this problem will not arise.

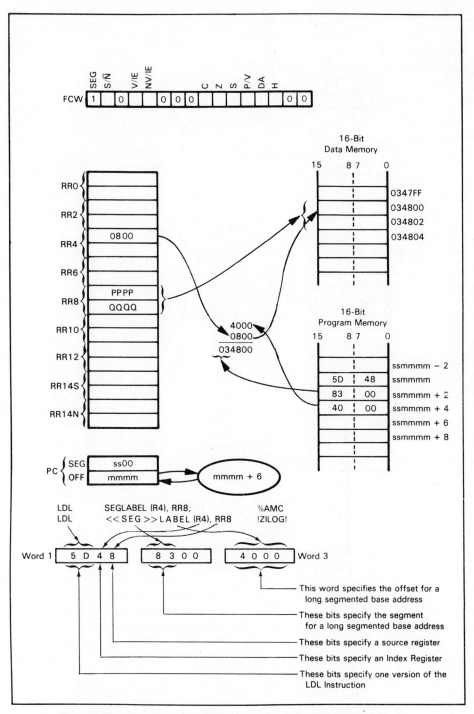

Figure 3-65. Execution of the LDL Instruction in Long Segmented Mode

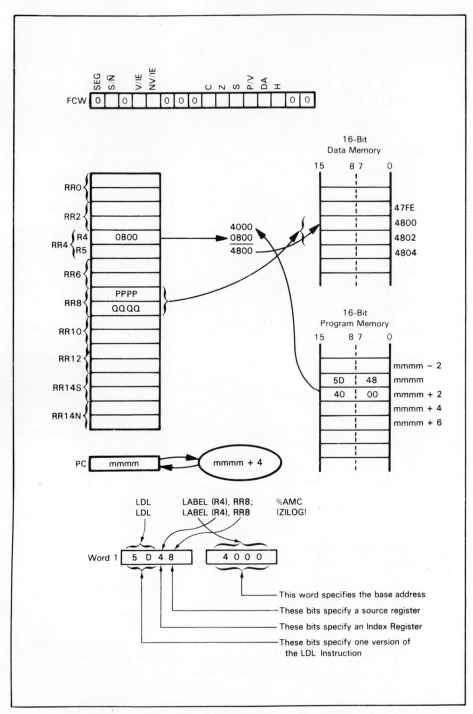

Figure 3-66. Execution of the LDL Instruction in Non-Segmented Mode

LDM - Load Multiple Words

This is the general format for the LDM instruction:

Addressing Options		
dst	**src**	**num**
R	IR	IM
R	DA	IM
R	X	IM
IR	R	IM
DA	R	IM
X	R	IM

LDM   dst,src,num

The symbols dst and src are destination and source operands, respectively. One must be a 16-bit CPU register, specified using direct register addressing; the other must be a 16-bit memory word, specified using register indirect, direct, or direct indexed addressing.

The symbol num is a 4-bit immediate data value that may range from 1 to 16; it is encoded as (num-1) in the instruction object code. Thus operand values range from 0 for 1 through F_{16} for 16.

When the LDM instruction is executed, a block of 16-bit words is transferred from the source to the destination. The symbol num specifies the number of 16-bit words in the block. CPU registers are accessed by ascending numbers, with register R0 following R15. Memory words are accessed in order of ascending memory addresses; the memory address specified in the instruction object code is the beginning memory address — and therefore the lowest memory address for the accessed block.

For the two cases where data is transferred from memory to CPU registers, or from CPU registers to memory, LDM instruction object codes may be illustrated as follows:

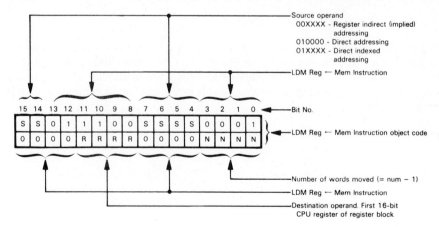

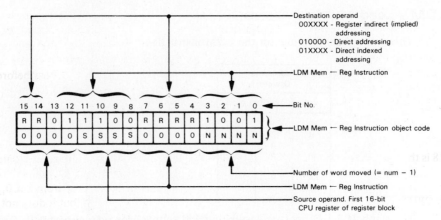

No status flags are modified by the LDM instruction.

Figure 3-67 illustrates execution of the instruction:

```
LDM     LABEL,R12,8;      % AMC syntax
LDM     LABEL,R12,#8      ! Zilog syntax !
```

This instruction shows eight words of data being moved from CPU registers to memory. CPU registers are, in order of access, R12, R13, R14, R15N, (assuming normal mode), R0, R1, R2, and R3. These registers' contents are moved to data memory words with addresses beginning at 4000_{16}.

The following LDM instruction would move data in the opposite direction:

```
LDM     R12,LABEL,8;      % AMC syntax
LDM     R12,LABEL,#8      ! Zilog syntax !
```

If you use register indirect addressing, and you specify the address register as the first CPU register of a block, then an LDM instruction that moves data from CPU registers to data memory will leave the address of the first data memory word within this word. For example, consider the following LDM instruction:

```
LDM     R8^,R8,8;         % AMC syntax
LDM     @R8,R8,#8         ! Zilog syntax !
```

R8 has been specified as the first register of an 8 CPU register block; it is also the implied memory address register. If register R8 were to contain 4000_{16} (and we choose this number arbitrarily), then memory word 4000_{16} would contain its own address, 4000_{16}, while the next sequential memory words would receive the contents of registers R9 through R15.

A reverse move from memory to CPU registers can use register indirect addressing, and include the indirect address register within the block of destination CPU registers. The fact that a new value will be loaded from memory into the implied memory address register will have no effect on the way in which data memory is addressed. This is because the LDM instruction computes the implied address before the first data transfer occurs, and subsequently ignores any new data that might get loaded into the implied memory address register. Consider the following instruction:

```
LDM    R8,R8^,8    % AMC syntax
LDM    R8,@R8,#8   ! Zilog syntax !
```

R8 is the implied memory address register; it is also the first CPU register to receive data from memory. Suppose R8 initially holds the value $84C0_{16}$. Then the first event to occur when the LDM instruction is executed will move the contents of memory word $84C0_{16}$ to CPU register R8. This would appear to modify the memory address, but it does not, since CPU execution logic holds the address originally read from R8, and ignores the new value loaded into R8.

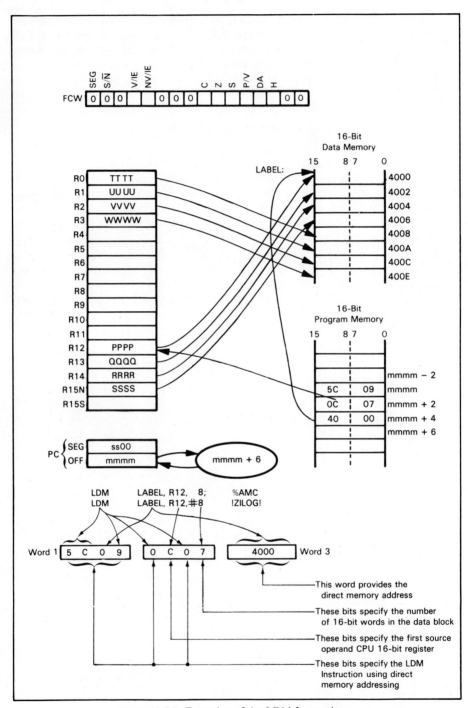

Figure 3-67. Execution of the LDM Instruction

LDPS — Load Program Status And Jump

LDPS is a privileged instruction.
This is the general format for the LDPS instruction:

Addressing Options
src
IR DA X

LDPS   src

The symbol src is a source operand which can be specified using register indirect (implied), direct or direct indexed memory addressing.

When the LDPS instruction is executed, data taken from memory words addressed by the source operand are loaded into the Flag and Control Word and the Program Counter. However, the new Flag and Control Word contents do not become active until the beginning of the next instructions' execution. The next instruction will be at the memory location addressed by the new Program Counter contents.

In non-segmented mode, two words of data are read from memory; in segmented mode, four words are read from memory. Memory words are read in the following sequence:

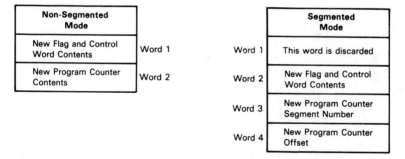

Thus the LDPS instruction executes a program jump while re-initializing all program status flags. Indirect memory addressing is used by program jump logic, since the memory location addressed by the source operand contains the jump address.

The LDPS instruction object code may be illustrated as follows:

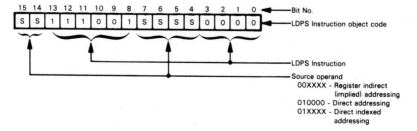

All status flags are modified by the LDPS instruction; however the new status flag settings do not become effective until the beginning of the next instructions execution.

We illustrated execution of the LDPS instruction in Figure 3-24, when describing Z8000 addressing modes. Figure 3-24 illustrates the LDPS instruction executed in segmented mode. Figure 3-65 illustrates the following LDPS instruction, executed in non-segmented mode:

```
LDPS    NEWDATA;        % AMC
LDPS    NEWDATA         ! Zilog !
```

Direct memory addressing has been used by the LDPS instruction in Figure 3-68. The label NEWDATA is shown with the value 4800_{16}. The contents of memory word 4800_{16} are loaded into the Flag and Control Word; the contents of memory word 4802_{16} are loaded into the Program Counter, causing the next instruction to be taken from memory location ZZZZ.

The LDPS instruction has been designed to transfer control between different program execution environments. For example, you might use LDPS to jump from system programs executing in system mode, to application programs executing in normal mode. You might also use LDPS to execute non-segmented programs in a segmented Z800l system.

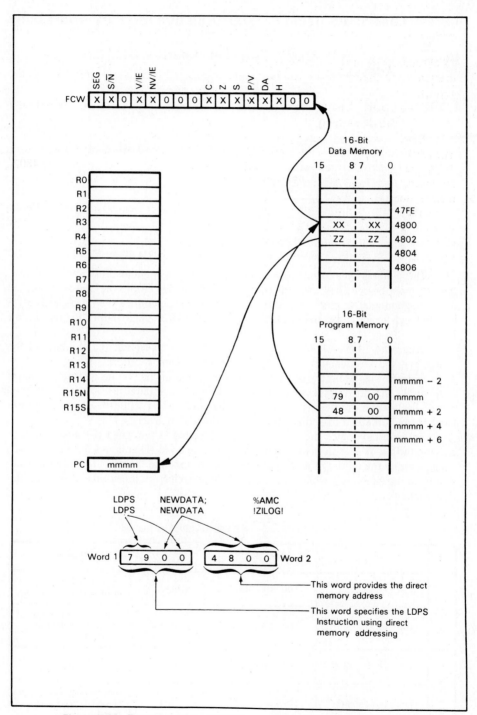

Figure 3-68. Execution of the LDPS Instruction in Non-Segmented Mode

LDR — Load Word Using Program Relative Memory Addressing

LDRB — Load Byte Using Program Relative Memory Addressing

LDRL — Load Long Word Using Program Relative Memory Addressing

This is the general format for the LDR, LDRB, and LDRL instructions:

Addressing Options	
dst	src
R	PR
PR	R

LDR   dst,src
LDRB dst,src
LDRL dst,src

The symbols dst and src are destination and source operands, respectively. One of the two must be specified using direct register addressing, while the other is specified using program relative memory addressing. Direct register addressing must specify a 16-bit CPU register for LDR, an 8-bit CPU register for LDRB, and a 32-bit CPU register for LDRL.

When the LDR, LDRB, or LDRL instruction is executed, the contents of the source operand are transferred to the destination operand location.

A 16-bit signed binary displacement is provided in the second instruction object code word. The program relative memory address is computed by adding this signed binary displacement to the contents of the Program Counter, after the program counter has been incremented to address the next sequential instruction.

To external logic, the data transfer occurring when an LDR instruction is executed will look like an instruction fetch machine cycle. That is to say, status signals which identify the nature of each machine cycle for external logic will report an instruction fetch machine cycle while data is being transferred from the source to the destination operand.

Table 3-17. Syntax of Load Relative Instruction

	AMC	Zilog	Address Mode	Meaning
Load Register	LDR R6,LABEL^;	LDR R6,LABEL	R,PR	Load R6 from memory at address LABEL
Load Register	LDR R6,$(#250);	LDR R6,$+%250	R,PR	Load R6 from memory 250_{16} bytes beyond this instruction
Load Memory	LDR LABEL^,R6;	LDR LABEL,R6	PR,R	Load memory at address LABEL from R6
Load Memory	LDR $(#250),R6;	LDR $+%250,R6	PR,R	Load memory 250_{16} bytes beyond this instruction from R6

The LDR, LDRB, and LDRL instructions' object codes may be illustrated as follows:

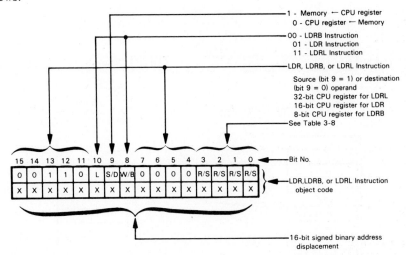

No status flags are modified by the LDR, LDRB, or LDRL instructions execution.

The LDR, LDRB, and LDRL instructions execute identically in segmented or non-segmented modes. In segmented mode, the program relative address is computed within the current program segment.

Figure 3-69 illustrates execution of the long word instruction:

```
LDRL      DLOC,RR4;        % AMC syntax
LDRL      DLOC,RR4         ! Zilog syntax !
```

The label DLOC is shown generating the displacement 8400_{16}. The assembler would automatically calculate a displacement based on the location of the LDRL instruction, as compared to the location of the label DLOC. In this case, a negative displacement is illustrated; it computes the address $mmmm - 7BFC_{16}$ as follows:

$$8400_{16} = -7C00_{16}$$
$$-7C00_{16} + 0004_{16} = -7BFC_{16}$$

Thus the 32-bit contents of Register RR4 are transferred to the long memory word located $7BFC_{16}$ bytes before the LDRL instruction's object code. The label must be within $+32771$ and -32764 bytes of the LDR instruction.

Table 3-18 shows the difference between AMC and Zilog notations for absolute forms of the LDRL instruction.

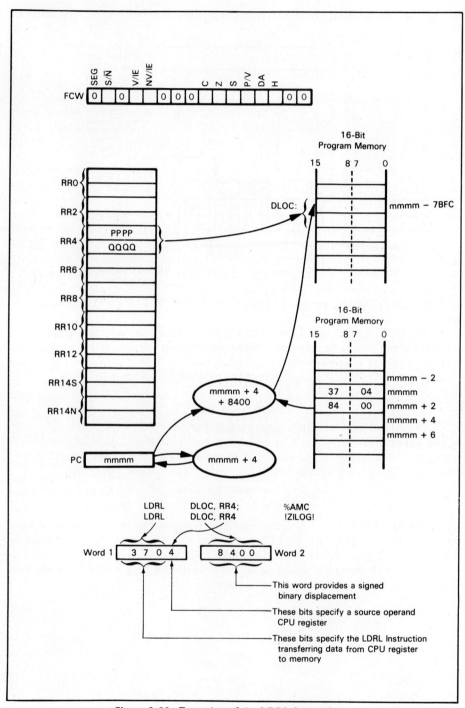

Figure 3-69. Execution of the LDRL Instruction

MBIT — Multi-Micro Bit Test

MBIT is a privileged instruction.
This is the format for the MBIT instruction:

MBIT

MBIT has no operands.

When the MBIT instruction is executed, the Sign status is set or reset to reflect the level of a special handshaking control input signal called Micro-In (MI). The Sign status is cleared if a high signal is being input at MI; the sign status is set if a low input is being input at MI.

The MBIT instruction is used in complex Z8000 configurations where two or more microprocessors can access a single shared resource (for example, a memory module). Some means must be devised to ensure that one microprocessor at a time accesses the shared resource. A variety of "handshaking protocols" serve this purpose; this subject is covered in detail in Chapter 13. One simple handshaking protocol assumes that a microprocessor can access a shared resource if it is receiving a high MI input, whereas a low MI input means that another microprocessor is currently accessing the shared resource — which is therefore unavailable. The MBIT instruction supports this simple protocol by setting S to 1 if MI is being input low, and by resetting S to 0 if MI is being input high.

The MBIT instruction's object code may be illustrated as follows:

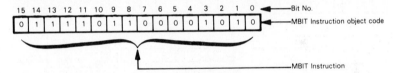

When the MBIT instruction is executed, the Sign status is modified to reflect the MI signal input level as described above; the Z status is left undefined. No other status flags are modified.

Program logic will execute an MBIT instruction, then test the sign status. A negative result (S = 1) means that the shared resource is unavailable. A positive result means that the shared resource is available. This handshaking protocol program logic is illustrated by the following instruction sequence:

```
                                ! Zilog syntax !
        MBIT                    ! Test MI input !
        JP      MI,NA           ! Input not available. Branch !
        -                       ! to NA !
        -               The instruction sequence here is executed
        -               if the shared resource is available
NA:             Beginning here is the instruction sequence to be
                executed when the shared resource is not available.
```

MREQ — Multi-Micro Request

MREQ is a privileged instruction.
This is the format for the MREQ instruction:

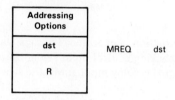

The symbol dst must be specified as a 16-bit CPU register using direct register addressing.

MREQ is used in complex Z8000 configurations where two or more microprocessors can access a single shared resource (for example, a memory module). Some means must be devised to assure that one microprocessor at a time accesses the shared resource. A variety of handshaking protocols serve this purpose; this subject is covered in detail in Chapter 13. MREQ is used in conjunction with the MI and MO signals to implement one possible handshaking protocol.

The MREQ instruction object code may be illustrated as follows:

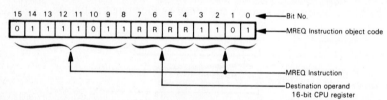

When the MREQ instruction is executed, the Sign and Zero status flags are modified. No other status flags are affected.

A microprocessor that executes the MREQ instruction requests shared resource access only when the shared resource is not being used by another microprocessor. If the shared resource is being used by another microprocessor, then the microprocessor executing the MREQ instruction does not even bother to request access. If the microprocessor executing the MREQ instruction finds that the shared resource is not being used by another microprocessor, it will request access, but the access request will only be acknowledged if a higher priority microprocessor does not request access simultaneously. The microprocessor executing the MREQ instruction thus detects one of three possible conditions following execution of MREQ; these three conditions are:

1. The shared resource is busy; no access request was made.

2. The shared resource is available, but the access request was denied.

3. The shared resource is available and the access request was granted.

Instructions executed following MREQ test for the conditions above using the sign and Zero statuses as follows:

1. Z and S are both 0. No access request was made.

2. Z = 1 and S = 0. An access request was made, but it was not granted.

3. Z and S are both 1. An access request was made and granted.

We will now examine the actual event sequences accompanying the various MREQ options.

First consider the case where the shared resource is busy and no access request is made. When MREQ executes, it first tests the level of the signal input at MI. If this signal is low, then MREQ logic assumes that the shared resource is busy and no access request is to be made. MREQ resets the Z and S statuses to 0, outputs a high signal at MO, then terminates execution. This may be illustrated as follows:

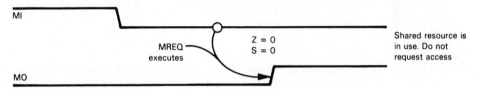

Next consider a high MI input which causes a shared resource access to be requested. When MREQ executes, if it detects a high input at MI, then it assumes that the shared resource is available and access may be requested. To request access, MREQ outputs a low signal at MO, then decrements the destination register contents to 0. The Destination register contents are decremented once every 7 clock periods. This gives external logic time to receive the low MO output and return an appropriate MI input.

After the Destination register has decremented to 0, MREQ instruction logic tests the MI input level. If MI is still being received high, then MREQ assumes that the access request has been denied. The Z status is set to 1, the Sign status is reset to 0, MO is output high again, and instruction execution ceases. This may be illustrated as follows:

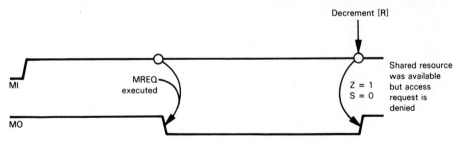

If after decrementing the Counter Register to 0, the MREQ instruction detects a low input at MI, then instruction logic assumes that the shared resource access request has been acknowledged. The Z and S statuses are both set to 1, and MO continues to be output low. This may be illustrated as follows:

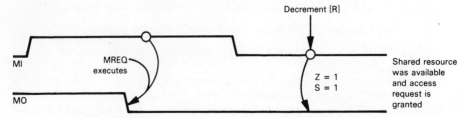

Literature published by Z8000 manufacturers is very confusing when it describes the MI and MO signals. This is because "low" signals are described corresponding to pin settings of 1, while "high" signals are described corresponding to pin settings of 0. In fact, logic internal to the Z8000 does transmit what appears to be a 1 bit in order to output a low MO signal, while it transmits what appears to be a 0 bit in order to output a high MO signal. Conversely, when MI is input low, Z8000 logic appears to receive a 1 bit, while it appears to receive a 0 bit when MI is input high. But this switch is irrelevant. You neither know nor care what bit level is detected by Z8000 logic for MI and MO. You are only interested in the levels of these two signals as they actually exist — and then only if you are a logic designer. If you are a programmer, you are only concerned with the status flag setting after executing the multi-micro instructions.

MRES — Multi-Micro Reset

MRES is a privileged instruction.
This is the format for the MRES instruction:

MRES

MRES has no operands.

When the MRES instruction is executed, a high signal is output via MO. Nothing else happens.

When two or more microprocessors can access a single shared resource (for example, a memory module), then a microprocessor outputs MO high if it does not wish to access the shared resource.

The MRES instructions' object code may be illustrated as follows:

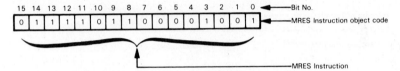

No status flags are modified by the MRES instruction.
See Chapter 13 for a discussion of the MRES instruction.

MSET — Multi-Micro Set

MSET is a privileged instruction.

This is the format for the MSET instruction:

MSET

MSET has no operands.

When the MSET instruction is executed, a low signal is output via MO. Nothing else happens.

When two or more microprocesses can access a single shared resource (for example, a memory module), then a microprocessor which is accessing the shared resource outputs MO low.

The MSET instructions object code may be illustrated as follows:

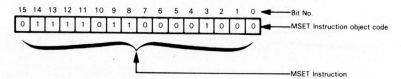

No status flags are modified by the MSET instruction.

See Chapter 13 for a discussion of the MSET instruction.

MULT — Multiply Words

MULTL — Multiply Long Words

This is the general format for the MULT and MULTL instructions:

Addressing Options	
dst	**src**
R	R
R	IM
R	IR
R	DA
R	X

MULT   dst,src
MULTL   dst,src

The symbol dst is a destination operand which must be specified using direct register addressing. A 32-bit CPU register must be specified for MULT; a 64-bit register must be specified for MULTL.

The symbol src is a source operand which can be specified using any standard operand addressing method (see Figure 3-26). A 16-bit operand is specified for MULT; a 32-bit operand is specified for MULTL.

The source and destination operands are both treated as twos complement signed binary numbers. Initially the low-order half of the destination operand CPU register contains the multiplicand; it is multiplied by the multiplier, which is the source operand. The product is returned in the destination operand. The high-order half of the destination operand does not participate in the multiplication and its contents are overwritten.

On some early production Z8000 chips MULTL gives incorrect results if refresh is enabled. See Table 3-18 at the end of this chapter for more information.

MULT and MULTL instruction object codes may be illustrated as follows:

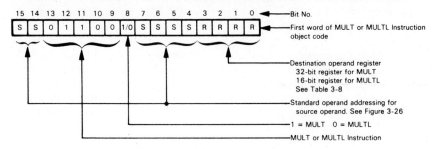

The MULT and MULTL instructions modify the C, Z, S, and V status flags.

The Carry status (C) is set if the product will not fit within the initial source/destination operand space. For MULT the product must have a value between -2^{15} and $+2^{15}-1$. For MULTL the product must have a value between -2^{31} and $+2^{31}-1$. If the product lies within these limits, then C is reset to 0; C is set to 1 otherwise. This makes the Carry status useless to program logic, since its value has nothing to do with the validity of the result.

The Overflow status (P/V) is always reset to 0.

The Zero status (Z) is set if a zero product is generated; it is reset otherwise.

The S status reports the sign of the product.

MULT and MULTL instruction execution is illustrated in Figures 3-70 and 3-71, respectively.

Figure 3-71 illustrates execution of the following MULT instructon:

```
MULT    RR4,LABEL;      % AMC syntax
MULT    RR4,LABEL       ! Zilog syntax !
```

Using the operands illustrated in Figure 3-70, Status flags will be modified as follows:

> C = 1 since the product will not fit within R5; the product is valid, nevertheless, because it will fit within the RR4, the designated product register.
>
> Z = 0 since the product is not zero
>
> S = 0 since the product is positive
>
> P/V = 0 since this status is always reset to 0

The MULT instruction in Figure 3-70 uses direct addressing to specify the multiplier. LABEL is shown with the value 8200_{16} — the direct address of the memory word from which the multiplier value 0200_{16} is taken. The multiplicand, 4000_{16}, is taken from the low-order half of RR4. The product is returned in RR4, 0080_{16} is loaded into R4, the high-order half of RR4, while 0000_{16} is loaded into R5, erasing the prior multicand value.

The MULTL instruction illustrated in Figure 3-71 is directly equivalent to the MULT instruction illustrated in Figure 3-70. Once again direct addressing is used to identify the multiplier, which now occupies two memory words, since 32-bit values are being multiplied. RQ4 is the destination operand, therefore RR6 holds the multicand, which is subsequently erased when the product is returned to RR4 and RR6.

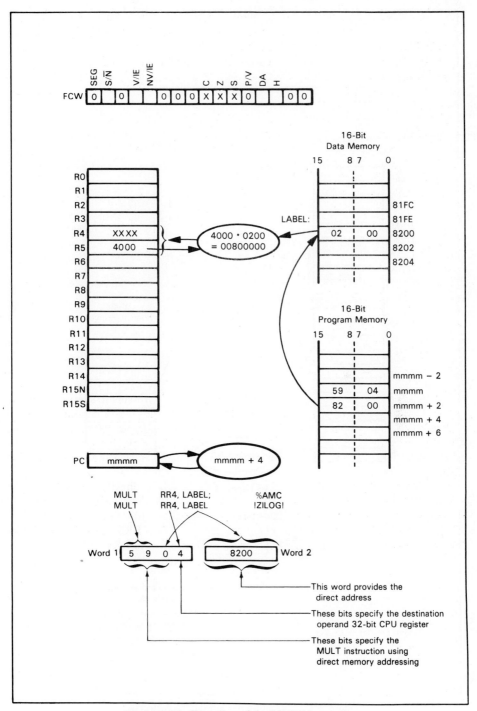

Figure 3-70. Execution of the MULT Instruction

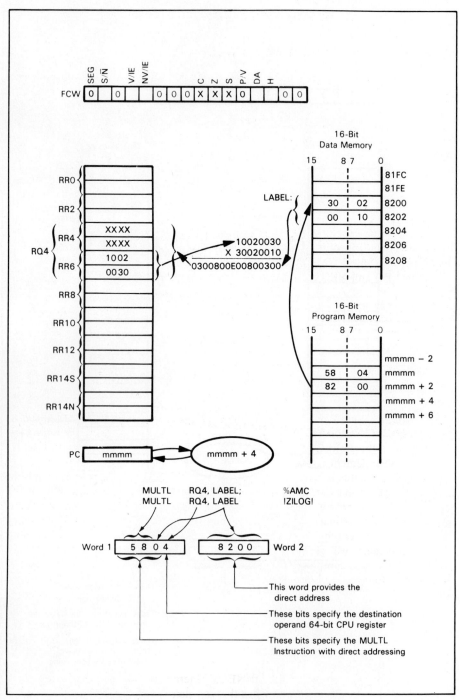

Figure 3-71. Execution of the MULTL Instruction

NEG — Twos Complement a 16-Bit Word

NEGB — Twos Complement a Byte

This is the general format for the NEG and NEGB assembly language instructions:

Addressing Options		
dst	NEG	dst
R IR DA X	NEGB	dst

The symbol dst is a destination operand which can be specified using any of the standard operand identification methods, with the exception of immediate addressing. The contents of the destination operand are twos complemented.

The NEG and NEGB instructions' object code may be illustrated as follows:

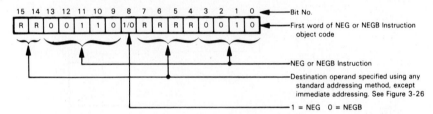

The C, Z, S and P/V statuses are modified by the NEG and NEGB instructions.

The Z and S status flags are modified in the standard way. Z is set to 1 if the twos complement of the destination operand is 0; it is reset to 0 otherwise. The high-order bit of the twos complement result is returned in the S status.

The Carry status is set to 1 to indicate a borrow, and it is reset to 0 if there is no borrow. Therefore the Carry status becomes the complement of any carry out of the high-order destination operand bit. If generating a twos complement causes a carry out of the high-order destination operand bit, then the Carry status is cleared; the Carry status is set whenever there is no carry out of the high-order bit. However, the only time a twos complement will generate a Carry is when the destination operand is zero, in which case the twos complement will also be zero. For NEG and NEGB this may be illustrated as follows:

	Word	Byte
Original value	0000	00
Ones complement	FFFF	FF
	1	1
Twos complement	0000	00
Carry	1	1

Thus, C is reset to 0 when NEG or NEGB generates a zero result, and C is reset to 1 otherwise. This makes the Carry status the complement of the Zero status.

The P/V status reports the special case where 8000_{16} is twos complemented by NEG, or 80_{16} is twos complemented by NEGB. In both cases the result equals the initial operand. For NEG and NEGB this may be illustrated as follows:

	NEG	NEGB
Original value =	8000	80
Ones complement =	7FFF	7F
	1	1
Twos complement =	8000	80

P/V is set to 1 when NEG generates an 8000_{16} result, or NEGB generates a 80_{16} result. P/V is reset to 0 otherwise.

When the instruction:

```
NEG    R3;              % AMC syntax
NEG    R3               ! Zilog syntax !
```

is executed, the contents of 16-bit register R3 is twos complemented. If R3 originally contains $423A_{16}$, this is what happens:

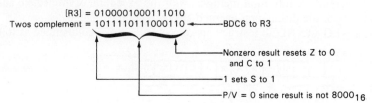

The NEGB instruction:

```
NEGB   #423A^;          % AMC syntax
NEGB   %423A            ! Zilog syntax !
```

will complement the contents of the memory byte with address $423A_{16}$. If this memory byte initially contains $3A_{16}$, this is what happens when the NEGB instruction is executed:

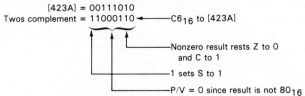

NOP — No Operation

This is the format for the NOP instruction:

NOP

The NOP instruction has no operands. No operation is performed when NOP executes. The instruction is used to introduce time delays or to reserve space in program memory. NOP takes 7 clock periods to execute.

The NOP instruction's object code may be illustrated as follows:

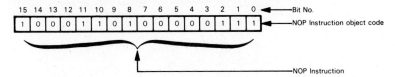

No Status flags are modified by the NOP instruction.

OR — Logically OR Words

ORB — Logically OR Bytes

This is the general format for the OR and ORB instructions:

Addressing Options			
dst	**src**		
R	R	OR	dst,src
R	IM	ORB	dst,src
R	IR		
R	DA		
R	X		

The symbol dst is a destination operand which must be specified using direct register addressing. A 16-bit CPU register must be specified for OR; an 8-bit CPU register must be specified for ORB.

The symbol src is a source operand which can be specified using any standard operand addressing method (see Figure 3-26).

The source and destination operands are logically ORed. The result is returned in the destination operand CPU register. The prior contents of the destination register are lost.

The OR and ORB instructions' object code may be illustrated as follows:

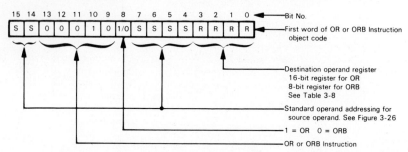

The Z and S status flags are modified by the OR and ORB instructions. In addition, the ORB instruction modifies the P/V status to reflect the parity of the result byte. (P = 1 for even parity, 0 for odd parity.)

Figure 3-72 illustrates execution of the ORB instruction:

```
ORB     RL2,R2^;       % AMC syntax
ORB     RL2,@R2        ! Zilog syntax !
```

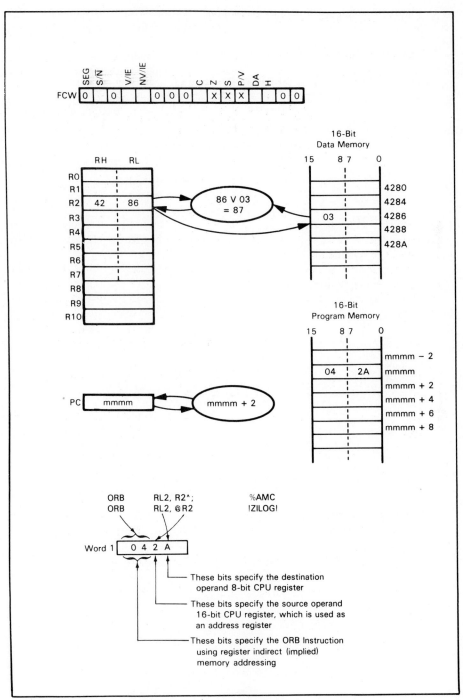

Figure 3-72. Execution of the ORB Instruction

Figures 3-5 and 3-10 illustrate execution of AND and ANDB instructions. Equivalent OR and ORB instructions execute identically, but perform different logical operations.

The ORB instruction illustrated in Figure 3-72 modifies the source operand indirect address. This is because 16-bit register R2 provides the address of a memory byte whose contents are ORed with RL2, the low-order byte of the address. This is what happens when the ORB instruction illustrated in Figure 3-72 is executed:

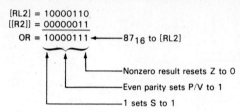

OTDR — Output Word Decrement and Repeat

OTDRB — Output Byte Decrement and Repeat

The OTDR and OTDRB instructions are privileged.

These two instructions are identical to INDR and INDRB, respectively, except that a block of data is output from memory via an I/O port, instead of being input via an I/O port to memory.

See OUT and OUTB for a description of output instructions. See INDR and INDRB for logic variations applicable to OTDR and OTDRB.

The OTDR and OTDRB instructions' object code may be illustrated as follows:

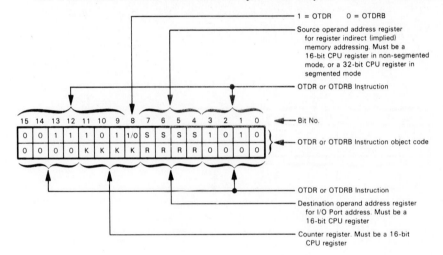

OTIR — Output Word Increment and Repeat

OTIRB — Output Byte Increment and Repeat

The OTIR and OTIRB instructions are privileged.

These two instructions are identical to INIR and INIRB, respectively, except that a block of data is output from memory via an I/O port, instead of being input via an I/O port to memory.

See OUT and OUTB for a description of output instructions. See INIR and INIRB for logic variations applicable to OTIR and OTIRB.

The OTIR and OTIRB instructions' object code may be illustrated as follows:

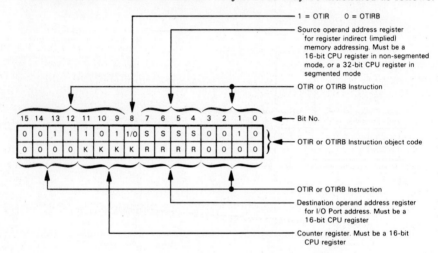

OUT — Output a Word

OUTB — Output a Byte

The OUT and OUTB instructions are privileged.
This is the general format for the OUT and OUTB instructions:

Addressing Options	
dst	**src**
IR	R
DA	R

OUT   dst,src
OUTB   dst,src

The symbol dst is a destination operand identifying an I/O port. A 16-bit I/O port address is generated using direct addressing, or register indirect (implied) addressing. Therefore 65536 I/O ports can be addressed. OUTB must address an odd numbered port.

The symbol src is a source operand which must be specified using direct register addressing. A 16-bit CPU register must be specified for OUT; and an 8-bit CPU register must be specified for OUTB.

When the OUT or OUTB instruction is executed, data is transferred from the CPU register selected by the source operand, to the I/O port addressed by the destination operand. OUT transfers a word of data from a 16-bit CPU register to an I/O port. OUTB transfers a byte of data from an 8-bit CPU register to an it I/O port.

The OUT and OUTB instructions have two object code formats, which may be illustrated as follows:

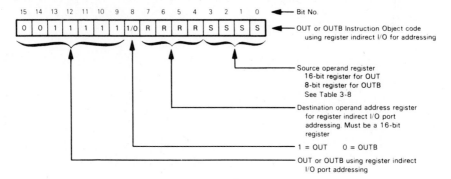

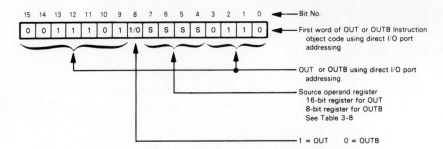

No status flags are modified by the OUT or OUTB instructions.

Figure 3-73 illustrates execution of the following OUT instruction:

```
OUT     R3,R0          % AMC syntax
OUT     @R3,R0         ! Zilog syntax !
```

This is the OUT equivalent of the IN instruction illustrated in Figure 3-49.

This instruction causes 16 bits of data, illustrated generally in Figure 3-70 as PPPP, to be transferred from a 16-bit register R0, to the I/O port selected by the address 0400_{16}.

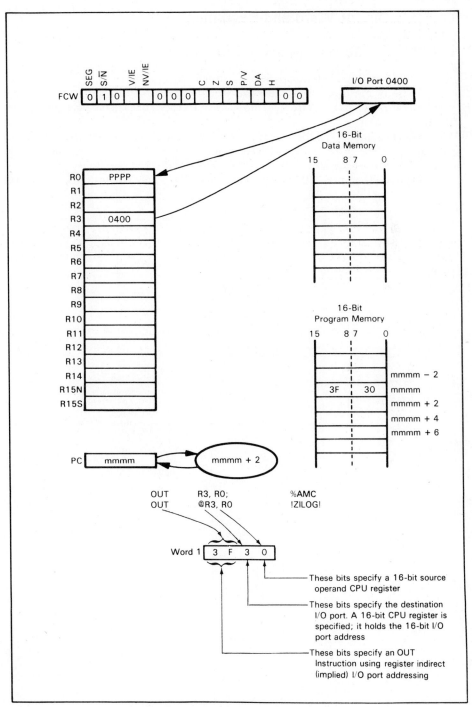

Figure 3-73. Execution of the OUT Instruction

OUTD — Output Word and Decrement

OUTDB — Output Byte and Decrement

OUTD and OUTDB are privileged instructions.

These two instructions are identical to INDR and INDRB, respectively, except that a block of data is output from memory via an I/O port, instead of being input via an I/O port to memory.

See OUT and OUTB for a description of output instructions. See IND and INDB for logic variations applicable to OUTD and OUTDB. The IND instruction illustrated in Figure 3-51 is the equivalent of the OUTD instruction.

The OUTD and OUTDB instructions' object code may be illustrated as follows:

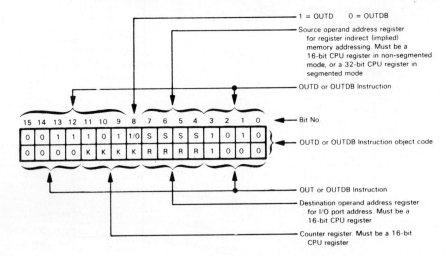

OUTI — Output Word and Increment

OUTIB — Output Byte and Increment

OUTI and OUTIB are privileged instructions.

These two instructions are identical to INI and INIB, respectively, except that a block of data is output from memory via an I/O port, instead of being input via an I/O port to a memory.

See OUT and OUTB for a description of output instructions. See INI and INIB for logic variations applicable to OUTI and OUTIB. The INI instruction illustrated in **Figure 3-52** is the equivalent of an OUTI instruction.

The OUTI and OUTIB instructions' object code may be illustrated as follows:

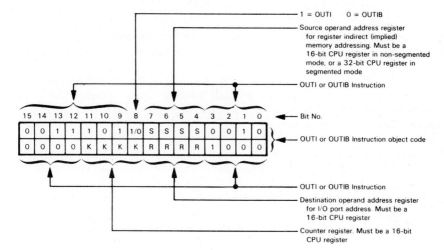

POP — Pop a Word

POPL — Pop a Long Word

This is the general format for the POP and POPL instructions:

Addressing Options	
dst	src
R	IRI
IR	IRI
DA	IRI
X	IRI

POP   dst,src
POPL   dst,src

The symbol dst is a destination operand which can be specified using any standard operand addressing method with the exception of immediate addressing. (See Figure 3-26.)

The symbol src is a source operand which must be specified using register (implied) memory addressing. The selected address register functions as a Stack Pointer; therefore the address is incremented after the source operand has been accessed. Any CPU register may be specified with the exception of R0 in non-segmented mode or RR0 in segmented mode.

When the POP instruction is executed, a memory word (for POP) or a long word (for POPL) is popped from the Stack and loaded into the destination operand memory location.

The Z8000 Stack begins at its highest memory address. The stack grows to lower memory addresses. The stack pointer always points to the entry currently on the top of the stack. Following each POP, therefore, the Stack address is incremented, thereby selecting the new top of Stack location; this is the entry directly below the value popped from the Stack. Since the Stack is origined at the highest Stack address, the entry "below" the value popped will have the next higher Stack address. That is why the source operand address is incremented. POP increments the stack (source operand) address by 2; POPL increments this address by 4.

POPL pops the high-order word first, then the low-order word, so that a long word is expected to appear in the stack in the same order in which it will appear in a double register or elsewhere in memory after the POPL.

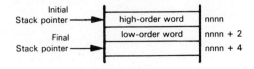

The POP and POPL instructions' object codes may be illustrated as follows:

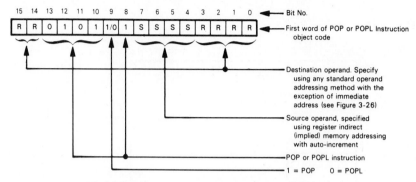

No status flags are modified by the POP or POPL instruction.

Figure 3-74 illustrates execution of the POP instruction:

```
POP     BASE(R5),RR8^;      % AMC syntax
POP     |BASE|(R5),@RR8     ! Zilog syntax !
```

This instruction is illustrated executing in segmented mode. The equivalent POPL instruction:

```
POPL    R5^,R9^;            % AMC syntax
POPL    @R5,@R9             ! Zilog syntax !
```

is illustrated in Figure 3-75, executing in non-segmented mode.

There are some restrictions placed on the registers which can be selected for source and destination operand addressing.

R0 cannot be selected as the Stack Pointer in non-segmented mode.

RR0 cannot be selected as the Stack Pointer in segmented mode.

For POPL the same register cannot be specified in the source and destination operand addressing logic.

The POP instruction illustrated in Figure 3-74 uses very sensible addressing options given the nature of the operations performed by a POP instruction. Destination data memory is identified using base indexed addressing. The assumption here is that a number of contiguous memory words may be popped from the Stack to data memory. Therefore, the data memory address is actually provided by Index register R5, while the base address specifies the segment only. A short-segmented base address is used; the short-segmented base address offset is 00. More often than not a short-segmented base address will provide a 00 offset within the selected segment if an Index register is used to compute the offset portion of the address.

The Stack Pointer itself is contained in 32-bit Register RR8. Only the offset word of the address is incremented. PPPP is used to illustrate any 16-bit data word transferred from Stack memory location 060400_{16} to data memory location 040800_{16}. After the POP instruction in Figure 3-74 has been executed, the Stack Pointer will be left addressing Stack memory word 060402_{16}.

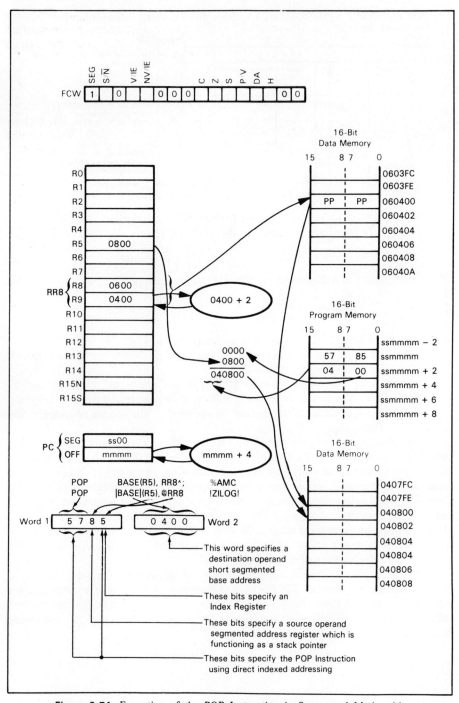

Figure 3-74. Execution of the POP Instruction in Segmented Mode with a Short Segmented Address

A non-segmented version of the POP instruction, illustrated in Figure 3-75, does not need base indexed addressing. Since the base portion of the address computation specifies the segment number only, a non-segmented POP instruction could use register indirect addressing as follows:

```
POP       R5^,RR8^;        % AMC syntax
POP       @R5,@RR8         ! Zilog syntax !
```

Figure 3-75 illustrates the POPL version of the non-segmented POP instruction shown above. R5 still provides the destination data memory address, but register indirect addressing is used since no base address is required. Since a long word is being moved from stack memory to data memory, the Stack Pointer is incremented by 4.

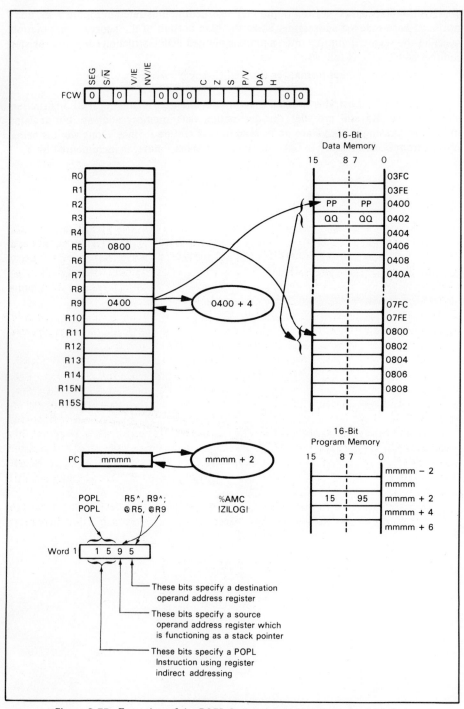

Figure 3-75. Execution of the POPL Instruction in Non-Segmented Mode

PUSH — Push Word

PUSHL — Push Long Word

This is the general format for the PUSH and PUSHL instructions:

Addressing Options	
dst	src
IRD	R
IRD	IR
IRD	DA
IRD	X
IRD	IM

PUSH   dst,src
PUSHL   dst,src

The symbol dst is a destination operand which must be specified using register indirect addressing. A 16-bit CPU register must be specified in non-segmented mode; a 32-bit CPU register must be specified in segmented mode. The specified address register will function as a Stack pointer; therefore the address is decremented before the destination operand is accessed. Any register may be specified with the exception of R0 in non-segmented or RR0 in segmented mode.

The symbol src is a source operand which can be specified using any standard operand addressing method. Immediate addressing can be specified for PUSH only, as a special case. (See Figure 3-26 for standard operand addressing methods.)

When the PUSH or PUSHL instruction is executed, a memory word (for PUSH) or long word (for PUSHL) is pushed onto the Stack from the source operand data memory location. The Z8000 Stack begins at its highest memory address. The stack grows toward lower memory addresses. The stack pointer always points to the entry on the top of the stack. Before each PUSH, therefore, the stack address is decremented, selecting the next available location on the stack. The source operand is stored at this location. After the PUSH or PUSHL instruction has been executed, the CPU register functioning as the Stack Pointer is left addressing the current "top" of Stack. PUSH decrements the stack (destination operand) address by 2; PUSHL decrements this address by 4.

PUSHL pushes the low-order word first, then the high-order word, so that the long word appears in the stack in the same order in which it appeared in a double register or elsewhere in memory before the PUSHL.

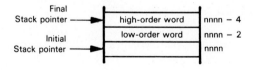

The PUSH and PUSHL instructions' object codes may be illustrated as follows:

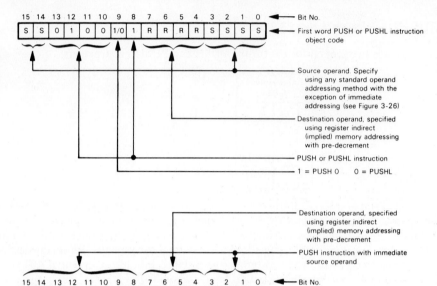

No status flags are modified by the PUSH or PUSHL instruction.

Some restrictions are placed on the registers which may be used to compute source and destination operand addresses.

R0 cannot be used as the Stack Pointer in non-segmented mode.

RR0 cannot be used as the Stack Pointer in segmented mode.

The PUSHL instruction does not allow the same register to be specified in the source and destination address computation.

Figures 3-76 and 3-77 illustrate PUSH versions of the POP instructions illustrated in Figures 3-74 and 3-75. The PUSH instructions illustrated are:

```
PUSH    RR8^,BASE(R5);      % AMC syntax
PUSH    @RR8,|BASE|(R5)     ! Zilog syntax !

PUSHL   R9^,R5^;            % AMC syntax
PUSHL   @R9,@R5             ! Zilog syntax !
```

For a discussion of addressing logic, refer to the POP instruction description.

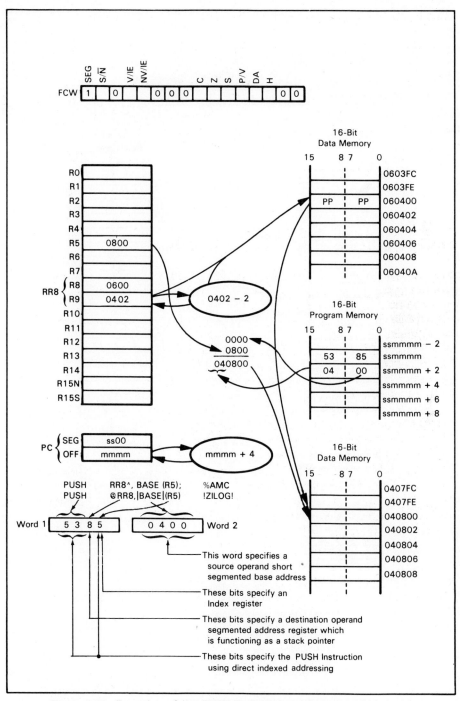

Figure 3-76. Execution of the PUSH Instruction in Segmented Mode with Short Segmented Address

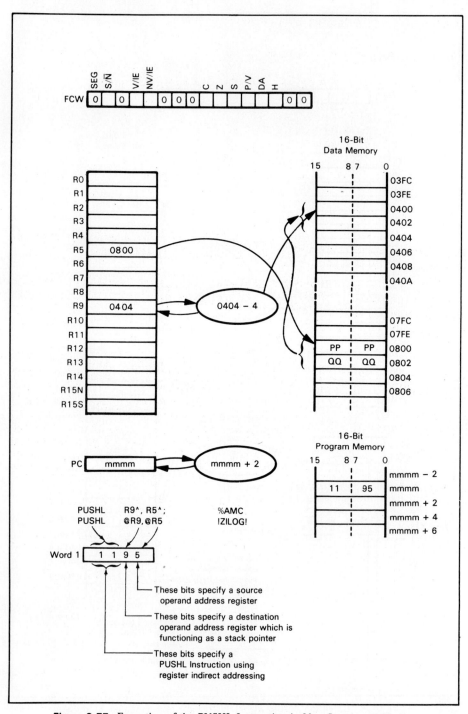

Figure 3-77. Execution of the PUSHL Instruction in Non-Segmented Mode

RES — Reset a Bit in a Word

RESB — Reset a Bit in a Byte

This is the general format for the RES and RESB instructions.

Addressing Options	
dst	src
R	IM
IR	IM
DA	IM
X	IM
R	R

RES dst,src
RESB dst,src

The symbol dst is a destination operand which can be specified using any standard operand addressing method with the exception of immediate addressing. (See Figure 3-26.)

The symbol src is a source operand which is normally specified as an immediate data value, but can also be specified using direct register addressing. In the latter case, any 16-bit CPU register must be specified for RES, but one of the eight 16-bit CPU registers R0-R7 must be specified for RESB. If the source operand is a CPU register, the destination operand must also be a CPU register.

When the RES or RESB instruction is executed, one bit of the destination word (for RES) or byte (for RESB) is reset to 0. The source operand specifies the number of the bit which is to be reset. Usually the source operand is specified as an immediate data value; in this case, the source operand can have a value between 0 and 15 for RES, or it can range between 0 and 7 for RESB. The source operand can be a CPU register, but only if the destination operand is a CPU register also. For RESB, the three low-order bits of the source operand CPU register identify the bit number in the destination operand CPU register which will be reset to 0. For RES, the four low-order bits of the source operand CPU register identify the bit number in the destination operand CPU register which is to be reset to 0.

The RES and RESB instruction object codes may be illustrated as follows:

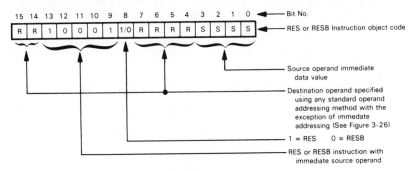

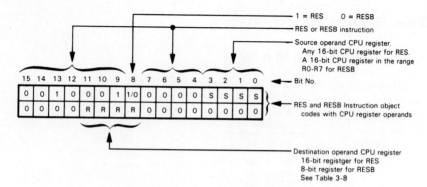

No status flags are modified by the RES or RESB instruction.
When the instruction:

```
RES     #4020^,3;       % AMC syntax
RES     %4020,#3        ! Zilog syntax !
```

is executed, bit 3 of memory word with address 4020_{16} is reset to 0.
When the instruction:

```
RESB    RH3,R2;         % AMC syntax
RESB    RH3,R2          ! Zilog syntax !
```

is executed, the bit of Register RH3 specified by Register R2 is reset to 0. The low-order three bits of Register R2 specify the bit within Register RH3 which will be reset to 0. For example, if Register R2 contains 0003, then bit 3 of Register RH3 will be reset to 0.

The RES and RESB instructions number bits as illustrated throughout this book, with the low-order bit being bit number 0, and the high-order bit being bit number 7 for a byte, or 15 for a word.

RESFLG — Reset Status Flags

This is the general format for the RESFLG instruction:

RESFLG flags

The word "flags" may be the designation for one or more of the status flags: Carry, Zero, Sign, Parity, and Overflow. The Zilog and AMC assemblers use different abbreviations for the statuses:

Status	Zilog Syntax	AMC Syntax
Carry	C	CY
Zero	Z	ZR
Sign	S	SGN
Parity*	P	PY
Overflow*	V	OV

RESFLG resets to 0 the identified status bits of the Flag and control word. You can list the status flags in any sequence.

The RESFLG instruction's object code may be illustrated as follows:

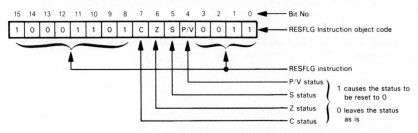

The status flags modified by the RESFLG instruction will depend on the flags specified in the operand field. No flags other than those specifically identified are modified.

The instruction:

```
RESFLG   ZR;            % AMC syntax
RESFLG   Z              ! Zilog syntax
```

will reset just the zero status. Other statuses are not modified. On the other hand, the instruction:

```
RESFLG   PY,SGN,ZR,CY;  % AMC syntax
RESFLG   P,S,Z,C        ! Zilog syntax !
```

will reset all four statuses to 0.

RET — Return From Subroutine

This is the general format for the RET instruction:

```
RET    cc
```

The symbol cc is a condition code. The symbol cc can have any of the mnemonics listed in the code column of Table 3-4, or can be omitted.

When the RET instruction is executed, the status conditions corresponding to the condition code specified by cc are compared with status flag settings in the Flag and Control Word. If there is a status match, a return from subroutine occurs. If there is no status match, the next sequential instruction is executed. If a return from subroutine occurs, a return address is popped from the Stack into the Program Counter. In non-segmented mode, Register R15 is treated as the Stack Pointer and a single word is popped from the top of the Stack into the Program Counter. In segmented mode, Register RR14 is treated as the Stack pointer. First the top word of the Stack is popped into the Program Counter Segment; then the next word is popped into the Program Counter Offset.

The RET instruction's object code may be illustrated as follows:

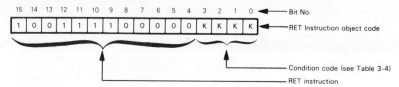

No status flags are modified by the RET instruction.

Figure 3-78 illustrates execution of the instruction:

```
RET    CY;              % AMC syntax
RET    C                ! Zilog syntax !
```

This instruction is shown executing in non-segmented mode. It executes a return from subroutine if the Carry status is 1.

If the RET instruction illustrated above were executed in segmented mode, the offset portion of the Stack Pointer address shown in Register R15 would be incremented by 4 rather than 2; also, the contents of memory words 0400_{16} and 0402_{16} would be loaded into the Segment and Offset registers, respectively, of the Program Counter.

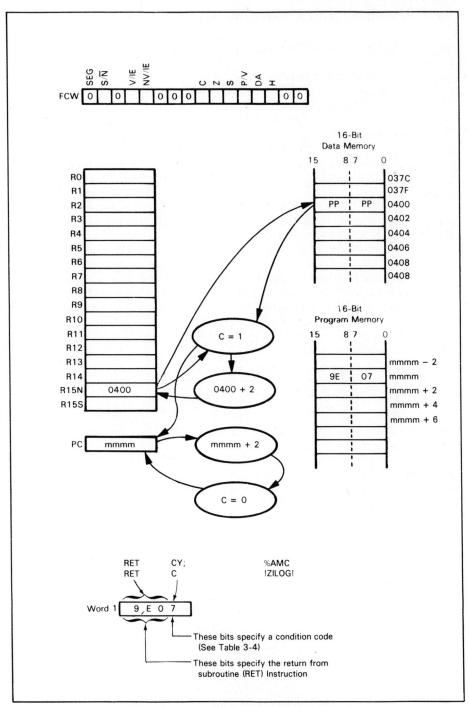

Figure 3-78. Execution of the RET Instruction

RL — Rotate Word Left and into Carry

RLB — Rotate Byte Left and into Carry

This is the general format for the RL and RLB instructions:

Addressing Options	
dst	n
R	IM

RL   dst,n
RLB   dst,n

The symbol dst is a destination operand which must be specified using direct register addressing. A 16-bit CPU register must be specified for RL; an 8-bit CPU register must be specified for RLB.

The symbol n is an integer digit which may be 1 or 2; no other values are allowed. The symbol n may be absent, in which case a value of 1 is assumed.

The RL and RLB instructions, when executed, rotate the contents of the destination CPU register to the left. A 16-bit CPU register's contents are rotated for RL; an 8-bit CPU register's contents are rotated for RLB. Register contents are rotated left one bit position if n is 1, or 2 bit positions if n is 2. In each case the value shifted out of the high-order bit, and into the low-order bit, is also shifted into the Carry status. This may be illustrated as follows:

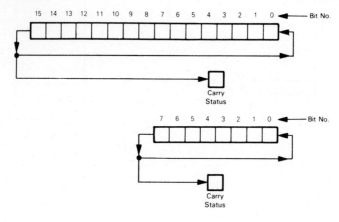

The RL and RLB instructions' object codes may be illustrated as follows:

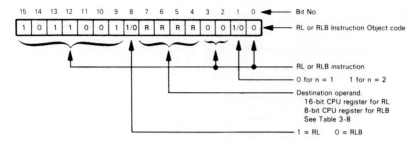

The RL and RLB instructions modify the C, Z, S, and V status flags.

The Carry status (C) receives the high-order bit being rotated into bit position 0.

The Zero status (Z) is modified in the standard fashion; it is set to 1 if the register contents are zero after the rotation has been performed; it is cleared otherwise. Note that a rotate operation cannot generate a zero result unless the original register contents were also zero.

The Sign status (S) acquires the value of the high-order bit after the rotation has been performed.

The Overflow status (P/V) is set if the value of the high-order bit changes during any rotation step. The Overflow status is reset otherwise. For example, if the high-order bit is initially 0, then P/V will be set to 1 if the high-order bit is ever 1 during a one or two bit rotation.

When the RL instruction:

```
RL      R3,2;           % AMC syntax
RL      R3,#2           ! Zilog syntax !
```

is executed, if register R3 initially contains $423A_{16}$, this is what happens:

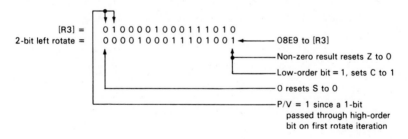

RLC — Rotate Word Left Through Carry

RLCB — Rotate Byte Left Through Carry

This is the general format for the RLC and RLCB instructions:

Addressing Options	
dst	src
R	IM

RLC   dst,n
RLCB   dst,n

The symbol dst is a destination operand which must be specified using direct register addressing. A 16-bit CPU register must be specified for RLC; an 8-bit CPU register must be specified for RLCB.

The symbol n is an integer digit which may be 1 or 2; no other values are allowed. The symbol n may be absent, in which case a value of 1 is assumed.

The RLC and RLCB instructions, when executed, rotate the contents of the destination CPU register and the Carry status to the left through the Carry status. A 16-bit CPU register's contents are rotated for RL; an 8-bit CPU register's contents are rotated for RLCB. Register contents are rotated left one bit position if n is 1, or 2 bit positions if n is 2. At each rotation step each case the Carry status is shifted into the low-order bit, and the high-order bit is shifted into the Carry status. This may be illustrated as follows:

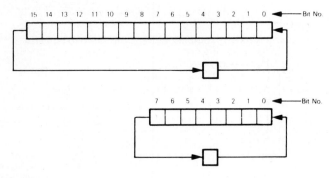

The RLC and RLCB instructions' object codes may be illustrated as follows:

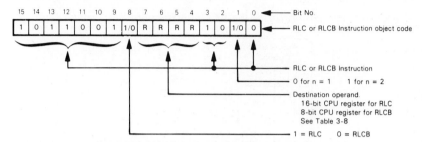

The RLC and RLCB instructions modify the C, Z, S, and V status flags.

The Carry status (C) receives the rotated high-order bit.

The Zero status (Z) is modified in the standard fashion; it is set to 1 if the register contents are zero after the rotation has been performed; it is cleared otherwise.

The Sign status (S) acquires the value of the high-order bit, after the rotation has been performed.

The Overflow status (P/V) is set if the value of the high- order bit changes during any rotation step. The Overflow status is reset otherwise. For example, if the high-order bit is initially 0, then P/V will be set to 1 if the high-order bit is ever 1 during a one or two bit rotation.

When the RLC instruction:

```
RLC     R3,2;           % AMC syntax
RLC     R3,#2           ! Zilog syntax !
```

is executed, if register R3 originally contains $423A_{16}$ and the Carry status is set, this is what happens:

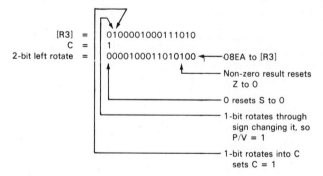

RLDB — Rotate Left BCD

This is the general format for the RLDB instruction:

Addressing Options	
dst	src
R	R

RLDB   dst,src

The symbols dst and src are destination and source operands which must both be specified as 8-bit CPU registers.

When the RLDB instruction is executed, a binary coded decimal rotation to the left occurs as follows:

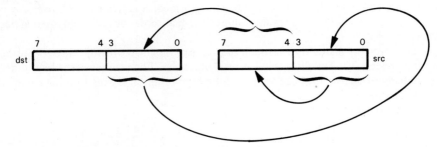

You cannot specify the same CPU register as the destination and the source operand; if you do, the result is unpredictable.

This is the RLDB instruction's object code:

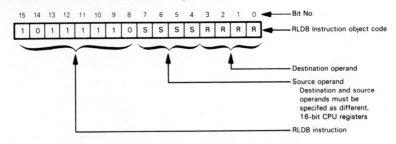

The RLDB instruction modifies the Z and S status flags.

The Zero status (Z) is set if the destination operand CPU register contains 0 after the RLDB instruction has been executed; the Zero status is reset otherwise. Note, however, that the four high-order bits of the destination register are not modified by the RLDB instruction.

The sign status (S) acquires the value of the destination operand CPU register high-order bit. Note, again that this bit is not modified by the RLDB instruction.

When the RLDB instruction:

```
RLDB      RH3,RL3;        % AMC syntax
RLDB      RH3,RL3         ! Zilog syntax !
```

is executed, if RH3 initially contains 39_{16} and RL3 initially contains 42_{16}, this is what happens:

```
[RH3] =  39
[RL3] =  42

RLDB  → 3429 {  34₁₆ to [RH3]
              {  29₁₆ to [RL3]

Z = 0 since [RH3] is not zero
S = 0 since [RH3] high-order bit = 0
P/V is undefined.
```

The RLDB instruction is used to left shift binary coded decimal data.

RR — Rotate Word Right and into Carry

RRB — Rotate Byte Right and into Carry

This is the general format for the RR and RRB instructions:

Addressing Options	
dst	n
R	IM

RR dst,n
RRB dst,n

  The symbol dst is a destination operand which must be specified using direct register addressing. A 16-bit CPU register must be specified for RR; an 8-bit CPU register must be specified for RRB.

  The symbol n is an integer digit which may be 1 or 2; no other values are allowed. The symbol n may be absent, in which case a value of 1 is assumed.

  The RR and RRB instructions, when executed, right rotate the contents of the destination CPU register to the right. A 16-bit CPU register's contents are rotated for RR; an 8-bit CPU register's contents are rotated for RRB. Register contents are rotated right one bit position if n is 1, or 2 bit positions if n is 2. In each case the value shifted out of the low-order bit, and into the high-order bit, is also shifted into the Carry status. This may be illustrated as follows:

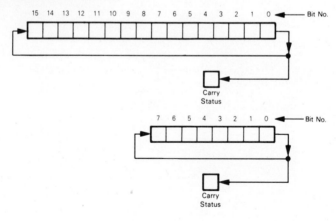

The RR and RRB instructions' object codes may be illustrated as follows:

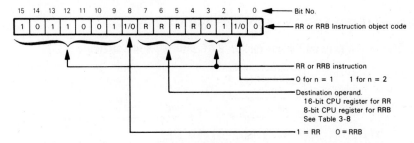

The RR and RRB instructions modify the C, Z, S, and V status flags.

The Carry status (C) receives the low-order bit being rotated into the high-order bit position.

The Zero status (Z) is modified in the standard fashion; it is set to 1 if the register contents are zero after the rotate has been performed; it is cleared otherwise. Note that a rotate operation cannot generate a zero result unless the original register contents were also zero.

The Sign status (S) acquires the value of the high-order bit, after the rotate has been performed.

The Overflow status (P/V) is set if the value of the high-order bit changes during any rotation step. The Overflow status is reset otherwise. For example, if the high-order bit is initially 0, then P/V will be set to 1 if the high-order bit is ever 1 during a one or two bit rotate.

When the RR instruction:

```
RR      R3,2;           % AMC syntax
RR      R3,#2           ! Zilog syntax !
```

is executed, if register R3 initially contains $423A_{16}$, this is what happens:

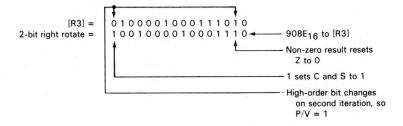

RRC — Rotate Word Right Through Carry

RRCB — Rotate Byte Right Through Carry

This is the general format for the RRC and RCB instructions:

Addressing Options	
dst	n
R	IM

RRC   dst,n
RRCB   dst,n

The symbol dst is a destination operand which must be specified using direct register addressing. A 16-bit CPU register must be specified for RRC; an 8-bit CPU register must be specified for RRCB.

The symbol n is an integer digit which may be 1 or 2; no other values are allowed. The symbol n may be absent, in which case a value of 1 is assumed.

The RRC and RRCB instructions, when executed, rotate the contents of the destination CPU register and the Carry status to the right through the Carry status. A 16-bit CPU register's contents are rotated for RRC; an 8-bit CPU register's contents are rotated for RRCB. Register contents are rotated right one bit position if n is 1, or 2 bit positions if n is 2. At each rotation step the Carry status is shifted into the high-order bit, and the low-order bit is shifted into the Carry status. This may be illustrated as follows:

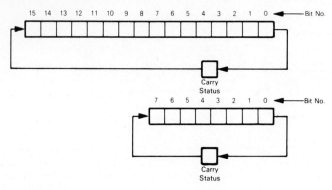

The RRC and RRCB instructions' object codes may be illustrated as follows:

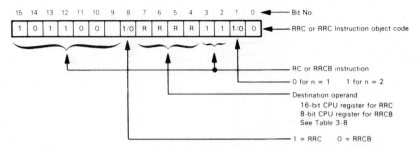

The RRC and RRCB instructions modify the C, Z, S, and V status flags.

The Carry status (S) receives the rotated low-order bit.

The Zero status (Z) is modified in the standard fashion; it is set to 1 if the register contents are zero after the rotate has been performed; it is cleared otherwise.

The Sign status (S) acquires the value of the high-order bit, after the rotate has been performed.

The Overflow status (P/V) is set if the value of the high-order bit changes during any rotation step. The Overflow status is reset otherwise. For example, if the high-order bit is initially 0, then P/V will be set to 1 if the high-order bit is ever 1 during a one or two bit rotate.

When the RRC instruction:

```
RRC     R3,2;           % AMC syntax
RRC     R3,#2           ! Zilog syntax !
```

is executed, if register R3 originally contains $423A_{16}$ and the Carry status is set, this is what happens:

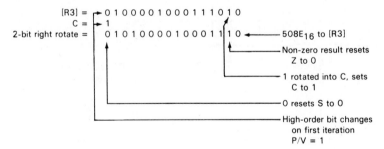

RRDB — Rotate Right BCD

This is the general format for the RRDB instruction:

Addressing Options	
dst	src
R	R

RRDB   dst,src

The symbols dst and src are destination and source operands which must both be specified as 8-bit CPU registers.

When the RRDB instruction is executed, a binary coded decimal left shift occurs as follows:

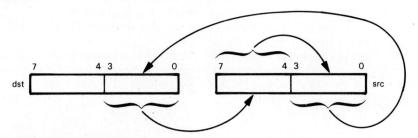

You cannot specify the same CPU register as the destination and the source operand; if you do, the result is unpredictable.

This is the RRDB instruction's object code:

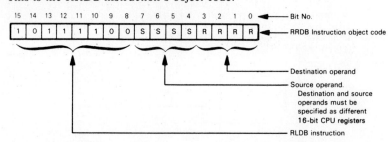

The RRDB instruction modifies the Z and S status flags.

The Zero status (Z) is set if the destination operand CPU register contains 0 after the RDB instruction has been executed; the Zero status is reset otherwise. However, note that the four high-order bits of the destination operand are not modified by the RRDB instruction.

The Sign status (S) acquires the value of the destination operand CPU register high-order bit. Note again that this bit is not modified by the RRDB instruction.

When the RRDB instruction:

```
RRDB      RH3,RL3;          % AMC syntax
RRDB      RH3,RL3           ! Zilog syntax !
```

is executed, if RH3 initially contains 39_{16} and RL3 initially contains 42_{16}, this is what happens:

$$[RH3] = 39$$
$$[RL3] = 42$$

$$RRDB \quad 3294 \begin{cases} 32_{16} \text{ to [RH3]} \\ 94_{16} \text{ to [RL3]} \end{cases}$$

Z = 0 since [RH3] is not zero
S = 0 since [RH3] high-order bit = 0
P/V is undefined.

The RRDB instruction is used to right shift binary coded decimal data.

SBC — Subtract Words With Borrow, Register-To-Register

SBCB — Subtract Bytes With Borrow, Register-To-Register

This is the general format for the SBC and SBCB instructions:

```
SBC      dst,src
SBCB     dst,src
```

The symbols dst and src are the destination and source operands respectively; they must both be specified as CPU registers using direct register addressing. 16-bit CPU registers must be specified for SBC; 8-bit CPU registers must be specified for SBCB. The contents of the source register, plus the Carry status, are subtracted from the destination register, whose prior contents are lost. The source operand is not modified.

An anomaly of the Z8000 instruction set is the fact that SBC and SBCB are the only subtract with borrow instructions. These two instructions can only subtract the contents of CPU registers; they do not allow either the source or the destination operand to be specified as a memory location.

The SBC and SBCB instructions' object codes may be illustrated as follows:

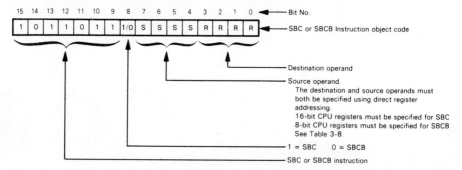

The C, Z, S, and P/V status flags are modified by the SBC and SBCB instructions. In addition, the SBCB instruction modifies the H status and sets the D status to 1.

The Z and S status flags are modified in the standard fashion. C and H status logic is inverted, to signal borrows. C and H are set if there is no carry out of the high-order bit (for C), or out of bit position 3 (for H). C and H are reset if there is a carry out of these bit positions.

The P/V status is set if an arithmetic overflow occurs; the P/V status is reset otherwise. An arithmetic overflow is assumed if the operands were of opposite signs, and the sign of the result is the same as the sign of the source operand.

SBC and SBCB instruction execution is not illustrated; instead see Figures 3-27 and 3-28 which illustrate very similar ADC and ADCB instructions. Remember SBCB sets D to 1.

Consider the SBC instruction:

```
SBC      R4,R7;          % AMC syntax
SBC      R4,R7           ! Zilog syntax !
```

Suppose Register R4 initially contains $276A_{16}$ while Register R7 contains $A3B0_{16}$ and the Carry status is set to 1. This is what happens when the SBC instruction illustrated above is executed:

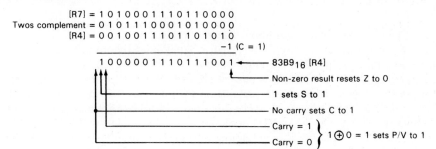

Remember, C = 1 signifies a borrow during the previous operation; therefore, the minuend (in R7) must be reduced by 1, which is equivalent to subtracting 1 from the difference.

SC — System Call

This is the general format for the SC instruction:

SC   data

The word data is an 8-bit immediate data value.

When the SC instruction is executed, a variation of the interrupt acknowledgement procedure occurs. The current Program Counter value, incremented to address the next sequential instruction, is pushed onto the Stack; then the current Flag and Control word is pushed onto the Stack; finally the System Call instruction object code itself is pushed onto the Stack. New Flag and Control word and Program Counter values are then read from the System Call locations in the Z8000 interrupt vector.

The System Call instruction always pushes data onto the System Stack; that is to say, the System Stack Pointer is used, irrespective of whether the System Call instruction is executed out of system mode or normal mode. Furthermore, the Z8001 always uses the two-word, segmented System Stack Pointer, irrespective of whether the SC instruction is executed in segmented or non-segmented mode.

The Z8002 takes a new one-word Program Counter value from an interrupt vector whose memory address is computed using the New Program Status Area Pointer (PSAP), as follows:

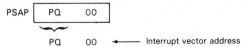

P and Q are any hexadecimal digits; they are taken from the high-order byte of NPSAP and they become the high order byte of the interrupt vector address. The low-order byte of the interrupt vector address is always $0C_{16}$ for a system call.

The Z8001 takes a new two-word Program Counter value, a Program Counter Segment and a Program Counter Offset, from two memory words whose memory addresses are computed using a segmented New Program Status Area Pointer as follows:

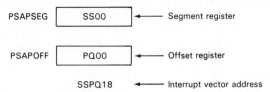

S, P, and Q are any hexadecimal digits; they provide the segment number and the high-order byte for the interrupt vector address, as illustrated above. The low-order byte of the interrupt vector address is always 18_{16}.

The SC instruction leaves the S/N status set to 1, so that the next instruction will be executed in system mode. For the Z8001, the SC instruction leaves the SEG status set to 1, so that the next instruction will be executed in segmented mode.

The SC instruction's object code is left at the top of the Stack as an identifier. Subsequent program logic will pop this word off the Stack and identify the nature of the system call by examining the 8-bit data value provided in the SC instruction operand.

The SC instruction's object code may be illustrated as follows:

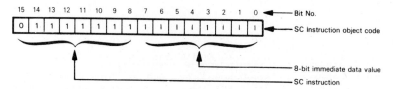

Figure 3-79 illustrates the execution of the SC instruction:

```
SC      DATA;       % AMC syntax
SC      #DATA       ! Zilog syntax !
```

The new Program Counter value is arbitrarily shown equal to $C800_{16}$. The next instruction executed will therefore be taken from memory location $C800_{16}$. The S/N status is set to 1 after the Flag and Control Word has been pushed onto the Stack.

The Z8001 version of the same SC instruction is illustrated in Figure 3-80. Figure 3-80 arbitrarily shows the System Stack Pointer in memory segment 20_{16}, the new Program Counter segment value equal to 03, and the new Program Status Area Pointer in arbitrary segment tt. Instruction execution logic is otherwise identical to Figure 3-79.

Only the SEG and N/S status flags are modified by the SC instruction. Both these status flags are set to 1 for the Z8001. The Z8002 has no SEG status; therefore only its N/S status is set to 1.

SC instruction execution is illustrated in Figures 3-79 and 3-80, for the Z8002 and Z8001 respectively.

The 8-bit immediate data value provided by the SC instruction is shown generally as PP in both figures.

In Figure 3-79 the system stack pointer is shown arbitrarily holding the value 8000_{16}. Since Z8000 stacks begin at the highest memory address, each push causes the Stack Pointer to be decremented by 2, before the word to be stored in the Stack is written into the current "top of stack" memory location. Since the incremented Program Counter value, mmmm + 2, is the first word saved, it is written onto memory location $7FFE_{16}$. The Flag and Control Word is saved next in memory location $7FFC_{16}$. Finally the SC instruction object code is written into memory word $7FFA_{16}$ — which becomes the new "top of system stack". This is the location addressed by CPU register R15S when the SC instruction has completed execution.

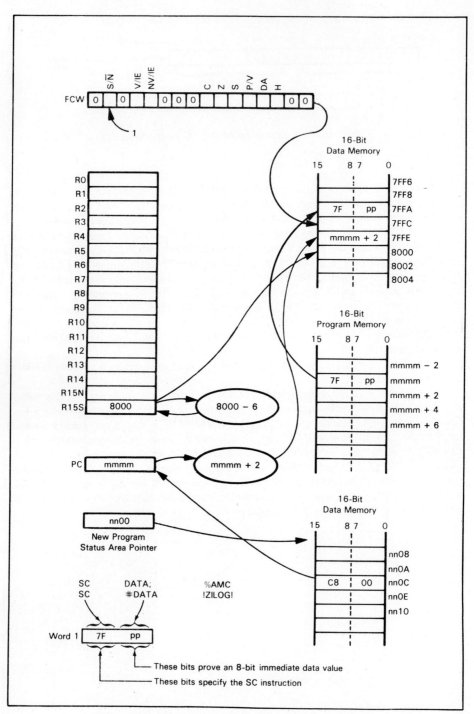

Figure 3-79. Execution of the SC Instruction for the Z8002

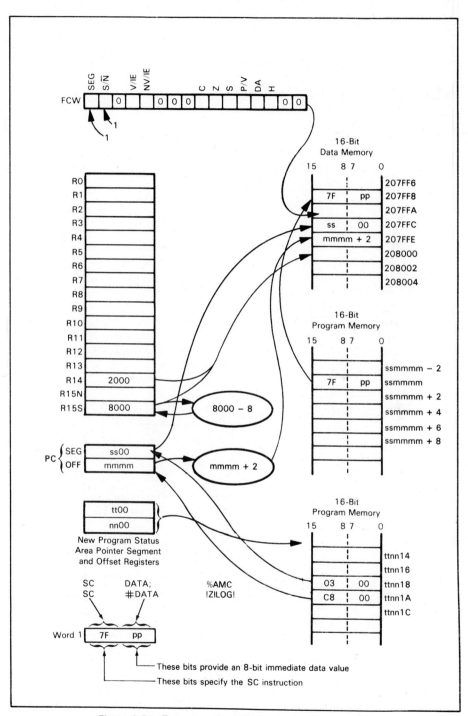

Figure 3-80. Execution of the SC Instruction for the Z8001

SDA — Arithmetic Shift Word

SDAB — Arithmetic Shift Byte

SDAL — Arithmetic Shift Long Word

This is the general format for the SDA, SDAB, and SDAL instructions:

Addressing Options	
dst	src
R	R

```
SDA     dst,src
SDAB    dst,src
SDAL    dst,src
```

The symbol dst is a destination operand which must be specified using direct register addressing. A 16-bit CPU register must be specified for SDA; an 8-bit CPU register must be specified SDAB; a 32-bit CPU register must be specified for SDAL.

The symbol src is a source operand which must be specified as a 16-bit CPU register using direct register addressing.

The SDA, SDAB, and SDAL instructions perform left or right arithmetic shifts on the contents of the destination operand CPU register. Single bit left and right arithmetic shifts may be illustrated for 8-bit, 16-bit and 32-bit CPU registers as follows:

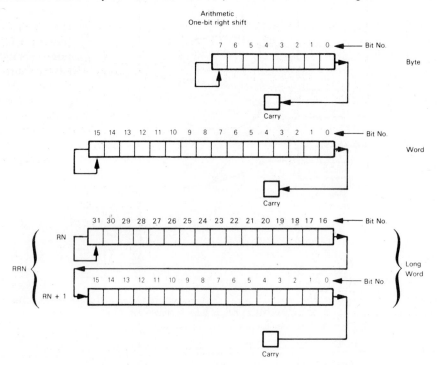

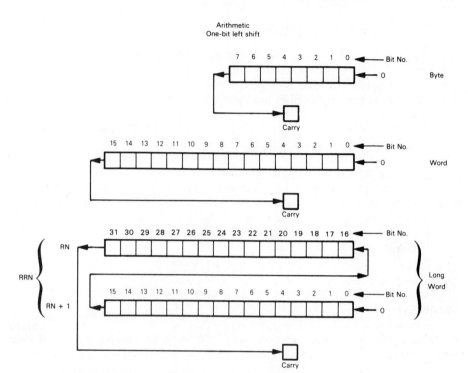

The source operand 16-bit CPU register specifies the number of shifts which are to be performed, together with the direction of the shift. If the source operand CPU register contains a negative number, a right shift is performed. If the source operand CPU register contains a positive number, a left shift is performed. For SDAB the source operand CPU register may contain values ranging between −8 and +8. For SDA, values ranging between −16 and +16 are allowed. For SDAL, shift specifications ranging between −32 and +32 are legal. Shift specifications outside of the allowed range cause undefined results. A shift specification of 0 is allowed; this leaves the destination operand CPU register contents unaltered, but Status flags are modified.

SDA, SDAB, and SDAL instructions' object codes may be illustrated as follows:

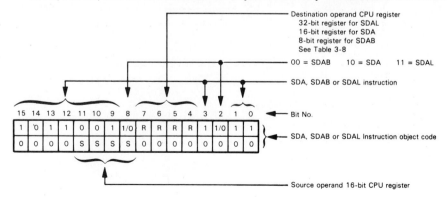

The SDA, SDAB, and SDAL instructions modify the C, Z, S, and P/V status flags.

The Carry status (C) will hold the last bit shifted out of the destination operand CPU register. If a zero shift is specified, the Carry status is not modified.

The Zero status (Z) is set to 1 if the destination operand CPU Register contains a zero value after the specified shift has been performed. The Zero status is reset to 0 otherwise.

The Sign status is set equal to the high-order bit of the destination operand CPU register, after the shift has been performed.

The Overflow status (P/V) is set to 1 if the destination operand high-order bit changes during any shift step. If the high-order bit never changes, the Overflow status is reset to 0. The high-order bit cannot change on a right shift, since the right shift propagates the high-order bit to the right; therefore, the right shift always resets P/V to 0. The arithmetic left shift does modify the high-order bit. If the left shift ever changes the content of the high-order bit, on any step of a multi-step shift, the P/V status is set to 1.

Consider the SDA instruction:

```
SDA     R7,R0;          % AMC syntax
SDA     R7,R0           ! Zilog syntax !
```

If CPU register R7 initially contains $C23A_{16}$, and R0 holds $FFFD_{16}$ ($= -3$), then when the illustrated instruction is executed, this is what happens:

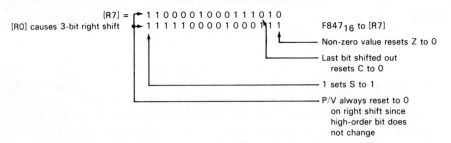

If R0 contained $+3$, the following 3-bit left shift would be performed:

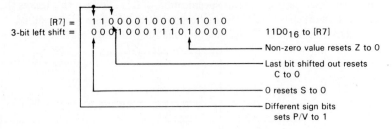

SDL — Logical Shift Word

SDLB — Logical Shift Byte

SDLL — Logical Shift Long Word

This is the general format for the SDL, SDLB, and SDLL instructions:

Addressing Options	
dst	src
R	R

SDL   dst,src
SDLB   dst,src
SDLL   dst,src

The symbol dst is a destination operand which must be specified using direct register addressing. A 16-bit CPU register must be specified for SDL; an 8-bit CPU register must be specified for SDLB; a 32-bit CPU register must be specified for SDLL.

The symbol src is a source operand which must be specified as a 16-bit CPU register using direct register addressing.

The SDL, SDLB, and SDLL instructions perform left or right logical shifts on the contents of the destination operand CPU register. A single bit right logical shift may be illustrated for 8-bit, 16-bit and 32-bit CPU registers as follows:

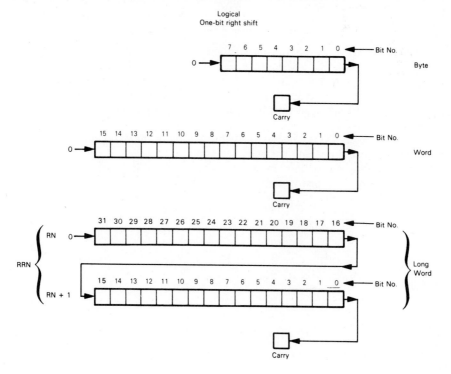

There is no difference between arithmetic and logical left shifts. The one-bit arithmetic left shift illustrated for the SDA/SDAB/SDAL instructions is also a one-bit logical left shift.

The source operand 16-bit CPU register specifies the number of shifts which are to be performed, together with the direction of the shift. If the source operand CPU register contains a negative number, a right shift is performed. If the source operand CPU register contains a positive number, a left shift is performed. For SDLB the source operand CPU register may contain values ranging between -8 and $+8$. For SDL values ranging between -16 and $+16$ are allowed. For SDLL shift specifications ranging between -32 and $+32$ are legal. Shift specifications outside of the allowed range cause undefined results. A shift specification of 0 is allowed; this leaves the destination operand CPU register contents unaltered, but Status flags are modified.

SLD, SDLB, and SDLL instructions' object codes may be illustrated as follows:

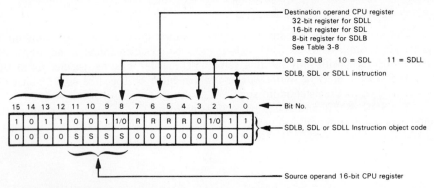

The SDL, SDLB, and SDLL instructions modify the C, Z, S, and P/V statuses.

The Carry status (C) will hold the last bit shifted out of the destination operand CPU register. If a zero shift is specified, the Carry status is not modified.

The Zero status (Z) is set to 1 if the destination operand CPU register contains a zero value after the specified shift has been performed. The Zero status is reset to 0 otherwise.

The Sign status (S) is equal to the high-order bit of the destination operand CPU register after the shift operand has been performed.

The Overflow status (P/V) is modified, but its value is undefined.

Consider the SDL instruction:

```
SDL     R7,R0;          % AMC syntax
SDL     R7,R0           ! Zilog syntax !
```

If CPU register R7 initially contains $C23A_{16}$, and R0 holds $FFFD_{16}$ ($= -3$), then when the illustrated instruction is executed, this is what happens:

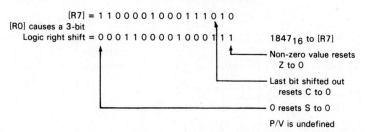

If R0 contains $+3$, the execution of the SDL instruction will be identical to the previously illustrated SDA instruction, except that the value of P/V is undefined.

SET — Set a Bit in a Word

SETB — Set a Bit in a Byte

This is the general format for the SET and SETB instructions:

Addressing Options	
dst	**src**
R	IM
IR	IM
DA	IM
X	IM
R	R

SET   dst,src
SETB   dst,src

The symbol dst is a destination operand which can be specified using any standard operand addressing method with the exception of immediate addressing. (See Figure 3-26.)

The symbol src is a source operand which is normally specified as an immediate data value, but can also be specified using direct register addressing. In the latter case, any 16-bit CPU register can be specified for RES, but one of the eight 16-bit CPU registers R0-R7 must be specified for RESB. If the source operand is a CPU register, the destination operand must also be a CPU register.

When the SET or SETB instruction is executed, one bit of the destination word (for SET) or byte (for SETB) is set to 1. The source operand specifies the number of the bit which is to be set. Usually the source operand is specified as an immediate data value; in this case, the source operand can have a value between 0 and 15 for SET, or it can range between 0 and 7 for SETB. The source operand can be a CPU register, but only if the destination operand is a CPU register also. For SETB, the three low-order bits of the source operand CPU register identify the bit number in the destination operand which will be set to 1. For SET, the four low-order bits of the source operand CPU register identify the bit number in the destination operand which is to be set to 1.

The SET and SETB instruction object codes may be illustrated as follows:

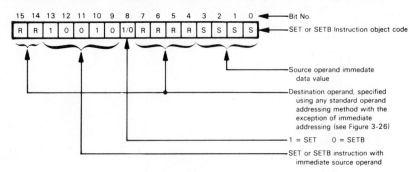

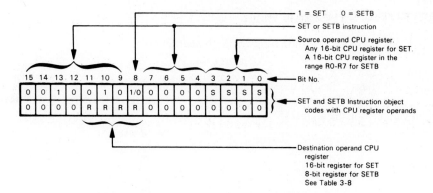

No status flags are modified by the SET or SETB instruction.

When the instruction:

```
SET     #4020^,3;        % AMC syntax
SET     %4020,#3         ! Zilog syntax !
```

is executed, bit 3 of the memory word with address 4020_{16} is set to 1.

When the instruction:

```
SETB    RH3,R2;          % AMC syntax
SETB    RH3,R2           ! Zilog syntax !
```

is executed, the bit of 8-bit Register RH3 specified by 16-bit Register R2 is set to 1. The low-order three bits of Register R2 specify the bit within Register RH3 which will be set to 1. For example, if Register R2 contains 0003, then bit 3 of Register RH3 will be set to 1.

The SET and SETB instructions number bits as illustrated throughout this book, with the low-order bit being bit number 0, and the high-order bit being bit number 7 for a byte, or 15 for a word.

SETFLG — Set Status Flags

This is the general format for the SET instruction:

SETFLG flags

The word "flags" may be the designation for one or more of the status flags: Carry, Zero, Sign, Parity, and Overflow. The Zilog and AMC assemblers use different abbreviations for the statuses:

Status	Zilog Syntax	AMC Syntax
Carry	C	CY
Zero	Z	ZR
Sign	S	SGN
Parity*	P	PY
Overflow*	V	OV

*Parity and Overflow are the same flag.

SETFLG sets to 1 the identified status bits of the Flag and Control word. You can list the status flags in any sequence.

The SETFLG instruction's object code may be illustrated as follows:

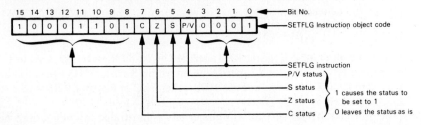

The status flags modified by the SETFLG instruction will depend on the flags specified in the operand field. No flags other than those specifically identified are modified.

The instruction:

```
SETFLG    ZR;              % AMC syntax
SETFLG    Z                ! Zilog syntax !
```

will set just the Zero status. Other statuses are not modified. On the other hand, the instruction:

```
SETFLG    PY,SGN,ZR,CY;    % AMC syntax
SETFLG    P,S,Z,C          ! Zilog syntax !
```

will set all four status flags to 1.

SIN — Special Input Word

SINB — Special Input Byte

SIND — Special Input Word and Decrement

SINDB — Special Input Byte and Decrement

SINDR — Special Input Word, Decrement and Repeat

SINDRB — Special Input Byte, Decrement and Repeat

SINI — Special Input Word and Increment

SINIB — Special Input Byte and Increment

SINIR — Special Input Word, Increment and Repeat

SINIRB — Special Input Byte, Increment and Repeat

The Z8000 special input instructions are identical to the normal input instructions, except that a "special input" status signal is output by the Z8000 microprocessor during the special input machine cycle, and that byte forms of special input instructions must address an even numbered port.

The special input instructions are intended to be used with external memory management hardware. See Chapter 13 for a discussion of memory management.

For descriptions of the special input instructions, see the corresponding normal input instruction descriptions given earlier in this chapter, as follows:

SIN/SINB see IN/INB. Note that the IN and INB instructions have two formats; one format specifies the I/O port using register indirect addressing; the other format specifies the I/O port using direct addressing. The SIN and SINB instructions specify the I/O port using direct addressing only.

SIND/SINDB see IND/INDB

SINDR/SINDRB see INDR/INDRB

SINI/SINIB see INI/INIB

SINIR/SINIRB see INIR/INIRB

Instruction object codes for the special input instructions are, in every case, identical to the equivalent normal input instructions' object code, except that for the special input instructions the low-order bit of the first instruction object code word is 1.

SLA - Arithmetic Left Shift Word

SLAB — Arithmetic Left Shift Byte

SLAL — Arithmetic Left Shift Long Word

The SLA/SLAB/SLAL instructions execute exactly the same operations as the left shift portion of the SDA/SDAB/SDAL, or the SDL/SDLB/SDLL instructions. However, SLA/SLAB/SLAL specify the number of bit positions to be shifted via an immediate source operand.

This is the general format for the SLA, SLAB, and SLAL instructions:

Addressing Options		SLA dst,data
dst	data	SLA dst,data
		SLAB dst,data
R	IM	SLAL dst,data

The symbol dst is a destination operand which must be specified using direct register addressing. A 16-bit CPU register must be specified for SLA; an 8-bit CPU register must be specified SLAB; a 32-bit CPU register must be specified for SLAL.

The symbol data is an immediate source operand; its value must lie between 0 and 8 for SLAB, between 0 and 16 for SLA, and between 0 and 32 for SLAL. The word data may be omitted, in which case a value of 1 is assumed.

The SLA, SLAB, and SLAL instructions perform left arithmetic shifts, which are identical to left logical shifts, on the contents of the destination operand CPU register. A single bit left shift is illustrated for 8-bit, 16-bit, and 32-bit CPU registers in the SDA/SDAB/SDAL instruction description.

The immediate source operand specifies the number of left shifts to be performed. Shift specifications outside of the allowed range cause undefined results. A shift specification of 0 is allowed; this leaves the destination operand CPU register contents unaltered, but Status flags are modified.

SLA, SLAB, and SLAL instructions' object codes may be illustrated as follows:

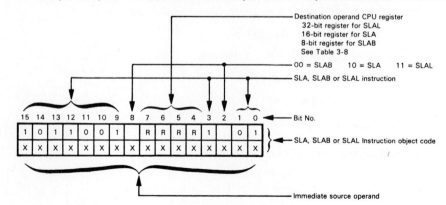

The SLA, SLAB, and SLAL instructions modify the C, Z, S, and P/V status flags.

The Carry status (C) will hold the last bit shifted out of the destination operand CPU register. If a zero shift is specified then the Carry status is not modified.

The Zero status (Z) is set to 1 if the destination operand CPU register contains a zero value after the specified shift has been performed. The Zero status is reset to 0 otherwise.

The Sign status (S) is equal to the high-order bit of the destination operand CPU register after the shift operand has been performed.

The Overflow status (P/V) is set to 1 if the destination operand high-order bit changes during any shift step. If the high-order bit never changes, then the Overflow status is reset to 0.

The SLA instruction:

```
SLA     R7,3;          % AMC syntax
SLA     R7,#3          ! Zilog syntax !
```

is equivalent to the SDA instruction:

```
SDA     R7,R0;         % AMC syntax
SDA     R7,R0          ! Zilog syntax !
```

when R0 contains 3. This is illustrated in the preceding SDA instruction description.

SLL — Logical Left Shift Word

SLLB — Logical Left Shift Byte

SLLL — Logical Left Shift Long Word

THE SLL/SLLB/SLLL instructions are identical in every way to the SLA/SLAB/SLAL instructions which we just described, except that the SLLL/SLLB/SLLL instructions leave the P/V status undefined. For descriptions of SLL, SLLB and SLLL, therefore, see SLA, SLAB and SLAL, respectively.

SLL, SLLB and SLLL instruction object codes may be illustrated as follows:

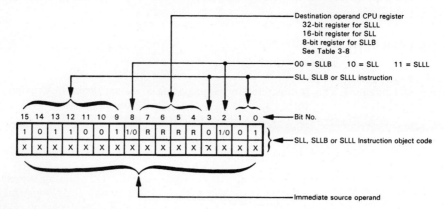

SOTDR — Special Output Word, Decrement and Repeat

SOTDRB — Special Output Byte, Decrement and Repeat

SOTIR — Special Output Word, Increment and Repeat

SOTIRB — Special Output Byte, Increment and Repeat

SOUT — Special Output Word

SOUTB — Special Output Byte

SOUTD — Special Output Word and Decrement

SOUTDB — Special Output Byte and Decrement

SOUTI — Special Output Word and Increment

SOUTIB — Special Output Byte and Increment

The special output instructions are identical to the equivalent output instructions, except that the Z8000 microprocessor outputs a "special output" status during system output machine cycles, and that the byte forms of special output instructions must address an even numbered port.

The special output instructions are intended to be used with external memory management hardware. See Chapter 13 for a discussion of memory management.

For descriptions of the special output instructions, see the equivalent output instruction descriptions given earlier in this chapter, as follows:

SOTDR/SOTDRB see OTDR/OTDRB

SOTIR/SOTIRB see OTIR/OTIRB

SOUT/SOUTB see OUT/OUTB.

Note, however, that the OUT and OUTB instructions have two versions, where the source operand I/O port may be specified using register indirect addressing or direct addressing. The SOUT/SOUTB instructions are only available with direct addressing used to specify the source operand I/O port.

SOUTD/SOUTDB see OUTD/OUTDB

SOUTI/SOUTIB see OUTI/OUTIB

System output instruction object codes are identical to equivalent normal output instruction object codes except that for system output instructions the low-order bit of the first object code word is 1.

SRA — Arithmetic Right Shift Word

SRAB — Arithmetic Right Shift Byte

SRAL — Arithmetic Right Shift Long Word

The SRA/SRAB/SRAL instructions execute exactly the same operations as the right shift portion of the SDA/SDAB/SDAL instructions; however, SRA/SRAB/SRAL specify the number of bit positions to be shifted via an immediate source operand.

This is the general format for the SRA, SRAB, and SRAL instructions:

Addressing Options	
dst	data
R	IM

SRA	dst,data
SRAB	dst,data
SRAL	dst,data

The symbol dst is a destination operand which must be specified using direct register addressing. A 16-bit CPU register must be specified for SRA; an 8-bit CPU register must be specified SRAB; a 32-bit CPU register must be specified for SRAL.

The word data is an immediate source operand; its value must lie between 0 and 8 for SRAB, between 0 and 16 for SRA, and between 0 and 32 for SRAL. The word data may be omitted, in which case a value of 1 is assumed.

The SRA, SRAB, and SRAL instructions perform right arithmetic shifts on the contents of the destination operand CPU register. A single bit right arithmetic shift is illustrated for 8-bit, 16-bit and 32-bit CPU registers in the SDA/SDAB/SDAL instruction description.

The immediate source operand specifies the number of right shifts to be performed. Shift specifications outside of the allowed range cause undefined results. A shift specification of 0 is allowed; this leaves the destination operand CPU register contents unaltered, but Status flags are modified.

SRA, SRAB, and SRAL instructions' object codes may be illustrated as follows:

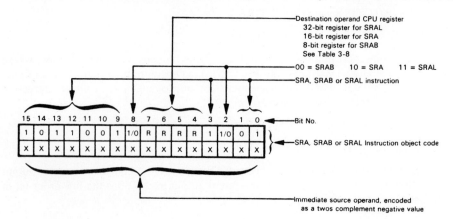

The word data is specified as a positive number in the operand field of the SRA/ SRAB/SRAL instruction, but this positive number is recorded in the second word of the instruction object code in its twos complement form. This is compatible with the shift magnitude and direction format used by the SDA and SDL instructions.

The SRA, SRAB, and SRAL instructions modify the C, Z, S, and P/V statuses.

The Carry status (C) will hold the last bit shifted out of the destination operand CPU register. If a zero shift is specified, the Carry status is not modified.

The Zero status (Z) is set to 1 if the destination operand CPU register contains a zero value after the specified shift has been performed. The Zero status is reset to 0 otherwise.

The Sign status is equal to the high-order bit of the destination operand CPU register after the shift operand has been performed.

The Overflow status is reset to 0. This is because the high-order bit of the destination operand never changes during an arithmetic right shift.

Consider the SRA instruction:

```
SRA     R7,3;           % AMC syntax
SRA     R7,#3           ! Zilog syntax !
```

is equivalent to the instruction:

```
SDA     R7,R0;          % AMC syntax
SDA     R7,R0           ! Zilog syntax !
```

when R0 contains FFFD (-3). This option is illustrated in the preceding SDA instruction description.

SRL — Logical Right Shift Word

SRLB — Logical Right Shift Byte

SRLL — Logical Right Shift Long Word

This is the general format for the SRL, SRLB, and SRLL instructions:

Addressing Options	
dst	data
R	IM

SRL   dst,data
SRLB   dst,data
SRLL   dst,data

The symbol dst is a destination operand which must be specified using direct register addressing. A 16-bit CPU register must be specified for SRL; an 8-bit CPU register must be specified SRLB; a 32-bit CPU register must be specified for SRLL.

The word data is an immediate source operand; its value must lie between 0 and 8 for SRLB, between 0 and 16 for SRL, and between 0 and 32 for SRLL. The word data may be omitted, in which case a value of 1 is assumed.

The SRL, SRLB, and SRLL instructions perform right logical shifts on the contents of the destination operand CPU register. A single bit right logical shift is illustrated for 8-bit, 16-bit and 32-bit CPU registers in the SDL/SDLB/SDLL instruction description.

The immediate operand specifies the number of right shifts to be performed. Shift specifications outside of the allowed range cause undefined results. A shift specification of 0 is allowed; this leaves the destination operand CPU register contents unaltered, but Status flags are modified.

SRL, SRLB, and SRLL instructions' object codes may be illustrated as follows:

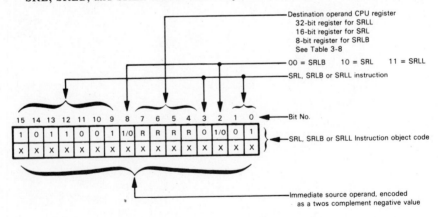

The word data is specified as a positive number in the operand field of the SRL/ SRLB/SRLL instruction, but this positive number is recorded in the second word of the instruction object code in its twos complement form. This is compatible with the shift magnitude and direction format used by the SDA and SDL instructions.

The SRL, SRLB, and SRLL instructions modify the C, Z, and S statuses. The P/V status is left undefined.

The Carry status (C) will hold the last bit shifted out of the destination operand CPU register. If a zero shift is specified then the Carry status is not modified.

The Zero status (Z) is set to 1 if the destination operand CPU register contains a zero value after the specified shift has been performed. The Zero status is reset to 0 otherwise.

The Sign status (S) is equal to the high-order bit of the destination operand CPU register bit after the shift operand has been performed.

The Overflow status (P/V) is modified, but its value is undefined.

Consider the SRL instruction:

```
SRL     R7,3;           % AMC syntax
SRL     R7,#3           ! Zilog syntax !
```

This instruction executes the same operation as:

```
SDL     R7,R0;          % AMC syntax
SDL     R7,R0           ! Zilog syntax !
```

when R0 contains $FFFD_{16}$ (-3). This SRL instruction's execution is identical to the SDL illustration.

SUB — Subtract Words

SUBB — Subtract Bytes

SUBL — Subtract Long Words

This is the general format for the SUB, SUBB, and SUBL instructions:

Addressing Options			
dst	src		
R	R	SUB	dst,src
R	IM	SUBB	dst,src
R	IR	SUBL	dst,src
R	DA		
R	X		

The symbol dst is a destination operand which must be specified using direct register addressing. A 16-bit CPU register must be specified for SUB; an 8-bit CPU register must be specified for SUBB; a 32-bit CPU register must be specified for SUBL.

The symbol src is a source operand which can be specified using any standard operand addressing method (see Figure 3-26).

The source and destination operands are both assumed to be twos complement, signed binary numbers. When SUB, SUBB, or SUBL instruction is executed, the source operand is subtracted from the destination operand using twos complement signed binary arithmetic. The result is returned in the destination operand CPU register whose prior contents are lost. The source operand is not modified.

The SUB, SUBB, and SUBL instructions' object code may be illustrated as follows:

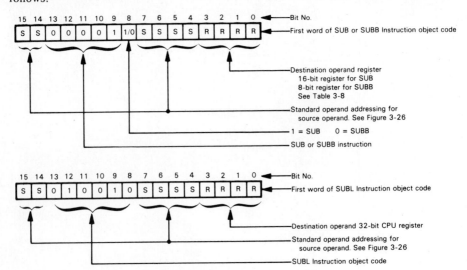

The C, Z, S and P/V status flags are modified by the SUB, SUBB and SUBL instructions. In addition, the SUBB instruction modifies the H status and sets the DA status to 1.

All status flags are modified in the standard way except for the Carry status (C) whose logic is inverted to indicate a borrow. If twos complement addition generates a Carry out of the high-order bit, this is interpreted as a "no-borrow" and the Carry status is reset. When no carry is generated out of the high-order bit, the Carry status is set to indicate a borrow.

There is not a conceptual difference between subtract instruction logic and add instruction execution logic. For illustrations of SUB, SUBB, and SUBL instructions, therefore, see the equivalent ADD, ADDB, and ADDL instructions which are illustrated in Figures 3-29, and 3-30. Remember that SUBB sets DA to 1.

Consider execution of the SUB instruction:

```
SUB       R3,R4^;          % AMC syntax
SUB       R3,@R4           ! Zilog syntax !
```

If register R3 initially contains $862A_{16}$, and the memory word addressed by Register R4 initially contains $216A_{16}$, this is what happens when the SUB instruction illustrated above is executed:

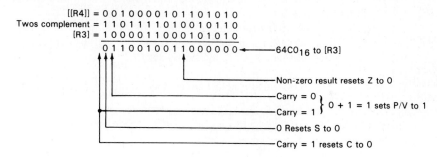

TCC — Test Condition Code and Return Result in a Word Register

TCCB — Test Condition Code and Return Result in a Byte Register

This is the general format for the TCC and TCCB instructions:

Addressing Options		
dst	TCC	cc,dst
	TCCB	cc,dst
R		

The symbol dst is a destination operand which must be specified using direct register addressing. A 16-bit CPU register must be specified for TCC; an 8-bit CPU register must be specified for TCCB.

The symbol cc is a condition code which must equal one of the mnemonics shown in the code column of Table 3-4.

When the TCC or TCCB instruction is executed, the condition code specified by cc is compared to status flag settings in the Flag and Control Word. If there is a match, the low-order bit of the destination CPU register is set to 1; otherwise this bit is left unaltered.

The TCC and TCCB instruction object codes may be illustrated as follows:

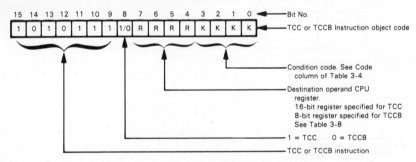

No status flags are modified by the TCC or TCCB instruction.

The TCCB instruction:

```
TCCB    ZR,RH0 ;        % AMC syntax
TCCB    Z,RH0           ! Zilog syntax !
```

will set the low-order bit of RH0 to 1 if the Zero status is set to 1. The low-order bit of RH0 will be left unaltered otherwise.

TEST — Test a Word

TESTB — Test a Byte

TESTL — Test a Long Word

This is the general format for the TEST, TESTB and TESTL instructions:

Addressing Options
dst
R IR DA X

```
TEST    dst
TESTB   dst
TESTL   dst
```

The symbol dst is a destination operand which can be specified using any standard operand addressing method with the exception of immediate addressing. (See Figure 3-26.)

The three TEST instructions modify status flags based on the contents of their destination operands. Status flags reflect the result of ORing the destination operand with zero.

The three TEST instructions' object codes may be illustrated as follows:

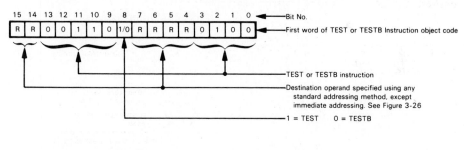

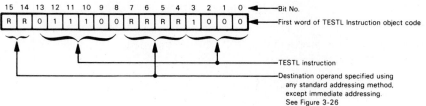

The Z and S status flags are modified by all three TEST instructions. In addition, TESTB modifies the P/V status to reflect the parity of the destination operand; P/V is set to 1 for even parity and reset to 0 for odd parity.

When the instruction:

```
TEST    #4800^;      % AMC syntax
TEST    %4800        ! Zilog syntax !
```

if memory word 4800_{16} contains $423A_{16}$ this is what happens:

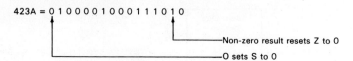

The following TESTB instruction:

```
TESTB   SEGADDR;          % AMC syntax
TESTB   <<%30>>%4800      ! Zilog syntax !
```

will test byte 4800_{16} in segment 30_{16}. If this byte contains $3A_{16}$, statuses will be modified as follows:

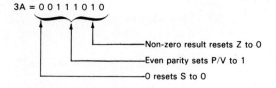

TRDB — Translate and Decrement

This is the general format for the TRDB instruction:

Addressing Options		
dst	**src**	**r**
IR	IR	R

TRDB   dst,src,r

The symbol dst and src are destination and source operand address registers. 16-bit address registers must be specified in non-segmented mode; 32-bit address registers must be specified in segmented mode.

The symbol r is a Counter Register. A 16-bit CPU register must be specified using direct register addressing.

The TRDB instruction has been designed to translate 8-bit characters from one code to another. The destination address register identifies the character to be changed. The source address register identifies the base (lowest memory address) of a byte table containing the new character codes. The contents of the addressed destination byte are treated as an unsigned 8-bit index into the translation table. The sum of this index and the source operand address identifies a byte in the translation table whose contents replaces the original destination byte. The destination address register and Counter Register are both decremented by 1. This leaves the destination register addressing the next sequential byte to be translated. When the Counter Register decrements to 0, the Overflow status is set to 1. The Overflow status is cleared otherwise.

8-bit CPU register RH1 is used by the TRDB instruction. RH1 contents are left undefined when TRDB completes execution.

The TRDB instructions object code may be illustrated as follows:

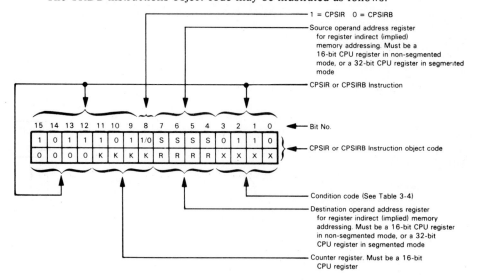

The TRDB instruction modifies the Overflow status. This status is set to 1 when the Counter Register decrements to 0; it is reset to 0 otherwise. The Zero status is left undefined. Other status flags are not affected.

Figure 3-81 illustrates execution of the TRDB instruction:

```
TRDB      R2^R12^,R8;       % AMC syntax
TRDB      @R2,@R12,R8       ! Zilog syntax !
```

Figure 3-81 illustrates a translation table that converts ASCII characters to their EBCDIC equivalents. Every translation table address is computed by adding an ASCII character code to 8000_{16}. Therefore 8000_{16} becomes the translation table base address; it is held in R12, the source operand address register. Every byte in the translation table corresponds to an ASCII character; the character whose ASCII code, added to 8000_{16}, generates the translation table byte address. Every byte in the translation table contains the EBCDIC code for its corresponding ASCII character.

The TRDB instruction requires the presence of some translation table such as the one illustrated in Figure 3-81.

The TRDB instruction in Figure 3-81 arbitrarily shows a destination address of 4004_{16}; there is no special significance to this address. At memory location 4004_{16} the value 44_{16} is to be found; this happens to be the ASCII code for "D". When the TRDB instruction is executed, the original contents of the destination memory location, in this case 44_{16}, is added to the source base address, 8000_{16}. The sum, 8044_{16}, addresses an entry in the translation table. This entry contains the value $C4_{16}$, which is loaded into the destination operand byte, overwriting 44_{16}, the original destination operand. $C4_{16}$ is the EBCDIC code for "D". Thus the contents of memory byte 4004_{16} has been translated from an ASCII code to its EBCDIC code.

The destination operand address 4004_{16} is decremented, along with the contents of counter register R8. Thus R2 addresses the next sequential destination data memory byte and the Counter Register indicates that 27_{16} bytes remain to be processed.

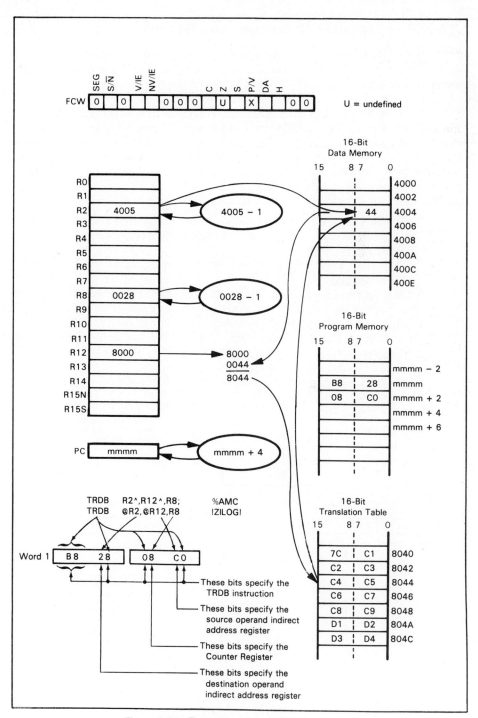

Figure 3-81. Execution of the TRDB Instruction

TRDRB — Translate Decrement and Repeat

The TRDRB instruction is identical to the TRDB instruction which we just described, except that TRDRB continues to re-execute until the counter register contents decrement to zero.

This is the general format for the TRDRB instruction:

Addressing Options		
dst	src	r
IR	IR	R

TRDRB   dst,src,r

The symbols dst and src are destination and source operand address registers. A 16-bit CPU register must be specified in non-segmented mode; a 32-bit CPU register must be specified in segmented mode.

The symbol r is a counter register. A 16-bit CPU register must be specified using direct register addressing.

TRDRB instruction execution is identical to TRDB, except that TRDRB continues to re-execute until the Counter Register contents decrements to zero. Thus a block of contiguous bytes is translated by a single execution of the TRDRB instruction. The Counter Register identifies the number of bytes in the data block to be translated. The first translated destination byte has the highest memory address and the last translated destination byte has the lowest memory address.

The TRDRB instruction object code may be illustrated as follows:

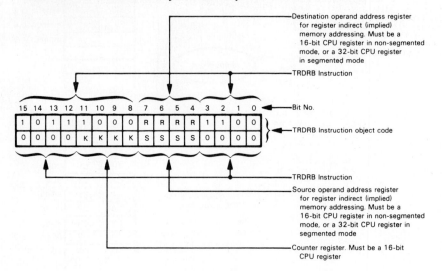

The TRDRB instruction leaves the Z status undefined. The Overflow status will be set to 1 when the TRDRB instruction completes execution.

Like TRDB, TRDRB leaves an undefined value in 8-bit register RH1. Prior contents of register RH1 are lost.

The TRDRB equivalent of the TRDB instruction illustrated in Figure 3-81 is:

```
TRDRB    R2^,R12^,R8;     % AMC syntax
TRDRB    @R2,@R12,R2      ! Zilog syntax !
```

The single TRDRB instruction is equivalent to the instruction pair:

```
LOOP:    TRDB    R2^,R12^,R8;     % AMC syntax
         JR      NOV,LOOP;

LOOP:    TRDB    @R2,@R12,R8      ! Zilog syntax !
         JR      NOV,LOOP
```

With reference to Figure 3-81, the equivalent TRDRB instruction, when executed once, would translate an entire block of ASCII characters to their EBCDIC equivalents, whereas the TRDB instruction would have to be re-executed once for each translated character. Conversely, if characters need to be processed additionally during translation, instructions can be inserted appropriately between TRDB and JR; but the TRDRB instruction must be allowed to execute to its conclusion.

Once a TRDRB instruction starts to execute, it could conceivably continue executing for a long time if it were translating a long string. This could present interrupt logic with problems. In order to prevent any such problems, the Z8000 allows interrupts to be acknowledged between each iterative execution of the TRDRB instruction. Furthermore, the Program Counter value saved during the interrupt acknowledgement process is the address of the TRDRB instruction, so that execution of this instruction will continue from the point of interrupt, after the interrupt has been serviced. Seven clock periods must be added to the TRDRB instruction's execution time to account for each interrupt acknowledged during the instruction's execution.

TRIB — Translate Byte and Increment

The TRIB instruction is identical to TRDB, except that TRIB increments the destination address which TRDB decrements.

This is the general format for the TRDB instruction:

Addressing Options		
dst	**src**	**r**
IR	IR	R

TRIB   dst,src,r

The symbols dst and src are destination and source operand address registers. 16-bit address registers must be specified in non-segmented mode; 32-bit address registers must be specified in segmented mode.

The symbol r is a Counter Register. A 16-bit CPU register must be specified using direct register addressing.

The TRIB instruction has been designed to translate 8-bit characters from one code to another. The destination address register identifies the character to be changed. The source address register identifies the base (lowest memory address) of a byte table containing the new character codes. The contents of the addressed destination byte are treated as an unsigned 8-bit index into the translation table. The sum of this index and the source operand address identifies a byte in the translation table whose contents replace the original destination byte. The destination address is incremented by 1. The Counter Register is decremented by 1. This leaves the destination register addressing the next sequential byte to be translated. When the Counter Register decrements to 0, the Overflow status is set to 1. The Overflow status is cleared otherwise.

8-bit CPU register RH1 is used by the TRIB instruction. RH1 contents are left undefined when TRIB completes execution.

The TRIB instructions' object code may be illustrated as follows:

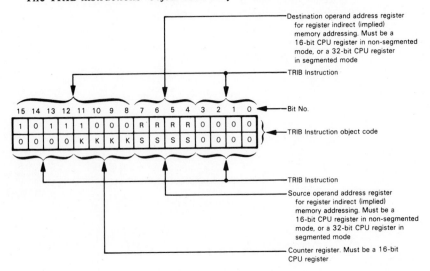

The TRIB instruction modifies the Overflow status. This status is set to 1 when the Counter Register decrements to 0; it is reset to 0 otherwise. The Zero status is left undefined. Other status flags are not affected.

This is the TRIB version of the TRDB instruction illustrated in Figure 3-81:

```
TRIB     R2^,R12^,R8;     % AMC syntax
TRIB     @R2,@R12,R8      ! Zilog syntax !
```

The only difference between the two instructions is that register R2 contents will be incremented for TRIB, where it is shown being decremented for TRDB. This means that the destination bytes are translated in the opposite direction. The next destination byte to be translated will be at the next higher memory address.

TRIRB — Translate Decrement and Repeat

The TRIRB instruction is identical to the TRDRB instruction, except that TRIRB increments the destination address which TRDRB decrements.

The TRIRB instruction is also identical to the TRIB instruction, which we just described, except that TRIRB continues to re-execute until the Counter Register contents decrements to zero.

This is the general format for the TRIRB instruction:

Addressing Options		
dst	src	r
IR	IR	R

TRIRB   dst,src,r

The symbols dst and src are destination and source operand address registers. A 16-bit CPU register must be specified in non-segmented mode; a 32-bit CPU register must be specified in segmented mode.

The symbol r is a counter register. A 16-bit CPU register must be specified using direct register addressing.

TRIRB instruction execution is identical to TRIB, except that TRIRB continues to re-execute until the Counter Register content decrements to zero. Thus a block of contiguous bytes are translated by a single execution of the TRIRB instruction. The Counter Register identifies the number of bytes in the data block to be translated. The first translated destination byte has the lowest memory address and the last translated destination byte has the highest memory address.

The TRIRB instruction object code may be illustrated as follows:

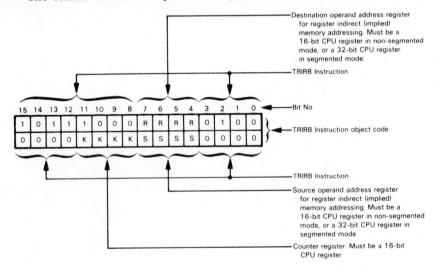

The TRIRB instruction leaves the Z status undefined. The Overflow status will be left set to 1 when the TRIRB instruction completes execution.

Like TRIB, TRIRB leaves an undefined value in 8-bit register RH1. Prior contents of RH1 are lost.

The TRIRB equivalent of the TRDB instruction illustrated in Figure 3-81 is:

```
          TRIRB    R2^,R12^,R8;      % AMC syntax
          TRIRB    @R2,@R12,R8       ! Zilog syntax !
```

The single TRIRB instruction is equivalent to the instruction pair:

```
LOOP:     TRIB     R2^,R12^,R8;      % AMC syntax
          JR       NOV,LOOP;

LOOP:     TRIB     @R2,@R12,R8       ! Zilog syntax !
          JR       NOV,LOOP
```

With reference to Figure 3-81, the equivalent TRIRB instruction, when executed once, would translate an entire block of ASCII characters to their EBCDIC equivalents, whereas the TRDB instruction would have to be re-executed once for each translated character. Conversely, if characters need to be processed additionally during translation, instructions can be inserted appropriately between TRIB and JR; but the TRIRB instruction must be allowed to execute to its conclusion. The TRIRB instruction would translate a block of contiguous bytes.

Once a TRIRB instruction starts to execute, it could conceivably continue executing for a long time if it were translating a long string. This could present interrupt logic with problems. In order to prevent any such problems, the Z8000 allows interrupts to be acknowledged between each iterative execution of the TRIRB instruction. Furthermore, the Program Counter value saved during the interrupt acknowledgement process is the address of the TRIRB instruction, so that execution of this instruction will continue from the point of interrupt, after the interrupt has been serviced. Seven clock periods must be added to the TRIRB instruction's execution time to account for each interrupt acknowledged during the instruction's execution.

TRTDB — Translate Test and Decrement

This instruction is identical to TRDB except that the selected translation table byte is loaded into 8-bit register RH1; the destination memory location is not modified.

This is the general format for the TRTDB instruction:

Addressing Options		
src1	src2	r
IR	IR	R

TRTDB   src1,src2,r

The symbols src1 and src2 are a pair of memory address registers. 16-bit CPU registers must be specified in non-segmented mode; 32-bit CPU registers must be specified in segmented mode.

The symbol r is a counter register which must be specified as a 16-bit CPU register.

The TRTDB instruction uses a translation table of the type described for the TRDB instruction. When the TRTDB instruction is executed, a translation table address is computed by summing the address specified in src2 with the contents of the memory byte addressed by src1. The contents of the addressed translation table byte is loaded into 8-bit register RH1. The source operands themselves are not modified. The Z status is set to 1 if RH1 contains 0; the Z status is reset to 0 otherwise.

The src1 address register and the Counter Register contents are both decremented by 1. If the Counter Register contains 0 after being decremented, the Overflow status is set to 1; the Overflow status is reset to 0 otherwise.

The TRTDB instruction object code may be illustrated as follows:

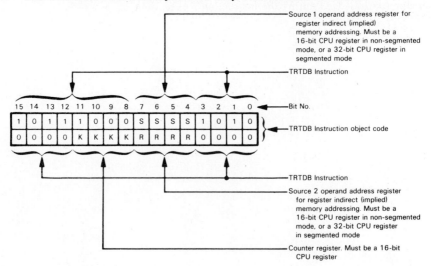

The TRTDB instruction modifies the Z and P/V status flags as described earlier. Other status flags are not modified.

Figure 3-82 illustrates the following TRTDB instruction:

```
TRTDB    R2^,R12^,R8;      % AMC syntax
TRTDB    @R2,@R12,R8       ! Zilog syntax !
```

This is the TRTDB version of the TRDB instruction illustrated in Figure 3-81. The only difference between these two instructions is that $C4_{16}$, the value read out of the translation table, is loaded into 8-bit register RH1, instead of being loaded into memory byte 4004_{16}. Also, the Zero status (Z) is modified, in this case being reset to 0, to reflect a non-zero value read out of the translation table.

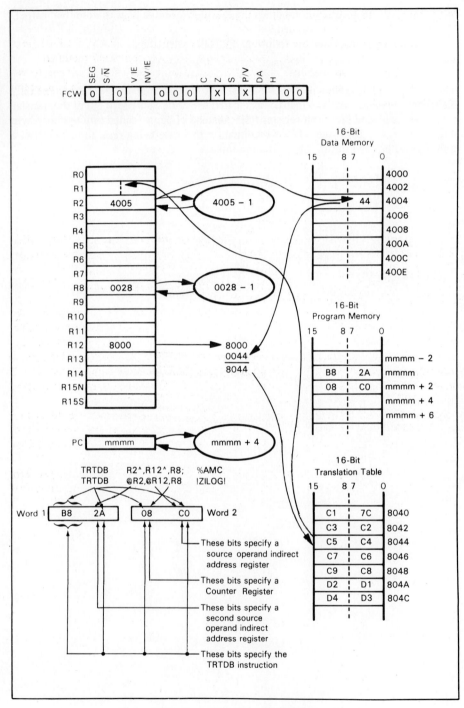

Figure 3-82. Execution of the TRTDB Instruction

TRTDRB — Translate Test Decrement and Repeat

TRTDRB is identical to TRDRB except that the selected translation table byte is loaded into 8-bit register RH1; the destination memory location is not modified.

TRTDRB is also identical to TRTDB except that TRTDRB continues to re-execute until the Counter Register decrements to zero, or a zero byte is read out of the translation table.

This is the general format for the TRTDRB instruction:

Addressing Options		
src1	src2	r
IR	IR	R

TRTDRB   src1,src2,r

The symbols src1 and src2 are a pair of memory address registers. 16-bit CPU registers must be specified in non-segmented mode; 32-bit CPU registers must be specified in segmented mode.

The symbol r is a Counter Register which must be specified as a 16-bit CPU register.

The TRTDRB instruction uses a translation table of the type described for the TRDB instruction. When the TRTDRB instruction is executed, a translation table address is computed by summing the address specified in src2 with the contents of the memory byte addressed by src1. The contents of the addressed translation table byte is loaded into 8-bit register RH1. The source operands themselves are not modified. The Z status is set to 1, and instruction execution ceases if RH1 contains 0; the Z status is reset to 0 otherwise.

The src1 address register and the Counter Register contents are both decremented by 1. If the counter register contains 0 after being decremented, the Overflow status is set to 1 and instruction execution ceases; the Overflow status is reset to 0 otherwise.

Instruction execution continues until the Z status is set to 1, identifying a zero byte read out of the translation table, or the Overflow status is set to 1, when the Counter Register contents decrements to 0.

The TRTDRB instruction object code may be illustrated as follows:

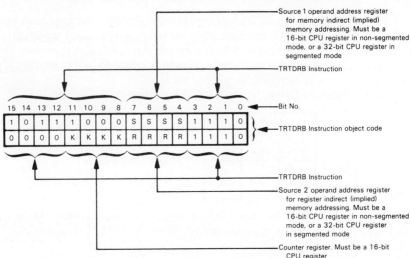

The TRTDRB instruction modifies the Z and P/V statuses as described earlier. Other status flags are not modified.

The TRTDRB instruction:

```
TRTDRB  @R2,@R12,R8
```

is the TRTDRB version of the TRTDB instruction illustrated in Figure 3-82. The only difference between these two instructions is that TRTDRB continues executing until a zero byte is read out of the translation table, which causes the Z status to be set to 1, or the Counter Register decrements to zero, which causes the P/V status to be set to 1. Thus the TRTDRB instruction sequence:

```
TRTDRB  @R2,@R12,R8      ! Zilog syntax !
JR      Z,ZBYTE          ! Zero byte detected !
                         ! Counter decremented to zero !

TRTDRB  R2^,R12^,R8;     % AMC syntax
JR      Z,ZBYTE;
```

replaces the longer TRTDB sequence:

```
LOOP:   TRTDB   @R2,@R12,R8      ! Zilog syntax !
        JR      Z,ZBYTE          ! Zero byte detected !
        JR      NOV,LOOP         ! Return if Counter not zero !
                                 ! Counter decremented to zero !

LOOP:   TRTDB   R2^,R12^,R8;     % AMC syntax
        JR      ZR,ZBYTE
        JR      NOV,LOOP
```

Once a TRTDRB instruction starts to execute, it could conceivably continue executing for a long time if it were translating a long string with few zero test bytes. This would present interrupt logic with problems. In order to prevent any such problems, the Z8000 allows interrupts to be acknowledged between each iterative execution of the TRTDRB instruction. Furthermore, the Program Counter value saved during the interrupt acknowledge process is the address of the TRTDRB instruction, so that execution of this instruction will continue from the point of interrupt, after the interrupt has been serviced. Seven clock periods must be added to the TRTDRB instruction's execution time to account for each interrupt acknowledged during the instruction's execution.

TRTIB — Translate Test and Increment

The TRTIB instruction is identical to TRIB except that the selected translation table byte is loaded into 8-bit register RH1; the destination memory location is not modified.

TRTIB is also identical to TRTDB, except that TRTIB increments the source byte memory address that is decremented by TRTDB.

This is the general format for the TRTIB instruction:

Addressing Options		
src1	src2	r
IR	IR	R

TRTIB   src1,src2,r

The symbols src1 and src2 are a pair of memory address registers. 16-bit CPU registers must be specified in non-segmented mode; 32-bit CPU registers must be specified in segmented mode.

The symbol r is a counter register which must be specified as a 16-bit CPU register.

The TRTIB instruction uses a translation table of the type described for the TRDB instruction. When the TRTIB instruction is executed, a translation table address is computed by summing the address specified in src2 with the contents of the memory byte addressed by src1. The contents of the addressed translation table byte is loaded into 8-bit register RH1. The source operands themselves are not modified. The Z status is set to 1 if RH1 contains 0 the Z status is reset to 0 otherwise.

The src1 address register is incremented by 1. The Counter Register is decremented by 1. If the Counter Register contains 0 after being decremented, the Overflow status is set to 1; the Overflow status is reset to 0 otherwise.

The TRTIB instruction object code may be illustrated as follows:

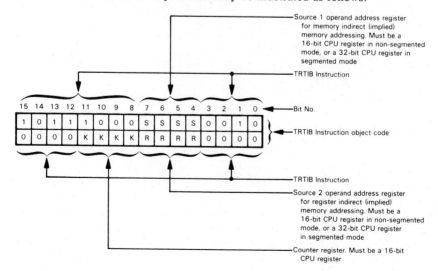

The TRTIB instruction modifies the Z and P/V statuses as described earlier. Other statuses are not modified.

The following TRTIB instruction:

```
TRTIB    R2^R12^,R8;      % AMC syntax
TRTIB    @R2,@R12,R8      ! Zilog syntax !
```

is the TRTIB version of the TRTDB instruction illustrated in Figure 3-82. The only difference between these two instructions is that TRTIB increments address register R2, whereas TRTDB decrements this address register, as illustrated in Figure 3- 82.

TRTIRB — Translate Test Increment and Repeat

TRTIRB is identical to TRIRB except that the selected translation table byte is loaded into 8-bit register RH1; the destination memory location is not modified.

TRTIRB is also identical to TRTIB, except that TRTIRB continues to re-execute until the Counter Register contents decrement to zero, or a zero byte is read out of the translation table.

This is the general format for the TRTIRB instruction:

Addressing Options		
src1	src2	r
IR	IR	R

TRTIRB   src1,src2,r

The symbols src1 and src2 are a pair of memory address registers. 16-bit CPU registers must be specified in non-segmented mode; 32-bit CPU registers must be specified in segmented mode.

The symbol r is a Counter Register which must be specified as a 16-bit CPU register.

The TRTIRB instruction uses a translation table of the type described for the TRDB instruction. When the TRTIRB instruction is executed, a translation table address is computed by summing the address specified in src2 with the contents of the memory byte addressed by src1. The contents of the addressed translation table byte are loaded into 8-bit register RH1. The source operands themselves are not modified. The Z status is set to 1, and instruction execution ceases, if RH1 contains 0; the Z status is reset to 0 otherwise.

The src1 address register is incremented by 1. The Counter Register is decremented by 1. If the Counter Register contains 0 after being decremented the Overflow status is set to 1 end instruction execution ceases; the Overflow status is reset to 0 otherwise.

Instruction execution continues until the Z status is set to 1, identifying a zero byte read out of the translation table, or the Overflow status is set to 1, when the Counter Register contents decrements to 0.

The TRTIRB instruction object code may be illustrated as follows:

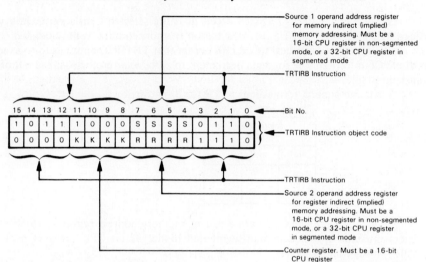

The TRTIRB instruction modifies the Z and P/V status flags as described earlier. Other status flags are not modified.

The TRTIRB instruction:

```
TRTIRB  @R2,@R12,R8
```

is the TRTIRB version of the TRTDB instruction illustrated in Figure 3-82. There are two differences between these two instructions. One difference is that TRTIRB continues executing until a zero byte is read out of the translation table, which causes the Z status to be set to 1, or the Counter Register decrements to zero, at which time the P/V status is set to 1. The other difference is that TRTIRB increments the Counter register, while TRTDB decrements this register.

The TRTIRB sequence:

```
        TRTIRB  @R2,@R12,R8     ! Zilog syntax !
        JR      Z,ZBYTE         ! Zero byte detected !
                                ! Counter decrements to zero !

        TRTIRB  R2^,R12^,R8;    % AMC syntax
        JR      ZR,ZBYTE;
```

replaces the longer TRTIB sequence:

```
LOOP:   TRTIB   @R2,@R12,R8     ! Zilog syntax !
        JR      Z,ZBYTE         ! Zero byte detected !
        JR      NOV,LOOP        ! Return if Counter not zero !
                                ! Counter decrements to zero !

LOOP:   TRTIB   R2^,R12^,R8;    % AMC syntax
        JR      ZR,ZBYTE
        JR      NOV,LOOP
```

Once a TRTIRB instruction starts to execute, it could conceivably continue executing for a long time if it were translating a long string with few zero test bytes. This could present interrupt logic with problems. In order to prevent any such problems, the Z8000 allows interrupts to be acknowledged between each iterative execution of the TRTIRB instruction. Furthermore, the Program Counter value saved during the interrupt acknowledge process is the address of the TRTIRB instruction, so that execution of this instruction will continue from the point of interrupt, after the interupt has been serviced. Seven clock periods must be added to the TRTIRB instruction's execution time to account for each interrupt acknowledged during the instruction's execution.

TSET — Test and Set a Word

TSETB — Test and Set a Byte

This is the general format for the TSET and TSETB instructions:

Addressing Options
dst
R
IR
DA
X

TSET   dst
TSETB   dst

The symbol dst is a destination operand which can be specified using any standard operand addressing method with the exception of immediate addressing.

When the TSET or TSETB instruction is executed, the Sign status acquires the value of the high-order destination operand bit. The destination operand is then filled with 1 bits. The Z8000 does not allow any other access to this bit during the execution of the instruction.

TSET and TSETB provide a method for independently executing programs to syncronize their activities, for example references to shared data. With TSET, you can test data flag to see if another program has set it, and also set the flag at the same time. Without this instruction your program might test the flag and find it to be zero, then get interrupted before setting it. The interrupting program might also test the flag, find it to be zero, and set it. After the interrupt your program would proceed as if the flag were still zero.

The TSET and TSETB instructions' object codes may be illustrated as follows:

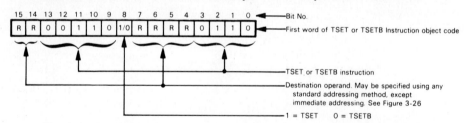

Only the Sign status (S) is modified by the TSET and TSETB instructions.

An interrupt request or a bus request from an external device is not honored while a TSET or TSETB instruction is being executed. This guarantees that the entire instruction will execute without the possibility of the destination operand being changed during execution of the instruction.

If the destination operand is in memory shared with one or more other microprocessors, TSET and TSETB do not prevent access by the other micprocessors. In this case, you must use the multi-micro instructions.

The use of the multi-micro instructions is described in detail in Chapter 13.

XOR — Logically Exclusive OR Words

XORB — Logically Exclusive OR Bytes

This is the general format for the XOR and XORB instructions:

Addressing Options	
dst	**src**
R	R
R	IM
R	IR
R	DA
R	X

XOR   dst,src
XORB   dst,src

The symbol dst is a destination operand which must be specified using direct register addressing. A 16-bit CPU register must be specified for XOR; an 8-bit CPU register must be specified for XORB.

The symbol src is a source operand which can be specified using any standard operand addressing method (see Figure 3-26).

The source and destination operands are logically exclusive ORed. The result is returned in the destination operand CPU register whose prior contents are lost.

The XOR and XORB instructions' object code may be illustrated as follows:

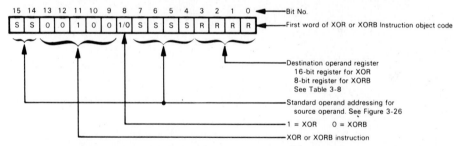

The Z and S status flags are modified by the XOR and XORB instructions. In addition, the XORB instruction modifies the P/V status to reflect the parity of the result byte (P = 1 for even parity, 0 for odd parity).

Figure 3-72 illustrates execution of the ORB instruction:

```
ORB     RL2,R2^;        % AMC syntax
ORB     RL2,@R2         ! Zilog syntax !
```

The equivalent XOR instruction is:

```
XORB    RL2,R2^;        % AMC syntax
XORB    RL2,@R2         ! Zilog syntax !
```

Figures 3-5 and 3-10 illustrate execution of AND and ANDB instructions. Equivalent XOR and XORB instructions execute identically, but perform different logical operations.

The XORB instruction illustrated above modifies the source operand indirect address. This is because 16-bit register R2 provides the address of a memory byte whose contents are ORed with RL2, the low-order byte of the address. If R2 initially contains 4286_{16}, and memory word 4286_{16} contains 03_{16}, this is what happens when the XORB instruction illustrated above is executed:

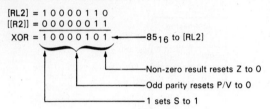

EXTENDED INSTRUCTIONS

Certain object codes have been reserved for use in extending the Z8000 instruction set. An extended instruction code may cause a trap so that the desired instruction can be executed in software, or the code may be recognized and executed by a device external to the Z8000 CPU. Such a device is known as an Extended Processing Unit (EPU).

If the EPA bit of the Flag and Control Word is zero, an extended instruction code causes an Extended Processing trap. If the EPA bit is one, the CPU expects external logic to execute the extended instruction. In this case the CPU will fetch the entire instruction and perform any address calculations required by the addressing mode of the instruction. The CPU will also control any data transfer required by the instruction. The Extended Processing Unit (EPU) is expected to complete the processing required by the instruction. (Note: If the EPA bit of the Flag and Control Word is zero, the unimplemented object codes 0E and 4E also cause an Extended Processing trap.)

The following instruction descriptions cover only the CPU's role in execution of the extended instructions. The remaining operations are determined by the EPU; for example, an EPU might perform floating point arithmetic. Since the particulars of EPU operation are system-dependent, we will not discuss EPU operation in this book.

There may be up to four EPUs in a system. The desired EPU is selected by a two-bit identifier field in the instruction. In the general format of each instruction we show specification of an EPU with the symbol EPUn, where n represents a number between 0 and 3.

Extended instructions which transfer data between an EPU and memory may use any standard memory addressing mode except immediate. Extended instructions which load data to or from CPU registers use the Register addressing mode.

The assembler format for each extended instruction provides for an 8-bit immediate constant. This constant becomes part of the object code and is meant to be interpreted by the EPU. Our general format for each instruction uses the symbol data 8 to represent this constant.

The descriptions assume the EPA bit of the Flag and Control word is 1; if it is zero, the instruction will cause an Extended Processing trap. What happens after the trap depends on software.

Extended processing instructions are a new feature which is not implemented on early production chips. Table 3-18 and the accompanying text explain which chips lack extended processing.

XCTL — Internal EPU Operation

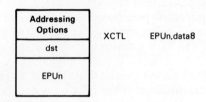

The CPU treats this instruction as a NOP. The EPU interprets the opcode and performs an internal operation.

The object code may be illustrated as follows:

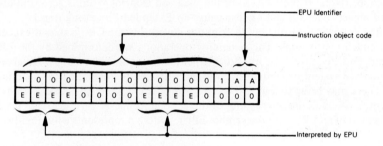

No flags are modified by this operation.

XLDCTL — Load EPU From Flags

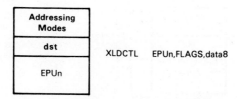

The Flags (bits 0-7) of the CPU Flag and Control word are transferred to the specified EPU.

The object code may be illustrated as follows:

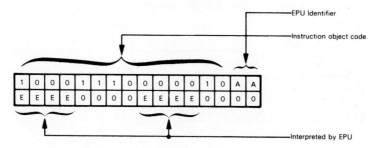

No flags are modified by this operation.

XLDCTL — Load Flags from EPU

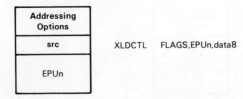

Addressing Options	
src	XLDCTL FLAGS,EPUn,data8
EPUn	

The Flags (Bits 0-7) of the CPU Flag and Control word are loaded with data provided by the specified EPU.

The contents of CPU register R0 are undefined after execution of this instruction. The object code may be illustrated as follows:

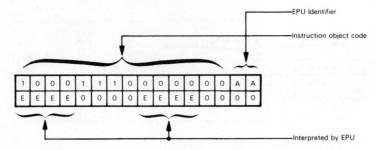

All the status flags are modified by this instruction.

XLDM — Load CPU Registers from EPU

Addressing Options	
src	**dst**
EPUn	R

XLDM   dst,EPUn,num,data8

A specified number of words of data are transferred from the specified EPU to CPU registers starting with register dst. CPU registers are loaded consecutively; R0 follows R15.

The object code may be illustrated as follows:

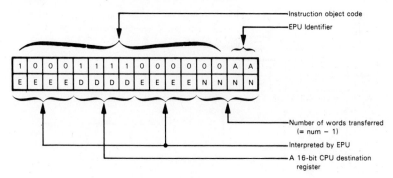

No flags are modified by this operation.

XLDM — Load EPU from CPU Registers

Addressing Modes	
src	**dst**
R	EPUn

XLDM   EPUn,src,num,data8

The contents of a specified number of CPU registers starting with the register src are transferred to the specified EPU. CPU register contents are transferred consecutively; R0 follows R15.

The object code may be illustrated as follows:

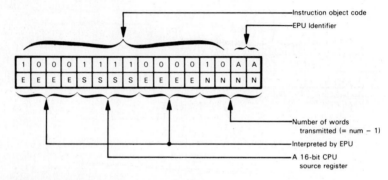

No flags are modified by this operation.

XLDM — Load EPU from Memory

Addressing Modes	
src	dst
IR	EPUn
DA	EPUn
X	EPUn

XLDM   EPUn,src,num,data8

The CPU computes the effective address and controls a specified number of data word transfers from memory to the specified EPU.

The object code may be illustrated as follows:

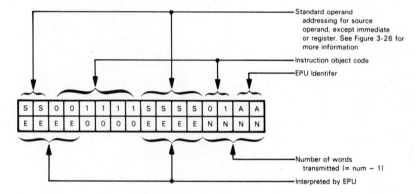

No flags are modified by this operation.

XLDM — Load Memory from EPU

Addressing Modes	
src	**dst**
EPUn	IR
EPUn	DA
EPUn	X

XLDM   dst,EPUn,num,data8

The CPU computes the effective address and controls a specified number of data word transfers from the specified EPU to memory.

The object code may be illustrated as follows:

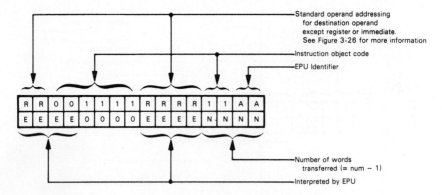

No flags are modified by this operation.

Early Production Z8000 Microprocessors

As is always the case with complex integrated circuits, early production Z8000 microprocessor chips do not operate exactly as specified. This was mentioned in the descriptions of the affected instructions. Table 3-18 summarizes this information and suggests ways to get around the problems.

Which instructions do not work properly depends on which version of the Z8000 chip is in your microprocessor. To find out which version you have, look at the markings on the top of the chip. In addition to the manufacturer's trademark and part number, a copyright notice, and possibly a batch number, you will find a date-of-manufacture code which looks either like this:

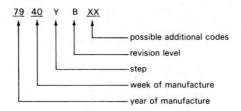

or like this:

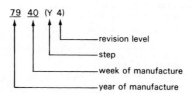

It is the "step" which will tell you problems your chip has. Zilog and AMD chips of the same step should have identical characteristics from the programmer's point of view. The first sample chips made were designated step Z. It is unlikely that you will have one of these chips. The first production chips shipped were step Y. Few of these were shipped; they were mostly for evaluation purposes. Most early production chips were step W. In the summer of 1980, step V chips were delivered. Manufacturers plan for all known problems to be corrected in the step V chips.

If you find an "early production" step Y or W chip in your microcomputer, consult Table 3-18 to learn its limitations.

Table 3-18. Early Production Problems

Instruction	Step	Problem	Suggestion
DAB	Y	P/V flag is set.	Don't rely on previous value of P/V being preserved.
	Y	S flag is not set.	Don't rely on value of S. Test the result.
DIV DIVL	Y	V flag is not set correctly.	Don't rely on value of V. You may need to check the operands to determine if overflow will occur.
	Y	Divide by zero causes the next instruction to execute incorrectly.	Check for zero before dividing.
DJNZ	Y	This instruction does not execute correctly.	Use DBJNZ or use DEC and JP.
JP JR	W,Y	If a jump is executed in non-segmented mode, the internally stored PC segment may be changed. The PC segment will then be incorrect if the SEG flag is set to return to segmented mode.	Execute a System Call and trap to a system routine to return to segmented mode. A correct segment number will be loaded from the Program Status Area.
	W,Y	If an interrupt occurs in normal mode during an instruction which has R14n or RR14n as the destination register, the result will be loaded into R14s or RR14s.	Do not load R14n in normal mode. In a segmented mode routine load the normal mode stack pointer.
MULTL	W,Y	MULTL may give incorrect results if refresh is enabled.	If your microcomputer runs with refresh enabled, either do not use MULTL, or use it in the following process sequence: Disable interrupts, disable refresh, MULTL, enable refresh, enable interrupts.
Extended Instructions	W,Y	This is a new feature, first implemented on V step chips.	

4

Simple Programs

The only way to learn assembly language programming is through experience. The next six chapters of this book contain examples of simple programs that perform actual microprocessor tasks. You should read each example carefully and try to execute the program on a Z8000-based microcomputer. Finally, you should work the problems at the end of each chapter and run the resulting programs to ensure that you understand the material.

You should use the examples as guidelines for solving the problems at the end of each chapter. Be sure to run your solutions on a Z8000-based microcomputer to ensure that they are correct.

This chapter contains some very elementary programs.

EXAMPLE FORMAT

Each program example in this and in subsequent chapters contains the following parts:

- A title that describes the general problem

- A statement of purpose that describes the task which the program performs and the memory locations used

- A sample problem with data and results

- A flowchart if the program logic is complex

- The source program assembly language listing

- The object program hexadecimal, machine language listing

- Explanatory notes that discuss the instructions and methods used in the program

Each program example is written and assembled as a stand-alone program module, referred to as a "procedure." Each program is assigned a name which identifies the chapter within which the program occurs, and the sequential position of the program within the chapter. This may be illustrated generally as follows:

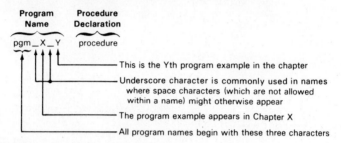

X and Y represent any decimal numbers. Thus the declaration:

    pgm _ 6 _ 3   procedure

names the third program example in Chapter 6.

The program listings in this book will show the object code program alongside the source program — this is a common assembler output format. For example, here is a portion of program 4-1:

Memory Address	Object Code		Source Program	
4604	4100	ADD	R0,%6002	!Add second !
4606	6002			
4608	6F00	LD	%6004,R0	!Store result !
460A	6004			

The four-digit number starting in the far left column of each line is the hexadecimal address of the first byte of object code shown on that line. In the first line above, 4604 is the address of the first object code byte of the four-byte ADD R0,%6002 instruction; the hexadecimal object code for this instruction is 4100 6002, and the first byte, 41, is in location 4604. The first two bytes of object code are shown on the same line as the instruction, and the next two bytes are shown, along with their first address, on the next line. Thus location 4605 contains the byte 00 — we infer this from the fact that 00 follows the byte in address 4604 — and locations 4606 and 4607 hold the bytes 60 and 02, respectively. The letters, numbers, and words to the right of the object code are the assembly language fields which were described in Chapter 2. These fields comprise the source program.

If you wish to assemble these examples on your microcomputer, key in the source statements only; do not enter the addresses or object codes, since the assembler program will generate them. You will also need to enter some assembler directives (for example, to tell the assembler where to start program addresses). We show some of these directives, but the ones you use will be determined by your assembler and the requirements of your microcomputer's operating system.

If you wish to execute the program examples without assembling source code, you can key the object code into the specified addresses. Before you do this, however, make sure that you will not be trying to load areas of memory reserved for the monitor or operating system. To avoid such problems, you may need to change addresses before you load the programs. As we will discuss in guideline 7 below, you may also need to change the instruction at the end of the program.

Source Program

The source programs in the examples have been constructed as follows:

1. Standard Zilog Z8000 assembler notation is used, as summarized in Chapter 3. AMC notation is not used.

2. The forms in which data and addresses appear are selected for clarity rather than for consistency. We use hexadecimal numbers for memory addresses, instruction codes, and BCD data; decimal for numeric constants; binary for logical masks; and ASCII for characters.

3. Frequently used instructions and programming techniques are emphasized.

4. Examples illustrate tasks that microprocessors perform in communications, instrumentation, computers, business equipment, industrial, and military applications.

5. Detailed comments are included.

6. Simple and clear structures are emphasized, but programs are written as efficiently as possible within this guideline. Notes accompanying programs often describe more efficient procedures.

7. Programs use consistent memory allocations. Each program starts in memory location 4600_{16} and ends with the HALT instruction. If your microcomputer has no monitor and no interrupts, you may prefer to end programs with an endless loop instruction such as

        HERE: JR   HERE

8. Programs use standard Zilog assembler directives. We introduced assembler directives conceptually in Chapter 2. When first examining programming examples, you can ignore assembler directives if you do not understand them. Assembler directives do not contribute to program logic, which is what you will be trying to understand initially; but they are a necessary part of every assembly language program, so you will have to learn how to use them before you write any executable programs. Including assembler directives in all program examples will help you become familiar with the functions they perform. We show the assembler directives in lower-case letters; actual Z8000 instructions, labels, and operands are shown in upper case.

Some Z8000-based microcomputers may require that the program end with a RET instruction, or a JP instruction with a specific destination address to return control to the monitor. Also, the memory space allocated to user programs and data will vary from one microcomputer to the next. Consult your microcomputer user's manual to determine where memory has been allocated for user programs and data.

PROGRAM INITIALIZATION

All of the programming examples presented in Chapter 4, and in subsequent chapters, pay particular attention to the correct initialization of constants and operands. Often this requires additional instructions that may appear superfluous, in that they do not contribute directly to the solution of the stated problem. Nevertheless, correct initialization is emphasized since the Z8000 is a powerful microprocessor that will be used frequently in complex applications that are intolerant of programming shortcuts introduced in the interest of local expediency.

We want to stress correct initialization; that is why we are going to emphasize this aspect of problems.

SPECIAL CONDITIONS

For the same reasons that we emphasize correct initialization, we also pay particular attention to special conditions that can cause a program to fail. Empty lists and zero indexes are two of the most common circumstances overlooked in sample problems. **It is critically important** for microprocessors in general, and powerful 16-bit microprocessors in particular, **that you learn with your very first program to anticipate unusual circumstances; they frequently cause your program to fail.** You must build in the necessary programming steps to account for these potential problems.

USE OF THE STACK

When introducing the Z8000 in Chapter 1, we stated that the Z8000 is a stack-oriented microprocessor. The Z8000 will likely have a specific area of memory set aside for a single stack, much as any other microprocessor would. However, the versatility of the PUSH and POP instructions suggests their use for simple data memory reference. Therefore, programming examples will frequently use POP instructions to fetch data from memory, and PUSH instructions to return results to memory, simply because PUSH and POP are efficient memory reference instructions. It also means that data memory can be visualized as a collection of innumerable small stacks.

PROGRAMMING GUIDELINES FOR SOLVING PROBLEMS

Use the following guidelines in solving the problems at the end of each chapter:

1. Comment each program so that others can understand it. The comments can be brief and ungrammatical. They should explain the purpose of a section or instruction in the program, but should not describe the operation of instructions; that description is available in manuals. You do not have to comment each statement or explain the obvious. You may follow the format of the examples but provide less detail.

2. Emphasize clarity, simplicity, and good structure in programs. While programs should be reasonably efficient, do not worry about saving a single byte of program memory or a few microseconds.

3. Make programs reasonably general. Do not confuse parameters (such as the number of elements in any array) with fixed constants (such as π or ASCII C).

4. Never assume fixed initial values for parameters.

5. Use assembler notation as shown in the examples and defined in Chapter 3.

6. Use hexadecimal notation for addresses. Use the clearest possible form for data.

7. If your microcomputer allows it, start all programs in memory location 4600_{16} and use memory locations starting with 6000_{16} for data and temporary storage. Use location 8000_{16} as the base of the stack. Otherwise, establish equivalent addresses for your microcomputer and use them consistently. Again, consult the user's manual.

8. Use meaningful names for labels and variables; e.g., SUM or CHECK rather than X, Y, or Z.

9. Execute each program on your microcomputer. There is no other way of ensuring that your program is correct. We have provided sample data with each problem. Be sure that the program works for special cases.

PROGRAM EXAMPLES

4-1. 16-Bit Addition

Purpose: Add the contents of memory location 6000_{16} to the contents of memory location 6002_{16}. Place the result into memory location 6004_{16}.

Sample Problem:

```
            (6000)  =  201E
            (6002)  =  0774
   Result:  (6004)  =  2792
```

Program 4-1a:

```
                  internal
                    pgm_4_la   procedure
                  entry
                      $abs     IBASE

      4600 6100       LD       R0,%6000      ! Get first number !
      4602 6000
      4604 4100       ADD      R0,%6002      ! Add second !
      4606 6002
      4608 6F00       LD       %6004,R0      ! Store result !
      460A 6004
      460C 7A00       HALT

      460E         end    pgm_4_la
```

This solves the problem in three steps. The first instruction loads Register R0 with the value in location 6000; the next instruction adds the value in location 6002 to Register R0; the last instruction takes the resulting value in R0 and stores it in location 6004.

All three of these instructions contain addresses to determine the source or destination of the data. On the non-segmented Z8000, the addresses are 16 bits long (32 bits on the segmented machine). The address immediately follows the instruction code.

The fact that the ADD instruction can add the contents of a memory word to a register demonstrates one of the most important differences between 8-bit and 16-bit microprocessors. An 8-bit machine typically has a small set of instructions that operate on memory. Most Z8000 instructions have at least one operand that can be taken from a memory location.

This simple example demonstrates some important programming techniques. First, there is register indirect addressing. Registers can be used to hold addresses as well as data. If we set Register 2 to contain 6000, we can use it as a pointer to data. This is called implied, or register indirect, addressing. Another version of our 16-bit addition example is shown in program 4-1b.

Program 4-1b:

```
            internal
                pgm_4_lb procedure
                entry
                    $abs     IBASE
    4600 7602           LDA     R2,%6000        ! Set up data area pointer !
    4602 6000
    4604 2120           LD      R0,@R2          ! First number !
    4606 A921           INC     R2,#2           ! Point to second !
    4608 0120           ADD     R0,@R2          ! Add together !
    460A A921           INC     R2,#2           ! Point to result location !
    460C 2F20           LD      @R2,R0          ! Store result !
    460E 7A00           HALT

    4610            end pgm_4_lb
```

The first instruction points R2 to location 6000. In the instructions that follow, @R2 refers to the memory location whose address is in R2. Note that R2 is advanced by 2 each time. This is because word addresses are always even. Byte addresses may be even or odd.

Using register indirect addressing in this example appears to be more work than it is worth. We use three instructions to maintain the pointer register. But note that the object program is only one word longer. This is because instructions that reference memory using register indirect addressing are only one word long. The extra word for the address is not needed. Compare the object code produced for the LD and ADD instructions in the two versions. Do you see what bits indicate what type of addressing mode is used?

4-2. Using a Stack

Now we will use the addition example to demonstrate the use of a stack and the two basic stack instructions: PUSH and POP. There can be as many stacks as there are registers on the Z8000. But R15 (RR14 on the segmented version) is the dedicated stack pointer. Several instructions use the dedicated stack pointer implicitly, most notably CALL and RET, which are covered more completely in Chapter 10. Many of our examples will assume values have been placed on the R15 (RR14) stack, and will often return values there, too. This is in keeping with common programming practices in many software systems on the Z8000 and other similar machines. Let us restate the problem to incorporate the stack.

Purpose: Add the contents of the top of the stack and the second value on the stack. Place the result onto the stack.

Sample Problem:

```
              R15    =  7FFC     8000 - 4
             (7FFC)  =  201E
             (7FFE)  =  0774
   Result:   R15     =  7FFE     7FFC + 4 - 2
             (7FFE)  =  2792
```

In all our examples, we use location 8000 as the base of the stack. This means that the locations lower than 8000 are used as stack storage. When the stack is empty, R15 will contain 8000. Note, then, that location 8000 itself is never used. If it ever is used, or R15 goes higher than 8000, this is an error condition called stack underflow. Stack overflow occurs when the stack is so full (the stack pointer is so low) that it exceeds its allotted storage and causes other data or program space to be overwritten.

Program 4-2:

```
                    internal
                      pgm_4_2 procedure
                      entry
                          $abs      IBASE

   4600 97F0            POP       R0,@R15      ! R0 <- (7FFC); R15 <- R15+2 !
   4602 97F1            POP       R1,@R15      ! R1 <- (7FFE); R15 <- R15+2 !
   4604 8110            ADD       R0,R1
   4606 93F0            PUSH      @R15,R0      ! R15 <- R15-2; (7FFE) <- R0 !
   4608 7A00            HALT

   460A            end       pgm_4_2
```

The two POP instructions load operands from the stack. The PUSH instruction returns the sum to the stack. Note that the original contents of location 7FFE are lost. In addition, although the value is not changed by this program, the contents of location 7FFC should also be considered lost. By the rules of stack usage, whenever a value is popped off the stack, the contents of that location should be considered invalid. One reason for this is that an interrupt may cause something to be pushed onto the stack between the execution of any two instructions. (This topic is covered fully in Chapter 12.)

4-3. Setting Up the Stack

When you are solving the problems at the end of each chapter, or trying the given examples on your microcomputer, you will often have to set up the stack with sample data. This can be done by hand on most microcomputers. It may also be done by a program. We will expand the above example with some instructions that set up the stack pointer and the stack contents to prepare for the sample problem.

Purpose: Initialize the stack pointer to 8000. Push the values 0774_{16} and $201E_{16}$ onto the stack.

Program 4-3:

```
               internal
                  pgm_4_3 procedure
                  entry
                     $abs     IBASE

    4600  760F       LDA      R15,%8000       ! Initialize stack pointer !
    4602  8000
    4604  0DF9       PUSH     @R15,#%0774      ! Push the two parameters !
    4606  0774
    4608  0DF9       PUSH     @R15,#%201E
    460A  201E
    460C  97F0       POP      R0,@R15          ! Parameters to registers !
    460E  97F1       POP      R1,@R15
    4610  8110       ADD      R0,R1
    4612  93F0       PUSH     @R15,R0          ! Result to stack !
    4614  7A00       HALT

    4616           end      pgm_4_3
```

This example violates one of the programming guidelines previously set forth: do not assume fixed values for operands.

The first two PUSH instructions use immediate operands. Immediate operands are denoted by the   symbol. Note the resulting object code. Note also that LD R15, %8000 achieves the same result as the LDA instruction. However, the two forms would not be the same on a segmented machine. If we were initializing our stack to segment 3, offset 8000, the two forms would be:

```
       LDA      RR14,<<3>>%8000

                 or

       LDL      RR14,#%83008000
```

Obviously, the LDA is quite useful here.

If you are using an AMC assembler, you will use names to represent segmented addresses; you could also use the LDL instruction to load a numeric constant segmented address.

4-4. Ones Complement

Purpose: Form the ones complement of the contents of the top of the stack. Place the result onto the stack.

Sample Problem:

```
        R15   =  7FFE
      (7FFE)  =  0FF2
Result:  R15   =  7FFE
      (7FFE)  =  F00D
```

Program 4-4:

```
              internal
              pgm_4_4 procedure
              entry
                   $abs    IBASE

4600 97F0          POP     R0,@R15        ! Fetch value !
4602 8D00          COM     R0
4604 93F0          PUSH    @R15,R0        ! Store result !
4606 7A00          HALT

4608          end      pgm_4_4
```

COM is an instruction that inverts each bit of its destination. The sample data may be easier to see in binary:

```
0FF2 = 0000111111110010
F00D = 1111000000001101
```

Actually, the source program is much simpler if we don't use POP and PUSH. What single instruction replaces the three used in the program?

4-5. Shift Left One Bit

Purpose: Shift the value on the top of the stack left one bit. Place the result onto the top of the stack.

Sample Problems:

a.	R15	= 7FFE	
	(7FFE)	= 289B	0010 1000 1001 1011 binary
Result:	R15	= 7FFE	
	(7FFE)	= 5136	0101 0001 0011 0110 binary
b.	(7FFE)	= 80F8	1000 0000 1111 1000 binary
Result:	(7FFE)	= 01F0	0000 0001 1111 0000 binary

Program 4-5:

```
          internal
            pgm_4_5 procedure
            entry
                $abs     IBASE

4600 97F2           POP     R2,@R15
4602 B329           SLA     R2              ! Shift left one position !
4604 0001
4606 93F2           PUSH    @R15,R2
4608 7A00           HALT

460A          end       pgm_4_5
```

The SLA instruction, without a second operand, shifts the destination register left one position. The same instruction can be used to shift a register from 0 to 16 positions. The number of positions is the second operand.

On a machine as powerful as the Z8000, there are often many ways to perform the same operation. Except for different flag results, the following sequences all produce the same result in R2 as SLA R2 generated:

```
          ADD     R2,R2
          SLL     R2

          LDK     R1,#1
          SDA     R2,R1

          RL      R2,#1
          RES     R2,#0
```

How many others can you find? Which of those presented will execute the fastest?

4-6. Word Disassembly

Purpose: Divide the low-order byte of the value on the top of the stack into two 4-bit nibbles and store them on the stack. The low-order four bits of the byte will be in the low-order four bits of the first word pushed onto the stack. The high-order four bits of the byte will be in the low-order four bits of the second (and top) stack word.

Sample Problem:

```
              R15   =  7FFE
            (7FFE)  =  004D

Result:       R15   =  7FFC
            (7FFC)  =  0004
            (7FFE)  =  000D
```

Program 4-6a:

```
              internal
                 pgm_4_6a procedure
                 entry
                      $abs     IBASE

  4600 97F2       POP     R2,@R15          ! Data is in low byte of R2 !
  4602 8C28       CLRB    RH2              ! Clear high byte !
  4604 A121       LD      R1,R2            ! Second copy of data byte !
  4606 0609       ANDB    RL1,#%(2)00001111 ! Clear second nibble !
  4608 0F0F
  460A 93F1       PUSH    @R15,R1          ! Only the low 4 bits in R1 !
  460C B2A1       SRLB    RL2,#4           ! 2nd nibble to low 4 bits !
  460E FFFC
  4610 93F2       PUSH    @R15,R2          ! R2 contains the high... !
  4612 7A00       HALT                     ! ...4 bits, shifted right !

  4614         end     pgm_4_6a
```

This is an example of byte manipulation. The Z8000 has no "pop byte" or "push byte" instructions, so the required stack byte must be separated from the top stack word.

Byte Register RL2 is the least significant eight bits of Word Register R2. CLRB RH2 clears the high-order eight bits of R2. The ANDB instruction performs a logical AND function on the two operands. Can you find a way to combine CLRB and ANDB into a single instruction?

The SRLB (shift right logical byte) instruction shifts RL1 four bit positions to the right. Could we have used SRAB in its place? Also consider the RRDB instruction.

This program has not been made any more complex by introducing stack accesses. Consider the following non-stack version.

Sample Problem:

              (7FFE) = XX4D (X can have any value)

Result: (7FFC) = 0004
         (7FFE) = 000D

Program 4-6b:

```
              internal
                pgm_4_6b procedure
                entry
                      $abs      IBASE
4600 7608             LDA       R8,%7FFE        ! Set up pointer !
4602 7FFE
4604 2181             LD        R1,@R8          ! Data in low byte !
4606 8C18             CLRB      RH1             ! Zero high byte !
4608 A112             LD        R2,R1
460A 0701             AND       R1,##000F       ! R1 holds low-order nibble !
460C 000F
460E B321             SRL       R2,#4           ! R2 holds high-order nibble !
4610 FFFC
4612 2F81             LD        @R8,R1          ! Return results !
4614 6F82             LD        -2(R8),R2
4616 FFFE
4618 7A00             HALT

461A             end       pgm_4_6b
```

It is just as long as the stack version.

4-7. Find Larger of Two Numbers

Purpose: Find the larger of the two values on the top of the stack. Place the result onto the top of the stack. Assume the values are unsigned numbers.

Sample Problems:

```
    a.                      R15   =  7FFC
                          (7FFC)  =  2012
                          (7FFE)  =  520E

         Result:           R15   =  7FFE
                          (7FFE)  =  520E

    b.                      R15   =  7FFC
                          (7FFC)  =  2012
                          (7FFE)  =  E025

         Result:           R15   =  7FFE
                          (7FFE)  =  E025
```

Program 4-7:

```
                    internal
                      pgm_4_7 procedure
                      entry
                        $abs     IBASE

4600 97F0                 POP     R0,@R15
4602 97F1                 POP     R1,@R15
4604 8B10                 CP      R0,R1
4606 EF01                 JR      UGE,FIN      ! Is R0 larger than R1? !
4608 A110                 LD      R0,R1        ! If no, move larger to R0 !
460A 93F0        FIN:     PUSH    @R15,R0
460C 7A00                 HALT

460E              end     pgm_4_7
```

The Compare instruction, CP, sets the flags as if the source, R1, were subtracted from the destination, R0. The JR instruction transfers control to the statement labeled FIN if R0 is greater than or equal to R1. Otherwise, the next instruction, LD, is executed. At FIN, R0 always contains the larger of the two values.

Notice that we used "UGE," not "GE." The condition names that begin with "U" are unsigned; the others assume signed twos complement numbers. To change the program to operate on signed numbers, simply change the UGE to GE:

```
                        -
                        -
                        -
                        CP      R0,R1
                        JR      GE,FIN
                        -
                        -
                        -
```

Try this program on your microcomputer both ways with the values in sample problem b.

Dealing with compares and jumps is an important part of programming the Z8000. Don't confuse the sense of the CP instruction. After a compare the relation tested is: destination condition source. For example, if the condition is "less than" then you test for destination less than source. Become familiar with all of the conditions and their meanings. Unsigned compares are very useful when comparing two addresses.

4-8. Indirect Memory Addressing

Purpose: Load a data word into a register using indirect memory addressing.

Sample Problem:

```
                    (6000)  =  5000
                    (5000)  =  FFFF

        Result:     (RO)    =  FFFF
```

Program 4-8:

```
                internal
                   pgm_4_8 procedure
                   entry
                        $abs     IBASE

    4600 7601           LDA      R1,%6000        ! Rl points to the address !
    4602 6000
    4604 2111           LD       R1,@R1          ! Now R1 points to the data !
    4606 2110           LD       R0,@R1          ! Data is now in R0 !
    4608 7A00           HALT

    460A                end      pgm_4_8
```

Very few microprocessors offer indirect memory addressing. The Z8000 creates the equivalent of indirect memory addressing via the instruction:

```
            LD       RN,@RN
```

If RN initially contains the direct memory address, it will finally contain the indirect memory address.

Try reproducing indirect addressing, with pre-indexing and with post-indexing as described in *An Introduction to Microcomputers: Volume 1.*[1]

PROBLEMS

4-1. 64-Bit Data Transfer

Purpose: Move the contents of memory locations 6000 through 6006 to locations 6800 through 6806.

Sample Problem:

	(6000)	=	3E2A
	(6002)	=	42A1
	(6004)	=	21F2
	(6006)	=	60A0
Result:	(6800)	=	3E2A
	(6802)	=	42A1
	(6804)	=	21F2
	(6806)	=	60A0

4-2. 16-Bit Subtraction

Purpose: Subtract the contents of location 6002 from the contents of location 6000.

Sample Problem:

	(6000)	=	3977
	(6002)	=	2182
Result:	(6000)	=	17F5

4-3. Shift Right Three Bits

Purpose: Shift the contents of memory location 6000 right three bits. Clear the three most significant bit positions.

Sample Problem:

a.	(6000)	=	415D
Result:	(6000)	=	082B
b.	(6000)	=	C15D
Result:	(6000)	=	182B

4-4. Clear Long Word

Purpose: Clear the long word (32 bits) that begins at location 6000. (Long format means that location 6000 contains the most significant 16 bits and locaion 6002 contains the least significant 16 bits.)

Note that the Z8000 contains no CLRL instruction, although plans for later versions of the Z8000 include this instruction.

4-5. Word Assembly

Purpose: Combine the low four bits of each of the four consecutive bytes beginning at location 6000 into one 16-bit word. The value at 6000 goes into the most significant nibble of the result; the value at 6003 becomes the least significant nibble. Store the result in location 6004.

Sample Problem:

```
            (6000)  =  0C
            (6001)  =  02
            (6002)  =  06
            (6003)  =  09

Result:     (6004)  =  C269
```

4-6. Find Smallest of Three Numbers

Purpose: Locations 6000, 6002, and 6004 each contain an unsigned number. Store the smallest of these numbers in location 6006.

Sample Problem:

```
            (6000)  =  9125
            (6002)  =  102C
            (6004)  =  7040

Result:     (6006)  =  102C
```

4-7. 64-Bit Addition

Purpose: Add the 64-bit value starting at location 6000 to the 64-bit value starting at
location 6008.

Sample Problem:

```
              (6000)  =  12A2
              (6002)  =  E640
              (6004)  =  F210   12A2E640F2100123
              (6006)  =  0123
              (6008)  =  0010
              (600A)  =  19BF   001019BF40023F51
              (600C)  =  4002
              (600E)  =  3F51

Result:       (6008)  =  12B3
              (600A)  =  0000   12B3000032124074
              (600C)  =  3212
              (600E)  =  4074
```

Sample Answer:

```
        LDA     R8,%6008
        POPL    RR4,@R8
        POPL    RR6,@R8
        ADDL    RR6,%6004
        PUSHL   @R8,RR6
        LDL     RR0,%6000
        ADC     R5,R1
        PUSH    @R8,R5
        ADC     R4,R0
        PUSH    @R8,R4
```

4-8. Sum of Squares

Purpose: Calculate the squares of the contents of byte locations 6000 and 6001 and add them together. Place the result into the word at location 6002.

Sample Problem:

$$(6000) \ = \ 07$$
$$(6001) \ = \ 32$$

Result: $(6002) \ = \ 09F5$

That is, $7^2 + 50^2 = 49 + 2500 = 2549$ (Decimal)

same as $7^2 + 32^2 = 31 + 9C4 = 9F5$ (Hexadecimal)

Hint: the following instruction multiplies the value in R1 by itself:

```
MULT      RR0,R1
```

Sample Answer:

```
CLR       R3
LDB       RL3,%6000
MULT      RR2,R3
CLR       R1
LDB       RL1,%6001
MULT      RR0,R1
ADD       R3,R1
LD        %6002,R3
```

4-9. Shift Left Variable Number of Bits

Purpose: Shift the contents of memory location 6000 left. The number of positions to shift should be popped off the R15 stack. The low-order bits should be cleared.

Sample Problems:

a.

```
        R15  =  7FFE
      (7FFE) =  0003      Shift left 3 positions
      (6000) =  182B
```

Result:
```
        R15  =  8000
      (6000) =  C158
```

b.

```
        R15  =  7FFE
      (7FFE) =  0010      Shift left 16 positions
      (6000) =  182B
```

Result:
```
        R15  =  8000
      (6000) =  0000
```

Sample Answer:

```
POP       R0,@R15
LD        R1,%6000
SDA       R1,R0
LD        %6000,R1
```

REFERENCES

1. A. Osborne, *An Introduction to Microcomputers: Volume 1 — Basic Concepts,* second edition (Berkeley: Osborne/McGraw-Hill, 1980), Chapter 6.

5

Simple Program Loops

The program loop is used to reexecute a sequence of instructions. Loops have four sections:

1. The initialization section, which establishes starting values for counters, address registers (pointers) and other variables.

2. The processing section, which contains the instruction sequence to be reexecuted.

3. The loop control section, which updates counters and pointers for the next iteration.

4. The concluding section, which analyzes and stores results.

Sections 1 and 4 are executed once. Sections 2 and 3 may be executed many times. Therefore, **loop execution time will depend primarily on execution time of Sections 2 and 3,** which should execute as quickly as possible. Do not worry about the execution time of Sections 1 and 4. **A typical program loop flowchart is shown in Figure 5-1. The positions of the processing and loop control sections may be reversed as shown in Figure 5-2.** The processing section in Figure 5-1 is always executed at least once, while the processing section in Figure 5-2 may not be executed at all. Figure 5-1 seems more natural, but Figure 5-2 is often more efficient and avoids the problem of what to do when there is no data (a bugaboo for computers, and the frequent cause of silly situations like the computer dunning someone for a bill of $0.00).

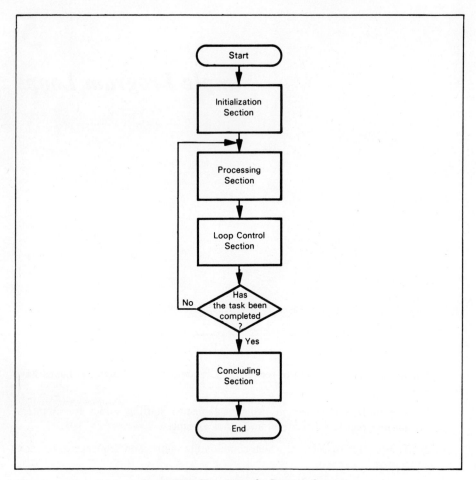

Figure 5-1. Flowchart of a Program Loop

The loop structure can be used to process entire blocks of data. To accomplish this, the program must increment an address register after each iteration so that the address register points to the next element in the data block. The next iteration will then process data in the next memory location.

Register indirect memory addressing is the key to processing a block of data, since it allows you to vary the actual memory address by changing the contents of registers. Indexed addressing generates more object code and requires more execution time, but may be handy when processing more than one block of data. Note that direct addresses are in program memory, which means they cannot be changed if programs are in read-only memory, or are to be shared.

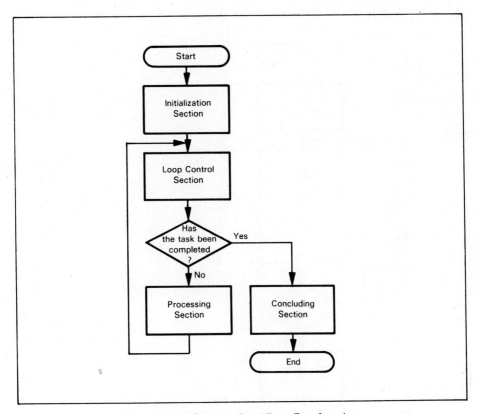

Figure 5-2. A Program that Allows Zero Iterations

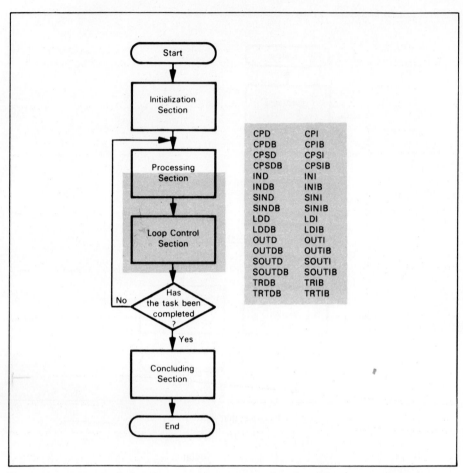

Figure 5-3. Decrement and Increment Variations of String Handling Instructions

PROGRAM LOOP INSTRUCTIONS

A number of Z8000 instructions have variations that provide some or all of the logic needed by a program loop. These instructions are summarized in Table 5-1.

Table 5-1. Z8000 Instructions with Loop Variations

Instruction	Decrement String Address(es)	Increment String Address(es)	Decrement Address(es) and repeat	Increment Address(es) and repeat
Compare CP CPB	CPD CPDB CPSD CPSDB	CPI CPIB CPSI CPSIB	CPDR CPDRB CPSDR CPSDRB	CPIR CPIRB CPSIR CPSIRB
Input IN INB SIN SINB	IND INDB SIND SINDB	INI INIB SINI SINIB	INDR INDRB SINDR SINDRB	INIR INIRB SINIR SINIRB
Load LD LDB	LDD LDDB	LDI LDIB	LDDR LDDRB	LDIR LDIRB
Output OUT OUTB SOUT SOUTB	OUTD OUTDB SOUTD SOUTDB	OUTI OUTIB SOUTI SOUTIB	OTDR OTDRB SOTDR SOTDRB	OTIR OTIRB SOTIR SOTIRB
Translate	TRDB	TRIB	TRDRB	TRIRB
Translate and test	TRTDB	TRTIB	TRTDRB	TRTIRB

The input, load, output, translate, and translate and test instructions use three CPU registers:

```
INST      @RD,@RS,RC
```

INST is the operation.

RD is the Destination Indirect Address register.

RS is the Source Indirect Address register.

RC is the Iteration Counter register.

The compare instructions use three CPU registers and a condition code:

```
INST      RD,@RS,RC,CC
```

INST is the instruction mnemonic.

RD is the Destination Operand register.

RS is the Source Indirect Address register.

RC is the Iteration Counter register.

CC is the Condition Code.

Remember, the relation tested is: destination condition source.

The Decrement (e.g., CPD) and Increment (e.g., CPI) variations provide the "Loop Control Section" **logic** shown in Figures 5-1 and 5-2; they also provide that part of the "Processing Section" implemented by the base instruction (e.g., CP). **Figure 5-3 illustrates logic for Decrement and Increment instruction variations.**

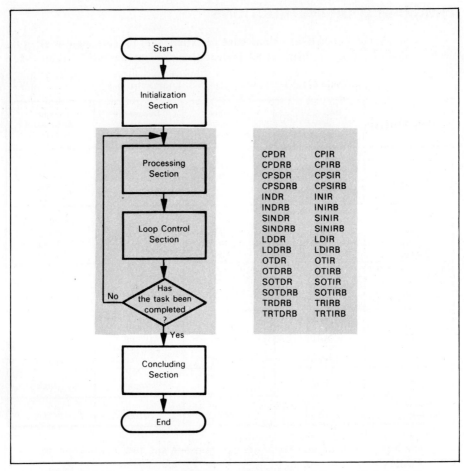

Figure 5-4. Decrement and Repeat, and Increment and Repeat Variations of
String Handling Instructions

The **Decrement and Repeat (e.g., CPDR) and Increment and Repeat (e.g.,
CPIR) variations provide the "Processing Section," the "Loop Control Section,"
and the "Has the task been completed?" logic** shown in Figure 5-1 (but not 5-2). Of
necessity, the "Processing Section" can do no more than the operations performed by
the base instruction (e.g., CP). **Figure 5-4 illustrates logic for these instruction variations.**

PROGRAM EXAMPLES

5-1. 16-Bit Sum of Data

Purpose: Calculate the sum of a series of numbers. The length of the series is in location 6000. The series begins in memory location 6002. Store the sum on the stack. Assume that the sum is a 16-bit number so that you can ignore carries.

Sample Problem:

(6000)	=	0003
(6002)	=	2040
(6004)	=	1C22
(6006)	=	0242
R15	=	8000

Result: R15 = 7FFE

(7FFE)	=	(6002) + (6004) + (6006)
	=	2040 + 1C22 + 0242
	=	3EA4

There are three operands to be summed since (6000) = 3.

Flowchart 5-1:

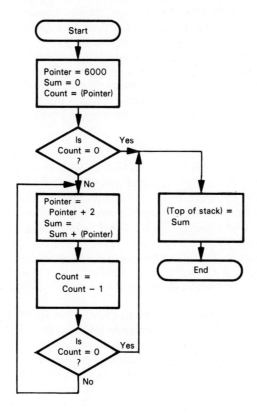

Program 5-1:

```
                internal
                    pgm_5_1 procedure              ! Sum of data !
                    entry
                        $abs    IBASE
    4600 7602           LDA     R2,%6000           ! Data pointer !
    4602 6000
    4604 8D18           CLR     R1                 ! Sum !
    4606 2120           LD      R0,@R2             ! Length !
    4608 8D04           TEST    R0                 ! Check for empty block !
    460A E604           JR      Z,DONE
    460C A921   SUM:    INC     R2,#2              ! Advance to next WORD !
    460E 0121           ADD     R1,@R2             ! Sum next element !
    4610 AB00           DEC     R0                 ! Keep count !
    4612 EEFC           JR      NZ,SUM
    4614 93F1   DONE:   PUSH    @R15,R1            ! Store sum on stack !
    4616 7A00           HALT

    4618            end     pgm_5_1
```

The initialization section of the program consists of the first three instructions; they initialize the counter and data pointer. The next two instructions ensure that the program works if the list is empty.

The processing section of the program is the single instruction ADD R1,@R2.

The loop control section of the program consists of the instructions INC R2,#2 and DEC R0. INC updates the data pointer so that the next iteration adds the next number to the sum. Note that the pointer must be advanced by 2 since we are dealing with word values. DEC R0 decrements the iteration counter.

The instruction JR NZ,SUM causes a branch if the Zero flag is zero. The offset part of the JR is a twos complement number, which is multiplied by two and added to the address of the memory location immediately following the JR. The offset in the JR instruction is a number of *words*, not bytes. (Can an instruction begin at an odd address?) In this case, the required jump is from memory location 4614 to memory location 460C. So the offset is:

$$460C - 4614 = FFF8 \text{ bytes}$$

using twos complement notation. Converted to an 8-bit word displacement, FFF8 becomes $0.5 \times (F8) = FC$, again using twos complement notation.

If the Zero flag is one (set), the CPU executes the next instruction in sequence (i.e., PUSH). The Zero status tested by the JR instruction is generated by the execution of the preceding DEC R0 instruction. JR NZ,LOOP causes a jump to LOOP if DEC R0 does not produce a zero result.

Since the JR instruction offset is only one byte long, such jumps can go no further than 127 words forward or 128 words backwards (actually 128 words forward or 127 backwards, since the count starts at the end of the instruction). Longer jumps must use the JP instruction.

Because loop control logic occurs so frequently, the Z8000 has an instruction (DJNZ) which combines operations performed by DEC and JR. DJNZ (Decrement and Jump on Not Zero) decrements a counter register, then executes a branch if the counter register contents are not zero. The next sequential instruction is executed if the counter register has decremented to zero. In fact, there are two Decrement and Jump on Not Zero instructions: DJNZ decrements a 16-bit counter register; DBJNZ decrements an 8- bit counter register. The two instructions execute identically otherwise.

In this example program, we could replace the last four instructions with these three instructions:

```
                DJNZ    R0,LOOP
        DONE:   PUSH    @R15,R1
                HALT
```

which has the object form:

```
        4610 F083         DJNZ    R0,LOOP
        4612 93F1  DONE:  PUSH    @R15,R1
        4614 7A00         HALT
```

This change saves one word of memory. Note that, unlike the JR instruction, the DJNZ offset is an *unsigned* number which is *subtracted* from the program counter. Therefore DJNZ (and DBJNZ) can only jump backwards up to 126 words from the beginning of the instruction.

Program logic usually decrements iteration counters rather than incrementing them. If you decrement an iteration counter, you can use the number of iterations as the initial counter value; the Zero flag is then set to 1 when the counter decrements from 1 to 0. If you increment a counter, then you must initially load the complement of the number of iterations into the counter; the Zero flag will be set to 1 when the counter increments from FFFF (or FF) to 0. Try rewriting the program using INC R0 in the place of DEC R0.

The order of instructions is often very important. DEC R0 must immediately precede JR NZ,LOOP, otherwise the zero result set by DEC R0 could be changed by an intervening instruction. INC R2, #2 must precede ADD R1,@R2 or else the first number added to the sum would be the contents of memory location 6000.

5-2. 32-Bit Sum of Data

Purpose: Calculate the sum of a series of 16 numbers. The length of the series is in location 6000. The series begins in memory location 6002. Store the sum as a long word (32 bits) on the stack. Take carries into account.

Sample Problem:

```
            (6000)  =  0003
            (6002)  =  8040
            (6004)  =  BC22
            (6006)  =  7242
              R15   =  8000

Result:   8040 + BC22 + 7242 = 0001AEA4

              R15   =  7FFC
            (7FFC)  =  0001
            (7FFE)  =  AEA4
```

Program 5-2a:

```
                     internal
                       pgm_5_2a procedure          ! 32 bit sum of data !
                     entry
                             $abs     IBASE

     4600 7602              LDA    R2,%6000
     4602 6000
     4604 8D58              CLR    R5                ! Low order sum !
     4606 8D48              CLR    R4                ! High order sum !
     4608 2120              LD     R0,@R2            ! Length !
     460A 8D04              TEST   R0                ! Empty? !
     460C E605              JR     Z,DONE
     460E A921     SUM32:   INC    R2,#2             ! Next word !
     4610 0125              ADD    R5,@R2            ! Add to low order sum !
     4612 EF01              JR     NC,STEP           ! Was carry set? !
     4614 A940              INC    R4                ! Yes, add 1 to high order !
     4616 F085     STEP:    DJNZ   R0,SUM32          ! Repeat till end of block !
     4618 91F4     DONE:    PUSHL  @R15,RR4          ! Push R4 R5 long word !
     461A 7A00              HALT

     461C          end      pgm_5_2a
```

This program differs from the 16-bit addition in detail only. Since a 32-bit sum is to be generated, two 16-bit CPU registers must be cleared initially. There is no CLRL (clear long word) instruction. The two halves of a 32-bit CPU register are cleared, and used to create the 32-bit sum, so that the result can be stored using a single PUSHL instruction. The processing section now has three instructions (ADD, JR and INC).

The two new instructions (JR and INC) increment the high- order result word if the sum in the low-order result word overflows.

JR NC,STEP causes a jump to memory location STEP if the carry = 0. Thus, if there is no carry from the 16-bit addition, the program jumps around the statement that increments the most significant bits of the sum. The relative offset for JR NC,STEP is:

$$\frac{\begin{array}{r} 4616 \\ -4614 \end{array}}{02 \text{ bytes} = 01 \text{ words}}$$

Flowchart 5-2:

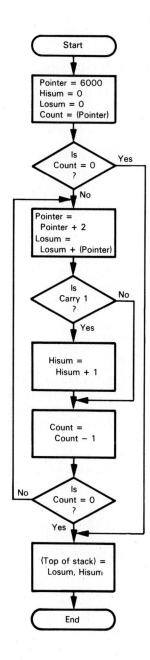

The relative offset for DJNZ R0,SUM32 is:

$$
\begin{array}{r}
4618 \\
-460E \\
\hline
\end{array}
$$
$$
\text{0A bytes = 05 words}
$$

The long form of the ADD instruction could simplify the program, but the list contains 16-bit values; we must do some extra work to make the value look like a long word.

Program 5-2b:

```
                internal
                    pgm_5_2b procedure          ! 32 bit sum with ADDL !
                entry
                    $abs      IBASE

4600 7602           LDA       R2,%6000
4602 6000
4604 8D68           CLR       R6              ! High crder of every value !
4606 8D58           CLR       R5              ! Low order sum !
4608 8D48           CLR       R4              ! High order sum !
460A 2120           LD        R0,@R2          ! Length !
460C 8D04           TEST      R0              ! Empty? !
460E E604           JR        Z,DONE
4610 A921  SUM32:   INC       R2,#2           ! Next word !
4612 2127           LD        R7,@R2          ! Value to RR6 high order 0 !
4614 9664           ADDL      RR4,RR6
4616 F084           DJNZ      R0,SUM32        ! Repeat till end of block !
4618 91F4  DONE:    PUSHL     @R15,RR4        ! Push R4 R5 long word !
461A 7A00           HALT

461C                end       pgm_5_2b
```

We clear R6 so that the high-order 16 bits of RR6 are always 0. We don't need to clear it each time through the loop since it never changes.

This change decreases the number of instructions in the loop, and perhaps makes the program easier to understand. However, does it make the loop itself run faster? The first loop takes 25 or 29 cycles:

INC	4 cycles
ADD	4 cycles
JR	6 cycles
(INC)	(4 cycles) not always executed
DJNZ	11 cycles
	25 (29) cycles

The second version takes 29 cycles:

INC	4 cycles
LD	7 cycles
ADDL	8 cycles
DJNZ	11 cycles
	29 cycles

The first version is faster. We will often find cases like this on the Z8000. A single, more powerful instruction often takes longer to execute than two or more simpler instructions that perform the same task. In this case, the extra time is taken by the LD instruction, which is required to set up a 32-bit operand for the more powerful ADDL instruction.

5-3. Number of Negative Elements

Purpose: Determine the number of negative elements in a string of 16-bit memory words. Negative elements are identified by a 1 in the most significant bit position. The length of the string is in memory word 6000. The string elements are stored in memory starting at memory word 6002. Place the number of negative elements at the top of the stack.

Sample Problem:

```
            (6000)  =  0006
            (6002)  =  2026
            (6004)  =  5120
            (6006)  =  COCO
            (6008)  =  77F9
            (600A)  =  FFF0
            (600C)  =  0240
              R15   =  8000

Result:     R15   =  7FFE
            (7FFE)  =  0002, since 6006 and 600A contain numbers
                          with an MSB (sign) of 1.
```

Program 5-3a:

```
             internal
                 pgm_5_3a procedure          ! Count elements < 0 !
             entry
                   $abs    IBASE

4600 7602            LDA     R2,%6000
4602 6000
4604 8D18            CLR     R1               ! No. of negative elements !
4606 2120            LD      R0,@R2           ! Length !
4608 8D04            TEST    R0               ! Empty? !
460A E605            JR      Z,DONE
460C A921   NNEG:    INC     R2,#2            ! Advance to next WORD !
460E 0D24            TEST    @R2
4610 ED01            JR      PL,NONEG         ! Positive or negative? !
4612 A910            INC     R1               ! Count it if negative !
4614 F085   NONEG:   DJNZ    R0,NNEG
4616 93F1   DONE:    PUSH    @R15,R1          ! Return no. of elements < 0 !
4618 7A00            HALT

461A                 end     pgm_5_3a
```

The TEST @R2 instruction sets the S (Sign) flag if bit 15 (MSB) of the source is set; it is cleared otherwise.

Could we have used JR GE,NONEG instead of JR PL,NONEG? In most cases yes, but only because we know the V (Overflow) flag is cleared by the INC R2,#2 instruction. What happens if our data starts at location 7FFE? Or what if the program were rewritten to use byte instead of word data? (Hint: the TESTB instruction sets the P flag, which is the same as V.)

Condition codes GE, GT, LE, LT, EQ and NE should be used only when signed binary numbers are Compared, or after execution of a signed binary arithmetic operation.

Flowchart 5-3:

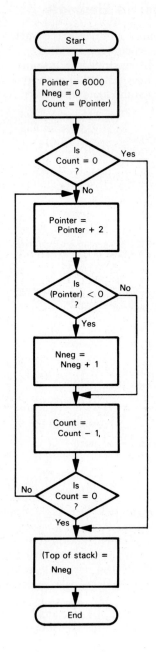

Use PL, MI, Z and NZ after a TEST or a logical operation. Use the unsigned conditons (UGE, etc.) after comparing two addresses, or other unsigned numbers.

We could replace:

```
            TEST     @R2
            JR       PL,NONEG
```

with

```
            BIT      @R2,#15
            JR       Z,NONEG
```

The BIT instruction tests the specified bit in the destination. If the bit is zero, the Z flag is set; if the bit is one, the Z flag is zero. The low-order bit is bit 0; 15 is the high-order bit of a word. Does this change the execution time?

We can use the CPI instruction in our program, which now takes the form shown in program 5-3b.

Program 5-3b:

```
                internal
                     pgm_5_3b  procedure          ! Count elements < 0 !
                entry
                          $abs       IBASE

     4600 8D38            CLR      R3              ! Compare each with 0 !
     4602 7602            LDA      R2,%6002        ! Start of element list !
     4604 6002
     4606 8D18            CLR      R1              ! Number of elements < 0 !
     4608 6100            LD       R0,%6000        ! Number of elements !
     460A 6000
     460C 8D04            TEST     R0              ! Empty? !
     460E E607            JR       Z,DONE
     4610 BB20    NNEG:   CPI      R3,@R2,R0,LT    ! Is next element negative? !
     4612 0031
     4614 E402            JR       OV,LAST         ! Jump if done with list !
     4616 A910            INC      R1              ! Count it if negative !
     4618 E8FB            JR       NNEG
     461A EE01    LAST:   JR       NZ,DONE         ! Was the last element < 0? !
     461C A910            INC      R1
     461E 93F1    DONE:   PUSH     @R15,R1         ! Return no. of elements < 0 !
     4620 7A00            HALT

     4622         end     pgm_5_3b
```

This program generates more object code, and takes longer to execute than program 5-3a; once again this emphasizes that you are frequently better off using simple instructions. Check for yourself. For the two programs 5-3a and 5-3b compare the number of object code words for the entire program, and the number of execution clock periods within the loop.

You can replace the CPI instruction with the equivalent CPIR instruction; the program does not change otherwise. Now the program will execute faster within the loop. Check for yourself.

5-4. Find Maximum

Purpose: Find the largest element in a block of data bytes. The length of the block is in memory location 6000 and the block begins in memory location 6001. Store the maximum value (as a word) on the stack. Assume that all numbers in the block are 8-bit unsigned binary values.

Sample Problem:

```
                    (6000) = 05
                    (6001) = 67
                    (6002) = 79
                    (6003) = 15
                    (6004) = E3
                    (6005) = 72
                     R15   = 8000

        Result:      R15   = 7FFE
                    (7FFE) = 00E3, since this is the largest of the five
                                   unsigned numbers.
```

Program 5-4:

```
                internal
                     pgm_5_4 procedure          ! Find maximum value !
                     entry
                         $abs     IBASE

    4600 7602                LDA    R2,%6000
    4602 6000
    4604 8C88                CLRB   RL0          ! Maximum value !
    4606 2020                LDB    RH0,@R2      ! Length !
    4608 8C04                TESTB  RH0
    460A E605                JR     Z,DONE
    460C A920     MAX:       INC    R2           ! Next element !
    460E 0A28                CPB    RL0,@R2      ! Larger than previous max? !
    4610 EF01                JR     UGE,MSTEP
    4612 2028                LDB    RL0,@R2      ! Yes, make it new max !
    4614 F005     MSTEP:     DBJNZ  RH0,MAX
    4616 93F0     DONE:      PUSH   @R15,R0      ! Return maximum value !
    4618 7A00                HALT

    461A              end       pgm_5_4
```

Since 0 is the smallest unsigned binary number, RL0 is set to 0; the first non-zero 8-bit value in the list will be loaded into RL0; subsequent 8-bit values will be loaded into RL0 only if they are larger than the current contents of RL0.

Before reading further, rewrite the program using RH1 as the counter instead of RH0.

Flowchart 5-4:

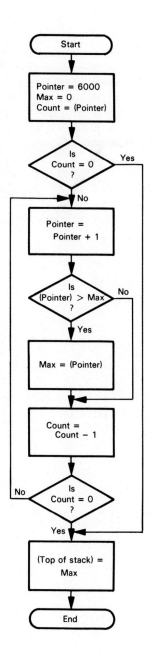

The last step in the program demonstrates the use of a programming "trick." We push R0 onto the stack without clearing the high-order byte. This can be done because we know the DBJNZ has left a 0 in RH0. This is called a "trick" because it makes use of a subtle side effect of a seemingly unrelated operation. Using tricks like this is generally a bad practice. Did you notice this problem when rewriting the program to use RH1, or did you push whatever happend to be in RH0? Tricks detract from program clarity, and lend themselves to program errors. You, or another person, might want to change the program at a later date; this subtlety is easily overlooked. The savings that a trick like this yields are seldom great enough to justify the resulting lack of clarity. At worst, tricks should be noted in the comments; at best, add redundant instructions to improve clarity and structure:

```
MSTEP:  DBJNZ    RH0,MAX
DONE:   CLRB     RH0                     ! Turn max into 16-bit word  !
        PUSH     @R15,R0
        HALT
```

5-5. Find Maximum Using Indexed Addressing

Purpose: This problem can be used to illustrate indexed addressing. Instead of storing the value of the maximum element on the stack, suppose the element number is to be stored on the stack. In this case 0003 should be pushed onto the stack since the fourth number in the block is the largest. If the block of numbers is empty, we will store -1 on the stack.

Sample Problems:

```
a.              (6000)  =  05
                (6001)  =  67
                (6002)  =  79
                (6003)  =  15
                (6004)  =  E3
                (6005)  =  72
                   R15  =  8000

     Result:    R15   =  7FFE
                (7FFE)  =  0003, since (6001 + 0003) is
                           the largest value, E3.

b.              (6000)  =  00
                   R15  =  8000

     Result:    R15   =  7FFE
                (7FFE)  =  FFFF, since the list is empty.
```

Program 5-5a:

```
           internal
                pgm_5_5a procedure          ! Return index of max value !
                entry
                     $abs     IBASE

4600 2101            LD       R1,#%FFFF      ! R1 is index of max !
4602 FFFF
4604 6100            LD       R0,%6000       ! Length !
4606 6000
4608 8D04            TEST     R0
460A E60C            JR       Z,DONE
460C A910            INC      R1             ! Index of first element !
460E BD21            LDK      R2,#1          ! Index of second element !
4610 AB00            DEC      R0             ! Check for only 1 element !
4612 E608            JR       EQ,DONE
4614 602B   IXMAX:   LDB      RL3,%6001(R2)  ! Fetch next element !
4616 6001
4618 4A1B            CPB      RL3,%6001(R1)  ! Larger than previous max? !
461A 6001
461C E701            JR       ULT,IXSTEP
461E A121            LD       R1,R2          ! Yes, use as new max !
4620 A920   IXSTEP:  INC      R2             ! Advance to next element !
4622 F088            DJNZ     R0,IXMAX
4624 93F1   DONE:    PUSH     @R15,R1        ! Return index of max !
4626 7A00            HALT

4628            end       pgm_5_5a
```

Flowchart 5-5:

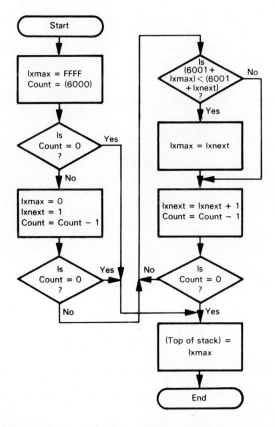

Note that the initialization is fairly complicated. This is because there are two degenerate cases to handle: an empty list and a list of only one element. (A block of numbers is frequently referred to as a list.)

The instructions LDB RL3,%6001(R2) and CPB RL3,%6001(R1) make use of indexed addressing. Remember, if R2 contains 4, %6001(R2) references location 6001 + 0004 = 6005.

A typical point of confusion is the 0th element in a list. A list of length 5 consists of 5 elements with indexes 0 through 4. This becomes important when the program is written to index backwards. Example program 5-5b shows an example.

Program 5-5b:

```
                internal
                   pgm_5_5b procedure        ! Max index backwards !
                entry
                     $abs      IBASE

   4600 6102        LD         R2,%6000       ! Length is last index + 1 !
   4602 6000
   4604 A121        LD         R1,R2          ! Set up max index (+ 1) !
   4606 AB10        DEC        R1             ! Real index of last element !
   4608 AB20        DEC        R2             ! Index of 2nd to last (+ 1) !
   460A E208        JR         LE,DONE        ! If 1 or 0 elements !
   460C 601B IXMAX: LDB        RL3,%6001(R1)  ! Pick up next element !
   460E 6001
   4610 4A2B        CPB        RL3,%6001-1(R2) ! Note R2 is index + 1 !
   4612 6000
   4614 EB02        JR         UGT,IXSTEP
   4616 A121        LD         R1,R2          ! Use as nex max !
   4618 AB10        DEC        R1             ! We don't want index + 1 !
   461A F288 IXSTEP: DJNZ      R2,IXMAX       ! Next element !
   461C 93F1 DONE:  PUSH       @R15,R1
   461E 7A00        HALT

   4620             end        pgm_5_5b
```

Convince yourself that the program works for 0 or 1 elements. (Hint: look at the status bits modified by DEC, and how they are interpreted by the LE condition.)

We could replace:

```
        LD      R2,%6000
        LD      R1,R2
        DEC     R1
        DEC     R2
        JR      LE,DONE
```

with

```
        LD      R2,%6000
        DEC     R2
        JR      LE,DONE
        LD      R1,R2
```

but the extra DEC instruction is, perhaps, worth including since it makes program logic easier to follow.

The instruction

```
        CPB     RL3,%6001-1(R2)
```

is the same as

```
        CPB     RL3,%6000(R2)
```

However, we wanted to emphasize that R2 is actually the index + 1. This allows the DJNZ instruction to be used with R2.

5-6. Normalize a Binary Number

Purpose: Shift the contents of memory location 6000 left until the most significant bit of the number is 1. Store the result in location 6002. Store the number of left shifts required in location 6004. If the contents of memory location 6000 are zero, clear both 6002 and 6004.

Note: This is equivalent to converting a number to a scientific notation. For example:

$$0.0057 \rightarrow 5.7 \times 10^{-3}$$

Sample Problems:

a.		(6000)	=	2022
	Result:	(6002)	=	8088
		(6004)	=	0002
b.		(6000)	=	0001
	Result:	(6002)	=	8000
		(6004)	=	000F
c.		(6000)	=	0000
	Result:	(6002)	=	0000
		(6004)	=	0000
d.		(6000)	=	C123
	Result:	(6002)	=	C123
		(6004)	=	0000

Program 5-6:

```
          internal
                pgm_5_6 procedure          ! Justify a Binary Fraction !
          entry
                    $abs     IBASE
4600 6100           LD       R0,%6000      ! Get data !
4602 6000
4604 8D18           CLR      R1            ! Count number of shifts !
4606 8D04           TEST     R0
4608 E604           JR       Z,DONE        ! Simple if value is 0 !
460A E503           JR       MI,DONE       ! If already justified !
460C A910  JUST:    INC      R1            ! Count shifts !
460E 8100           ADD      R0,R0         ! Shift left one position !
4610 EDFD           JR       PL,JUST       ! Repeat till sign bit is on !
4612 6F00  DONE:    LD       %6002,R0      ! Store justified number !
4614 6002
4616 6F01           LD       %6004,R1      ! Store number of shifts !
4618 6004
461A 7A00           HALT

461C          end       pgm_5_6
```

Flowchart 5-6:

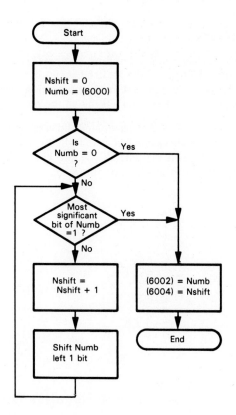

It is ironic that the Z8000 has 12 different shift and rotate instructions, yet ADD provides the only left shift with a one-word object code.

Note the two separate tests for zero and minus:

```
TEST    R0
JR      Z , DONE
JR      MI , DONE
```

As noted earlier, these two could not be combined into a JR LE,DONE because we do not know the state of the V (Overflow) flag.

PROBLEMS

5-1. Checksum of Data

Purpose: Calculate the checksum of a list of 8-bit numbers. The length of the list is in memory location 6000_{16} and the list itself begins in memory location 6001_{16}. Store the checksum in the first memory location following the list. The checksum is formed by Exclusive-ORing all the numbers in the list.

    Note: Checksums are often used by paper tape and cassette systems to ensure that data has been read correctly. A checksum calculated when reading the data is compared to a checksum that is stored with the data. If the two checksums do not agree, the system will usually either indicate an error, or automatically read the data again.

Sample Problem:

$$
\begin{aligned}
(6000) &= 03 \\
(6001) &= 28 \\
(6002) &= 55 \\
(6003) &= 26
\end{aligned}
$$

$$
\begin{aligned}
\text{Result:}\quad (6004) &= (6001) \oplus (6002) \oplus (6003) \\
&= 28 \oplus 55 \oplus 26 \\
&= \begin{array}{c} 0\,0\,1\,0\,1\,0\,0\,0 \\ \oplus\ 0\,1\,0\,1\,0\,1\,0\,1 \\ \hline 0\,1\,1\,1\,1\,1\,0\,1 \\ \oplus\ 0\,0\,1\,0\,0\,1\,1\,0 \\ \hline 0\,1\,0\,1\,1\,0\,1\,1 \end{array} \\
&= 5B
\end{aligned}
$$

5-2. Number of Zero, Positive, and Negative Numbers

Purpose: Determine the number of zero, positive (most significant bit zero, but entire number not zero) and negative (most significant bit 1) elements in a block. The length of the block is in memory location 6000. Place the number of negative elements in memory location 6800, the number of zero elements in memory location 6802, and the number of positive elements in memory location 6804.

Sample Problem:

$$
\begin{aligned}
(6000) &= 0006 \\
(6002) &= 7602 \\
(6004) &= 8D48 \\
(6006) &= 2120 \\
(6008) &= 0000 \\
(600A) &= E605 \\
(600C) &= 0004
\end{aligned}
$$

$$
\text{Result:}\quad \text{2 negative, 1 zero, 3 positive, so}
$$

$$
\begin{aligned}
(6800) &= 0002 \\
(6802) &= 0001 \\
(6804) &= 0003
\end{aligned}
$$

5-3. Find Minimum

Purpose: Find the smallest element in a block of byte data. The length of the block is in memory location 6000 and the block itself begins in memory location 6001. Store the minimum value on the stack as a word with the high byte 0. Assume that the numbers in the block are 8-bit unsigned numbers.

Sample Problem:

```
        R15   =  8000
      (6000)  =  05
      (6001)  =  65
      (6002)  =  79
      (6003)  =  15
      (6004)  =  E3
      (6005)  =  72
```

Result: R15   = 7FFE
         (7FFE) = 15, since this is the smallest of the
                    five unsigned numbers.

5-4. Count 1 Bits

Purpose: Determine how many bits in memory location 6000 are one and place the result in memory location 6002.

Sample Problem:

```
      (6000)  =  B794 = 1011011110010100
```
Result: (6002) = 0009

5-5. Find Element with Most 1 Bits

Purpose: Determine which element in a block of data words has the highest number of bits that are one. The length of the block is in location 6000 and the block itself begins in location 6002. Place the value with the most 1 bits on the stack. If two or more values have the same number of 1 bits, use the earliest element in the list.

Sample Problem:

```
        R15   =  8000
      (6000)  =  0005
      (6002)  =  6779 = 0110011101111001
      (6004)  =  15E3 = 0001010111100011
      (6006)  =  68F2 = 0110100011110010
      (6008)  =  8700 = 1000011100000000
      (600A)  =  592A = 0101100100101010
```

Result: R15   = 7FFE
         (7FFE) = 6779, since this element is the first
                    one in the list to have ten 1 bits.

6

Character Coded Data

Microprocessors often handle character-coded data. Keyboards, teletypewriters, communications devices, displays, and computer terminals expect or provide character-coded data; so do many instruments, test systems, and controllers. The most commonly used character code is ASCII. Baudot and EBCDIC are found less frequently. We will assume all of our character-coded data to be 7-bit ASCII, with the eighth (most significant) bit zero (see Table 6-1).

HANDLING DATA IN ASCII

Some principles to remember when handling ASCII-coded data are:

1. **The codes for the numbers and letters form ordered subsequences.** The codes for the decimal numbers are 30_{16} through 39_{16} so that you can convert between decimal and ASCII using simple addition. The codes for the upper-case letters are 41_{16} through $5A_{16}$ so you can order alphabetically by sorting data in increasing numeric order.

2. **The computer draws no distinction between printing and non-printing characters.** Only I/O devices make that distinction.

3. **An ASCII device will handle only ASCII characters.** To print a 7 on an ASCII printer, the microprocessor must send 37_{16} to the printer; 07_{16} is the 'bell' character. Similarly, the microprocessor will receive the character 9 from an ASCII keyboard as 39_{16}; 09_{16} is the 'tab' character.

Table 6-1. Hex-ASCII Characters

Hex LSD \ Hex MSD	0	1	2	3	4	5	6	7
0	NUL	DLE	SP	0	@	O	`	p
1	SOH	DC1	!	1	A	Q	a	q
2	STX	DC2	"	2	B	R	b	r
3	ETX	DC3	#	3	C	S	c	s
4	EOT	DC4	$	4	D	T	d	t
5	ENQ	NAK	%	5	E	U	e	u
6	ACK	SYN	&	6	F	V	f	v
7	BEL	ETB	'	7	G	W	g	w
8	BS	CAN	(	8	H	X	h	x
9	HT	EM	)	9	I	Y	i	y
A	LF	SUB	*	:	J	Z	j	z
B	VT	ESC	+	;	K	[	k	{
C	FF	FS	,	<	L	\	l	|
D	CR	GS	-	=	M	]	m	}
E	SO	RS	.	>	N	∧	n	~
F	SI	US	/	?	O	—	o	DEL

4. **Some ASCII devices do not use the full character set.** For example, control characters and lower-case letters may be ignored; sometimes they are printed as spaces or question marks. Some devices print upper-case letters when they receive codes for lower-case letters.

5. **Some widely used ASCII characters are:**

   $0A_{16}$ - line feed (LF)
   $0D_{16}$ - carriage return (CR)
   20_{16} - space (SP)
   $3F_{16}$ - ? (question mark)
   $7F_{16}$ - rubout or delete character

6. **Each ASCII character occupies seven bits.** This allows a large character set, but it is wasteful when a small character subset, such as the decimal numbers, is being represented. An 8-bit byte, for example, can hold just one ASCII-coded decimal digit but it can hold two BCD-coded digits.

Most assembly languages have features that make character-coded data easy to handle. In Zilog's PLZ/ASM assembly language, quotation marks around a character indicate the character's ASCII value. For example,

```
        LDB     RL0,#'A'
```

is the same as

```
        LDB     RL0,#%41
```

The first form is preferable for several reasons. It increases the readability of the instruction; it also avoids errors that may result from looking up a value in a table. The program does not depend on ASCII as the character set, since the assembler handles the conversion using whatever code has been designed into it. Each of the most common non-printing ASCII characters has a special symbol representing its value. '%R' is carriage return ($0D_{16}$), '%L' is line feed and '%Q' is a quotation mark. Strings of characters in data also have a convenient syntax. To define a message "MSG":

```
        GLOBAL
            MSG ARRAY [* BYTE] := 'This is the message%R'
```

the byte at address MSG will contain 54_{16} ('T'), followed by the values of the other characters.

PROGRAM EXAMPLES

6-1. Length of a String of Characters

Purpose: Determine the length of a string of ASCII characters (seven bits plus most significant bit zero). The string starts in memory location 6001, and the end of the string is marked by a carriage return character ('CR', $0D_{16}$). Place the length of the string (excluding the carriage return) into memory location 6000.

Sample Problems:

a. (6001) = 0D

Result: (6000) = 00, since the first character is a carriage return.

b.
(6001) = 52 'R'
(6002) = 41 'A'
(6003) = 54 'T'
(6004) = 48 'H'
(6005) = 45 'E'
(6006) = 52 'R'
(6007) = 0D CR

Result: (6000) = 06

Flowchart 6-1a:

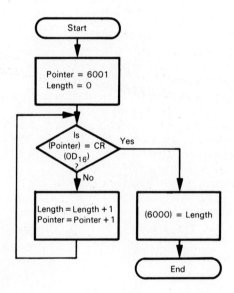

Program 6-1a:

```
                internal
                  pgm_6_1a procedure
                  entry
                       $abs    IBASE

  4600 7601            LDA     R1,%6001        ! Point to start of string !
  4602 6001
  4604 8C88            CLRB    RL0             ! Count chars in RL0 !
  4606 0C11    LOOP:   CPB     @R1,#'%R'       ! Look for ASCII CR !
  4608 0D0D
  460A E603            JR      EQ,DONE
  460C A910            INC     R1              ! Advance pointer !
  460E A880            INCB    RL0             ! Count another char !
  4610 E8FA            JR      LOOP
  4612 6E08    DONE:   LDB     %6000,RL0       ! Store length at beginning !
  4614 6000
  4616 7A00            HALT

  4618           end   pgm_6_1a
```

The carriage return character, 'CR', is just another ASCII code ($0D_{16}$) as far as the computer is concerned. The fact that this character causes an output device to perform a control function rather than print a symbol does not affect the computer.

The Compare instruction, CPB, sets the flags as if the carriage return code had been subtracted from the destination operand, but leaves the carriage return character in the source register for later comparisons. The Zero (Z) flag is affected as follows:

Z = 1   if the character in the string is a carriage return
Z = 0   if it is not a carriage return

The condition code EQ tests for Z = 1.

The instruction INC adds 1 to the string length counter in Register RL0. CLRB RL0 initializes this counter to zero before the loop begins. Remember to initialize variables before using them in a loop.

Unlike other program loops we have shown, this loop does not terminate when a counter decrements to zero or reaches a maximum value. The computer will simply continue examining characters until it finds a carriage return. It is good programming practice to place a maximum count in a loop like this to avoid problems with erroneous strings that do not contain a carriage return. What would happen if the example program were used with such a string?

Note that by rearranging the logic and changing the initial conditions, you can shorten the program and decrease its execution time. If we adjust the flowchart so that the program increments the string length before it checks for the carriage return, only one Jump instruction is necessary instead of two. See flowchart 6-1b and program 6-1b.

Flowchart 6-1b:

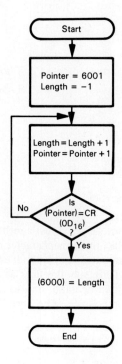

Program 6-1b:

```
            internal
              pgm_6_1b procedure
              entry
                  $abs      IBASE

4600 7601         LDA       R1,%6001-1       ! Point to string start - 1 !
4602 6000
4604 C8FF         LDB       RL0,#-1          ! Start char counter at -1 !
4606 A880  LOOP:  INCB      RL0              ! Count previous char !
4608 A910         INC       R1               ! Point to next char !
460A 0C11         CPB       @R1,#'%R'        ! Look for ASCII CR !
460C 0D0D
460E EEFB         JR        NE,LOOP          ! Keep going till found !
4610 6E08         LDB       %6000,RL0        ! Store length at beginning !
4612 6000
4614 7A00         HALT

4616         end      pgm_6_1b
```

This version of the program is shorter and faster. The shortest and fastest version makes use of one of the Z8000's repeating instructions: CPIRB (compare byte, increment and repeat). This is shown in Program 6-1c.

Program 6-1c:

```
                    internal
                      pgm_6_1c procedure
                    entry
                        $abs       IBASE

    4600 7601           LDA       R1,%6001        ! Point to start of string !
    4602 6001
    4604 C80D           LDB       RL0,#'%R'       ! Search object: ASCII CR !
    4606 2102           LD        R2,#%100        ! R2 counts down till CR found
    4608 0100                                     ! Stop search after 256 chars !
    460A BA14           CPIRB     RL0,@R1,R2,EQ   ! Scan string for the CR !
    460C 0286
    460E 8CA0           COMB      RL2             ! Get actual char count !
    4610 6E0A           LDB       %6000,RL2       ! Store length at beginning !
    4612 6000
    4614 7A00           HALT

    4616            end       pgm_6_1c
```

The CPIRB instruction performs these steps:

1. RL0 is compared to the byte pointed to by R1.

2. If they are equal, the Z flag is set to 1; it is reset (0) if they are not equal.

3. R1 is incremented.

4. R2 is decremented; if 0, the V flag (overflow) is set.

5. If the Z flag is 0 and the V flag is 0, the instruction is repeated. If either is set, control passes to the next instruction.

The instruction repeats until the byte addressed by R1 is equal to RL0, or until the Count register, R2, goes to zero. Note that any condition can be used in place of EQ. Any condition code can be used in the CPIRB instruction, yet the Z flag is set when the condition is met. This use of the Z flag can be confusing. We will see another example of this in a later program.

Since the instruction decrements the Count register, we must do a calculation to get the string length. Convince yourself that the COMB instruction achieves the desired result. (Hint: check first if it works for length 0, then length 1.)

Since there are two conditions that cause the CPIRB instruction to terminate, it is usually followed by a JR instruction to determine why it stopped. However, in this example, if there is no CR in the first 256 bytes, R2 will be 0 and we will store 255 (FF_{16}) as the length, so we don't need to check whether the counter went to zero.

6-2. Find First Non-Blank Character

Purpose: Search a string of ASCII characters (seven bits plus most significant bit 0) for a non-blank character. The string starts in memory location 6000. Place the address of the first non-blank character on the stack. The blank character code is 20_{16} in ASCII.

Sample Problems:

<table>
<tr><td>a.</td><td></td><td>(6000)</td><td>=</td><td>37</td><td>'7'</td></tr>
<tr><td></td><td></td><td>R15</td><td>=</td><td>8000</td><td></td></tr>
<tr><td></td><td>Result:</td><td>R15</td><td>=</td><td>7FFE</td><td></td></tr>
<tr><td></td><td></td><td>(7FFE)</td><td>=</td><td>6000</td><td></td></tr>
<tr><td>b.</td><td></td><td>(6000)</td><td>=</td><td>20</td><td>SP</td></tr>
<tr><td></td><td></td><td>(6001)</td><td>=</td><td>20</td><td>SP</td></tr>
<tr><td></td><td></td><td>(6002)</td><td>=</td><td>20</td><td>SP</td></tr>
<tr><td></td><td></td><td>(6003)</td><td>=</td><td>46</td><td>'F'</td></tr>
<tr><td></td><td></td><td>(6004)</td><td>=</td><td>20</td><td>SP</td></tr>
<tr><td></td><td></td><td>R15</td><td>=</td><td>8000</td><td></td></tr>
<tr><td></td><td>Result:</td><td>R15</td><td>=</td><td>7FFE</td><td></td></tr>
<tr><td></td><td></td><td>(7FFE)</td><td>=</td><td colspan="2">6003, since the three previous memory locations all contain blanks.</td></tr>
</table>

To shorten the program, as described in example 6-1, we alter the initial conditions so that the loop control section precedes the processing section.

Flowchart 6-2:

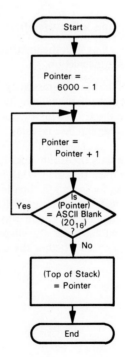

Program 6-2:

```
              internal
                  pgm_6_2 procedure
                  entry
                       $abs      IBASE
    4600 7601          LDA       R1,%6000-1     ! Point to string start - 1 !
    4602 5FFF
    4604 A910   LOOP:  INC       R1             ! Move pointer to next char !
    4606 0C11          CPB       @R1,#' '       ! Look for ASCII space !
    4608 2020
    460A E6FC          JR        EQ,LOOP        ! Go till non-blank found !
    460C 93F1          PUSH      @R15,R1        ! Addr of first non-blank !
    460E 7A00          HALT

    4610          end       pgm_6_2
```

Note that we used LDA R1,%6000 − 1 rather than LDA R1,%5FFF. The first form draws attention to the fact that this is the beginning address minus 1.

Try rewriting this program using the CPIRB instruction. Remember that the Pointer register is incremented even after the condition is met.

6-3. Replace Leading Zeros with Blanks

Purpose: Edit a string of ASCII decimal characters by replacing all leading zeros with blanks. The string starts in memory location 6001; assume that it consists entirely of ASCII-coded decimal digits. The length of the string is in memory location 6000.

Sample Problems:

a.
(6000)	=	01
(6001)	=	36 '6'

The program leaves the string unchanged, since the leading digit is not zero.

b.
(6000)	=	08
(6001)	=	30 '0'
(6002)	=	30 '0'
(6003)	=	38 '8'

Result:	(6001)	=	20 SP
	(6002)	=	20 SP
	(6003)	=	38 '8'

The two leading ASCII zeros have been replaced by ASCII blanks.

You will frequently want to edit decimal strings before they are printed or displayed to improve their appearance. Common editing tasks include eliminating leading zeros, justifying numbers, adding signs or other identifying markers, and rounding. Clearly, printed numbers like 0006 or $27.34382 can be confusing and annoying.

Here the loop has two exits — one if the processor finds a nonzero digit and the other if it has examined the entire string.

All digits in the string are assumed to be ASCII; that is, the digits are 30_{16} through 39_{16} rather than the ordinary decimal 0 to 9. The conversion from decimal to ASCII is simply a matter of adding 30_{16} to the decimal digit.

You may have to be careful, when blanking zeros, to leave one zero in the case in which all digits are zero. How would you do this?

Flowchart 6-3:

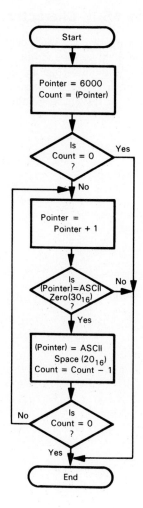

Program 6-3:

```
                internal
                pgm_6_3 procedure
                entry
                    $abs      IBASE

    4600 760A           LDA     R10,%6000        ! Point to length of string !
    4602 6000
    4604 20AF           LDB     RL7,@R10         ! Length to RL7 !
    4606 8CF4           TESTB   RL7
    4608 E607           JR      Z,DONE           ! Finished if length is 0 !
    460A A9A0   LOOP:    INC     R10              ! Move pointer to next char !
    460C 0CA1           CPB     @R10,#'0'        ! Look for ASCII zero !
    460E 3030
    4610 EE03           JR      NE,DONE          ! No, we're done !
    4612 0CA5           LDB     @R10,#' '        ! Replace the '0' with a blank !
    4614 2020
    4616 FF07           DBJNZ   RL7,LOOP         ! Stop if string is all zeros !
    4618 7A00   DONE:    HALT

    461A            end     pgm_6_3
```

6-4. Add Even Parity to ASCII Characters

Purpose: Add even parity to a string of 7-bit ASCII characters. The length of the string is in memory location 6000 and the string itself begins in memory location 6001. Place even parity in the most significant bit of each character by setting the most significant bit to 1 if that makes the total number of 1 bits in the word an even number, or leaving it 0 if the character already has an even number of 1 bits.

Sample Problem:

	(6000)	=	06
	(6001)	=	31
	(6002)	=	32
	(6003)	=	33
	(6004)	=	34
	(6005)	=	35
	(6006)	=	36
Result:	(6001)	=	B1
	(6002)	=	B2
	(6003)	=	33
	(6004)	=	B4
	(6005)	=	35
	(6006)	=	36

Flowchart 6-4:

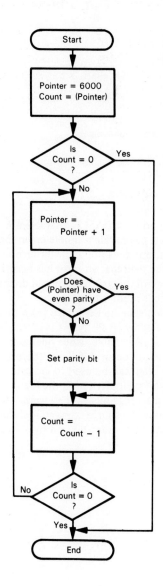

Program 6-4:

```
                internal
                    pgm_6_4 procedure
                    entry
                        $abs     IBASE

    4600 7606           LDA      R6,%6000      ! Point to length byte !
    4602 6000
    4604 206D           LDB      RL5,@R6       ! Length to RL5 !
    4606 8CD4           TESTB    RL5           ! Watch for zero length string !
    4608 E605           JR       Z,DONE
    460A A960  LOOP:    INC      R6            ! Point to next char !
    460C 0C64           TESTB    @R6           ! Set P flag correctly !
    460E E401           JR       PE,NSET       ! Jump if parity even !
    4610 2467           SETB     @R6,#7        ! Set the parity bit if odd !
    4612 FD05  NSET:    DBJNZ    RL5,LOOP
    4614 7A00  DONE:    HALT

    4616           end      pgm_6_4
```

A parity bit is often added to ASCII characters before they are transmitted on noisy communications lines, to provide a simple error-checking facility. Parity checking detects all single-bit errors, but does not allow for error correction; that is, you can tell by checking the parity of the data that an error has occurred, but you cannot tell which bit was received incorrectly. All that the receiver can do is request retransmission. Parity checking will not detect most multi-bit errors.

The TESTB instruction sets the Parity flag (P) if there is an even number of 1 bits in the byte. The jump specified by JR PE,NSET is taken if parity is even. Note that P and V are the same flag. This is reasonable, since operations which set the Parity flag are those for which overflow cannot occur. Similarly, there is no need to check the parity of an arithmetic result, so the flag can be used to indicate overflow operations.

SETB @R6,#7 sets the parity bit (bit 7, the high-order bit) in the byte addressed by R6, while retaining all the other bits as they were. The SET, RES and BIT instructions all use the same format. The source operand is always the number of a bit. 0 is the low-order bit, while 7 is the high-order bit in a byte and 15 is the high-order bit of a word.

6-5. Compare Two Strings

Purpose: Compare two strings of ASCII characters to see if they are the same. The length of the first string is in memory location 6000, and is followed by the string. The length of the second string is in memory location 6400, and is followed by the string. If the two strings match, clear the top of the stack; otherwise, set the top of the stack to FFFF hex (all ones).

Sample Problems:

a.
```
        R15    =  8000
      (6000)   =  03
      (6001)   =  43  'C'
      (6002)   =  41  'A'
      (6003)   =  54  'T'
      (6400)   =  03
      (6401)   =  43  'C'
      (6402)   =  41  'A'
      (6403)   =  54  'T'
```

Result:
```
        R15    =  7FFE
      (7FFE)   =  0000, since the strings match
```

b.
```
        R15    =  8000
      (6000)   =  03
      (6001)   =  43  'C'
      (6002)   =  41  'A'
      (6003)   =  54  'T'
      (6400)   =  03
      (6401)   =  52  'R'
      (6402)   =  41  'A'
      (6403)   =  54  'T'
```

Result:
```
        R15    =  7FFE
      (7FFE)   =  FFFF, since the first characters in the
                 strings differ.
```

```
        R15    =  8000
      (6000)   =  03
      (6400)   =  04
```

Result:
```
        R15    =  7FFE
      (7FFE)   =  FFFF, since the strings are not the
                 same length.
```

Note: the matching process ends as soon as we find a difference. The rest of the strings need not be examined.

Flowchart 6-5a:

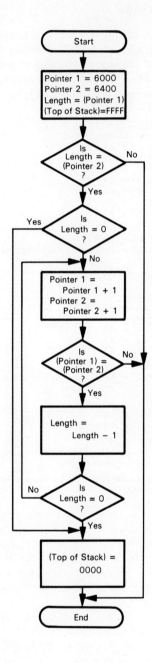

Program 6-5a:

```
              internal
                 pgm_6_5a procedure
                 entry
                    $abs    IBASE

  4600 760C           LDA    R12,%6000     ! Point R12 to 1st length !
  4602 6000
  4604 760D           LDA    R13,%6400     ! R13 points to other length !
  4606 6400
  4608 0DF9           PUSH   @R15,#%FFFF   ! Assume strings don't match !
  460A FFFF
  460C 20CA           LDB    RL2,@R12      ! RL2 is length counter !
  460E 0ADA           CPB    RL2,@R13      ! Are the lengths the same? !
  4610 EE09           JR     NE,DONE       ! No, then strings don't match !
  4612 8CA4           TESTB  RL2           ! Is the length 0? !
  4614 E606           JR     EQ,MATCH      ! Yes, then they do match !
  4616 A9C0    LOOP:  INC    R12           ! Advance both pointers !
  4618 A9D0           INC    R13
  461A 20C8           LDB    RL0,@R12
  461C 0AD8           CPB    RL0,@R13      ! Do the next chars match? !
  461E EE02           JR     NE,DONE       ! If not, the compare stops !
  4620 FA06           DBJNZ  RL2,LOOP
  4622 0DF8   MATCH:  CLR    @R15          ! Return 0 if strings match !
  4624 7A00   DONE:   HALT

  4626              end     pgm_6_5a
```

Matching strings of ASCII characters is an essential part of recognizing names or commands, identifying variables or operation codes in assemblers and compilers, finding files, and many other tasks.

The PUSH @R15, #%FFFF instruction has the effect of assuming there will be no match. If a match is found, the top of the stack is cleared. Had we not done it this way, the end of the program would have been more complicated:

```
                       .
                       .
                       .
                     DBJNZ   RL2,LOOP
           MATCH:    PUSH    @R15,#0
                     JR      LEAVE
           DONE:     PUSH    @R15,#%FFFF
           LEAVE:    HALT
```

Assuming a result is true until proven false, or false until proven true, is a common technique that simplifies many programs.

Note the CLR @R15 instruction. This illustrates that the top of the stack can be referenced by instructions other than PUSH and POP. The CLR instruction does not add a new element to the stack; R15 remains unchanged. The top element of the stack can be referenced by any instruction that can use indirect addressing. Note also that a byte instruction can be used to access the low-order byte of the value on top of the stack. Other values on the stack can be referenced with indexed addressing. CLR 2(R15) sets the second value on the stack to 0.

This program is much more complicated than it needs to be. First, note that we can treat the length bytes of the strings as if they were part of the string. If the lengths are unequal, the strings are unequal. This is done by adding 1 to the Length register during initialization. Then we must advance the pointers after the compare, not before.

Since we add 1 to the length, we no longer have to check for zero-length strings.

Flowchart 6-5b:

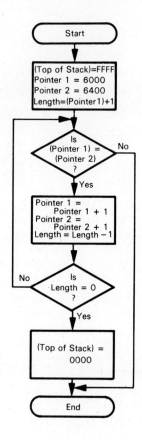

Program 6-5b:

```
              internal
                pgm_6_5b procedure
              entry
                    $abs      IBASE

4600 760C           LDA       R12,%6000      ! Point R12 to 1st length !
4602 6000
4604 760D           LDA       R13,%6400      ! R13 points to other length !
4606 6400
4608 0DF9           PUSH      @R15,#%FFFF    ! Assume strings don't match !
460A FFFF
460C 20CA           LDB       RL2,@R12       ! RL2 is length counter !
460E A8A0           INCB      RL2            ! Add one for the length byte !
4610 20C8    LOOP:  LDB       RL0,@R12
4612 0AD8           CPB       RL0,@R13       ! Are chars (or lengths) same? !
4614 EE04           JR        NE,DONE        ! If not, stop compare !
4616 A9C0           INC       R12            ! Advance both pointers !
4618 A9D0           INC       R13
461A FA06           DBJNZ     RL2,LOOP
461C 0DF8           CLR       @R15           ! Strings match so return 0 !
461E 7A00    DONE:  HALT

4620            end       pgm_6_5b
```

Program 6-5c:

```
              internal
                  pgm_6_5c procedure
                  entry
                       $abs      IBASE

4600 760C             LDA      R12,%6000      ! Point R12 to 1st string length !
4602 6000
4604 760D             LDA      R13,%6400      ! R13 points to other length !
4606 6400
4608 0DF9             PUSH     @R15,#%FFFF    ! Assume the strings don't match !
460A FFFF
460C BD21             LDK      R2,#1          ! To compare lengths, count... !
460E 00CA             ADDB     RL2,@R12       ! ...is string length plus 1 !
4610 BAD6             CPSIRB   @R12,@R13,R2,NE ! Stop if R2=0... !
4612 02CE                                     ! ...or the bytes differ !
4614 E601             JR       Z,DONE         ! Exit if 2 bytes didn't match !
4616 0DF8             CLR      @R15           ! Return 0 if the strings match !
4618 7A00   DONE:     HALT

461A              end        pgm_6_5c
```

If the lengths are unequal, the program terminates at the first iteration.

Since string search is such an important, common operation, the Z8000 has an instruction that performs it in one step. The CPSIRB (compare byte string, increment and repeat) instruction compares two strings until a condition is met or until the length counter goes to 0. The setup is almost the same as in the previous program, except that the length counter must be a word register.

The LDK R2,#1 (load constant) instruction is a shorter form of LD R2,#1. If the constant is between 0 and 15, the LDK instruction can be used. Since the constant can be encoded as the low-order four bits of the instruction, the word used to hold the immediate data for the LD instruction is saved. (Compare the execution time of LDK R2, #0 and CLR R2.)

The sequence

```
              LDK      R2,#1
              ADDB     RL2,@R12
```

is one word shorter than

```
              CLRB     RH2
              LDB      RL2,@R12
              INC      R2
```

The CPSIRB instruction operates as follows:

1. The byte addressed by R12 is compared to the byte addressed by R13.

2. If they are *not equal*, the Z flag is set.

3. R12 and R13 are both incremented.

4. R2 is decremented. If R2 is 0, the V flag is set.

5. If neither the Z flag nor the V flag is set, the operation repeats.

Take special note that in this case, the Z flag is set if the bytes are *not equal*. Regardless of what condition is used in the instruction, the Z flag is used to show that the condition was met by the last comparison.

PROBLEMS

6-1. Length of a Teletypewriter Message

Purpose: Determine the length of an ASCII message. All characters are 7-bit ASCII with MSB = 0. The string of characters in which the message is embedded starts in memory location 6001. The message itself starts with an ASCII STX character (02_{16}) and ends with ETX (03_{16}). Place the length of the message (the number of characters between the STX and the ETX but including neither) into memory location 6000.

Sample Problem:

```
(6001)  =  40
(6002)  =  02  STX
(6003)  =  47  'G'
(6004)  =  4F  'O'
(6005)  =  03  ETX
```

Result: (6000)   =   02, since there are two characters between
                      the STX in location 6002 and ETX in location 6005.

Note: PLZ/ASM has no special characters for ETX or STX. The following statements define symbolic constants:

```
CONSTANT
        STX = %02
        ETX = %03
INTERNAL
        prob_1  PROCEDURE
        .
        .
        .
        CPB     RL0,#ETX
        .
        .
        .
```

6-2. Find Last Non-Blank Character

Purpose: Search a string of ASCII characters for the last non-blank character. The string starts in memory location 6001 and ends with a carriage return character ($0D_{16}$). Place the index of the last non-blank character in memory location 6000.

Sample Problems:

a.
$$(6001) = 37 \quad '7'$$
$$(6002) = 0D \quad CR$$

Result: $(6000) = 00$, since the last (and only) non-blank character is in memory location 6001.

b.
$$(6001) = 20 \quad SP$$
$$(6002) = 41 \quad 'A'$$
$$(6003) = 20 \quad SP$$
$$(6004) = 48 \quad 'H'$$
$$(6005) = 41 \quad 'A'$$
$$(6006) = 54 \quad 'T'$$
$$(6007) = 20 \quad SP$$
$$(6008) = 20 \quad SP$$
$$(6009) = 0D \quad CR$$

Result: $(6000) = 05$

6-3. Truncate Decimal String to Integer Form

Purpose: Edit a string of ASCII decimal characters by replacing all digits to the right of the decimal point with ASCII blanks (20_{16}). The string starts in memory location 6001 and is assumed to consist entirely of ASCII-coded decimal digits and a possible decimal point $(2E_{16})$. The length of the string is in memory location 6000. If no decimal point appears in the string, assume that the decimal point is implicitly at the far right.

Sample Problems:

a.		(6000)	=	04
		(6001)	=	37 '7'
		(6002)	=	2E '.'
		(6003)	=	38 '8'
		(6004)	=	31 '1'
	Result:	(6001)	=	37 '7'
		(6002)	=	2E '.'
		(6003)	=	20 SP
		(6004)	=	20 SP
b.		(6000)	=	03
		(6001)	=	36 '6'
		(6002)	=	37 '7'
		(6003)	=	31 '1'
	Result:			Unchanged, as the number is assumed to be 671.

6-4. Check for Even Parity in ASCII Characters

Purpose: Check for even parity in a string of ASCII characters. The length of the string is in memory location 6000, and the string itself begins in memory location 6001. If the parity of all the characters in the string is correct, clear the top of the stack; otherwise, set the top of the stack to FFFF hex (all ones).

Sample Problems:

a.
(6000)	=	03
(6001)	=	B1
(6002)	=	B2
(6003)	=	33

Result:
R15	=	7FFE
(7FFE)	=	0000, since all characters have even parity.

b.
(6000)	=	03
(6001)	=	B1
(6002)	=	B6
(6003)	=	33
R15	=	8000

Result:
R15	=	7FFE
(7FFE)	=	FFFF, since the character in memory location 6002 does not have even parity.

6-5. Compare Two Strings

Purpose: Compare two strings of ASCII characters to see which is larger (i.e., which follows the other in alphabetical ordering). Both strings are the same length, and the length is in memory location 6000. The first string begins in memory location 6001 and the second begins in memory location 6401. If the first string is greater than or equal to the other string, clear the top of stack; otherwise, set the top of the stack to FFFF hex (all ones).

Sample Problems:

a.

R15	=	8000
(6000)	=	03
(6001)	=	43 'C'
(6002)	=	41 'A'
(6002)	=	54 'T'
(6401)	=	42 'B'
(6402)	=	41 'A'
(6403)	=	54 'T'

Result:

R15	=	7FFE
(7FFE)	=	0000, since CAT is 'larger' than BAT.

b.

R15	=	8000
(6000)	=	03
(6001)	=	43 'C'
(6002)	=	41 'A'
(6003)	=	54 'T'
(6401)	=	43 'C'
(6402)	=	41 'A'
(6403)	=	54 'T'

Result:

R15	=	7FFE
(7FFE)		0000, since the two strings are equal.

c.

R15	=	8000
(6000)	=	03
(6001)	=	43 'C'
(6002)	=	41 'A'
(6003)	=	54 'T'
(6401)	=	43 'C'
(6402)	=	4F 'O'
(6403)	=	44 'D'

Result:

R15	=	7FFE
(7FFE)	=	FFFF, since COD is 'larger' than CAT.

Does the program become more complex if the strings are not the same length and location 6400 contains the length of the second string?

7

Code Conversion

Code conversion is a continual problem in most microcomputer applications. Peripherals provide data in ASCII, BCD, or various special codes. The program must convert the data into some standard form for processing. Output devices may require data in ASCII, BCD, seven-segment, or other codes. Therefore, the program must convert the results to a suitable form after the processing is completed.

There are several ways to approach code conversion:

1. **Some conversions are best handled by algorithms involving arithmetic or logical functions.** But the program may have to handle some special cases separately.

2. **More complex conversions can be handled with lookup tables.** The lookup table method requires little programming and is easy to apply. However, the table may occupy a large amount of memory if the range of input values is large.

3. **Hardware is readily available for some conversion tasks.** Typical examples are decoders for BCD to seven-segment conversion and Universal Asynchronous Receiver/Transmitters (UARTs) for conversion between parallel and serial formats.

In most applications, the program should do as much as possible of the code conversion work. This saves parts and board space; it also increases reliability. Most code conversions are easy to program and require little execution time.

PROGRAM EXAMPLES

7-1. Hex to ASCII

Purpose: Convert the contents of memory location 6000 to an ASCII character. Memory location 6000 contains a single hexadecimal digit (the four most significant bits are zero). Store the ASCII character in memory location 6001.

Sample Problems:

a.	(6000)	=	0C	
Result:	(6001)	=	43	'C'
b.	(6000)	=	06	
Result:	(6001)	=	36	'6'

Flowchart 7-1:

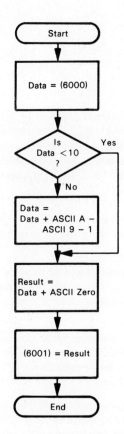

Program 7-1a:

```
            internal
                pgm_7_la procedure              ! Hex to ASCII !
                entry
                    $abs      IBASE

4600 6008           LDB      RL0,%6000         ! Get value; range 00-0F !
4602 6000
4604 0A08           CPB      RL0,#10           ! Is it in range 0-9? !
4606 0A0A
4608 E102           JR       LT,ZADD           ! Yes, simply add '0' !
460A 0008           ADDB     RL0,#'A'-'9'-1    ! No, make result 'A'-'F' !
460C 0707
460E 0008  ZADD:    ADDB     RL0,#'0'          ! Convert to final value !
4610 3030
4612 6E08           LDB      %6001,RL0         ! Store result !
4614 6001
4616 7A00           HALT

4618                end      pgm_7_la
```

In program 7-1a, the basic idea is to add ASCII 0 to all the hexadecimal digits. This addition converts the decimal digits correctly; however, there is a break between ASCII 9 (39 hex) and ASCII A (41 hex) which must be considered. This break must be added to the nondecimal digits A, B, C, D, E, and F. The first ADDB instruction does this. The offset 'A' — '9' — 1 is added to the contents of RL0. Can you explain why the offset is 'A' — '9' — 1? Another form of the offset is 'A' — 10 — '0'. We want to make the purpose of the terms as clear as possible in the assembly language listing. The extra assembly time is a very small price to pay for a large increase in clarity.

This routine could be used in a variety of programs; for example, monitor programs must convert hexadecimal digits to ASCII in order to display the contents of memory locations in hexadecimal on an ASCII printer or video display.

A (quicker) conversion method that requires no conditional jumps at all is program 7-1b, described by Allison in *Computer* magazine.[1]

Program 7-1b:

```
                internal
                    pgm_7_1b procedure           ! Hex to ASCII: Allison !
                entry
                    $abs       IBASE
   4600 6008       LDB    RL0,%6000             ! Get value; range 00-0F !
   4602 6000
   4604 0008       ADDB   RL0,#%90              ! Prepare for decimal adjust !
   4606 9090
   4608 B080       DAB    RL0                   ! Range 90-99... !
                                                ! ... or 00-06 with carry !
   460A C040       LDB    RH0,#%40              ! Constant for following add !
   460C B408       ADCB   RL0,RH0               ! Range C0-C9 or 41-47 !
   460E B080       DAB    RL0                   ! Range 30-39 or 41-47 !
   4610 6E08       LDB    %6001,RL0             ! Store ASCII character !
   4612 6001
   4614 7A00       HALT

   4616            end    pgm_7_1b
```

Try this program on some digits. Can you explain why it works?

The Carry flag is not affected by the LDB instruction, so the ADCB instruction adds in the carry if it is set by the DAB instruction.

This program could be shortened by one word if we take advantage of the fact that LDB RL0, #%90 is a single-word instruction. We could replace the first two instructions with

```
          LDB    RL0,#%90
          ADDB   RL0,%6000
```

7-2. Decimal to Seven-Segment

Purpose: Convert the contents of memory location 6000 to a seven-segment code in memory location 6001. If memory location 6000 does not contain a single decimal digit, clear memory location 6001.

A seven-segment code represents characters using the standard 8-bit byte. The high-order bit is always 0. The remaining bits are assigned to the seven segments of the standard display character; the assignments are specified by the manufacturer. There is no industry standard. Figure 7-1 illustrates one option, which we use in the program that follows. a, b, c, d, e, f, and g identify display segments. A segment is turned "on" by a 1 in the corresponding bit position; it is turned off by a 0 in the corresponding bit position. In Figure 7-1 bits are assigned in descending order, from bit 6 for segment g, to bit 0 for segment a.

Note that Figure 7-1 uses 7D for 6 rather than the alternative 7C (top bar off) to avoid confusion with lower case b, and 6F for 9 rather than 67 (bottom bar off) to match the style of the 6.

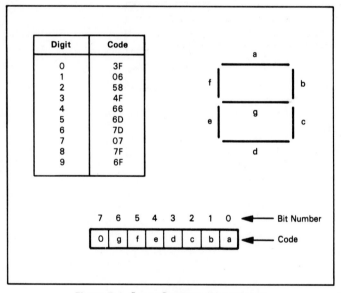

Figure 7-1. Seven-Segment Arrangement

Sample Problems:

a.		(6000)	=	03
	Result:	(6001)	=	4F
b.		(6000)	=	28
	Result:	(6001)	=	00

Flowchart 7-2:

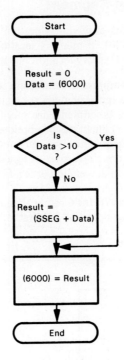

The address of the seven-segment code is the sum of base address SSEG and the index DATA.

Program 7-2:

```
              internal
                 pgm_7_2 procedure          ! BCD to seven segment !
              entry
                 $abs     IBASE

   4600 8D18      CLR    R1                 ! R1 is index; RH1 is result !
   4602 6009      LDB    RL1,%6000          ! Get BCD value in R1 !
   4604 6000
   4606 0A09      CPB    RL1,#10            ! Valid BCD? !
   4608 0A0A
   460A EF02      JR     UGE,DONE           ! No, result is 0 in RH1 !
   460C 6011      LDB    RH1,SSEG(R1)       ! Get 7 seg code from table !
   460E 6400
   4610 6E01 DONE: LDB   %6001,RH1          ! Store result (or 0) !
   4612 6001
   4614 7A00      HALT

   4616      end    pgm_7_2

              internal
                 $abs    %6400              ! Put translate table at 6400 !

   6400 3F  06  SSEG   ARRAY [10 BYTE] := [%3F %06 %5B %4F %66    ! 0-4 !
   6402 5B  4F                              %6D %7D %07 %7F %6F]   ! 5-9 !
   6404 66  6D
   6406 7D  07
   6408 7F  6F
```

The program calculates the memory address of the desired code by adding the index (i.e., the digit to be displayed) to the base address of the seven-segment code table. This procedure is known as a table lookup. No explicit instructions are required for the addition, since it is performed automatically in the indexed addressing modes.

The PLZ/ASM assembly language data declaration ARRAY, with an initialization list, places constant data in program memory. Such data may include tables, headings, error messages, prompting messages, format characters, thresholds, etc. The label attached to an ARRAY declaration is assigned the value of the address into which the first byte of data is placed.

The assembler simply places data for the table in memory. We put the table at 6400; but note that the table could have been placed anywhere in memory. The value used as the index would be different, but the remainder of the program would not change.

Tables are often used to perform code conversions that are more complex than the previous example. Such tables typically contain results organized according to the input data; e.g., the first entry is the code corresponding to the number zero.

Seven-segment displays provide recognizable forms of the decimal digits and a few letters and other characters. Calculator-type seven-segment displays are inexpensive, easy to multiplex, and use little power. However, the seven-segment coded digits are somewhat difficult to read.

The BCD to seven-segment program could be rewritten to use a translate instruction. Translate instructions assume that a number of conversions are to be performed. For example, suppose a string of BCD digits are to be converted to seven-segment code. The seven-segment code overwrites and replaces the BCD digit. The following procedure handles one character conversion:

```
LD      R1,BCD          ! BCD digit address              !
LDA     R2,SEVSEG       ! Seven-segment table base       !
LD      R3,COUNT        ! Character count                !
TRIB    @R1,@R2,R3      ! Translate BCD to seven-segment !
LD      BCD,R1          ! Save incremented address       !
LD      COUNT,R3        ! Save decremented word count    !
HALT
```

Typically, a routine such as the one illustrated above would not load and save addresses or character counts after each translation. These parameters would be held in registers until all characters have been translated. Note also that we do not check for a valid BCD digit. When translating a string of bytes, you would check the string for validity before beginning the translation. Can you write a validating program using the CPI or CPIR instructions?

7-3. ASCII to Decimal

Purpose: Convert the contents of memory location 6000 from an ASCII character to a decimal digit and store the result in memory location 6001. If the contents of memory location 6000 are not the ASCII representation of a decimal digit, set the contents of memory 6001 to FF_{16}.

Sample Problems:

a.		(6000)	=	37 (ASCII 7)
Result:	(6001)	=	07
b.		(6000)	=	55 (an invalid code, since it is not an ASCII decimal digit)
Result:	(6001)	=	FF

Flowchart 7-3a:

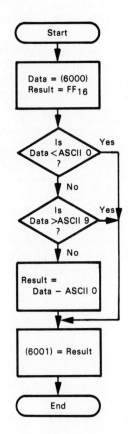

Program 7-3a:

```
                    internal
                        pgm_7_3a procedure        ! ASCII to decimal !
                        entry
                            $abs      IBASE

    4600  4C05              LDB       %6001,#%FF   ! Assume character not valid !
    4602  6001
    4604  FFFF
    4606  6008              LDB       RL0,%6000    ! Get ASCII character !
    4608  6000
    460A  0A08              CPB       RL0,#'0'     ! Valid digit? !
    460C  3030
    460E  E707              JR        ULT,DONE     ! Lower is invalid !
    4610  0A08              CPB       RL0,#'9'
    4612  3939
    4614  EB04              JR        UGT,DONE     ! Higher is invalid !
    4616  0208              SUBB      RL0,#'0'     ! Convert from ASCII !
    4618  3030
    461A  6E08              LDB       %6001,RL0    ! Store value; range 00-09 !
    461C  6001
    461E  7A00    DONE:     HALT

    4620                end       pgm_7_3a
```

Program 7-3a handles ASCII-coded characters like any other binary data. Note that the decimal digits and the letters form groups of consecutive codes. Strings of letters (like names) can be alphabetized by placing their ASCII representations in increasing numeric order (ASCII B = ASCII A + 1, for example).

Subtracting ASCII zero (30_{16}) from any ASCII decimal digit gives the BCD representation of that digit.

ASCII-to-decimal conversion is necessary when decimal numbers are being entered from an ASCII device like a teletypewriter or CRT terminal.

The program determines if the character lies in the range ASCII 0 to ASCII 9, inclusive. If so, the character is an ASCII decimal digit since the digits form a sequence. The ASCII character is converted to a decimal digit by subtracting 30_{16} (ASCII 0): e.g., ASCII 7 − ASCII 0 = 37 − 30 = 7.

The first comparison and the later subtraction could be combined into one step. This is shown in program 7-3b.

Program 7-3b:

```
                    internal
                        pgm_7_3b procedure        ! ASCII to decimal: II !
                        entry
                            $abs      IBASE

    4600  4C05              LDB       %6001,#%FF   ! Assume character not valid !
    4602  6001
    4604  FFFF
    4606  6008              LDB       RL0,%6000    ! Get ASCII character !
    4608  6000
    460A  0208              SUBB      RL0,#'0'     ! Convert from ASCII !
    460C  3030
    460E  E105              JR        LT,DONE      ! Less than '0' is invalid !
    4610  0A08              CPB       RL0,#9
    4612  0909
    4614  EA02              JR        GT,DONE      ! Higher than '9' is invalid !
    4616  6E08              LDB       %6001,RL0    ! Store value; range 00-09 !
    4618  6001
    461A  7A00    DONE:     HALT

    461C                end       pgm_7_3b
```

7-4. BCD to Binary

Purpose: Convert four BCD digits in memory locations 6000, 6001, 6002, and 6003 to a binary number in memory location 6004. The most significant BCD digit is in memory location 6000.

Sample Problems:

a.
$$
\begin{array}{ll}
(6000) & = 02 \\
(6001) & = 09 \\
(6002) & = 07 \\
(6003) & = 01
\end{array}
$$

Result: (6004) = $0B9B_{16}$ = 2971_{10}

b.
$$
\begin{array}{ll}
(6000) & = 09 \\
(6001) & = 07 \\
(6002) & = 00 \\
(6003) & = 02
\end{array}
$$

Result: (6004) = $25E6_{16}$ = 9702_{10}

Flowchart 7-4a:

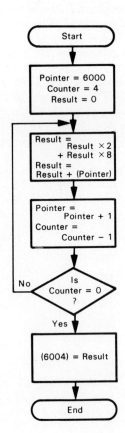

Program 7-4a multiplies each intermediate result by 10 by using the formula $10 x = 8 x + 2 x$. Multiplying by 2 requires one arithmetic left shift, and multiplying by 8 requires three such shifts.

Program 7-4a:

```
                 internal
                    pgm_7_4a procedure          ! 4 digit BCD to binary !
                    entry
                           $abs    IBASE
      4600 7601            LDA     R1,%6000      ! Pointer to high order BCD !
      4602 6000
      4604 2100            LD      R0,#4         ! 4 digits to process !
      4606 0004
      4608 8D28            CLR     R2            ! Final result !
      460A 8C38            CLRB    RH3           ! RL3 used for each digit !
      460C E805            JR      NOMULT        ! Skip multiply first time !
      460E 8122    BCLOOP: ADD     R2,R2         ! 2x !
      4610 A124            LD      R4,R2
      4612 B329            SLA     R2,#2         ! 8x = 2x * 4 !
      4614 0002
      4616 8142            ADD     R2,R4         ! 10x = 8x + 2x !
      4618 201B    NOMULT: LDB     RL3,@R1       ! BCD digit to R3 (RH3 is 0) !
      461A 8132            ADD     R2,R3         ! Add in next digit !
      461C A910            INC     R1            ! Point to next BCD digit !
      461E F089            DJNZ    R0,BCLOOP
      4620 2F12            LD      @R1,R2        ! Store result in 6004 !
      4622 7A00            HALT

      4624         end     pgm_7_4a
```

BCD entries are converted to binary in order to save on storage and to simplify calculations. However, the program time and space required for conversion may offset some of the advantages of binary storage and arithmetic.

BCD numbers require about 20% more storage than do binary numbers. Representing the numbers 0 to 999 requires three BCD digits (12 bits) but only 10 binary digits (since $2^{10} = 1024 \approx 1000$).

The program uses a word length ADD to add the BCD digit to the accumulated result. Had we used ADDB RL2,@R1, the program would not work for all values. Consider 0257. Before adding in the lowest digit, R2 would contain 0250, or 00FA. Adding 7 to the low byte of R2 yields FA + 07 = 01, and the high byte is still 0.

Note that the program skips the first multiply, since we know the initial value is 0.

Again we note that the fastest way to shift a value left one place on the Z8000 is with the ADD instruction. Two ADD instructions would also be faster than the SLA instruction.

We could also use the multiply instruction. The multiply instruction takes the destination operand from the low-order 16 bits of a double register, and places the result in the whole double register. In program 7-4b, we use RR2. That is, we multiply the value in R3 (low-order half of RR2) by 10 and get the result from RR2 (the R2-R3 pair).

Program 7-4b:

```
                  internal
                     pgm_7_4b procedure              ! 4 digit BCD to binary: II !
                  entry
                        $abs       IBASE
   4600 7601            LDA        R1,%6000          ! Pointer to high order BCD !
   4602 6000
   4604 2100            LD         R0,#4             ! 4 digits to process !
   4606 0004
   4608 8D38            CLR        R3                ! R3 used for final result !
   460A 8C48            CLRB       RH4               ! R4 used for each BCD digit !
   460C E802            JR         NOMULT            ! Skip multiply first time !
   460E 1902  BCLOOP:   MULT       RR2,#10           ! Multiply R3 by 10 !
   4610 000A
   4612 201C  NOMULT:   LDB        RL4,@R1           ! BCD digit to R4 (RH4 is 0) !
   4614 8143            ADD        R3,R4             ! Add in next digit !
   4616 A910            INC        R1                ! Point to next BCD digit !
   4618 F086            DJNZ       R0,BCLOOP
   461A 2F13            LD         @R1,R3            ! Store result in 6004 !
   461C 7A00            HALT

   461E            end     pgm_7_4b
```

Since we know the result is less than $FFFF_{16}$ (9,999 < 65,536), we can take the result from R3, the low-order half of RR2. Note that we didn't have to clear R2 before the multiply since the high-order half of RR2 is ignored by the MULT; it is only used for storing the result. If we compare the execution times of the two versions of the program, we see that each MULT takes 70 cycles, while the four instructions in the explicit version take 33. If we use two ADDs instead of the SLA, the explicit version takes 19 cycles. 51 cycles may be a high price to pay for saving three words of storage.

7-5. Binary Number to ASCII String

Purpose: Convert the 16-bit binary number on the top of the stack into 16 ASCII characters (either ASCII 0 or ASCII 1). Store the ASCII characters in memory locations 6000 through 600F (the most significant bit is in 6000).

Sample Problem:

```
        R15  =  7FFE
       (7FFE) =  31D2 = 0011000111010010

Result: R15  =  8000
       (6000) =  30  '0'
       (6001) =  30  '0'
       (6002) =  31  '1'
       (6003) =  31  '1'
       (6004) =  30  '0'
       (6005) =  30  '0'
       (6006) =  30  '0'
       (6007) =  31  '1'
       (6008) =  31  '1'
       (6009) =  31  '1'
       (600A) =  30  '0'
       (600B) =  31  '1'
       (600C) =  30  '0'
       (600D) =  30  '0'
       (600E) =  31  '1'
       (600F) =  30  '0'
```

Flowchart 7-5:

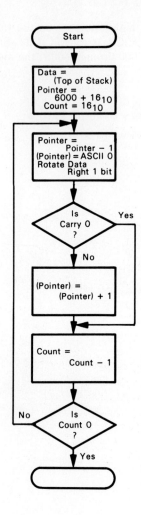

Program 7-5:

```
                internal
                        pgm_7_5 procedure              ! Binary to 16 ASCII digits !
                        entry
                            $abs        IBASE
    4600  97F1            POP     R1,@R15              ! Get value from stack !
    4602  7602            LDA     R2,%6000+16          ! Point past end of string !
    4604  6010
    4606  2100            LD      R0,#16               ! Repeat loop 16 times !
    4608  0010
    460A  AB20  CVLOOP:   DEC     R2                   ! Point to next lowest digit !
    460C  0C25            LDB     @R2,#'0'             ! Assume this bit is 0 !
    460E  3030
    4610  B314            RR      R1                   ! Get low bit to carry flag !
    4612  EF01            JR      NC,CVSTEP
    4614  2820            INCB    @R2                  ! Digit is 1 if carry set !
    4616  F087  CVSTEP:   DJNZ    R0,CVLOOP
    4618  7A00            HALT

    461A            end     pgm_7_5
```

The ASCII digits form a sequence so ASCII 1 = ASCII 0 + 1. The INCB (and INC) instruction can be used to directly increment the contents of a memory location. The savings here are that no explicit instructions are required to load the data from memory or to store the result back into memory. Nor are any registers disturbed.

Note that the string pointer, R2, starts at the end of the string and is decremented at the beginning of each step. We could just as easily have started R2 at $6000 + 15_{10}$ and decremented it after each step. We chose to decrement the pointer before each step.

When accessing data in this manner, note that the end of a string address is actually the address of the first byte not in the string. For example, the byte at $6000 + 16_{10}$ is not in the string of ASCII digits. Finally, note that $6000 + 16_{10}$ is more easily identified with a 16-unit string than $6000 + 15_{10}$.

This program could be improved in several ways. For instance, we could load a register with the value ASCII 0; that would shorten the loop by one word. We might also consider using the ADCB (add with carry byte) instruction to save the JR and INCB. But, unfortunately, the ADCB instruction only operates on a register, so the savings noted earlier from the INCB instruction would be lost.

7-6. Lower to Upper Case Alphabetic Conversion

Purpose: If memory location 6000 contains a lower-case ASCII character ('a' through 'z', 61_{16} through $7A_{16}$), convert it to upper case. If it is not a lower-case ASCII character, leave it unchanged.

Sample Problems:

		(6000)	=	6B	'k'
a.		(6000)	=	6B	'k'
	Result:	(6000)	=	4B	'K'
b.		(6000)	=	4B	'K'
	Result:	(6000)	=	4B	'K'
c.		(6000)	=	37	'7'
	Result:	(6000)	=	37	'7'

Program 7-6:

```
               internal
                   pgm_7_6 procedure          ! Lower to upper case !
               entry
                       $abs      IBASE

    4600 6008          LDB       RL0,%6000     ! Get ASCII char !
    4602 6000
    4604 0A08          CPB       RL0,#'a'      ! Is it in the range... !
    4606 6161
    4608 E707          JR        ULT,DONE
    460A 0A08          CPB       RL0,#'z'      ! ... 'a' through 'z' ? !
    460C 7A7A
    460E EB04          JR        UGT,DONE
    4610 0208          SUBB      RL0,#'a'-'A'  ! Yes, convert to upper case !
    4612 2020
    4614 6E08          LDB       %6000,RL0     ! Store converted value !
    4616 6000
    4618 7A00   DONE:  HALT

    461A           end      pgm_7_6
```

Conversion between upper- and lower-case alphabetic characters is a very common procedure. Note that each lower-case character differs from its upper-case counterpart by 20_{16}. Conversion from lower to upper case can be accomplished either by subtracting 20_{16} from the lower-case character, or by clearing the 20 bit (bit 5).

PROBLEMS

7-1. ASCII to Hex

Purpose: Convert the contents of memory location 6000 from an ASCII character to a hexadecimal digit and store the result in memory location 6001. Assume that memory location 6000 contains the ASCII representation of a valid hexadecimal digit (7 bits plus MSB 0).

Sample Problems:

a.
$$(6000) = 43 \ 'C'$$
Result: $(6001) = 0C$

b.
$$(6000) = 36 \ '6'$$
Result: $(6001) = 06$

7-2. Decimal to ASCII

Purpose: Convert the contents of memory location 6000 from a decimal digit to an ASCII character and store the result in memory location 6001. If the number in memory location 6000 is not a decimal digit, set the contents of memory location 6001 to an ASCII blank character (20_{16}).

Sample Problems:

a.
$$(6000) = 07$$
Result: $(6001) = 37 \ '7'$

b.
$$(6000) = 55$$
Result: $(6001) = 20 \ SP$

7-3. Binary to BCD

Purpose: Convert the contents of memory location 6000 to four BCD digits in memory locations 6002, 6003, 6004, and 6005 (most significant digit in 6002). The number in memory location 6000 is unsigned and less than 10000.

Sample Problem:

$$(6000) = 1C52 \ (7250 \ decimal)$$

Result:
$(6002) = 07$
$(6003) = 02$
$(6004) = 05$
$(6005) = 00$

7-4. ASCII String to Binary Number

Purpose: Convert the eight ASCII characters in memory locations 6000 through 6007 to an 8-bit binary number. Store the result as the low-order eight bits of the top word on the stack, with the high-order eight bits all zeros. If any of the characters in the string are other than ASCII 0 or ASCII 1, set the top word of the stack to $FFFF_{16}$.

Sample Problems:

a.
```
        R15    =  8000
      (6000)   =  31   '1'
      (6001)   =  31   '1'
      (6002)   =  30   '0'
      (6003)   =  31   '1'
      (6004)   =  30   '0'
      (6005)   =  30   '0'
      (6006)   =  31   '1'
      (6007)   =  30   '0'
```

Result:
```
        R15    =  7FFE
      (7FFE)   =  00D2
```

b.   Same as 'a.' except:
```
      (6005)   =  37   '7'
```

Result:
```
        R15    =  7FFE
      (7FFE)   =  FFFF
```

7-5. Hex Number to ASCII String

Purpose: Convert the 16-bit value on the top of the stack to four ASCII hex digits in memory locations 6000 through 6003 (most significant digit in location 6000).

Sample Problems:

a.
```
        R15    =  7FFE
      (7FFE)   =  3214
```

Result:
```
        R15    =  8000
      (6000)   =  33   '3'
      (6001)   =  32   '2'
      (6002)   =  31   '1'
      (6003)   =  34   '4'
```

b.
```
        R15    =  7FFE
      (7FFE)   =  F20A
```

Result:
```
        R15    =  8000

      (6000)   =  46   'F'
      (6001)   =  32   '2'
      (6002)   =  30   '0'
      (6003)   =  41   'A'
```

7-6. Upper to Lower Case Alphabetic Conversion

Purpose: Convert each upper-case alphabetic ASCII character in a string to lower case. The string begins in memory location 6000 and is terminated by an ASCII CR ($0D_{16}$).

Sample Problems:

a.

(6000)	=	43	'C'
(6001)	=	41	'A'
(6002)	=	54	'T'
(6003)	=	0D	CR

Result:

(6000)	=	63	'c'
(6001)	=	61	'a'
(6002)	=	74	't'
(6003)	=	0D	CR

b.

(6000)	=	20	SP
(6001)	=	43	'C'
(6002)	=	61	'a'
(6003)	=	74	't'
(6004)	=	32	'2'
(6005)	=	21	'!'
(6006)	=	0D	CR

Result:

(6000)	=	20	SP
(6001)	=	63	'c'
(6002)	=	61	'a'
(6003)	=	74	't'
(6004)	=	32	'2'
(6005)	=	21	'!'
(6006)	=	0D	CR

REFERENCES

1. D. R. Allison, "A Design Philosophy for Microcomputer Architectures," *Computer*, February 1977, pp. 35-41.

8

Arithmetic Problems

MULTIPLE-WORD AND DECIMAL ARITHMETIC

Much of the arithmetic in microprocessor applications consists of multiple-word binary or decimal manipulations. A decimal correction (decimal adjust) or some other means for performing decimal arithmetic is frequently the only arithmetic instruction provded besides basic addition and subtraction. When this is the case, you must implement other arithmetic operations with sequences of instructions. The Z8000, however, provides multiply and divide instructions for 16- and 32-bit binary arithmetic.

Multiple-precision binary arithmetic requires simple repetitions of the basic instructions. The Carry bit transfers information between words. Add with Carry and Subtract with Carry use the information from the previous arithmetic operations. You must be careful to clear the Carry before operating on the first words (obviously there is no carry into or borrow from the least significant bits).

Decimal arithmetic is a common enough task for microprocessors that most have special instructions for this purpose. These instructions may either perform decimal operations directly or correct the results of binary operations to the proper decimal form. Decimal arithmetic is essential in such applications as point-of-sale terminals, calculators, check processors, order entry systems, and banking terminals. The Z8000 provides instructions for addition and subtraction followed by adjustment to decimal form.

You can implement decimal multiplication and division as series of additions and subtractions, respectively, much as they are done by hand. Extra storage must be reserved for results, since a multiplication produces a result twice as long as the operands. A division similarly contracts the length of the result. Multiplications and divisions are time-consuming when done in software because of the repeated arithmetic and shift operations that are necessary.

PROGRAM EXAMPLES

8-1. 64-Bit Binary Addition

Purpose: Add two four-word binary numbers. The first number occupies memory locations 6000 through 6007, the second occupies locations 6200 through 6207. Place the sum in locations 6000 through 6007.

Sample Problem:

```
        (6000)  =  6A4D  ⎫
        (6002)  =  ED05  ⎬  6A4DED05A9376414
        (6004)  =  A937  ⎪
        (6006)  =  6414  ⎭

        (6200)  =  56C8  ⎫
        (6202)  =  46E6  ⎬  56C846E676C84AEA
        (6204)  =  76C8  ⎪
        (6206)  =  4AEA  ⎭

Result: (6000)  =  C116  ⎫
        (6002)  =  33EC  ⎬  C11633EC1FFFAEFE
        (6004)  =  1FFF  ⎪
        (6006)  =  AEFE  ⎭
```

Flowchart 8-1:

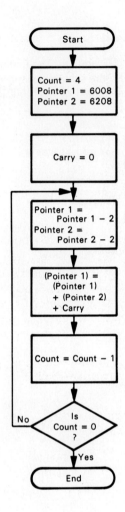

Program 8-1a:

```
                internal
                    pgm_8_la procedure              ! 64 bit ADD !
                    entry
                        $abs      IBASE

    4600 7604               LDA     R4,%6000 + 8    ! Address beyond end... !
    4602 6008                                       ! ...of 64 bit value !
    4604 7602               LDA     R2,%6200 + 8    ! Beyond end of second value !
    4606 6208
    4608 BD04               LDK     R0,#4           ! 4 loop iterations !
    460A 8D83               RESFLG  C               ! Clear carry for first ADC !
    460C AB41     LOOP:     DEC     R4,#2           ! Point to next... !
    460E AB21               DEC     R2,#2           ! ...more significant word !
    4610 2143               LD      R3,@R4
    4612 2121               LD      R1,@R2
    4614 B513               ADC     R3,R1           ! R3 <- R3 + R1 + (Carry) !
    4616 2F43               LD      @R4,R3          ! Store result !
    4618 F087               DJNZ    R0,LOOP         ! Repeat !
    461A 7A00               HALT

    461C           end       pgm_8_la
```

The instruction RESFLG clears (resets) the specified flag or flags. RESFLG C clears the Carry flag to prepare for the first ADC instruction. RESFLG C followed by an ADC or a rotate instruction is the most common use of the RESFLG instruction.

The ADC instruction, Add with Carry, adds the contents of the two registers. If the Carry flag is set, then 1 is added to the sum. This operation then sets the Carry flag appropriately. Note that no instruction in this program other than these two affects or uses the Carry flag.

A quick and elegant version of this same program, shown in program 8-1b, uses the powerful Z8000 LDM (load multiple) instruction.

Program 8-1b:

```
                internal
                    pgm_8_lb procedure              ! 64 bit add using LDM !
                    entry
                        $abs      IBASE

    4600 5C01               LDM     R0,%6000,#4     ! Load R0 - R3 with 1st value !
    4602 0003
    4604 6000
    4606 5C01               LDM     R4,%6200,#4     ! Load R4 - R7 with second !
    4608 0403
    460A 6200
    460C 9662               ADDL    RR2,RR6         ! Add low 32 bits !
    460E B551               ADC     R1,R5           ! Add rest 16 bits at a time... !
    4610 B540               ADC     R0,R4           ! ...plus previous step's carry !
    4612 5C09               LDM     %6000,R0,#4     ! Store result from R0 - R3 !
    4614 0003
    4616 6000
    4618 7A00               HALT

    461A           end       pgm_8_lb
```

This second version, aside from being much shorter, is more than twice as fast as the first version.

8-2. Add a 16-Bit Value to a Multiple Precision Value

Purpose: Location 6200 contains the length in words of a multiple precision value. The value itself occupies the consecutive memory locations immediately preceding 6200, with the least significant bits in memory location 61FE. Add the contents of memory location 6000 to this value. If there is a carry from the most significant bit, increase the length of the value by one word.

Sample Problems:

a.
$$\left.\begin{array}{l} (6000) = 872C \\ (61FC) = 6204 \\ (61FE) = A049 \\ (6200) = 0002 \end{array}\right\} \quad 6204A049$$

Result:
$$\left.\begin{array}{l} (61FC) = 6205 \\ (61FE) = 2775 \\ (6200) = 0002 \end{array}\right\} \quad 62052775$$

b.
$$\left.\begin{array}{l} (6000) = 872C \\ (61FC) = FFFF \\ (61FE) = A049 \\ (6200) = 0002 \end{array}\right\} \quad FFFFA049$$

Result:
$$\left.\begin{array}{l} (61FA) = 0001 \\ (61FC) = 0000 \\ (61FE) = 2775 \\ (6200) = 0003 \end{array}\right\} \quad 000100002775$$

Program 8-2a:

```
              internal
                 pgm_8_2a procedure     ! 16 bits to multi precision add !
              entry
                 $abs     IBASE

4600 7604        LDA      R4,%6200      ! End of multi precision value !
4602 6200
4604 2143        LD       R3,@R4        ! Length of value in words !
4606 6102        LD       R2,%6000      ! 16 bit value to be added !
4608 6000
460A 8D83        RESFLG   C             ! Clear carry for first ADC !
460C AB41  LOOP: DEC      R4,#2         ! Point to next higher word !
460E 2140        LD       R0,@R4
4610 B520        ADC      R0,R2         ! Add in value first time, or... !
                                        ! ...zero plus carry afterward !
4612 2F40        LD       @R4,R0        ! Store result !
4614 EF07        JR       NC,DONE       ! If no carry from the ADC, done !
4616 8D28        CLR      R2            ! Next time add 0 !
4618 F387        DJNZ     R3,LOOP       ! Fall through only if carry... !
                                        ! ...from high order word !
461A 4D45        LD       -2(R4),#1     ! New high order word !
461C FFFE
461E 0001
4620 6900        INC      %6200         ! Add one to length of value !
4622 6200
4624 7A00  DONE: HALT

4626          end      pgm_8_2a
```

Again, note that RESFLG and the ADC are the only instructions that affect the carry. The first time ADC is executed, we add the value in 6000 to the low-order word of the multiple precision number. All subsequent repetitions simply add 1 if the Carry flag is set. Other than the first repetition, is the Carry flag ever 0?

Unlike oth program loops that we have examined, this loop is executed less frequently than the instructions surrounding it. So rather than doing as much work as possible outside of the loop, in this case it is better to make the first add as quick as possible. Consider the variation shown in program 8-2b.

Since the INC instruction does not affect the carry bit, we need another way of detecting carry into the next position. We note that, since we are increasing the word by one, this case arises only when the value goes from $FFFF_{16}$ to 0. So the loop is repeated only when the INC causes a 0 result.

This procedure can produce a binary number of any length. Note that ten bits corresponds to about three decimal digits since $2^{10} = 1024 \approx 1000$. You can calculate the number of bits required to perform binary calculations with any decimal precision using the formula $N \times \frac{10}{3}$, where N represents the number of decimal digits. For example, a number containing 12 decimal digits will require $12 \times \frac{10}{3} = 40$ bits.

Program 8-2b:

```
            internal
            pgm_8_2b procedure          ! 16 bit to multi precision - II !
            entry
                $abs      IBASE
4600 7604         LDA     R4,%6200 - 2       ! Get pointer to low order word !
4602 61FE
4604 2140         LD      R0,@R4
4606 4100         ADD     R0,%600(           ! Add in 16 bit value !
4608 6000
460A 2F40         LD      @R4,R0             ! Store result !
460C EF0C         JR      NC,DONE            ! No carry, we're done !
460E 6103         LD      R3,%6200           ! Length of value in words !
4610 6200
4612 AB41  LOOP:  DEC     R4,#2              ! Point to next higher order val !
4614 AB30         DEC     R3
4616 E203         JR      LE,LONGER          ! Maybe need to lengthen value !
4618 2940         INC     @R4                ! Add carry to next higher word !
461A E6FB         JR      Z,LOOP             ! Repeat if carry out of word !
461C E804         JR      DONE
461E 0D45  LONGER: LD     @R4,#1             ! New high order word !
4620 0001
4622 6900         INC     %6200              ! Increase length !
4624 6200
4626 7A00  DONE:  HALT

4628          end     pgm_8_2b
```

8-3. Decimal Addition

Purpose: Add two multiple-byte BCD numbers. The length of the numbers (in bytes) is in memory location 6000. The numbers themselves start (most significant bits first) in memory locations 6001 and 6101. The sum replaces the number starting in memory location 6001.

Sample Problem:

```
        (6000)  =  04
        (6001)  =  36
        (6002)  =  70
        (6003)  =  19
        (6004)  =  85
        (6101)  =  12
        (6102)  =  66
        (6103)  =  34
        (6104)  =  59

Result: (6001)  =  49
        (6002)  =  36
        (6003)  =  54
        (6004)  =  44

that is,    36701985
          + 12663459
            49365444
```

The Decimal Adjust instruction (DAB) uses the Carry (C) and Half Carry (H) bits as follows:

1. If the sum of two digits is between 10 and 15, inclusive, six must be added to the binary sum to give the correct decimal result:

    ```
        0101 (5)
      + 1000 (8)
        1101 (D)
      + 0110
    0001 0011 (BCD 13, which is correct)
    ```

2. If the sum of two digits is 16 or more, the result is a proper BCD number, but six less than it should be:

    ```
        1000 (8)
      + 1001 (9)
    0001 0001 (BCD 11)
        + 0110
    0001 0111 (BCD 17, which is correct)
    ```

Six must be added in both situations. Case 1 can be recognized by the fact that the sum is not a BCD digit, it is between 10 and 15 (or A and F hexadecimal). Case 2 can be recognized only by the fact that the Carry (most significant digit) or Half Carry (least significant digit) has been set to 1; the result is a valid BCD number. DAB is the only instruction that uses the Half Carry status flag.

Flowchart 8-3:

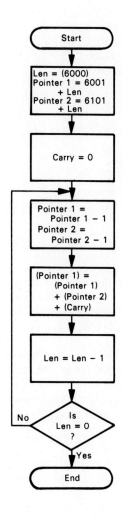

Program 8-3:

```
                internal
                    pgm_8_3 procedure          ! BCD multi precision add !
                entry
                    $abs    IBASE

4600 8C18           CLRB    RH1
4602 6009           LDB     RL1,%6000          ! Length of values into R1 !
4604 6000
4606 7616           LDA     R6,%6001(R1)       ! Point to end of values !
4608 6001
460A 7614           LDA     R4,%6101(R1)
460C 6101
460E 8D83           RESFLG  C
4610 AB60   LOOP:   DEC     R6                 ! Point to next higher byte !
4612 AB40           DEC     R4
4614 206D           LDB     RL5,@R6            ! Values to RL5 and RL3 !
4616 204B           LDB     RL3,@R4
4618 B4DB           ADCB    RL3,RL5            ! DAB might have set carry !
461A B0B0           DAB     RL3                ! Decimal adjust value !
461C 2E6B           LDB     @R6,RL3            ! Store result !
461E F188           DJNZ    R1,LOOP
4620 7A00           HALT

4622            end     pgm_8_3
```

The Z8000 microprocessor distinguishes between Add instructions (ADDB, ADCB) and Subtract instructions (SUBB, SBCB) by setting the Decimal Adjust status flag. This allows the DAB instruction to correctly change binary addition into BCD addition and binary subtraction into BCD subtraction. See Table 3-12 for details of the DAB instruction's operation.

DAB can be used only after instructions that properly affect the Carry and Half Carry. You cannot use DAB after INC (since INC does not affect the Carry), DEC, or any word or long word instruction.

This procedure can add decimal (BCD) numbers of any length. Four binary digits are required for each decimal digit, so ten-digit accuracy requires:

$$10 \times 4 = 40 \text{ bits}$$

as opposed to 33 bits in the case of pure binary data. This is essentially five 8-bit words instead of four. The decimal procedure also takes a little longer per word because of the extra DAB instruction.

8-4. 16-Bit Binary Multiplication

Purpose: Multiply the 16-bit unsigned number in memory location 6000 by the 16-bit unsigned binary number in memory location 6002. Place the 16 most significant bits of the result in memory location 6004. Place the 16 least significant bits in memory location 6006.

Sample Problems:

```
        a.                    (6000)  =  0003
                             (6002)  =  0005

              Result:  (6004)  =  0000
                             (6006)  =  000F

        or in decimal, 3 × 5 = 15

        b.                    (6000)  =  706F
                             (6002)  =  0161

              Result:  (6004)  =  009B
                             (6006)  =  090F or 28783 × 353 = 10160399
```

First, we will show the solution using the Z8000 MULT instruction:

Program 8-4:

```
                 internal
                 pgm_8_4 procedure           ! 16 bit by 16 bit multiply !
                 entry
                      $abs     IBASE
   4600 6103        LD       R3,%6000        ! Multiplicand !
   4602 6000
   4604 6105        LD       R5,%6002        ! Multiplier !
   4606 6002
   4608 9952        MULT     RR2,R5
   460A 5D02        LDL      %6004,RR2       ! Store result !
   460C 6004
   460E 7A00        HALT

   4610             end      pgm_8_4
```

It is interesting to look at a binary multiplication routine for two reasons: first, we can compare the execution time of the routine with the MULT instruction; and second, most other microprocessors don't have multiply instructions and understanding multiplication is important.

8-5. A Binary Multiplication Algorithm

Purpose: Multiply the 16-bit unsigned number in memory location 6000 by the 16-bit unsigned binary number in memory location 6002. Place the 16 most significant bits of the result in memory location 6004. Place the 16 least significant bits in memory location 6006.

Sample Problems:

```
a.                    (6000)  =  0003
                      (6002)  =  0005

          Result:     (6004)  =  0000
                      (6006)  =  000F

          or in decimal, 3 × 5 = 15

b.                    (6000)  =  706F
                      (6002)  =  0161

          Result:     (6004)  =  009B
                      (6006)  =  090F or 28783 × 353 = 10160399
```

You can perform multiplication on a computer in the same way that you do long multiplication by hand. Since the numbers are binary, the only problem is whether to multiply by 0 or 1; multiplying by zero obviously gives zero as a result, while multiplying by one produces the same number you started with (the multiplicand). So each step in binary multiplication can be reduced to the following operation: if the current bit in the multiplier is 1, add the multiplicand to the partial product.

The only remaining problem is to ensure that you line everything up correctly each time. The following operations perform this task.

1. Shift the multiplier left one bit so that the bit to be examined is placed in the Carry.

2. Shift the product left one bit so that the next addition is lined up correctly.

To keep things simple, we will multiply two 8-bit values to produce a 16-bit result.

Step 1 - Initialization

> Product = 0
> Counter = 8

Step 2 - Shift Product so as to line up properly

> Product = 2 × Product (LSB = 0)

Step 3 - Shift Multiplier so bit goes to Carry

> Multiplier = 2 × Multiplier

Step 4 - Add Multiplicand to Product if Carry is 1

> If Carry = 1, Product = Product + Multiplicand

Step 5 - Decrement Counter and check for zero

> Counter = Counter - 1
> If Counter > 0 go to Step 2

Assuming the multiplier is 61_{16} and the multiplicand is $6F_{16}$, the algorithm works as follows.

Initialization:

Product	0000
Multiplier	61
Multiplicand	6F
Counter	08

After first iteration of steps 2-5:

Product	0000
Multiplier	C2
Multiplicand	6F
Counter	07
Carry from Multiplier	0

After second iteration:

Product	006F
Multiplier	84
Multiplicand	6F
Counter	06
Carry from Multiplier	1

After third iteration:

Product	014D
Multiplier	08
Multiplicand	6F
Counter	05
Carry from Multiplier	1

After fourth iteration:

Product	029A
Multiplier	10
Multiplicand	6F
Counter	04
Carry from Multiplier	0

After fifth iteration:

Product	0534
Multiplier	20
Multiplicand	6F
Counter	03
Carry from Multiplier	0

After sixth iteration:

Product	0A68
Multiplier	40
Multiplicand	6F
Counter	02
Carry from Multiplier	0

After seventh iteration:

Product	14D0
Multiplier	80
Multiplicand	6F
Counter	01
Carry from Multiplier	0

After eighth iteration:

Product	2A0F
Multiplier	00
Multiplicand	6F
Counter	00
Carry from Multiplier	1

Flowchart 8-5:

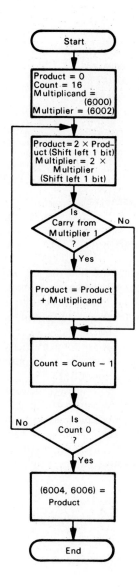

Program 8-5:

```
              internal
                  pgm_8_5 procedure        ! Long hand 16 bit by 16 bit... !
                  entry                    ! ...unsigned multiply !
                      $abs     IBASE

4600 9200             SUBL     RR0,RR0     ! Clear product !
4602 6103             LD       R3,%6000    ! Multiplier !
4604 6000
4606 8344             SUB      R4,R4       ! RR4 is multiplicand !
4608 6105             LD       R5,%6002
460A 6002
460C CE10             LDB      RL6,#16     ! Repeat loop 16 times !
460E 9600     LOOP:   ADDL     RR0,RR0     ! Double product !
4610 8133             ADD      R3,R3       ! Shift multiplier left 1 bit !
4612 EF01             JR       NC,STEP     ! If multiplier high bit = 1... !
4614 9640             ADDL     RR0,RR4     ! ...add multiplicand to product !
4616 FE05     STEP:   DBJNZ    RL6,LOOP    ! Repeat !
4618 5D00             LDL      %6004,RR0   ! Store result !
461A 6004
461C 7A00             HALT

461E          end     pgm_8_5
```

When we count clock cycles, we find the expected result. The MULT version takes 102 cycles. The long version takes 49 cycles outside of the loop, and $464 + 8 \times n$ (n = number of 1 bits in multiplier) cycles inside the loop.

We sacrificed some clarity for the sake of speed in this program. Instead of using the slower CLR instruction, we subtracted registers from themselves.

Do the two programs (8-4 and 8-5) produce exactly the same result for all values? Try multiplying 8000_{16} by 5. The software multiply routine gives the result 00028000_{16}. The hardware multiply gives the result $FFFD8000_{16}$. Both are correct. The software multiply (used in program 8-5) expects unsigned numbers: $8000_{16} = 32,768_{10}$. The Z8000 hardware multiply (used in program 8-4) expects signed twos complement numbers: $8000_{16} = -32,768_{10}$. The results have the same value ($32,768 \times 5$), but the result of the hardware multiply is negative: $-28000_{16} = FFFD8000_{16}$ in twos complement notation. Programs 8-4 and 8-5 work alike only for unsigned numbers less than 8000_{16}; larger numbers are treated as negative numbers by program 8-4.

FLOATING POINT NUMBERS

Floating point is a format frequently used to represent numbers in scientific and engineering applications. A floating point number has two parts, a mantissa and an exponent. This may be illustrated as follows:

$$(\text{Mantissa}) \times \text{Base}^{\text{Exponent}}$$

The mantissa provides the precision for the number; the exponent gives the number's magnitude. The base is 10 for decimal numbers, 2 for binary numbers, 16 for hexadecimal numbers, etc. For example, the decimal number 60200000 would be represented in floating point format as follows:

$$6.02 \times 10^7 \text{ or } 0.602 \times 10^8$$

A detailed discussion of floating point formats, and conversion between number bases, is available elsewhere.[1]

Since microprocessors are binary machines, floating point computations, like any other arithmetic, process binary numbers. For example, the binary number 101110010101 would be represented in binary floating point format as follows:

$$0.101110010101 \times 2^{1100}$$

A binary floating point number will be held in memory as two separate numbers; one number will be interpreted as the mantissa while the other is interpreted as the exponent. The mantissa will usually be larger. For example, a 32-bit long word can represent decimal numbers ranging up to $2^{32} - 1$, which equals 4294967295; this is nine decimal digits of precision, which is enough for nearly all applications. As the mantissa of a floating point number, $2^{32} - 1$ would represent the value 0.4294967295.

A byte can represent exponents in the range -128 to $+127$. What are the equivalent decimal exponents?

$$\text{If} \qquad 2^{127} = 10^X$$

$$\text{then} \qquad 127 \ln 2 = X \ln 10$$

$$\text{so} \qquad X = 127 \times \frac{\ln 2}{\ln 10} \approx 38$$

Another way to see this is to calculate 2^{127}, which is about 1.7×10^{38}.

A decimal exponent of 38 is sufficient to represent any number normally encountered. Frequently, a 16-bit exponent is specified so that all data will lie on word address boundaries.

NORMALIZING NUMBERS

A given value can have more than one representation in a floating point format. For example, $60.2 \times 10^5 = 6.02 \times 10^6 = .602 \times 10^7$. This poses a problem when comparing two floating point values. Floating point numbers become much more manageable when we ensure that, after computations are complete, the mantissa is within a specified range. A convenient form for decimal numbers is $1.0 >$ mantissa ≥ 0.1. We consider a binary number to be normalized when the high-order bit of the mantissa is 1.

A representation for zero is also a problem. $0 \times 2^{14} = 0 \times 2^{-30}$, but this could easily confuse a program that compares two numbers. In our representations, we will reserve the smallest signed exponent (80_{16} for 8 bits, 8000_{16} for 16 bits) with a zero mantissa to represent 0.

To normalize a binary number, shift the number left until the high-order bit is set. Decrement the exponent by 1 for each left shift of the mantissa.

8-6. Normalize a Floating Point Number

Purpose: Normalize a floating point binary number. The 32-bit mantissa is in locations 6000 through 6003. The high-order byte is in location 6000. After normalization the high-order mantissa bit must be 1. Adjust the 16-bit exponent which is held in memory locations 6004 and 6005. If the mantissa is zero, set the exponent to the smallest negative number.

Sample Problems:

a.
$$
\begin{aligned}
(6000) &= \text{023F} \\
(6002) &= \text{4260} \\
(6004) &= \text{000A}
\end{aligned} \Bigg\} \quad 0.23F4260 \times 2^A
$$

Result:
$$
\begin{aligned}
(6000) &= \text{8FD0} \\
(6002) &= \text{9800} \\
(6004) &= \text{0004}
\end{aligned} \Bigg\} \quad 0.8FD09800 \times 2^4
$$

b.
$$
\begin{aligned}
(6000) &= \text{0000} \\
(6002) &= \text{0000} \\
(6004) &= \text{000A}
\end{aligned} \Bigg\} \quad 0.0 \times 2^A
$$

Result:
$$
\begin{aligned}
(6000) &= \text{0000} \\
(6002) &= \text{0000} \\
(6004) &= \text{8000}
\end{aligned} \Bigg\} \quad 0.0
$$

Flowchart 8-6:

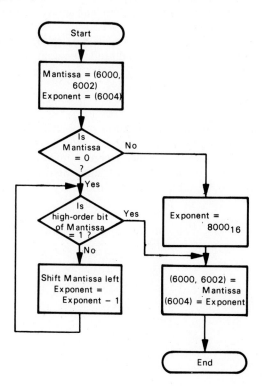

Program 8-6:

```
                    internal
                      pgm_8_6 procedure              ! Floating point normalize !
                    entry
                          $abs      IBASE
  4600 5C01              LDM       R2,%6000,#3      ! RR2 mantissa, R4 exponent !
  4602 0202
  4604 6000
  4606 9C28              TESTL     RR2
  4608 E605              JR        Z,ZERO           ! If mantissa 0, set exp to 8000 !
  460A E506              JR        MI,DONE          ! < 0 means normalized already !
  460C AB40    NORM:     DEC       R4               ! Decrease exponent !
  460E 9622              ADDL      RR2,RR2          ! Shift mantissa left one place !
  4610 EDFD              JR        PL,NORM          ! Repeat until sign bit is set !
  4612 E802              JR        DONE
  4614 2104    ZERO:     LD        R4,#%8000        ! Exp = 8000 if mantissa is 0 !
  4616 8000
  4618 5C09    DONE:     LDM       %6000,R2,#3
  461A 0202
  461C 6000
  461E 7A00              HALT

  4620           end       pgm_8_6
```

Note the use of the LDM instruction to load and store three 16-bit words at a time.

We have not yet considered the sign of the mantissa. Multiplication and division are easier if we hold the mantissa sign in a separate location, and always assume that the mantissa itself is an unsigned binary number.

If an 8-bit exponent is held in memory byte 6005 while the sign of the mantissa is held in memory byte 6004, can you rewrite the normalization program, assuming that the exponent is a signed 8-bit binary number?

ALIGNMENT (SCALING)

When two floating point numbers are to be added or subtracted, they must both have the same exponent. If the two numbers have unequal exponents, they must be aligned. The mantissa of the number with the smaller exponent must be right shifted, and 1 must be added to the exponent for each right shift, until the two exponents are equal. In texts on floating point arithmetic this alignment process is often called scaling.

8-7. Scale a Floating Point Number

Purpose: Align the smaller of two floating point numbers with the larger of the two numbers so that they both have the same exponent. If the smaller floating point number must be right shifted until the mantissa is 0, then set the exponent to 80_{16}. Each floating point number occupies three words of memory. The mantissa is held in the first two words of memory. The high-order byte of the last memory word holds the sign of the mantissa; 0 represents a positive mantissa while 1 represents a negative mantissa. The low-order byte of the third memory word holds an 8-bit signed twos complement binary exponent. The two floating point words are stored in memory beginning at locations 6000 and 6006.

Sample Problems:

a.
$$
\begin{array}{lll}
(6000) & = & 42A1 \\
(6002) & = & 362C \\
(6004) & = & 000A
\end{array} \Bigg\} \quad 0.42A1362C \times 2^A
$$

$$
\begin{array}{lll}
(6006) & = & 243C \\
(6008) & = & 621A \\
(600A) & = & 0105
\end{array} \Bigg\} \quad -0.243C621A \times 2^5
$$

Result:
$$
\begin{array}{lll}
(6000) & = & 42A1 \\
(6002) & = & 362C \\
(6004) & = & 000A
\end{array} \Bigg\} \quad 0.42A1362C \times 2^A
$$

$$
\begin{array}{lll}
(6006) & = & 0121 \\
(6008) & = & E310 \\
(600A) & = & 010A
\end{array} \Bigg\} \quad -0.0121E31 \times 2^A
$$

b.
$$
\begin{array}{lll}
(6000) & = & 42A1 \\
(6002) & = & 362C \\
(6004) & = & 000A
\end{array} \Bigg\} \quad 0.42A1362C \times 2^A
$$

$$
\begin{array}{lll}
(6006) & = & 243C \\
(6008) & = & 621A \\
(600A) & = & 01E0
\end{array} \Bigg\} \quad -0.243C621A \times 2^{-20}
$$

Result:
$$
\begin{array}{lll}
(6000) & = & 42A1 \\
(6002) & = & 362C \\
(6004) & = & 000A
\end{array} \Bigg\} \quad 42A1362C \times 2^A
$$

$$
\begin{array}{lll}
(6006) & = & 0000 \\
(6008) & = & 0000 \\
(600A) & = & 0080
\end{array} \Bigg\} \quad 0.0
$$

Flowchart 8-7:

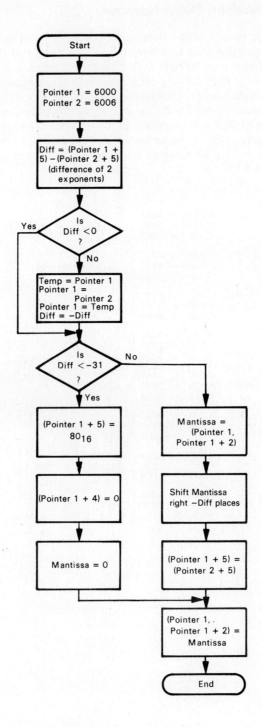

Program 8-7:

```
                    internal
                      pgm_8_7 procedure                ! Floating point scaling !
                    entry
                      $abs      IBASE
4600  7601            LDA       R1,%6000               ! R1 will point to smaller... !
4602  6000
4604  7602            LDA       R2,%6006               ! ...R2 to larger number !
4606  6006
4608  6018            LDB       RL0,%5(R1)             ! Difference of the exponents !
460A  0005
460C  4228            SUBB      RL0,%5(R2)
460E  0005
4610  E202            JR        LE,NEXT                ! If 1st is smaller, no exchange !
4612  AD21            EX        R1,R2                  ! Now R1 points to smaller !
4614  8C82            NEGB      RL0                    ! Ensure difference is negative !
4616  0A08   NEXT:    CPB       RL0,#-31               ! Is 1st too much smaller? !
4618  E1E1
461A  E10A            JR        LT,ZERO                ! Yes, treat smaller as if 0 !
461C  1414            LDL       RR4,@R1                ! Fetch smaller mantissa !
461E  B100            EXTSB     R0                     ! 16 bit exponent difference !
4620  B347            SDLL      RR4,R0                 ! Shift mantissa right !
4622  0000
4624  1D14            LDL       @R1,RR4
4626  6028            LDB       RL0,%5(R2)             ! Get larger exponent !
4628  0005
462A  6E18            LDB       %5(R1),RL0             ! Store in smaller exponent !
462C  0005
462E  7A00            HALT

4630  0D18   ZERO:    CLR       @R1                    ! Zero smaller number !
4632  4D18            CLR       %2(R1)
4634  0002
4636  4D15            LD        %4(R1),#%0080
4638  0004
463A  0080
463C  7A00            HALT

463E            end       pgm_8_7
```

This alignment or scaling program illustrates an interesting use of register indirect addressing. Since we do not know which of the two floating point numbers has the smaller exponent, the program begins by identifying this number, and then loading its address into R1, while the address of the number with the larger exponent is loaded into R2. For the rest of the program we can simply use register indirect addressing and avoid any more logic complications arising from the fact that either one of the two numbers might need to be scaled.

Note the use of the Shift Dynamic Logical instruction (SDLL). The number of bit positions to be shifted is equal to the difference between the two exponents. Since a right shift is to be performed, a negative shift count is required. Therefore if a positive difference between exponents is computed, the difference is negated. The EXTSB instruction propagates the sign bit of RL0 through RH0, allowing R0 to be used as the Shift Count register.

If the computed number of right shifts is 32 or more, a 0 result will be generated. Therefore, RL0 is compared with -31; if RL0 is less than -31, the number with the smaller exponent is set to zero.

FLOATING POINT ARITHMETIC

We will now examine floating point arithmetic.

To compare two floating point numbers, you must first compare the signs. If the signs are equal, then you must compare the exponents. If the exponents are equal, then you must compare the mantissas.

To add or subtract two floating point numbers, you must first scale the number with the smaller exponent using the routine previously illustrated. Then you add or subtract the mantissas, and finally you compute the sign of the result.

The exponent must be incremented following addition if the sum of the mantissas generates a carry. The mantissa must then be rotated right, moving the carry into the high-order bit and moving the low-order bit into the carry, which is then discarded. In the programs below, we use an alternate procedure, which is to shift the mantissas right one bit before adding them. This leaves the high-order bit clear, so that there can be no carry. Of course, the exponents must be increased by one to compensate for the shift.

Following subtraction, the result may have to be normalized to remove any leading zeros. If the mantissas are signed, you will have to test for carry or normalization following addition or subtraction, since adding a negative number is equivalent to subtraction, while subtracting a negative number is equivalent to addition.

To multiply two floating point numbers, you must multiply the mantissas and add the exponents. The product may need to be normalized.

To divide two floating point numbers, you must divide the mantissas and subtract the exponents. The quotient may need to be normalized.

8-8. Floating Point Arithmetic Comparison

Purpose: Compare two signed floating point numbers. Each floating point number occupies three 16-bit words: the first two 16-bit words contain a 32-bit unsigned mantissa. The first word contains the high-order 16 bits of the mantissa while the second word contains the low-order 16 bits. The high-order byte of the third word contains the sign of the mantissa; 1 represents a negative mantissa whereas 0 represents a positive mantissa. The low-order byte of the third word contains a signed binary exponent. The first floating point number is stored in memory locations 6000 through 6005. The second floating point number is stored in memory locations 6006 through 600B. The address of the larger word is to be returned on the top of the stack. If the two words are equal, return $FFFF_{16}$ on the top of the stack.

Sample Problem:

$$
\begin{aligned}
(6000) &= 423A \\
(6002) &= 617B \\
(6004) &= 010A
\end{aligned} \Bigg\} \; -0.423A617B \times 2^A
$$

$$
\begin{aligned}
(6006) &= 217C \\
(6008) &= A13A \\
(600A) &= 0004
\end{aligned} \Bigg\} \; 0.217CA13A \times 2^4
$$

$$R15 \;=\; 8000$$

Result:
$$
\begin{aligned}
R15 &= 7FFE \\
(7FFE) &= 6006
\end{aligned}
$$

Flowchart 8-8:

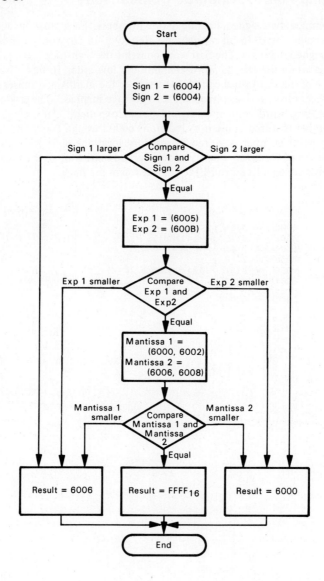

Program 8-8:

```
                internal
                    pgm_8_8 procedure              ! Floating point compare !
                entry
                    $abs      IBASE

    4600 5C01       LDM       R0,%6000,#3          ! Load first number into R0-R2 !
    4602 0002
    4604 6000
    4606 5C01       LDM       R4,%6006,#3          ! Second number to R4-R6 !
    4608 0402
    460A 6006
    460C 8A62       CPB       RH2,RH6              ! Compare signs !
    460E E10A       JR        LT,FIRST             ! 1st positive, 2nd negative !
    4610 EA0C       JR        GT,SECOND            ! 2nd positive, 1st negative !
    4612 8AEA       CPB       RL2,RL6              ! Compare exponents !
    4614 EA07       JR        GT,FIRST             ! 1st has larger exponent !
    4616 E109       JR        LT,SECOND
    4618 9040       CPL       RR0,RR4              ! Compare mantissas !
    461A EB04       JR        UGT,FIRST            ! First is larger !
    461C E706       JR        ULT,SECOND
    461E 0DF9       PUSH      @R15,#%FFFF          ! Numbers are equal !
    4620 FFFF
    4622 7A00       HALT
    4624 0DF9 FIRST:  PUSH    @R15,#%6000          ! First is larger !
    4626 6000
    4628 7A00       HALT
    462A 0DF9 SECOND: PUSH    @R15,#%6006          ! Second is larger !
    462C 6006
    462E 7A00       HALT

    4630            end       pgm_8_8
```

The comparison program uses two LDM instructions to load the two three-word floating point numbers into CPU registers. A single LDM instruction could be used, but the second mantissa would not get loaded into a 32-bit CPU register. Why is this a problem? Try rewriting the program to find out.

Often the representation of floating point numbers will be designed to use an even number of memory words so that 32-bit data can be loaded into 32-bit CPU registers more easily. If four words are used to represent each floating point number, there are a variety of ways in which the four words could be assigned. How would you assign this space? And why?

Notice the use of absolute addresses to identify floating point numbers. As we explained on numerous occasions, this is a very bad practice. A subroutine that compares two floating point numbers, providing they are stored in specific memory locations, is not nearly as useful as a subroutine that can compare two floating point numbers located anywhere in memory. While the use of absolute addresses makes the program easier to understand, remember this is a bad practice. Here are three ways in which the program could be made more general:

1. Place starting addresses for the two floating point numbers at the top of the stack.

2. Place starting addresses for the two floating point numbers in CPU registers; it is the responsibility of the program which calls the comparison procedure to load appropriate starting addresses into registers.

3. Place starting addresses for the two floating point numbers in dedicated memory locations, such as memory words 6000 and 6002.

Try rewriting the program using these three generalization techniques.

8-9. Floating Point Addition and Subtraction

Purpose: Add or subtract two floating point numbers. Floating point numbers occupy four words of memory as follows:

Lowest address — (word 1): Mantissa, high-order word ⎱ Unsigned binary number
(word 2): Mantissa, low-order word ⎰

(word 3): Mantissa sign. 1 = negative
0 = positive

Highest address — (word 4): Exponent (signed binary number)

This routine uses four parameters, which it expects to find in four words at the top of the stack, in the following sequence:

Top of stack: operation. 1 = subtract, 0 = add
Next on stack: Address of first floating point number
Next on stack: Address of second floating point number
Next on stack: Address for result floating point number

The addresses are the addresses of the high-order word of the mantissa.

Sample Problems:

a.

R15	=	7FF8
(7FF8)	=	0000	addition
(7FFA)	=	6000
(7FFC)	=	6008
(7FFE)	=	6400

(6000)	=	823A	
(6002)	=	281C	$0.823A281C \times 2^A$
(6004)	=	0000	
(6006)	=	000A	

(6008)	=	C121	
(600A)	=	4000	$0.C1214000 \times 2^6$
(600C)	=	0000	
(600E)	=	0006	

Result:

RI5	=	8000	
(6400)	=	8E4C	
(6402)	=	3C1C	$0.8E4C3C1C \times 2^A$
(6404)	=	0000	
(6406)	=	000A	

b.

R15	=	7FF8
(7FF8)	=	0001	subtraction
(7FFA)	=	6000
(7FFC)	=	6008
(800E)	=	6400

(6000)	=	823A	
(6002)	=	281C	$-0.823A281C \times 2^A$
(6004)	=	0001	
(6006)	=	000A	
(6008)	=	C121	
(600A)	=	4000	$-0.C1214000 \times 2^6$
(600C)	=	0001	
(600E)	=	0006	

Result:

R15	=		
(6400)	=	EC50	
(6402)	=	2838	$-0.EC502838 \times 2^9$
(6404)	=	0001	
(6406)	=	0009	

Flowchart 8-9:

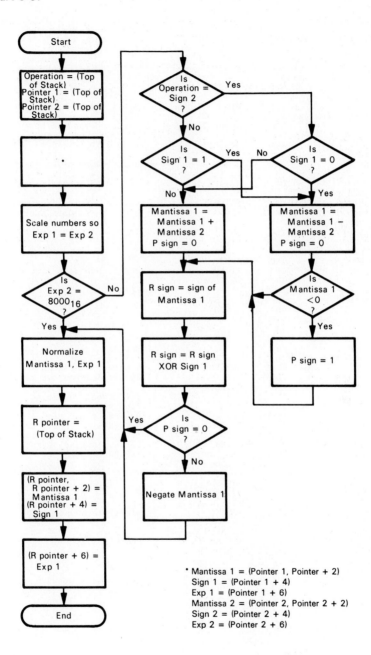

* Mantissa 1 = (Pointer 1, Pointer + 2)
 Sign 1 = (Pointer 1 + 4)
 Exp 1 = (Pointer 1 + 6)
 Mantissa 2 = (Pointer 2, Pointer 2 + 2)
 Sign 2 = (Pointer 2 + 4)
 Exp 2 = (Pointer 2 + 6)

Program 8-9:

```
              external
                 SCALE     procedure          ! Routine to scale numbers !
                 NORMAL    procedure          ! Routine to normalize a number !

              internal
                 pgm_8_9 procedure            ! Floating point add & subtract !
              entry
                 $abs      IBASE

4600  97FA              POP     R10,@R15       ! R10 = 0 for add, 1 for sub !
4602  95FC              POPL    RR12,@R15      ! R12 & R13 operand addresses !
4604  1CC1              LDM     R0,@R12,#4     ! First operand to R0 - R3 !
4606  0003
4608  1CD1              LDM     R4,@R13,#4     ! Second to R4 - R7 !
460A  0403
460C  5F00              CALL    SCALE          ! Scale numbers in registers !
460E  0000*
4610  0B07              CP      R7,#%8000      ! If second number is zero... !
4612  8000
4614  E61F              JR      EQ,DONE        ! ... result is first number !
4616  B305              SRLL    RR0            ! Right shift both mantissas !
4618  FFFF
461A  A930              INC     R3             ! Increment both exponents !
461C  B345              SRLL    RR4
461E  FFFF
4620  A970              INC     R7
4622  8B6A              CP      R10,R6         ! Add or subtract mantissas? !
4624  E603              JR      EQ,EQUAL
4626  8D24              TEST    R2
4628  E606              JR      Z,FLSUB
462A  E802              JR      FLADD
462C  8D24      EQUAL:  TEST    R2
462E  EE03              JR      NZ,FLSUB
4630  9640      FLADD:  ADDL    RR0,RR4        ! Add mantissas !
4632  8D98              CLR     R9             ! Use R9 as RR0 sign indicator !
4634  E804              JR      RESSIGN
4636  9240      FLSUB:  SUBL    RR0,RR4        ! Subtract mantissas !
4638  8D98              CLR     R9             ! Sign indicator for result !
463A  ED01              JR      PL,RESSIGN
463C  A990              INC     R9             ! 1 if result negative !
463E  8D88      RESSIGN:CLR     R8             ! Find sign of result !
4640  9C08              TESTL   RR0            ! Set R8 to RR0 sign !
4642  ED01              JR      PL,SIGN        ! Result sign equals RR0 sign !
4644  A980              INC     R8             ! If first FP number is < 0... !
4646  8982      SIGN:   XOR     R2,R8          ! ...use inverse of RR0 sign !
4648  8D94              TEST    R9             ! If RR0 is negative, negate it !
464A  E604              JR      Z,DONE
464C  8D12              NEG     R1
464E  8D00              COM     R0
4650  EF01              JR      NC,DONE
4652  A900              INC     R0
4654  5F00      DONE:   CALL    NORMAL         ! Normalize number in R0 - R3 !
4656  0000*
4658  97F8              POP     R8,@R15
465A  1C89              LDM     @R8,R0,#4      ! Store result !
465C  0003
465E  7A00              HALT

4660              end     pgm_8_9
```

The floating point addition and subtraction program illustrated above is a little more complex than most presented in this book. However, there are relatively few points where the logic is complex. This is the basic algorithm:

1. Positive mantissas are either added or subtracted.

2. The mantissas are right shifted one bit to create space for a carry from the high-order bit.

3. The sign of the result is computed based on the sign of the first floating point number and the sign of the result of adding or subtracting the mantissas.

Three pieces of information determine whether the second mantissa will be added to the first mantissa or subtracted from it. These three pieces of information are the operation as specified at the top of the stack, and the signs of the two mantissas.

Bear in mind that the two mantissas (A and B below) are positive numbers; their signs are held in separate sign words. The following algorithm therefore determines whether addition or subtraction is to be performed, and what the sign of the result will be:

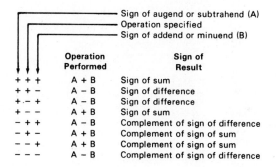

	Operation Performed	Sign of Result
+ + +	A + B	Sign of sum
+ + −	A − B	Sign of difference
+ .− +	A − B	Sign of difference
+ − −	A + B	Sign of sum
− + +	A − B	Complement of sign of difference
− + −	A + B	Complement of sign of sum
− − +	A + B	Complement of sign of sum
− − −	A − B	Complement of sign of difference

Sign of augend or subtrahend (A)
Operation specified
Sign of addend or minuend (B)

If the logic shown above is not obvious, try various cases to prove it for yourself.

By right shifting the two positive mantissas one bit before adding or subtracting, we simplify subsequent logic; logic could become quite complex if we had to worry about carries and overflows. The 1-bit right shift ensures that addition cannot generate a carry out, while subtraction cannot generate an overflow. Notice the use of the result sign indicator, which is set or reset within the separate logic paths of addition and subtraction. This prevents a high-order bit set to 1 following addition from being interpreted as a sign bit, whereas a high-order bit set to 1 during subtraction should be interpreted as a sign bit.

There are a number of places in the floating point addition/subtraction routine where we could save instructions. For example, R9 could be cleared initially, and then set if subtraction generates a negative result. But the penalty would be a program that is harder to read. Can you find other places in the program where instructions could be eliminated? Is it worth shortening the program if it makes the logic harder to follow?

8-10. Floating Point Multiplication and Division

Purpose: Multiply two floating point numbers. Each floating point number occupies four memory words as follows:

Lowest address   (word 1) : Mantissa, high-order word   Unsigned binary number
                           (word 2) : Mantissa, low-order word
                           (word 3) : Mantissa sign. 1 = negative
                                          0 = positive

Beginning addresses for the multiplier, multiplicand, and product are held at the top of the stack as follows:

Top of stack : Address of multiplier (or dividend)
Next on stack : Address of multiplicand (or divisor)
Next on stack : Address of product (or quotient)

Sample Problem:

$$
\begin{array}{rcl}
\text{R15} & = & \text{7FFA} \\
\text{(7FFA)} & = & \text{6000} \\
\text{(7FFC)} & = & \text{6008} \\
\text{(800E)} & = & \text{6400}
\end{array}
$$

$$
\left.
\begin{array}{rcl}
\text{(6000)} & = & \text{8001} \\
\text{(6002)} & = & \text{0800} \\
\text{(6004)} & = & \text{0000} \\
\text{(6006)} & = & \text{000A}
\end{array}
\right\} \quad 0.800108 \times 2^A
$$

$$
\left.
\begin{array}{rcl}
\text{(6008)} & = & \text{C000} \\
\text{(600A)} & = & \text{0401} \\
\text{(600C)} & = & \text{0001} \\
\text{(600E)} & = & \text{0004}
\end{array}
\right\} \quad -0.C0000401 \times 2^4
$$

Result:
$$
\left.
\begin{array}{rcl}
\text{R15} & = & \text{8000} \\
\text{(6400)} & = & \text{C001} \\
\text{(6402)} & = & \text{9000} \\
\text{(6404)} & = & \text{0001} \\
\text{(6406)} & = & \text{000D}
\end{array}
\right\} \quad -0.C0019 \times 2^D
$$

Flowchart 8-10:

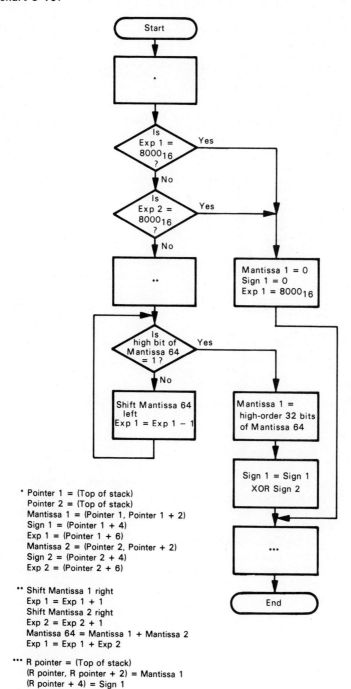

* Pointer 1 = (Top of stack)
  Pointer 2 = (Top of stack)
  Mantissa 1 = (Pointer 1, Pointer 1 + 2)
  Sign 1 = (Pointer 1 + 4)
  Exp 1 = (Pointer 1 + 6)
  Mantissa 2 = (Pointer 2, Pointer + 2)
  Sign 2 = (Pointer 2 + 4)
  Exp 2 = (Pointer 2 + 6)

** Shift Mantissa 1 right
  Exp 1 = Exp 1 + 1
  Shift Mantissa 2 right
  Exp 2 = Exp 2 + 1
  Mantissa 64 = Mantissa 1 + Mantissa 2
  Exp 1 = Exp 1 + Exp 2

*** R pointer = (Top of stack)
  (R pointer, R pointer + 2) = Mantissa 1
  (R pointer + 4) = Sign 1
  (R pointer + 6) = Exp 1

Program 8-10a:

```
              internal
              pgm_8_10a procedure
              entry
                     $abs      IBASE
  4600 95FC           POPL     RR12,@R15       ! Addresses in R12, R13 !
  4602 1CC1           LDM      R0,@R12,#4      ! Multiplier in R0 - R3 !
  4604 0003
  4606 1CD1           LDM      R4,@R13,#4      ! Multiplicand in R4 - R7 !
  4608 0403
  460A 0B03           CP       R3,#%8000       ! Test for zero multiplier !
  460C 8000
  460E E616           JR       EQ,ZERO
  4610 0B07           CP       R7,#%8000       ! Test for zero multiplicand !
  4612 8000
  4614 E613           JR       EQ,ZERO
  4616 940A           LDL      RR10,RR0        ! Will get product in RQ8 !
  4618 B3A5           SRLL     RR10            ! Shift both operands right... !
  461A FFFF
  461C A930           INC      R3              ! ...to ensure sign bits off !
  461E B345           SRLL     RR4
  4620 FFFF
  4622 A970           INC      R7
  4624 9848           MULTL    RQ8,RR4
  4626 8173           ADD      R3,R7           ! Sum exponents !
  4628 8D84           TEST     R8
  462A E608           JR       Z,ZERO          ! If valid, should be non-zero !
  462C AB30    NORM:  DEC      R3              ! Dec exponent for each shift !
  462E B3A8           RLC      R10             ! Shift R8-R9-R10 left... !
  4630 B398           RLC      R9
  4632 B388           RLC      R8
  4634 EDFB           JR       PL,NORM         ! ...until high bit is set !
  4636 9480    STORE: LDL      RR0,RR8         ! Use high order 32 bits !
  4638 8962           XOR      R2,R6           ! Generate product sign !
  463A E804           JR       DONE
  463C 9200    ZERO:  SUBL     RR0,RR0         ! Set result to 0 !
  463E 8D28           CLR      R2
  4640 2103           LD       R3,#%8000
  4642 8000
  4644 97FD    DONE:  POP      R13,@R15        ! Result address !
  4646 1CD9           LDM      @R13,R0,#4
  4648 0003
  464A 7A00           HALT

  464C          end       pgm_8_10a
```

The multiplicand could be accessed in memory; it does not need to be loaded into Registers R4 through R7. Try rewriting the multiplication program in this fashion. How much shorter is the program? What about the length of the object program, and program execution time?

Note the use of the Exclusive-OR instruction to generate the sign of the product. The mantissas are treated as unsigned positive numbers. Therefore the sign of the product will be positive if the mantissas have the same signs, but it will be negative if the mantissa signs differ.

Program 8-10b:

```
                constant
                    ZERODIVISOR := %FF

                external
                    NORMAL procedure

                internal
                    pgm_8_10b procedure       ! Floating point divide !
                    entry
464C 95FC               POPL    R12,@R15         ! R12 & R13 operand addresses !
464E 1CC1               LDM     R0,@R12,#4       ! Dividend to R0 - R3 !
4650 0003
4652 1CD1               LDM     R4,@R13,#4       ! Divisor to R4 - R7 !
4654 0403
4656 0B03               CP      R3,#%8000        ! Test for zero dividend !
4658 8000
465A E616               JR      EQ,ZERO
465C 0B07               CP      R7,#%8000        ! Zero divisor is an error !
465E 8000
4660 E612               JR      EQ,ZERODIV
4662 9408               LDL     RR8,RR0          ! Will get quotient in RQ8 !
4664 92AA               SUBL    RR10,RR10        ! Start with low order 0 !
4666 B345               SRLL    RR4              ! Ensure divisor sign bit off !
4668 FFFF
466A A970               INC     R7
466C B385       DSCALE: SRLL    RR8              ! Ensure high order dividend...
466E FFFF
4670 B3AC               RRC     R10              ! ...is not negative... !
4672 A930               INC     R3
4674 9048               CPL     RR8,RR4
4676 EAFA               JR      GT,DSCALE        ! ...and is less than divisor !
4678 9A48               DIVL    RQ8,RR4
467A 8373               SUB     R3,R7            ! Subtract exponents !
467C 94A0               LDL     RR0,RR10         ! Quotient to RR0 !
467E 5F00               CALL    NORMAL           ! Normalize number in R0-R3 !
4680 0000*
4682 8962               XOR     R2,R6            ! Generate quotient sign !
4684 E805               JR      DONE
4686 7FFF       ZERODIV:SC      #ZERODIVISOR     ! Error if divide by 0 !
4688 9200       ZERO:   SUBL    RR0,RR0          ! Set result to 0 !
468A 8D28               CLR     R2
468C 2103               LD      R3,#%8000
468E 8000
4690 97FD       DONE:   POP     R13,@R15         ! Result address !
4692 1CD9               LDM     @R13,R0,#4
4694 0003

4696            end     pgm_8_10b
```

A program to divide two floating point numbers is almost identical to the multiplication procedure. The only difference is that the dividend mantissa is divided by the divisor mantissa, and the divisor exponent is subtracted from the dividend exponent. Also, default conditions may differ. A zero dividend will generate a zero quotient, but a zero divisor is an error condition; it will frequently generate a software trap.

Program 8-10b is a floating point division variation of the floating point multiplication procedure.

The normalization subroutine assumes that the floating point number which is to be normalized is held in R0-R3.

Try modifying this program to return the remainder. Should it also be returned as a floating point number?

PROBLEMS

8-1. Multiple Precision Binary Subtraction

Purpose: Subtract one multiple-word number from another. The length in words of both numbers is in memory location 6000. The numbers themselves start (most significant bits first) in memory locations 6002 and 6102, respectively. The difference replaces the number starting in memory location 6002. Subtract the number starting in 6102 from the one starting in 6002.

Sample Problem:

(6000)	=	0003	
(6002)	=	2F5B	
(6004)	=	47C3	
(6006)	=	306C	
(6102)	=	14DF	
(6104)	=	85B8	
(6106)	=	03BC	
Result: (6002)	=	1A76	
(6004)	=	C206	
(6006)	=	2C60	

That is,
$$\begin{array}{r} 2F5B47C3306C \\ -\ 14DF85B803BC \\ \hline 1A7BC20B2CB0 \end{array}$$

8-2. Decimal Subtraction

Purpose: Subtract one multiple-word decimal (BCD) number from another. The length in bytes of both numbers is in memory byte 6000, the numbers themselves start (most significant digits first) in memory locations 6001 and 6101, respectively, and the difference replaces the number starting in 6001. Subtract the number starting in 6101 from the one starting in 6001.

Sample Problem:

(6000)	=	04
(6001)	=	36
(6002)	=	70
(6003)	=	19
(6004)	=	85
(6101)	=	12
(6102)	=	66
(6103)	=	34
(6104)	=	59
Result: (6001)	=	24
(6002)	=	03
(6003)	=	85
(6004)	=	26

That is,
$$\begin{array}{r} 36701985 \\ -\ 12663459 \\ \hline 24038526 \end{array}$$

8-3. 32-Bit by 32-Bit Multiply

Purpose: Multiply the value in memory locations 6000 (high-order) and 6002 by the value in memory locations 6004 and 6006. Do the multiply twice: first use the MULTL instruction and place the result in the four words starting at memory location 6008; then use a shift and add method as in the earlier example and place the result in the four words starting at memory location 6010.

Sample Problem:

	(6000)	=	0024
	(6002)	=	68AC
	(6004)	=	0328
	(6006)	=	1088
Result:	(6008)	=	0000
	(600A)	=	72EC
	(600C)	=	B8C2
	(600E)	=	5B60
	(6010)	=	0000
	(6012)	=	72EC
	(6014)	=	B8C2
	(6016)	=	5B60

Note: On many early versions of the Z8000, the MULTL instruction worked incorrectly. This exercise can help you determine if the instruction performs correctly on your machine.

8-4. Floating Point Sort

Purpose: Sort a list of 4-word floating point numbers into ascending order. The number of floating point numbers is in location 6000. The first number begins in location 6002. The numbers are in the format used by program 8-8.

Sample Problem:

$$(6000) = 0003$$

$$\left.\begin{array}{l} (6002) = C121 \\ (6004) = 4000 \\ (6006) = 0000 \\ (6008) = FFFA \end{array}\right\} \quad 0.C1214000 \times 2^{-6}$$

$$\left.\begin{array}{l} (600A) = 823A \\ (600C) = 281C \\ (600E) = 0000 \\ (6010) = 000A \end{array}\right\} \quad 0.823A281C \times 2^{A}$$

$$\left.\begin{array}{l} (6012) = 8E4C \\ (6014) = 3C1C \\ (6016) = 0001 \\ (6018) = 000A \end{array}\right\} \quad -0.8E4C3C1C \times 2^{A}$$

Result:

$$\left.\begin{array}{l} (6002) = 8E4C \\ (6004) = 3C1C \\ (6006) = 0001 \\ (6008) = 000A \end{array}\right\} \quad -0.8E4C3C1C \times 2^{A}$$

$$\left.\begin{array}{l} (600A) = C121 \\ (600C) = 4000 \\ (600E) = 0000 \\ (6000) = FFFA \end{array}\right\} \quad 0.C1214000 \times 2^{-6}$$

$$\left.\begin{array}{l} (6002) = 823A \\ (6004) = 281C \\ (6006) = 0000 \\ (6008) = 000A \end{array}\right\} \quad 0.823A281C \times 2^{A}$$

Note: This program could also operate on a list of pointers to floating point numbers. The cumbersome exchanges could then be avoided.

9

Tables and Lists

Tables and lists are two of the basic data structures used with all computers. We have already seen tables used to perform code conversions and arithmetic. Tables may also be used to identify or respond to commands and instructions, linearize data, provide access to files or records, define the meaning of keys or switches, and choose among alternate programs. Lists are usually less structured than tables. Lists may record tasks that the processor must perform, messages or data that the processor must record, or conditions that have changed or should be monitored. Tables are a simple way of making decisions or solving problems, since no computations or logical functions are necessary. The task, then, reduces to organizing the table so that the proper entry is easy to find. Lists allow the execution of sequences of tasks, the preparation of sets of results, and the construction of interrelated data files (or data bases). Problems include how to add elements to a list and remove elements from it.

Consistent with the Z8000 stack-oriented data handling logic demonstrated throughout this book, this chapter assumes that temporary data resides at the top of a stack. Although R15 (the official stack pointer) is used to access temporary data, remember that any register (with the exception of R0) can substitute for R15. Should you choose not to handle temporary data via secondary stacks, the programming examples presented in this chapter are easily modified; simply replace PUSH and POP instructions with appropriate LD instructions.

PROGRAMMING EXAMPLES

9-1. Add an Entry to a List

Purpose: Add the value on the top of the stack to a list if it is not already present in the list. The length of the list is in location 6000. The list itself begins in the next location, 6002.

Sample Problems:

a.

R15	=	7FFE (Stack Pointer)
(7FFE)	=	16B2
(6000)	=	0004
(6002)	=	5376
(6004)	=	7618
(6006)	=	138A
(600A)	=	21DC

Result:	R15	=	8000
	(6000)	=	0005
	(600C)	=	16B2

The entry is added to the list since it is not already present. The length of the list is increased by 1.

b.

R15	=	7FFE
(7FFE)	=	16B2
(6000)	=	0004
(6002)	=	5376
(6004)	=	7618
(6006)	=	16B2
(600A)	=	21DC

Result: No change to the list, since the entry is already present.

Flowchart 9-1:

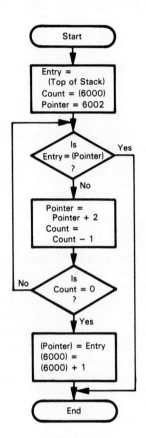

Program 9-1a:

```
              internal
                pgm_9_la procedure
                entry
                     $abs      IBASE

    4600 97F0           POP     R0,@R15      ! Search object !
    4602 7602           LDA     R2,%6000     ! Pointer to list !
    4604 6000
    4606 9723           POP     R3,@R2       ! First element is length !
    4608 0B20  AGAIN:   CP      R0,@R2       ! Search object in R0 !
    460A E605           JR      EQ,DONE      ! Done if already there !
    460C A921           INC     R2,#2        ! Bump to next WORD element !
    460E F384           DJNZ    R3,AGAIN     ! Length Counter !
    4610 2F20           LD      @R2,R0       ! Insert object at end of list !
    4612 6900           INC     %6000        ! Increase length !
    4614 6000
    4616 7A00  DONE:    HALT

    4618           end       pgm_9_la
```

We could also use the block search instruction, CPIR, as follows.

Program 9-1b:

```
              internal
                 pgm_9_1b procedure
                 entry
                    $abs        IBASE

4600 97F0              POP     R0,@R15        ! Search object !
4602 7602              LDA     R2,%6000       ! Pointer to list !
4604 6000
4606 9723              POP     R3,@R2         ! First element is length !
4608 BB24              CPIR    R0,@R2,R3,EQ   ! Search the list !
460A 0306
460C E603              JR      Z,DONE         ! If zero, the object was found !
460E 2F20              LD      @R2,R0         ! Insert object at end of list !
4610 6900              INC     %6000          ! Increase length !
4612 6000
4614 7A00    DONE:     HALT

4616              end     pgm_9_1b
```

Remember that CPIR automatically repeats the comparison until the length register (R3) is zero or until a true comparison occurs (R0 = @R2).

Clearly, this method of adding elements is very inefficient if the list is long. We could improve the procedure by limiting the search to part of the list or by ordering the list. **We could limit the search by using the entry to get a starting point in the list. This method is called "hashing,"** and is much like selecting a starting page in a dictionary or directory on the basis of the first letter in an entry.

We could order the list by numerical value. The search could then end when the list values went beyond the entry (larger or smaller, depending on the ordering technique used). A new entry would have to be inserted properly, and all the other entries would have to be moved down in the list.

The program could be restructured to use two tables. One table could provide a starting point in the other table; for example, the search point could be based on the most or least significant 4-bit digit in the entry.

Programs 9-1a and 9-1b do not work if the length of the list could be zero (what happens?). We could avoid this problem by checking the length initially. The initialization procedure would then be:

```
                 .
                 .
                 .
              POP     R3,@R2         ! First element is length !
              TEST    R3
              JR      Z,INSERT
                 .
                 .
                 .
    INSERT:   LD      @R2,R0         ! Add entry to end of list !
```

If each entry has more than two words, a pattern-matching program is needed. The program must proceed to the next entry if a match fails. The program must skip over the last part of the current entry once a mismatch is found. Try rewriting the program to handle this case.

9-2. Check an Ordered List

Purpose: Check the value on the top of the stack to see if it is in an ordered list. The length of the list is in memory location 6000; the list itself begins in memory location 6002 and consists of unsigned binary numbers in increasing order. If the value on the stack is in the list, leave the index of its entry on the top of the stack; if the value is not found, set the top of the stack to $FFFF_{16}$.

Sample Problems:

a.

```
          R15  =  7FFE   (Stack pointer)
        (7FFE)  =  5376
        (6000)  =  0004
        (6002)  =  138A
        (6004)  =  21DC
        (6006)  =  5376
        (600A)  =  8618
```

Result: (7FFE) = 0004

The top of stack is set to 0004 because location 6006 (6002 + 0004) contains the search object.

b.

```
          R15  =  7FFE
        (7FFE)  =  46B2
        (6000)  =  0004
        (6002)  =  138A
        (6004)  =  21DC
        (6006)  =  5376
        (600A)  =  8618
```

Result: (7FFE) = FFFF

The top of the stack is set to $FFFF_{16}$ because the search object is not in the list.

Program 9-2a:

```
                internal
                pgm_9_2a procedure
                entry
                        $abs      IBASE

    4600 97F0           POP       R0,@R15         ! Search object !
    4602 6103           LD        R3,%6000        ! Length of list !
    4604 6000
    4606 AB30           DEC       R3              ! Index range 0 to (n-1) !
    4608 E507           JR        MI,MISSING      ! Not found if list empty !
    460A 8133           ADD       R3,R3           ! Form WORD index !
    460C 4B30   AGAIN:  CP        R0,%6002(R3)    ! Use R3 as index into list !
    460E 6002
    4610 E605           JR        EQ,DONE         ! Object found? !
    4612 EB02           JR        UGT,MISSING     ! Not in list if > element !
    4614 AB31           DEC       R3,#2           ! Next element !
    4616 E9FA           JR        GE,AGAIN        ! Through with list when < 0 !
    4618 2103   MISSING:LD        R3,#%FFFF       ! FFFF on stack if not found !
    461A FFFF
    461C 93F3   DONE:   PUSH      @R15,R3         ! Index on stack if found !
    461E 7A00           HALT

    4620                end       pgm_9_2a
```

Flowchart 9-2:

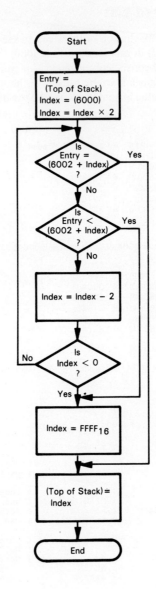

The searching process takes advantage of the fact that elements are ordered. Once we find an element smaller than the entry, the search is over, since subsequent elements will be even smaller. You may want to try an example to convince yourself that the procedure works.

As in the previous problem, any method of choosing a good starting point will speed up the search. **One method starts in the middle of the list, determines which half of the list the entry is in, then divides the half into halves, etc. This method is called a binary search,** since it divides the remaining part of the list in half following each test.[1] The best method is to divide the table into thirds and begin the search at one or the other of the boundaries between thirds. This is a close approximation of the Fibonacci search.

Program 9-2a works if the length is zero since we test for zero length when forming the word index.

This example demonstrates the use of indexed addressing. The instruction CP R0,%6002(R3) has the same effect as:

```
ADD     R3,#%6002    SLL     R1,2         ! Multiply R1 by 4  !
CP      R0,@R3       LDPS    %6000(R1)    ! Load new status and jump  !
```

Of course the ADD would change R3 and could not be repeated.

Also note that an unsigned comparison, UGT, is made. In the sample problems, a comparison using GT will not work correctly since the last entry in the list, 8618, has its sign bit set. Unsigned compares are particularly useful when dealing with addresses, which are always unsigned.

Note that the two JR instructions can be replaced by a JR UGE, ... This will speed up execution of the loop. Here is the resulting program:

```
        .
        .
        .
AGAIN:   CP     R0,%6002(R3)   ! Use R3 as index into list            !
         JR     UGE,LPEXIT     ! Done if found or greater than        !
TST:     DEC    R3,#2          ! Next element                         !
         JR     GE,AGAIN       ! Through with list when < 0           !
LPEXIT:  JR     EQ,DONE        ! If found, leave R3 alone             !
         LD     R3,#%FFFF      ! Leave FFFF on stack if not found     !
DONE:    PUSH   @R15,R3        ! Leave index on stack if found        !
         HALT
```

The JR at LPEXIT always fails when the list is exhausted.

The CPDR block search instructions are not as useful when dealing with indexed addresses. However, we can rewrite the program to eliminate indexed addressing, then use CPDR, as shown in program 9-2b.

Program 9-2b:

```
            internal
                  pgm_9_2b procedure
                  entry
                        $abs     IBASE
4600 97F0             POP      R0,@R15          ! Search object !
4602 6103             LD       R3,%6000         ! Length of list !
4604 6000
4606 A132             LD       R2,R3            ! Form word index in R2 !
4608 8122             ADD      R2,R2
460A E607             JR       Z,MISSING        ! Stop if zero length list !
460C 0102             ADD      R2,#%6002-2      ! Compute end of list address !
460E 6000
4610 BB2C             CPDR     R0,@R2,R3,UGE    ! Search for value... !
4612 030F                                      ! ...equal or smaller !
4614 4B20             CP       R0,2(R2)         ! Was it equal? !
4616 0002
4618 E602             JR       EQ,DONE
461A 2102     MISSING:LD       R2,#%FFFF+%6000  ! If not found, push FFFF !
461C 5FFF
461E 0302     DONE:   SUB      R2,#%6000        ! Form index !
4620 6000
4622 93F2             PUSH     @R15,R2          ! Index or FFFF !
4624 7A00             HALT

4626                  end      pgm_9_2b
```

9-3. Remove an Element from a Queue

Purpose: Memory location 6000 contains the address for the head of a queue. Push the address of the first element (head) of the queue onto the stack. Update the queue to remove the element. Each element in the queue is one word long and contains the address of the next element in the queue. The last element in the queue contains zero to indicate that there is no next element.

Queues are used to store information in sequence of access. The queue is a first-in, first-out (FIFO) data structure; i.e., elements are removed from the queue in the same order in which they are entered. Operating systems place tasks in queues so that they will be executed in the proper order. I/O drivers transfer data to or from queues to ensure that the data will be transmitted or handled in the proper order. Buffers are queued so that it becomes easy to find the next available buffer in a storage pool. Queues may also be used to link requests for storage, timing, or I/O, and to ensure that requests are satisfied in the correct order.

In real applications, each element in the queue will typically contain a large amount of information and/or storage space, in addition to providing the address which links each element to the next one.

Sample Problems:

a.		R15	=	8000	Stack pointer
		(6000)	=	6020	Address of first element in queue
		(6020)	=	6060	First element in queue
		(6060)	=	60A0	
		(60A0)	=	0000	Last element in queue
	Result:	R15	=	7FFE	
		(7FFE)	=	6020	Address of element removed from queue
		(6000)	=	6060	Address of new first element in queue
b.		R15	=	8000	
		(6000)	=	0000	Empty queue
	Result:	R15	=	7FFE	
		(7FFE)	=	0000	No element available from queue

Flowchart 9-3:

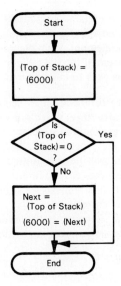

Program 9-3:

```
                internal
                  pgm_9_3 procedure
                  entry
                      $abs      IBASE

  4600 53F0           PUSH      @R15,%6000      ! Push head of queue !
  4602 6000
  4604 0DF4           TEST      @R15            ! Is rest of queue empty? !
  4606 E604           JR        EQ,DONE
  4608 21F3           LD        R3,@R15         ! No, remove first element !
  460A 2133           LD        R3,@R3
  460C 6F03           LD        %6000,R3
  460E 6000
  4610 7A00   DONE:   HALT

  4612              end       pgm_9_3
```

Queuing can handle lists that are not stored sequentially in memory, since each element in the queue contains the address of the next element. Such lists ensure that you handle data or tasks in the proper order. You can change variables or fill in program definitions in the correct sequence using a queued list. Queued lists require some extra storage, but elements are easily added or deleted.

The stack-oriented Z8000 architecture is well-suited to lists. Using R15 (the official Z8000 stack pointer) or any other register (except R0), a single PUSH instruction moves data from the queue to the current stack.

It may be useful to maintain pointers to both ends of the queue rather than just its head. This simplifies the addition of a new element to the queue. It also allows the data structure to be used in either a first-in first-out manner or in a last-in first-out manner, depending on whether new elements are added to the head or the tail. How would you change the program example so that memory location 6002 contains the address of the last element (tail) of the queue?

9-4. Eight-Bit Sort

Purpose: Sort an array of unsigned binary 8-bit numbers into descending order. The length of the array is in location 6000 and the array itself begins in the next location, 6001. Therefore the array has 255 or fewer elements.

Sample Problem:

	(6000)	=	06
	(6001)	=	2A
	(6002)	=	B5
	(6003)	=	60
	(6004)	=	3F
	(6005)	=	D1
	(6006)	=	19
Result:	(6001)	=	D1
	(6002)	=	B5
	(6003)	=	60
	(6004)	=	3F
	(6005)	=	2A
	(6006)	=	19

A simple sorting technique works as follows:

Step 1 — Clear a flag INTER.

Step 2 — Examine each consecutive pair of numbers in the array. If any are out of order, exchange them and set INTER.

Step 3 — After the entire array has been examined, if INTER = 1, then return to Step 1; otherwise finished.

INTER will be set if any consecutive pair of numbers is out of order. Therefore, if INTER = 0 at the end of a pass through the entire array, the array is in proper order.

This sorting method is referred to as a "bubble sort." It is an easy algorithm to implement. However, other sorting techniques should be considered when sorting long lists where speed is important.[2]

The technique operates as follows in a simple case. Let us assume that we want to sort an array into descending order; the array has four elements: 12, 03, 15, 08.

1st Iteration:

Step 1 — INTER = 0

Step 2 — Final order of the array is:

12

15

08

03

since the second pair (03,15) is
exchanged and so is the third pair (03,08). INTER = 1.

Step 3 — Since INTER = 1, another iteration is required.

2nd Iteration:

    Step 1 — INTER = 0

    Step 2 — Final order of the array is:

           15

           12

           08

           03

           since the first pair (12,15) is exchanged. INTER = 1.

    Step 3 — Since INTER = 1, another iteration is required.

3rd Iteration:

    Step 1 — INTER = 0

    Step 2 — The elements are already in order, so no exchanges are necessary and INTER remains zero.

    Step 3 — Since INTER = 0, we are finished.

Flowchart 9-4:

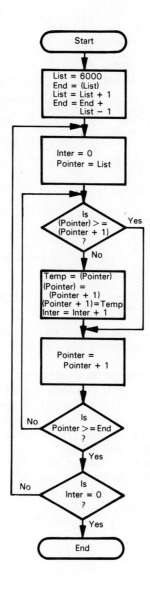

Program 9-4a:

```
                internal
                    pgm_9_4a procedure
                    entry
                        $abs    IBASE

    4600 7604           LDA     R4,%6000        ! Pointer to length !
    4602 6000
    4604 204A           LDB     RL2,@R4         ! Length !
    4606 8C28           CLRB    RH2             ! High order half of length = 0 !
    4608 A940           INC     R4              ! Now point to list !
    460A 8142           ADD     R2,R4
    460C AB20           DEC     R2              ! R2 now points to end of list !
    460E 8C88   SORT:   CLRB    RL0             ! Count interchanges !
    4610 A141           LD      R1,R4           ! R1 is roving list pointer !
    4612 2010   NEXT:   LDB     RH0,@R1
    4614 A910           INC     R1
    4616 0A10           CPB     RH0,@R1         ! Compare next pair !
    4618 EF04           JR      UGE,NOSW        ! If correct order, no change !
    461A 2C10           EXB     RH0,@R1         ! Exchange the two elements !
    461C 6C10           EXB     RH0,-1(R1)
    461E FFFF
    4620 A880           INCB    RL0             ! Count interchanges !
    4622 8B21   NOSW:   CP      R1,R2           ! Past end of list? !
    4624 E7F6           JR      ULT,NEXT        ! No, keep going !
    4626 8C84           TESTB   RL0             ! Any changes made? !
    4628 EEF2           JR      NE,SORT
    462A 7A00           HALT

    462C            end     pgm_9_4a
```

The program must reduce the end pointer (R2) by 1 because the last element has no successor. Before starting each sorting pass, we must be careful to reinitialize the pointer and the interchange flag.

Previous examples in this chapter used counters to control loops. In this example we compare addresses. This avoids decrementing the counter on each step. It is interesting to note what happens if there are fewer than two elements in the list. Although the results are not as tragic as they would be if we used counters, the results are incorrect nevertheless. Actually, checking for this case is quite simple. We simply insert JR NOSW before the statement labeled NEXT.

Two equal elements in the array must not be exchanged; if they are, the exchange will occur on every pass and the program will never end.

We can rewrite the bubble sort program to use indexed addressing. This generates a program with fewer instructions; but more two-word instructions are needed, therefore the object progams are of approximately equal length. Program 9-4b is a variation that uses indexed addressing.

Program 9-4b:

```
                internal
                   pgm_9_4b procedure
                entry
                   $abs      IBASE

4600 8C88    SORT:   CLRB    RL0              ! Count swaps in RL0 !
4602 600A            LDB     RL2,%6000        ! Load list length !
4604 6000
4606 8C28            CLRB    RH2              ! R2 is the index register !
4608 E80A            JR      NOSW             ! Test for null list !
460A 6020    NEXT:   LDB     RH0,%6001(R2)    ! Get next byte !
460C 6001
460E 4A20            CPB     RH0,%6001-1(R2)  ! Compare with previous byte !
4610 6000
4612 E305            JR      ULE,NOSW         ! If correct order, no change !
4614 6C20            EXB     RH0,%6001-1(R2)  ! Exchange the two elements !
4616 6000
4618 6C20            EXB     RH0,%6001(R2)
461A 6001
461C A880            INCB    RL0              ! Increment swap counter !
461E AB20    NOSW:   DEC     R2               ! Decrement index !
4620 EAF4            JR      GT,NEXT          ! Repeat till 1 element left !
4622 8C84            TESTB   RL0              ! Were there any swaps? !
4624 EEED            JR      NZ,SORT          ! Yes, do another iteration !
4626 7A00            HALT

4628            end     pgm_9_4b
```

Note that this variation of the bubble sort program starts at the end of the array (with the largest memory address) and works back to the start of the array (with the smallest memory address).

There have been entire books written on sorting and searching, so a discussion of sorting methods would be beyond our scope. However, there is one variation that should be considered. At the end of every step, we know that the smallest element is at the end of the list. Therefore the number of pairs we need to compare decreases by one each step. (Try a few examples to convince yourself this is true. Do you see how the method gets its name?) What simple change to the program would take advantage of this?

9-5. Using a Jump Table

Purpose: Use the value on the top of the stack as an index to a jump table starting at location 6000. Each entry in the jump table contains an address. The program should transfer control to the address with the appropriate index; that is, if the index is 6, the program jumps to address entry #6 in the table. (Note that we start counting with entry #0.)

Sample Problem:

```
           R15   =   7FFE
         (7FFE)  =   0002
         (6000)  =   4740
         (6002)  =   47A6
         (6004)  =   47D0
         (6006)  =   4620
         (6008)  =   4854
```

Result: PC   =   47D0   since that is entry #2 in the jump table.

Flowchart 9-5:

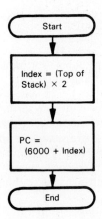

This last box results in a transfer of control to the address obtained from the table.

Program 9-5:

```
                internal
                pgm_9_5 procedure
                entry
                     $abs      IBASE

4600  97F1           POP       R1,@R15        ! Get index !
4602  8111           ADD       R1,R1          ! Form word index !
4604  6111           LD        R1,%6000(R1)   ! Get address from jump table !
4606  6000
4608  1E18           JP        @R1            ! Transfer to address !

460A            end       pgm_9_5
```

The jump table replaces a whole series of compare and jump operations. The program is compact, efficient, and easily changed or extended. A program that accesses the jump table could be used to access several different tables by putting the start address of the table in a register and using base indexed addressing.

The index must be multiplied by 2 to give the correct word index. Were this program intended for a segmented machine (Z8001), the index would have to be doubled again, since addresses are two words long.

Note that Register R0 cannot be used in place of Register R1, since R0 cannot be an index register, nor can it be used in an indirect jump.

The instruction JP@R1, which transfers the contents of register R1 to the program counter, is an indirect jump. This instruction sometimes causes confusion because of its "level of indirection." If we compare the action of JP@R1 with LD R0,@R1, we see that in the case of JP @R1, the program counter receives the value in R1; R0 receives the value pointed to by R1 in the LD instruction. What would have happened if we had replaced the last two instructions in the program with JP %1000(R1)?

Most of the previous examples made use of the JR instruction. Wherever we used the JR instruction, we could have replaced it with a JP instruction. The JR instruction cannot jump outside of the range -254 to $+256$ bytes from the start of the JR instruction. In addition, the JR instruction cannot be used with register indirect or indexed addressing. The JP instruction uses an extra word of program memory when used with a direct address.

Jump tables are used when one of several routines must be executed. This occurs, for example, when commands are decoded, programs are selected, or I/O devices chosen. Most higher level languages have a computed GO TO statement which uses jump table logic.

Do not overlook the LDPS instruction when creating jump table logic. LDPS loads two words of data per table entry; one word provides new status, the other is the jump table address. Assuming the index is in R1, these two instructions suffice:

```
SLL     R1,#2                  ! Multiply R1 by 4 !
LDPS    %6000(R1)              ! Load new status and jump !
```

PROBLEMS

9-1. Remove an Entry From a List

Purpose: Remove the value on the top of the stack from a list if the value is present. The length of the list is in memory location 6000 and the list itself begins in memory location 6002. Move entries up one position if below a removed entry, and reduce the length of the list by 1.

Sample Problems:

a.

R15	=	7FFE	
(7FFE)	=	D010	Entry to be removed
(6000)	=	0004	Length of list
(6002)	=	C121	First element in list
(6004)	=	A346	
(6006)	=	3A64	
(6008)	=	6C20	

Result:	R15	=	8000

No change to the list, since the entry is not in the list. Note that the value was popped from the stack, so R15 has changed.

b.

R15	=	7FFE	
(7FFE)	=	D010	
(6000)	=	0004	Length of list
(6002)	=	C121	First element in list
(6004)	=	D010	
(6006)	=	3A64	
(6008)	=	6C20	

Result:	R15	=	8000	
	(6000)	=	0003	Length reduced by 1
	(6002)	=	C121	
	(6004)	=	3A64	Other elements in list moved up one position
	(6006)	=	6C20	

The entry is removed from the list and the ones below it are moved up one position. The length of the list is reduced by 1.

9-2. Add an Entry to an Ordered List

Purpose: Insert the value on the top of the stack into an ordered list if it is not already there. The length of the list is in memory location 6000. The list itself begins in memory location 6002 and consists of unsigned binary numbers in increasing order. Place the new entry in the correct position in the list, move down the elements below it, and increase the length of the list by 1.

Sample Problems:

a.

R15	=	7FFE
(7FFE)	=	7010	Entry to be added to list
(6000)	=	0004	Length of list
(6002)	=	0037	First element in list
(6004)	=	5322
(6006)	=	A101
(6008)	=	C203

Result:

R15	=	8000
(6000)	=	0005	Length of list increased by 1
(6002)	=	0037
(6004)	=	5322
(6006)	=	7010	New entry
(6008)	=	A101	Other elements moved down one position
(600A)	=	C203

b.

R15	=	7FFE
(7FFE)	=	7010
(6000)	=	0004	Length of list
(6002)	=	0037	First element in list
(6004)	=	5322
(6006)	=	7010
(6008)	=	C203

Result: R15 = 8000

No change in the list since the entry is already in the list.

9-3. Add an Element to a Queue

Purpose: Add the value on the top of the stack to a queue. The address of the first queue element is in memory location 6000. Each element in the queue contains either the address of the next element in the queue or zero if there is no next element. The new element is placed at the end (tail) of the queue; the new element's address will be in the element that was at the end of the queue. The new element will contain zero to indicate that it is now at the end of the queue.

Sample Problem:

```
        R15   =  7FFE
       (7FFE) =  60A0
       (6000) =  6020   Pointer to head of queue
       (6020) =  6030
       (6030) =  0000   Last element in queue

Result: R15   =  8000
       (6000) =  6020
       (6020) =  6030
       (6030) =  60A0   Old last element points to new last element
       (60A0) =  0000   New last element
```

How would you add an element to the queue if memory location 6002 contained the address of the tail of the queue (the last element)?

9-4. Four-Byte Sort

Purpose: Sort a list of 4-byte entries into descending order. The first three bytes in each entry are an unsigned key with the first byte being the most significant. The fourth byte is additional information and should not be used to determine the sort order, but should be moved along with its key. The number of entries in the list is a word in location 6000. The list itself begins in location 6002.

Sample Problem:

(6000)	=	0004	4 entries in list
(6002)	=	41	Beginning of first entry key
(6003)	=	42	
(6004)	=	43	End of first entry key
(6005)	=	07	First entry additional information
(6006)	=	4A	Beginning of second entry
(6007)	=	4B	
(6008)	=	4C	
(6009)	=	13	
(600A)	=	4A	Beginning of third entry
(600B)	=	4B	
(600C)	=	41	
(600D)	=	37	
(600E)	=	44	Beginning of fourth entry
(600F)	=	4B	
(6010)	=	41	
(6011)	=	3F	

Result:	(6002)	=	4A	
	(6003)	=	4B	
	(6004)	=	4C	
	(6005)	=	13	End of first entry
	(6006)	=	4A	
	(6007)	=	4B	
	(6008)	=	41	
	(6009)	=	37	End of second entry
	(600A)	=	44	
	(600B)	=	4B	
	(600C)	=	41	
	(600D)	=	3F	End of third entry
	(600E)	=	41	
	(600F)	=	42	
	(6010)	=	43	
	(6011)	=	07	End of last entry

The data in the unsorted entries are 'ABC',%07; 'JKL',%13; 'JKA',%37; 'DKA',%3F.

9.5 Using a Jump Table with a Key

Purpose: Use the value on the top of the stack as the key to a jump table starting in memory location 6000. Each entry in the jump table contains a 16-bit identifier followed by a 16-bit address to which the program should transfer control if the key is equal to that identifier.

Sample Problem:

R15	=	7FFE	
(7FFE)	=	4142	
(6000)	=	434B	First key
(6002)	=	4900	First transfer address
(6004)	=	4142	Second key
(6006)	=	4940	
(6008)	=	4558	Third key
(600A)	=	4A20	

Result: PC   =   4940,   since that address corresponds to key value 4142.

Is the CPIR instruction useful in this program? Can you think of a way to restructure the program so that the CPIR instruction would help? (Hint: use two separate tables.) What happens when the key is not found?

REFERENCES

1. D. Knuth, *The Art of Computer Programming, Volume III: Sorting and Searching* (Reading, Mass.: Addison-Wesley, 1978).

    D. Knuth, "Algorithms," *Scientific American*, April 1977, pp. 63-80.

2. K. J. Thurber and P.C. Patton, *Data Structures and Computer Architecture* (Lexington, Mass.: Lexington Books, 1977).

3. J. Hemenway and E. Teja, "Data Structures — Part 1," *EDN*, March 5, 1979, pp. 89-92.

4. B.W. Kernighan and P.J. Plauger, *The Elements of Programming Style* (New York: McGraw-Hill, 1978).

5. K.A. Schember and J.R. Rumsey, "Minimal Storage Sorting and Searching Techniques for RAM Applications," *Computer*, June 1977, pp. 92-100.

6. "Sorting 30 Times Faster with DPS," *Datamation*, February 1978, pp. 200-203.

7. L.A. Leventhal, "Cut Your Processor's Computation Time," *Electronic Design*, August 16, 1977, pp. 82-89.

8. J.B. Peatman, *Microcomputer-Based Design* (New York: McGraw-Hill, 1977), Chapter 7.

10

Subroutines

Programs such as the ones illustrated in this book rarely stand alone; usually they constitute a small part of a much larger program. Small programs, such as the ones we have illustrated, each typically perform a single task. This task may need to be executed by a variety of large programs; conversely, a single large program may need to execute one task many times.

How do we package a small program so that it can be used frequently by a single large program, or by many different large programs? We package the small program as a subroutine.

SUBROUTINE INSTRUCTIONS

Nearly every microprocessor has instructions designed specifically to handle subroutines. Usually a Call instruction and a Return instruction serve this purpose. A Call instruction causes program logic to branch to a subroutine; this is done in a fashion that allows the Return instruction to branch back to the point that directly follows the Call.

For this to be possible, **the Call instruction saves the address of the next sequential instruction in some suitable memory location (usually at the top of the stack), then branches to the subroutine's "entry point."** A subroutine's entry point is the address of the subroutine instruction which gets executed first. This is not necessarily the first instruction in the subroutine.

The Return instruction loads the program counter with the address which the Call instruction saved. This causes program execution to resume with the instruction that follows the Call; it does not matter where in addressable memory the Call instruction resides.

The Call instruction must be part of the program that calls the subroutine. The Return instruction must be part of the subroutine.

The Z8000 has two Call instructions, CALL and CALR; they differ only in the memory addressing method used to identify the subroutine entry point. Also, CALR generates a one-word instruction object code, whereas CALL may have as many as three object code words.

The Z8000 Call instruction pushes the address of the next sequential instruction onto the stack. This is referred to as the "Return Address." The Return instruction pops the return address into the program counter. Z8000 Call instructions offer a very broad range of addressing modes by which the subroutine entry point can be identified.

The Z8000 Return instruction, RET, is conditional; the return can be executed unconditionally, or only when specified status conditions are met.

If you do not understand programming logic associated with subroutines, an elementary discussion of this topic is available elsewhere.[1]

SUBROUTINE PARAMETERS

The programs illustrated in this book all use memory addresses and/or data to perform their assigned tasks. For example, a procedure that manipulates data in some fashion may need to know the starting memory address where the data is held, plus the number of data items present. **Information which a calling program passes to a subroutine is referred to as "subroutine parameters."**

The way in which parameters are passed to a subroutine represents one of the most important aspects of subroutine organization. This is because subroutines become more useful as they become more general purpose. For example, if a subroutine that operates on data requires a fixed number of data items to be present in a nonvarying area of memory, the subroutine will not be very useful. The execution time and program space which the calling routine expends preparing data for the subroutine may exceed the execution time and program space required by the subroutine itself. Furthermore, when a number of subroutines are called by a single program (and this is the rule rather than the exception) the specific requirements of one subroutine will quickly start to conflict with specific requirements of other subroutines, generating a memory management nightmare. Our goal, therefore, should be to make subroutines as non-restricting as possible.

The first and simplest method of passing parameters to a subroutine is via CPU registers. Before calling a subroutine, the calling program could load memory addresses, counters and other data into CPU registers. For example, suppose a subroutine operates on two data buffers of equal length. The subroutine might specify that the length of the two data buffers must be in CPU Register R0, while the two data buffer beginning addresses are in CPU Registers R2 and R4. The calling program would then call the subroutine as follows:

```
LD      R0,#BUFL        ! Length of buffers in R0            !
LDA     R2,BUFA         ! Buffer A beginning address in R2 !
LDA     R4,BUFB         ! Buffer B beginning address in R4 !
CALL    SUBR            ! Call subroutine                    !
```

The advantage of this parameter passing method is that the subroutine finds its parameters in CPU registers, ready to use. The disadvantage of this parameter passing method is that the CPU registers in which the subroutine expects to find its parameters may be used by the calling program for totally different purposes. The calling program must then vacate registers required by the subroutine before loading them with parameters. Just as memory management can become a nightmare when different subroutines compete indiscriminately for memory, so the assignment of CPU registers can become a nightmare when they are used too freely in competing ways.

Another common method of passing parameters to a subroutine is to push the parameters onto the stack. Using this parameter passing technique, the subroutine call illustrated above would occur as follows:

```
PUSH    @R15,#BUFL      ! Push buffer length                 !
PUSH    @R15,#BUFA      ! Then two buffer starting addresses !
PUSH    @R15,#BUFB      ! onto stack                         !
CALL    SUBR
```

The subroutine must begin by loading parameters into CPU registers, as follows:

```
SUBR:   PUSHL   @R15,RR0        ! Save prior contents of CPU Registers !
        PUSH    @R15,R2         ! ...used by subroutine                !
        LD      R2,8(R15)       ! Buffer B starting address in R2      !
        LD      R1,10(R15)      ! Buffer A starting address in R1      !
        LD      R0,12(R15)      ! Buffer length in R0                  !
```

The subroutine must save prior register contents before using any CPU register. Otherwise the calling program would be required to vacate the CPU registers used by a called subroutine; this approach is awkward because the calling program needs to know which registers the subroutine uses, and if the subroutine is changed to include another register, then all the calling programs would have to be changed.

Passing parameters to a subroutine via the stack is very general purpose in that neither the calling program nor the subroutine places any restrictions on memory utilization or CPU register assignments. But it takes execution time and program memory to include the instructions that place parameters on the stack and subsequently retrieve these parameters.

Parameters that are to be passed to a subroutine can be listed directly after the subroutine call. The subroutine must then modify the return address at the top of the stack in addition to fetching the parameters. Using this technique our example would be modified as follows:

```
        CALL    SUBR
        WVAL    BUFL        ! Buffer length !
        WVAL    BUFA        ! Buffer A starting address  !
        WVAL    BUFB        ! Buffer B starting address  !
                            ! Subroutine returns here    !
```

The subroutine saves prior contents of CPU registers, then loads parameters and adjusts the return address as follows:

```
SUBR:   PUSHL   @R15,RR0    ! Subroutine uses R0, R1, R2, R3 !
        PUSHL   @R15,RR2                                     !
        LD      R3,8(R15)   ! Return address points to BUFL  !
        POP     R0,@R3      ! BUFL                           !
        POP     R1,@R3      ! BUFA                           !
        POP     R2,@R3      ! BUFB                           !
        LD      8(R15),R3   ! Adjust return address          !
```

This parameter passing technique has the advantage of being easy to read. It has the disadvantage of requiring parameters to be fixed when the program is written. A modification which allows parameters to vary uses an address pointer following the subroutine call. The pointer addresses an area of read/write memory where the parameters are actually found. This may be illustrated as follows:

```
        CALL    SUBR
        WVAL    PARAM       ! Beginning address of parameters  !
          .
          .
          .

PARAM:  ARRAY   [3 WORD]    ! Store BUFL, BUFA, and BUFB !     !
                            ! in this space !                  !

SUBR:   PUSHL   @R15,RR0    ! SUBR uses R0, R1, R2, R3         !
        PUSHL   @R15,RR2                                       !
        LD      R2,8(R15)   ! Return address points to PARAM   !
        POP     R3,@R2      ! Get parameters starting address  !
                            ! ...and update return address     !
        LD      8(R15),R2   ! Replace corrected return address !
        POP     R0,@R3      ! BUFL to R0                        !
        POP     R1,@R3      ! BUFA to R1                        !
        POP     R2,@R3      ! BUFB to R2                        !
```

Parameters held in a separate area of memory are frequently referred to as a "parameter block." In the illustration above, PARAM is the beginning address for a three-word parameter block. The parameter block address could be passed to the subroutine via the stack, as follows:

```
        PUSH    @R15,#PARAM ! Parameter block address to stack !
        CALL    SUBR
```

The subroutine would fetch parameters as follows:

```
SUBR:   PUSHL   @R15,RR0    ! Subroutine uses R0, R1, R2, R3 !
        PUSHL   @R15,RR2                                     !
        LD      R3,8+2(R15) ! Parameter block address        !
        POP     R0,@R3      ! Parameter to CPU registers      !
        POP     R1,@R3                                        !
        POP     R2,@R3
        INC     8+2(R15),#2 ! Correct return address !
```

RETURN VALUES

Results generated by a subroutine can be returned to the calling program in several ways. Often, the subroutine simply performs an operation on the data whose address was passed into the subroutine. For example, on receiving the address of an ASCII string in R2, a subroutine might convert each lower-case character in the string to upper case. The calling program knows where to find the converted data; the subroutine does not need to return any additional data to the calling program.

If a subroutine does need to return parameters to the calling program, it can do so using CPU registers. For example, if a subroutine is passed the address of an ASCII string in R2, it could return the length of the string in R1.

A subroutine can return values on the stack. Using the Z8000, this is very common. We will show several examples of this method. Returning parameters on the stack is made more complicated by the fact that the CALL instruction causes the program counter contents to be stored on the top of the stack. So we often have to do some extra processing if the number of parameters transmitted to the subroutine at the top of the stack is not the same as the number of data items returned.

Subroutines can return data to the calling program in a variety of ways, each of which may be well suited to a different set of circumstances. **We recommend that you use the stack or CPU registers to return parameters whenever possible.**

Experienced assembly language programmers quickly find that assembly language programs are written most efficiently by making extensive use of subroutines. Whenever you write a subroutine for one program you should make it as general purpose as possible; then you will be able to use the same subroutine in another program, thereby reducing the time needed to write that program. Soon you will build up a library of subroutines, some of which you have written yourself, while others are collected from co-workers, manufacturers, or the literature. Every assembly language programmer should strive to develop a good library of useful and general purpose subroutines.

Reentrant and Recursive Subroutines

Reentrant subroutines and recursive subroutines are two classes of subroutines that need special mention.

A subroutine is reentrant if it can be interrupted, then called by the interrupting program, giving correct results for the interrupting program and the interrupted program. It is important that standard subroutines be reentrant in any interrupt-based microcomputer system, otherwise interrupt service routines would not be able to use standard subroutines. It is easy to write reentrant subroutines for many microprocessors; it is particularly easy to do so with the Z8000. Call and Return instructions use the stack, which is automatically reentrant. The only additional requirement for reentrancy is that the subroutine use CPU registers or the stack to store temporary data. If the subroutine uses any fixed memory locations to store temporary data, then it ceases to be reentrant; if the subroutine is interrupted in mid-execution and then reexecuted, temporary data generated prior to the interrupt will be destroyed by the interrupt time reexecution.

A subroutine is recursive if it can call itself. To be recursive a subroutine must also be reentrant. A subroutine is also said to be recursive if it calls a second subroutine, which in turn calls the first subroutine again. Two such subroutines are said to be mutually recursive. Recursive subroutines are used most frequently in the computation of complex arithmetic functions.

DOCUMENTATION

Subroutine listings must provide enough information in comments so that users need not examine the subroutine's internal structure. Among the necessary specifications are:

- A description of the purpose of the subroutine

- A list of input and output parameters

- Registers and memory locations used. Identify any that change.

- A sample case

If these guidelines are followed, the subroutine will be easy to use.

In general, a subroutine should not change the contents of calling program registers, unless a register is used to return a parameter. Many subroutines begin by saving on the stack the contents of all CPU registers used by the subroutine. Register contents must be restored before returning to the calling program. The powerful LDM instruction is often used to save and restore blocks of registers.

PROGRAM EXAMPLES

Examples in this chapter assume that the stack and stack pointer have already been initialized. Instructions that load an address into the stack pointer or clear the stack prior to use are not shown. If you wish to establish your own stack area, remember to save any prior stack pointer and to restore it in order to produce a proper return at the end of your program.

To save a prior stack pointer, use the instruction LD addr,R15 (or LDL addr, RR14 on a Z8001). To restore the prior stack pointer, use the instruction LD R15,addr (or LDL RR14,addr on a Z8001).

If a RET instruction ends a program, instead of the HALT instruction used in our examples, the following setup procedure can be used to save the prior stack and set up a new stack beginning at 8000.

Program:

```
               internal
                     stack_init procedure       ! Stack init and return !
                     entry
                            $abs      %8004

      8004 6F0F    ENTRYP: LD       %8002,R15      ! Save prior stack pointer !
      8006 8002
      8008 760F            LDA      R15,%8002      ! Set up our stack !
      800A 8002
      800C 5F00            CALL     MAIN
      800E 4600
      8010 610F            LD       R15,%8002      ! Restore stack !
      8012 8002
      8014 9E08            RET                     ! Return to prior program !

      8016            end       stack_init
```

The "prior program" is usually a monitor program. The monitor program is executed following system startup, and all main programs return to the monitor upon concluding execution.

The program illustrated above saves the monitor stack pointer, sets up the main program's stack pointer, and then calls the main program. The stack base for the main program is then 8000. When the main program has completed execution, it can execute a RET (instead of the HALT used in our examples), which returns control to the setup routine, which restores the monitor stack pointer, then returns control to the monitor.

10-1. Hex to ASCII

Purpose: Convert the contents of RL0 from a hexadecimal digit to an ASCII character. Assume that the original contents of RL0 form a valid hexadecimal digit.

Sample Problems:

a.	RL0	=	0C	
Result:	RL0	=	43	'C'
b.	RL0	=	06	
Result:	RL0	=	36	'6'

Flowchart 10-1:

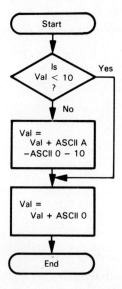

The calling program gets the data from memory location 6000, calls the conversion subroutine, and stores the result in memory location 6001.

Program 10-1:

```
              internal
                  pgm_10_1 procedure        ! Convert (6000) to ASCII hex !
                  entry
                      $abs    IBASE

4600 6008     MAIN:   LDB    RL0,%6000      ! Get data: range is 00 - 0F !
4602 6000
4604 5F00             CALL   HEXDIGIT       ! Get ASCII digit into RL0 !
4606 460E
4608 6E08             LDB    %6000,RL0      ! Store result !
460A 6000
460C 7A00             HALT

              !* Subroutine HEXDIGIT
               *
               * Purpose: HEXDIGIT converts a hexadecimal digit to an ascii
               *          character
               *
               * Initial conditions:  RL0 contains a value in the range
               *                       00 - 0F
               * Final conditions:     RL0 contains an ASCII character in
               *                       the range '0' - '9' or 'A' - 'F'
               *
               * Registers changed:    RL0 is the only register to be
               *                       affected
               *
               * Sample case: Initial conditions: 6 in RL0
               *                       Final conditions:   '6' (36 hex) in RL0
               *!
              HEXDIGIT:
460E 0A08             CPB    RL0,#%0A       ! Decimal digit or hex letter? !
4610 0A0A
4612 E102             JR     LT,ADDZ
4614 0008             ADDB   RL0,#'A'-'0'-%0A ! Offset for letters !
4616 0707
4618 0008     ADDZ:   ADDB   RL0,#'0'       ! Convert to ASCII by adding '0' !
461A 3030
461C 9E08             RET

461E          end      pgm_10_1
```

The CALL instruction saves the program counter (the address of the instruction following the CALL) on the stack, and then places the subroutine starting address in the program counter. The procedure is:

Step 1 - Decrement the stack pointer by 2

Step 2 - Save the program counter in the top word of the stack

Step 3 - Place the subroutine start address in the program counter.

The RET instruction reverses the process:

Step 1 - Place the value on the top of stack in the program counter

Step 2 - Increment the stack pointer by 2.

On the segmented Z8001, the address is two words long, so the stack pointer (RR14) changes by 4 instead of 2.

The calling program consists of three steps: placing the data in the register, calling the subroutine, and storing the result in memory. The subroutine is reentrant since it uses no data memory.

10-2. Hex Word to ASCII String

Purpose: Convert the value in memory location 6000 to four ASCII hex digits in memory locations 6002 through 6005. Perform the task using a subroutine that is passed the four hex digit value and the string address.

Sample Problem:

```
                (6000)  =  4CD0

        Result: (6002)  =  34  '4'
                (6003)  =  43  'C'
                (6004)  =  44  'D'
                (6005)  =  30  '0'
```

Program 10-2:

```
                internal
                    pgm_10_2 procedure       ! 16 bit value to 4 ASCII hex digits !
                entry
                    $abs     IBASE

4600 0DF9   MAIN:   PUSH    @R15,#%6002     ! Address of space for 4... !
4602 6002                                   ! ...ASCII characters !
4604 53F0           PUSH    @R15,%6000      ! Value to be converted !
4606 6000
4608 5F00           CALL    B2HEX           ! Binary to ASCII hex !
460A 460E
460C 7A00           HALT                    ! ASCII string now at 6002-6005 !

            !* Subroutine B2HEX
             *
             * Purpose: Convert a 16 bit value to 4 ASCII hex digits
             *
             * Initial conditions:   The first parameter on the stack is
             *                        the value; the second parameter is
             *                        the address of the string to be built
             * Final conditions:      The hex string occupies 4 succesive
             *                        bytes beginning with the address
             *                        passed as the second parameter
             *
             * Register usage:        No registers are affected, and the
             *                        call parms are popped from the stack
             *
             * Sample case:     Initial conditions: 4CD0 at top of stack,
             *                        then 6002
             *                  Final conditions:   The string "4CD0" in
             *                        ASCII occupies locations 6002-6005
             *!
460E 93F2   B2HEX:  PUSH    @R15,R2         ! Save R2, R1 and R0 !
4610 91F0           PUSHL   @R15,RR0
4612 C004           LDB     RH0,#4          ! Loop counter: 4 digits !
4614 61F1           LD      R1,6+2(R15)     ! Get value !
4616 0008
4618 61F2           LD      R2,6+4(R15)     ! Get string address !
461A 000A
461C A923           INC     R2,#4           ! Point past last byte !
461E A098   LOOP:   LDB     RL0,RL1         ! Low order value byte to RL0 !
4620 0608           ANDB    RL0,#%0F        ! Low order nibble to RL0 !
4622 0F0F
4624 DFF5           CALR    HEXDIGIT        ! ASCII digit to RL0 !
4626 AB20           DEC     R2
4628 2E28           LDB     @R2,RL0         ! Store next digit !
462A B311           SRL     R1,#4           ! Next nibble to low 4 bits !
462C FFFC
462E F009           DBJNZ   RH0,LOOP        ! Repeat for all 4 digits !
4630 95F0           POPL    RR0,@R15        ! Restore R0, R1 and R2 !
4632 97F2           POP     R2,@R15
4634 57FF           POP     4(R15),@R15     ! Move the return addr down !
4636 0004
4638 A9F1           INC     R15,#2          ! Remove the second parameter !
463A 9E08           RET
```

```
          !* Subroutine HEXDIGIT
          *
          * Purpose: HEXDIGIT converts a hexadecimal digit to an
          *                   ASCII character
          *
          * Initial conditions:  RL0 contains a value in the range
          *                       00 - 0F
          * Final conditions:     RL0 contains an ASCII character in
          *                       the range '0' - '9' or 'A' - 'F'
          *
          * Registers changed:    RL0 is the only register to be affected
          *
          * Sample case: Initial conditions: 6 in RL0
          *                    Final conditions:   '6' (36 hex) in RL0
          *!
          HEXDIGIT:
463C 0A08           CPB     RL0,#%0A          ! Decimal digit or hex letter? !
463E 0A0A
4640 E102           JR      LT,ADDZ
4642 0008           ADDB    RL0,#'A'-'0'-%0A ! Offset for letters !
4644 0707
4646 0008  ADDZ:    ADDB    RL0,#'0'          ! Convert to ASCII by adding '0' !
4648 3030
464A 9E08           RET

464C              end    pgm_10_2
```

The main program pushes the destination address and the four hexadecimal digit value on the stack, then calls the subroutine.

The first part of the B2HEX subroutine performs initialization: registers are saved, parameters are fetched, and local parameters (such as the loop counter) are initialized.

The PUSHL instruction is an efficient way of saving R0 and R1 at the same time. When fetching parameters from the stack, we use indexed addressing to index past the three saved registers (offset 6) plus the return address (offset 2). After the registers are saved, the stack looks like this:

```
              R15    =  7FF4
            (7FF4)   =  saved R0
            (7FF6)   =  saved R1
            (7FF8)   =  saved R2
            (7FFA)   =  return address: 6(R15)
            (7FFC)   =  value parameter: 6 + 2(R15)
            (7FFE)   =  address parameter: 6 + 4(R15)
```

The next part of the subroutine is the processing section. We gladly make use of the HEXDIGIT subroutine, since it is already written and tested. Note that we use the Call Relative instruction, CALR, to call the HEXDIGIT subroutine. The object code for this instruction is only one word long. Compare it with the CALL instruction in the main program, which requires two words. The low-order 12 bits of the CALR instruction make up a signed word offset. The instruction following the CALR is at memory location 4628. HEXDIGIT is at location 463E. So the offset is:

```
              463E
             -4628
              0016 bytes = 000B words
```

Each of the four hex digits is isolated using the SRL instruction and the subsequent ANDB.

The last part of the program takes care of the subroutine exit. First, the registers that were saved on the stack are restored. Note that since R2 was the first register pushed, it is the last popped. A stack is often described as a last-in first-out (LIFO) structure. It is a good programming practice to always push registers in descending order (i.e., R2 before R1 before R0), and therefore pop them in ascending order. Always doing it the same way whenever you program will make your programs easier to understand and less error prone.

Pushing in descending order is better than ascending order because the Load Multiple instruction, LDM, is often used to push and pop registers from the stack. The LDM instruction stores the registers in memory with the lowest numbered register occupying the lowest address. The two PUSH instructions could be replaced by the following sequence:

```
DEC      R15,#6           ! Make room for 3 registers !
LDM      @R15,R0,#3       ! Store R0-R2                !
```

Registers can be restored as follows:

```
LDM      R0,@R15,#3       ! Restore R0-R2             !
INC      R15,#6           ! Pop the three values      !
```

The order of the operations is important, and is in keeping with the rules for stack usage outlined in Chapter 4.

The sequence

```
POP      4(R15),@R15
INC      R15,#2
```

is used to remove the two parameters from the stack without destroying the return address. The action of POP 4(R15), @R15 has the same effect on the stack as

```
POP      R0,@R15
LD       2(R15),R0
```

In our example we don't want to destroy the contents of R0. Here is a picture of the stack before and after the POP and INC.

```
R15      7FFA:    460C             (return address)
         7FFC:    4CD0             (value parameter)
         7FFE:    6002             (address parameter)

         after:

         7FFA:    xxxx
         7FFC:    xxxx
         7FFE:    460C             (return address)
```

10-3. 64-Bit Add

Purpose: Add the 64-bit (4-word) value contained in memory locations 6008 through
600F to the 64-bit value in memory locations 6000 through 6007. Place the
result in memory locations 6000 through 6007.

Sample Problem:

```
        (6000)  =  0420
        (6002)  =  147A
        (6004)  =  EB52
        (6006)  =  9CB8
        (6008)  =  3020
        (600A)  =  EB85
        (600C)  =  2047
        (600E)  =  3118

Result: (6000)  =  3441
        (6002)  =  0000
        (6004)  =  0B99
        (6006)  =  CDD0
```

Program 10-3:

```
             internal
               pgm_10_3 procedure          ! Add 64-bit values at 6000 and 6008 !
               entry
                    $abs    IBASE

4600 0DF9   MAIN:  PUSH    @R15,#%6000      ! Address of augend !
4602 6000
4604 0DF9          PUSH    @R15,#%6008      ! Address of addend !
4606 6008
4608 5F00          CALL    ADD64            ! Place result at 6000 !
460A 460E
460C 7A00          HALT

            !* Subroutine ADD64
             *
             * Purpose: Add two 64 bit (4 word) values
             *
             * Initial conditions:  The stack contains two addresses: the
             *                      augend (destination) is pushed first;
             *                      then the addend
             * Final conditions:    The augend is replaced by the sum of
             *                      the augend and addend
             *
             * Register usage:      No registers are affected, and both
             *                      parameters are popped from the stack.
             *
             * Sample case: 6000 - 6007 = 147A258B00C91100
             *              6008 - 600F = 652A9011661000F0
             *              6000 is pushed; 6008 is pushed
             *       Result: 6000 - 6007 = 79A4B59C66D911F0
             *!

460E DFEC   ADD64:  CALR    RPUSH           ! Save R0 - R14 !
4610 61F8           LD      R8,30+2(R15)    ! Address of addend !
4612 0020
4614 61FA           LD      R10,30+4(R15)   ! Address of augend... !
4616 0022                                   ! ...and destination !
4618 1C81           LDM     R0,@R8,#4       ! Addend to R0-R3 !
461A 0003
461C 1CA1           LDM     R4,@R10,#4      ! Augend to R4-R7 !
461E 0403
4620 9626           ADDL    RR6,RR2         ! Add low-order 32 bits !
4622 B515           ADC     R5,R1           ! Next 16 bits !
4624 B504           ADC     R4,R0           ! High order 16 bits !
4626 1CA9           LDM     @R10,R4,#4      ! Store result in augend !
4628 0403
```

```
462A 61F0          LD      R0,30(R15)        ! Move return address !
462C 001E
462E 6FF0          LD      30+4(R15),R0
4630 0022
4632 DFF5          CALR    RPOP              ! Restore R0 - R14 !
4634 A9F3          INC     R15,#4            ! Delete 2 parameters !
4636 9E08          RET

          !* Subroutines RPUSH and RPOP
          *
          * Purpose: RPUSH saves R14 through R0 on the stack
          *          RPOP restores R0 through R14 from the stack
          *
          * No registers are changed. The condition code flags are
          *     not affected.
          *
          * After a call to RPUSH, the return address is at offset 30
          *     from the top of the stack
          *!

4638 2DFE  RPUSH:  EX      R14,@R15          ! Save R14, get return address !
463A 76FF          LDA     R15,-28(R15)      ! Reserve room for 14 other regs !
463C FFE4
463E 1CF9          LDM     @R15,R0,#14       ! Store R0 - R13 !
4640 000D
4642 93FE          PUSH    @R15,R14          ! Leave return address on stack !
4644 61FE          LD      R14,28(R15)       ! Restore R14 !
4646 001C
4648 9E08          RET

464A 97FE  RPOP:   POP     R14,@R15          ! Save return address !
464C 1CF1          LDM     R0,@R15,#14       ! Restore R0 - R13 !
464E 000D
4650 76FF          LDA     R15,28(R15)       ! Remove values from stack !
4652 001C
4654 2DFE          EX      R14,@R15          ! Restore R14 & push return addr !
4656 9E08          RET

4658            end     pgm_10_3
```

The actual addition process was demonstrated in Chapter 8. The interesting part of this example is the register save and restore. Many large programs and programming systems make use of routines like this one. LDA instructions are used to avoid modifying condition codes. LDA R15,−28(R15) has the same effect on R15 as SUB R15,#28 but the SUB instruction affects the condition codes.

Subroutine RPUSH saves the contents of CPU registers R0-R14 on the stack. But RPUSH must leave the return address at the top of the stack. Therefore R14 is first placed on the stack by exchanging its contents with the return address. The stack pointer is decremented by 28 to bypass space that will be occupied by 14 CPU registers; then the remaining CPU registers are written into the reserved space. Finally, the return address, now held in R14, is placed at the top of the stack. Subroutine RPOP simply reverses this logic sequence.

10-4. Length of a Message

Purpose: Determine the length of a string of ASCII characters. The string starts in memory location 6001. The end of the string is marked by a carriage return character ($0D_{16}$). Place the length of the string (excluding the carriage return) in memory location 6000.

Sample Problems:

a.

(6001) = 0D

Result: (6000) = 00

b.

(6001)	=	52	'R'
(6002)	=	41	'A'
(6003)	=	54	'T'
(6004)	=	48	'H'
(6005)	=	45	'E'
(6006)	=	52	'R'
(6007)	=	0D	CR

Result: (6000) = 06

Flowchart 10-4:

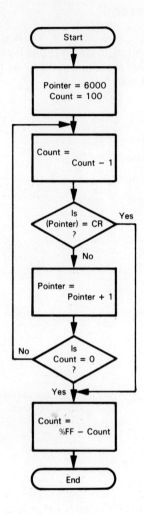

Program 10-4:

```
            internal
                pgm_10_4 procedure          ! Determine length of ... !
                entry                       ! ...an ASCII string !
                    $abs    IBASE

4600 0DF9   MAIN:   PUSH    @R15,#%6001     ! Pass string address !
4602 6001
4604 5F00           CALL    STRLEN
4606 4610
4608 97F0           POP     R0,@R15         ! Receive length !
460A 6E08           LDB     %6000,RL0       ! Store length !
460C 6000
460E 7A00           HALT

            !* Subroutine STRLEN
            *
            * Purpose: determine the length of a string of ASCII
            *          characters terminated by a carriage return
            *
            * Initial conditions:  The address of the first byte
            *                       in the string is pushed
            * Final conditions:    The length of the string (excluding
            *                       the carrige return) is returned on
            *                       the stack. If the first 255 bytes
            *                       contain no carriage return, FF hex
            *                       is returned
            *!

4610 91F2   STRLEN: PUSHL   @R15,RR2        ! Save R3, R2 and R1 !
4612 93F1           PUSH    @R15,R1
4614 61F3           LD      R3,6+2(R15)     ! Address of string !
4616 0008
4618 2102           LD      R2,#%100        ! Max length !
461A 0100
461C C90D           LDB     RL1,#'%R'       ! Search object: ASCII CR !
461E BA34           CPIRB   RL1,@R3,R2,EQ   ! Scan for CR !
4620 0296
4622 8CA0           COMB    RL2             ! Length of string to R2 !
4624 6FF2           LD      6+2(R15),R2     ! Return length !
4626 0008
4628 97F1           POP     R1,@R15         ! Restore R1, R2 and R3 !
462A 95F2           POPL    RR2,@R15
462C 9E08           RET

462E                end     pgm_10_4
```

This program is similar to one in Chapter 6. A more complete explanation of the CPIRB instruction and the effect of the COMB instruction can be found there.

This subroutine has the same number of parameters and return values. In this case, no extra stack management is required. The two previous examples both had two parameters and no return values. The next example has no stack parameters and one return value.

10-5. Find Minimum Value in a List

Purpose: Memory location 6002 contains the length of a list of unsigned 16-bit values that begins in memory location 6004. Place the minimum value from the list into memory location 6000.

Sample Problem:

$$
\begin{aligned}
(6002) &= 0004 \\
(6004) &= 1024 \\
(6006) &= 6006 \\
(6008) &= 4000 \\
(600A) &= 1014
\end{aligned}
$$

Result: (6000) = 1014

Flowchart 10-5:

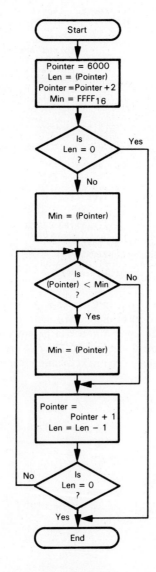

Program 10-5:

```
                internal
                    pgm_10_5 procedure          ! Find minimum value in a list !
                entry
                        $abs     IBASE

 4600 760A    MAIN:   LDA      R10,%6002        ! Put string address into R10 !
 4602 6002
 4604 5F00            CALL     MINVAL           ! Returns minimum on stack !
 4606 460E
 4608 57F0            POP      %6000,@R15       ! Store minimum value !
 460A 6000
 460C 7A00            HALT


              !* Subroutine MINVAL
              *
              * Purpose: Find the minimum value in a list of unsigned
              *          word values
              *
              * Initial conditions:   R10 contains the address of the first
              *                        word in the list. The first value
              *                        value in the list must be the number
              *                        of words in the list
              * Final conditions:     The minimum value in the list will
              *                        on the top of the stack. If the list
              *                        is empty, FFFF hex will be returned.
              *
              * No registers other than the stack pointer are changed by
              *          this subroutine
              *!

 460E 13FF    MINVAL: PUSH     @R15,@R15        ! Make room for return value !
 4610 91FA            PUSHL    @R15,RR10        ! Save R11, R10 and R9 !
 4612 93F9            PUSH     @R15,R9
 4614 97A9            POP      R9,@R10          ! Get length of list !
 4616 210B            LD.      R11,##FFFF       ! Assume largest possible val !
 4618 FFFF
 461A 8D94            TEST     R9               ! Empty list? !
 461C E607            JR       EQ,DONE
 461E 21AB            LD       R11,@R10         ! Assume first value is min !
 4620 BBA4    LOOP:   CPIR     R11,@R10,R9,UGT  ! Search for R11 > val !
 4622 09BB
 4624 EE03            JR       NZ,DONE          ! End of list? !
 4626 61AB            LD       R11,-2(R10)      ! Get new minimum !
 4628 FFFE
 462A ECFA            JR       NOV,LOOP         ! Continue if not at end of list !
 462C 6FFB    DONE:   LD       6+2(R15),R11     ! Store minimum in stack !
 462E 0008
 4630 97F9            POP      R9,@R15          ! Restore R9, R10 amd R11 !
 4632 95FA            POPL     RR10,@R15
 4634 9E08            RET

 4636            end     pgm_10_5
```

The main program begins by setting up R10 to point to the length word in the string. After the subroutine returns, the minimum value is on the stack.

The first instruction in the subroutine reserves a word on the stack beneath the return address. The instruction POP R9, @R10 is a more efficient version of

```
LD    R9,@R10
INC   R10,#2
```

The instruction immediately before the CPIR loads R11 with the first value in the list. Since R11 already contained FFFF, that instruction could have been omitted and the subroutine would have produced the same results. However, the CPIR would have stopped after the first iteration almost every time the routine was called. One instruction is a small price for this increase in efficiency. Whenever possible, the repeating instructions should be set up to execute with a minimum number of interruptions.

The case in which the last value in the list is the minimum is interesting. When this happens, the Z flag is set by CPIR. But since the length register went to zero, the V (Overflow) flag is also set. Had we tested the V flag before the Z flag, this case would have been missed.

10-6. String Comparison

Purpose: Locations 6000 and 6002 each contain the address of an ASCII string. The first byte of each string is its length. If the strings match, clear location 6002. If they differ, leave location 6002 holding its prior contents.

This program could be used to delete identical entries from a large list, such as a mailing list.

Sample Problems:

a.
(6000)	=	6100	
(6002)	=	6140	
(6100)	=	03	
(6101)	=	43	'C'
(6102)	=	41	'A'
(6103)	=	54	'T'
(6140)	=	03	
(6141)	=	43	'C'
(6142)	=	41	'A'
(6143)	=	54	'T'

Result: (6002) = 0000, since the two strings match

b.
(6100)	=	03	
(6101)	=	43	'C'
(6102)	=	41	'A'
(6103)	=	54	'T'
(6140)	=	03	
(6141)	=	43	'C'
(6142)	=	41	'A'
(6143)	=	52	'R'

Result: No change, since the strings do not match

c.
(6100)	=	03	
(6101)	=	43	'C'
(6102)	=	41	'A'
(6103)	=	54	'T'
(6140)	=	05	
(6141)	=	43	'C'
(6142)	=	41	'A'
(6143)	=	52	'T'
(6144)	=	43	'C'
(6145)	=	48	'H'

Result: No change, since the strings do not match

Flowchart 10-6:

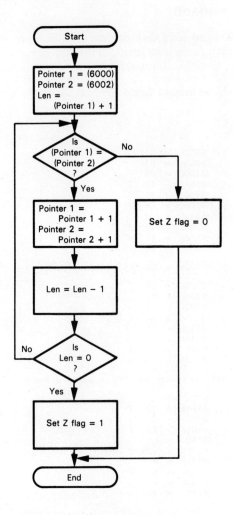

Program 10-6:

```
                internal
                    pgm_10_6 procedure
                    entry
                        $abs      IBASE
4600 760C   MAIN:   LDA     R12,%7000      ! Set up another stack !
4602 7000
4604 53C0           PUSH    @R12,%6000     ! Address of first string !
4606 6000
4608 53C0           PUSH    @R12,%6002     ! Address of second string !
460A 6002
460C 5F00           CALL    PMATCH         ! Compare the two strings !
460E 4618
4610 EE02           JR      NZ,FIN         ! Z flag is set if match !
4612 4D08           CLR     %6002          ! Delete second if they match !
4614 6002
4616 7A00   FIN:    HALT
```

```
            !* Subroutine PMATCH
            *
            * Purpose: Determine if two strings are identical
            *
            * Initial conditions:   R12 is a stack pointer. The top
            *                       two values on this stack are each
            *                       addresses of byte strings. The first
            *                       byte of each string is its length
            * Final conditions:     If the two strings match, the Z flag
            *                       is set to 1; it is 0 if the two
            *                       strings differ
            *
            * Register usage:  The two values are popped off the R12 stack
            *!
```

```
4618 91F2   PMATCH: PUSHL   @R15,RR2       ! Save R3, R2 and R1 !
461A 93F1           PUSH    @R15,R1
461C 95C2           POPL    RR2,@R12       ! R2 & R3 point to the strings !
461E 8D18           CLR     R1
4620 2029           LDB     RL1,@R2
4622 A910           INC     R1             ! Length + 1 !
4624 BA36           CPSIRB  @R2,@R3,R1,NE  ! Scan for unequal bytes !
4626 012E
4628 8D45           COMFLG  Z              ! Set Z flag if strings match !
462A 97F1           POP     R1,@R15        ! Restore R1, R2 and R3 !
462C 95F2           POPL    RR2,@R15
462E 9E08           RET

4630                end     pgm_10_6
```

The CPSIRB instruction compares successive bytes of the two strings until two bytes don't match or until the length register becomes 0. Note that for our purposes, the length byte can be considered part of the string. Doing this also saves us the work of testing for a zero length string, since we know that there is always a length byte.

If the strings match, the CPSIRB stops executing with the V flag set to 1 and the Z flag set to 0. If the strings aren't the same, the Z flag is set to 1. This is exactly the opposite from what is desired in the Z flag. So the COMFLG instruction serves us perfectly; it reverses the sense of the Z flag. Note that none of the instructions that follow it affect the Z flag, so the main program can test the Z flag with a JR instruction upon return.

If the subroutine had required more registers, we could have used the RPUSH and RPOP subroutines shown earlier. These routines do not affect the Z flag.

This subroutine demonstrates the use of a second stack. In this case, R12 is a pointer to a stack that contains the parameters for the subroutine. This simplifies the subroutine greatly. The disadvantage is that memory must be set aside for this second stack, and a second register must be dedicated to being a stack pointer.

PROBLEMS

Write both a calling program for the sample problem and at least one properly documented subroutine.

10-1. ASCII Hex to Binary

Purpose: Convert the contents of RL0 from the ASCII representation of a hexadecimal digit to the 4-bit binary representation of the digit. Place the result into RL0.

Sample Problems:

a.		RL0	= 43	'C'
	Result:	RL0	= 0C	
b.		RL0	= 36	'6'
	Result:	RL0	= 06	

10-2. ASCII Hex String to Binary Word

Purpose: Convert the four ASCII characters starting in memory location 6002 into a 16-bit binary value. Store the value in location 6000. Write a subroutine that takes the string address from the stack and returns the value on the stack. (This subroutine can use the subroutine written for problem 10-1.)

Sample Problem:

(6002)	= 42	'B'
(6003)	= 32	'1'
(6004)	= 46	'F'
(6005)	= 30	'0'
Result: (6000)	= B1F0	

10-3. Test for Alphabetic Character

Purpose: If the ASCII character in location 6000 is an alphabetic (upper or lower case), set location 6001 to FF_{16}; otherwise set it to 0. Use a subroutine that returns its result using the condition code flags.

Sample Problems:

a.	(6000)	= 47	'G'
	(6001)	= FF	
b.	(6000)	= 40	'@'
	(6001)	= 00	
c.	(6000)	= 6A	'j'
	(6001)	= FF	

10-4. Scan to Next Non-Alphabetic

Purpose: Memory location 6000 contains the address of an ASCII string. Place the address of the first non-alphabetic character in this string in memory location 6002.

Sample Problems:

a.	(6000)	=	6100	
	(6100)	=	43	'C'
	(6101)	=	61	'a'
	(6102)	=	74	't'
	(6103)	=	0D	CR
Result:	(6002)	=	6103	
b.	(6000)	=	6100	
	(6100)	=	32	'2'
	(6101)	=	50	'P'
	(6102)	=	49	'I'
	(6103)	=	0D	CR
Result:	(6002)	=	6100	

10-5. Check Even Parity

Purpose: Location 6001 contains the length in bytes of a string that begins at location 6002. If each byte in the string has even parity, set location 6000 to 0; if one or more bytes have odd parity, set location 6000 to FF_{16}.

Sample Problems:

a.	(6001)	=	3
	(6002)	=	47
	(6003)	=	AF
	(6004)	=	18
Result:	(6000)	=	00
b.	(6001)	=	3
	(6002)	=	47
	(6003)	=	AF
	(6004)	=	19
Result:	(6000)	=	FF, since 19 = 00011001 has odd parity

10-6. Compare Two Strings

Purpose: Write a subroutine, and a main program that tests it, to compare two ASCII strings. The first byte in each string is its length. Return the information in the condition codes: i.e., S flag set if the first string is lexically less than ("prior to") the second, Z flag set if the strings are equal, no flags set if the second is prior to the first. Note that "ABCD" is lexically greater than "ABC".

REFERENCES

1. A. Osborne, *An Introduction to Microcomputers: Volume 1 — "Basic Concepts"*, second edition, (Osborne/McGraw Hill, 1980), Chapter 6.

11

Input/Output

"Input/Output" describes the transfer of data between a microprocessor and "external" logic or devices. A typical microcomputer system communicates with external devices such as a terminal keyboard and display; there may also be a printer, disk drives, and sundry similar devices. A microprocessor-based control system might communicate with temperature and pressure sensors and controllers, inputting data via analog-to-digital converters, and outputting data via digital-to-analog converters.

The very nature of input/output requires the microprocessor to communicate with a broad variety of external logic and devices that may have little or nothing in common; **yet programs that control I/O data transfer are all very similar conceptually. This is because all I/O is channeled through a very few kinds of I/O devices.** For the Z8000, **two special I/O devices will suffice; the Z80-PIO and the Z80-SIO.** These two devices are described later in this chapter. Similar devices have been announced which are tailored for the Z8000: the Z8036 CIO and the Z8030 SCC. However these devices are not yet in production (Summer 1980). Programming these devices will be similar to programming the Z80-PIO and Z80-SIO. The general principles explained in this chapter are the same.

Using standard devices greatly simplifies the task of I/O programming. It does not matter whether the microprocessor is receiving input from a keyboard or an analog-to-digital converter; it will appear to receive the data from a Z80-PIO. Data output, likewise, will be directed to an "I/O port" for an incredible variety of output operations.

The parameters that make I/O programs differ from one another are: data transfer rates, data interpretations, and the types of control/status information that are exchanged during any data transfer.

Interrupts and direct memory access are not described in this chapter, although they are referred to tangentially. Interrupts are described in Chapter 12. We do not discuss details of direct memory access in this book.

I/O programming, reduced to its most basic components, consists of reading data from I/O ports and writing data to I/O ports. I/O ports have addresses; so do memory locations. In fact, some microcomputer systems address I/O ports as though they were memory locations; but standard Z8000 microcomputer systems do not, and in this chapter we will not. We are not going to concern ourselves with the way I/O ports acquire their I/O port addresses. We leave that discussion to a more hardware oriented book. Instead we will describe the competing needs of the microprocessor and the external device, and how you write programs to match these needs at the I/O interface.

I/O AND MEMORY

In theory, the transfer of data to or from an I/O device is similar to the transfer of data to or from memory. In fact, we can consider memory as just another I/O device. The memory is, however, special for the following reasons:

1. It operates at almost the same speed as the microprocessor.

2. It uses the same type of signals as the CPU. The only circuits usually needed to interface memory to the CPU are line drivers, receivers, and level translators.

3. It requires no special formats or control signals other than the standard read and write pulses.

4. It automatically latches data sent to it. This means that it captures the data when it is sent by the CPU (or I/O device) and holds it in internal registers until it is needed by the I/O device or CPU.

5. Its word length is compatible with the microprocessor.

Most I/O devices do not have such convenient features. They may operate at speeds much slower than the processor; for example, some teletypewriters can transfer only 10 characters per second, while a slow processor can transfer 10,000 characters per second. The range of speeds is also very wide — sensors may provide one reading per minute, while video displays or floppy disks may transfer 250,000 bits per second. Furthermore, I/O devices may require continuous signals (motors or thermometers), currents rather than voltages (teletypewriters), or voltages at far different levels than the signals used by the processor (gas-discharge displays). I/O devices may also require special formats, protocols, or control signals. Their word lengths may be much shorter or much longer than any word length handled by the microprocessor. These variations make the design of I/O hardware difficult. Each peripheral presents its own special interfacing problem.

I/O DEVICE CATEGORIES

We can roughly separate I/O devices into three categories, based on their data transfer rates:

1. Slow devices that change state no more than once per second. Changing their states typically requires milliseconds or longer. Such devices include lighted displays, switches, relays, and mechanical sensors and actuators.

2. Medium-speed devices that transfer data at rates of 1 to 10,000 bits per second. Such devices include keyboards, printers, card readers, paper tape readers and punches, cassettes, ordinary communications lines, and many analog data acquisition systems.

3. High-speed devices that transfer data at rates of over 10,000 bits per second. Such devices include magnetic tapes, magnetic disks, high-speed line printers, high-speed communications lines, and video displays.

INTERFACING SLOW DEVICES

Slow I/O device interfaces are simple. Few control signals are necessary unless devices are multiplexed, i.e., several are handled from one port, as shown in Figures 11-1 to 11-4. Often data will change in a short time and must be latched. Latching input data means putting the data presented by an external device into a register where it can be kept until the CPU is ready for it. Latching output data means transferring data from the CPU to a register outside the CPU where it can be kept during the time the external device needs it.

Input data from slow devices need not be latched, since it remains stable over a long time interval. Output data must, of course, be latched. The only problems with input are transitions that occur while the computer is reading the data. One-shots, cross-coupled latches, or software delay routines can smooth the transitions.

A single port can handle several slow devices. Figure 11-1 shows a demultiplexer that automatically directs the next output data to the next device by counting output operations. Figure 11-2 shows a control port that provides select inputs to a demultiplexer. The data outputs here can come in any order, but an additional output instruction is necessary to change the state of the control port. Output demultiplexers are commonly used to drive several displays from the same output port. Figures 11-3 and 11-4 show the same alternatives for an input multiplexer.

Note the differences between input and output with slow devices:

1. Input data need not be latched, since the input device holds the data for an enormous length of time by computer standards. Output data must be latched, since the output device will not respond to data that is present for only a few CPU clock cycles.

2. Input transitions cause problems because of their duration; brief output transitions cause no problems because the output devices (or the observers) react slowly.

3. The major constraints on input are reaction time and responsiveness; the major constraints on output are response time and observability.

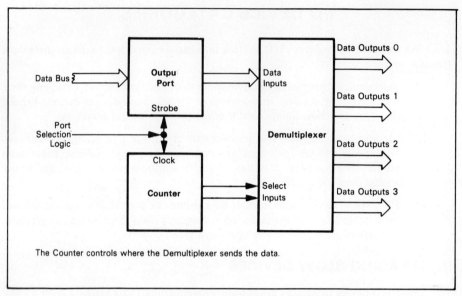

Figure 11-1. An Output Demultiplexer Controlled by a Counter

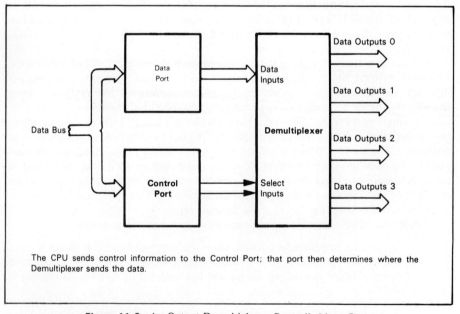

Figure 11-2. An Output Demultiplexer Controlled by a Port

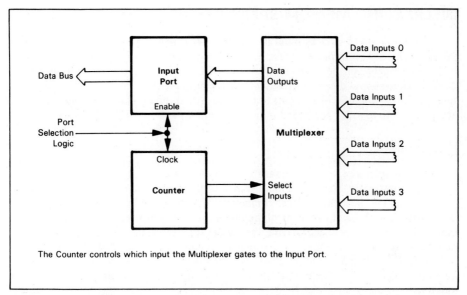

Figure 11-3. An Input Multiplexer Controlled by a Counter

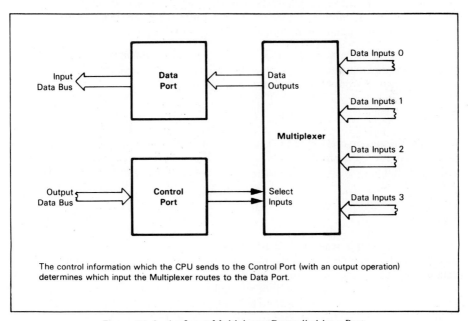

Figure 11-4. An Input Multiplexer Controlled by a Port

INTERFACING MEDIUM-SPEED DEVICES

Medium-speed devices must be synchronized with the processor clock in some fashion. The CPU cannot treat these devices as if they held their data forever, or always had data available on demand. Instead, the CPU must be able to determine when a device has new input data, or is ready to receive output data. It must also have a way of telling a device that new output data is available or that the previous input data has been accepted. Note that the peripheral may be or contain another microprocessor.

Handshake

The handshake is the standard unclocked means of I/O communication used by a microprocessor. Here the sender indicates the availability of data to the receiver and transfers the data; the receiver completes the handshake by acknowledging receipt of the data. The receiver may control the operation by initially requesting the data or by indicating its readiness to accept data; the sender then sends the data and completes the handshake by indicating that data is available. In either case, the sender knows that the transfer has been completed successfully and the receiver knows when new data is available. Figures 11-5 and 11-6 show typical input and output operations using handshaking.

There are several ways of providing the handshake signals. Among these are:

1. Separate dedicated I/O lines. The processor may handle these as additional I/O ports, through special lines, or via interrupts. The Z8000 does not have I/O control lines, but the Z80 Parallel Input/Output device (or PIO) does.

2. Special patterns on the I/O lines. These may be single start and stop bits or entire characters or groups of characters. The patterns must be easy to distinguish from background noise or inactive states.

Polling

An alternative method to the typical I/O operations using handshaking, called polling, has the CPU check the status of all I/O devices before initiating any I/O operation. But polling can occupy a large amount of processor time if there are many I/O devices.

Strobe

We often call a separate I/O line that indicates the availability of data or the occurrence of a transfer a "strobe line." A signal on this line may, for example, clock data into a latch or read data from a buffer.

Many peripherals transfer data at regular intervals, i.e., synchronously. Here the only problem is starting the process by lining up to the first input or marking the first output. In some cases, the peripheral provides a clock input from which the processor can obtain timing information.

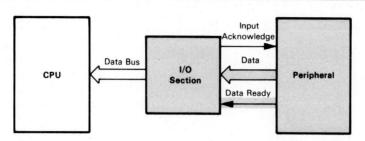

a. Peripheral provides data and Data Ready signal to computer I/O section.

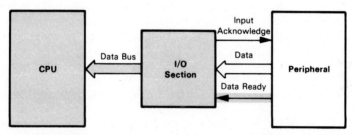

b. CPU reads Data Ready signal from I/O section (this may be a hardware, interrupt connection).

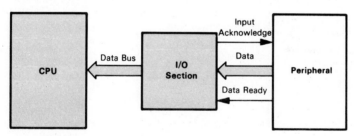

c. CPU reads data from I/O section.

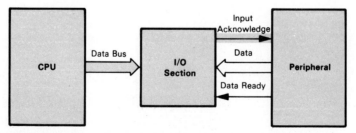

d. CPU sends Input Acknowledge signal to I/O section which then provides Input Acknowledge signal to Peripheral (this may be a hardware connection).

Figure 11-5. An Input Handshake

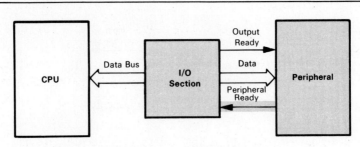

a. Peripheral provides Peripheral Ready signal to computer I/O section.

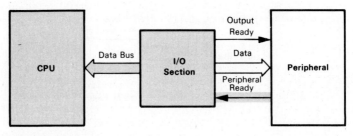

b. CPU reads Peripheral Ready signal from I/O section (this may be a hardware, e.g., interrupt connection).

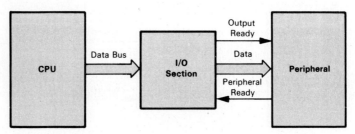

c. CPU sends data to Peripheral.

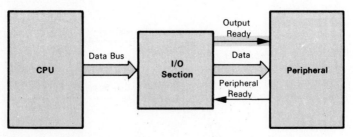

d. CPU sends Output Ready signal to Peripheral (this may be a hardware connection).

Figure 11-6. An Output Handshake

Reducing Transmission Errors

Transmission errors are a problem with medium-speed devices. Several methods can lessen the likelihood of such errors; they include:

1. Sampling input data at the center of the transmission interval in order to avoid edge effects; that is, keep away from the edges where the data is changing.

2. Sampling each input several times and using majority logic such as best three out of five.[1]

3. Generating and checking parity; an extra bit is used that makes the number of 1 bits in the correct data either even or odd.

4. Using other error detecting and correcting codes such as checksums, LRC (longitudinal redundancy check), and CRC (cyclic redundancy check).[2]

INTERFACING HIGH-SPEED DEVICES

High-speed devices that transfer more than 10,000 bits per second require special methods. The usual technique is to construct a special-purpose controller that transfers data directly between the memory and the I/O device. This process is called direct memory access (DMA). The DMA controller must force the CPU off the bus, provide addresses and control signals to the memory, and transfer the data. Such a controller will be fairly complex. Programming for direct memory access is dependent on the particular controller and is not discussed in this book.

TIMING INTERVALS (DELAYS)

One problem that we will face throughout the discussion of input/output is the generation of time delays. Such delays are necessary to debounce mechanical switches (to smooth their irregular transitions), to provide pulses with specified lengths and frequencies for displays, and to provide timing for devices that transfer data regularly (for example, a teletypewriter that sends or receives one bit every 9.1 ms).

We can produce time delays in several ways:

1. In hardware with one-shots or monostable multivibrators. These devices produce a single pulse of fixed duration in response to a pulse input.

2. In a combination of hardware and software with a flexible programmable timer such as the Z80-CTC Counter-Timer Circuit[3] or the counter/timers in the new Z8036 CIO.[4] The CTC can provide timing intervals of various lengths with a variety of starting and ending conditions.

3. In software with delay routines. These routines use the processor as a counter. This is possible since the processor has a stable clock reference, but it clearly underutilizes the processor. However, delay routines require no additional hardware and often use processor time that would otherwise be wasted.

Which of these three methods is chosen depends on the application. The software method is inexpensive but may overburden the processor. Programmable timers are relatively expensive, but they are easy to interface and may be able to handle many complex timing tasks.

BASIC SOFTWARE DELAY

A simple delay routine works as follows:

Step 1.   Load a register with a specified value.
Step 2.   Decrement the register.
Step 3.   If the result of Step 2 is not zero, repeat Step 2.

This routine does nothing except use time. The amount of time used depends on the execution time of the instructions used. The maximum length of the delay is limited by the size of the register; however, one routine can be placed inside another routine that uses another register, and so on.

Example 11-1 uses Register R1 to provide delays measured in 1 millisecond increments.

PROGRAM EXAMPLE

11-1. Delay Program

Purpose: The program provides a delay of 1 ms.

Program 11-1a:

```
            internal
                 pgm_11_1a procedure
                 entry
                     $abs    IBASE

4600 2101   DELAY:  LD      R1,#MSCNT       ! Get count for 1 ms delay !
4602 018F
4604 AB10   DLY1:   DEC     R1              ! Execute 2 instructions... !
4606 EEFE           JR      NZ,DLY1         ! ...until counter goes to 0 !
4608 7A00   NEXT:   HALT

460A                end     pgm_11_1a
```

The value of MSCNT depends on the speed of the CPU and the memory cycle. Program 11-1a budgets its time as follows:

			Clock Periods	Number of Times Executed
DELAY:	LD	R1,#MSCNT	7	1
DLY1:	DEC	R1	4	MSCNT
	JR	NZ,DLY1	6	MSCNT

If the Z8000 clock period is x microseconds, then the time delay introduced by the loop illustrated above will be:

$$(7 + 10 \times MSCNT \times X$$

The standard Z8000 clock period is 250 ns; therefore x is 0.25 and the computed time delay is:

$$(1.75 + 2.5 \times MSCNT) \text{ microseconds}$$

If MSCNT is 400_{10} (190_{16}) then the time delay is one millisecond plus 1.75 microseconds. If MSCNT is 399_{10} ($18F_{16}$) then the time delay is one millisecond minus 0.75 microseconds. 1.75 microseconds represents a 0.175% error in a one millisecond time interval. Before you attempt to eliminate this small error, or the smaller error introduced by MSCNT = 399_{10}, you should assure yourself that your clock signal is not introducing even larger errors. For example, if your clock signal is accurate to 0.2%, eliminating smaller errors in a delay loop is not very productive. Program 11-1g will allow you to compute a delay of exactly 1 millisecond, given an exact 250 nanosecond clock.

Program 11-1b:

```
            internal
                pgm_11_1b procedure
                entry
                        $abs        IBASE

    4600 2101   DELAY:  LD      R1,#0       ! Use 7 clock periods !
    4602 0000
    4604 AD11           EX      R1,R1       ! Use 6 clock periods !
    4606 2101           LD      R1,#398     ! Counter for 1 ms delay !
    4608 018E
    460A AB10   DLY1:   DEC     R1
    460C EEFE           JR      NZ,DLY1
    460E 7A00   NEXT:   HALT

    4610        end     pgm_11_1b
```

The one millisecond delay routine will be imbedded in a larger program that loads and decrements another register (we have chosen R2). Do not forget that these outer instructions will also contribute to the time delay. Here is one possibility:

Flowchart 11-1:

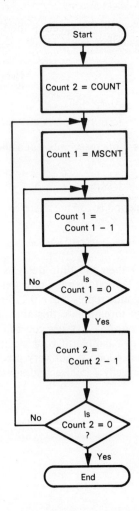

Program 11-1c:

```
                internal
                   pgm_ll_lc procedure
                   entry
                           $abs      IBASE

      4600 2102   TIME:   LD      R2,#COUNT        ! Milliseconds counter !
      4602 000E
      4604 2101   DELAY:  LD      R1,#0            ! 1 ms delay !
      4606 0000
      4608 AD11           EX      R1,R1
      460A 2101           LD      R1,#398
      460C 018E
      460E AB10   DLY1:   DEC     R1
      4610 EEFE           JR      NZ,DLY1
      4612 F288           DJNZ    R2,DELAY         ! Repeat the 1 ms delay !
      4614 7A00   NEXT:   HALT

      4616            end     pgm_ll_lc
```

The LD R2,#COUNT introduces a one time, 7-clock-period delay. The DJNZ instruction adds 11 clock periods to each millisecond. We will have to put up with the 7-clock-period delay introduced by the LD R2,#COUNT instruction, but do you see how we can replace DJNZ with instructions that will add 20 clock periods to each millisecond, then eliminate this addition by loading 396 into R1?

Z8000 I/O INSTRUCTIONS

The Z8000 microprocessor has an extensive set of Input/Output instructions. All I/O instructions use 16-bit device addresses, thus allowing up to 65,536 input ports and 65,536 output ports. An I/O device may occupy several I/O addresses; for example, each Z80 PIO (as we will describe later in this chapter) occupies four output port addresses and four input port addresses. Furthermore, I/O devices which transfer a byte (8 bits) of data at a time will generally have odd addresses in a Z8000 system. Thus effective I/O space may be smaller than the address range.

All I/O instructions have a byte version that transfers eight bits of data, and a word version that transfers sixteen bits of data.

The I/O instructions can be grouped as follows:

1. Double-word instructions that use absolute addressing. IN Rn,PORT and OUT PORT,Rn transfer eight or sixteen bits of data between any register and the port addressed by the second word of the instruction object code.

2. Single-word instructions that use register indirect addressing. IN Rn, @Rm and OUT @Rm,Rn transfer eight or sixteen bits of data between the specified register and the port addressed indirectly via 16-bit register Rm (which can be any register except R0).

3. Block I/O instructions. INI and OUTI transfer eight or sixteen bits of data between the memory location addressed indirectly by a 16-bit (non-segmented) or 32-bit (segmented) register and the port addressed indirectly by a 16-bit register. Both instructions then increment the indirect memory address and decrement a counter which is also held in a 16-bit register. The V flag is set if the counter decrements to zero; it is reset otherwise. IND and OUTD are the same instructions except that they decrement the indirect memory address instead of incrementing it.

4. Repeated Block I/O instructions. INIR and OTIR repeat the effects of INI and OUTI, respectively, until the counter is decremented to zero. INDR and OTDR have the same relationship to IND and OUTD.

5. Special I/O instructions. Every instruction has a "special" version that activates a special I/O control signal but is otherwise identical. You should consult your microcomputer user's manual before using special I/O instructions. They may be used in some special way, they may function like the normal I/O equivalent instruction, or they may be unusable. They are intended for use with the Z8010 Memory Management Unit described in Chapter 13.

You should note the following features of these groups of instructions:

1. Double-word instructions with absolute addressing.

    -   Data is always transferred to or from an 8-bit CPU register for INB or OUTB, or a 16-bit CPU register for IN or OUT.

    -   No status flags are affected.

    -   The port address is encoded as part of the instruction and cannot be changed easily.

2. Single-word instructions with register indirect addressing.

    -   INB and OUTB transfer 8-bit data to or from any 8-bit CPU register. IN and OUT transfer 16-bit data to or from any 16-bit CPU register. The I/O port address is held in any 16-bit CPU register with the exception of R0.

    -   No status flags are modified.

    -   Since the I/O port address is in a 16-bit CPU register, it can be used as a parameter by an I/O subroutine (or I/O driver). Thus several different applications could use one I/O driver, or one application could use one I/O driver to service several similar I/O devices.

3. Block I/O instructions.

    -   Data is always transferred between a block of memory locations and an I/O port. Memory locations are addressed indirectly by any 16-bit (non-segmented) or 32-bit (segmented) CPU register with the exception of R0. An 8-bit block I/O instruction will access 8-bit memory locations. 16-bit memory locations are accessed by 16-bit block I/O instructions.

    -   Z (Zero) status is left undefined. The P/V (parity/overflow) status is set to 1 when the counter decrements to zero; it is reset to 0 otherwise. No other status flags are affected.

    -   The I/O Port address is specified indirectly by any 16-bit CPU register with the exception of register R0. Therefore the I/O port address can be a parameter for an I/O driver.

    -   The counter is held in a 16-bit CPU register. Any 16-bit CPU register, including R0, can be used.

I/O INSTRUCTION EXAMPLES

Here are some examples of the various I/O instructions without any timing considerations:

1. Load Register R0 from 16-bit Input Port 2.

    a. Using absolute addressing:

    ```
    IN      R0,2
    ```

    b. Using register indirect addressing via R1:

    ```
    LD      R1,#2
    IN      R0,@R1
    ```

2. Store the contents of Register RL0 in 8-bit Output Port 5.

    a. Using absolute addressing:

    ```
    OUTB    5,RL0
    ```

    b. Using register indirect addressing via R1:

    ```
    LD      R1,#5
    OUTB    @R1,RL0
    ```

3. Load memory location 6000 from 8-bit Input Port 3.

    a. Using absolute addressing:

    ```
    INB     RL0,3           ! Get Data    !
    LDB     %6000,RL0       ! Store Data  !
    ```

    b. Using register indirect addressing:

    ```
    LD      R1,#3           ! Port Number !
    INB     RL0,@R1         ! Get Data    !
    LDB     %6000,RL0       ! Store Data  !
    ```

    c. Using block I/O:

    ```
    LD      R3,#1           ! Count               !
    LD      R1,#3           ! Port Number         !
    LD      R2,#%6000       ! Memory Destination  !
    INIB    @R2,@R1,R3      ! Get Data            !
    ```

4. Store the contents of memory location 6000 in 8-bit Output Port 5.

    a. Using absolute addressing:

    ```
    LDB     RL0,%6000       ! Load Data !
    OUTB    5,RL0           ! Send Data !
    ```

    b. Using register indirect addressing:

    ```
    LD      R1,#5           ! Port Number !
    LDB     RL0,%6000       ! Load Data   !
    OUTB    @R1,RL0         ! Send Data   !
    ```

    c. Using block I/O:

    ```
    LD      R3,#1           ! Count         !
    LD      R1,#5           ! Port Number   !
    LD      R2,%6000        ! Memory Source !
    OUTIB   @R1,@R2,R3      ! Send Data     !
    ```

5. Load memory bytes 6000 through 6007 from 8-bit Input Port 3.

    a. Using absolute addressing:

```
         LDA     R1,%6000        ! Starting Address of Data !
         LDB     RL3,#8          ! Count = 8                 !
INBYTE:  INB     RL0,3           ! Get Data                  !
         LDB     @R1,RL0         ! Store in Memory           !
         INC     R1              ! Count                     !
         DBJNZ   RL3,INBYTE      ! Repeat until done         !
```

    b. Using block I/O:

```
         LDA     R1,%6000        ! Starting Address of Data !
         LD      R3,#8           ! Byte Counter = 8          !
         LD      R2,#3           ! Port Number               !
INBYTE:  INIB    @R1,@R2,R3      ! Get Data into Memory      !
         JR      NOV,INBYTE      ! Repeat until done         !
```

    c. Using repeated block I/O:

```
         LDA     R1,%6000        ! Starting Address of Data !
         LD      R3,#8           ! Byte Counter = 8          !
         LD      R2,#3           ! Port Number               !
         INIRB   @R1,@R2,R3      ! Get Data into Memory      !
```

6. Send the contents of memory locations 6000 through 6007 to 8-bit Output Port 5.

    a. Using absolute addressing:

```
         LDA     R1,%6000        ! Starting Address of Data !
         LDB     RL3,#8          ! Count                     !
OTBYTE:  LDB     RL0,@R1         ! Load from Memory          !
         OUTB    #5,RL0          ! Send Data                 !
         INC     R1              ! Next data word            !
         DBJNZ   RL3,OTBYTE      ! Repeat until done         !
```

    b. Using block I/O:

```
         LDA     R1,%6000        ! Starting Address of Data !
         LD      R3,#8           ! Count                     !
         LD      R2,#5           ! Port Number               !
OTBYTE:  OUTIB   @R2,@R1,R3      ! Send Data from Memory     !
         JR      NOV,OTBYTE      ! Repeat until done         !
```

    c. Using repeated block I/O:

```
         LDA     R1,%6000        ! Starting Address of Data !
         LD      R3,#8           ! Count                     !
         LD      R2,#5           ! Port Number               !
         OTIRB   @R2,@R1,R3      ! Send Data from Memory     !
```

Using Block I/O Instructions

Note that the repeated Block I/O instructions operate continuously. You cannot modify timing between transfers. Thus these instructions cannot be used unless the peripheral operates at the same speed as the processor, or timing is handled separately in hardware. Ways to handle timing in hardware include forcing the processor into wait states or buffering the data.

Examples of I/O programming in this chapter usually use instructions with absolute addressing. You can easily replace the instructions with register indirect addressing as long as you remember to initialize the I/O port address. We will occasionally identify applications for the Block I/O instructions.

PROGRAM EXAMPLES

11-2. A Pushbutton Switch

We will illustrate interfacing a single pushbutton switch (or a single-pole, single-throw (SPST) switch) to a Z8000 microprocessor. The pushbutton is a mechanical switch that provides a single contact closure (i.e., a logic zero) while pressed.

Figure 11-7 shows the circuitry required to interface the pushbutton. It uses one bit of a PIO, which also acts as a buffer; no latch is needed, since the pushbutton remains closed for many CPU clock cycles. Pressing the button grounds the PIO input bit. The pullup resistor ensures that the input bit is 1 if the button is not being pressed.

We will perform two tasks with this circuit. They are:

a. Set a memory location based on the state of the button.

b. Count the number of times that the button is pressed.

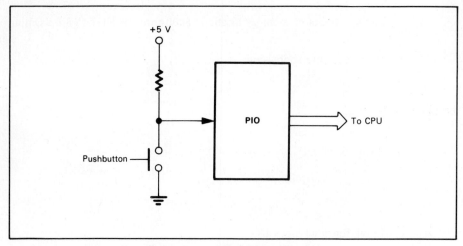

Figure 11-7. A Pushbutton Circuit

Task 1: Determine switch position.

Purpose: Set memory location 6000 to one if the button is not being pressed, and to zero if it is being pressed.

Sample Cases:

1. Button open (not pressed)
   Result = (6000) = 01

2. Button closed (pressed)
   Result = (6000) = 00

Flowchart:

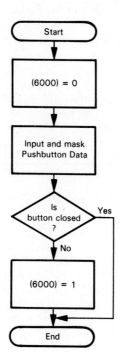

Program 11-2a:

```
                constant
                    MASK := %08                      ! Button connected to bit 3 !

                internal
                    pgm_11_2a procedure
                    entry
                         $abs    IBASE

    4600  C84F          LDB     RL0,#%4F             ! Make port A input !
    4602  3A86          OUTB    PIOADR+5,RL0
    4604  FF25
    4606  8C08          CLRB    RH0                  ! Assume button closed !
    4608  3A84          INB     RL0,PIOADR+1         ! Read button position !
    460A  FF21
    460C  0608          ANDB    RL0,#MASK            ! Mask off unneeded bits !
    460E  0808
    4610  E601          JR      Z,DONE               ! Is button bit 0 (closed)? !
    4612  A800          INCB    RH0                  ! No, indicate open !
    4614  6E00  DONE:   LDB     %6000,RH0            ! Store result !
    4616  6000
    4618  7A00          HALT

    461A          end     pgm_11_2a
```

The port addresses depend on how the PIO is connected in your microcomputer. The PIO control lines are not used in this example. In fact, we could place the A side of the PIO in the control mode with the starting sequence:

```
LD      R0,#%FFCF       ! Make Port A Control !
OUTB    PIOADR+5,RL0
OUTB    PIOADR+5,RH0
```

MASK depends on the bit to which the pushbutton is connected; it has a one in the button position and zeros elsewhere.

Button Position (Bit Number)	Mask	
	Binary	Hex
0	00000001	01
1	00000010	02
2	00000100	04
3	00001000	08
4	00010000	10
5	00100000	20
6	01000000	40
7	10000000	80

The program can use the bit test instruction to determine the button's state. For example, if bit 6 is connected to the button, we could use:

```
INB     RL0,PIOADR+1    ! Read button position  !
BITB    RL0,#6          ! Is button closed (0)? !
JR      NZ,DONE         ! If closed, then done   !
```

Task 2: Count switch closures.

Purpose: Count the number of button closures by incrementing location 6000 after each closure.

Sample Case:

Pressing the button ten times after the start of the program should give:

$$(6000) = 0A_{16}$$

In order to count the number of times that the button has been pressed, we must be sure that each closure causes a single transition. However, a mechanical pushbutton does not produce a single transition for each closure, because the mechanical contacts bounce back and forth before settling into their final positions. We can use a one-shot to eliminate the bounce or we can handle it in software.

The program can debounce the pushbutton by waiting after detecting a closure. The required delay is called the debouncing time; it is part of the specifications for the pushbutton. Typical values are a few milliseconds. The program should not examine the pushbutton during this period because it might mistake bounces for new closures. The program may either enter a delay routine like the one described previously, or simply perform other tasks for the specified amount of time.

Even after debouncing, the program must still wait for the present closure to end before looking for a new closure. This procedure avoids double counting. The following program uses a software delay of 1 ms to debounce the pushbutton. You may want to try varying the delay or eliminating it entirely to see what happens. To run this program, you must enter the delay subroutine into memory starting at location 4800.

Flowchart 11-2:

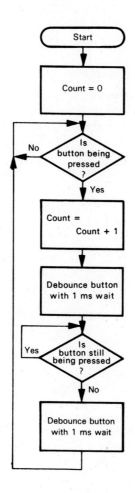

Program 11-2b:

```
            constant
                BUTTON := 3                        ! Button connected to bit 3 !


            internal
                pgm_11_2b procedure
                entry
                    $abs      IBASE
4600 C84F               LDB       RL0,#%4F         ! Port A input !
4602 3A86               OUTB      PIOADR+5,RL0
4604 FF25
4606 7601               LDA       R1,%6000
4608 6000
460A 0C18               CLRB      @R1              ! Initially set count to 0 !
460C 3A84     OPEN:     INB       RL0,PIOADR+1     ! Read button !
460E FF21
4610 A683               BITB      RL0,#BUTTON      ! Is it closed (0)? !
4612 EEFC               JR        NZ,OPEN          ! No, wait until it is !
4614 2810               INCB      @R1              ! Count the closure !
4616 5F00               CALL      DELAY            ! Wait 1 ms to debounce !
4618 4800
461A 3A84     CLOSED:   INB       RL0,PIOADR+1
461C FF21
461E A683               BITB      RL0,#BUTTON      ! Is button still closed? !
4620 E6FC               JR        Z,CLOSED         ! Wait until it is released !
4622 5F00               CALL      DELAY            ! Debounce opening !
4624 4800
4626 E8F2               JR        OPEN             ! Look for next closure !


4628           end      pgm_11_2b
```

The three instructions beginning with the label CLOSED are used to determine when the switch reopens.

Clearly we do not really need a PIO for this simple interface. An addressable tri-state buffer would do the job at far lower cost.

The Z8000 has two handshaking control signals (MI and MO) that are used by microprocessors to communicate with each other in large, multi-CPU configurations. In a single Z8000 configuration MI can be used to receive a single bit input such as the pushbutton switch we are describing. MO can be used to generate a single bit output. There are four instructions that manage MI and MO; they are: MBIT, MREQ, MRES and MSET. MBIT tests the MI input level and reports it in the sign status; **if the pushbutton switch is connected to MI, then our Task 1 program could be rewritten as follows:**

```
                LDA       R1,%6000       ! Marker = 0                  !
                CLRB      @R1
                MBIT                     ! Read button position  !
                JR        MI,DONE        ! Is button closed (0)? !
                INCB      @R1            ! No, marker = 1              !
        DONE:   HALT
```

Can you rewrite Task 2 using MBIT? Also try rewriting Task 2 using MREQ; it automatically handles the debouncing delay for you, but you will need to make some assumptions regarding MO. See Chapter 13 for more information on these signals.

11-3. A Toggle Switch

We will illustrate a single-pole, double-throw (SPDT) toggle switch interfaced to a Z8000 microprocessor. The toggle is a mechanical device that is in either one of two positions, or is moving between the positions.

Figure 11-8 shows the circuitry required to interface the switch. Like the pushbutton, the switch uses one bit of a Z8000 PIO. Unlike the button, the switch may be left in either position. Typical program tasks are to determine the switch position and to see if the position has changed. Either a one-shot with a pulse length of a few milliseconds or a pair of cross-coupled NAND gates (see Figure 11-9) can debounce a mechanical switch.

The circuits will produce a single step or pulse in response to a change in switch position even if the switch bounces before settling into its new position.

We will perform two tasks involving this circuit. They are:

1. Set a memory location to 1 when the switch is closed.

2. Set a memory location to 1 when the state of the switch changes.

Task 1: Wait for switch to close.

Purpose: Memory location 6000 is 0 until the switch is closed, at which time it is set to 1. The processor clears memory location 6000, waits for the switch to close, then sets memory location 6000 to 1.

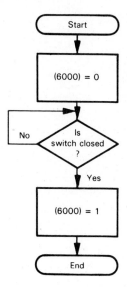

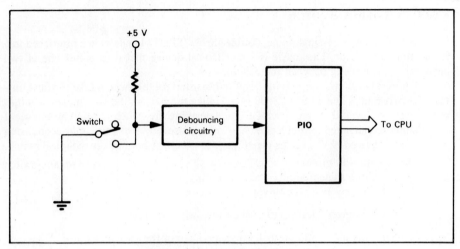

Figure 11-8. A Toggle Switch Circuit

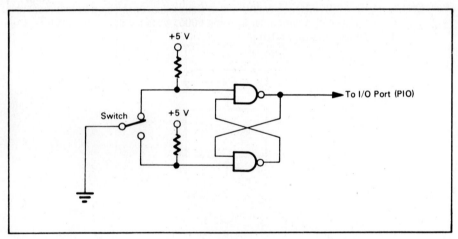

Figure 11-9. A Debounce Circuit Based on Cross-Coupled NAND Gates

Program 11-3a:

```
              internal
                 pgm_ll_3a procedure
                 entry
                    $abs    IBASE

    4600 C84F          LDB     RL0,#%4F          ! Port A output !
    4602 3A86          OUTB    PIOADR+5,RL0
    4604 FF25
    4606 4C08          CLRB    %6000             ! Set marker to zero !
    4608 6000
    460A 3A84   OPEN:  INB     RL0,PIOADR+1
    460C FF21
    460E A683          BITB    RL0,#BUTTON       ! Is switch closed? !
    4610 EEFC          JR      NZ,OPEN           ! No, wait for closure !
    4612 6800          INCB    %6000             ! Yes, marker = 1 !
    4614 6000
    4616 7A00          HALT

    4618         end      pgm_ll_3a
```

Task 2: Wait for switch to change.

Purpose: Memory location 6000 remains 0 until the switch position changes; i.e., the processor waits until the switch changes, then sets memory location 6000 to 1.

Flowchart:

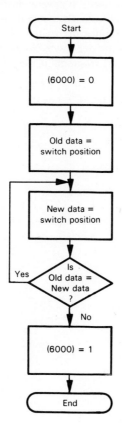

Program 11-3b:

```
                internal
                   pgm_11_3b procedure
                entry
                   $abs      IBASE

4600 C84F               LDB      RL0,#%4F        ! Port A output !
4602 3A86               OUTB     PIOADR+5,RL0
4604 FF25
4606 4C08               CLRB     %6000           ! Marker = 0 !
4608 6000
460A 3A84               INB      RL0,PIOADR+1    ! Get old switch position !
460C FF21
460E 0608               ANDB     RL0,#MASK       ! Isolate button bit !
4610 0808
4612 3A04       SRCH:   INB      RH0,PIOADR+1    ! Get new switch position !
4614 FF21
4616 0600               ANDB     RH0,#MASK
4618 0808
461A 8A80               CPB      RH0,RL0         ! Has the button changed? !
461C E6FA               JR       EQ,SRCH         ! No, keep waiting !
461E 6800               INCB     %6000           ! Changed, so set marker = 1 !
4620 6000
4622 7A00               HALT

4624            end      pgm_11_3b
```

A Subtract or Exclusive-OR could replace the Compare in the program. The Exclusive-OR would be especially useful if several switches were attached to the same PIO, since it would produce a 1 bit for each switch that changed state. How would you rewrite this program so as to debounce the switch in software? Assume the switch is wired as in Figure 11-8, but with the debounce circuit replaced by a direct connection. Also, how would you rewrite these programs if the switch were connected to the MI input?

11-4. A Multiple-Position (Rotary, Selector, or Thumbwheel) Switch

We will interface a multiple-position switch to a microprocessor. The lead corresponding to the switch position is grounded (logic zero), while the other leads are high (logic ones).

Figure 11-10 shows the circuitry required to interface an 8-position switch. The switch uses all eight data bits of one PIO data port. Typical tasks are to determine the position of the switch and to check whether or not that position has changed. Two special situations must be handled:

1. The switch is temporarily between positions so that no leads are grounded.

2. The switch has not yet reached its final position.

The first of these situations can be handled by waiting until the input is not all ones, i.e., until a switch lead is grounded. We can handle the second situation by examining the switch again after a delay (such as 1 or 2 seconds) and only accepting the input when it remains the same. We can also use another switch (i.e., a Load switch) to tell the processor when the selector switch should be read.

We will perform two tasks using the circuit illustrated in Figure 11-10. These are:

a. Monitor the switch until it is in a definite position, then determine the position and store its binary value in a memory location.

b. Wait for the position of the switch to change, then store the new position in a memory location.

If the switch is in a position, the lead from that position is grounded through the common line. In an actual circuit, pullup resistors would be required on the input lines to ensure that they are read as logic ones when they are not grounded.

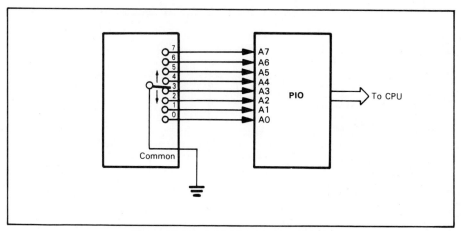

Figure 11-10. A Multiple-Position Switch

Task 1: Determine switch position.

Purpose: The program waits for the switch to be in a specific position and then places the number of that position into memory location 6000.

Table 11-1 contains the data inputs corresponding to the various switch positions. This scheme is inefficient, since it requires eight bits to distinguish among eight different positions.

A TTL or MOS encoder could reduce the number of bits needed. Figure 11-11 shows a circuit using the 74LS148 TTL 8-to-3 encoder.[8] We attach the switch outputs in inverse order, since the 74LS148 device has active-low inputs and outputs. The output of the encoder circuit is a 3-bit representation of the switch position. Many switches include encoders so that their outputs are coded, usually as a BCD digit (in negative or active-low logic). In an actual circuit, pullup resistors would be required on the input lines to ensure that they are read as logic ones when not grounded.

Since the encoder produces active-low outputs, switch position 5, which is attached to input 2, produces an output of 2 in negative logic (010), which corresponds to 5 in positive logic (101). You may want to verify the double negative for yourself.

Table 11-1. Data Input vs. Switch Position

Switch Position	Data Input	
	Binary	Hex
0	11111110	FE
1	11111101	FD
2	11111011	FB
3	11110111	F7
4	11101111	EF
5	11011111	DF
6	10111111	BF
7	01111111	7F

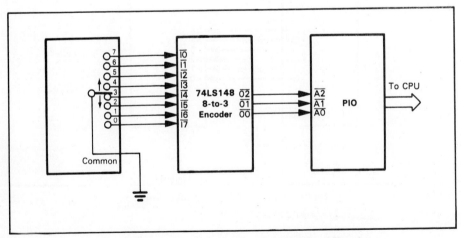

Figure 11-11. A Multiple-Position Switch with an Encoder

Flowchart:

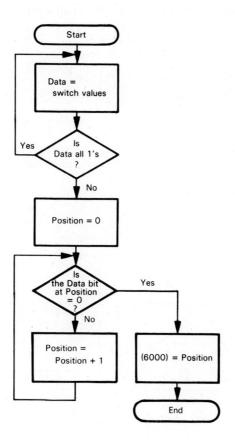

Program 11-4a:

```
            internal
              pgm_11_4a procedure
              entry
                    $abs      IBASE

4600 C84F            LDB      RL0,#%4F        ! Port A input !
4602 3A86            OUTB     PIOADR+5,RL0
4604 FF25
4606 3A84   CHKSW:   INB      RL0,PIOADR+1    ! Get switch data !
4608 FF21
460A 0A08            CPB      RL0,#%FF        ! Is switch between stops? !
460C FFFF
460E E6FB            JR       EQ,CHKSW        ! No, wait for a position !
4610 8D18            CLR      R1              ! Start searching at bit 0 !
4612 2601   CHKPOS:  BITB     RL0,R1          ! Test next bit in RL0 !
4614 0800
4616 E602            JR       Z,DONE          ! If bit = 0, position is found !
4618 A910            INC      R1              ! Check next bit !
461A E8FB            JR       CHKPOS
461C 6F01   DONE:    LD       %6000,R1        ! Store switch position !
461E 6000
4620 7A00            HALT

4622        end      pgm_11_4a
```

Suppose that a faulty switch or defective PIO results in the input always being FF. How would you change the program to detect this error?

There is an unconditional jump, JR CHKOS, in the source program. Can you change the initial conditions so as to make this instruction unnecessary?

This example assumes that the switch is debounced in hardware. How would you change the program to debounce the switch in software?

What shift or rotate instructions could you use in place of BITB to detect the 0 bit?

Task 2: Wait for switch position to change.

Purpose: The program waits for the switch position to change and then waits until the switch reaches its new position. The program decodes the new position and places it in memory location 6000.

Flowchart:

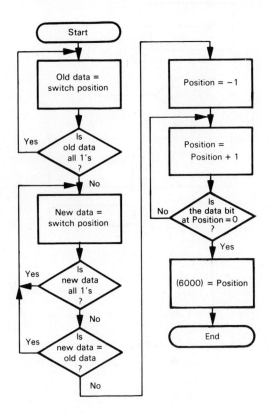

Program 11-4b:

```
            internal
                pgm_11_4b procedure
                entry
                    $abs     IBASE

4600 C84F           LDB      RL0,#%4F           ! Port A input !
4602 3A86           OUTB     PIOADR+5,RL0
4604 FF25
4606 3A04   FIRST:  INB      RH0,PIOADR+1       ! Read switch !
4608 FF21
460A 0A00           CPB      RH0,#%FF           ! Is it between stops? !
460C FFFF
460E E6FB           JR       EQ,FIRST           ! Wait for a position !
4610 3A84   SECOND: INB      RL0,PIOADR+1       ! Get new switch data !
4612 FF21
4614 0A08           CPB      RL0,#%FF           ! Is switch between stops? !
4616 FFFF
4618 E6FB           JR       EQ,SECOND
461A 8A08           CPB      RL0,RH0            ! Is position same as before? !
461C E6F9           JR       EQ,SECOND          ! Wait for it to change !
461E 2101           LD       R1,#%FFFF          ! Start switch position at -1 !
4620 FFFF
4622 A910   CHKPOS: INC      R1
4624 2601           BITB     RL0,R1             ! Find switch position !
4626 0800
4628 EEFC           JR       NZ,CHKPOS          ! Skip the 1 bits !
462A 6F01           LD       %6000,R1           ! Store the switch position !
462C 6000
462E 7A00           HALT

4630                end      pgm_11_4b
```

An alternative method for determining if the switch is in a position is:

```
            SECOND:  INB      RL0,PIOADR+1
                     COMB     RL0
                     JR       Z,SECOND
```

Why does this work? What happens to the input data?

11-5. A Single LED

Here we interface a single light-emitting diode to a Z8000 microprocessor. The LED can be attached so that either a logic zero or a logic one turns it on.

Figure 11-12 shows the circuitry required to interface an LED. The LED lights when its anode is positive with respect to its cathode (a). Therefore, you can either light the LED by grounding the cathode and having the computer supply a one to the anode (b) or by connecting the anode to +5 volts and having the computer supply a zero to the cathode (c). Using the cathode is the most common approach. The LED is brightest when it operates from pulsed currents of about 10 to 50 mA applied a few hundred times per second. LEDs have a very short turn-on time (in the microsecond range) so they are well suited to multiplexing (operating several from a single port). LED circuits usually need integrated circuit or transistor drivers and current-limiting resistors. MOS devices normally cannot drive LEDs directly and make them bright enough for easy viewing.

Note: The PIO has an output latch on both ports. However, the B port is normally used for output, since it has somewhat more drive capability. In particular, the B port outputs are capable of driving Darlington transistors: they provide 1.5 mA minimum at 1.5 V. Darlington transistors are high-gain transistors capable of switching large amounts of current at high speed; they are useful in driving solenoids, relays, and other devices.

Task: Turn the light on or off.

Purpose: The program turns a single LED either on or off.

a.   Send a logic one to the LED (turn a positive display on or a negative display off).

Program 11-5:

```
                    constant
                        LED1BIT := %(2)00000100      ! The LED is bit 2 !
                        LED     := 2                  ! The LED bit position !

                    internal
                        pgm_11_5 procedure
                        entry
                            $abs    IBASE

                    INILED:                           ! Light LED initially !
        4600 C8CF           LDB     RL0,#%CF          ! Port B control !
        4602 3A86           OUTB    PIOADR+7,RL0
        4604 FF27
        4606 8C88           CLRB    RL0               ! All B lines output !
        4608 3A86           OUTB    PIOADR+3,RL0
        460A FF23
        460C C804           LDB     RL0,#LED1BIT      ! Data for LED !
        460E 3A86           OUTB    PIOADR+3,RL0      ! Send data to LED !
        4610 FF23
        4612 7A00           HALT

                    ONLED:                            ! Light LED again !
        4614 3A84           INB     RL0,PIOADR+3      ! Get old data !
        4616 FF23
        4618 A482           SETB    RL0,#LED          ! Turn on LED bit !
        461A 3A86           OUTB    PIOADR+3,RL0      ! Send data to LED !
        461C FF23
        461E 7A00           HALT

        4620            end     pgm_11_5
```

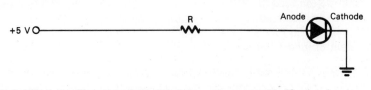

a. Basic LED circuitry. The resistor R should limit the maximum current to 50 mA and the average current to 10 mA.

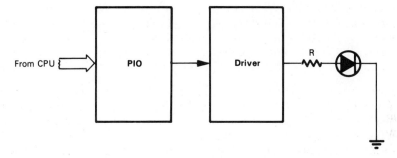

b. Interfacing an LED with positive logic. A logic '1' from the CPU turns the LED on.

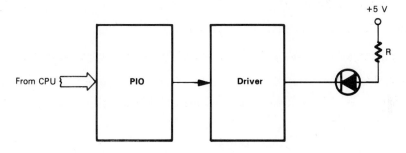

c. Interfacing an LED with negative logic. A logic '0' from the CPU turns the LED on.

Figure 11-12. Interfacing an LED

Note that we can read the PIO Data Output register when the PIO is in the output mode. We can also read any combination of input data and Data Output register contents when the PIO is in the control mode; the combination is defined by the assignment of inputs and outputs.

b. Send a logic zero to the LED (turn a positive display off or a negative display on).

The differences are that the constant LED1BIT must be replaced by its logical complement LED0BIT and SETB RL0,#LED must be replaced by RESB RL0, #LED. LED0BIT would be defined by:

```
constant
        LED0BIT := %(2)11111011
```

11-6. Seven-Segment LED Display

We illustrate interfacing a seven-segment LED display to a Z8000 microprocessor. The display may be either common-anode (negative logic) or common-cathode (positive logic).

Figure 11-13 shows the circuitry required to interface a seven-segment display. Each segment may have one, two, or more LEDs attached in the same way. There are two ways of connecting the displays. One is tying all the cathodes together to a positive voltage supply (see Figure 11-14b); this is a "common-anode" display, and a logic zero at the cathode lights a segment. So the common-cathode display uses positive logic and the common-anode display negative logic. Either display requires appropriate drivers and resistors.

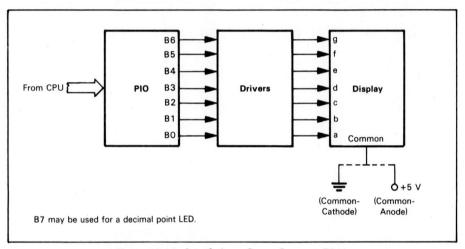

Figure 11-13. Interfacing a Seven-Segment Display

The common line from the display is tied either to ground or to +5 volts. The display segments are customarily labeled:

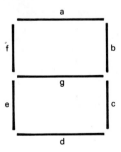

Bit 7 is always zero and the others are g, f, e, d, c, b, and a in decreasing order of significance (bits 6 to 0).

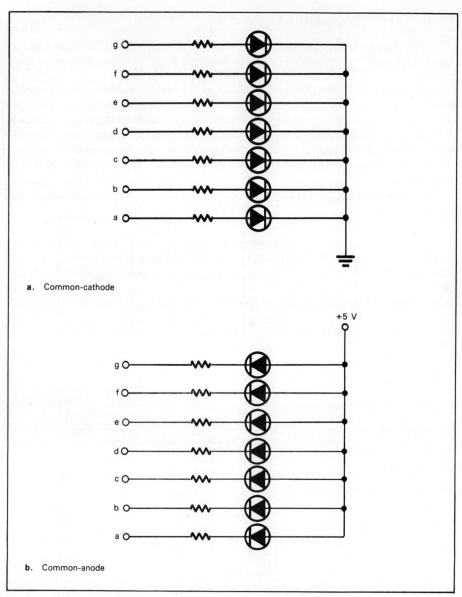

a. Common-cathode

b. Common-anode

Figure 11-14. Seven-Segment Display Organization

Table 11-2. Seven-Segment Representations of Decimal Numbers

Number	Hexadecimal Representation	
	Common-cathode	Common-anode
0	3F	40
1	06	79
2	5B	24
3	4F	30
4	66	19
5	6D	12
6	7D	02
7	07	78
8	7F	00
9	67	18
Bit 7 is always zero and the others are g, f, e, d, c, b, and a in decreasing order of significance (bits 6 to 0).		

The seven-segment display is widely used because it contains the smallest number of separately controlled segments that can provide recognizable representations of all the decimal digits (see Figure 11-15 and Table 11-12). Seven-segment displays can also produce some letters and other characters (see Table 11-3). Better representations require a substantially larger number of segments and more circuitry.[9] Since seven-segment displays are so popular, low-cost seven-segment decoder/drivers have become widely available. The most popular devices are the 7447 common-anode driver and the 7448 common-cathode driver;[10] these devices have Lamp Test inputs (that turn all the segments on) and blanking inputs and outputs (for blanking leading or trailing zeros).

Table 11-3. Seven-Segment Representations of Letters and Symbols

	Letter / Character	Hexadecimal Representation	
		Common-cathode	Common-anode
Upper-case Letters	A	77	08
	C	39	46
	E	79	06
	F	71	0E
	H	76	09
	I	06	79
	J	1E	61
	L	38	47
	O	3F	40
	P	73	0C
	U	3E	41
	Y	66	19
Lower-case Letters and Special Characters	b	7C	03
	c	58	27
	d	5E	21
	h	74	0B
	n	54	2B
	o	5C	23
	r	50	2F
	u	1C	63
	-	40	3F
	?	53	2C

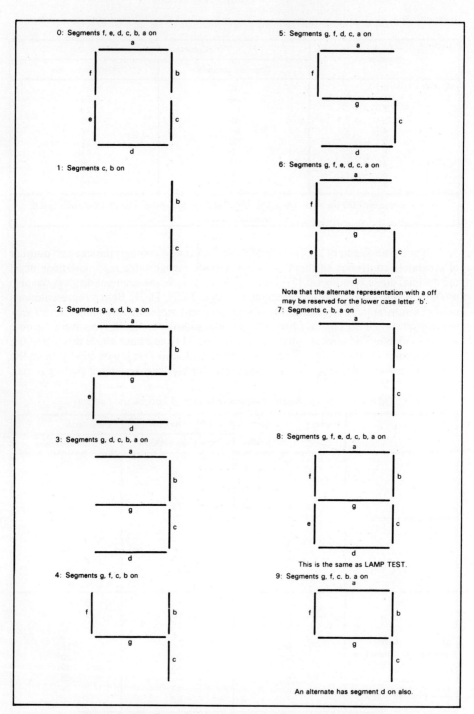

Figure 11-15. Seven-Segment Representation of Decimal Digits

Task 1: Display a decimal digit.

Purpose: Display the contents of memory location 6000 on a seven-segment display if it contains a decimal digit. Otherwise, blank the display.

Sample Problems:

 a. (6000) = 05
 Result is 5 on the display

 b. (6000) = 66
 Result is a blank display

Flowchart:

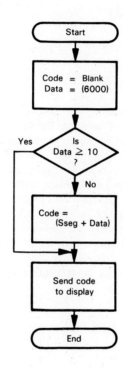

Program 11-6a:

```
                internal
                    pgm_11_6a procedure
                    entry
                         $abs      IBASE

    4600  C80F           LDB       RL0,#%0F         ! Port B output !
    4602  3A86           OUTB      PIOADR+7,RL0
    46C4  FF27
    4606  C800           LDB       RL0,#BLANK       ! Seven segment blank code !
    4608  6009           LDB       RL1,%6000        ! Get data to be displayed !
    460A  6000
    460C  0A09           CPB       RL1,#10          ! Valid decimal digit? !
    460E  0A0A
    4610  EA03           JR        GT,DSPLY         ! No, show a blank !
    4612  8C18           CLRB      RH1              ! Make R1 an index register !
    4614  6018           LDB       RL0,SSEG(R1)     ! Get seven segment code !
    4616  6200
    4618  3A86   DSPLY:  OUTB      PIOADR+3,RL0     ! Send code to display !
    461A  FF23
    461C  7A00           HALT

    461E           end       pgm_11_6a
```

SSEG is a direct address identifying the first byte of a table that contains seven-segment codes. The program logic assumes that the number identifying the character to be displayed can also serve as the index into the seven-segment codes table. Try creating this table for the characters listed in Tables 11-2 and 11-3.

Several displays may be multiplexed, as shown in Figure 11-16. A brief strobe on the B RDY line clocks the counter and directs data to the next display. Note that B RDY is tied directly back to $\overline{\text{B STB}}$; i.e., the ready line essentially provides its own acknowledgment. The internal timing of the PIO is such that this connection results in a strobe with a duration of one clock period. Such a brief strobe is exactly what the counter requires. RESET starts the decimal counter at 9 so that the first output operation clears the counter and directs data to the first display.

The following program uses the delay routine to pulse each of ten common-cathode displays for 1 ms.

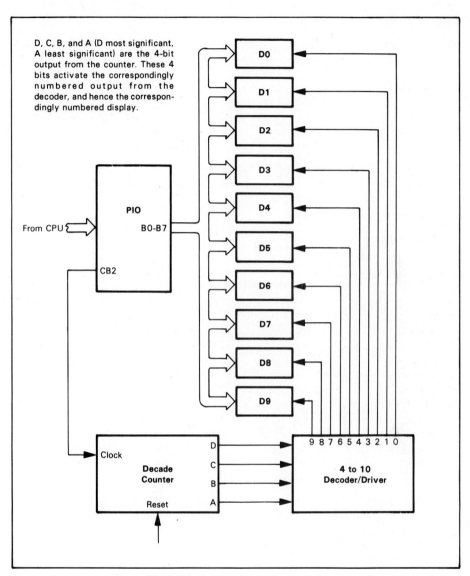

Figure 11-16. Multiplexed Seven-Segment Displays

Task 2: Display ten decimal digits.

Purpose: Display the contents of memory locations 6000 through 6009 on ten 7-segment displays that are multiplexed with a counter and a decoder.

Sample Problem:

```
(6000)  =  66
(6001)  =  3F
(6002)  =  7F
(6003)  =  7F
(6004)  =  06
(6005)  =  5B
(6006)  =  07
(6007)  =  4F
(6008)  =  6D
(6009)  =  7D
```

Display reads 4088127356

Program 11-6b:

```
                external
                DELAY procedure
                internal
                pgm_11_6b procedure
                entry
                     $abs    IBASE

4600 C80F            LDB     RL0,#%0F        ! Port B output !
4602 3A86            OUTB    PIOADR+7,RL0
4604 FF27
4606 7601            LDA     R1,%6000        ! First data address !
4608 6000
460A 2102            LD      R2,#PIOADR+3    ! I/O port address !
460C FF23
460E 2103            LD      R3,#10          ! Get character count !
4610 000A
4612 3A12    DSPLY:  OUTIB   @R2,@R1,R3      ! Send data to display !
4614 0328
4616 5F00            CALL    DELAY           ! Wait 1 ms !
4618 0000*
461A ECFB            JR      NOV,DSPLY       ! Return for more characters !
461C 7A00            HALT

461E            end     pgm_11_6b
```

This program assumes that the P/V status is not modified by the DELAY subroutine. INC and DEC do; DJNZ does not. If you cannot guarantee the P/V status across subroutine DELAY, how would you modify the program?

Note that I/O Port B must operate in output mode since the circuit uses handshaking port signals.

THE Z80 PARALLEL I/O DEVICE (PIO)

A variety of serial and parallel I/O devices can handle I/O transfers for the Z8000. We will describe (and use) just one parallel I/O device, the Z80-PIO,[5] and one serial I/O device, the Z80-SIO.[6] Should your microcomputer use different devices, your I/O programs will differ from those described in this chapter in detail but not concept.

A parallel I/O device, as its name would imply, transfers parallel data: in the case of the Z80-PIO, eight bits at a time. A serial I/O device, in contrast, transfers data one bit at a time.[7]

The Z80-PIO has two parallel I/O ports together with latches, buffers, flip-flops and other logic circuits needed for simple handshaking and interfacing. Fortunately you do not need to concern yourself with any of this logic. To write I/O programs you need only understand the operating options of the Z80-PIO. **Some** of these **options must be specified during an initialization phase** of your program, when you prepare the Z80-PIO for subsequent use. **Other options affect the way you write program steps that actually transmit or receive data.**

Figure 11-17 is a block diagram illustrating Z80-PIO logic. The device contains two nearly identical 8-bit ports — A, which is usually an input port, and B, which is usually an output port. Port A can also be used as a bidirectional port. Each port contains the following (see Figure 11-18):

- An 8-bit Data Output register

- An 8-bit Data Input register

- A 2-bit Mode Control register, which indicates whether the corresponding data pins are inputs (1) or outputs (0) in the control mode

- Two control lines (STB and RDY) that are configured by the Mode Control register. These lines can serve as the handshaking signals shown in Figures 11-5 and 11-6.

- A 2-bit Mask Control register (used only in the control mode) that determines the active polarity of the port lines and whether they will be logically ORed or ANDed to form an interrupt signal

- An 8-bit Mask register (used only in the control mode) that determines which port lines will be monitored to form the interrupt signal

- An 8-bit Vector Address register used with the interrupt system

- A 1-bit Interrupt Enable register which determines whether the port will generate interrupt requests

For now, we will be concerned only with the Mode Control registers, the Input and Output registers, and the control lines. We will discuss the interrupt-related features of the PIO in Chapter 12.

Operating options are specified by Control and Mask register bit settings. The assignment of most of these bits is more or less arbitrary; before using them you simply look them up in this chapter, or in Chapter 12.

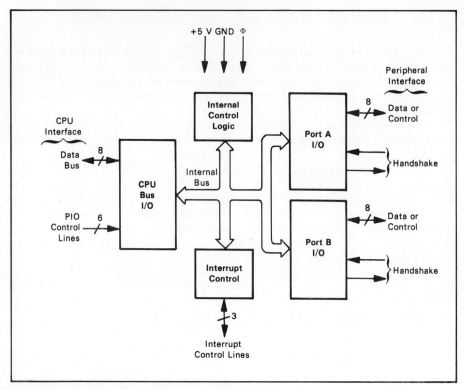

Figure 11-17. PIO Block Diagram

PIO ADDRESSES

Each PIO occupies four input port addresses and four output port addresses.
The B/A SEL (Port B or A select) and C/D SEL (Control or Data Select) lines choose
one of the four ports, as described in Table 11-4. Most often, designers attach address
bit A1 to the B/A SEL input and address bit A2 to the C/D SEL input. The PIO then
occupies four consecutive odd port addresses as described in the last column of Table
11-4. Only odd addresses are used so that the eight data lines can be connected to bits 0-
7 of the Z8000 CPU data bus. During byte I/O, the Z8000 uses data bus bits 0-7 for odd
I/O port addresses and bits 8-15 for even I/O port addresses.

16-bit I/O ports can be configured using paired PIO devices. A single 16-bit I/O
Port A will then be configured from the two A I/O ports of the two PIO devices; a single
16-bit I/O port B will be configured from the two B ports. Address bit A0 must select
one or the other of the paired PIO devices, while A1 connects to both B/A SEL inputs,
A2 connects to both C/D SEL inputs, and the paired PIO devices have the same device
select code. 16-bit I/O ports will then be addressed in 8-bit halves, just as 16-bit memory
words are addressed as 8-bit halves. Table 11-4 illustrates this alternative addressing.

There are more internal control registers than there are port addresses. **All control registers associated with one I/O port are accessed via a single I/O port address.**
For this to be possible some of the bits written to a control register are used as additional
address bits, as summarized in Table 11-5.

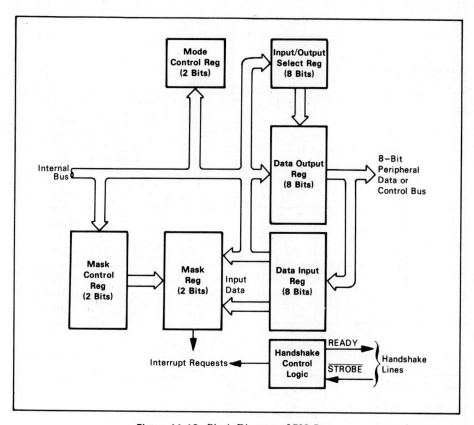

Figure 11-18. Block Diagram of PIO Port

Table 11-4. Z80-PIO Addresses

C/D SEL Address Line A1	B/A SEL Address Line A2	8-Bit Ports		16-Bit Ports	
		Register Addressed	Port Address	Register Addressed	Port Address
0	0	Data Register A	PIOADD + 1	Data Register A High-order byte	PIOADD
				Data Register A Low-order byte	PIOADD + 1
0	1	Data Register B	PIOADD + 3	Data Register B High-order byte	PIOADD + 2
				Data Register B Low-order byte	PIOADD + 3
1	0	Control Register A	PIOADD + 5	Control Register A High-order byte	PIOADD + 4
				Control Register A Low-order byte	PIOADD + 5
1	1	Control Register B	PIOADD + 7	Control Register B High-order byte	PIOADD + 6
				Control Register B Low-order byte	PIOADD + 7

Table 11-5. Addressing of PIO Control Registers

Register	Addressing
Mode Control	D3 = D2 = D1 = D0 = 1
Input/Output Control	Next Word if Mode Control Sets Mode 3
Mask Control Register	D3 = 0, D2 = D1 = D0 = 1
Interrupt Mask Register	Next Word if Mask Control Register is Loaded with D4 = 1
Interrupt Enable	D3 = D2 = 0, D1 = D0 = 1
Interrupt Vector	D0 = 0

Set Mode

M1	M0	Mode
0	0	Output
0	1	Input
1	0	Bidirectional
1	1	Bit Control

M1	M0	X	X	1	1	1	1

When selecting Mode 3, the next word must set the I/O Register:

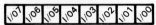

I/O = 1 sets bit to Input
I/O = 0 sets bit to Output

PIO Mode	Meaning	Control Word	
		(Binary)	(Hex)
0	Output	00001111	0F
1	Input	01001111	4F
2	Bidirec- tional	10001111	8F
3	Control	11001111	CF

Note that bits 4 and 5 are not used and could have any values.

Figure 11-19. Mode Control for the Z80 PIO

PIO MODE CONTROL

You set the PIO operating mode by writing a control word with the form shown in Figure 11-19. Note that bits D5 and D4 are not used. When power is turned on, the PIO is in mode 1 (input).

We may summarize the modes as follows:

1. **Mode 0 — OUTPUT from microprocessor to peripheral.**

   Writing data into the port Output register latches the data and causes it to appear on the port data bus. The Ready (RDY) line goes high to indicate Data Ready; it remains high until the peripheral sends a rising edge on the STROBE ($\overline{STB}$) line to indicate Data Accepted (or Device Ready). The rising edge of $\overline{STB}$ causes an interrupt if the interrupt has been enabled.

2. **Mode 1 — INPUT to microprocessor from peripheral.**

   The peripheral latches data into the Port Input register. The STROBE ($\overline{STB}$) signal is low, indicating Data Ready. The rising edge of $\overline{STB}$ causes an interrupt (if enabled) and deactivates RDY. When the CPU reads the data, RDY goes high to indicate Data Accepted (or Input Port Ready). Note that the PIO allows the peripheral to strobe data into the register regardless of the state of RDY. Therefore your program or the hardware must handle the problem of overrun, i.e., new data being placed into the register before the old data is read.

3. **Mode 2 — BIDIRECTIONAL between microprocessor and peripheral.**

   This mode uses all four handshake lines, so it is allowed only on Port A. The Port A RDY and $\overline{STB}$ signals are used for output control and the Port B RDY and $\overline{STB}$ signals are used for input control. The only difference between this mode and a combination of modes 0 and 1 is that data from the Port A Output register is placed on the port data lines only when $\overline{A\ STB}$ is low. This allows the Port A bus to be used bidirectionally. $\overline{A\ STB}$ is interpreted as Output Data Accepted and $\overline{B\ STB}$ is interpreted as Input Data Ready. Note that the B side control signals are governed by Input Register A in this mode.

4. **Mode 3 — CONTROL.**

   This mode does not use the RDY and $\overline{STB}$ signals. It is intended for status and control applications in which each bit has an individual meaning. When mode 3 is selected, the next control word sent to the PIO defines the directions of the port data bits. A '1' in a bit position makes the corresponding bus line an input, while a '0' makes it an output.

Note that the mode numbers have mnemonic value:

   0 — Output

   1 — Input

   2 — Bidirectional

Features of PIO Modes

Note the following features of the PIO modes:

1. In modes 0, 1, and 2 the peripheral indicates Data Ready or Data Accepted (Device Ready) with a rising edge on the $\overline{\text{STB}}$ line. This edge also causes an interrupt if the interrupt is enabled.

2. In modes 0, 1, and 2 the PIO indicates Data Ready or Data Accepted (Input Port Ready) by sending RDY high. This signal remains high until the next rising edge of $\overline{\text{STB}}$.

3. Only Port A can be used bidirectionally. If Port A is in mode 2 (bidirectional), Port B can only be in mode 3 (control) since no handshake lines are available for Port B.

4. The control mode (3) is the only mode in which the Input/Output Control register is used. Otherwise, the entire port is used for either input or output.

5. There is no way for the processor to determine if a pulse has occurred on $\overline{\text{STB}}$ if interrupts are not being used. The PIO is designed for use in interrupt-driven rather than polling systems (see Chapter 12). $\overline{\text{STB}}$ should be tied low if it is not being used.

6. The processor cannot directly control the RDY lines. The RDY line on a port goes high when data is transferred to or from the port and goes low on the rising edge of $\overline{\text{STB}}$.

7. The contents of the Data Output register can be read if the port is in the output or bidirectional mode. If the port is in the control mode, the output register data from the lines assigned as outputs can be read. The contents of control registers cannot be read.

8. If the RDY output is tied to the STB input on a port in the output mode, RDY will go high for one clock period after each output operation. This brief pulse can be used to multiplex displays as shown in Figure 11-1.

As Table 11-5 shows, a data word written to a Z80 PIO control register may contain further addressing information. P0 = 0 causes data bits D7-D0 to be loaded into the Interrupt Vector Address register. D3 = 0, D2 = D1 = D0 = 1 causes data bits D6 and D5 to be loaded into the Mask Control register and data bit D7 to be loaded into the Interrupt Enable register. If D4 = 1, the next control word is loaded into the Interrupt Mask register.

D3 = D2 = 0, D1 = D0 = 1 causes data bit D7 to be loaded into the Interrupt Enable register. D3 = D2 = D1 = D0 = 1 causes the data bits D7 and D6 to be loaded into the Mode Control register. If D7 = D6 = 1 (control mode), the next control word is loaded into the Input/Output Control register.

Since external addresses are shared, you must be sure to handle operations in the correct sequence. The meaning of a particular output instruction will vary with its position in the control output sequence. Therefore you should document the PIO configuration in detail in the program. The device is complex, and a reader of the program is unlikely to be able to make much sense out of the sequence of operations that configures it.

Usually the control registers of the PIO are loaded just once in the initialization phase of the program. The rest of the program uses PIO data registers only.

CONFIGURING THE PIO

A program must select required PIO options by writing appropriate codes to the various control registers. This selection (or configuration) is usually part of an initialization routine.

When power is turned on, the PIO comes up in the input mode with all interrupts disabled and control signals reset (low) except the Vector Address registers. However, the PIO does not necessarily return to the reset state when the microprocessor is reset. PIO configuration requires two steps:

1. Establish the mode of operation by writing appropriate control words to the Mode Control register. Interrupt control as well as I/O mode information may have to be sent.

2. If in mode 3, establish the directions of the I/O pins by writing a control word to the Input/Output Control register. This word must follow the control word that selected mode 3.

Let us now look at some examples of configuring a PIO without interrupts:

1. Output Port:

        LDB   RL0,#%(2)00001111   ! Make Port B output !
        OUTB   PIOADD+7,RL0

2. Input Port:

        LDB   RL0,#%(2)01001111   ! Make Port A input   !
        OUTB   PIOADD+5,RL0

3. Bidirectional Port:

        LDB   RL0,#%(2)10001111   ! Make Port A bidirectional !
        OUTB   PIOADD+5,RL0

Remember that only Port A can be bidirectional and that Port B must then be a control port.

4. Control Port, All Inputs:

        LDB   RL0,#%(2)11001111   ! Make Port A control !
        OUTB   PIOADD+5,RL0
        LDB   RL0,#%0FF   ! All bits inputs   !
        OUTB   PIOADD+5,RL0

5. Control Port, All Outputs:

        LDB   RL0,#%(2)11001111   ! Make Port A control !
        OUTB   PIOADD+7,RL0
        CLRB   RL0   ! All bits outputs   !
        OUTB   PIOADD+7,RL0

6. Control Port, Bidirectional

```
        LD      RL0,#%(2)11001111    ! Make Port A control !
        OUT     PIOADD+5,RL0
        LD      RL0,#%(2)01100010    ! Bits 1,5,6, inputs  !
                                     ! -- 0,2,3,4,7 out-   !
                                     ! puts                !
        OUT     PIOADD+5,RL0
```

You will rarely specify immediate binary data; we have done so above so that control codes are easier to understand. For example, "1. Output Port" would more likely be encoded as follows:

```
        LDB     RL0,#%0F         ! Make Port B output !
        OUTB    PIOADD+7,RL0
```

An even better method would be to use symbolic constants you have defined in the documentation part of the program:

```
        LDB     RL0,PIOOUT
        OUTB    PIOADD+PIOB+PIOCNTL,RL0
```

Also, when two bytes need to be output, as in 4, 5, and 6, consider this alternative:

```
        LD      R0,#%FFCF        ! Make Port A Control with !
                                 ! all input bits           !
        OUTB    PIOADD+5,RL0
        OUTB    PIOADD+5,RH0
```

If PIO devices have been configured in pairs to generate 16-bit I/O ports, then identical control codes must be output to each control register of the pair. To ensure this, load a 16-bit register with the same 8-bit code in each register half, **then execute a 16-bit OUT instruction.** Here are some examples:

1. 16-Bit Output Port:

```
        LD      R0,#%0F0F        ! Make Port B Output !
        OUT     PIOADD+6,R0
```

3. 16-Bit Bidirectional Port:

```
        LD      R0,#%8F8F        ! Make Port A bidirectional !
        OUT     PIOADD+4,R0
```

6. 16-Bit Control Port. Lines 1, 5, 6, 8, 9, 11 Inputs; Lines 0, 2, 3, 4, 7, 10, 12, 13, 14, 15 Outputs:

```
        LD      R0,#%CFCF        ! Make Port A Control !
        OUT     PIOADD+4,R0
        LD      R0,#%0B62        ! Define input and    !
                                 ! output lines        !
        OUT     PIOADD+4,R0
```

Note that the two halves of 16-bit data need not be identical when Control port lines are being defined as input or output. This is because there is no reason why pin assignments need to be the same in the two halves of a 16-bit Control port.

COMPLEX I/O DEVICES

More complex I/O devices differ from simple keyboards, switches, and displays in these ways:

1. They transfer data at higher rates.

2. They may have their own internal clocks and timing.

3. They produce status information and require control information, as well as transferring data.

Because of their higher data rates, you cannot handle these I/O devices casually. If the processor does not provide the appropriate service, the system may miss input data or produce erroneous output data. You are therefore working under much more exacting constraints than in dealing with simple devices. Interrupts are a convenient method for handling complex I/O devices, as we shall see in Chapter 12.

Synchronizing with I/O Devices

Peripherals such as keyboards, teletypewriters, cassettes, and floppy disks produce their own internal timing. These devices provide streams of data, separated by specific timing intervals. The computer must synchronize the initial input or output operation with the peripheral clock and then provide the proper interval between subsequent operations. A simple delay loop like the one shown previously can produce the timing interval. The synchronization may require one or more of the following procedures:

1. **Detecting a clock or strobe line transition which the peripheral provides for timing purposes.** A simple approach would be to tie the strobe to PIO $\overline{STB}$ input and respond to a change in the interrupt ($\overline{INT}$) output by executing an interrupt service routine. In a system that uses polling instead of interrupts, the strobe must connect to an input port and be latched if necessary. If the strobe is latched, a circuit must clear the latch as part of the subsequent input or output transfer.

2. **Finding the center of the time interval during which the data is stable.** Data should be sampled at the center of the pulse, not at the edges, where the data may be changing. The center of a pulse occurs one-half of a transmission interval after the edge. Sampling data at the pulse center also means that small timing errors have little effect on the accuracy of the reception.

3. **Recognizing a special starting code.** This is easy if the code is a single bit or if it occurs at a known time. The procedure is more complex if the code is long, or if it can start at any time.

4. **Sampling the data several times.** This reduces the probability of receiving data incorrectly from noisy lines. Majority logic (such as best 3 out of 4, or 5 out of 8) can be used to decide on the actual data value.

Control and Status Information

Reception is more difficult than transmission, since the computer must interpret timing information generated by the peripheral. The computer provides timing and formatting during transmission. In addition to data and timing, peripherals may require control information that selects modes of operation, starts or stops processes, clocks registers, enables buffers, chooses formats or protocols, provides operator displays, counts operations, or identifies the type and priority of the operation. The peripheral provides status information that indicates mode of operation, readiness of devices, presence of error conditions, format of protocol in use, and other states or conditions.

Microprocessors transmit and receive data, control, and status information in the same way; but there are big differences in the way each is interpreted. **As compared to data, control and status information seldom changes.** Data has a constant word size. Control or status information may be single bits, digits, words, or multiple words. Often single bits or short fields are combined and handled by a single input or output port.

Combining status and control information into bytes reduces the total number of I/O port addresses used by the peripherals. However, the combination does mean that individual status input bits must be separately interpreted and control output bits must be separately set. The procedures for isolating status bits and setting or resetting control bits are as follows:

Separating Out Status Bits:

Step 1.   Read status data from the peripheral.

Step 2.   Logical AND with a mask (the mask has ones in bit positions that must be examined and zeros elsewhere)

Step 3.   Shift the separated bits to the least significant bit positions (one or two bits may be shifted into sign and carry)

Setting and Clearing Bits:

Step 1.   Read prior control information

Step 2.   Use SET and RES instructions to set or reset bits; or use masks and the AND and OR instructions (to set bits, OR a mask with ones in the positions to be set and zeros elsewhere; to reset bits, AND a mask with zeros in the positions to be reset and ones elsewhere)

Step 3.   Send new control information to the peripheral

Here are some examples of separating and combining status bits:

1. A 3-bit field in bit positions 2 through 4 of PIO data is a scaling factor. Place that factor into RL0.

    ```
    ! Read status data from input port   !

    INB     RL0,PIOADR+1    ! Read status data              !

    ! Mask off scaling factor and shift  !

    ANDB    RL0,#%1C        ! Mask scaling factor           !
    SRLB    RL0,#2          ! Shift twice to normalize      !
    ```

2. Register RL0 contains a 2-bit field that must be placed into bit positions 3 and 4 of a PIO data register.

    ```
    ! Move data to field positions              !

    SLLB    RL0,#3          ! Shift data to bit positions   !
                            ! 3 and 4                       !
    ANDB    RL0,#%18        ! Clear out other bits          !

    ! Combine new field positions with old data !

    INB     RH0,PIOADDR+1   ! Get old data                  !
    AND     RH0,#%E7        ! Clear bits 3 and 4            !
    ORB     RL0,RH0         ! Combine new and old data      !
    OUTB    PIOADR+1,RL0    ! Output combined data          !
    ```

Documenting Status and Control Transfers

Documentation is a serious problem in handling control and status information. The meanings of status inputs or control outputs are seldom obvious. You should clearly indicate the purposes of input and output operations in the comments, e.g., "Check if reader is on," "Choose even parity option," or "Activate bit rate counter." The bit manipulation, Logical, and Shift instructions will otherwise be very difficult to remember, understand or debug.

PROGRAM EXAMPLES

11-7. An Unencoded Keyboard

Purpose: Recognize a key closure from an unencoded 3 × 3 keyboard and place the number of the key that was pressed into register RL0.

Keyboards are just collections of switches (see Figure 11-20). Small numbers of keys are easiest to handle if each key is attached separately to a bit of an input port. Interfacing the keyboard is then the same as interfacing a set of switches.

Keyboards with more than eight keys require more than one input port and therefore multibyte operations. This is particularly wasteful if the keys are logically separate, as in a calculator or terminal keyboard where a user will only strike one at a time. The number of input lines required may be reduced by interconnecting the keys as a matrix, as shown in Figure 11-21. Now each key represents a potential connection between a row and a column. The keyboard matrix requires n + m external lines, where n is the number of rows and m is the number of columns. This compares to n × m external lines if each key is independent. Table 11-6 compares the number of keys required by typical configurations.

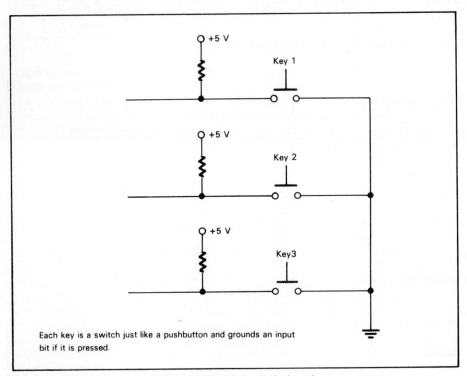

Each key is a switch just like a pushbutton and grounds an input bit if it is pressed.

Figure 11-20. A Small Keyboard

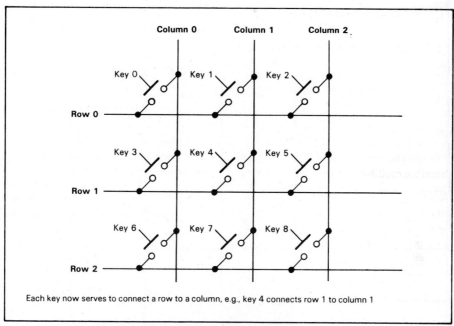

Figure 11-21. A Keyboard Matrix

Table 11-6. Comparison Between Independent Connections and Matrix Connections for Keyboards

Keyboard Size	Number of Lines with Independent Connections	Number of Lines with Matrix Connections
3 × 3	9	6
4 × 4	16	8
4 × 6	24	10
5 × 5	25	10
6 × 6	36	12
6 × 8	48	14
8 × 8	64	16

Program logic detects a depressed key by executing a keyboard scan. Keyboard scan logic uses the fact that a depressed key connects a row to a column at the matrix point corresponding to the key position. If a row is grounded, therefore, a depressed key will also ground the connected column. Program logic grounds a row by writing a 0 to the I/O port bit that connects to the row. Program logic executes a keyboard scan by grounding rows one at a time and examining columns by reading bit levels at I/O port pins connected to the columns. If a 0 bit is detected, then the depressed key has been located; it is at the junction of the row grounded by writing a 0 bit, and the column detected as grounded by reading a 0 bit.

For keyboard scan logic to work, rows must be connected to I/O port output pins and columns must be connected to I/O port input pins. One possible configuration is illustrated in Figure 11-22.

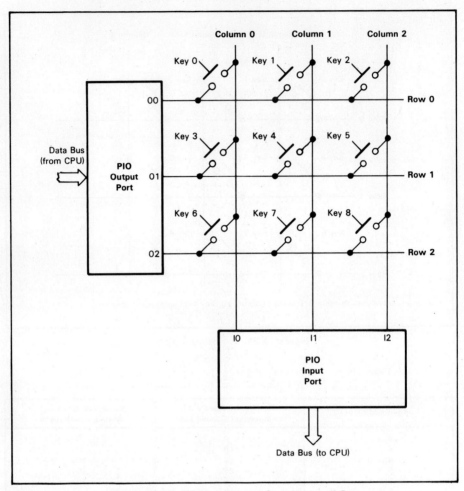

Figure 11-22. I/O Arrangement for a Keyboard Scan

Task 1: Determine key closure.

Purpose: Wait for a key to be pressed.

The procedure is as follows:

1. Ground all the rows by writing 0 to all the output bits.

2. Get the column inputs by reading the input port

3. Return to Step 1 if all bits corresponding to input columns are 1.

Flowchart:

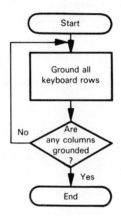

Program 11-7a:

```
             internal
                pgm_11_7a procedure
                entry
                   $abs      IBASE

4600 2100          LD        R0,#%4F0F      ! Port A input, Port B output !
4602 4F0F
4604 3A06          OUTB      PIOADR+5,RH0
4606 FF25
4608 3A86          OUTB      PIOADR+7,RL0
460A FF27
460C 8D08          CLR       R0             ! Ground all KB rows by... !
460E 3A86          OUTB      PIOADR+3,RL0   ! ...writing 0s to each !
4610 FF23
4612 3A84 KEYWAIT:INB        RL0,PIOADR+1   ! Read KB column levels !
4614 FF21
4616 0606          ANDB      RL0,#7         ! Isolate column bits !
4618 0707
461A 0A08          CPB       RL0,#7         ! Are any columns grounded ? !
461C 0707
461E E6F9          JR        EQ,KEYWAIT     ! Wait for one line to go 0 !
4620 7A00          HALT

4622             end       pgm_11_7a
```

PIO Port B is the keyboard output port. Port A is the input port.

Masking off unassigned column bits eliminates problems caused by unknown states of unused input lines.

We could generalize the routine by using labels for the output and masking patterns. Consider the following constants:

```
constant
    ALLG    :=      %F8
    OPEN    :=      %07
```

If ALLG and OPEN are used to specify keyboard masks, then by assigning new values to ALLG and OPEN, and reassembling the program, any new keyboard configuration could be accommodated.

Of course, one port of a PIO is all that is really necessary for a 3 × 3 or 4 × 4 keyboard. Try rewriting the program so that it uses only Port A. The PIO must be placed into the control mode so that lines can be individually selected as inputs or outputs.

Task 2: Identify key.

Purpose: Identify a depressed key and place the number of the key in Register R0.

The procedure is as follows:

1. Set the key number to −1. Set a counter to the number of rows.

2. Ground a row by sending a 0 to the grounded row and 1 to other rows. (Ground row 0 first).

3. Update the output pattern by shifting the zero bit left one position.

4. Fetch the column inputs by reading the input port.

5. If any column inputs are zero, proceed to Step 8.

6. Advance the key number to the start of the next row by adding the number of columns (i.e., number of keys in a row) to the current key number.

7. Decrement the row counter. Go to Step 2 if any rows have not been scanned, otherwise go to Step 10.

8. Add 1 to the key number. Shift column inputs right one bit and to the Carry flag.

9. If Carry = 1, return to Step 8.

10. End of program.

Flowchart:

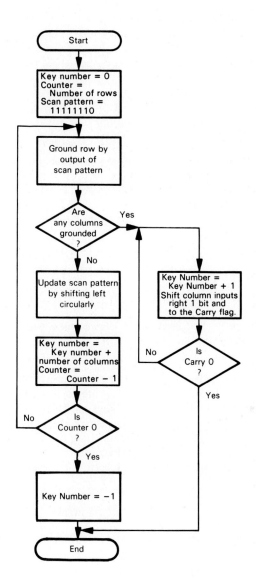

Program 11-7b:

```
            internal
                 pgm_ll_7b procedure
            entry
                 $abs     IBASE

  4600 2100         LD     R0,#%4F0F        ! Port A input, Port B output !
  4602 4F0F
  4604 3A06         OUTB   PIOADR+5,RH0
  4606 FF25
  4608 3A86         OUTB   PIOADR+7,RL0
  460A FF27
  460C 2101         LD     R1,#%0303        ! RH1 number of rows... !
  460E 0303                                 ! ...RL1 number of columns !
  4610 2102         LD     R2,#%FE07        ! RH2 scan pattern, RL2 KB mask !
  4612 FE07
  4614 C8FF         LDB    RL0,#%FF         ! Start counting keys at -1 !
  4616 3A26  FROW:  OUTB   PIOADR+1,RH2     ! Scan a row !
  4618 FF21
  461A B2A0         RLB    RL2              ! Update pattern for next row !
  461C 3A04         INB    RH0,PIOADR+3     ! Get keyboard column data !
  461E FF23
  4620 86A0         ANDB   RH0,RL2          ! Mask column bits !
  4622 8AA0         CPB    RH0,RL2          ! Test for grounded column bits !
  4624 EE04         JR     NZ,FCOL          ! Figure which key is grounded !
  4626 8098         ADDB   RL0,RL1          ! Advance key number to next row !
  4628 F10A         DBJNZ  RH1,FROW         ! Examine next row !
  462A C8FF         LDB    RL0,#%FF         ! No depressed key found !
  462C E803         JR     DONE
  462E A880  FCOL:  INCB   RL0              ! Increment key number !
  4630 B204         RRB    RH0              ! Is this column grounded? !
  4632 EFFD         JR     NC,FCOL          ! No, next key !
  4634 7A00  DONE:  HALT

  4636        end    pgm_ll_7b
```

Each time a row scan fails, we must add the number of columns to the key number so as to move past the present row (try it on the keyboard in Figure 11-22).

What is the result of the program if no keys are being pressed? Note the extra INCB RL0 instruction which differentiates between no keys pressed and the last key being pressed. What is the final value in RL0 for these two cases?

An alternative approach uses a PIO port in control mode, so that input and output lines can coexist. Program logic would then proceed as follows:

1. Ground all the columns and save the row inputs.

2. Ground all the rows and save the column inputs.

3. Use the row and column inputs together to determine the key number from a table.

Try to write a program using this procedure.

This program can be generalized by using names to specify the number of rows, the number of columns, and the masking pattern.

11-8. An Encoded Keyboard

Purpose: Fetch data, when it is available, from an encoded keyboard that provides a strobe with each keystroke.

An encoded keyboard provides a unique code for each key. It is internal circuitry that scans the keyboard and identifies depressed keys; it is therefore more expensive than an unencoded keyboard, but it is easier to program.

Encoded keyboards may use diode matrices, TTL encoders, or MOS encoders. The codes may be ASCII, EBCDIC, or a custom code.

The encoding circuitry may also debounce the keys and handle two or more keys depressed at the same time. This is referred to as "rollover." If one key is depressed, and then another is depressed before the first is released, rollover logic treats this as two separate keystrokes, in the sequence that they were first depressed. Simple rollover handles two simultaneously depressed keys only, losing third and subsequent simultaneous keystrokes. More complex rollover logic separates a number of simultaneously depressed keys.

The encoded keyboard also provides a strobe with each data transfer. The strobe signals that a new closure has occurred. Figure 11-23 shows the interface between an encoded keyboard and the Z8000 microprocessor. The rising edge of the strobe latches the data into the input port. We also tie the strobe to one pin of I/O Port B so that the CPU can determine when a strobe has occurred.

We have assumed in the program that the strobe signal is long enough for the CPU to handle it in software. If it is not, the signal will have to be latched and cleared (with RDY) when the input or output transfer occurs.

You may have to watch the polarity of the strobe, since the PIO always reacts to a rising edge. An inverter gate may be necessary.

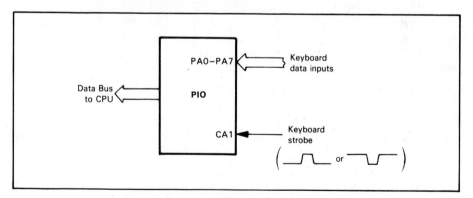

Figure 11-23. I/O Interface for an Encoded Keyboard

Task: Input from keyboard.

Purpose: Wait for the rising edge of a strobe at the B port of a PIO and then place the data from Port A into Register RL0.

Flowchart:

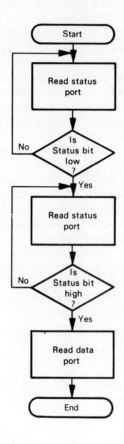

Program 11-8:

```
                internal
                   pgm_11_8 procedure
                   entry
                        $abs      IBASE

4600 2100               LD        R0,#%4FCF          ! Port A input, Port B control !
4602 4FCF
4604 3A06               OUTB      PIOADR+5,RH0
4606 FF25
4608 3A86               OUTB      PIOADR+7,RL0
460A FF27
460C C8FF               LDB       RL0,#%FF           ! Make all port B lines input !
460E 3A86               OUTB      PIOADR+7,RL0
4610 FF27
4612 3A84      SRCHL:   INB       RL0,PIOADR+3       ! Get status from port B !
4614 FF23
4616 A684               BITB      RL0,#4             ! Has line gone low? !
4618 EEFC               JR        NZ,SRCHL           ! No, wait until it does !
461A 3A84      SRCHH:   INB       RL0,PIOADR+3       ! Examine bit 4 port B again !
461C FF23
461E A684               BITB      RL0,#4             ! Has it gone high? !
4620 E6FC               JR        Z,SRCHH            ! No, wait until it does !
4622 3A84               INB       RL0,PIOADR+1       ! Rising edge found, fetch data !
4624 FF21
4626 7A00               HALT

4628           end       pgm_11_8
```

If the CPU repeats this routine, it will not get another character until the next rising edge occurs on the strobe line. A continuing high level on the strobe line will be ignored.

The LDB RL0, #%FF instruction could be replaced by an EXTS instruction that loads FF into RH0. Do you see why? Try rewriting the two relevant instructions to accommodate this variation.

11-9. Digital-to-Analog Converter

Purpose: Send data to an 8-bit digital-to-analog converter, which has an active-low latch enable.

Digital-to-analog converters produce the continuous signals required by meters, amplifiers, servomechanisms, and other electrical and mechanical output devices. Typical converters consist of switches and resistor ladders with the appropriate resistance values.[11]

Figure 11-24 illustrates the 8-bit Signetics NE5018 D/A converter, which contains an on-chip 8-bit parallel data input latch. A low level on the $\overline{LE}$ (Latch Enable) input gates the input data into the latches, where it remains after $\overline{LE}$ goes high.

Figure 11-25 illustrates an interface between the D/A converter and a Z8000 microprocessor. Here Port A of the PIO is used to generate the Latch Enable signal. The RDY line from the PIO could be tied to the $\overline{STB}$ line to form a pulse lasting one clock cycle, however, one clock cycle may not be long enough, since the NE5018 requires a 400 ns pulse. Furthermore, the polarity is the opposite of that needed by the NE5018.

Note that the PIO latches the output data. The data therefore remains stable during and after the conversion. The converter typically requires only a few microseconds to produce an analog output. Thus, the converter latch could be left enabled if the port were not used for any other purpose.

In applications where eight bits of resolution are not enough, higher precision converters can be used.

Task: Output to converter.

Purpose: Send the data in memory byte 6000 to the converter.

Flowchart:

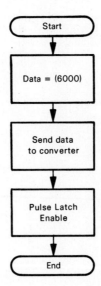

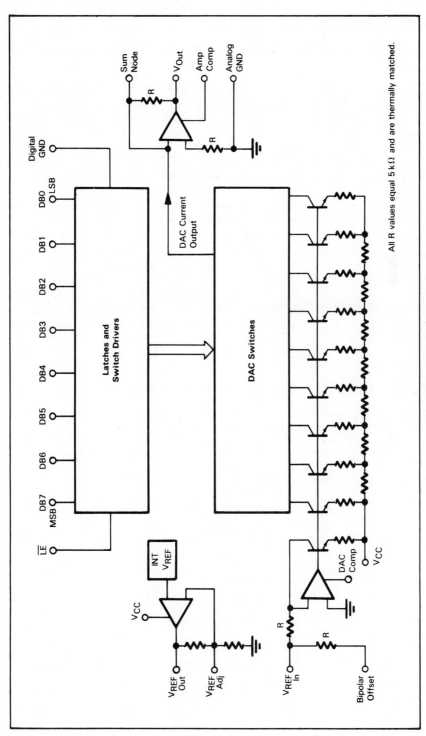

Figure 11-24. Signetics NE5018 D/A Converter

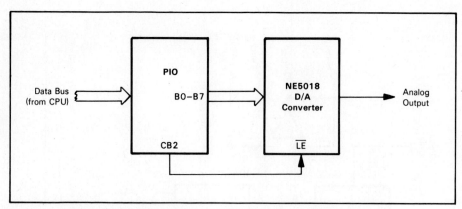

Figure 11-25. I/O Interface for an 8-Bit Digital-to-Analog Converter

Program 11-9:

```
                internal
                pgm_11_9 procedure
                entry
                        $abs    IBASE

4600 2100       LD      R0,#%CF00       ! Port A control, 8 lines output !
4602 CF00
4604 3A06       OUTB    PIOADR+5,RH0
4606 FF25
4608 3A86       OUTB    PIOADR+5,RL0
460A FF25
460C C80F       LDB     RL0,#%0F        ! Port B output !
460E 3A86       OUTB    PIOADR+7,RL0
4610 FF27
4612 6008       LDB     RL0,%6000       ! Get data !
4614 6000
4616 3A86       OUTB    PIOADR+3,RL0    ! Send data to D/A converter !
4618 FF23
461A 3A84       INB     RL0,PIOADR+1    ! Don't change other lines !
461C FF21
461E A284       RESB    RL0,#4          ! Send bit 4 low... !
4620 3A86       OUTB    PIOADR+1,RL0
4622 FF21
4624 A484       SETB    RL0,#4          ! ...then high !
4626 3A86       OUTB    PIOADR+1,RL0
4628 FF21
462A 7A00       HALT

462C            end     pgm_11_9
```

We could use the automatic brief strobe from B ACK if the Latch Enable were active-high (and if this strobe were long enough when B ACK is tied back to $\overline{\text{B STB}}$). The program would then be:

```
LDB     RL0,#%0F        ! Make Port B output  !
OUTB    PIOADR+7,RL0
LDB     RL0,%6000       ! Data                !
OUTB    PIOADR+3,RH0
HALT
```

An inverter gate could produce an active-low signal. Note how many fewer instructions are necessary.

Often a program will transmit a sequence of data values to a DAC. The DAC will translate the data sequence into an equivalent, continuous analog signal. How would you modify the program to output a sequence of bytes from the data memory?

11-10. Analog-to-Digital Converter

Purpose: Fetch data from an 8-bit analog-to-digital converter. It requires an Initiate Conversion pulse to start the conversion process and has a Data Valid line to indicate the availability of valid data.

Analog-to-digital converters receive continuous signals produced by various types of sensors and transducers.[12] The converter produces digital values corresponding to the sampled analog input. The microprocessor reads these digital values.

One form of analog-to-digital converter is the successive approximation device, which makes a direct 1-bit comparison during each clock cycle. Such converters are fast but have little noise immunity. Dual slope integrating converters are another form of analog-to-digital converter. These devices take longer but are more resistant to noise. Other techniques, such as the incremental charge balancing technique, are also used.

Older analog-to-digital converters usually require some external analog and digital circuitry, although complete units are becoming available at low cost.

Figure 11-26 shows the 8-bit Teledyne Semiconductor 8703 A/D converter. The device contains a result latch and tristate data outputs. A pulse on the Initiate Conversion line starts conversion of the analog input; after about two milliseconds the result will go to the output latches, and the Data Valid output will indicate this by switching first low and then high. Data is read from the latches by applying '0' to the $\overline{\text{ENABLE}}$ input.

Figure 11-27 shows the interface between the Z8000 microprocessor and the 8703 converter.[13] Port B generates an Initiate Conversion pulse (active-high) of sufficient length. The Data Valid signal is tied to $\overline{\text{A STB}}$ so that Data Valid going low and then high will latch the converted data into Port A. The Data Valid signal is also tied to a bit of Port B so that the CPU can determine its value. The important edge on the Data Valid line is the low-to-high edge, which indicates the completion of the conversion. As with the encoded keyboard, additional circuitry will be necessary if the pulse on Data Valid is too short to be handled in software. Note that we are using Port B here for both status and control.

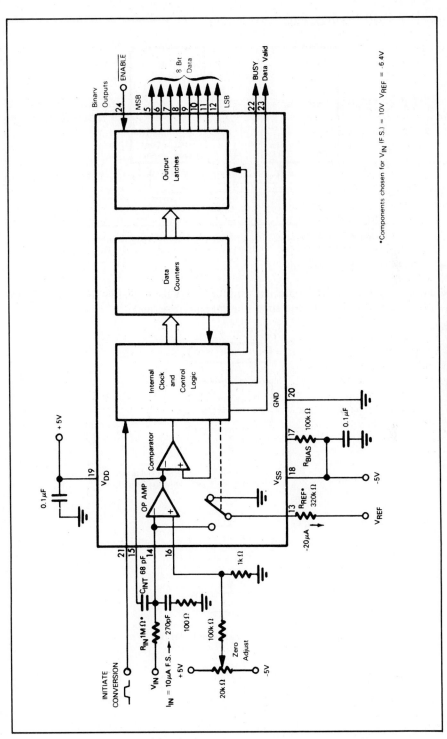

Figure 11-26. Teledyne 8703 A/D Converter

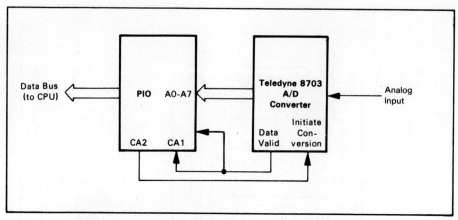

Figure 11-27. Interface for an 8-bit Analog-to-Digital Converter

Task: Input from converter.

Purpose: Start the conversion process, wait for Data Valid to go low and then high, and then read the data and store it in memory byte 6000.

Flowchart:

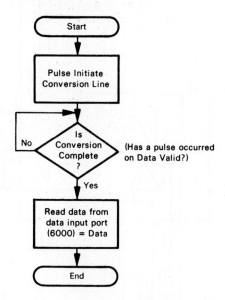

The PIO serves as a parallel data port, a status port, and a control port.

Program 11-10:

```
              internal
                pgm_11_10 procedure
                entry
                   $abs     IBASE
4600 C84F          LDB      RL0,#%4F        ! Port A input !
4602 3A86          OUTB     PIOADR+5,RL0
4604 FF25
4606 2100          LD       R0,#%CF0F       ! Port B control... !
4608 CF0F
460A 3A06          OUTB     PIOADR+7,RH0    ! ...with B0-3 input... !
460C FF27
460E 3A86          OUTB     PIOADR+7,RL0    ! ...B4-7 output !
4610 FF27
4612 3A84          INB      RL0,PIOADR+3    ! Save other port B lines... !
4614 FF23
4616 A485          SETB     RL0,#5          ! ...& set "initiate conversion" !
4618 3A86          OUTB     PIOADR+3,RL0
461A FF23
461C A285          RESB     RL0,#5          ! Toggle the bit !
461E 3A86          OUTB     PIOADR+3,RL0
4620 FF23
4622 3A84  WTLOW:  INB      RL0,PIOADR+3    ! Data valid (bit 2) gone low? !
4624 FF23
4626 A682          BITB     RL0,#2
4628 EEFC          JR       NZ,WTLOW        ! No, wait !
462A 3A84  WTHI:   INB      RL0,PIOADR+3    ! Wait for it to go high again !
462C FF23
462E A682          BITB     RL0,#2
4630 E6FC          JR       Z,WTHI
4632 3A84          INB      RL0,PIOADR+1    ! Fetch data on rising edge !
4634 FF21
4636 6E08          LDB      %6000,RL0       ! Store data from converter !
4638 6000
463A 7A00          HALT

463C              end     pgm_11_10
```

How would you modify the program to receive a long stream of data from the ADC?

11-11. A Teletypewriter (TTY)

We will demonstrate the transfers of data to and from a standard 10-character-per-second serial teletypewriter.

The common teletypewriter transfers serial asynchronous data as follows:

1.   The line is normally in the one state (high).

2.   A Start bit (low, or zero bit) precedes each character.

3.   The character is usually 7-bit ASCII with the least significant bit transmitted first.

4.   A Parity bit may follow the character; the combined parity of the character and this bit may be even or odd, or the Parity bit may be fixed at zero or one.

5.   Two stop bits (high, or one bit) follow each character.

Figure 11-28 shows this format. Note that eleven bits are transmitted for each character; only seven contain data. Since the data rate is ten characters per second, the bit rate is 10×11, or 110 baud. Each bit therefore has a width of 1/110 of a second, or about 9.1 milliseconds. This is an average width; the teletypewriter does not maintain it accurately.

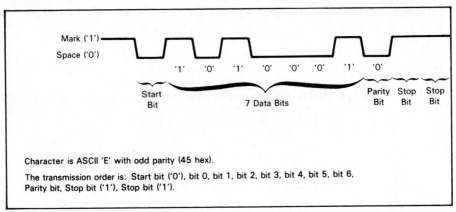

Figure 11-28. Teletypewriter Data Format

For a teletypewriter to communicate properly with a computer, the following procedures are necessary: receive data from the teletypewriter, and transmit data to the teletypewriter.

Task 1: Read data.

Purpose: Fetch data from a teletypewriter through bit 7 of a PIO data port and place the data into memory location 6000. For procedure, see Figure 11-29. Assume that the serial port is bit 7 of the PIO and that no parity or framing check is necessary.

Program 11-11a:

```
                external
                    DHALF procedure
                    DFULL procedure
                internal
                    pgm_11_11a procedure
                    entry
                            $abs        IBASE

    4600  2100              LD      R0,#%004F       ! Port A input, clear RH0 !
    4602  004F
    4604  3A86              OUTB    PIOADR+5,RL0
    4606  FF25
    4608  3A84  WTSTART:INB  RL0,PIOADR+1    ! Read serial data line !
    460A  FF21
    460C  A687              BITB    RL0,#7          ! Wait for the 0 start bit !
    460E  EEFC              JR      NZ,WTSTART
    4610  5F00              CALL    DHALF           ! Delay one half bit time !
    4612  0000*
    4614  5F00              CALL    TTYRCV          ! Get character in RH0 !
    4616  461E
    4618  6E00              LDB     %6000,RH0       ! Store character in memory !
    461A  6000
    461C  7A00              HALT

    461E            end     pgm_11_11a


                global
                    TTYRCV procedure        ! Returns 7 bit character in RH0 !
                    entry

    461E  93F1              PUSH    @R15,R1
    4620  C908              LDB     RL1,#8          ! RL1 counts number of bits !
    4622  5F00  RCVBIT: CALL  DFULL             ! Delay 1 bit time !
    4624  0000*
    4626  3A14              INB     RH1,PIOADR+1    ! Next bit please !
    4628  FF21
    462A  B211              SLLB    RH1             ! Shift bit 7 into carry... !
    462C  0001
    462E  B20C              RRCB    RH0             ! ...then into high order RH0 !
    4630  F908              DBJNZ   RL1,RCVBIT      ! Get all 8 bits into RH0 !
    4632  8C04              TESTB   RH0             ! Done, check parity !
    4634  EC00*             JR      PO,PERR         ! Odd parity is an error !
    4636  5F00              CALL    DFULL           ! Wait for stop bit !
    4638  0000*
    463A  3A14              INB     RH1,PIOADR+1
    463C  FF21
    463E  A617              BITB    RH1,#7          ! Should be a 1 !
    4640  E600*             JR      Z,FRERR         ! Framing error if not !
    4642  5F00              CALL    DFULL           ! Repeat for second stop bit !
    4644  0000*
    4646  3A14              INB     RH1,PIOADR+1
    4648  FF21
    464A  A617              BITB    RH1,#7
    464C  E600*             JR      Z,FRERR
    464E  A207              RESB    RH0,#7          ! Strip off parity bit !
    4650  97F1              POP     R1,@R15
    4652  9E08              RET

    4658            end     TTYRCV
```

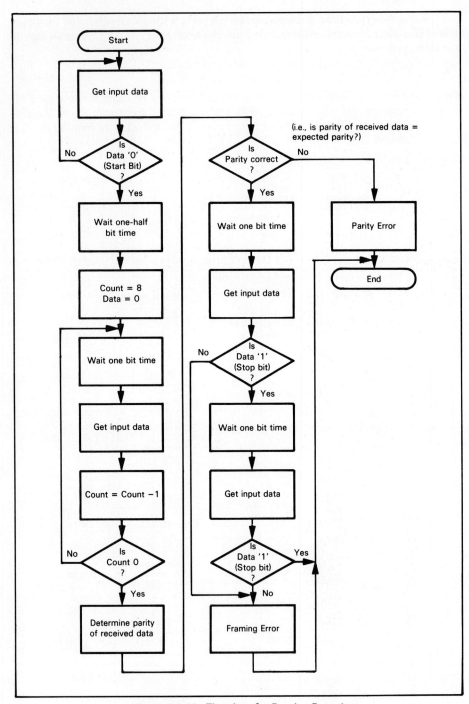

Figure 11-29. Flowchart for Receive Procedure

DHALF is a subroutine that executes a 4.05 millisecond delay. DFULL is a subroutine that executes a 9.1 millisecond delay. To be precise, these delays would have to be less than 4.05 and 9.1 milliseconds by the execution time of surrounding instructions. But this timing error is insignificant; it represents microseconds of error within milliseconds of delay. The cumulative error is still insignificant since synchronization restarts with the start bit of each character. Therefore the maximum error is the accumulation of eleven single bit timing errors.

DHALF and DFULL could both use subroutine DELAY to generate required time delays. Can you modify DELAY to increase the standard delay to 1.01 milliseconds? Then a simple multiple will allow DHALF to compute 4.04 milliseconds, while DFULL computes 9.09 milliseconds.

Branches are shown to parity error (PERR) and framing error (FRERR) routines which we will not concern ourselves with for now. Our parity error logic arbitrarily assumes even parity as correct.

Task 2: Write data.

Purpose: Transmit data to a teletypewriter through bit 0 of a PIO data register. The data is in memory location 6000.

Figure 11-30 flowcharts the transmit data procedure outlined below:

Step 1.   Transmit a Start bit (i.e., a zero).

Step 2.   Transmit the seven data bits, starting with the least significant bit.

Step 3.   Generate and transmit the Parity bit (assume even parity).

Step 4.   Transmit two Stop bits (i.e., two logic ones).

The transmission routine must wait one bit time between each operation.

Program 11-11b:

```
                external
                   DFULL procedure
                internal
                   pgm_11_11b procedure
                   entry
                      $abs       IBASE
4600 C80F             LDB        RL0,#%0F      ! Make port A output !
4602 3A86             OUTB       PIOADR+5,RL0
4604 FF25
4606 6008             LDB        RL0,%6000     ! Get character to be sent !
4608 6000
460A 8C84             TESTB      RL0           ! Must have even parity !
460C E401             JR         PE,PAROK
460E A487             SETB       RL0,#7
4610 C003   PAROK:    LDB        RH0,#3        ! 11 bits in R0: 2 stop bits... !
4612 B301             SLL        R0            ! ...(ones) and one start... !
4614 0001                                      ! ...bit (zero) !
4616 C90B             LDB        RL1,#11       ! Number of bits to send !
4618 3A86   TBIT:     OUTB       PIOADR+1,RL0  ! Transmit next bit !
461A FF21
461C B301             SRL        R0
461E FFFF
4620 5F00             CALL       DFULL         ! Delay one bit time !
4622 0000*
4624 F907             DBJNZ      RL1,TBIT
4626 7A00             HALT

4628             end       pgm_11_11b
```

DFULL is the same delay subroutine we used to receive a character.

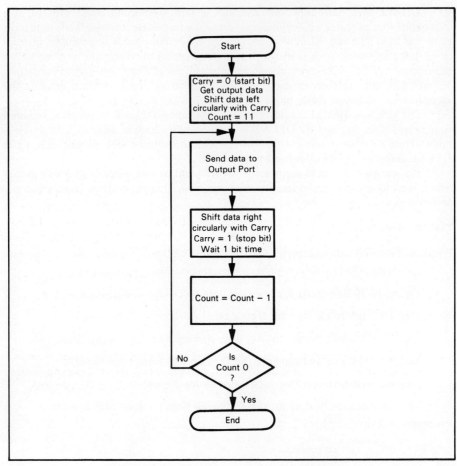

Figure 11-30. Flowchart for Transmit Procedure

UART/USART

These procedures are sufficiently common and complex to merit a special LSI device: the UART, or Universal Asynchronous Receiver/Transmitter.[14] The UART provides the entire logic interface between a microprocessor transferring parallel data, and external logic transferring serial data. Typical UART capabilities include:

1. Ability to handle various character sizes (usually 5 to 8 bits), parity options, and numbers of Stop bits (usually 1, 1-1/2, and 2).

2. Indicators for framing errors, parity errors, and "overrun errors" (failure to read a character before another one is received).

3. RS-232[15] control signals; i.e., a Request-to-Send (RTS) output signal that indicates the presence of data to communications equipment and a Clear-to-Send (CTS) input signal that indicates, in response to RTS, the readiness of the communications equipment. There may be provisions for other RS-232 signals, such as Data Carrier Detect (DCD), Received Signal Quality, Data Set Ready (DSR), or Data Terminal Ready (DTR).

4. Tristate data lines and control compatibility with a microprocessor.

5. Clock options that allow the UART to sample incoming data several times in order to detect false Start bits and other errors.

6. Interrupt facilities and controls.

UARTs are inexpensive ($5 to $50, depending on features) and easy to use.

The USART is another serial I/O device; it can handle both synchronous and asynchronous serial data transfers.[18] One such device, the Z80-SIO, is described next.

THE Z80 SERIAL INPUT/OUTPUT DEVICE (SIO)

Logic of the Z80 Serial Input/Output device, or SIO, is illustrated in Figure 11-31. It can serve a variety of communications functions, but we will only discuss its use as a simple asynchronous receiver/transmitter.[17]

The SIO has two complete serial I/O channels (A and B) which can both receive and transmit serial data (see Figure 11-32). Channels that can receive and transmit simultaneously are called full-duplex. Alternatives include half-duplex (able to transmit and receive, but not at the same time), and simplex (receive-only or transmit-only).

SIO ADDRESSES

An SIO occupies four input port addresses and four output port addresses. The B/$\overline{\text{A}}$ (Channel B or A select) and C/$\overline{\text{D}}$ (Control or Data Select) lines choose one of the four ports as described in Table 11-7. Most often, designers attach address bit A1 to the B/$\overline{\text{A}}$ input and address bit A2 to the C/$\overline{\text{D}}$ input. The SIO then occupies four consecutive odd port addresses as described in the last column of Table 11-7. This is done so that the eight data lines of the SIO can be connected to data lines 0-7 of the CPU data bus. I/O instructions with an odd port address use these lines.

SIO REGISTERS

As with the PIO, SIOs have more control registers than addresses. In fact, each SIO has eight registers in each channel for control and three registers for status. Figure 11-33 diagrams each control or Write register; Figure 11-34 diagrams each status or Read register. Write Register 0 contains three bits that direct the next transfer to or from another register. Note, in Figure 11-33, that these three bits occupy the three least significant bit positions; zeros in the other bit positions indicate a control byte that has no function other than addressing.

Write Registers

The Z80 SIO contains eight registers in each channel that are programmed (written into) by the system software to configure the functional personality of each channel. All Write registers, with the exception of Write Register 0, require two bytes to be properly programmed. The first byte contains three bits that point to the selected register (D0-D2); the second byte is the actual control byte that is being written to that register to configure the SIO.

Write Register 0 is a special case. RESET (either internal command or external input) will initialize the SIO to Write Register 0. All basic commands (CMD2-CMD0) and CRC controls (CRC0, CRC1) can be accessed with a single byte using Write Register 0.

When addressing any other Write register, the basic commands (CMD2-CMD0) and the CRC controls (CRC0, CRC1) may be included in the first control byte, so that maximum system control and flexibility is maintained.

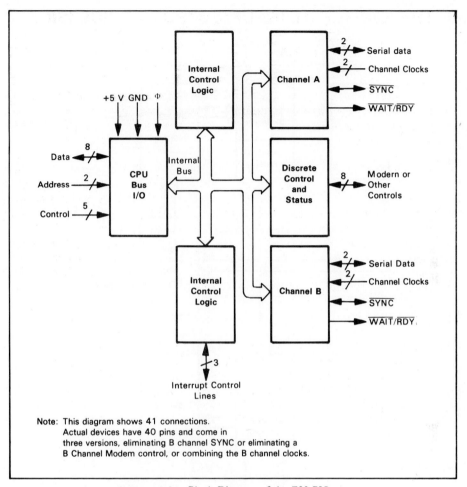

Figure 11-31. Block Diagram of the Z80 PIO

Table 11-7. SIO Addresses

Control or Data Select	Channel B or A Select	Register Addressed	Port Address
0	0	Data Register A	SIOADD + 1
0	1	Data Register B	SIOADD + 3
1	0	Control A	SIOADD + 5
1	1	Control B	SIOADD + 7

The port addresses assume that C/$\overline{\text{D}}$ is tied to A2 and B/$\overline{\text{A}}$ to A1

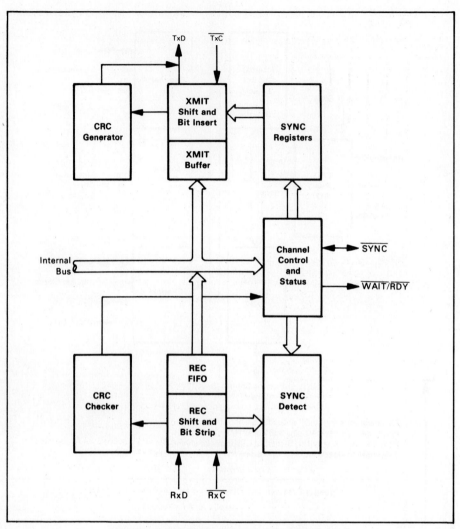

Figure 11-32. Block Diagram of the SIO Channel

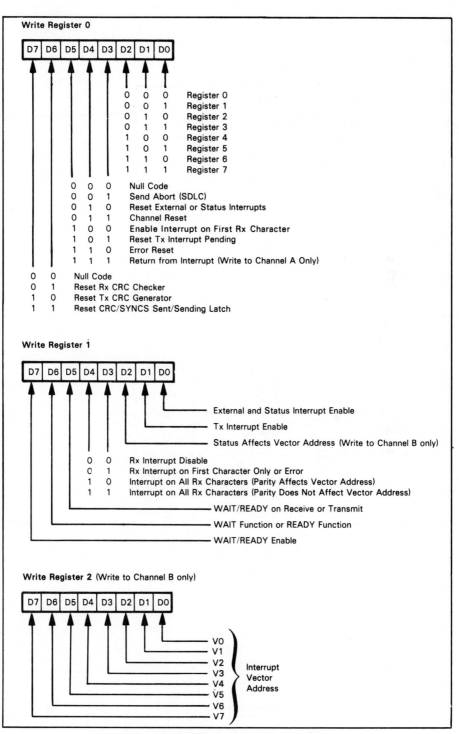

Figure 11-33. SIO Control or Write Registers

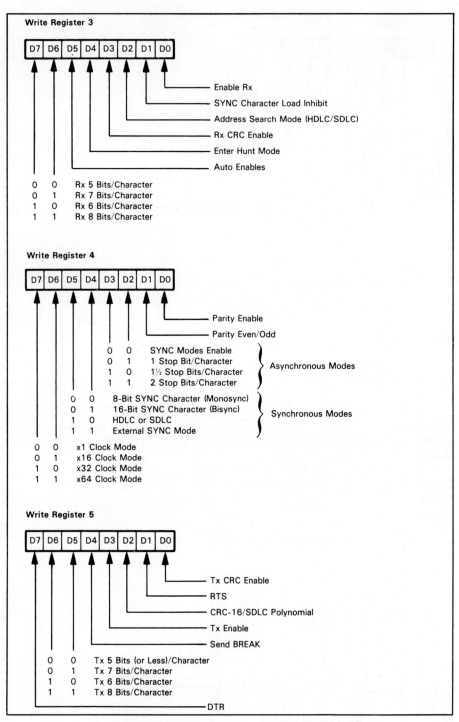

11-33. SIO Control or Write Registers (Continued)

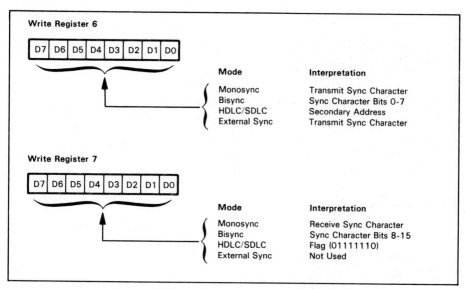

Write Register 6

| D7 | D6 | D5 | D4 | D3 | D2 | D1 | D0 |

Mode	Interpretation
Monosync	Transmit Sync Character
Bisync	Sync Character Bits 0-7
HDLC/SDLC	Secondary Address
External Sync	Transmit Sync Character

Write Register 7

| D7 | D6 | D5 | D4 | D3 | D2 | D1 | D0 |

Mode	Interpretation
Monosync	Receive Sync Character
Bisync	Sync Character Bits 8-15
HDLC/SDLC	Flag (01111110)
External Sync	Not Used

11-33. SIO Control or Write Registers (Continued)

Read Registers

The Z80 SIO contains three registers that can be read to obtain the status of each channel. Status information includes error conditions, interrupt vector, and standard communication interface protocol signals. To read the contents of a selected Read register, the system software must first write to the SIO a byte containing pointer information (D0-D2) in exactly the same manner as in a Write register operation. Then, by issuing a READ operation, the contents of the addressed Read/Status register can be read by the Z8000 CPU.

The real power in this type of command structure is that the programmer has complete freedom, after pointing to the selected register, of either reading or writing to initialize or test that register. By designing software to initialize the Z80 SIO in a modular, structured fashion, the programmer can use the powerful Z8000 Block I/O instructions to significantly simplify and speed his software development and debugging.

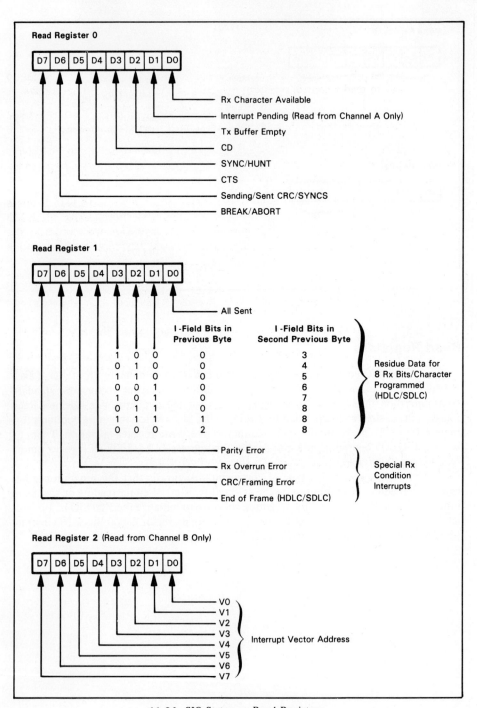

11-34. SIO Status on Reed Registers

SPECIAL FEATURES OF THE SIO

Note the following special features of the SIO:

1. Input and Output instructions address physically distinct registers. There is no way to read a control register's contents or write into the status registers.

2. All control registers for a channel share a single port address. Two bytes must be output to change the contents of any control register other than Register 0.

3. Reset initializes the SIO to Write Register 0. It also disables both receivers and transmitters, deactivates all control signals, and disables all interrupts. We will discuss the SIO interrupt system in Chapter 12.

4. The SIO must be configured before it can be used. The easiest way to do this is by placing the required bytes into a table and using the repeated Block I/O instruction. The table must include both the bytes needed to address the various registers and the data that must be placed into them. A typical routine would be:

```
LD      R3,#LENGTH      ! Number of Words in Control Table  !
LD      R1,#PORT+5      ! Control Port Address              !
LD      R2,#SRCBUF      ! Start of Control Table            !
OTIRB   @R1,@R2,R3      ! Configure SIO                     !
```

Bytes must be output since the Z80-SIO receives byte data only.

5. The RS-232 signals are all active-low. However, the SIO control bits for these signals are active-high (i.e., a logic '1' in a control bit sets an RS-232 signal low).

6. The SIO requires an external clock. Asynchronous communications at 110 baud use a 1760 Hz clock with X16 mode.

7. The Data Ready (Rx Character Available) flag is bit 0 of Read Register 0. The Peripheral Ready (Tx Buffer Empty) flag is bit 2 of Read Register 0.

8. Error status bits (parity, overrun, and framing) are in Read Register 1.

PROGRAM EXAMPLES

11-12. Teletypewriter Interface Using the SIO

Task 1: Read data.

Purpose: Receive data from a teletypewriter through an SIO and place the data into memory location 6000. The data is 7-bit ASCII with odd parity.

Program 11-12a:

```
              internal                    ! Z80 SIO commands !
                SRCBUF   ARRAY[* BYTE] := [ ! Port A initialization !
6000 04                      %04          ! Select write register 4 !
6001 41                      %41          ! x16 clock mode, odd parity !
6002 03                      %03          ! Select write register 3 !
6003 41                      %41          ! 7 bit chars, enable receiver !
6004 00                      %00          ! Select read register 0 !
                          ]
              internal
                pgm_11_12a procedure
                entry
                      $abs    IBASE

4600 2103            LD      R3,#SIZEOF SRCBUF   ! Length of initialization !
4602 0005
4604 7602            LDA     R2,SRCBUF      ! Pointer to initialization data !
4606 6000
4608 2101            LD      R1,#SIOADR+5   ! Initialize SIO channel A !
460A FF45
460C 3A22            OTIRB   @R1,@R2,R3
460E 0310
4610 3A84    WAITD:  INB     RL0,SIOADR+5   ! Read status register 0 !
4612 FF45
1614 A680            BITB    RL0,#0         ! Is character ready? !
4616 E6FC            JR      Z,WAITD
4618 3A84            INB     RL0,SIOADR+1   ! Read data from channel A !
461A FF41
461C 6E08            LDB     %6000,RL0      ! Store into memory !
461E 6000
4620 7A00            HALT

4622         end     pgm_11_12a
```

The program loads Write Register 4 as follows:

Bits 7 and 6 = 01 to select X16 clock mode (1760 Hz clock must be supplied)

Bit 1 = 0 to select odd parity

Bit 0 = 1 to enable parity checking

The program loads Write Register 3 as follows:

Bits 7 and 6 = 01 for 7 bits per character

Bit 0 = 1 to enable the receiver

The received data status bit is bit 0 of Read Register 0.
Note that any errors found will be reported in Read Register 1 as follows:

Bit 6 = 1 for a framing error (no stop bit)

Bit 5 = 1 for an overrun error (more data received before previous data read)

Bit 4 = 1 for a parity error

Try adding an error checking routine to the program. Set memory byte 6001 as follows:

= 0 if no errors occurred

= 1 if a parity error occurred

= 2 if an overrun error occurred

= 4 if a framing error occurred.

If more than one error occurs, store the sum of the error codes.

Note that the receiver always checks for one stop bit. Some teletypewriters send one and one-half stop bits. This will not cause any problem; it will simply delay the next start bit.

Task 2: Write data.

Purpose: Send data from memory location 6000 to a teletypewriter using SIO channel A. The data is 7-bit ASCII with odd parity.

Program 11-12b:

```
                internal
                SRCBUF   ARRAY[* BYTE] := [   ! Z80 SIO commands !
                                             ! Port A initialization !
6000 04                  %04                 ! Select write register 4 !
6001 4D                  %4D                 ! x16 clock, odd, 2 stop bits !
6002 05                  %05                 ! Select write register 5 !
6003 41                  %41                 ! 7 bit characters... !
                                             ! ...enable transmitter !
6004 00                  %00                 ! Select read register 0 !
                         ]

                internal
                pgm_11_12b procedure
                entry
                     $abs     IBASE

4600 2103            LD       R3,#SIZEOF SRCBUF   ! Initialize channel A !
4602 0005
4604 7602            LDA      R2,SRCBUF
4606 6000
4608 6101            LD       R1,SIOADR+5
460A FF45
460C 3A22            OTIRB    @R1,@R2,R3
460E 0310
4610 3A84   WAITR:   INB      RL0,SIOADR+5       ! Read status register 0 !
4612 FF45
4614 A682            BITB     RL0,#2             ! Transmitter ready? !
4616 E6FC            JR       Z,WAITR
4618 6008            LDB      RL0,%6000          ! Character to transmit !
461A 6000
461C 3A86            OUTB     SIOADR+1,RL0
461E FF41
4620 7A00            HALT

4622            end     pgm_11_12b
```

The program sets up Write Register 4 as follows:

Bits 7 and 6 = 01 to select X16 clock mode (1760 Hz clock must be supplied)

Bits 3 and 2 = 11 to add 2 stop bits to each character

Bit 1 = 0 to select odd parity

Bit 0 = 1 to enable parity generation

The program sets up Write Register 5 as follows:

Bits 6 and 5 = 01 for 7 bits per character

Bit 3 = 1 to enable the transmitter

The transmitter status bit is bit 2 of Read Register 1.

STANDARD INTERFACES

Other standard interfaces besides the TTY current-loop and RS-232 can also be used to connect peripherals to the Z8000 microcomputer. Popular ones include:

1. The serial R-449 interface, used with RS-422 or RS-423.[18]

2. The 8-bit parallel General Purpose Interface Bus, also known as IEEE-488 or Hewlett-Packard Interface Bus (HPIB).[19]

3. The S-100 or Altair/Imsai hobbist bus.[20] This bus can be used as an 8-bit or 16-bit bus.

4. The Intel Multibus.[21] This is another 8-bit bus that can be expanded to handle 16 bits in parallel.

The S-100 and Multibus differ from the others listed in that they are "motherboard" busses which connect circuit boards within a single chassis. Such a bus connects peripheral interface control logic to the central processor and memory; a different interface (either a custom job or one of the standards we have mentioned) connects the peripheral device itself to the interface card in this microcomputer chassis.

OTHER INTERFACE DEVICES

There are a variety of other interface devices which you are likely to encounter in Z8000 based microcomputer systems. We do not describe additional devices in this chapter since they introduce no new programming concepts, rather they provide additional interfacing capabilities. Descriptions of these additional devices would be more appropriate in a book describing harware design.

The Z8034 UPC Universal Peripheral Controller[22] provides a peripheral interface like that provided by the Z80-PIO and Z80-SIO. However, the UPC is itself a fully programmable high speed microprocessor suitable for interfacing a wide range of devices with complex control requirements and high data rates.

The 8255 programmable peripheral interface and the Z8036 CIO[23] are two parallel interface devices you are likely to encounter as alternatives to the Z80-PIO.

Additional serial I/O devices include USARTs, which might be looked upon as direct replacements for the Z80-SIO. But there are also SDLC and HDLC receiver/transmitters, such as the Z8030 SCC[24], which receive and transmit serial I/O data using the more recent SDLC and HDLC protocols.[25]

PROBLEMS

11-1. An On-Off Pushbutton

Purpose: Each closure of the pushbutton complements (inverts) all the bits in memory location 6000. The location initially contains zero. The program should continuously examine the pushbutton and complement location 6000 with each closure. You may wish to complement a display output port instead, so as to make the results easier to see.

Sample Case:

Location 6000 initially contains zero.

The first pushbutton closure changes location 6000 to FF_{16}, the second changes it back to zero, the third back to FF_{16}, etc. Assume that the pushbutton is debounced in hardware. How would you include debouncing in your program?

11-2. Debouncing a Switch in Software

Purpose: Debounce a mechanical switch by waiting until two readings, taken a debounce time apart, give the same result. Assume that the debounce time (in ms) is in memory location 6000 and place the switch position into memory location 6001.

Sample Problem:

(6000) = 03 causes the program to wait 3 ms
between readings

11-3. Control for a Rotary Switch

Purpose: Another switch serves as a Load switch for a four-position unencoded rotary switch. The CPU waits for the Load switch to close (be zero), and then reads the position of the rotary switch. This procedure allows the operator to move the rotary switch to its final position before the CPU tries to read it. The program should place the position of the rotary switch into memory location 6000. Debounce the Load switch in software.

Sample Problem:

Place rotary switch in position 2. Close Load switch.

Result: (6000) = 02

11-4. Record Switch Positions on Lights

Purpose: A set of eight switches should have their positions reflected in eight LEDs. That is to say, if the switch is closed (zero), the LED should be on, otherwise the LED should be off. Assume that the CPU output port is connected to the cathodes of the LEDs.

Sample Problem:

SWITCH 0	CLOSED
SWITCH 1	OPEN
SWITCH 2	CLOSED
SWITCH 3	OPEN
SWITCH 4	OPEN
SWITCH 5	CLOSED
SWITCH 6	CLOSED
SWITCH 7	OPEN

Result:

LED 0	ON
LED 1	OFF
LED 2	ON
LED 3	OFF
LED 4	OFF
LED 5	ON
LED 6	ON
LED 7	OFF

How would you change the program so that a switch attached to bit 7 of Port A of PIO #2 determines whether or not the displays are active (i.e., if the control switch is closed, the displays attached to Port B reflect the switches attached to Port A; if the control switch is open, the displays are always off)? A control switch is useful when the displays may distract the operator, as in an airplane.

How would you change the program so as to make the control switch an on-off pushbutton; that is, each closure reverses the previous state of the displays? Assume that the displays start in the active state and that the program examines and debounces the pushbutton before sending data to the displays.

11-5. Count on a Seven-Segment Display

Purpose: The program should count from 0 to 9 continuously on a seven-segment display, starting with zero.

Hint: Try different timing lengths for the displays and see what happens. When does the count become visible? What happens if the display is blanked part of the time?

11-6. Separating Closures from an Unencoded Keyboard

Purpose: The program should read entries from an unencoded 3 × 3 keyboard and place them into an array. The number of entries required is in memory location 6000 and the array starts in memory location 6001.

Separate one closure from the next by waiting for the current closure to end. Remember to debounce the keyboard (this can be simply a 1 ms wait).

Sample Problem:

```
            (6000)  =  04
Keys pressed are 7, 2, 2, 4

Result:  (6001)  =  07
         (6002)  =  02
         (6003)  =  02
         (6004)  =  04
```

11-7. Read a Sentence from an Encoded Keyboard

Purpose: The program should read entries from an ASCII keyboard (7 bits with a zero Parity bit) and place them into an array until it receives an ASCII period (hex 2E). The array starts in memory location 6000. Each entry is marked by a strobe as in the example given under An Encoded Keyboard.

Sample Problem:

Keys pressed are H, E, L, L, O, and period.

```
Result:  (6000)  =  48  H
         (6001)  =  45  E
         (6002)  =  4C  L
         (6003)  =  4C  L
         (6004)  =  4F  O
         (6005)  =  2E  .
```

11-8. A Variable Amplitude Square Wave Generator

Purpose: The program should generate a square wave, as shown in the figure below, using a D/A converter. Memory location 6000 contains the scaled amplitude of the wave, memory location 6001 the length of a half cycle in milliseconds, and memory location 6002 the number of cycles.

Assume that a digital output of 80_{16} to the converter results in an analog output of zero volts. In general, a digital output of D results in an analog output of $(D-80)/80 \times -V_{REF}$ volts.

Sample Problem:

$$(6000) = A0 \text{ (hex)}$$
$$(6001) = 04$$
$$(6002) = 03$$

Result:

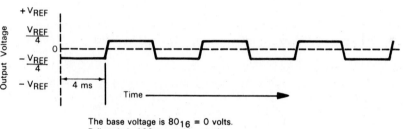

The base voltage is 80_{16} = 0 volts.
Full scale is 100_{16} = $-V_{REF}$ volts.
So $A0_{16} = (A0-80)/80 \times (-V_{REF}) = -V_{REF}/4$

The program produces 3 pulses of amplitude $V_{REF}/4$ with a half cycle length of 4 ms.

11-9. Averaging Analog Readings

Purpose: The program should take four readings from an A/D converter ten milliseconds apart and place the average in memory location 6000. Assume that the A/D conversion time can be ignored.

Sample Problem:

Readings are (hex) 86, 89, 81, 84

Result: (6000) = 85

11-10. A 30 Character-per-Second Terminal

Purpose: Modify the transmit and receive routines of the example given under A Teletypewriter to handle a 30 cps terminal that transfers ASCII data with one stop bit and even parity. How could you write the routines to handle either terminal depending on a flag bit in memory location 6060; e.g., (6060) = 0 for the 30 cps terminal, (6060) = 1 for the 10 cps terminal?

REFERENCES

1. J. Barnes and V. Gregory, "Use Microcomputers to Enhance Performance with Noisy Data," *EDN*, August 20, 1976, pp. 71-72.

2. R. Swanson, "Understanding Cyclic Redundancy Codes," *Computer Design*, November 1975, pp. 93-99; and J. E. McNamara, *Technical Aspects of Data Communication*, Digital Equipment Corp., Maynard, Mass. 1977.

3. A. Osborne and J. Kane, *An Introduction to Microcomputers: Volume2 — Some Real Microprocessors*, Chapter 7. Osborne/McGraw-Hill, 1980.

4. Zilog, Inc. "Z8036 CIO Technical Manual."

5. Further information on the Z80-PIO appears in Reference 3 and in Zilog, Inc. "Z80-PIO Technical Manual" Pub. 30-0008-01, 1977.

6. The SIO is discussed more completely in:

   J. Kane and A. Osborne, *An Introduction to Microcomputers: Volume 3 — Some Real Support Devices*, Chapter C4. Osborne/McGraw-Hill, 1980.

   Zilog, Inc. "Z80-SIO Technical Manual" Pub. 03-3033-01, August 1978.

   The following reference describes use of the SIO as a data link controller:

   A. J. Weissberger, "Data-Link Control Chips: Bringing Order to New Protocols," *Electronics*, June 8, 1978, pp. 104-112.

7. A. Osborne, *An Introduction to Microcomputers: Volume 1 — Basic Concepts*, Chapter 5. Osborne/McGraw-Hill, 1980.

8. *The TTL Data Book for Design Engineers*, Texas Instruments, Inc., P.O. Box 5012, Dallas, Texas 75222, 1976.

9. E. Dilatush, "Special Report: Numeric and Alphanumeric Displays," *EDN*, February 5, 1978, pp. 26-35.

10. See Reference 8.

11. E. R. Hnatek, *A User's Handbook of D/A and A/D Converters*, Wiley, New York, 1976.

12. Ibid.

13. See Also D. Guzeman, "Marry You up to Monolithic A/Ds," *Electronic Design*, January 18, 1977, pp. 82-86.

14. For a discussion of UARTs, see P. Rony et al., "The Bugbook IIa," E and L Instruments Inc., 61 First Street, Derby, CT. 06418; or D. G. Larsen et al., "INWAS: Interfacing with Asynchronous Serial Mode," *IEEE Transactions on Industrial Electronics and Control Instrumentation*, February 1977, pp. 2-12. Also see McNamara, Reference 2.

15. The official RS-232 standard is available as: Electronic Industries Association, "Interface between Data Terminal Equipment and Data Communications Equipment Employing Serial Binary Data Interchange," EIA RS-232C August, 1969. You can find introductory descriptions of RS-232 in G. Pickles, "Who's Afraid of RS-232?," *Kilobaud*, May 1977, pp. 50-54 and in C. A. Ogdin, "Microcomputer Busses — Part II," *Mini-Micro Systems*, July 1978, pp. 76-80. Ogdin also describes the newer RS-449 standard.

16. See Reference 7.

17. See Reference 6.

18. Electronic Industries Association, "Electrical Characteristics of Balanced Voltage Digital Interface Circuits," *EIA RS-422*, April 1975.

    Electronic Industries Association, "Electrical Characteristics of Unbalanced Voltage Digital Interface Circuits," *EIA RS-423*, April 1975.

    Electronic Industries Association, "General Purpose 37-Position and 9-Position Interface for Data Terminal Equipment and Data Circuit Terminating Equipment Employing Serial Binary Data Interchange," *EIA RS-449*, November 1977.

    D. Morris, "Revised Data Interface Standards," *Elecronic Design*, September 1, 1977, pp. 138-141.

19. Institute of Electrical and Electronic Engineers, "IEEE Standard Digital Interface for Programmable Instrumentation," *IEEE Std 488-1975-ANSI MC 1.1-1975*.

    J. B. Peatman, *Microcomputer-Based Design*, McGraw-Hill, New York, 1977; D. C. Loughry and M. S. Allen, "IEEE Standard 488 and Microprocessor Synergism," *Proceedings of the IEEE*, February 1978, pp. 162-172.

20. K. A. Elmquist, H. Fullmer, D. B. Gustavson, and G. Morrow, "Standard Specification for S-100 Bus Interface Devices," *Computer*, July 1979, pp. 28-52.

21. T. Rolander, "Intel Multibus Interfacing," *Intel Application Note AP-28*, Intel Corporation, Santa Clara, CA., 1977.

22. Zilog, Inc. "Z8034 UPC Technical Manual."

23. See Reference 4.

24. Zilog, Inc. "Z8030 SCC Technical Manual."

25. A large number of serial I/O devices of all types are described in:

    J. Kane and A. Osborne, *An Introduction to Microcomputers: Volume 3 — Some Real Support Devices*, Section C. Osborne/McGraw-Hill, 1980.

    Chapter C1 of that book provides an overview of the SDLC and HDLC protocols.

12

Interrupts

Interrupts provide external logic with a means of modifying the sequence in which programs are executed by a microprocessor.

Without interrupts, external logic has no way of directly controlling program execution sequences. Without interrupts, an external device that requires execution of some specific program must attract the microprocessor's attention by modifying some suitable external status flag. The external logic must then wait until the microprocessor gets around to checking the status flag. This is referred to as "polling." Polling is frequently used in simple microcomputer configurations. But polling will not work when an external device needs the microprocessor's immediate attention. By the time the microprocessor gets around to checking the external device's status flag it may be too late. Data that the external device had ready for the microprocessor may have been overwritten; information the external device needed from the microprocessor may not have arrived in the allotted time; or perhaps the microprocessor has continued to execute some I/O operation long after the external device detected a fatal error and tried to report it. These are three typical examples of situations where external logic must take an active role, forcing the microprocessor to stop whatever it is doing and attend to some more pressing need. Interrupts are the mechanism used by external logic to achieve this goal.

INTERRUPT ENABLE

External logic transmits interrupt requests to the microprocessor via appropriate signals, generally referred to as "Interrupt Request" signals. The microprocessor tests these interrupt request signals once during the execution of every instruction. Some interrupts can be enabled or disabled under program control; others cannot. The microprocessor ignores a disabled interrupt request; it services an enabled interrupt requests as follows:

1. It stops executing the current program.

2. It executes a special program that caters to the needs of the interrupting external logic.

3. It continues executing the current program from the point where the interrupt occurred.

Interrupt Acknowledgment

Step 1 above is frequently referred to as the Interrupt Acknowledge step. During an interrupt acknowledgment the microprocessor must save the program counter and the Flag and Control Word contents on the stack. The program counter addresses the next sequential instruction; this is the instruction which would have been executed had the interrupt not occurred. This is also the instruction which will be executed as soon as the interrupt has been serviced in Step 3. For Step 2, execution branches to a special program dedicated to a particular interrupt being acknowledged.

Interrupt Service Routine

The program executed on behalf of the acknowledged interrupt is referred to as an interrupt service routine. This routine normally begins by saving additional information, information that was not automatically saved during the acknowledgment process. For example, the contents of all CPU registers are frequently pushed onto the stack before any register contents are modified by the body of the interrupt service routine. The interrupt service routine then performs operations required by the acknowledged interrupt.

Return from Interrupt

Finally, in Step 3, a return from interrupt occurs; this is the exact inverse of the interrupt acknowledgment process. If the interrupt service routine saved any additional information before starting to execute, then it will restore this information before triggering the actual return from interrupt. For example, if the interrupt service routine initially saved the contents of all CPU registers on the stack, then it will restore all these registers' contents from the stack. A "Return-from-Interrupt" instruction is then executed; it restores the program counter and Flag and Control Word contents that were saved during the acknowledgment process, causing the interrupted program to continue execution from the point where it was interrupted. This sequence may be illustrated as follows:

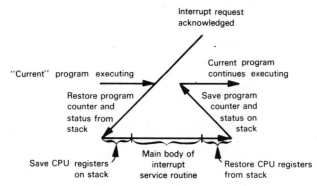

An interrupted program is not affected in any way by the occurrence of the interrupt, except that there is a pause in program execution. The interrupted program appears to enter a state of "suspended animation," at the end of which it continues execution, unaffected by the interrupt process per se.

The repeated Z8000 instructions (such as CPIR) test and acknowledge enabled interrupts between repeated executions; therefore once **an interrupt request** occurs, **if enabled,** the interrupt **will be serviced no more than one instruction execution time later.**

Why use interrupts? Interrupts allow events to receive fast microprocessor attention. An alarm, a power failure, the end of a specified time delay, a fast peripheral's need to transmit or receive data, these are all candidates for interrupt logic. The only alternative would be for the microprocessor to execute a program that polled each potential interrupt source. That could be very time consuming and might easily result in important events being missed.

NON-MASKABLE INTERRUPTS

Some interrupts are so important that they cannot be disabled. These are called non-maskable interrupts. A microprocessor will always acknowledge and service a non-maskable interrupt, whatever it is doing when the interrupt request occurs. **Non-maskable interrupts are frequently used to flag a power failure;** a microprocessor can usually execute a few hundred instructions between the time a power failure is detected and the time when insufficient power remains to operate the microprocessor. These instructions can "tidy up" the program, enabling an orderly restart when power is turned on again.

MASKABLE INTERRUPTS

Interrupts that can be disabled or enabled are referred to as maskable interrupts. All interrupts encountered during normal program execution should be maskable interrupts.

The interrupt event sequence itself is valuable. Therefore microprocessors frequently allow the event sequence to be triggered by logic internal to the microprocessor. This can occur in one of two ways:

1. **A condition detected during instruction execution may trigger** an event sequence that is equivalent to **an interrupt request; this is called a software trap.** For example, if an unknown instruction object code is fetched from memory, the microprocessor might respond by executing a trap.

2. Many microprocessors have one or more **instructions that are designed to cause an interrupt sequence to occur.** These **are referred to as software interrupts.**

INTERRUPT PRIORITY

A microprocessor may receive many different interrupt requests; this being the case, **two or more simultaneous interrupt requests may occur. Which one is to be serviced first? Interrupt priority logic answers this question.** Interrupt priority logic applies only during the interrupt acknowledgment step; it does not apply over the entire period that the interrupt is being serviced. For example, if two interrupt requests occur simultaneously, and the higher priority interrupt request is acknowledged, then the interrupt service routine executed on behalf of the higher priority interrupt must keep the lower priority interrupt disabled. If the higher priority interrupt service routine does not keep the lower priority interrupt disabled, the lower priority interrupt will be acknowledged within the higher priority interrupt service routine. This may be illustrated as follows:

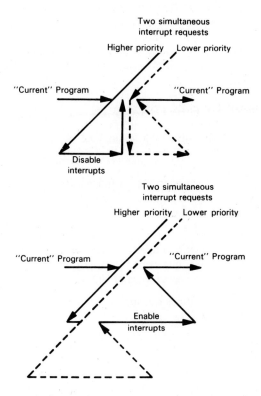

Once the higher priority interrupt's service routine starts executing, only the lower priority interrupt request is pending, as shown in the above illustrations. Being the only interrupt request, it will be acknowledged, even within the higher priority interrupt's service routine, if interrupts are enabled.

VECTORING

Once an interrupt has been acknowledged, there are two ways in which the microprocessor can identify the source of the interrupt. **If the interrupt is vectored then no identification process is required,** since the acknowledgment sequence handles this identification step. Each vectored interrupt has one interrupt service routine, and the interrupt acknowledgment process includes some mechanism for identifying this interrupt service routine.

POLLING

In simpler cases two or more devices may share a single interrupt request. Then the microprocessor has to poll the devices sharing the single interrupt request in order to determine which one (or more) is actually requesting an interrupt. The microprocessor reads Status register contents at the various devices — which is what the microprocessor would do if there were no interrupts. So why interrupt? Because the interrupt triggers the polling sequence. Without the interrupt the microprocessor would have to poll continuously, or on some scheduled basis that might, from time to time, not be frequent enough.

DISADVANTAGES OF INTERRUPTS

There are some disadvantages to using interrupts; they include:

1. Interrupts require additional hardware external to the microprocessor.

2. Once an interrupt has been acknowledged, it must still be serviced by the normal process of executing a program. Interrupts have no inherent speed advantages equivalent to the speed advantages offered by giving external devices direct memory access.

3. Interrupts are difficult to debug since they are random events which occur sporadically; for example, when an I/O operation is complete or following error conditions. The occurrence of I/O completion or errors is unpredictable.

4. Interrupt service routines can spend a lot of time saving and restoring the contents of CPU registers.

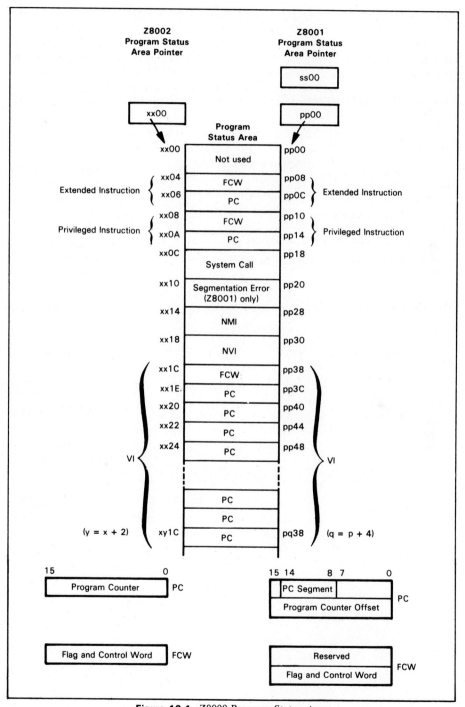

Figure 12-1. Z8000 Program Status Area

THE Z8000 INTERRUPT SYSTEM

The Z8000 microprocessor has a very complete set of external interrupts and several internal interrupts, all supported by extensive interrupt handling logic. The following interrupts are available:

1. **Software interrupts.** Execution of the System Call instruction (SC) generates a software interrupt.

2. **Software traps.** There are two software traps. An extended instruction trap occurs whenever the Z8000 CPU is presented with the instruction object code of an extended instruction while the EPA bit of the Flag and Control Word is zero. A privileged instruction trap occurs whenever the Z8000 attempts to execute a privileged instruction in normal mode.

3. **Non-maskable interrupt**

4. **Maskable, vectored interrupt**

5. **Maskable, non-vectored interrupt**

6. **Segmentation trap**

Other software traps which are desirable but are not provided by the Z8000 include:

1. Arithmetic errors, such as overflow or division by zero. The Z8000 program must test the flags.

2. Illegal addressing, such as using an odd address for a jump or for a word or long word memory reference; or using a register number other than the defined ones in a multiple-word register operation. The Z8000 jump goes to the next lower even address; the result of the other instructions is undefined.

3. Undefined instruction, that is, a combination of object code bits which specifies a disallowed addressing mode or is not defined as an instruction (e.g., 0C03). The Z8000 result is undefined.

Any possible externally detected condition may be handled by any of the external interrupts 3 to 5 above. Almost 200,000 distinct external interrupts may be easily identified. Interrupt 6 is reserved for memory management errors, and is supported only by the Z8001. It is discussed in Chapter 13.

PROGRAM STATUS AREA

Z8000 interrupt logic assumes the existence in memory of a Program Status Area; this memory area is illustrated in Figure 12-1. The base address in memory for the Program Status Area is held in the Program Status Area Pointer register; you initialize this register using an appropriate LDCTL instruction. Here are appropriate instruction sequences for the Z8002 and the Z8001:

```
! Initialize program status area for the Z8002            !
            LDA     R0,BASEADDR     ! BASEADDR is a name   !
                                    ! representing         !
            LDCTL   PSAP,R0         ! the base address     !
            HALT


! Initialize program status area for the Z8001            !
            LDA     RR0,NPSADR      ! NPSADR is a name      !
                                    ! representing ...      !
            LDCTL   PSAPSEG,R0      ! ...the segmented base !
                                    ! address               !
            LDCTL   PSAPOFF,R1
            HALT
```

The Program Status Area contains information used by interrupt acknowledgment logic; for all interrupts, acknowledgment logic transfers control to an appropriate interrupt service routine using an address taken from the Program Status Area.

Z8000 INTERRUPT ACKNOWLEDGMENT

When the Z8000 microprocessor acknowledges an interrupt, the following event sequence occurs:

1. The first word of the next instruction's object code is fetched in the usual way, as if no interrupt was being acknowledged. This instruction object code is discarded and the program counter is not incremented. The discarded instruction will be fetched again, after the interrupt has been serviced, becoming the first instruction to be executed following the return from interrupt. This aborted instruction fetch requires three clock periods.

2. Following the aborted instruction fetch an interrupt acknowledge machine cycle is executed. During the interrupt acknowledge machine cycle the interrupting device sends the Z8000 microprocessor a 16-bit data word which the microprocessor interprets as an interrupt identifier. This is an automatic event; no program steps are required to make it happen. Normally the interrupt acknowledge machine cycle lasts for 10 clock periods, but it may sometimes last longer.

3. Current contents of the program counter and the Flag and Control Word are pushed onto the stack. The identifier is then pushed onto the stack. New values are loaded into the Flag and Control Word and the program counter, these new values being taken from the Program Status Area. For the Z8002 and the Z8001, information is pushed onto the stack in the following sequences:

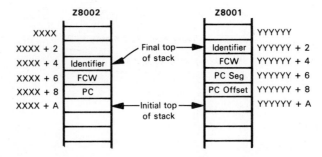

Note carefully that you do not write any instructions to enable the interrupt acknowledgment operations described above. The interrupt service routine entered after Step 3 simply assumes that information will be at the top of the stack, as illustrated. The interrupt service routine entered after Step 3 is identified by an entry address stored in the Program Status Area. At the same time data taken from the Program Status Area is loaded into the Flag and Control Word; this determines status conditions that will apply upon entry into the interrupt service routine.

Vectored and non-vectored interrupts are separately enabled and disabled via the VI and NVI bits of the Flag and Control Word. Therefore **the Flag and Control Word, as stored in the Program Status Area, determines whether interrupts will be enabled or disabled when the interrupt service routine begins execution.** Normally an interrupt service routine will begin execution with interrupts disabled. Therefore the VI and NVI bits of Flag and Control Words stored in the Program Status Area will be 0.

Interrupt service routines do not need to reenable interrupts before returning
control to the main program. When a Return-from-Interrupt instruction is executed,
the program counter and the Flag and Control Word values saved on the stack are
returned to their respective CPU registers. **The returning Flag and Control Word determines whether interrupts will be enabled or disabled following the Return-from-
Interrupt.**

We will now examine the specific acknowledgment sequence associated with each
interrupt type supported by the Z8000 microprocessor.

System Call Interrupt Acknowledgment

A software interrupt is executed in response to a System Call instruction. This
instruction has the following source and object code:

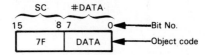

The one-word object code becomes the interrupt identifier; therefore, it will be at
the top of the stack when the System Call interrupt service routine begins execution.
The System Call instruction takes new values for the program counter and the Flag and
Control Word from these specific memory locations within the Program Status Area:

Z8002

[FCW]   from xx0C
[PC]   from xx0E

Z8001

[FCW]   from sspp1A
[PC Segment]   from sspp1C
[PC Offset]   from sspp1E

(See Figure 12-1.)

Suppose the Program Status Area begins at memory address 0200_{16}. The System Call software interrupt service routine is entered at memory location $3C80_{16}$, in system mode, with all interrupts disabled and status flags reset to 0. You could initialize the Program Status Area for a Z8002 as follows:

```
LDA      R1,%0200        ! Initialize PSAP          !
LDCTL    PSAP,R1
LD       %C(R1),#%4000   ! Initialize System Call !
                         ! service                 !
LD       %E(R1),#%3C80   ! routine FCW and entry   !
                         ! address                 !
HALT
```

For a Z8001 the sequence would be:

```
LDA      RR2,<<0>>%0200
LDCTL    PSAPOFF,R2
LDCTL    PSAPSEG,R3      ! PSAP in Segment 0         !
LD       %1A(RR2),#%4000 ! FCW                       !
LD       %1C(RR2),#0     ! Service Routine Segment !
LD       %1E(RR2),#%3C80 ! and entry                 !
```

These initialization instructions would be executed once, during system initialization, shortly after your program begins execution. In some microcomputers the Program Status Area will be permanently defined and held in read-only memory.

The System Call interrupt service routine can recognize up to 256 different System Call instructions. Remember, the SC instruction has an 8-bit immediate operand that appears in the low-order byte of the SC instruction's object code. The SC instruction's object code is treated as the interrupt identifier, therefore it appears on the top of the stack when the System Call interrupt service routine begins execution. Instructions at the beginning of the interrupt service routine could branch to different procedures for each of the 256 different SC instructions as follows:

```
! System Call interrupt service routine                      !
        ENTER:  LD      R1,@R15     ! Load identifier into R1 !
                CLRB    RH1         ! Convert R1 into a jump  !
                                    ! table index             !
                SLL     R1
                LD      R1,JTABL(R1) ! Load start address from !
                                     ! jump table              !
                JP      @R1          ! Jump to selected procedure !
                 .
                 .
                 .

! Start of jump table holding addresses for individual       !
! procedures executed on behalf of SC instructions           !
                internal
        JTABL ARRAY [256 WORD]:= [
                ADDR0
                ADDR1
                ADDR2
                 .
                 .
                 .
                ]
```

Software Trap Interrupt Acknowledgment

The extended instruction and privileged instruction software traps, when acknowledged, give control to different interrupt service routines. Each trap has its own entries in the Program Status Area from which new program counter and Flag and Control Word contents are taken. This portion of the Program Status Area may be illustrated as follows:

	Z8002		**Z8001**	
Illegal instruction:	[FCW]	from xx04	[FCW]	from sspp0A
	[PC]	from xx06	[PC Segment]	from sspp0C
			[PC Offset]	sspp0E
Privileged instruction:	[FCW]	from xx08	[FCW]	from sspp12
	[PC]	from xx0A	[PC Segment]	from sspp14
			[PC Offset]	from sspp16

(See Figure 12-1.)

The privileged instruction trap occurs if a program attempts to execute a privileged instruction in normal mode. The privileged instruction trap identifier is the first word of the object code for the privileged instruction which caused the software trap to occur. A privileged instruction software trap routine can use the identifier, together with the saved program counter value, to locate the normal mode program which was attempting to execute a privileged instruction. This can be useful when debugging a program that is being developed, or it can be used as part of program security logic in a working system.

An extended instruction trap occurs if a program attempts to execute an extended instruction with the EPA bit of the Flag and Control Word set to zero. The following instruction object codes are defined as extended instruction operation codes:

```
0Fxx
4Fxx
8Exx
8Fxx
```

The symbol xx represents any two hexadecimal digits. Following an extended instruction interrupt, one of these object codes will be at the top of the stack. This trap could be used to allow simulation of an instruction not available on the microcomputer.

Non-Maskable and Non-Vectored Interrupts

When a non-maskable interrupt or a maskable non-vectored interrupt is acknowledged, control transfers to a single interrupt service routine using a unique set of entries in the Program Status Area, which can be illustrated as follows:

		Z8002		Z8001	
Non-maskable interrupt:	[FCW]	from xx14	[FCW]	from sspp2A
	[PC]	from xx16	[PC Segment]	from sspp2C
			[PC Offset]	from sspp2E
Non-vectored interrupt:	[FCW]	from xx18	[FCW]	from sspp32
	[PC]	from xx1A	[PC Segment]	from sspp34
			[PC Offset]	from sspp36

Both the non-maskable interrupt and the maskable non-vectored interrupt return a 16-bit identifier which is provided by the external device requesting the interrupt. The maskable non-vectored interrupt is usually shared by a number of devices capable of requesting an interrupt. These devices use the identifier to identify themselves. The interrupt service routine executed for the non-vectored interrupt will examine the identifier and use it to identify the requesting device.

When more than one emergency condition can generate a non-maskable interrupt, the microprocessor will use the identifier to determine which condition caused the non-maskable interrupt to occur.

Let us look at non-vectored interrupt program logic in more detail. Suppose the non-vectored interrupt service routine entry point is at memory location NVIR; it must be entered in system mode, with interrupts disabled and all status flags reset to 0. The Program Status Area would be initialized as follows:

```
! Initialize non-vectored interrupt in program status area            !
         LD      NPSAP+%18,#%4000    ! NPSAP is a name            !
                                     ! identifying                !
         LD      NPSAP+%1A,#NVIR     ! the program status         !
                                     ! area starting address !
```

Suppose devices requesting a non-vectored interrupt each have a dedicated interrupt service routine. How is the microprocessor to identify the interrupt service routine? A good method would be for the interrupt service routine's entry address to be the sum of the identifier, and the contents of an Index register. Changing the value in the Index register would allow for changes in the memory location of the group of non-vectored interrupt service routines; but the routines would have to be moved as a group. Here are the instructions that would select the correct service routine:

```
! Entry point for all non-vectored interrupts                 !
       NVIR:   LD      R2,@R15        ! Get identifier            !
               LDA     R2,NVIX(R2)    ! First routine address + !
                                      ! identifier                !
       JP      @R2
```

Do not pop the identifier off the stack; this will be done by the IRET instruction, to be described later.

There is a more flexible way of computing the interrupt service routine's entry address. Let devices requesting a non-vectored interrupt return an index in the identifier. The index should start at 0 for the first device, then increment by 2 for subsequent devices. We will use a jump table to compute the procedure starting address as follows:

```
! Entry point for all non-vectored interrupts             !
        NVIR:   LD      R1,@R15         ! Get identifier    !
                LD      R1,JTABL(R1)
                JP      @R1             ! Jump to procedure !
                .
                .
                .
! Start of non-vectored interrupts entry address table     !
                internal
        JTABL ARRAY   [256 WORD]:= [
                      ADDR0
                      ADDR1
                      ADDR2
                      .
                      .
                      .
                      ]
```

Vectored Interrupt Acknowledgment

When a vectored interrupt request is acknowledged, the Z8000 microprocessor transfers control directly to one of 256 interrupt service routines. The low-order byte of the identifier word returned by the acknowledged device (yy) is used to perform this vectoring step as follows:

For the Z8002: New PC comes from xx1E + (yy × 2)
New FCW comes from xx1C

For the Z8001: New PC comes from sspp3C + (yy × 4)
New FCW comes from sspp3A

This may be illustrated as follows:

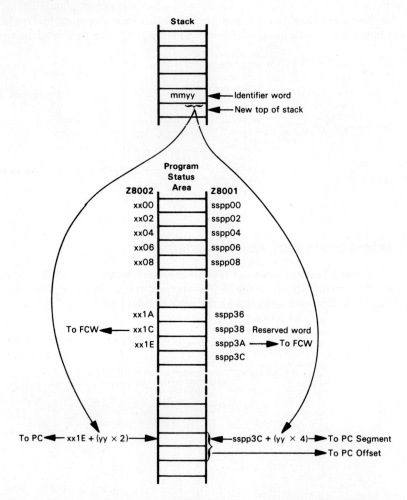

As illustrated above, all vectored interrupts take the same new Flag and Control Word from the Program Status Area. The new program counter contents, however, are selected using the low-order byte of the identifier as an index into the Program Status Area.

INTERRUPT IDENTIFIERS

We can summarize identifier interpretations for the different Z8000 interrupts as follows:

Interrupt	Identifier
System Call	zzzz
Extended Instruction Trap	zzzz
Privileged Instruction Trap	zzzz
Non-Maskable Interrupt	xxxx
Non-Vectored Interrupt	xxxx
Vectored Interrupt	xxyy
Segmentation Error Trap	xxxx

The summary given above lists the identifier contents as a sequence of four hexadecimal digits. Letters are used as follows:

The symbol xxxx represents device dependent information; Z8000 interrupt logic does not specify the way in which this data will be interpreted.

The symbol yy is an offset used to generate an address in the program status area.

The symbol zzzz represents the first word of the object code of the instruction causing the interrupt or trap.

INTERRUPT PRIORITIES

When the Z8000 detects two or more simultaneous interrupt requests, it uses the following priority in order to determine which interrupt to acknowledge:

- Software interrupt or trap (highest priority)

- Non-maskable interrupt

- Segmentation error trap (for the Z8001 only)

- Maskable vectored interrupt

- Maskable non-vectored interrupt (lowest priority)

Note that only one of the software interrupts or traps can exist at any time since each is the product of a different instruction's execution, and only one instruction can be executed at any time. That is why software traps and interrupts are grouped together in the highest priority category.

RETURN FROM INTERRUPT

You must use the Return-from-Interrupt instruction (IRET) to return from an interrupt service routine to the interrupted program. Every interrupt service routine must include one or more Return-from-Interrupt (IRET) instructions. When IRET is executed, this is what happens:

1. The identifier is popped from the stack and discarded.

2. The Flag and Control Word is popped from the stack and loaded into the FCW register; but the new FCW contents do not become effective until the next instruction begins execution.

3. The saved program counter contents are popped from the stack and loaded into the program counter, effecting the actual return from interrupt.

Do not enable microprocessor interrupts before executing IRET. The data word popped into the FCW register determines whether vectored and/or non-vectored interrupts will be enabled after the Return-from-Interrupt.

THE Z8000 RESET

Z8000 reset logic is very similar to non-maskable interrupt logic. A Z8000 microcomputer system is reset to initialize all portions of the system before restarting program execution from the lowest level starting point. Following a reset, prior contents of the program counter and the Flag and Control Word are not saved on the stack. But new values for these registers are taken from the beginning of program memory, as follows:

Z8002		Z8001	
[FCW]	from 0002	[FCW]	from 0002
[PC]	from 0004	[PC Segment]	from 0004
		[PC Offset]	from 0006

This is very similar to the standard interrupt acknowledgment process.

Z80 PIO INTERRUPT LOGIC

The Z80 PIO which we described in Chapter 11 has two I/O ports; each I/O port has its own interrupt logic with these component parts:

1. **An 8-bit Interrupt Vector Address register.** The contents of this register are returned to the Z8000 as the low-order byte of the identifier word during an interrupt acknowledgment. The low-order bit of the Interrupt Vector register must be 0. If the PIO is connected to a vectored interrupt this value is used as an index into the Program Status Area.

2. **An Interrupt Enable bit.** This bit can be used by the microprocessor to enable or disable the I/O port's interrupt logic.

3. **An Interrupt Control register.** Contents of this register determine the circumstances that will cause an interrupt request to be generated by the I/O port.

4. **An Interrupt Mask register.** Individual data lines can generate interrupt requests at an I/O port that is operating in control mode. The Interrupt Mask register selects the data lines capable of generating interrupt requests.

INTERRUPT VECTOR ADDRESS REGISTER

The Interrupt Vector Address register at each I/O port is selected by writing to the I/O Port Control address. An 8-bit data value must be written to the Interrupt Vector Address register; the low-order bit of the data value must be 0 in order to select the Interrupt Vector Address register. (Recall that different locations are accessed via the single I/O port control address; the low-order bits of the data written to the I/O port control address determine which location is selected.)

From our discussion of Z8000 vectored interrupts, recall that the low-order byte of the identifier is left shifted (one bit for the Z8002, or two bits for the Z8001) before being used as an index into the Program Status Area. Since the Z80 PIO always has a 0 in the low-order bit of each I/O port interrupt vector address, alternate entries in the Program Status Area will be used. For example, suppose the two I/O ports of a particular Z80 PIO have the adjacent values $3C_{16}$ and $3E_{16}$ in their Interrupt Vector Address registers. A Z8002 will compute Program Status Area addresses as follows:

$$xx1E + 3C \times 2 = xx96$$
$$xx1E + 3E \times 2 = xx9A$$

The address in $xx98_{16}$ has been skipped.

Z80 PIO MODES

The Z80 PIO generates interrupt requests in different ways for different modes. Z80 PIO modes are described in Chapter 11.

Mode 0 Interrupts

In Mode 0 either I/O port generates an interrupt request when external logic acknowledges having received data output.

Mode 1 Interrupts

In Mode 1 either I/O port generates an interrupt request when external logic transmits a new data word to the I/O port.

Mode 2 Interrupts

In Mode 2 an I/O Port A interrupt request is generated when external logic acknowledges having received data output via I/O Port A; an I/O Port B interrupt request is generated when external logic transmits input data to I/O Port A.

Interrupt Enable/Disable Control Code

You must enable or disable interrupt logic associated with an I/O port; each I/O port has its own interrupt enable/disable logic. The interrupt control code is output to the control address of each I/O port. Control code bits are interpreted as follows:

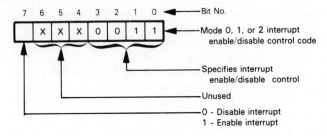

Mode 3 Interrupts

When an I/O port is operating in Mode 3, you must write a special Mode 3 control code, optionally followed by a mask code. These two outputs are directed to the control address for the I/O port. The Mode 3 interrupt control code is interpreted as follows:

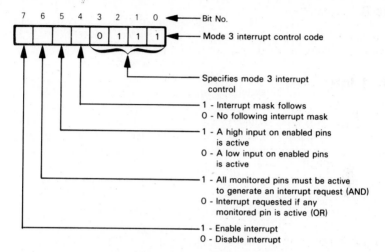

If bit 4 of the Mode 3 control code is 1, then the next byte written to the control address is interpreted as a mask identifying the data lines of the Mode 3 I/O port which are to be monitored for interrupts. Mask bits are interpreted as follows:

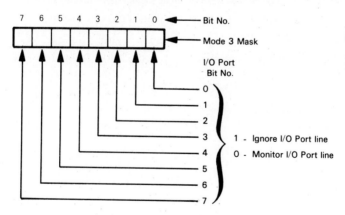

Z80 PIO INTERRUPT CONFIGURATION

We will now look at some Z80 PIO configuration programming examples.

Suppose I/O Port B is to be initialized as an output port (Mode 0), with interrupts enabled and an interrupt vector of 80_{16}; initialization requires these instructions:

```
LDB     RL0,#%0F      ! Make Port B output      !
OUTB    PIOADR+7,RH0  ! Port B control address  !
LD      R0,#%8083
OUTB    PIOADR+7,RH0  ! Vector Address 80       !
OUTB    PIOADR+7,RL0  ! Enable interrupts       !
```

An interrupt request will be generated when external logic acknowledges data received from I/O Port B.

If I/O Port A is bidirectional (Mode 2) then I/O Port B must be operated in control mode (Mode 3). I/O Port A has interrupts enabled and an interrupt vector address of 40_{16}. I/O Port B has interrupts enabled; an interrupt occurs when lines 1, 3, and 5 are all high. The Port B interrupt vector address is 42_{16}. Initialization requires these instructions:

```
LDB     RL0,#%8F      ! Make Port A bidirectional !
OUTB    PIOADR+5,RL0  ! Port A control address     !
LD      R0,#%4083
OUTB    PIOADR+5,RH0  ! Vector address 40          !
OUTB    PIOADR+5,RL0  ! Enable interrupts          !
LD      R0,#%CF2A
OUTB    PIOADR+7,RH0  ! Make Port B control        !
OUTB    PIOADR+7,RH0  ! with pins 1, 3, and 5      !
                      ! inputs                     !
LD      R0,#%F72A
OUTB    PIOADR+7,RH0  ! Enable interrupt when all  !
                      ! high, mask follows         !
OUTB    PIOADR+7,RL0  ! Monitor lines 1, 3, and 5  !
```

Try rewriting this instruction sequence using OUTIRB. Does it save execution time or memory space?

Z80 PIO INTERRUPT PRIORITY

If interrupt requests occur simultaneously at I/O Ports A and B, then the I/O Port A interrupt request has priority.

When two or more Z80 PIO devices are present in a single microcomputer system, daisy chained **interrupt priority** logic is frequently employed. The Z80 PIO design provides for this, but how it is implemented **is a function of the way in which Z80 PIO devices have been connected in your particular microcomputer configuration.** You should therefore check the documentation provided with your microcomputer to determine whether the information which follows applies to your case.

When any Z80 PIO I/O port's interrupt request is acknowledged, the Z80 PIO device outputs a signal which permanently disables interrupt requests from all lower priority Z80 PIO devices. Lower priority Z80 PIO device interrupt requests remain disabled until the higher priority Z80 PIO device removes its disable signal. This occurs when the Z80 PIO device receives an interrupt acknowledgment. Z80 PIO devices were originally designed as support parts for the Z80 microprocessor. Therefore Z80 PIO devices assume that they have received an interrupt acknowledgment when they detect a Z80 Return-from-Interrupt instruction (RETI) being executed. Unfortunately the Z8000 microprocessor has no equivalent logic, nor is it possible to simulate a Z80 RETI instruction using Z8000 program steps only. Some additional external hardware is required. Depending on the nature of this hardware, you will have to execute one or more Z8000 instructions in order to provide the Z80 PIO device with its interrupt acknowledgment. For example, the standard Z8000 development system provided by Zilog requires seven instructions to be executed; this sequence causes external hardware to provide the Z80 PIO device with its interrupt acknowledgment. The way in which you create an interrupt acknowledgment for Z80 PIO devices will depend on the way your microcomputer system has been designed, and whether your microcomputer system does indeed use Z80 PIO devices for its parallel I/O ports.

Z80 SIO INTERRUPT LOGIC

The Z80 SIO device was introduced in Chapter 11. **The Z80 SIO device has very complex interrupt logic.** There are forty different ways in which interrupt requests can be generated by the Z80 SIO device; interrupt requests which are active at any time depend on operating options which you specify by writing appropriately to seven Write registers. You subsequently monitor operations by reading from the device's three Read registers. But the complexities of the Z80 SIO device all pertain to the different types of serial I/O protocols which are supported; they have no impact whatsoever on programming techniques for using the device. Therefore **in the discussion that follows we will examine only the routine interrupt servicing steps for the Z80 SIO device. A detailed description of this device can be found elsewhere.**[6]

Transmitter interrupts are enabled by writing 1 to bit 1 of Write Register 1. Each of the two channels has its own Write Register 1; transmitter interrupts must be enabled or disabled separately for each channel.

Each Z80 SIO channel's Read and Write registers are written via the channel's control port. Read Register 0 and Write Register 0 are normally selected. However, if you write any other register number to the three low-order bits of Write Register 0, then the next access will select the register identified in the three low-order bits of Write Register 0; the three low-order bits of Write Register 0 are then reset to 0. While this may sound complicated, from the programmer's viewpoint it is quite straightforward. Just assume that the first time you write to a Z80 SIO control channel register, or read from it, you will access Write Register 0 or Read Register 0. To access any other register, first write the other register's number, then execute another write or read. For example, the following instruction writes data to Write Register 0 of Channel A:

```
        LDB     RL0,#DATA
        OUTB    SIOADR+5,RL0    ! Channel A control address !
```

To enable transmitter interrupts by writing to Write Register 1, as described previously, execute these instructions:

```
        LDB     RL0,#1
        OUTB    SIOADR+5,RL0    ! Select Channel A Write   !
                                ! register 1               !
        LDB     RL0,#2
        OUTB    SIOADR+5,RL0    ! Write to Channel A Write !
                                ! register 1               !
! The next write to SIOADR+5 will select Write Register 0 again  !
```

If you wish to read from Read Register 2 execute these two instructions:

```
        LDB     RL0,#2
        OUTB    SIOADR+5,RL0    ! Select Channel A Read     !
                                ! Register 2                !
        INB     RL0,SIOADR+5    ! Input from Read Register 2 !
```

Receiver interrupts are enabled and disabled by writing appropriately to bits 3 and 4 of Write Register 1 at each channel. In addition to enabling and disabling interrupts these two bits specify the receive condition which generates an interrupt request as follows:

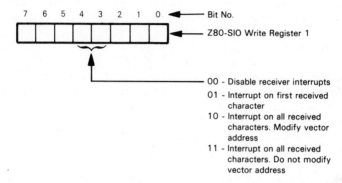

The Z80 SIO device has an 8-bit interrupt vector address which is returned as the low-order byte of the identifier following an interrupt acknowledge. The Z80 SIO device does not return any high-order identifier byte. The high-order identifier byte will be defined by logic specific to your microcomputer system, or it will be undefined. One interrupt vector address is shared by both channels of the Z80 SIO device. This address is held in Write Register 2 of Channel B. There is no Channel A Write Register 2.

If you use non-vectored interrupts to service a single Z80 SIO device, instructions at the beginning of the interrupt service routine can read the identifier from the top of the stack to determine what caused the interrupt.

If there is more than one Z80 SIO device in your configuration, and the priority logic is not connected, then you will have to determine which device requested the interrupt. You can poll Z80 SIO devices by reading Read Register 0 of Channel A at each Z80 SIO device. Bit 1 of this register will be set to 1 if there is an active interrupt request anywhere in the device. Subsequently, you should read the Interrupt Vector Address register contents directly from the Z80 SIO device by reading the contents of Read Register 2 of Channel B. Do not read the identifier from the top of the stack. Two or more Z80 SIO devices may have requested interrupts simultaneously. Without performing further analysis you will not know which device's vector address is on top of the stack.

The following instruction sequence polls four Z80 SIO devices with adjacent I/O port addresses. On detecting a device with an active interrupt request, this program fetches the vector address, returning the device number in RH1 and the vector address in RL1.

```
        LDA     R2,SIOADR4+5    ! Load largest Port A control !
                                ! address                     !
        LDB     RH1,#4          ! Load device number (4 to 1) !
LOOP:   INB     RL0,@R2         ! Poll device                 !
        BITB    RL0,#1          ! Test interrupt request bit  !
        JR      NZ,FOUND        ! Active interrupt found       !
        DEC     R2,#8           ! Decrement address for next  !
                                ! device                      !
        DBJNZ   RH1,LOOP        ! Decrement device number.    !
                                ! Return if not zero          !
        CLRB    RL1             ! Therefore no SIO interrupt   !
                                ! requests                    !
        HALT
FOUND:  INC     R2,#2           ! Interrupt found. Select     !
                                ! Port B                      !
        LDB     RL1,#2
        OUTB    @R2,RL1         ! Select Register 2           !
        INB     RL1,@R2         ! Interrupt Vector Address     !
        HALT
```

Try rewriting this program to poll a variable number of Z80 SIO devices, where the number of devices is represented by a name. Return a list of all Z80 SIO devices with active interrupt requests; the list should consist of 16-bit words having the following format:

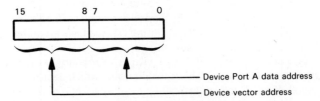

Push these words onto a data stack addressed by Register R1. Return the number of stack entries in Register RL0.

When both channels of a Z80 SIO device request interrupts simultaneously, Channel A interrupts have priority over Channel B interrupts.

We will not discuss programming aspects of Z80 SIO interrupt service routines. The programming logic itself is very simple; you have to clear interrupt conditions by writing to appropriate registers and you must read or transmit data in a routine fashion. The hard part is understanding the serial I/O protocol being supported by the Z80 SIO device.

PROGRAM EXAMPLES

12-1. A Startup Interrupt

Purpose: Following a reset, the program performs initialization steps, then waits for a PIO interrupt to occur before starting actual operations.

Following a reset, the processor fetches a program status from low memory and transfers program control to the specified address. On the Z8001 the status occupies four words beginning at segment 0, offset 0. (The first word of the status is not used by current production chips.) On the Z8002, the status occupies two words beginning at address 2.

When a reset occurs, the program should initialize the stack pointer, enable the startup interrupt, then execute a HALT instruction. Remember that a reset disables microprocessor interrupts and power-on disables all PIO interrupts. In flowchart 12-1, hardware inputs an interrupt request to initiate the startup.

Flowchart 12-1:

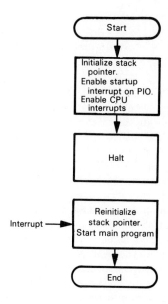

Program 12-1:

```
              internal
                     $abs     2                    ! RESET program status: Z8002 !
    0002 4000 RESFCW  WORD := %4000                ! FCW: interrupts disabled !
    0004 0006 RESPC   WORD := RESET                ! PC: the reset program !

              internal
                     pgm_12_1 procedure
                     entry
                     $abs     6
    0006 760F RESET:  LDA     R15,%8000            ! Initialize stack pointer !
    0008 8000
    000A 2100         LD      R0,#%4F83
    000C 4F83
    000E 3A06         OUTB    PIOADR+5,RH0         ! PIO port A input mode !
    0010 FF25
    0012 3A86         OUTB    PIOADR+5,RL0         ! Interrupts enabled !
    0014 FF25
    0016 7C04         EI                           ! Enable processor interrupts !
    0018 7A00         HALT                         ! Wait for first interrupt !

              ! Interrupt service routine: !

                     $abs     INTRP

    4200 760F         LDA     R15,%8000            ! Reinitialize stack !
    4202 8000
    4204 5E08         JP      START                ! Enter main program !
    4206 4600

    4208              end     pgm_12_1
```

First we enable the startup-of-PIO interrupt, then we execute the EI instruction to enable CPU interrupts. Remember, reset automatically disables Z8000 CPU interrupts.

The program executed following the reset must initialize the stack pointer, since the program counter contents will be pushed onto the stack with the next interrupt. We show the service routine reinitializing the stack pointer after the next interrupt, and before the actual startup routine is executed. Instead we could increment the stack pointer by 4 to bypass the current stack contents.

The exact location of the interrupt service routine varies with the microcomputer. If your microcomputer has no monitor, you can start the interrupt service routine wherever you wish. Of course, you should place the routine so that it does not interfere with fixed addresses or with other programs.

Most microcomputers do have a monitor. A monitor is a program which provides the lowest level, most primitive interface between the microcomputer and a user. Often the monitor is held in read-only memory; its execution is triggered by a reset. In our example, the startup PIO interrupt will probably reexecute the monitor. The monitor is a conversational program, with commands that let you execute other programs, then return to the monitor. This may be done by CALLing the program, or an interrupt may be used to exit from the monitor to the program you wish to execute. This requires that you enter an execution address (probably from a keyboard), then trigger an interrupt request, possibly by depressing a control key. There are many ways in which this logic could be implemented. The execution address could be held in an Index register, for example, in which case the interrupt service routine might begin with the instruction:

```
              JP      @Rn                ! Enter identified program !
```

You might want to exit the monitor to execute a user-defined program, as described above, or to execute a program out of a permanent library. Programs in such a library perform a variety of routine tasks, such as editing, assembling, compiling, etc. We could hold execution addresses for library programs in an address list. Suppose RL0 holds 0 if a library program is to be executed, or 1 if a user program is to be executed. R1 holds the library program number, or the user program execution address. This is how the monitor might select the program to be executed:

```
        TESTB   RL0               ! User program?               !
        JR      NZ,PROG           ! Yes                         !
        LD      R1,LIBADR(R1)     ! No. Get library address     !
PROG:   JP      @R1
LIBADR:                           ! Library program execution   !
                                  ! addresses stored here        !
```

12-2. A Keyboard Interrupt

Purpose: The computer waits for a keyboard interrupt and places the data from the keyboard into memory location 6000.

Sample Problem:

Keyboard data = 06

Result: (6000) = 06

Flowchart 12-2:

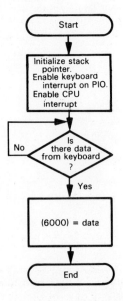

There is nothing in the main program that pertains specifically to the keyboard interrupt; it is shown to illustrate the interrupt process. In this instance, the JR HERE endless loop will be interrupted by the keyboard interrupt service routine, among others.

Instead of returning to JR HERE, you might want to return elsewhere. To return to the instruction following JR HERE increment the return address by 2, since JR HERE has two object code bytes. This single instruction appearing before IRET will suffice (for the Z8002):

```
INC     4(R15),#2        ! Increment return PC !
```

What single instruction is needed for the Z8001? What instructions would you add to give a completely new address?

Since the Z8000 does not automatically save registers' contents during an interrupt acknowledgment, you can use them to pass parameters and results between the main program and the interrupt service routine. This is, however, a dangerous practice that should be avoided in all but the most trivial programs. In most applications, the processor is using its registers during normal program execution; having the interrupt service routines randomly change the contents of one or more registers would surely cause

Program 12-2a:

```
                internal
                    pgm_12_2a procedure
                    entry
                        $abs     IBASE

        ! Main Program !

4600 760F               LDA      R15,%8000        ! Initialize stack !
4602 8000
4604 2101               LD       R1,#%4F83
4606 4F83
4608 3A16               OUTB     PIOADR+5,RH1     ! PIO port A input mode !
460A FF25
460C 3A96               OUTB     PIOADR+5,RL1     ! Enable interrupts !
460E FF25
4610 7C04               EI                        ! Enable processor interrupts !
4612 E8FF      HERE:    JR       HERE             ! Loop until PIO interrupts !

        ! Keyboard interrupt service routine !

4614 93F0               PUSH     @R15,R0          ! Save a register !
4616 3A84               INB      RL0,PIOADR+1     ! Read character !
4618 FF21
461A 6E08               LDB      %6000,RL0        ! Store into memory !
461C 6000

                ! (PIO interrupt acknowledgement sequence here) !

461E 97F0               POP      R0,@R15
4620 7B00               IRET                      ! Enable interrupts upon exit !

4622           end      pgm_12_2a
```

havoc. In general, no interrupt service routine should ever alter any register unless that register's contents are saved prior to its alteration and restored at the completion of the routine.

Note that you must not explicitly reenable microprocessor interrupts at the end of the service routine. The IRET instruction restores the interrupt enable status in effect at the time of the interrupt. The special PIO interrupt acknowledgment sequence deactivates the interrupt signal so that the same interrupt is not serviced again.

An alternative approach, shown in program 12-2b, would have the main program initialize a keyboard buffer. The interrupt service routine will store keyboard input in the buffer until a carriage return character is detected or the buffer fills up.

Can you see how the INIB and CPB instructions work? Try rewriting the program so that an INB instruction loads data from Port A to RL0. Do you save object code or execution time?

When the processor receives a carriage return, it leaves the interrupt system disabled while it handles the line using a program entered at LPROC.

An alternative approach would be to fill another buffer while LPROC handles the first one; this approach is called double buffering.

In a real application, the CPU could perform other tasks between interrupts. It could, for instance, edit, move, or transmit a line from one buffer while the interrupt was filling another buffer.

Program 12-2b:

```
                    internal
                       pgm_12_2b procedure
                       entry
                               $abs      IBASE

                    ! Main Program !

      4600 760F              LDA       R15,%8000         ! Initialize stack !
      4602 8000
      4604 2101              LD        R1,#%4F83
      4606 4F83
      4608 3A16              OUTB      PIOADR+5,RH1      ! PIO port A input mode !
      460A FF25
      460C 3A96              OUTB      PIOADR+5,RL1      ! Enable interrupts !
      460E FF25
                             ! Complete line returns to next instruction. Main !
                             ! program falls through first time !
      4610 4D05      LININIT:LD        %6000,#KEYBUF     ! Buffer starting address !
      4612 6000
      4614 6000
      4616 4D05              LD        %6002,#SIZEOF KEYBUF   ! Length of buffer !
      4618 6002
      461A 0050
      461C 7C04              EI                          ! Enable processor interrupts !
      461E E8FF      HERE:   JR        HERE              ! Loop until PIO interrupts !

                    ! Keyboard interrupt service routine !

      4620 93F1              PUSH      @R15,R1           ! Save R1, R2 and R3 !
      4622 91F2              PUSHL     @R15,RR2
      4624 6101              LD        R1,%6000          ! Next free byte in buffer !
      4626 6000
      4628 6102              LD        R2,%6002          ! Remaining space in buffer !
      462A 6002
      462C 2103              LD        R3,#PIOADR+1      ! Port address !
      462E FF21
      4630 3A30              INIB      @R1,@R3,R2        ! Next byte into buffer !
      4632 0218
                             ! (PIO interrupt acknowledgement sequence here) !

      4634 8D24              TEST      R2                ! End of buffer? !
      4636 E60B              JR        EQ,LPROC
      4638 4C11              CPB       -1(R1),#CR        ! Was last character CR? !
      463A FFFF
      463C 0D0D
      463E E607              JR        EQ,LPROC          ! Yes !
      4640 6F01              LD        %6000,R1          ! No, update pointer !
      4642 6000
      4644 6F02              LD        %6002,R2
      4646 6002
      4648 95F2              POPL      RR2,@R15          ! Restore registers !
      464A 97F1              POP       R1,@R15
      464C 7B00              IRET                        ! Re-enable interrupts on exit !

              LPROC:  ! (Process complete line) !

      464E 95F2              POPL      RR2,@R15
      4650 97F1              POP       R1,@R15
      4652 A9F5              INC       R15,#6            ! Remove status (PC etc)... !
                                                        ! ...pushed by interrupt !
      4654 5E08              JP        LININIT           ! Set up for next line !
      4656 4610

      4658              end       pgm_12_2b
```

12-3. A Printer Interrupt

Purpose: The computer waits for a printer interrupt and sends a data byte from memory location 6000 to the printer.

Sample Problem:

$$(6000) = 51_{16}$$

Result: Printer receives a 51_{16} (ASCII Q) when it is ready.

Program 12-3a:

```
                internal
                    pgm_12_3a procedure
                    entry
                        $abs     IBASE

                ! Main program !

    4600 760F           LDA      R15,%8000        ! Set up stack !
    4602 8000
    4604 2100           LD       R0,#%0F83
    4606 0F83
    4608 3A06           OUTB     PIOADR+5,RH0     ! PIO Port A output !
    460A FF25
    460C 3A86           OUTB     PIOADR+5,RL0     ! Interrupts enabled !
    460E FF25
    4610 7C04           EI
    4612 E8FF  HERE:    JR       HERE

                ! Interrupt service routine !

    4614 93F0           PUSH     @R15,R0
    4616 6008           LDB      RL0,%6000        ! Get data to be sent !
    4618 6000
    461A 3A86           OUTB     PIOADR+1,RL0     ! Send byte to printer !
    461C FF21

                ! (PIO interrupt acknowledgement steps here) !

    461E 97F0           POP      R0,@R15
    4620 7B00           IRET

    4622            end      pgm_12_3a
```

Here, as with the keyboard, you could have the printer continue to interrupt until it transferred an entire line of text. The main program and the service routine are shown in program 12-3b.

Program 12-3b:

```
                internal
                    pgm_12_3b procedure
                    entry
                        $abs    IBASE

              ! Main Program !

  4600 760F       LDA     R15,%8000       ! Initialize stack !
  4602 8000
  4604 2101       LD      R1,#%0F83
  4606 0F83
  4608 3A16       OUTB    PIOADR+5,RH1    ! PIO port A output mode !
  460A FF25
  460C 3A96       OUTB    PIOADR+5,RL1    ! Enable interrupts !
  460E FF25

                ! Complete line returns to next instruction. Main !
                ! program falls through first time !

  4610 4D05  LININIT:LD   %6000,#LPBUF    ! Buffer starting address !
  4612 6000
  4614 6000
  4616 4D05       LD      %6002,#SIZEOF LPBUF ! Length of buffer !
  4618 6002
  461A 0050
  461C 7C04       EI                      ! Enable processor interrupts !
  461E E8FF  HERE:   JR    HERE            ! Loop until PIO interrupts !

              ! Printer interrupt service routine !

  4620 91F0       PUSHL   @R15,RR0        ! Save R0 and R1 !
  4622 6101       LD      R1,%6000        ! Next free byte in buffer !
  4624 6000
  4626 2018       LDB     RL0,@R1         ! Get next character !
  4628 3A86       OUTB    PIOADR+1,RL0    ! Send to printer !
  462A FF21

                ! (PIO interrupt acknowledgement sequence here) !

  462C 0A08       CPB     RL0,#CR         ! Watch for carriage return !
  462E 0D0D
  4630 E607       JR      EQ,LPROC
  4632 6900       INC     %6000           ! Advance to next character !
  4634 6000
  4636 6B00       DEC     %6002           ! Adjust length !
  4638 6002
  463A E602       JR      EQ,LPROC        ! Watch for end of buffer !
  463C 95F0       POPL    RR0,@R15
  463E 7B00       IRET

              LPROC:  ! (End of line processing takes place here) !

  4640 95F0       POPL    RR0,@R15
  4642 A9F5       INC     R15,#6          ! Remove status (PC etc.)... !
                                          ! ...pushed by interrupt !
  4644 E8E5       JR      LININIT

  4646          end     pgm_12_3b
```

Note that this program is simpler than the equivalent keyboard program. It is also shorter and will execute faster. So beware of complex instructions.

Comments following the equivalent keyboard program also apply to this printer program.

12-4. A Real-Time Clock Interrupt

Purpose: The computer waits for an interrupt from a real-time clock.

A real-time clock simply provides a regular series of pulses. The interval between the pulses can be used as a time reference. Real-time clock interrupts can be counted to give any multiple of the basic time interval. A real-time clock can be produced by dividing down the CPU clock, by using a separate timer or a programmable timer like the Z80-CTC or Z8036 CIO, or by using external sources such as the AC line frequency.

Note the tradeoffs involved in determining the frequency of the real-time clock. A high frequency (say 10 kHz) allows the creation of a wide range of time intervals of high accuracy. On the other hand, the overhead involved in counting real-time clock interrupts may be considerable. The choice of frequency depends on the precision and timing requirements of your application. The clock may, of course, consist partly of hardware; a counter may count high frequency pulses and interrupt the processor only occasionally. A program will have to read the counter to measure time to high accuracy.

Synchronizing operations with the real-time clock is not straightforward. Clearly, the time interval will not be precise if the CPU starts the measurement randomly during a clock period, rather than exactly at the beginning of a clock period. Some ways to synchronize operations are:

1. Start the CPU and clock together. A reset or a startup interrupt can start the clock as well as the CPU.

2. Allow the CPU to start and stop the clock under program control.

3. Use a high-frequency clock so that an error of less than one clock period will be small.

4. Line up the clock (by waiting for a change in some signal or an interrupt) before starting the measurement.

A real-time clock interrupt should have very high priority, since the precision of the timing intervals will be affected by any delay in servicing the interrupt. Usually the real-time clock is the highest priority interrupt, except for power failure. The clock interrupt service routine is generally kept extremely short so that it does not interfere with other CPU activities.

a. Wait for Real-Time Clock

Program 12-4a:

```
                internal
                   pgm_12_4a procedure
                   entry
                        $abs     IBASE
   4600 760F           LDA       R15,%8000
   4602 8000
   4604 2100           LD        R0,#%4F83
   4606 4F83
   4608 3A06           OUTB      PIOADR+5,RH0    ! PIO Port A input mode !
   460A FF25
   460C 3A86           OUTB      PIOADR+5,RL0    ! Interrupts enabled !
   460E FF25
   4610 7C04           EI
   4612 E8FF   HERE:   JR        HERE

                   ! Real time clock interrupt service routine !

   4614 7A00           HALT                      ! Clock interrupt !

   4616               end        pgm_12_4a
```

Program 12-4a reduces the real-time clock concept to its most trivial case. A real-time clock interrupt occurs on the rising edge of a PIO STROBE signal at Port A. The main program executes the JR HERE instruction waiting for the real-time clock interrupt. This interrupt halts the microprocessor.

If the real-time clock interrupt is to be useful, the interrupt service routine must do something useful; and the main program will do more than prepare for the interrupt.

The next problem is a small step in the direction of usefulness.

b. Count 10 Real-Time Clock Interrupts

Program 12-4b:

```
                    internal
                        pgm_12_4b procedure
                        entry
                            $abs    IBASE

                    ! Main Program !

  4600 760F             LDA     R15,%8000
  4602 8000
  4604 2100             LD      R0,#%4F83
  4606 4F83
  4608 3A06             OUTB    PIOADR+5,RH0    ! PIO Port A input mode !
  460A FF25
  460C 3A86             OUTB    PIOADR+5,RL0    ! Interrupts enabled !
  460E FF25
  4610 4D05             LD      %6000,#10       ! Initialize clock counter !
  4612 6000
  4614 000A
  4616 7C04             EI
  4618 4D04    WTTEN:   TEST    %6000           ! 10 interrupts yet? !
  461A 6000
  461C EEFD             JR      NZ,WTTEN        ! No, wait !
  461E 7A00             HALT                    ! Yes, done !

                    ! Real time clock interrupt service: !

  4620 6B00             DEC     %6000           ! Count interrupts !
  4622 6000
  4624 7B00             IRET

  4626            end      pgm_12_4b
```

The interrupt service routine shown in program 12-4b merely updates the counter in memory location 6000. The main program continues to execute.

A more realistic real-time clock interrupt routine could maintain real time in several memory locations. For example, the following routine uses addresses 6000 through 6003 as follows:

> 6000 - hundredths of seconds
> 6001 - seconds
> 6002 - minutes
> 6003 - hours

We assume that the interrupt is triggered by a 100 Hz clock.

Flowchart 12-4b:

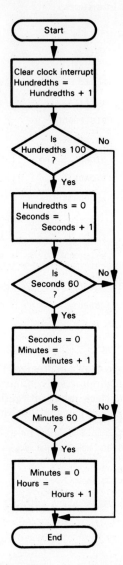

The "Count 10 Real-Time Clock Interrupts" main program is used here, however memory locations 6000 through 6003 are cleared using the two instructions:

```
CLR     %6000
CLR     %6002
```

The interrupt service routine is shown in program 12-4c.

Program 12-4c:

```
                internal
                  pgm_12_4c procedure
                entry
                    $abs      IBASE

  4600 91F0         PUSHL     @R15,RR0
  4602 7601         LDA       R1,%6004        ! Pointer to time data !
  4604 6004
  4606 5400         LDL       RR0,%6000       ! Fetch 4 bytes of time data !
  4608 6000
  460A A800         INCB      RH0             ! Hundredths of a second !
  460C 0A00         CPB       RH0,#100        ! Count up to 99 !
  460E 6464
  4610 E70C         JR        ULT,DONE
  4612 8C08         CLRB      RH0             ! At 100, reset and bump secs !
  4614 A880         INCB      RL0
  4616 0A08         CPB       RL0,#60         ! 60 seconds in an minute !
  4618 3C3C
  461A E707         JR        ULT,DONE
  461C 8C88         CLRB      RL0
  461E A810         INCB      RH1             ! Increment minutes !
  4620 0A01         CPB       RH1,#60         ! 60 minutes in an hour !
  4622 3C3C
  4624 E702         JR        ULT,DONE
  4626 8C18         CLRB      RH1
  4628 A890         INCB      RL1             ! Increment the hour !
  462A 5D00  DONE:  LDL       %6000,RR0       ! Return time to memory !
  462C 6000
  462E 95F0         POPL      RR0,@R15
  4630 7B00         IRET

  4632         end       pgm_12_4c
```

A main program can now compute delays by testing the time as stored in memory. The following routine causes a 300 ms delay in the main program:

```
              LDB     RL0,%6000       ! Get current hundredths of !
                                      ! a second                  !
              ADDB    RL0,#30         ! Add 30                     !
              CPB     RL0,#100        ! If the sum is more than    !
                                      ! 100 ...                    !
              JR      ULT,WT30
              SUBB    RL0,#100        ! ...then normalize          !
      WT30:   CPB     RL0,%6000       ! Desired time reached?      !
              JR      NE,WT30         ! No, wait                   !
```

Of course, the program could perform other tasks and check the elapsed time only occasionally. How would you produce a delay of seven seconds? Of three minutes?

Sometimes you may want to keep time either as BCD digits or as ASCII characters. How would you revise the program to handle these alternatives?

You can disable the clock interrupt (or any other interrupt) when it is no longer needed in any of the following ways:

1. By executing a DI VI instruction in the main program. This disables all vectored interrupts.

2. By clearing bit 7 of the Interrupt Control Word for the Z80 PIO I/O port. This disables interrupts at the selected I/O port only.

3. By changing the VI status bits in the Flag and Control Word stored on the stack, before returning from the interrupt service routine. However, it is a dangerous practice to modify a main program's interrupt enable/disable status from within an interrupt service routine; the main program can no longer assume that it knows which interrupts are or are not enabled. You are asking for trouble.

12-5. A Teletypewriter Interrupt

Purpose: The computer waits for a character to be received from a teletypewriter and stores the character in memory location 6000.

a.   Using an SIO (7-bit characters with odd parity)

Program 12-5a:

```
                internal
                  pgm_12_5a procedure
                  entry
                    $abs      IBASE

      ! Main Program !

4600 2100           LD        R0,#%0441
4602 0441
4604 3A06           OUTB      SIOADR+5,RH0      ! Select write register 4 !
4606 FF45
4608 3A86           OUTB      SIOADR+5,RL0      ! x16 clock, odd parity !
460A FF45
460C 2100           LD        R0,#%0341
460E 0341
4610 3A06           OUTB      SIOADR+5,RH0      ! Select write register 3 !
4612 FF45
4614 3A86           OUTB      SIOADR+5,RL0      ! 7 bit characters... !
4616 FF45                                       ! ...enable receiver !
4618 2100           LD        R0,#%0118
461A 0118
461C 3A06           OUTB      SIOADR+5,RH0      ! Select write register 1 !
461E FF45
4620 3A86           OUTB      SIOADR+5,RL0      ! Interrupt every character !
4622 FF45
4624 7C04           EI
4626 E8FF  HERE:    JR        HERE

      ! Teletypewriter interrupt service routine: !

4628 93F0           PUSH      @R15,R0
462A 3A84           INB       RL0,SIOADR+1      ! Get character from SIO !
462C FF41
462E 6E08           LDB       %6000,RL0         ! Store in memory !
4630 6000
4632 97F0           POP       R0,@R15
4634 7B00           IRET

4636                end       pgm_12_5a
```

We could use the OTIRB instruction to initialize a Z80 SIO channel in the main program. Assuming that the six bytes 044103410118 are stored in memory, beginning at address SIOINIT, these instructions will initialize Channel A:

```
         LD     R1,#SIOADR+5     ! Load Channel A control !
                                 ! address               !
         LDA    R2,SIOINIT       ! Load data base address !
         LD     R0,#6            ! Load number of bytes  !
         OTIRB  @R1,@R2,R0
```

These four instructions occupy 8 words of object code; add 6 bytes for the data and we have a total of 11 object code words. Nine instructions, occupying 12 object code bytes, are replaced.

The service routine in program 12-5a assumes that only the receive interrupt from one channel of the SIO has been enabled. Otherwise, further decoding will be required based on control bits D2, D3, and D4 of Write Register 0 (see the discussion of SIO interrupts earlier in this chapter). Alternatively, the routine will have to examine the status bits in Read Register 0 to determine the activity. The key status bits are:

Bit 0 - Receive Character Available — 1 when at least one character is available in the receive buffers.

Bit 1 - Interrupt Pending (Read from Channel A only) — 1 if any interrupt is pending in the entire SIO.

Bit 2 - Transmit Buffer Empty — 1 if all characters in the transmit buffer have been sent.

The program establishes the SIO registers as follows:

Write Register 4:

Bit 7 = 0, bit 6 = 1 for X16 clock mode
Bit 1 = 0 to select odd parity
Bit 0 = 1 to enable parity generation

Write Register 3:

Bit 7 = 0, bit 6 = 1 to select 7-bit characters
Bit 0 = 1 to enable the receiver

Write Register 1:

Bit 4 = 1, bit 3 = 1 to produce an interrupt on all received characters with parity errors not affecting the vector address sent to the CPU during interrupt acknowledgment.

The CPU clears the Received Character Available bit by reading a character from the SIO Data register. The Interrupt Pending bit is cleared automatically when the interrupt is serviced.

If we use bit 7 of Z80 PIO Port A to receive serial data, as we did in Chapter 11, the programs needed to input data from the teletypewriter are shown in program 12-5b.

Program 12-5b:

```
                external
                    TTYRCV procedure

                internal
                    pgm_12_5b procedure
                    entry
                        $abs    IBASE

            ! Main Program !

4600 2100          LD       R0,#%CF80
4602 CF80
4604 3A06          OUTB     PIOADR+5,RH0      ! Port A is control !
4606 FF25
4608 3A86          OUTB     PIOADR+5,RL0      ! Bit 7 is input !
460A FF25
460C 2100          LD       R0,#%977F
460E 977F
4610 3A06          OUTB     PIOADR+5,RH0      ! Enable int on start bit (0) !
4612 FF25
4614 3A86          OUTB     PIOADR+5,RL0      ! Mask out bits 0-6 !
4616 FF25
4618 7C04          EI
461A E8FF   HERE:  JR       HERE

            ! Teletypewriter interrupt service routine !

461C 030F          SUB      R15,#30           ! Room for 15 registers !
461E 001E
4620 1CF9          LDM      @R15,R0,#15       ! Save R0-R15 !
4622 000E
4624 C807          LDB      RL0,#%07
4626 3A86          OUTB     PIOADR+5,RL0      ! Disable start bit interrupt !
4628 FF25
462A 5F00          CALL     TTYRCV            ! Fetch data from TTY !
462C 0000*
462E C883          LDB      RL0,#%83
4630 3A86          OUTB     PIOADR+5,RL0      ! Enable start bit interrupt !
4632 FF25
            ! (PIO interrupt acknowledgement sequence here) !

4634 1CF1          LDM      R0,@R15,#15       ! Restore registers !
4636 000E
4638 010F          ADD      R15,#30
463A 001E
463C 7B00          IRET

463E          end      pgm_12_5b
```

Subroutine TTYRCV receives data from the teletypewriter; it is part of program 11-11a. It is good programming practice for subroutines to save and restore the contents of all CPU registers they use. This is particularly important for subroutines called by interrupt service routines.

The programs in program 12-5b assume that the monitor initializes the stack pointer. Otherwise it will have to be loaded in the main program.

The signal edge used to cause the interrupt is very important here. An interrupt must occur when the data line changes from the normal MARK or '1' state to the SPACE or '0' state, since this transition identifies the start of the transmisson.

The service routine must disable the PIO interrupt, since otherwise each '1'-to-'0' transition in the character will cause an interrupt. Of course, you must reenable the PIO interrupt after the entire character has been read.

Note the use of the PIO in the control mode:

1. The PIO is placed in the control mode by establishing Mode 3.

2. The next control word defines which data lines are to be inputs ('1') and which are to be outputs ('0').

3. The interrupt control word has, besides the usual enable in bit 7,

> bit 6 = 0 to perform a logical OR of the monitored data lines for an interrupt (not used in this case, since only one line is monitored)

> bit 5 = 0 to define the active polarity of the data lines as low (for the start bit in this case)

> bit 4 = 1 to indicate that a mask word follows.

4. The next control word contains the interrupt masks. Only those port lines with a mask bit of zero will be monitored for generating an interrupt.

The next result is for an interrupt to be generated if bit 7 is zero or changes from one to zero. Note that further interrupts occur only when the status of the bits being monitored changes.

Here again, the PIO could be configured by using a table and the repeated block output instruction.

PROBLEMS

12-1. Wait for an Interrupt

Purpose: The computer waits for a PIO interrupt to occur, then executes the endless loop instruction:

```
HERE:    JR      HERE
```

until the next interrupt occurs.

12-2. A Keyboard Interrupt

Purpose: The computer waits for a 4-digit entry from a keyboard and places the digits into memory locations 6000 through 6003 (first one received in 6000). Each digit entry causes an interrupt. The fourth entry should also result in the disabling of the keyboard interrupt.

Sample Problem:

```
                  Keyboard data =  04, 06, 01, 07

       Result:     (6000)  =  04
                   (6001)  =  06
                   (6002)  =  01
                   (6003)  =  07
```

12-3. A Printer Interrupt

Purpose: The computer sends four characters from memory locations 6000 to 6003 (starting with 6000) to the printer. Each character is requested by an interrupt. The fourth transfer also disables the printer interrupt.

12-4. A Real-Time Clock Interrupt

Purpose: The computer clears memory location 6000 initially and then complements memory location 6000 each time the real-time clock interrupt occurs.

How would you change the program so that it complements memory location 6000 after every ten interrupts? How would you change the program so that it leaves memory location 6000 at zero for ten clock periods, FF_{16} for five clock periods, then zero again for ten, and so on continuously? You may want to change a display rather than memory location 6000 so that it will be easier to see.

12-5. A Teletypewriter Interrupt

Purpose: The computer receives TTY data from an interrupting SIO and stores the characters in a buffer starting in memory location 6000. The process continues until the computer receives a carriage return ($0D_{16}$).

Assume that the characters are 7-bit ASCII with odd parity. How would you change your program to use a PIO? Assume that subroutine TTYRCV is available, as in the example. Include the carriage return as the final character in the buffer.

REFERENCES

1. You may want to review the discussion of interrupts in A. Osborne, *An Introduction to Microcomputers: Volume 1 — Basic Concepts*. Osborne/McGraw-Hill, 1980.

2. For a discussion of designing with interrupts, see R. L. Baldridge, "Interrupts Add Power, Complexity to Microcomputer System Design," *EDN*, August 5, 1977, pp. 67-73.

3. See A. Osborne and J. Kane, *An Introduction to Microcomputers: Volume 2 — Some Real Microprocessors*, Osborne/McGraw-Hill, 1980.

4. See reference 3 and L. Leventhal, *8080A/8085 Assembly Language Programming*, Osborne/McGraw-Hill, 1978.

5. R. L. Baldridge, "Interrupts Add Power, Complexity to Microcomputer System Design," *EDN*, August 5, 1977, pp. 67-73.

   R. M. Pond, "Let Microprocessors Communicate," *Electronic Design*, November 8, 1977, pp. 88-90.

   M. Shima, and R. Blacksher, "Improved Microprocessor Interrupt Capability," *Electronic Design*, April 26, 1978, pp. 96-100.

   W. J. Weller, *Practical Microcomputer Programming: the Z80*, Northern Technology Books, Evanston, Ill., 1978.

   A. W. Winston and T. B. Smith, "Use of the Z-80 in Data Collection and Control," *IECI '78 Proceedings — Industrial Applications of Microprocessors*, March 20-22, 1978, pp. 208-14.

6. J. Kane and A. Osborne, *An Introduction to Microcomputers: Volume 3 — Some Real Support Devices*, Chapter C4. Osborne/McGraw-Hill, 1978.

7. Zilog, Inc., *Z80-SIO Technical Manual*, Pub. 03-3033-01, August 1978.

8. The Proceedings of the IEEE's Industrial Electronics and Control Instrumentation Group's Annual Meeting on "Industrial Applications of Microprocessors" contains many interesting articles. Volumes (starting with 1975) are available from IEEE Service Center, CP Department, 445 Hoes Lane, Piscataway, NJ 08854.

13
Large Configurations

In this chapter we will look at system programming aspects of large Z8000 microcomputer configurations. Two subjects are covered:

1. Using the Z8010 memory management unit with a Z8001 microprocessor.

2. Use of the multi-micro instructions in multi-CPU configurations.

Programming aspects of memory management and multiple-CPU configurations are very dependent on hardware design, and programming rules will vary from one Z8000 microcomputer system to the next. Consequently, this chapter looks at the fundamental capabilities of the Z8010 memory management unit and at multi-micro instructions, rather than examining large computer system software concepts as they might apply to any specific configuration.

Z8010 MEMORY MANAGEMENT UNIT

MEMORY ADDRESS TRANSLATION

Memory management units translate logical memory addresses into physical memory addresses.

The effective memory address computed by a microprocessor memory reference instruction is a logical memory address. The memory address actually received by a memory device is a physical address.

For most microprocessors, including the Z8002, logical and physical memory addresses are identical. The effective memory address computed by a Z8002 memory reference instruction is also the physical memory address received by the memory device. Given a maximum Z8002 addressing range of 65,536 bytes, memory management is simply not a problem, and no useful purpose would be served if we inserted some means of converting Z8002 logical memory addresses into different physical memory addresses.

But the Z8001 computes 23-bit, segmented memory addresses, capable of addressing 128 65,536-byte segments, for a total addressing range that exceeds eight million bytes. In addition, the Z8001 distinguishes between system mode and normal mode memory references. These references may be directed to different parts of physical memory, extending the addressing range to over 16 million bytes. **Memory management becomes a problem given such a large memory space.** If we separate logical and physical memory addresses, then a programmer can use all 16 million bytes of addressable memory; a memory management unit can ensure that only physical memory which is actually present gets addressed. The Z8010 memory management unit[1] performs this task for a Z8001 microprocessor.

The Z8010 provides for 24-bit physical memory addresses, so over 16 million bytes of physical memory can be accessed by a Z8001 system.

The Z8010 translates memory addresses on a segment-by- segment basis. Logical segments can be placed anywhere in physical memory. For example, memory segment 0A has the logical addressing range 0A0000 through 0AFFFF. The Z8010 could be programmed to actually access physical memory locations 028000 through 037FFF on encountering memory addresses in logical segment 0A.

Each Z8010 memory management unit can translate addresses for 64 segments. Therefore a Z8001 microcomputer system needs two Z8010 memory management units in order to translate addresses for 128 logical segments. In fact, up to eight Z8010 memory management units can connect to a single Z8001 microprocessor. Memory management units in excess of two are added for programming convenience, to allow separation of program, data, and stack references, or to meet the needs of multi-CPU configuration logic.

Base Address

Each **Z8010 memory management unit has 64 base address registers into which you must write base addresses** for each physical segment. The segment number computed by a Z8001 memory reference instruction selects the base address that is to be used in the address translation. For example, if a Z8001 memory reference instruction computes an effective memory address in segment 0A, then the eleventh base address register within the Z8010 memory management unit will provide the physical memory base address. This base address will be 028000 to meet the needs of our previous illustration. In fact, each Z8010 base address is assumed to represent the high-order 16 bits of a 24-bit base address; the low-order 8 bits of the 24-bit base address are always 00. The 16-bit logical address offset is added to this base address to generate the actual physical address.

The **Z8010 receives as inputs the logical segment number and the high-order byte of the 16-bit offset computed by a Z8001 memory reference instruction;** the low-order byte of the offset bypasses the Z8010 memory management unit. Therefore each address translation may be illustrated as follows:

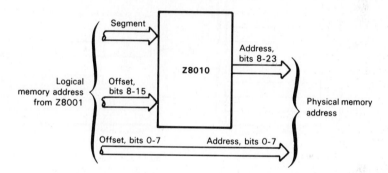

The Z8010 memory management unit creates physical addresses as follows:

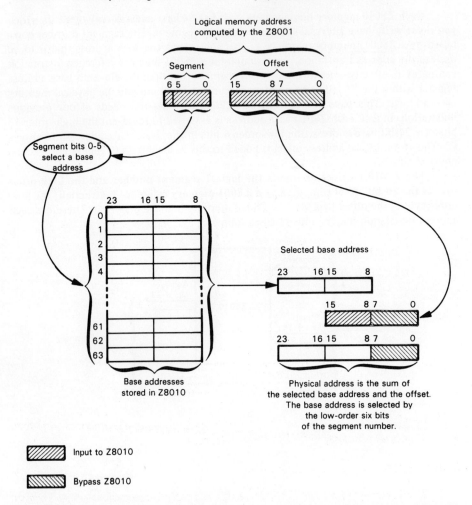

The high-order bit (bit 6) of the segment number does not participate in the address calculation performed by the Z8010. To use the full addressing range, the microcomputer must contain two Z8010s. The high-order bit of the segment number would then select one of the Z8010s.

SEGMENT DESCRIPTOR REGISTERS

The base addresses illustrated above are stored in segment descriptor registers. **Each Z8010 memory management unit has 64 segment descriptor registers,** which are addressed by the segment number computed by a Z8001 memory reference instruction. Segment descriptor registers may be illustrated as follows:

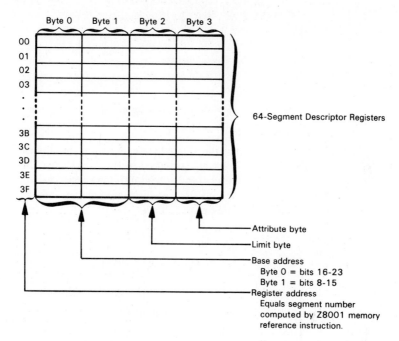

Let us examine the Attribute and Limit bytes of the segment descriptor registers. We have already described the base address bytes.

Limit Byte

The Limit byte specifies the addressable range for the segment. Values between 0 and FF_{16} may be written into the Limit byte; they specify segment sizes ranging from 1 to 256 256-byte blocks. Therefore a physical segment's size can increase in 256-byte increments from a minimum size of 256 bytes to a maximum size of 65,536 bytes.

If any value smaller than FF_{16} is written into the Limit byte of the Descriptor register, then some addresses computed for the segment by Z8001 memory reference instructions will be illegal.

Normally the Limit byte selects valid addresses beginning at the lowest address in the segment. For example, if $0F_{16}$ is written into the Limit byte, then this particular physical segment is limited to sixteen 256-byte memory blocks. The first 4096 bytes of the segment will be accessible. This may be illustrated as follows:

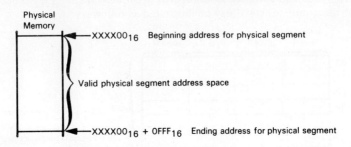

Optionally you may specify that the Limit byte apply from the highest memory address down. Stack segments are normally specified in this way, since Z8000 stacks originate at their highest memory address, and spread into lower memory addresses as the stack grows. If the Limit byte contains $0F_{16}$, as illustrated above, then a stack segment would create valid physical addresses as follows:

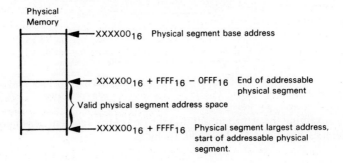

Attribute Byte

The Attribute byte of the Segment Descriptor register can be used to further restrict segment access. Attribute byte bits are interpreted as follows:

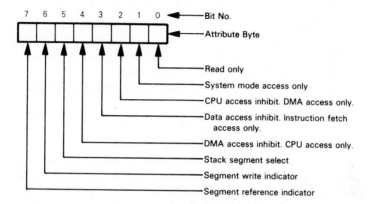

Attribute byte bit positions are "true" when set to 1, and "false" when reset to 0. Each Attribute byte describes a single segment. An attempt to access memory in violation of the restrictions set in the Attribute byte generates a segmentation trap interrupt request. In a properly designed Z8001 microcomputer system, if an attempt to access memory causes a segmentation trap, the memory access will be suppressed. This will prevent memory from being changed in violation of the restrictions in the Attribute byte.

Attribute byte bits 0 through 5 are control bits. Bits 6 and 7 are status bits.

Bit 0, when set to 1, allows the associated segment to be read but not written into.

Bit 1, if set to 1, allows the segment to be accessed in system mode only.

Bit 2, when set to 1, prevents any CPU access of the segment; direct memory accesses are allowed.

Bit 3, when set to 1, allows the segment to be accessed during instruction fetch machine cycles only. Therefore instructions, immediate data, and program relative data (LDR instruction) can be fetched from the segment, but other data cannot be accessed.

Bit 4, when set to 1, is the inverse of bit 2; the segment can be accessed by the CPU, but direct memory accesses are denied.

Remember, any of the conditions specified by bit 0 through 4, if contravened, cause a segmentation trap interrupt request. Also, in a properly designed Z8001 microcomputer system, the accompanying illegal memory access is suppressed.

Bit 5 of the Attribute byte, when set to 1, specifies a stack segment. As described earlier, a stack segment is originated at the segment's highest segment address, and the Limit byte specifies a memory space descending from this highest memory address. Whenever the last 256-byte block of a stack segment is written into, a warning segmentation trap interrupt request is generated. This segmentation trap is referred to as a warning trap because the memory access does occur, but program logic is alerted to the fact that the stack is running out of available memory.

Attribute byte **bit 6** is set to 1 whenever the associated segment is accessed by a write machine cycle. **Bit 7** is set to 1 when the associated segment is referenced, either by a read or a write machine cycle.

Bits 6 and 7 of the Attribute byte are not the only status indicators within the Z8010 memory management unit; there are six additional status registers which an interrupt service routine will interrogate following a segmentation trap. We will describe these status registers later, when discussing segmentation trap interrupt service routines.

CONTROL REGISTERS

You configure the Z8010 memory management unit by executing I/O instructions that access Z8010 internal registers. The I/O port address specified by the I/O instruction is interpreted partially as a command and partially as a device identifier. Table 13-1 summarizes Z8010 commands.

The Z8001 has a set of special I/O instructions that are intended for the Z8010 memory management unit. In your particular Z8001 microcomputer system, whether you use normal I/O instructions or special I/O instructions to access the Z8010 memory management unit will depend on how your microcomputer system has been designed.

Three control registers specify Z8010 devices' select logic and Segment Descriptor register addressing. The three control registers are:

- The Mode register

- The Segment Descriptor Address register

- The Segment Descriptor Selection Counter register

The Mode register controls the way in which the Z8010 memory management unit is selected. Register bit assignments may be illustrated as follows:

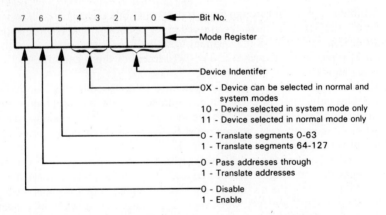

Bits 7 and 6 enable the Z8010 memory management unit and control its operation. Bit 7 is a master enable bit. This bit must be set to 1 for the Z8010 to operate. If the Z8010 is operating, then bit 6 determines whether addresses are translated or simply passed through.

If bit 6 is 1, then addresses are translated. If bit 6 is 0, then addresses are passed through unmodified. The segment number is passed through in bits 22-16 of the physical address; bit 23 is set to 0. Normally bit 6 of the Mode register will be 1.

Mode register bits 3, 4, and 5 control Z8010 selection logic.

Bit 5 determines which set of 64 segments the Z8010 memory management unit translates. Recall that the Z8001 generates a 7-bit segment number, representing 128 segments. Each Z8010 memory management unit translates 64 segments. If Mode register bit 5 is 1, then the Z8010 requires the high-order Segment bit to be 1, in which case it translates segment numbers 64 through 127. If bit 5 is 0, then the high-order segment bit must be 0, in which case the memory management unit translates segment numbers 0 through 63.

Mode register **bits 3 and 4** let you specify different memory management units in system and normal modes. If bit 3 is 0, then the memory management unit ignores the Z8001 mode setting. If bit 3 is 1, then bit 4 determines the mode to which this memory management unit will respond; if bit 3 is 1 and bit 4 is 0, the memory management unit will only translate addresses in system mode. If bits 3 and 4 are both 1, the memory management unit will only translate addresses in normal mode.

It is important to differentiate between bits 3 and 4 of the Mode register and bit 1 of the Attribute byte. The Mode register determines the circumstances under which the entire memory management unit will operate. In contrast, the Attribute byte determines the type of memory accesses that will be allowed, on a sector-by-sector basis. Clearly, Attribute byte bit 1 is logically related to Mode register bits 3 and 4; for example, Attribute byte bit 1 cannot specify any segment as accessible in system mode only, if the Mode register simultaneously specifies that the entire memory management unit could translate only normal mode addresses.

Mode register **bits 0, 1, and 2** hold a device number which affects the identifier word that is returned during the segmentation trap interrupt acknowledgment sequence. This identifier does not contribute in any way to memory management unit device select logic. For example, when you execute I/O instructions in order to access memory management unit registers, bits 0, 1, and 2 of the Mode register do not determine the device's I/O port number. These three bits are used only during the interrupt acknowledgment process.

When you execute an I/O instruction that writes data to a memory management unit, or reads data from it, you always access a byte register. If the accessed byte register is one of the Segment Descriptor register bytes, then **you must use the Segment Descriptor Address register to select a Segment Descriptor register. The Descriptor Selection Counter register identifies the byte within the Segment Descriptor register to be selected.** These two registers may be illustrated as follows:

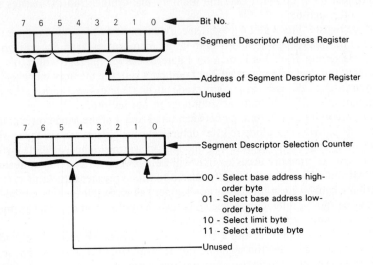

You will not normally write into the Descriptor Selection Counter register. Commands that access a Segment Descriptor register byte automatically modify Descriptor Selection Counter register bits to indicate the byte being accessed.

CONFIGURING Z8010 MEMORY MANAGEMENT UNITS

We will use special I/O instructions to configure Z8010 memory management units. If your microcomputer requires normal I/O instructions instead of special I/O instructions, this will not affect program logic.

Z8010 memory management units are accessed as I/O ports. There is no "natural" way in which I/O port numbers are assigned to Z8010 memory management units; **you will have to read your microcomputer's documentation to discover how Z8010 devices are addressed in your particular case.**

In a small Z8001 microcomputer system where a single Z8010 memory management unit is present, the device may need no I/O port address. If special I/O instructions are used only to access the Z8010 memory management unit, and nowhere else, then the "special" I/O instruction status can also serve as device select logic. On the other hand, if two Z8010 memory management units are present, where one translates addresses for segments 0 through 63, while the other translates addresses for segments 64 through 127, then each Z8010 memory management unit will require its own unique I/O port address.

Z8010 I/O port addresses appear in the low-order byte of the 16-bit I/O port number. The high-order byte of the I/O port number is interpreted as a command. For details, see Table 13- 1.

13-1. Z8010 Memory Management Unit Instructions

Type	I/O Port Number	Register Accessed	Z8000 Command Interpretation		
			Read ?	Write ?	Other Operations
C	00NN	Mode Control	X	X	None
C	01NN	Segment Descriptor Address	X	X	None
S	02NN	Violation Type	X		None
S	03NN	Violation Segment Number	X		None
S	04NN	Violation Offset	X		None
S	05NN	Bus Status	X		None
S	06NN	Instruction Segment Number	X		None
S	07NN	Instruction Offset	X		None
D	08NN	Segment Descriptor Base Address*	X	X	None
D	09NN	Segment Descriptor Limit Byte	X	X	None
D	0ANN	Segment Descriptor Attribute Byte	X	X	None
D	0BNN	Segment Descriptor**	X	X	None
D	0CNN	Segment Descriptor Base Address*	X	X	Increment Segment Descriptor Address Register
D	0DNN	Segment Descriptor Limit Byte	X	X	Increment Segment Descriptor Address Register
D	0ENN	Segment Descriptor Attribute Byte	X	X	Increment Segment Descriptor Address Register
D	0FNN	Segment Descriptor**	X	X	Increment Segment Descriptor Address Register
	10NN	Not Implemented			
S	11NN	Violation Type			Reset entire register
	12NN	Not Implemented			
S	13NN	Violation Type			Reset bit 6, SWW Flag
S	14NN	Violation Type			Reset bit 7, Fatal Flag
D	15NN	Attribute Byte of all Segment Descriptor Registers			Set bit 1 in all Inhibit CPU access
D	16NN	Attribute Byte of all Segment Descriptor Registers			Set bit 4 in all Inhibit DMA access
	17NN	Not Implemented			
C	1FNN / 20NN	Descriptor Selection Counter	X	X	None
	21NN				
	FFNN	Not Implemented			

C - Control register access instructions
D - Data register access instructions
S - Status register access instructions
NN - I/O port number to select a particular Z8010

* Alternate executions access the high-order byte, then the low-order byte.

** Repeated executions access base address high-order byte, then base address low-order byte, then limit byte, then attribute byte.

Configuration of the Z8010 is likely to be one of the first programs executed after a Z8001 microcomputer system is powered up, since all subsequent memory accesses will be affected by the way memory management units are configured. Moreover, while memory management units are disabled, no memory addresses are output — in which case memory receives only the low-order byte of any memory address. Every microcomputer will have a procedure for handling Z8010 initialization. We will assume that some portion of memory bypasses the memory management unit when the microcomputer is first turned on, allowing execution of a small program that gets the configuration process started. The first step might be to configure one Z8010 memory management unit so that it is enabled, but does not translate addresses. Here is the appropriate instruction sequence:

```
LDB     RL0,#%80        ! Initialization code !
SOUTB   %0000,RL0       ! Output to Mode register !
```

After these two instructions have been executed, one memory management unit will be enabled, but will transmit addresses as computed, without translation. This allows the rest of the configuration routine to be stored in some portion of memory that is addressed without memory address translation. If two Z8010 memory management units are present, then one might be enabled without address translation, while the other is disabled. Here is an appropriate instruction sequence:

```
LDB     RL0,#%00        ! Disable MMU 1 !
SOUTB   %0001,RL0
LDB     RL0,#%80        ! Enable MMU 0 without translation !
SOUTB   %0000,RL0
```

I/O port addresses %0000 and %0001 are illustrated. The high-order byte (00) selects the Mode Control register (see Table 13-1). The low-order byte (00 or 01) selects a memory management unit.

Suppose a full complement of eight memory management units are connected to a Z8001 microprocessor. The first memory management unit might be enabled without address translation, while the remaining seven units are disabled, as follows:

```
LDB     RL0,#%00        ! Disable MMU 1 through 7 !
SOUTB   %0001,RL0
SOUTB   %0002,RL0
SOUTB   %0003,RL0
SOUTB   %0004,RL0
SOUTB   %0005,RL0
SOUTB   %0006,RL0
SOUTB   %0007,RL0
LDB     RL0,#%80        ! Enable MMU 0 without translation !
SOUTB   %0000,RL0
```

You should disable memory management units that need to be disabled before enabling one memory management unit; this prevents any unknown MMU register contents from causing strange address translations.

Note that the SOUT instruction has no register indirect I/O port addressing variation. If eight memory management units are present, eight SOUT instructions must be executed, as illustrated above.

PROGRAM EXAMPLES

13-1. Translate Segment 00 Addresses

Purpose: Configure a Z8010 memory management unit to translate addresses in segment 00. The segment is to be accessed in system mode only, with DMA accesses inhibited. The physical segment size is 65,536 bytes and the physical base address is 028000. The Z8010 is programmed using special I/O instructions; it is addressed as I/O port 00.

Since the segment is accessed in system mode with DMA inhibited, 12_{16} must be written into the Segment Descriptor register's Attribute byte, and $C8_{16}$ must be written into the Mode Control register; this sets the device number to 0 in the three low-order Mode Control register bits. FF_{16} must be loaded into the limit byte.

Program 13-1:

```
                internal
                pgm_13_1 procedure
                entry
                        $abs      IBASE
4600 C880       LDB     RL0,#%80       ! Enable MMU, no translation !
4602 3A87       SOUTB   %0000,RL0      ! To MMU Mode register !
4604 0000
4606 C800       LDB     RL0,#%00       ! Segment Descriptor... !
                                       ! ...Register number !
4608 3A87       SOUTB   %0100,RL0      ! To Segment Descriptor... !
460A 0100
                                       ! ...Address register !
460C 2100       LD      R0,#%0280      ! Segment 00 base address !
460E 0280
4610 3A07       SOUTB   %0800,RH0      ! To Segment Descriptor... !
4612 0800
4614 3A87       SOUTB   %0800,RL0      ! ...high order byte... !
4616 0800
                                       ! ...then low order byte !
4618 2100       LD      R0,#%12FF
461A 12FF
461C 3A07       SOUTB   %0900,RH0      ! Attribute byte is 12 !
461E 0900
4620 3A87       SOUTB   %0A00,RL0      ! Limit byte is FF !
4622 0A00
4624 C8C8       LDB     RL0,#%C8       ! Enable MMU with translation !
4626 3A87       SOUTB   %0000,RL0      ! To MMU Mode Register !
4628 0000
462A 7A00       HALT

462C            end     pgm_13_1
```

13-2. Initialize Segment Descriptor Registers

Purpose: Configure a Z8010 memory management unit. All 64 Segment Descriptor registers must be initialized. Segment Descriptor register initialization data is held in data tables origined at memory location 6000. Data is held in the following byte sequence:

Program 13-2a:

```
              internal
              pgm_13_2a procedure
              entry
                 $abs     IBASE

4600 C880        LDB      RL0,#%80        ! Enable MMU, no translation !
4602 3A87        SOUTB    %0000,RL0       ! To MMU Mode register !
4604 0000
4606 7601        LDA      R1,%6000        ! Data address !
4608 6000
460A 2102        LD       R2,#64*4        ! Byte count !
460C 0100
460E C800        LDB      RL0,#%00
4610 3A87        SOUTB    %0100,RL0       ! To Segment Descriptor... !
4612 0100                                 ! ...Address register !
                 ! Set up I/O port pointer registers !
4614 2103        LD       R3,#%0800       ! Base address port !
4616 0800
4618 2104        LD       R4,#%0900       ! Limit byte port !
461A 0900
461C 2105        LD       R5,#%0E00       ! Attribute byte port and... !
461E 0E00                                 ! ...increment segment... !
                                          ! ...descriptor addr command !
4620 3A13  LOOP: SOUTIB   @R3,@R1,R2      ! Base address high byte !
4622 0238
4624 3A13        SOUTIB   @R3,@R1,R2      ! Base address low byte !
4626 0238
4628 3A13        SOUTIB   @R4,@R1,R2      ! Limit byte !
462A 0248
462C 3A13        SOUTIB   @R5,@R1,R2      ! Attribute byte, increment... !
462E 0258                                 ! ...segment descriptor addr !
4630 ECF7        JR       NOV,LOOP        ! Repeat for each segment !
4632 C8C0        LDB      RL0,#%C0        ! Enable MMU with translation !
4634 3A87        SOUTB    %0000,RL0
4636 0000
4638 7A00        HALT

463A             end      pgm_13_2a
```

Program 13-2a does not define any segment characteristics. Definitions will depend on the data actually stored in the initialization table.

By using command codes $0B_{16}$ and $0F_{16}$, we can make our initialization program shorter, as shown in program 13-2b.

Program 13-2b:

```
                  internal
                    pgm_13_2b procedure
                  entry
                       $abs     IBASE

4600 C880            LDB      RL0,#%80
4602 3A87            SOUTB    %0000,RL0       ! Enable MMU without translation !
4604 0000
4606 7601            LDA      R1,%6000        ! Data address !
4608 6000
460A 2102            LD       R2,#64          ! 64 segments to initialize !
460C 0040
460E C800            LDB      RL0,#%00
4610 3A87            SOUTB    %0100,RL0       ! Segment Descriptor... !
4612 0100                                     ! ...Address register !
                     ! Set up I/O port pointers !
4614 2103            LD       R3,#%0B00       ! Descriptor all fields I/O port !
4616 0B00
4618 2104            LD       R4,#%0F00       ! Descriptor all fields port... !
461A 0F00                                     ! ...and increment segment... !
                                              ! ...descriptor addr command !
461C 2105   LOOP:    LD       R5,#3
461E 0003
4620 3A13            SOTIRB   @R3,@R1,R5      ! 2 bytes of base address... !
4622 0530                                     ! ...and limit byte !
4624 3A13            SOUTIB   @R4,@R1,R2      ! Attribute byte, increment... !
4626 0248                                     ! ...descriptor register !
4628 ECF9            JR       NOV,LOOP        ! Repeat for each segment !
462A C8C0            LDB      RL0,#%C0        ! Enable MMU with translation !
462C 3A87            SOUTB    %0000,RL0
462E 0000
4630 7A00            HALT

4632            end       pgm_13_2b
```

If initialization data is held in this sequence:

    64   16-bit base addresses
    64   Limit bytes
    64   Attribute bytes

can you rewrite the configuration program using commands 08, 0C, 0D, and 0E?

Once a memory management unit has been configured, you can at any time modify a specific segment's translation parameters by writing new data to the appropriate Segment Descriptor register. For example, suppose segment $0A_{16}$ has been configured as a stack segment, with 20_{16} in the Limit byte. Can you write a short program to increase the physical segment size by writing 28_{16} into the Limit byte?

SEGMENTATION TRAP ACKNOWLEDGMENT

Once a Z8010 memory management unit has been configured and enabled, it operates without program intervention until a warning or error condition occurs, at which time a segmentation trap interrupt request is generated.

An error condition will cause a segmentation trap interrupt request; the memory access causing the error condition will be denied in a properly designed Z8000 microcomputer system. Error conditions occur when a memory access references a location beyond the addressing range specified by the segment's Limit byte, or when the memory access is of a type that has been declared illegal in the segment's Attribute byte.

A warning segmentation trap interrupt request occurs when you write into the last 256-byte block of a segment that has been specified as a stack segment. Remember, the last 256-byte block of a stack segment has the smallest memory addresses within the segment.

Violation Type Status Register

The interrupt service routine executed by the Z8001 microprocessor in response to a segmentation trap **can read the contents of six Z8010 status registers** in order to determine why the segmentation trap occurred. **The Violation Type Status register is the most important** of the six; its bits are set and reset as follows:

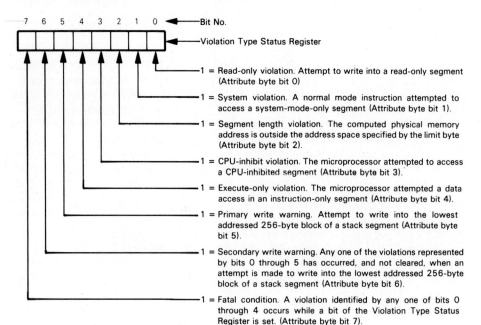

A 1 in any Violation Type Status register bit represents an error condition.

Violation Type Status register bits 1 through 5 report violations corresponding to bits 1 through 4 of a Segment Attribute and a violation of the Limit byte. We will examine these bits first.

If an instruction attempts to write into a read-only segment, then bit 0 is set.

If a segment is reserved for system mode accesses only, then any attempt to access the segment in a normal mode will cause bit 1 to be set.

If the physical address computed by the Z8010 memory management unit falls outside of the addressing range specified by the segment's Limit byte, then bit 2 is set.

A segment can be off limits to any CPU access; only direct memory accesses are then allowed. If the microprocessor attempts to address this segment, then bit 3 will be set.

A segment can be set aside for instruction accesses only. An attempt to read data out of the segment, or to write data into it, will cause bit 4 to be set.

Bit 5 is set when the microprocessor writes into the lowest addressed 256-byte block of a stack segment. This is referred to as a primary write warning.

Violation Type Status register bits 6 and 7 report violations which occur while servicing a segmentation trap.

If the microprocessor attempts to write into the lowest addressed 256-byte block of a stack segment while pushing data onto the stack during a segmentation trap interrupt acknowledgment, then a secondary write warning (SWN) is flagged; Violation Type Status register bit 6 is set.

Bit 7 is set if any violation represented by status bits 1 through 4 is detected while a segmentation trap is being serviced. This is a fatal error.

If a secondary write warning or a fatal error occurs, no further errors are detected, nor are any further segmentation trap interrupts requested until the conditions already reported have been serviced and the Violation Type Status register has been cleared.

A segment can be off limits to DMA access; only CPU accesses are then allowed. If a DMA device attempts to access this segment, no segmentation trap occurs; there is not much the CPU could do in this case. A signal is provided by the Z8010 which the computer designer should use to suppress the off limits DMA access.

The remaining five status registers attempt to identify the memory access attempt which caused the segmentation trap to occur. Unfortunately the exact location of the offending instruction cannot be reported by the Z8010 memory management unit, since it does not receive the entire logical address output by the Z8001 microprocessor. Only the logical segment number and high-order offset byte are received. These are reported for the memory access that caused the segmentation trap to occur, and for the most recent instruction fetch. These four registers may be illustrated as follows:

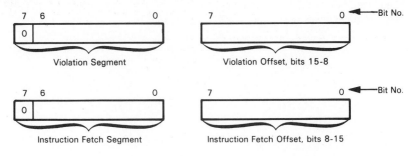

Violation Segment   Violation Offset, bits 15-8

Instruction Fetch Segment   Instruction Fetch Offset, bits 8-15

Table 13-2. CPU Status in MMU Bus Cycle Status Register

Bus Cycle Status Bits 0-3	CPU Operation
0000	Internal operation
0001	Memory refresh
0010	I/O reference
0011	Special I/O reference
0100	Segmentation trap acknowledgment
0101	Non-maskable interrupt acknowledgment
0110	Non-vectored interrupt acknowledgment
0111	Vectored interrupt acknowledgment
1000	Data memory request
1001	Stack memory request
1010	Data memory request (EPU)
1011	Stack memory request (EPU)
1100	Instruction memory request
1101	Instruction fetch, first word
1110	CPU/EPU transfer
1111	Reserved

If an instruction fetch caused the segmentation trap, then the Violation and Instruction Segment/Offset registers will contain the same addresses.

The last of the six status registers is the Bus Cycle Status register. Its bits are interpreted as follows:

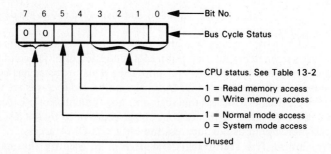

CPU status reported in bits 0 through 3 can be decoded as shown in Table 13-2. Bit 4 identifies the violation as having occurred during a read or a write access. Bit 5 reports the violation as having occurred while the microprocessor was in system or normal mode.

The Z8001 microprocessor acknowledges a segmentation trap by transferring control to an appropriate interrupt service routine. The actual acknowledgment sequence is identical for a segmentation trap or any other interrupt; this acknowledgment sequence was described in Chapter 12.

The identifier word returned by a memory management unit during the segmentation trap interrupt has one bit set in the high-order byte. The device ID written into bits 0 through 2 of the Mode Control register selects the identifier bit which will be set. You should assume that **the low-order byte of the identifier is indeterminate.** Thus the identifier word returned by a memory management unit may be illustrated as follows:

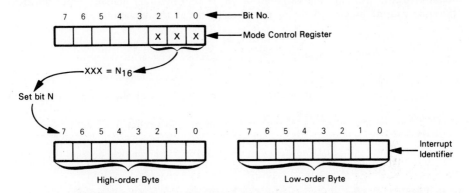

In a Z8001 microcomputer system that has more than one memory management unit, the segmentation trap interrupt service routine must first identify the memory management unit that requested the interrupt. This is done using the high-order identifier byte. More than one MMU may have requested a segmentation trap. In this case, more than one bit will be set in the high-order byte of the identifier.

One method of identifying the unit or units requesting the trap uses the BIT instruction; this routine allows interrupt service routine entry points to be anywhere in memory. Here is the instruction sequence:

```
        ! Segmentation trap. Identify acknowledged MMU !

        LDB     RL0,@R15        ! Read high-order identifier byte !
        CLRB    RH0
        LD      R1,#7           ! Use R1 as bit identifier !
LOOP:   BITB    RL0,R1          ! Test next bit !
        JR      NZ,FOUND        ! Look for a 1 bit !
        DBJNZ   RL1,LOOP        ! Decrement bit counter and... !
                                ! ...test next bit !
FOUND:  SLL     R1              ! Shift bit number left one bit !
        LD      R1,JTABLE(R1)   ! Use as jump table index !
        CALL    @R1             ! Call the addressed subroutine !
        IRET

JTABLE:                         ! Eight interrupt service routine... !
                                ! ...entry points are stored here !
```

   The interrupt service routine executed for a particular memory management unit should begin by reading the Violation Type Status register. First test bit 7, the fatal condition status. Next test bit 6, the secondary write warning status. If neither bit 7 nor bit 6 is set, then use bits 0 through 5 to identify the condition which caused the segmentation trap. Assuming that special I/O instructions are used to access the memory management unit, and I/O Port Address 2 selects the memory management unit being acknowledged, the following variation of the second memory management unit identification routine illustrated above will correctly detect the violation type:

```
           ! Identify Violation Type !

           SINB     RL0,%0202       ! Violation type status from MMU 2 !
           CLRB     RH0
           LD       R1,#7           ! Use R1 as bit identifier !
LOOP:      BITB     RL0,R1          ! Test next bit !
           JR       NZ,VIOLATION    ! 1 bit means found the violation !
           DEC      R1
           JR       GE,LOOP
           IRET                     ! There are no errors !
VIOLATION:
           SLL      R1              ! Form index into jump table !
           LD       R1,JTABLE(R1)   ! Violation type routine address !
           CALL     @R1
           IRET

JTABLE:                            ! Eight violation type interrupt... !
                                   ! ...serivce routine entry... !
                                   ! ...addresses are stored here !
```

   The Violation Type Status register must be reset. However, bits should not be reset until the error condition has been serviced. For example, if you reset bit 7 of the Violation Type Status register as the first step in the fatal condition interrupt service routine, then another fatal condition segmentation trap could occur immediately, and that would not be productive. You would probably be repeatedly interrupted at that point and never proceed. After the fatal condition has been serviced, reset bit 7 of the Violation Type Status register using the instruction:

```
           SOUTB    %1402,RLn       ! Reset MMU 2 Fatal status flag !
```

   RLn can be any register since no data is actually received by the memory management unit. The low-order byte of the I/O port address (02) can have any value that selects the memory management unit being reset. After the fatal condition has been serviced, you must return to the instruction sequence illustrated previously to identify another violation type; remember, after a fatal condition or a secondary write warning has been serviced, another Violation Type Status register bit will still be set, and in need of service.

   The secondary warning status bit is reset using the following instruction:

```
           SOUTB    %1300,RLn       ! Reset MMU 0 Secondary !
                                    ! Write Warning status !
```

   After all violations have been serviced, reset the entire Violation Type Status register using the following instruction:

```
           SOUTB    %1104,RLn       ! Reset MMU 4 Violation Type !
                                    ! status register !
```

The way in which you service any segmentation trap will depend entirely on your own memory management program logic. Remember, you can obtain some information regarding the source of the segmentation trap by reading the remaining five status registers. You do this using a SINB instruction as follows:

```
SINB    RL0,%0n00       ! Read MMU 0 Status Register n !
```

Any 8-bit register can replace RL0. The symbol n represents one of the digits 3 through 7, which identifies the status register being read. For details, see Table 13-1.

MULTIPLE-CPU CONFIGURATIONS

Z8000 microprocessors have handshaking signals which are used to control access of any shared resource. For example, a memory device that can be accessed by two or more microprocessors is a shared resource. If two or more microprocessors were to access a shared memory simultaneously, the results could be disastrous. Therefore some type of external logic will be designed into any multi-microprocessor system to prevent simultaneous accesses from occurring.

Each microprocessor will use the MI input signal to find out if a shared resource is available. The microprocessor will use the MO output signal to request shared resource access. The four instructions MBIT, MREQ, MRES, and MSET manipulate these two signals.

Normally microprocessors will connect with a shared memory resource, or disconnect from it by enabling or disabling a memory management unit. As a programmer, you need not concern yourself with the details of logic interfaces, but your program must configure the memory management unit correctly, then enable and disable it at the proper time.

PROGRAM EXAMPLE

13-3. Request Shared Resource

Purpose: Disable a memory management unit which is accessed as Special I/O Port 2. Request shared resource access by setting the MO output signal. When access is granted via the MI signal, enable the memory management unit. When finished with the memory, reset the MO output signal.

Task 1: Use the MBIT, MRES, and MSET instructions

Task 2: Use the MREQ and MRES instructions

Flowchart 13-3:

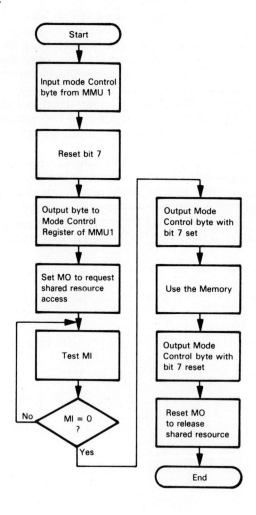

Program 13-3a:

```
                internal
                  pgm_13_3a procedure
                  entry
                      $abs     IBASE

4600 3A85             SINB     RL0,%0002        ! Input MMU 2 mode byte !
4602 0002
4604 A287             RESB     RL0,#7           ! Reset master enable bit !
4606 A080             LDB      RH0,RL0          ! Second version in RH0... !
4608 A407             SETB     RH0,#7           ! ...with master enable set !
460A 3A87             SOUTB    %0002,RL0        ! Ensure MMU disabled !
460C 0002
460E 7B08             MSET                      ! Request shared resource !
4610 7B0A    LOOP:    MBIT                      ! Test for resource available !
4612 EDFE             JR       PL,LOOP
4614 3A07             SOUTB    %0002,RH0        ! MMU 2 is available; enable it !
4616 0002
                      ! Use the memory !

4618 3A87             SOUTB    %0002,RL0        ! Disable MMU 2 !
461A 0002
461C 7B09             MRES                      ! Realease shared resource !
461E 7A00             HALT

4620             end      pgm_13_3a
```

Task 1, shown in program 13-3a, is very straightforward. The MSET instruction sets MO; this is assumed to constitute a shared resource request. When MI is 0 the resource is assumed to be available. MBIT reports the MI level in the S status. When the resource is available, MMU 1 is enabled. After using the resource, release it by resetting MO with the MRES instruction.

The task 2 program (program 13-3b) takes a slightly different approach. The MREQ instruction requests shared resource access by setting MO. If the shared resource is not available at this time, as indicated by MI, then instruction execution ends. If the shared resource appears to be available, MREQ computes a time delay by decrementing the contents of the destination register, then checks to make sure that the request for access to the shared resource was recognized and granted by the other processors.

The Z and S status flags report the results of MREQ instruction execution as follows:

If Z and S are both 0, then the shared resource was not available when requested.

If S is low, but Z is high, then the shared resource appeared to be available, but the request for access was denied.

If Z and S are both high, then the shared resource access request was granted.

Program 13-3b:

```
              constant
                  COUNT := %400                    ! Delay count for MREQ !

              internal
                  pgm_13_3b procedure
                  entry
                      $abs     IBASE

4600 3A85             SINB     RL0,%0002           ! Input MMU 2 mode byte !
4602 0002
4604 A287             RESB     RL0,#7              ! Reset master enable bit !
4606 A080             LDB      RH0,RL0             ! Second version in RH0... !
4608 A407             SETB     RH0,#7              ! ...with master enable set !
460A 3A87             SOUTB    %0002,RL0           ! Disable MMU 2 !
460C 0002
460E 2101             LD       R1,#COUNT           ! Delay counter for MREQ !
4610 0400
4612 7B1D             MREQ     R1
4614 E503             JR       MI,AVAILABLE
4616 E601             JR       Z,DENIED
4618 7A00             HALT                         ! MMU 2 not available !

                                                   ! MMU 2 available but denied !
              DENIED:
461A 7A00             HALT

              AVAILABLE:                           ! MMU 2 is available !
461C 3A07             SOUTB    %0002,RH0           ! Enable MMU 2 !
461E 0002

              ! Use the memory !

4620 3A87             SOUTB    %0002,RL0           ! Disable MMU 2 !
4622 0002
4624 7B09             MRES                         ! Release shared resource !
4626 7A00             HALT

4628          end     pgm_13_3b
```

REFERENCES

1. David Stevenson, *An Introduction to the Z8010 MMU Memory Management Unit — Tutorial Information.* Zilog, October 1979.

2. Zilog, Inc, *Z8010 MMU Technical Manual.*

14
Problem Definition and Program Design

In previous chapters we concentrated on writing short assembly language programs. This is an important topic, but it is only a small part of software development. Writing programs in assembly language is a major task for the beginner but it soon becomes simple. Integrating the programs into a working system is more difficult.

By now you should be familiar with standard methods for programming in assembly language on the Z8000 microprocessor. **The next four chapters will describe how to formulate tasks as programs and how to combine short programs to form a working system.**

STAGES OF SOFTWARE DEVELOPMENT

Software development involves many stages. Figure 14-1 illustrates the software development process. The following stages are shown:

1. Problem definition

2. Program design

3. Documentation

4. Coding

5. Debugging

6. Testing

7. Maintenance and Redesign

Each of these stages is important in the construction of a working system. Coding, the writing of programs in a form that the computer understands, is only one of the seven stages. In fact, **coding is usually the easiest stage.** The rules for writing computer programs are easy to learn. They vary somewhat from computer to computer, but the basic techniques remain the same. Few software projects run into trouble because of coding; coding is not the most time-consuming part of software development. Experts estimate that a programmer can write one to ten fully debugged and documented statements per day. Clearly, the mere coding of one to ten statements is hardly a full day's effort. On most software projects, coding occupies less than 25% of the programmer's time.

Measuring progress in the other stages is difficult. You can say that half of the program has been written, but you can hardly say that half of the errors have been removed or half of the problem has been defined. Timetables for such stages as program design, debugging, and testing are difficult to produce. Many days or weeks of effort may result in no clear progress. Furthermore, an incomplete job in one stage may result in tremendous problems later. For example, poor problem definition or program design can make debugging and testing very difficult. Time saved in one stage may be spent many times over in later stages.

Problem Definition

During problem definition you specify the task in terms of the requirements that it places on the computer. For example, what is necessary to make a computer control a tool, run a series of electrical tests, handle communications between a central computer and a remote terminal, solve a mathematical problem, or perform a data processing task? Problem definition requires that you determine the format and transfer rates for inputs and outputs, the amount and speed of processing that is needed, the computations to be performed, and the types of possible errors and their handling. Problem definition takes the vague idea of building a computer system and produces a definition of the tasks and requirements for the computer.

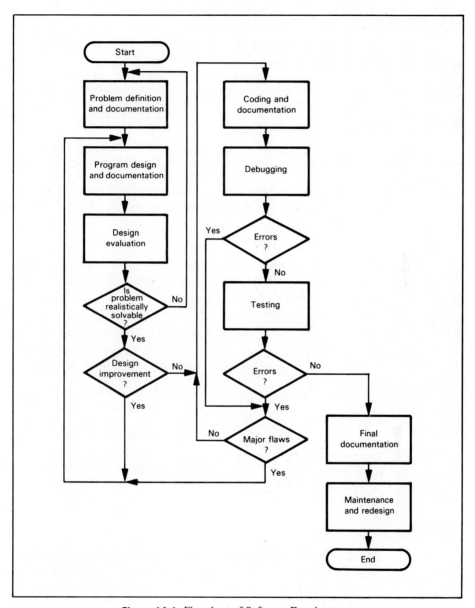

Figure 14-1. Flowchart of Software Development

Program Design

During program design you outline the computer program which will perform the tasks that have been defined. In the design stage, tasks are described in a way that is easily converted into a program. **Among the useful techniques in this stage are flowcharting, structured programming, modular programming, and top-down design.**

Documentation

Documentation is the description of the program in a form that users and maintenance personnel can understand. Documentation also allows the designer to develop a program library, so that subsequent tasks will be far simpler. Flowcharts, comments, memory maps, and library forms are some of the tools used in documentation. Documentation must begin early in the development process and continue throughout.

Coding

Coding involves writing the program in a form that the computer can either directly understand or translate. The form may be machine language, assembly language, or a high-level language.

Debugging

Debugging involves making the program do what the design specified that it would do. In this stage, you use such tools as breakpoints, traces, simulators, and, if necessary, logic analyzers. The end of the debugging stage is hard to define, since you never know when you have found the last error.

Testing

Testing, also referred to as program validation, **ensures that the program performs the overall system tasks correctly.** The designer uses simulators, exercisers, and various statistical techniques to measure the program's performance. This stage is like quality control for hardware.

Maintenance and Redesign

Maintenance and redesign include the servicing, improvement, and extension of the program. Clearly, the designer must be ready to handle field problems in computer-based equipment. Special diagnostic modes or programs and other maintenance tools may be required. The program may need to be upgraded or extended to meet new requirements or handle new tasks.

The rest of this chapter will consider only the problem definition and program design stages. Chapter 15 will discuss debugging and testing. Chapter 16 will discuss documentation, extension, and redesign. We will bring all the stages together using simple examples in Chapter 17.

PROBLEM DEFINITION

Typical microprocessor tasks require a lot of definition. For example, what must a program do to control a scale, a cash register, or a signal generator? Clearly, we have a long way to go just to define the tasks involved.

INPUTS

How do we start the definition? The obvious place to begin is with the inputs. **We should begin by listing all the inputs that the computer may receive in this application.**
Examples of inputs are:

- Data blocks from transmission lines

- Status words or data from peripherals

- Data from A/D converters

We may then ask the following questions about each input:

1. What is its form; i.e., what signals will the computer actually receive?

2. When is the input available and how does the processor know it is available? Does the processor have to request the input? Does the input provide its own clock?

3. How long is the input available?

4. How often does the input change, and how does the processor know that it has changed?

5. Does the input consist of a sequence or block of data? Is the order important?

6. What should be done if the data contains errors? These may include transmission errors, incorrect data, sequencing errors, extra data, etc.

7. What should be done if the processor makes a timing error?

8. Is the input related to other inputs or outputs?

OUTPUTS

Next define the outputs. **We must list all the outputs that the computer must produce.** Examples of outputs include:

- Data blocks to transmission lines
- Control words or data to peripherals
- Data to D/A converters

We may then ask the following questions about each output:

1. What is its form, i.e., what signals must the computer produce?

2. When must it be available, and how does the peripheral know it is available?

3. How long must it be available?

4. How often must it change, and how does the peripheral know that it has changed?

5. Is there a sequence of outputs?

6. What should be done to avoid transmission errors or to sense and recover from peripheral failures?

7. What should be done if the peripheral detects a transmission error or a timing failure by the processor?

8. How is the output related to other inputs and outputs?

PROCESSING SECTION

The processing section lies between reading input and sending output. Here **we must determine exactly how the computer must process the input data. The questions are:**

1. What is the basic procedure (algorithm) for transforming input data into output?

2. What time constraints exist? These may include data rates, delay times, the time constants of input and output devices, etc.

3. What memory constraints exist? Do we have limits on the amount of program memory or data memory, or on the size of buffers?

4. What standard programs or tables must be used? What are their requirements?

5. What special cases exist, and how should the program handle them?

6. How accurate must the results be?

7. How should the program handle processing errors or special conditions such as overflow, underflow, or loss of significance?

ERROR HANDLING

The way errors are handled is important in most applications. A well designed program must cope with all common errors; it must also detect malfunctions and less common errors. **Among the questions that the designer must ask at the definition stage are:**

1. What errors could occur?

2. Which errors are most likely? If a person operates the system, human error is the most common. Following human errors, communications or transmission errors are more common than mechanical, electrical, mathematical, or processor errors.

3. Which errors will not be immediately obvious to the system? A special problem is the occurrence of errors that the system or operator may not recognize as errors.

4. How can the system recover from errors with a minimum loss of time and data and yet be aware that an error has occurred?

5. Which errors or malfunctions have no immediately discernible impact on system behavior? How can these errors or malfunctions be identified for diagnostic purposes?

6. Which errors require special system procedures? For example, do parity errors require retransmission of data?

Another question is: How can the field technician systematically find the source of malfunctions without being an expert? Built-in test programs, special diagnostics, or signature analysis can help.[1]

HUMAN INTERACTION

Many microprocessor-based systems involve human interaction. **Human factors must be considered throughout the development process for such systems. Among the questions that the designer must ask are:**

1. What input procedures are most natural for the human operator?

2. Can the operator easily determine how to begin, continue and end the input operations?

3. How is the operator informed of procedural errors and equipment malfunctions?

4. What errors is the operator most likely to make?

5. How does the operator know that data has been entered correctly?

6. Are displays in a form that the operator can easily read and understand?

7. Is the response of the system adequate for the operator?

8. Is the system easy for the operator to use?

9. Is an inexperienced operator given adequate guidance?

10. Are there shortcuts and reasonable options for the experienced operator?

11. Can the operator always determine the state of the system, or reset it, after interruptions or distractions?

Building a system for people to use is difficult. The microprocessor can make the system more powerful, more flexible, and more responsive. However, the designer still must add the human touches that can greatly increase the usefulness and attractiveness of the system and the productivity of the human operator.[2]

EXAMPLES: PROBLEM DEFINITION

14-1. Response to a Switch

Figure 14-2 shows a simple system in which the input is from a single SPST switch and the output is to a single LED display. In response to a switch closure, the processor turns the display on for one second. This system should be easy to define.

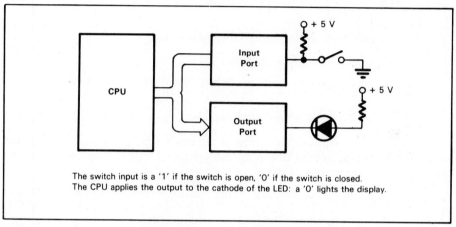

The switch input is a '1' if the switch is open, '0' if the switch is closed.
The CPU applies the output to the cathode of the LED: a '0' lights the display.

Figure 14-2. Switch and Light System

Input. Let us first examine the input and answer each of the questions previously presented:

1. The input is a single bit, which may be either '0' (switch closed) or '1' (switch open).

2. The input is always available and need not be requested.

3. The input is available for at least several milliseconds after the closure.

4. The input will seldom change more than once every few seconds. The processor has to handle only the bounce in the switch. The processor must monitor the switch to determine when it is closed.

5. There is no sequence of inputs.

6. The obvious input errors are switch failure, failure in the input circuitry, and the operator attempting to close the switch again before a sufficient amount of time has elapsed. We will discuss the handling of these errors later.

7. The input does not depend on any other inputs or outputs.

Output. The next requirement in defining the system is to examine the output. The answers to our questions are:

1. The output is a single bit which is '0' to turn the display on, '1' to turn if off.

2. There are no time constraints on the output. The peripheral does not need to be informed of the availability of data.

3. If the display is an LED, the data need be available for only a few milliseconds at a pulse rate of about 100 times per second. The observer will see a continuously lit display.

4. The data must change (go off) after one second.

5. There is no sequence of outputs.

6. The possible output errors are display failure and failure in the output circuitry.

7. The output depends only on the switch input and time.

Processing. The processing section is extremely simple. As soon as the switch input becomes a logic '0', the CPU turns the light on (a logic '0') for one second. No time or memory constraints exist.

Error Handling. Let us now look at the possible errors and malfunctions. These are:

1. Another switch closure before one second has elapsed

2. Switch failure

3. Display failure

4. Computer failure

Surely the first error is the most likely. The simplest solution is for the processor to ignore switch closures until one second has elapsed. This brief unresponsive period will hardly be noticeable to the human operator. Furthermore, ignoring the switch during this period means that no debouncing circuitry or software is necessary since the system will not react to the bounce anyway.

Clearly, the last three failures can produce unpredictable results. The display may stay on, stay off, or change state randomly. Some possible ways to isolate the failures would be:

- Lamp-test hardware to check the display; i.e., a button that turns the light on independently of the processor

- A direct connection to the switch to check its operation

- A diagnostic program that exercises the input and output circuits

If both the display and switch are working, the computer is at fault. A field technician with proper equipment can determine the cause of the failure.

14-2. A Switch-Based Memory Loader

Figure 14-3 shows a system that allows the user to enter data into any memory location in the microcomputer. One input port, DPORT, reads data from eight toggle switches. The other input port, CPORT, is used to read control information. There are three momentary switches: High Address, Low Address, and Data. The output is the value of the last completed entry from the data switches; eight LEDs are used for the display.

The system will also, of course, require various resistors, buffers, and drivers.

Input. We shall first examine the inputs. The characteristics of the switches are the same as in the previous example; however, here there is a distinct sequence of inputs, as follows:

1. The operator must set the data switches equal to the eight most significant bits of an address, then

2. press the High Address button. The high address bits will appear on the lights, and the program will interpret the data as the high byte of the address.

3. Then the operator must set the data switches equal to the value of the least significant byte of the address and

4. press the Low Address button. The low address bits will appear on the lights, and the program will consider the data to be the low byte of the address.

5. Finally, the operator must set the desired data into the data switches and

6. press the Data button. The display will show the data, and the program will store the data in the memory location with the previously entered address.

The operator may repeat the process to enter an entire program. Clearly, even in this simplified situation, we will have many possible sequences to consider. How do we cope with erroneous sequences and make the system easy to use?

Output. Output is no problem. After each input, the program sends to the displays the complement (since the displays are active-low) of the input bits. The output data remains the same until the next input operation.

Processing. The processing section remains quite simple. There are no time or memory constraints. The program can debounce the switches by waiting for a few milliseconds, and must provide complemented data to the displays.

Error Handling. The errors most likely to occur are operator mistakes. These include:

· Incorrect entries

· Incorrect order

· Incomplete entries: for example, forgetting the data

The system must be able to handle these problems in a reasonable way, since they are certain to occur in actual operation.

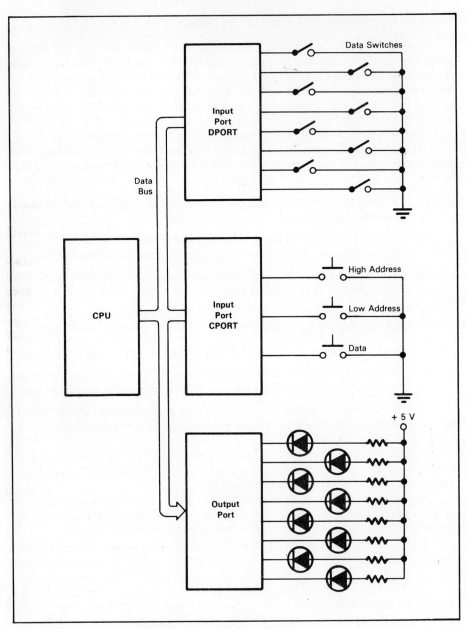

Figure 14-3. A Switch-Based Memory Loader

Equipment Failure. The designer must also consider the effects of equipment failure. Just as before, the possible difficulties are:

- Switch failure

- Display failure

- Computer failure

But in this case, we must pay more attention to how failures affect the system. A computer failure will presumably cause very unusual system behavior, and will be easy to detect. A display failure may not be immediately noticeable; a Lamp Test circuit would allow the operator to verify that the display is working. Note that we would like to test each LED separately, in order to diagnose output lines that are shorted together.

The operator may not immediately detect switch failure; however, the operator should soon notice it and establish which switch is faulty by a process of elimination.

Human Interaction. Consider again possible operator errors. The operator will presumably notice erroneous data as soon as it appears on the displays. What is a viable recovery procedure for the operator? Some of the options are:

1. The operator must complete the entry procedure: i.e., enter Low Address and Data if the error occurs in the High Address. Clearly, this procedure is wasteful and would only serve to annoy the operator.

2. The operator may restart the entry process by returning to the High Address entry steps. This solution is useful if the error was in the High Address, but forces the operator to reenter earlier data if the error was in the Low Address or Data stage.

3. The operator may enter any part of the sequence at any time by setting the Data switches with the desired data and pressing the corresponding button. This procedure allows the operator to make corrections at any point in in the sequence.

Procedure 3 above is always preferred over one that does not allow immediate error correction, has a variety of concluding steps, or enters data into the system without allowing the operator a final check. Any added complication in hardware or software will be justified by increased operator efficiency. You should always let the microcomputer do the tedious work and recognize arbitrary sequences; it never gets tired and never forgets what is in the operating manual.

Status lights are another helpful feature. Status lights let you define the meaning of the display. Three status lights, marked "High Address," "Low Address," and "Data," would let the operator know what had been entered without having to remember which button was pressed. The processor would have to monitor the sequence, but the added complication in software would simplify the operator's task. Clearly, three separate sets of displays plus the ability to examine a memory location would be even more helpful to the operator.

Although we have emphasized human interaction, machine or system interaction has many of the same characteristics. The microprocessor should do the work. If complicating the microprocessor's task makes error recovery simple and the causes of failure obvious, the entire system will work better and be easier to maintain. Note that you should not wait until after the software has been completed to consider system use and maintenance; instead, you should include these factors in the problem definition stage.

14-3. A Verification Terminal

Figure 14-4 is a block diagram for a simple credit-verification terminal. One input port receives data from a keyboard (see Figure 14-5); the other input port accepts verification data from a transmission line. One output port sends data to a set of displays (see Figure 14-6); another sends the credit card number to the central computer. A third output port turns on a "Ready" light whenever the terminal is ready to accept an inquiry, and a "Busy" light when the operator sends the information. The Busy light turns off when the response returns. Clearly, the input and output of data will be more complex than in the previous case, although the processing is still simple.

Additional displays may be useful to emphasize the meaning of the response. Many terminals use a green light for "Yes," a red light for "No," and a yellow light for "Consult Store Manager." Note that these lights will still have to be clearly marked with their meanings to allow for a new operator.

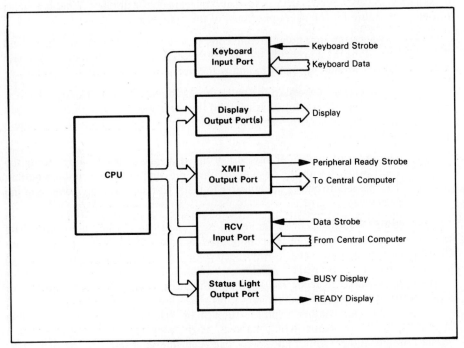

Figure 14-4. Block Diagram of a Verification Terminal

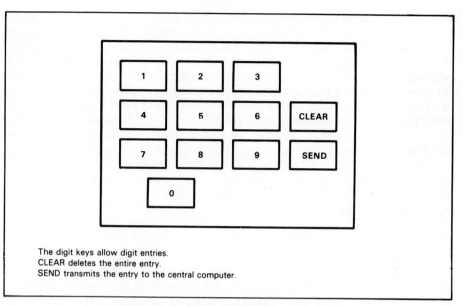

The digit keys allow digit entries.
CLEAR deletes the entire entry.
SEND transmits the entry to the central computer.

Figure 14-5. Verification Keyboard Terminal

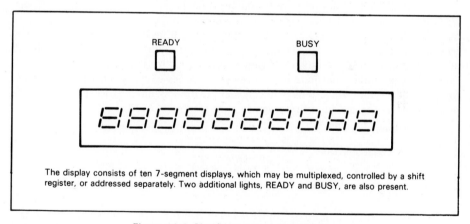

The display consists of ten 7-segment displays, which may be multiplexed, controlled by a shift register, or addressed separately. Two additional lights, READY and BUSY, are also present.

Figure 14-6. Verification Terminal Display

Input. Let us first look at the keyboard input. This is, of course, different from the switch input, since the CPU must have some way of distinguishing new data. We will assume that each key closure provides a unique hexadecimal code (we can code each of the 12 keys into one digit) and a strobe. The program will have to recognize the strobe and fetch the hexadecimal number that identifies the key. There is a time constraint, since the program cannot miss any data or strobes. The constraint is not serious, since the keyboard entries will be at least several milliseconds apart.

The transmission input similarly consists of a series of characters, each identified by a strobe (perhaps from a UART). The program will have to recognize each strobe and fetch the character. The data being sent across the transmission lines is usually organized into messages. A possible format for the input message is:

- Introductory characters, or header

- Terminal destination address

- Coded response (yes, no, or check)

- Ending characters, or trailer

The terminal will check the header, read the destination address, and see if the message is intended for it. If the message is for the terminal, the terminal accepts the data. The address could be (and often is) hard-wired into the terminal so that the terminal receives only messages intended for it. This approach simplifies the software at the cost of some hardware flexibility.

Output. The output is also more complex than in the earlier examples. If the displays are multiplexed, the processor must not only send the data to the display port but must also direct the data to a particular display. We will need either a separate control port or a counter and decoder to handle this. Time constraints include the pulse length and frequency required to produce a continuous display for the operator.

The communications output will consist of a series of characters with a particular format. The program will also have to consider the time required between characters. A possible format for the output message is:

- Header

- Terminal address

- Credit card number

- Trailer

A central communications computer may poll the terminals, checking for data ready to be sent.

Processing. The processing in this system involves many new tasks, such as:

- Identifying the control keys by number and performing actions that are specific to each control key.

- Adding the header, terminal address, and trailer to the outgoing message

- Recognizing the header and trailer in the returning message

- Checking the incoming terminal address

Note that none of the tasks involves any complex arithmetic or any serious time or memory constraints.

Error Handling. The number of possible errors in this system is, of course, much larger than in the earlier examples. Let us first consider the possible operator errors. These include:

- Entering the credit card number incorrectly

- Trying to send an incomplete credit card number

- Trying to send another number while the central computer is processing the previous one

Some of these errors are easily handled by correctly structuring the program. For example, the program should not accept the Send key until the credit card number has been completely entered, and it should ignore any additional keyboard entries until the response comes back from the central computer. Note that the operator will know that the entry has not been sent, since the Busy light will not go on. The operator will also know when the keyboard has been locked out (the program is ignoring keyboard entries), since entries will not appear on the display and the Ready light will be off.

Correcting Keyboard Errors. Incorrect entries are to be expected. If the operator recognizes an error, he can use the Clear key to make corrections. The operator would probably find it more convenient to have two Clear keys, one that clears the most recent key, and another that clears the entire entry. This allows the operator to recognize an error immediately, or late in the procedure. The operator should be able to correct errors immediately and have to repeat as few keys as possible. The operator will, however, make a certain number of errors without recognizing them. Most credit card numbers include a self-checking digit; the terminal could check the number before permitting it to be sent to the central computer. This step would save the central computer from wasting precious processing time checking the number. But the terminal must have some way of informing the operator of the error, perhaps by flashing one of the displays, or by providing some other special indicator that the operator is sure to notice.

Still another problem is how the operator knows that an entry has been lost or processed incorrectly. Some terminals simply unlock after a maximum time delay. The operator notes that the Busy light has gone off without an answer being received. The operator is then expected to try the entry again. After one or two retries, the operator should report the failure to supervisory personnel.

Correcting Transmission Errors. Many equipment failures are also possible. Besides the displays, keyboard, and processor, communications errors may now occur, or the central computer may fail.

The data transmission will probably include error checking and correcting procedures. Some possibilities are:

1. Parity checking provides an error detection facility but no correction mechanism. The receiver will need some way of requesting retransmission, and the sender will have to save a copy of the data until proper reception is acknowledged. Parity is very simple to implement.

2. Short messages may use more elaborate schemes. For example, the yes/no response to the terminal could be coded so as to provide error detection and correction capability.

3. An acknowledgement and a limited number of retries could trigger an indicator that would inform the operator of a communications failure (inability to transfer a message without errors) or central computer failure (no response at all to the message within a certain period of time). Such a scheme, along with the Lamp Test, would allow simple failure diagnosis.

A communications or central computer failure indicator should also "unlock" the terminal, i.e., allow it to accept another entry. This is necessary if the terminal will not accept entries while a verification is in progress. The terminal may also unlock after a certain maximum time delay. Certain entries could be reserved for diagnostics; i.e., certain credit card numbers could be used to check the internal operation of the terminal and test the displays.

REVIEW

Problem definition is as important a part of software development as it is of any other engineering task. Note that it does not require any knowledge of programming or computers; rather, it is based on an understanding of the system and sound engineering judgment. Microprocessors can offer flexibility that the designer can use to provide a range of features which were not previously available.

Problem definition is independent of any particular computer, computer language, or development system. It should, however, provide guidelines as to what type or speed of computer the application will require and what kind of hardware/software tradeoffs the designer can make. The problem definition stage is in fact independent of whether or not a computer is used at all, although a knowledge of the capabilities of the computer can help the designer in suggesting possible implementations of procedures.

PROGRAM DESIGN

During the program design stage the problem definition is formulated as a program. If the program is small and simple, this stage may involve little more than writing a one-page flowchart. If the program is large or complex, the program design may become quite elaborate.

We will discuss flowcharting, modular programming, structured programming, and top-down development. We will try to indicate the reasoning behind these methods, plus the advantages and disadvantages of each. We will not, however, advocate any particular method, since there is no evidence that one method is always superior to all others. You should remember that the goal is to produce a good working system, not to follow religiously the tenets of one methodology or another.

BASIC PRINCIPLES

All the methodologies have some obvious principles in common. Many of these are the same principles that apply to any kind of design, such as:

1. Proceed in small steps. Do not try to do too much at one time.

2. Divide large jobs into small, logically separate tasks. Make the sub-tasks as independent of one another as possible, so that they can be tested separately, with changes made in one task having as little impact as possible on other tasks.

3. Keep the flow of control as simple as possible so errors are easier to find.

4. Use pictorial or graphic descriptions as much as possible. They are easier to visualize than word descriptions. This is the great advantage of flowcharts. The layout of the program listing itself can be manipulated to add visual information.

5. Emphasize clarity and simplicity at first. You can improve performance (if necessary) once the system is working.

6. Proceed in a thorough and systematic manner. Use checklists and standard procedures.

7. Do not tempt fate. Avoid methods that you are not sure of, but if you must use them, be very careful. Watch for situations that might cause confusion, and clarify them as soon as possible.

8. Keep in mind that the system must be debugged, tested, and maintained. Plan for these later stages.

9. Use simple and consistent terminology and methods. Repetitiveness is no fault in program design, nor is complexity a virtue.

10. Have your design completely formulated before you start coding. Resist the temptation to start writing down instructions; it makes no more sense than making parts lists or laying out circuit boards before you know exactly what will be in the system.

11.   Be particularly careful of factors that may change. Make the implementation of likely changes as simple as possible.

Flowcharting

Flowcharting is certainly the best-known of all program design methods. Programming textbooks describe how programmers first write complete flowcharts and then start writing the actual program. In fact, few programmers have ever worked this way, and flowcharting has often been more of a joke or a nuisance to programmers than a design method. We will try to describe both the advantages and disadvantages of flowcharts, and show the place of this technique in program design.

The basic advantage of the flowchart is that it is a pictorial representation. People find such representations much more meaningful than written descriptions. The designer can visualize the whole system and see the relationships of the various parts. Logical errors and inconsistencies often stand out instead of being hidden in a printed page. At its best, the flowchart is a picture of th entire system.

Some of the more specific advantages of flowcharts are:

1.   Standard symbols exist (see Figure 14-7) so that flowcharting forms are widely recognized.

2.   Flowcharts can be understood by someone without a programming background.

3.   Flowcharts can be used to divide the entire project into sub-tasks. The flowchart can then be examined to measure overall progress.

4.   Flowcharts show the sequence of operations and can therefore aid in locating the source of errors.

5.   Flowcharting is widely used in areas other than programming.

6.   There are many tools available to aid in flowcharting, including programmer's templates and automated drawing packages.

These advantages are all important. There is no question that flowcharting will continue to be widely used. But **we should note some of the disadvantages of flowcharting** as a program design method, e.g.:

1.   Flowcharts are difficult to design, draw, or change in all but the simplest situations.

2.   There is no easy way to debug or test a flowchart.

3.   Flowcharts tend to become cluttered. Designers find it difficult to balance between the amount of detail needed to make the flowchart useful and the amount that makes the flowchart little better than a program listing.

4.   Flowcharts show only the program organization. They do not show the organization of the data.

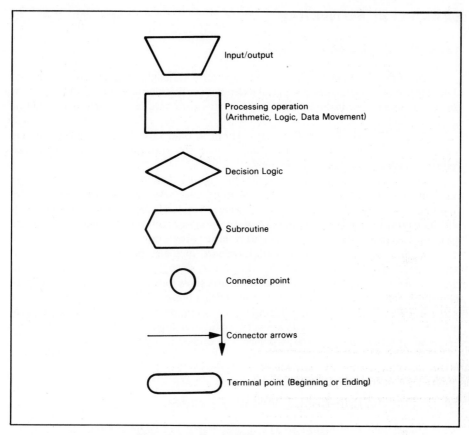

Figure 14-7. Standard Flowchart Symbols

5. Flowcharts do not help with hardware or timing problems or give hints as to where these problems might occur.

6. Flowcharts allow for highly unstructured design. Lines and arrows backtracking and looping all over the chart are the antithesis of good structured design principles.

Thus, flowcharting is a helpful technique that you should not try to extend too far. **Flowcharts are useful as program documentation, since they have standard forms and are comprehensible to non-programmers.** As a design tool, **however, flowcharts cannot provide much more than a starting outline; the programmer cannot debug a detailed flowchart,** and the flowchart is often more difficult to design than the program itself.

EXAMPLES: FLOWCHART

14-4. Response to a Switch

This simple task, in which a single switch turns on a light for one second, is easy to flowchart. In fact, such tasks are typical examples for flowcharting books, although they form a small part of most systems. The data structure here is so simple that it can be safely ignored.

Figure 14-8 shows the flowchart. There is little difficulty in deciding on the amount of detail required. The flowchart gives a straightforward picture of the procedure, which anyone could understand.

Note that the most useful flowcharts may ignore program variables and ask questions directly. Of course, compromises are often necessary here. **Two versions of the flowchart are sometimes helpful — one general version in layman's language, which will be useful to non-programmers, and one programmer's version in terms of the program variables, which will be useful to other programmers.**

A third type of flowchart, a data flowchart, may also be helpful. This flowchart serves as a cross-reference for the other flowcharts, since it shows how the program handles a particular type of data. Ordinary flowcharts show how the program proceeds, handling different types of data at different points. Data flowcharts, on the other hand, show how particular types of data move through the system, passing from one part of the program to another. Such flowcharts are very useful in debugging and maintenance, since errors most often show up as a particular type of data being handled incorrectly.

14-5. The Switch-Based Memory Loader

This system (see Figure 14-3) is considerably more complex than the previous example, and involves many more decisions. The flowchart (see Figure 14-9) is more difficult to write and is not as straightforward as the previous example. In this example, we face the fact that there is no way to debug or test the flowchart.

The flowchart in Figure 14-9 includes the improvements we suggested as part of the problem definition. Clearly, this flowchart is beginning to get cluttered and lose its advantages over a written description. If we add features that define the meaning of the entry with status lights, or allow the operator to check entries after completion, the flowchart will become even more complex. Writing the complete flowchart from scratch might become a formidable task, but the flowchart is useful documentation if it is developed as the program is written.

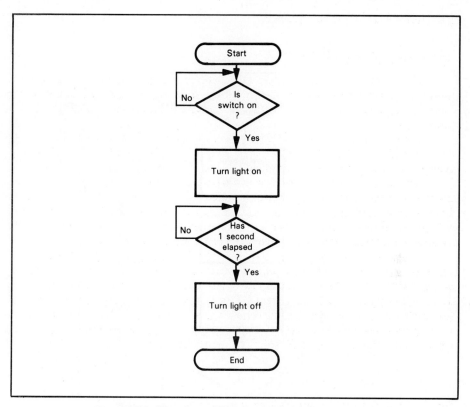

Figure 14-8. Flowchart of One-Second Response to a Switch

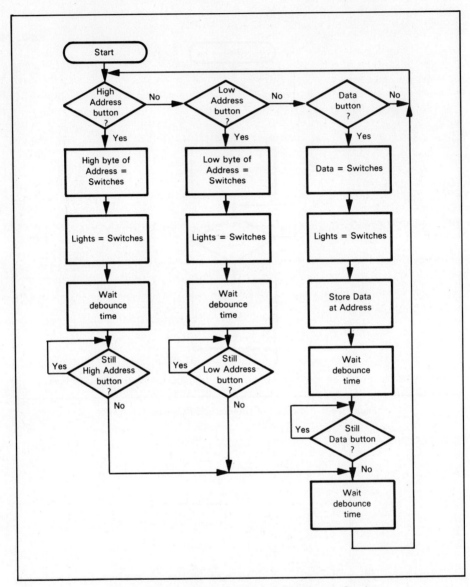

Figure 14-9. Flowchart of a Switch-Based Memory Loader

14-6. The Credit-Verification Terminal

In this application (see Figures 14-4 through 14-6), the flowchart will be even more complex than in the switch-based memory loader case. Here the best idea is to flowchart sections separately so that the flowcharts remain manageable. However, the presence of data structures (as in the multi-digit display and the messages) will make the gap between flowchart and program much wider.

Let us look at some of the sections. Figure 14-10 illustrates keyboard entry for the digit keys. The program must fetch the data after each strobe and place the digit into the display array if there is room for it. If there are already ten digits in the array, the program ignores the entry.

The actual program will have to handle displays and keyboard entry simultaneously. Note that either software or hardware must deactivate the keyboard strobe after the processor reads a digit.

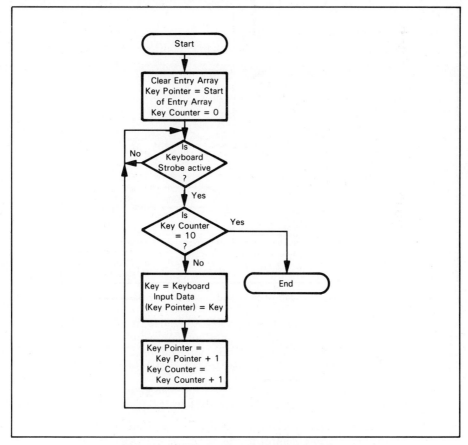

Figure 14-10. Flowchart of Keyboard Entry Process

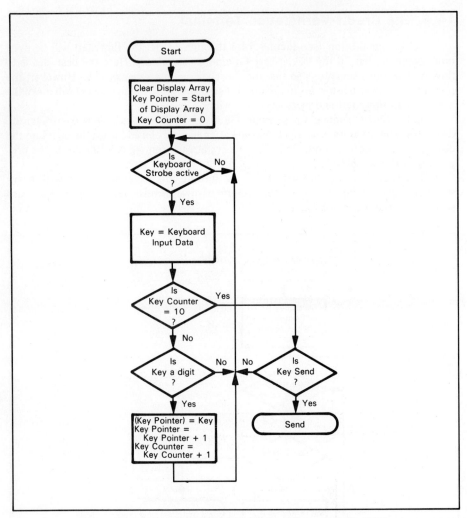

Figure 14-11. Flowchart of Keyboard Entry Process with Send Key

Figure 14-11 adds the Send key. This key, of course, is optional. The terminal could just send the data as soon as the operator enters a complete number. However, that would not give the operator a chance to check the entire entry. The flowchart with the Send key is more complex because there are two alternatives:

1. If the operator has not entered ten digits, the program must ignore the Send key and interpret other keys as valid data entry.

2. If the operator has entered ten digits, the program must respond to the Send key by transferring control to the Send routine. All other keys must be ignored.

Note that the flowchart has become much more difficult to organize and to follow. There is also no obvious way to check the flowchart.

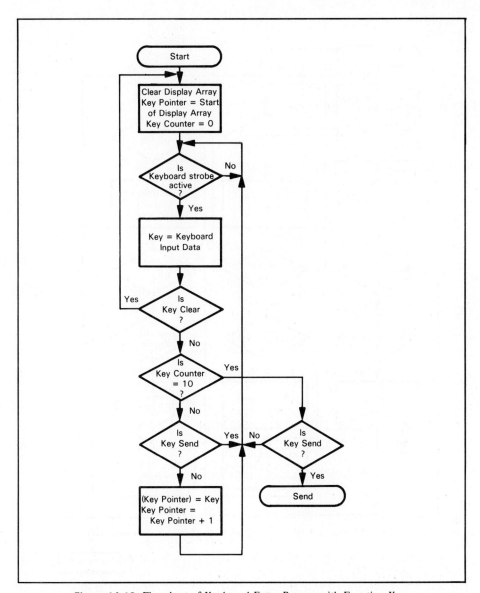

Figure 14-12. Flowchart of Keyboard Entry Process with Function Keys

Figure 14-12 shows the flowchart for keyboard entry with all the function keys. In this example, the flow of control is not simple. Some written description is necessary. The organization and layout of complex flowcharts requires careful planning. We have followed the process of adding features to the flowchart one at a time, but this still results in a large amount of redrawing. Again we should remember that throughout the keyboard entry process, the program must also refresh the displays if they are multiplexed and not controlled by hardware.

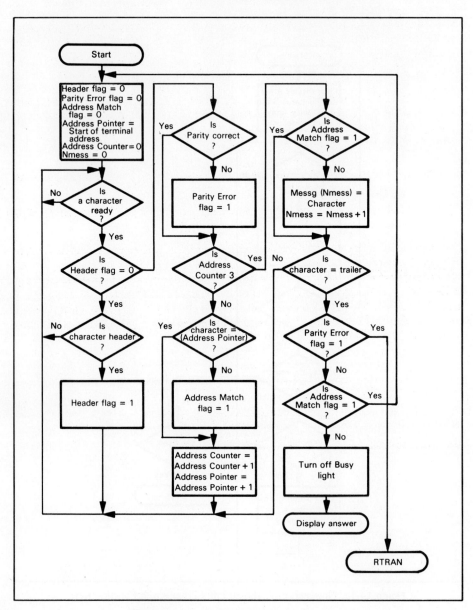

Figure 14-13. Flowchart of Receive Routine

Figure 14-13 is the flowchart for a receive routine. We assume that the serial/parallel conversion and error checking are done in hardware (e.g., by a UART). The processor must:

1. Look for the header (we assume that it is a single character).

2. Read the destination address (we assume that it is three characters long) and see if the message is meant for this terminal; i.e., if the three characters agree with the terminal address.

3. Wait for the trailer character.

4. If the message is meant for the terminal, turn off the Busy light and go to the Display Answer routine.

5. In the event of any errors, request retransmission by going to the RETRANS routine.

This routine involves a large number of decisions, and the flowchart is neither simple nor obvious.

Clearly, we have come a long way from the simple flowchart of the first example (Figure 14-8). Generating a complete set of flowcharts for the transaction terminal is a major task. It would consist of several interrelated charts with complex logic. Such an effort would be just as difficult as writing a preliminary program, and not as useful, since you could not check it on the computer.

MODULAR PROGRAMMING

Once programs become large and complex, flowcharting is no longer a satisfactory design tool. However, problem definition and flowcharting can help you divide the program into reasonable sub-tasks. **The division of the entire program into sub-tasks or modules is called "modular programming."** Most of the programs presented in earlier chapters would, typically, be modules within a large system program. **The problem a designer faces in modular programming is how to divide the program into modules, and how to put the modules together.**

The advantages of modular programming are obvious:

1. A single module is easier to write, debug, and test than an entire program.

2. A module can be used many times in one program; a module can also be used by many different programs. You can build up a library of standard modules, providing they are general purpose and perform common tasks.

3. Modular programming lets you use modules from your library. This reduces the amount of new code that must be generated and debugged.

4. Changes can be incorporated into one module rather than into the entire system.

5. Errors can often be isolated and then attributed to a single module.

6. Modular programming gives an idea of how much progress has been made and how much of the work is left.

The idea of modular programming is such an obvious one that its disadvantages are often ignored. These include:

1. Fitting the modules together can be a major problem, particularly if different people write the modules.

2. Modules require very careful documentation, since they may affect other parts of the program, such as data structures used by all the modules.

3. Testing and debugging modules separately is difficult, since other modules may produce the data used by the module being debugged and still other modules may use the results. You may have to write special programs (called "drivers") just to produce sample data and test the programs. These drivers require extra programming effort that is not useful in the final system.

4. Programs may be very difficult to divide into modules. If you make the division poorly, integration will be very difficult, since almost all errors and changes will involve several modules.

5. Modular programs often require extra time and memory, since the separate modules may repeat some functions.

Therefore, while modular programming is certainly an improvement over trying to write the entire program from scratch, it does have some disadvantages.

Important considerations include restricting the amount of information shared by modules, putting all the code that is affected by a single design decision into a single module, and restricting the access of one module by another.[3]

Principles of Modularization

An obvious problem is that there are no proven, systematic methods for dividing programs into modules. We should mention the following principles:[4]

1. As much as possible, data should not be referenced by more than one module. Furthermore, the structure or organization of related data should be completely defined within a single module. If this causes a module to become very large, you can break it up into sub-modules but the sub-modules should be accessible only through a common module.

2. If one module uses or depends on a second, but the second does not use or depend on the first, then the two modules must be separated. In other words, if you have a single module with two parts, where one part depends on the presence of the other, but the other part can also be used independently, then the two parts should be separated into individual modules.

3. Do not combine different tasks into a single module unless the tasks are used with approximately the same frequency and under approximately the same circumstances. When in doubt, break each task out into a separate module.

If a program is difficult to divide into modules, you may need to redefine the tasks that are involved. Too many special cases or too many variables that require special handling are typical signs of inadequate problem definition or poor program design.

EXAMPLES: MODULAR PROGRAMMING

14-7. Response to a Switch

This simple program can be divided into two modules. Module 1 waits for the switch to be turned on; in response it turns the light on. Module 2 provides the one second delay.

Module 1 is likely to be specific to the system, since it will depend on how the switch and light are attached. Module 2 will be generally useful, since many tasks require delays. Clearly, it would be advantageous to have a standard delay module that could provide delays of varying lengths. The module will require careful documentation so that you and other programmers will know how to specify the length of the delay, how to call the module, and what registers and memory locations the module affects.

A general version of Module 1 would be far less useful, since it would have to deal with different types of switches and lights, and various connections.

You would probably find it simpler to write a module for a particular configuration of switches and lights, rather than try to use a standard routine.

14-8. The Switch-Based Memory Loader

The switch-based memory loader is difficult to divide into modules, since all programming tasks depend on the hardware configuration, and the tasks are so simple that modules hardly seem worthwhile. The flowchart in Figure 14-9 suggests that one module might receive input when the operator presses a pushbutton.

Some other modules might be:

- A module that provides the delay required to debounce the switches

- A switch and display module that reads the data from the switches and sends it to the displays

- A Lamp Test module

Highly system-dependent modules such as the last two are unlikely to be generally useful. This example is not one in which modular programming offers great advantages.

14-9. The Credit-Verification Terminal

The verification terminal, on the other hand, lends itself very well to modular programming. The entire system can be divided into three main modules:

- Keyboard and display module

- Data transmission module

- Data reception module

A general keyboard and display module could handle many keyboard- and display-based systems. The sub-modules would perform such tasks as:

- Recognizing a new keyboard entry and fetching the data

- Clearing the array in response to a Clear key

- Entering digits into storage

- Looking for the terminator or Send key

- Displaying the digits

Although the key interpretations and the number of digits will vary, the basic entry, data storage, and data display processes will be the same for many programs. Function keys such as Clear would also be standard. Clearly, the designer must consider which modules will be useful in other applications, and pay careful attention to those modules.

The data transmission module could also be divided into such sub-modules as:

- Adding the header character

- Transmitting characters when the output line can handle them

- Generating delay times between bits or characters

- Adding the trailer character

- Checking for transmission failures; i.e., no acknowledgment or inability to transmit without errors.

The data reception module could include sub-modules which:

- Look for the header character

- Check the message destination address against the terminal address

- Store and interpret the message

- Look for the trailer character

- Generate bit or character delays.

Information Hiding Principle

Note here how important it is that each design decision (such as the bit rate, message format, or error-checking procedure) be implemented in only one module. A change in any of these decisions will then require changes only to that single module. All modules should be written so that they are totally unaware of the values chosen or the methods used in other modules. **An important concept here is the "information hiding principle,"[5] whereby modules share only information that is absolutely essential to getting the task done. Other information is hidden within a single module.**

Error handling is a typical context in which this principle should be employed. When a module detects a fatal error, it should not try to recover; instead, it should inform the calling module of the error status and allow that module to decide how to proceed. The reason is that the lower level module often lacks sufficient information to establish recovery procedures. For example, suppose that the lower level module is one that accepts numeric input from a user. This module expects a string of numeric digits terminated by a carriage return. Entry of a non-numeric character causes the module to terminate abnormally. Since the module does not know the context (i.e., is the numeric string an operand, a line number, an I/O unit number, or the length of a file?), it cannot decide how to handle an error. If the module always followed a single error recovery procedure, it would lose its generality and only be usable in those situations where that procedure was required.

Rules for Modular Programming

Modular programming can be very helpful if you abide by the following rules:

1. **Use modules of 20 to 50 lines.** Shorter modules are often a waste of time, while longer modules are seldom general and may be difficult to integrate.

2. **Try to make modules reasonably general.** Differentiate between common features like ASCII code or asynchronous transmission formats, which will be the same for many applications, and key identifications, number of displays, or number of characters in a message, which are likely to be unique to a particular application. Make the changing of the latter parameters simple. Major changes like different character codes should be handled by separate modules.

3. **Take extra time on modules** like delays, display handlers, etc. **that will be useful in other projects or in many different places in the present program.**

4. **Try to keep modules as distinct and logically separate as possible.** Restrict the flow of information between modules and implement each design decision in a single module.

5. **Do not try to divide simple tasks into modules** where rewriting the entire task may be easier than assembling or modifying the module.

STRUCTURED PROGRAMMING

How do you keep modules distinct and stop them from interacting? How do you write a program that has a clear sequence of operations so that you can isolate and correct errors? One answer is to use the methods known as "structured programming," whereby each part of the program consists of elements from a limited set of structures and each structure has a single entry and a single exit.

Figure 14-14 shows a flowchart of an unstructured program. If an error occurs in Module B, we have five possible sources for that error. Not only must we check each sequence, but we also have to make sure that any changes made to correct the error do not affect any of the other sequences. The usual result is that debugging is like wrestling an octopus. Every time you think the situation is under control, you encounter another loose tentacle.

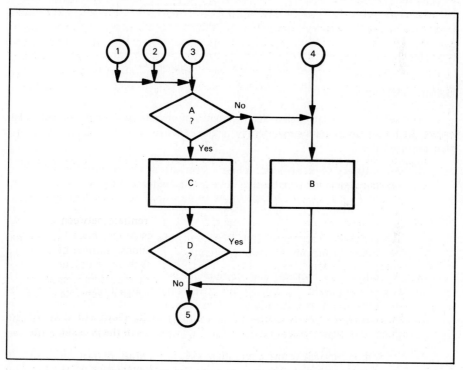

Figure 14-14. Flowchart of an Unstructured Program

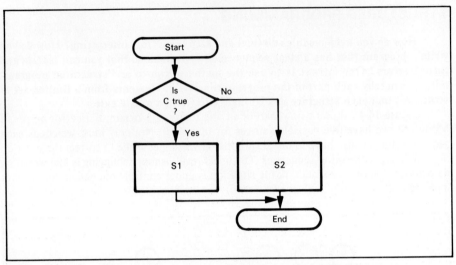

Figure 14-15. Flowchart of the Conditioned Structure

Basic Structures

The solution is to establish a clear sequence of operations so that you can isolate errors. Such a sequence uses single- entry, single-exit structures. **The basic structures that are needed are:**

1. **An ordinary sequence;** i.e., a linear structure in which statements or structures are executed consecutively. In the sequence:

   ```
   S1
   S2
   S3
   ```

   the computer executes S1 first, S2 second, and S3 third. S1, S2, and S3 may be single instructions or entire programs.

2. **A conditional structure.** The common one is "if C then S1 else S2," where C is a condition and S1 and S2 are statements or structures. The computer executes S1 if C is true, and S2 is C is false. Figure 14-15 shows the logic of this structure. Note that the structure has a single entry and a single exit; there is no way to enter or leave S1 or S2 other than through the structure.

   Some examples of the conditional structure are as follows:

   a. S2 included:

   ```
   if X > 0 then NPOS = NPOS + 1
        else NNEG = NNEG + 1
   ```

   Both S1 and S2 are single statements.

   b. S2 omitted:

   ```
   if X ≠ 0 then Y = 1/X
   ```

   Here no action is taken if the condition (X = 0) is false. S2 and "else" can be omitted in this case.

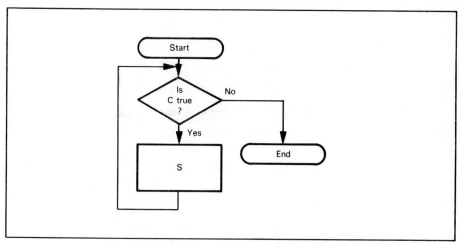

Figure 14-16. Flowchart of the Do-While-Loop Structure

3. A loop structure. The common loop structure is "while C do S," where C is a condition and S is a statement or structure. The computer checks C and executes S if C is true. This structure (see Figure 14-16) also has a single entry and a single exit. Note that the computer will not execute S at all if C is originally false, since the value of C is checked before S is executed.

Some examples of the do-while loop structure are as follows:

a. Form the sum of integers from 1 to N.

```
I = 0
SUM = 0
do while I < N
I = I + 1
SUM = SUM + I
end
```

The computer executes the loop as long as I < N. If N = 0, the program within the "do-while" is not executed at all.

b. Count characters in an array SENTENCE until you find an ASCII period.

```
NCHAR = 0
do while SENTENCE (NCHAR) ≠ PERIOD
NCHAR = NCHAR + 1
end
```

The computer executes the loop as long as the character in SENTENCE is not an ASCII period. The count is zero if the first character is a period.

In most structured programming languages, an alternative looping construct is provided. This construct is known as the do-until clause. Its basic structure is "do S until C" where C is a condition and S is a statement or structure. It is similar to the do-while construct except that the test of the looping condition C is performed at the end of the loop. Thus the loop is always executed at least once. This is illustrated by the flowchart in Figure 14-17. The common index-controlled or DO loop can be implemented as a special case of either of these two basic looping constructs.

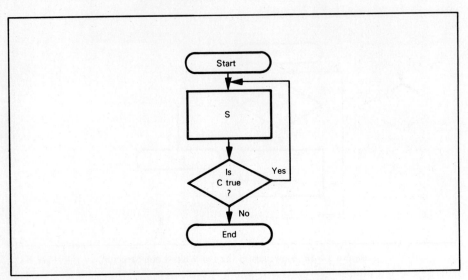

Figure 14-17. Flowchart of the Do-Until-Loop Structure

4. **A case structure.** Although not a primitive structure like sequential, if-then-else, and do-while, the case structure is so commonly used that we include it here as an adjunct to the basic structure descriptions. The case structure is "case I of S0, S1, . . ., Sn" where I is an index and S0, S1, . . ., Sn are statements or structures. If I is equal to zero then statement S0 is executed, if I is equal to 1 then statement S1 is executed, etc. Only one of the statements is executed. After execution of the selected statement, control passes to the next sequential statement following the case statement group. If I is greater than n (i.e., the number of statements in the case statement), then none of the statements in the case statement is executed, and control is passed directly to the next sequential statement following the case statement. This is illustrated by the flowchart in Figure 14-18.

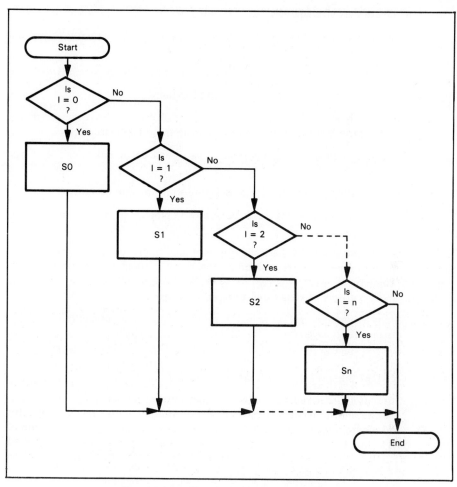

Figure 14-18. Flowchart of the Case Structure

Features

Note the following features of structured programming:

1. Only the three basic structures, and possibly a small number of auxiliary structures, are permitted.

2. Structures may be nested to any level of complexity so that any structure can, in turn, contain any of the structures.

3. Each structure has a single entry and a single exit.

The advantages of structured programming are:

1. The sequence of operations is simple to trace. This allows you to test and debug easily.

2. The number of structures is limited and the terminology is standardized.

3. The structures can easily be made into modules.

4. Theoreticians have proved that the given set of structures is complete; that is, all programs can be written in terms of the three basic structures.

5. The structured version of a program is partly self-documenting and fairly easy to read.

6. Structured programs are easy to describe with program outlines.

7. Structured programming has been shown in practice to increase programmer productivity.

Structured programming basically forces much more discipline on the programmer than does modular programming. The result is more systematic and better organized programs.

The disadvantages of structured programming are:

1. Many assemblers and some high-level languages do not accept the structures directly. The programmer therefore has to go through an extra translation stage to convert the structures to the language used. (Most languages and assemblers for the Z8000 do accept the structures: e.g., PLZ/ASM, MACRO8000, PLZ/SYS, PASCAL, and C.)

2. Structured programs often execute more slowly and use more memory than unstructured programs which have been carefully crafted to minimize time and memory use.

3. Limiting the structures to the three basic forms makes some tasks very awkward to perform. The completeness of the structures only means that all programs can be implemented with them; it does not mean that a given program can be implemented efficiently or conveniently.

4. The standard structures are often quite confusing; e.g., nested "if-then-else" structures may be very difficult to read, since there may be no clear indication of where the ones inside end. A series of nested "do-while" loops can also be difficult to read.

5. Structured programs consider only the sequence of program operations, not the flow of data. Therefore, the structures may handle data awkwardly.[6]

6. Few programmers are accustomed to structured programming. Many find the standard structures awkward and restrictive.

When to Use Structured Programming

We are neither advocating nor discouraging the use of structured programming. It is one way of systematizing program design. In general, structured programming is most useful in the following situations:

- Larger programs, perhaps exceeding 1000 instructions

- Applications in which memory usage is not critical

- Low-volume applications where software development costs, particularly testing and debugging, are important factors

- Applications involving string manipulation, process control, or other algorithms rather than simple bit manipulations.

Today we see the cost of memory decreasing, the average size of microprocessor programs increasing, and the cost of software development increasing. Therefore, methods like structured programming, which decrease software development costs for larger programs but sometimes use more memory, are becoming more valuable.

EXAMPLES: STRUCTURED PROGRAMMING

14-10. Response to a Switch

A structured version of this example is:

```
SWITCH = OFF
do while SWITCH = OFF
   READ SWITCH
   end
LIGHT = ON
   DELAY (1)
LIGHT = OFF
```

ON and OFF must have the proper definitions for the switch and light. We assume that DELAY is a module that provides a delay given by its parameter in seconds.

A statement in a structured program may actually be a subroutine. However, in order to conform to the rules of structured programming, the subroutine cannot have any exits other than the one that returns control to the main program.

Since "do-while" checks the condition before executing the loop, we set the variable SWITCH to OFF before starting. The structured program is straightforward, readable, and easy to check by hand. However, it would probably require somewhat more memory than an unstructured program, which would not have to initialize SWITCH and could combine the reading and checking procedures.

14-11. The Switch-Based Memory Loader

The switch-based memory loader is a more complex structured programming problem. We may implement the flowchart in Figure 14- 9 as follows (an "•" in the margin indicates a comment):

```
•
•   Initialize variables
•
HIADDRESS = 0
LOADDRESS = 0
•
•   This program uses a do-while construct with no condition
•   (called simply do-forever). Therefore, the system continually
•   executes the program contained in this do-while loop
•
do forever
•
•   Test for High Address button; perform the required processing
•   if it is on

    if HIADDRBUTTON = 1 then
      begin
        HIADDRESS = SWITCHES
        LIGHTS = SWITCHES
        do
          DELAY (DEBOUNCE TIME)
        until HIADDRBUTTON = 1
      end
•
•   Test for Low Address button; perform low address processing
•   if it is on

    if LOADDRBUTTON = 1 then
      begin
        LOADDRESS = SWITCHES
        LIGHTS = SWITCHES
        do
          DELAY (DEBOUNCE TIME)
        until LOADDRBUTTON ≠ 1
      end
•
•   Test for Data button, and store data into memory
•   if it is on.
•
    if DATABUTTON = 1 then
      begin
        DATA = SWITCHES
        LIGHTS = SWITCHES
        (HIADDRESS, LOADDRESS) = DATA
        do
          DELAY (DEBOUNCE TIME)
        until DATABUTTON = 1
      end
end
•
•   The last end above terminates the
•   do forever loop
•
```

Structured programs are not easy to write, but they can give a great deal of insight into the overall program logic. You can check the logic of the structured program by hand before writing any actual code.

14-12. The Credit-Verification Terminal

Let us look at the keyboard entry for the transaction terminal. We will assume that the display array is ENTRY, the keyboard strobe is KEYSTROBE, and the keyboard data is KEYIN. The structured program without the function keys is:

```
NKEYS = 10
·
·   Clear entry to start
·
   do while NKEYS > 0
     NKEYS = NKEYS – 1
     ENTRY(NKEYS) = 0
   end
·
·   Fetch a complete entry from keyboard
·
   do while NKEYS < 10
     if KEYSTROBE = ACTIVE then
       begin
         ENTRY(NKEYS) = KEYIN
         KEYSTROBE = INACTIVE
         NKEYS = NKEYS + 1
       end
   end
```

Adding the SEND key means that the program must ignore extra digits after it has a complete entry, and must ignore the SEND key until it has a complete entry. The structured program is:

```
NKEYS = 10
·
·   Clear entry to start
·
   do while NKEYS > 0
     NKEYS = NKEYS – 1
     ENTRY(NKEYS) = 0
   end
·
·   Wait for complete entry followed by Send key
·
   do while (KEY ≠ SEND) or (NKEYS ≠ 10)
     if KEYSTROBE = ACTIVE then
       begin
         KEY = KEYIN
         KEYSTROBE = INACTIVE
         if (NKEYS ≠ 10) and (KEY ≠ SEND) then
           begin
             ENTRY(NKEYS) = KEY
             NKEYS = NKEYS + 1
           end
       end
   end
```

Note the following features of this structured program.

1. The second if-then is nested within the first one, since keys are only entered after a strobe is recognized. If the second if-then were on the same level as the first, a single key could fill the entry, since its value would be entered into the array during each iteration of the do-while loop.

2. KEY need not be defined initially, since NKEYS is set to zero as part of the clearing of the entry.

Adding the CLEAR key would allow the program to clear the entry originally by simulating the pressing of CLEAR; i.e., by setting NKEYS to 10 and KEY to CLEAR before starting. The structured program must also clear only digits that have previously been filled. **The new structured program is:**

```
        .
        .   Simulate complete clearing
        .
    NKEYS = 10
    KEY = CLEAR

        .   Wait for complete entry and send key
        .
    do while (KEY ≠ SEND) or (NKEYS ≠ 10)
        .
        .   Clear entry if Clear key struck
        .
        if KEY = CLEAR then
          begin
            KEY = 0
            do while NKEYS > 0
              NKEYS = NKEYS - 1
              ENTRY(NKEYS) = 0
            end
          end

        .
        .   Get digit if entry is incomplete
        .
        if KEYSTROBE = INACTIVE then
          begin
            KEY = KEYIN
            KEYSTROBE = INACTIVE
            if (KEY < 10) and (NKEYS ≠ 10) then
              begin
                ENTRY(NKEYS) = KEY
                NKEYS = NKEYS + 1
              end
          end
    end
```

Note that the program resets KEY to zero when clearing the array, so that the operation is not repeated.

We can similarly build a structured program for the receive routine. An initial program could just look for the header and trailer characters. We will assume that RSTB is the indicator that a character is ready. **The structured program is:**

```
  .
  .  Clear Header flag to start
  .
HFLAG = 0
  .
  .  Wait for Header and Trailer
  .
do while (HFLAG = 0) or (CHAR ≠ TRAILER)
  .
  .  Get character if ready, look for Header
  .
    if RSTB = ACTIVE then
      begin
        CHAR = INPUT
        RSTB = INACTIVE
        if CHAR = HEADER then HFLAG = 1
      end
```

Now we can add the section that checks the message address against the three digits in the Terminal Address (TERMADDR). If any of the corresponding digits are not equal, the Address Match flag (ADDRMATCH) is set to 1.

```
  .
  .  Clear Header flag, Address Match flag, Address Counter to start
  .
HFLAG = 0
ADDRMATCH = 0
ADDRCTR = 0
  .
  .  Wait for Header, Destination Address and Trailer
  .
do while (HFLAG ≠ 0) or (CHAR ≠ TRAILER) or (ADDRCTR = 3)
  .
  .  Get character if ready
  .
    if RSTB = ACTIVE then
      begin
        RSTB = INACTIVE
        CHAR = INPUT
      end
  .
  .  Check for Terminal Address and Header
  .
    if (HFLAG = 1) and (ADDRCTR = 3) then
    if CHAR ≠ TERMADDR(ADDRCTR) then
      begin
        ADDRMATCH = 1
        ADDRCTR = ADDRCTR + 1
      end
    if CHAR = HEADER then HFLAG = 1
  end
```

The program must now wait for a header, a three-digit identification code, and a trailer. You must be careful of what happens during the iteration when the program finds the header, and of what happens if an erroneous identification code character is the same as the trailer.

A further addition can store the message in MESSG. NMESS is the number of characters in the message; if it is not zero at the end, the program knows that the terminal has received a valid message. We have not tried to minimize the logic expressions in this program.

```
·
·   Clear flags, counters to start
·
HFLAG = 0
ADDRMATCH = 0
NMESS = 0
·
·   Wait for Header, Destination Address and Trailer
·
do while (HFLAG 0) or (CHAR ≠ TRAILER) or (ADDRCTR ≠ 3)
·
·   Get character if ready
·
    if RSTB = ACTIVE then
        begin
            RSTB = INACTIVE
            CHAR = INPUT
        end
·   Read message if Destination Address = Terminal Address
·
    if (HFLAG = 1) and (ADDRCTR = 3) then
        if (ADDRMATCH = 0) and (CHAR = TRAILER) then
        begin
            MESSG(NMESS) = CHAR
            NMESS = NMESS + 1
        end
·
·   Check for Terminal Address
·
    if (HFLAG = 1) and (ADDRCTR ≠ 3) then
    if CHAR ≠ TERMADDR(ADDRCTR) then
        begin
            ADDRMATCH = 1
            ADDRCTR = ADDRCTR + 1
        end
·
·   Look for Header
·
    if CHAR = HEADER then HFLAG =1
end
```

The program checks for the identification code only if it found a header during a previous iteration. It accepts the message only if it has previously found a header and a complete, matching destination address. The program must work properly during the iterations when it finds the header, the trailer,and the last digit of the destination address. It must not try to match the header with the terminal address or place the trailer or the final digit of the destination address in the message. You might try adding the rest of the logic from the flowchart (Figure 14-13) to the structured program. Note that the order of operations is often critical. You must be sure that the program does not complete one phase and start the next one during the same iteration.

Terminators for Structures

The particular structures we have presented are not ideal and are often awkward. In addition, it can be difficult to distinguish where one structure ends and another begins, particularly if they are nested. Theorists may provide better structures in the future, or designers may wish to add some of their own. Some kind of terminator for each structure seems necessary, since indenting does not always clarify the situation. "End" is a logical terminator for the "do-while" loop. There is no obvious terminator, however, for the "if-then-else" statement; some theorists have suggested "endif" or "fi" ("if" backwards). Some languages make use of special symbols. The C programming language surrounds all of its structures with braces.

REVIEW OF STRUCTURED PROGRAMMING

Structured programming brings discipline to program design. It forces you to limit the types of structures you use and the sequence of operations. It provides single-entry, single-exit structures, which you can check for logical accuracy. Structured programming often makes the designer aware of inconsistencies or possible combinations of inputs. Structured programming is not a cure-all, but it does bring some order into a process that can be chaotic. The structured program should also aid in debugging, testing and documentation.

Structured programming is not simple. The programmer must not only define the problem adequately, but must also work through the logic carefully. This is tedious and difficult, but it results in a clearly written, working program.

We suggest the following rules for applying structured programming:

1. **Begin by writing a basic flowchart** to help define the logic of the program.

2. **Start with the "sequential," "if-then-else," and "do-while" constructs.** They are known to be a complete set; i.e., any program can be written in terms of these structures.

3. **Indent each level** a few spaces from the previous level, so that you will know which statements belong where.

4. **Use terminators for each structure;** e.g., "end" for the "do-while" and "endif" or "fi" for the "if-then-else." The terminators plus the indentation should make the program reasonably clear.

5. **Emphasize simplicity and readability.** Leave lots of spaces, use meaningful names, and make expressions as clear as possible. Do not try to minimize the logic at the cost of clarity.

6. **Use comments in the program** in an organized manner.

7. **Check the logic.** Try all the extreme cases or special conditions and a few sample cases. Any logical errors you find at this level will not plague you later.

TOP-DOWN DESIGN

The remaining problem is how to check and integrate modules or structures. Certainly we want to divide a large task into sub-tasks. But how do we check the sub-tasks in isolation and put them together? One standard procedure, called "bottom-up design," involves designing the bottom level or most detailed sub-tasks first. This requires extra work in testing and debugging and leaves the entire integration task to the end. **What we need is a method that allows testing and debugging in the actual program environment and allows step-wise system integration.**

This method is "top-down design." Here we start by writing the overall supervisor program. We replace the undefined sub-programs with program "stubs," temporary programs that may either record that they were entered, provide the answer to a selected test problem, or simply return. We then test the supervisor program to see that its logic is correct.

We proceed by expanding the stubs. Each stub will often contain sub-tasks, which we will temporarily represent as stubs. This process of expansion, debugging, and testing continues until all the stubs are replaced by working programs. Note that testing and integration occur at each level, rather than all at the end. No special driver or data generation programs are necessary. We get a clear idea of exactly where we are in the design. **Top-down design assumes modular programming, and is compatible with structured programming as well.**

One of the most important advantages of top-down design is that it allows design, coding, testing, and integration to proceed hand in hand. Often problems will occur during coding, testing, and integration that were not foreseen during design. You may have to go back and change the design. This could have drastic effects on parts of the program you throught were tested and integrated. **Top-down design gives you a chance to uncover and correct design errors before you have spent a great deal of time coding a flawed program.**

The disadvantages of top-down design are:

1. The overall design may not mesh well with system hardware.

2. It may be difficult to test the program without the actual input, output, or computations done by lower-level programs.

3. The design may not take good advantage of existing software.

4. Stubs may be difficult to write, particularly if they must work correctly in several different places.

5. Top-down design may not result in generally useful modules.

6. Errors at the top level can have catastrophic effects, whereas errors in bottom-up design are usually limited to a particular module.

In large programming projects, top-down design has been shown to greatly improve programmer productivity. However, almost all of these projects have used some bottom-up design in cases where the top-down method would have resulted in a large amount of extra work.

Top-down design is a useful tool that should not be followed to extremes. It provides the same discipline for system testing and integration that structured programming provides for program design. The method, however, has more general applicability, since it does not assume the use of programmed logic. However, top-down design may not result in the most efficient implementation.

EXAMPLES: TOP-DOWN DESIGN

14-13. Response to a Switch

The first structured programming example actually demonstrates top-down design as well. The program was:

```
SWITCH = OFF
do while SWITCH = OFF
  READ SWITCH
end
LIGHT = ON
DELAY 1
LIGHT = OFF
```

These statements are really stubs, since none of them is fully defined. For example, what does READ SWITCH mean? If the switch were one bit of input port SPORT, it really means:

```
SWITCH = INPUT(SPORT) and SMASK
```

where SMASK has a '1' bit in the appropriate position. The masking may, of course, be implemented with a Bit Test instruction.

Similarly, DELAY 1 actually means (if the processor itself provides the delay):

```
REG = COUNT
do while REG ≠ 0
  REG = REG − 1
end
```

COUNT is the appropriate number to provide a one-second delay. The expanded version of the program is:

```
SWITCH = 0
do while SWITCH = 0
  SWITCH = INPUT(SPORT) and MASK
end
LIGHT = ON
REG = COUNT
do while REG ≠ 0
  REG = REG − 1
end
LIGHT = NOT (LIGHT)
```

Certainly this program is more explicit, and could more easily be translated into actual instructions or statements.

14-14. The Switch-Based Memory Loader

This example is more complex than the first example, so we must proceed systematically. Here again, **the structured program contains stubs.**

For example, if the High Address button is one bit of input port CPORT, "if HIADDRBUTTON = 1" really means:

1. Input from CPORT

2. Complement

3. Logical AND with HAMASK.

where HAMASK has a '1' in the appropriate bit position and '0's elsewhere. Similarly the condition "if Data Button = 1" really means:

1. Input from CPORT

2. Complement

3. Logical AND with DAMASK.

So, the initial stubs could just assign values to the buttons, e.g.,

```
HIADDRBUTTON = 0
LOADDRBUTTON = 0
DATABUTTON = 0
```

A run of the supervisor program should show that it takes the implied "else" path through the "if-then-else" structures, and never reads the switches. Similarly, if the stub were:

```
HIADDRBUTTON = 1
```

the supervisor program should stay in the "do while HIADDRBUTTON = 1" loop waiting for the button to be released. Simple tests like these check the overall logic.

Note that **we can expand each stub and see if the expansion produces a reasonable overall result. Note how debugging and testing proceed in a straightforward and modular manner.** We expand the HIADDRBUTTON = 1 stub to:

```
CDATA = INPUT(CPORT)
HIADDRBUTTON = not (CDATA) and HAMASK
```

The program should wait for the High Address button to be closed. The program should then display the values of the switches on the lights. This run checks for the proper response to the High Address button.

We then expand the Low Address button module to:

```
CDATA = INPUT (PORT)
HIADDRBUTTON = not (CDATA) and LAMASK
```

With the Low Address button in the closed position, the program should display the values of the switches on the lights. This run checks for the proper response to the Low Address button.

Similarly, we can expand the Data button module and check for the proper response to that button. The entire program will then have been tested.

When all the stubs have been expanded, the coding, debugging, and testing stages will all be complete. Of course, we must know exactly what results each part of the program should produce. However, many logical errors will become obvious at each level without any further expansion.

14-15. The Credit-Verification Terminal

This example, of course, will have more levels of detail. **We could start with the following program** (see Figure 14-19 for a flowchart):

```
KEYBOARD
ACK = 0
do while ACK = 0
   TRANSMIT
   RECEIVE
end
DISPLAY
```

Here **KEYBOARD, TRANSMIT, RECEIVE, and DISPLAY are program stubs that will be expanded later.** The KEYBOARD stub, for example, could simply place a ten-digit verified number into the appropriate buffer.

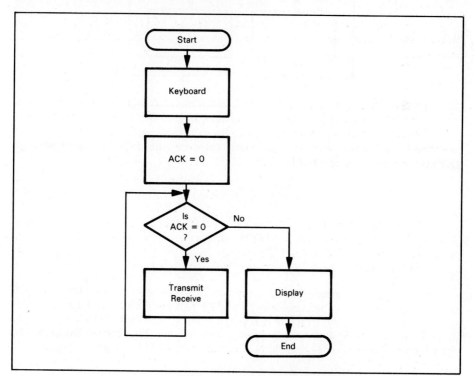

Figure 14-19. Initial Flowchart for Transaction Terminal

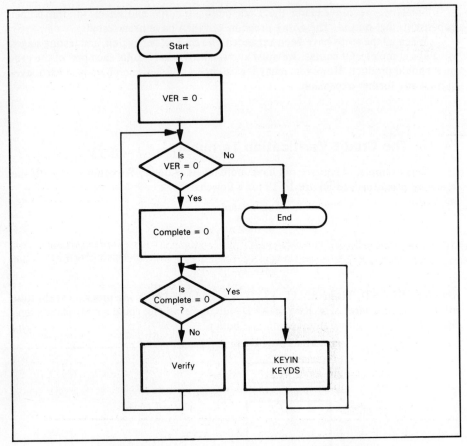

Figure 14-20. Flowchart for Expanded KEYBOARD Routine

The next stage of expansion could produce the following program for **KEYBOARD** (see Figure 14-20):

```
VER = 0
do while VER = 0
   COMPLETE = 0
   do while COMPLETE = 0
      KEYIN
      KEYDS
   end
   VERIFY
end
```

Here VER = 0 means that an entry has not been verified. COMPLETE = 0 means that the entry is incomplete. KEYIN and KEYDS are the keyboard input and display routines, respectively. VERIFY checks the entry. A stub for KEYIN would simply place a random entry (from a random number table or generator) into the buffer and set COMPLETE to 1.

We would continue by similarly expanding, debugging, and testing TRANSMIT, RECEIVE, and DISPLAY. Note that you should expand each program by one level, then go back and expand each program by another level, so that you do not perform the integration of an entire program at any one time. You must use your judgment in defining levels. Too small a step wastes time, while too large a step gets you back to the problems of system integration that top-down design is supposed to solve.

REVIEW OF TOP-DOWN DESIGN

Top-down design brings discipline to the testing and integration stages of program design. It provides a systematic method for expanding a flowchart or problem definition to the level required to actually write a program. It facilitates catching and correcting design errors. Together with structured programming, it forms a complete set of design techniques.

Like structured programming, top-down design is not simple. The designer must have defined the problem carefully and must work systematically through each level. Here again the methodology may seem tedious, but the payoff can be substantial if you follow the rules.

We recommend the following approach to top-down design:

1. Start with a basic flowchart.

2. Make the stubs as complete and as separate as possible using the principles of modular programming and information hiding.

3. Define precisely all the possible outcomes from each stub and select a set of test data to generate these outcomes.

4. Check each level carefully and systematically.

5. Use the structures from structured programming.

6. Expand all the stubs by one level at a time. Do not try to do too much in one step.

7. Watch carefully for common tasks and data structures.

8. Test and debug after expanding each stub. Do not try to do an entire level at a time.

9. Be aware of what the hardware can do. Do not hesitate to stop and do a little bottom-up design in order to get realistic input, output, or computations.

CHAPTER REVIEW

You should note that we have spent an entire chapter without mentioning any specific microprocessor or assembly language, and without writing a single line of actual code. Hopefully, though, you know a lot more about the examples than you would have if we had just asked you to write the programs at the start. Although we often think of the writing of computer instructions as a key part of software development, it is actually one of the easiest stages and, in a sense, one of the least important.

Once you have written a few programs, coding will become simple. You will soon learn the instruction set, recognize which insructions are really useful, and remember the common sequences that make up the largest part of most programs. You will then find that many of the other stages of software development remain difficult and have few clear rules.

We have suggested here some ways to systematize the important early stages. In the problem definition stage, you must define all the characteristics of the system — its inputs, outputs, processing, time and memory constraints, and error handling. You must particularly consider how the system will interact with the larger system of which it is a part, and whether that larger system includes computer peripherals, electrical equipment, mechanical equipment, or a human operator. You must start at this stage to make the system easy to use and maintain.

In the program design stage, several techniques can help you to systematically specify and document the logic of your program. Modular programming forces you to divide the total program into small, distinct modules. Structured programming provides a systematic way of defining the logic of those modules, while top- down design is a systematic method for integrating and testing them. Of course, no one can compel you to follow all of these techniques; they are, in fact, guidelines more than anything else. But they do provide a unified approach to design, and you should consider them a basis on which to develop your own approach.

REFERENCES

1. D. R. Ballard, "Designing Fail-Safe Microprocessor Systems," *Electronics*, January 4, 1979, pp. 139-43.

    "A Designer's Guide to Signature Analysis," Hewlett-Packard Application Note 222, Hewlett-Packard, Inc., Palo Alto, CA, 1977.

    E. S. Donn and M. D. Lippman, "Efficient and Effective Microcomputer Testing Requires Careful Preplanning." *EDN*, February 20, 1979, pp. 97-107 (includes self-test examples for 6502).

    G. Gordon and H. Nadig, "Hexadecimal Signatures Identify Troublespots in Microprocessor Systems," *Electronics*, March 3, 1977, pp. 89-96.

    M. Neil and R. Goodner, "Designing a Serviceman's Needs into Microprocessor-Based Systems," *Electronics*, March 1, 1979, pp. 122-28.

    W. Schweber and L. Pearce, "Software Signature Analysis Identifies and Checks PROMs," *EDN*, November 5, 1978, pp. 79-81.

    V. P. Srini, "Fault Diagnosis of Microprocessor Systems," *Computer*, January 1977, pp. 60-65.

2. For a brief discussion of human factors considerations, see G. Morris, "Make Your Next Instrument Design Emphasize User Needs and Wants," *EDN*, October 20, 1978, pp. 100-05.

3. D. L. Parnas (see the references below) has been a leader in the area of modular programming.

4. Collected by B. W. Unger (see reference below).

5. Formulated by D. L. Parnas.

6. However, see the following for guidance in applying structured programming concepts to the flow of data:

    C. A. R. Hoare, "Notes on Data Structuring" in Dahl, O. J., E.. Dijkstra, and C. A. R. Hoare, *Structured Programming*, Academic Press, New York, 1972.

    The following references provide additional information on problem definition and program design:

    N. Chapin, *Flowcharts*, Auerbach, Princeton, N. J., 1971.

    W. F. Dalton, "Design Microcomputer Software like Other Systems - Systematically," *Electronics*, January 19, 1978, pp. 97-101.

    E. W. Dijkstra, *A Discipline of Programming*, Prentice-Hall, Englewood Cliffs, N. J., 1976.

    M. H. Halstead, *Elements of Software Science*, American Elsevier, New York, 1977.

J. K. Hughes and J. I. Michtom, *A Structured Approach to Programming*, Prentice-Hall, Englewood Cliffs, N. J., 1977.

D. E. Morgan and D. J. Taylor, "A Survey of Methods for Achieving Reliable Software," *Computer*, February 1977, pp. 44- 52.

W. Myers, "The Need for Software Engineering," *Computer*, February 1978, pp. 12-25.

D. L. Parnas, "On the Criteria to be Used in Decomposing Systems into Modules," *Communications of the ACM*, December 1972, pp. 1053-58.

D. L. Parnas, "A Technique for the Specification of Software Modules with Examples," *Communications of the ACM*, May 1973, pp. 330-36.

M. Phister, Jr., *Data Processing Technology and Economics*, Santa Monica Publishing Co., Santa Monica, CA, 1976.

V. Schneider, "Prediction of Software Effort and Project Duration — Four New Formulas," *SIGPLAN Notices*, June 1978, pp. 49-59.

B. Shneiderman, et al., "Experimental Investigations of the Utility of Detailed Flowcharts in Programming," *Communications of the ACM*, June 1977, pp. 373-81.

R. C. Tausworthe, *Standardized Development of Computer Software*, Prentice-Hall, Englewood Cliffs, N. J., 1977.

B. W. Unger, "Programming Languages for Computer System Simulation," *Simulation*, April 1978, pp. 101-10.

N. Wirth, *Algorithms + Data Structures = Programs*, Prentice-Hall, Englewood Cliffs, N. J., 1976.

N. Wirth, *Systematic Programming: an Introduction*, Prentice- Hall, Englewood Cliffs, N. J., 1973.

E. U. Yourdon, *Techniques of Program Structure and Design*, Prentice-Hall, Englewood Cliffs, N. J., 1975.

15
Debugging and Testing

As we noted at the beginning of the previous chapter, debugging and testing are among the most time-consuming stages of software development. **Even though such methods as modular programming, structured programming, and top-down design can simplify programs and reduce the frequency of errors, debugging and testing are still difficult** because they are so poorly defined. The selection of an adequate set of test data is seldom a clear or scientific process. Finding errors sometimes seems like a game of "pin the tail on the donkey," except that the donkey is moving and the programmer must position the tail by remote control. Surely, few tasks are as frustrating as debugging programs.

This chapter will first describe the tools available to aid in debugging. It will then discuss basic debugging procedures, describe the common types of errors, and present some examples of program debugging. The last sections will describe how to select test data and test programs.

DEBUGGING

We will not do much more than describe the purposes of most of the debugging tools. There is very little standardization in this area, and not enough space to discuss all the devices and programs that are currently available. The examples should give you some idea of the uses, advantages, and limitations of particular hardware or software aids.

SIMPLE DEBUGGING TOOLS

The simplest debugging tools available are:

- A breakpoint facility
- A single-step facility
- A register dump program
- A memory dump program

Breakpoint

A breakpoint is a place at which the program will automatically halt or wait so that the user can examine the current status of the system. The program will usually not start again until the operator requests a resumption of execution. Breakpoints allow you to check, or pass through an entire section of a program. For example, to see if an initialization routine is correct, you can place a breakpoint at the end of it and run the program. You can then check memory locations and registers to see if the entire section is correct. But if the section is not correct, you'll still have to pin down the error, either with earlier breakpoints or with a single-step mode.

Breakpoints invariably use the interrupt system. Some microprocessors have a special software interrupt or trap facility that can act as a breakpoint. The Z8000 has no special facilities or instructions for this, so the extended instruction trap is sometimes used. The new program status for this trap is the second in the Program Status Area. On the Z8002 it occupies two words beginning at offset 4 into the Program Status Area; on the Z8001 it occupies four words beginning at offset 8. Chapter 12 describes the Program Status Area in detail.

Whether or not interrupt logic is used, a special program is executed in response to a breakpoint. The breakpoint program is executed as an interrupt service routine if interrupt logic is used; the breakpoint program is executed as a subroutine or system program otherwise.

The breakpoint routine might automatically print register contents as soon as it is executed, or the program may wait for the user to enter a command.

If the breakpoint routine is executed using interrupt logic, remember that the stack and the stack pointer will both be modified in the course of executing the breakpoint program.

The simplest method for inserting breakpoints is to replace the first word of the instruction with an extended instruction or to replace the instruction with a JP or CALL instruction. The extended instruction is preferable, since only a single word must be replaced, and the breakpoint will not overrun the subsequent instructions.

Many monitors have facilities for inserting and removing breakpoints implemented via some type of Jump instruction. Such breakpoints do not affect the timing of the program until the breakpoint is executed. However, note that this procedure will not work if part or all of the program is in ROM or PROM. Other monitors implement breakpoints by actually checking the address lines or the program counter in hardware or in software. This method allows breakpoints on addresses in ROM or PROM, but it may affect the timing if the address must be checked in software.

Single-Step

A single-step facility allows you to execute the program one instruction at a time. This type of facility often looks the same as inserting a breakpoint after each instruction.

There are many errors that single stepping cannot help you find. These include timing errors and errors in the interrupt or DMA systems. Furthermore, single stepping is very slow, typically executing a program at less than one millionth of the processor speed. To single-step through one second of real processor time would take more than ten days. Single stepping is useful only to check the logic of short instruction sequences.

Breakpoints and single-step mode complement each other. You can use breakpoints either to localize the error or to pass through sections that you know are correct. You can then do the detailed debugging in single-step mode. In some cases, breakpoints do not affect program timing; they can then be used to check input/output and interrupts.

Register Dump

A register dump utility on a microcomputer is a program that lists the contents of all the CPU registers. This information is usually not displayed by the microcomputer. The following routine will print the contents of all the registers on the system printer, if we assume that PRTHEX prints the contents of Register 0 as four hexadecimal digits. Figure 15-1 is a flowchart of the program and Figure 15-2 shows a typical result. We assume that the routine is entered with a CALL instruction that stores the old program counter at the top of the stack. An interrupt will store both the program counter and the Status register at the top of the stack.

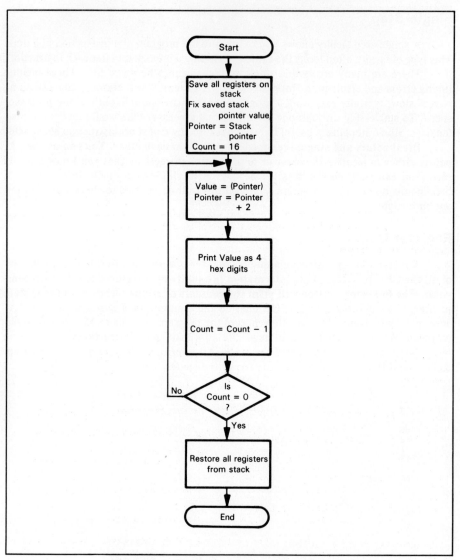

Figure 15-1. Flowchart of Register Dump Program

A605	R0
0100	R1
C549	R2
42C7	R3
0016	R4
17A0	R5
240A	R6
0061	R7
717C	R8
0000	R9
CCF9	R10
17F0	R11
A085	R12
0010	R13
6160	R14
7FF8	R15

Figure 15-2. Results of a Typical Z8000 Register Dump

Register Dump Program:

```
                external
                    PRTHEX procedure

                internal
                    PRREGS procedure
                    entry
                          $abs      IBASE
4600 030F            SUB     R15,#32          ! Room for 16 regs !
4602 0020
4604 1CF9            LDM     @R15,R0,#16      ! Store R0 - R15 !
4606 000F
4608 61F0            LD      R0,30(R15)       ! Get saved R15 !
460A 001E
460C 0100            ADD     R0,#32+2         ! Adjust to value before call !
460E 0022
4610 6FF0            LD      30(R15),R0       ! Return to stack for printing !
4612 001E
4614 A1F1            LD      R1,R15           ! Pointer to values !
4616 2102            LD      R2,#16           ! Number of registers to print !
4618 0010
461A 9710   LOOP:    POP     R0,@R1           ! Next register value !
461C 5F00            CALL    PRTHEX           ! Print out 4 hex characters !
461E 0000*
4620 F284            DJNZ    R2,LOOP
4622 1CF1            LDM     R0,@R15,#15      ! Restore R0 - R14 !
4624 000E
4626 010F            ADD     R15,#32          ! Throw away saved values !
4628 0020
462A 9E08            RET

462C               end     PRTHEX
```

Memory Dump

A memory dump is a program that lists the contents of memory on an output device (such as a printer). This is a more efficient way of examining data arrays or entire programs than just looking at single locations. However, very large memory dumps are not useful (except to supply scrap paper) because of the sheer mass of information that they produce. They may also take a long time to execute on a slow printer. **Small dumps may,** however, **provide the programmer with a reasonable amount of information that can be examined as a unit. Regular repetitions of data patterns or offsets of entire arrays are easily spotted in a dump.**

A general dump program is often rather difficult to write. Make sure that the ending memory address is not smaller than the starting memory address. A larger starting memory address might be treated as an error, or it may cause no output.

Since the speed of the memory dump depends on the speed of the output device, the efficiency of the routine seldom matters. **The following program will ignore cases where the starting address is larger than the ending address, and will handle memory blocks of any length.** We assume that the starting address is in Register 1 and the ending address is in Register 2.

```
4600 93F2   DUMP:   PUSH   @R15,R2
4602 91F0           PUSHL  @R15,RR0
4604 A310           RES    R1,#0        ! Make sure start ptr is even !
4606 E803           JR     ETEST        ! Test for trivial cases first !
4608 9710   LOOP:   POP    R0,@R1
460A 5F00           CALL   PRTHEX       ! Print value from R0 !
460C 0000*
460E 8B21   ETEST:  CP     R1,R2        ! Done yet? !
4610 E7FB           JR     ULT,LOOP
4612 95F0           POPL   RR0,@R15     ! Restore registers !
4614 97F2           POP    R2,@R15
4616 9E08           RET
```

Note that locations up to, but not including, the end address are printed.

Figure 15-3 shows the output from a dump of memory locations 6000 to 601F.

This routine correctly handles the case in which the starting and ending locations are the same (try it!). You will have to interpret the results carefully if the dump area includes the stack, since the dump subroutine itself uses the stack. PRTHEX may also change memory and stack locations.

6000	231F	6054	3728	3E00	
6008	6E42	3817	5944	9837	
6010	4736	2381	E1FF	FF5A	
6018	34ED	BCAF	FEFF	2702	

Figure 15-3. Results of a Typical Memory Dump

In a memory dump, the data can be displayed in a number of different ways. Common forms are ASCII characters or pairs of hexadecimal digits for 8-bit values, and four hexadecimal digits for 16-bit values. The format should be chosen based on the intended use of the dump. It is almost always easier to interpret an object code dump if it is displayed in hexadecimal form rather than ASCII form.

A common and useful dump format is illustrated here:

1000 54 68 65 20 64 75 60 70 /The dump/

Each line consists of three parts. The line starts with the hexadecimal address of the first byte displayed on the line. Following the address are eight or sixteen bytes displayed in hexadecimal form. Last is the ASCII representation of the same eight or sixteen bytes. Try rewriting the memory dump program so that it will print the address and the ASCII characters as well as the hexadecimal form of the memory contents.

MORE ADVANCED DEBUGGING TOOLS

The more advanced debugging tools that are most widely used are:

* **Simulator programs to check program logic**

* **Logic analyzers to check signals and timing**

Many variations of both these tools exist, and we will discuss only the standard features.

Software Simulator

The simulator is the computer equivalent of a pencil-and-paper computer. It **is a computer program that goes through the operating cycle of a computer, keeping track of the contents of all the registers, flags, and memory locations.** We could, of course, do this by hand, but it would require a large effort and close attention to the exact effects of each instruction. The simulator program never gets tired or confused, it never forgets an instruction or register, nor does it run out of paper.

Typical simulator features include:

* **A breakpoint facility.** Usually, breakpoints can be set to occur after a particular number of cycles have been executed, when a memory location or one of a set of memory locations is referenced, when the contents of a location or one of a set of locations are altered, or on other conditions.

* **Register and memory dump facilities** that display the contents of memory locations, registers, and I/O ports.

* **A trace facility** that prints the contents of particular registers or memory locations whenever the program changes or uses them.

* **A load facility** that allows you to set initial register and/or memory location contents, or change them during the simulation.

Some simulators can simulate input/output, interrupts, and even DMA. **The simulator has many advantages:**

1. It can provide a complete description of the status of the computer, since the simulator program is not restricted by pin limitations or other characteristics of the underlying circuitry.

2. It can provide breakpoints, dumps, traces, and other facilities, without using any of the simulated processor's memory space or control system. These facilities will therefore not interfere with the user program.

3. Programs, starting points, and other conditions are easy to change.

4. All the facilities of a large computer, including peripherals and software, are available to the microprocessor designer.

On the other hand, the simulator is limited by its software base and its separation from the real microcomputer. The major limitations are:

1. The simulator cannot cope with timing problems, since it operates at less than real-time execution speed. The simulator is usually quite slow. Reproducing one second of actual processor time may require hours of computer time.

2. The simulator cannot model the input/output section exactly since it cannot represent external hardware or interfaces accurately.

The simulator represents the software side of debugging; it has the typical advantages and limitations of a wholly software-based approach. The simulator can provide insight into program logic and other software problems, but often cannot help with timing, I/O, and hardware problems.

Logic Analyzer

The logic, or microprocessor, analyzer is the hardware solution to debugging. Basically, the analyzer is a parallel digital version of the standard oscilloscope. The analyzer displays information in binary, hexadecimal, or mnemonic form on a CRT, and has a variety of triggering events, thresholds, and inputs. Most analyzers also have a memory so that they can display the past contents of the busses.

The standard procedure is to set a triggering event, such as the occurrence of a particular address on the address bus or instruction on the data bus. For example, one might trigger the analyzer if the microcomputer tries to store data in a particular address, or execute an input or output instruction. One may then look at the sequence of events that preceded the breakpoint. **Common problems you can find in this way include short noise spikes (or glitches), incorrect signal sequences, overlapping waveforms, and timing or signaling errors. A software simulator could not be used to diagnose those errors.**

Logic analyzers offer numerous options; these include:

- Number of input lines. At least 32 are necessary to monitor a 16-bit data bus and a 16-bit address bus. Still more are necessary for control signals, clocks, and other important inputs.

- Amount of memory. Each previous state that is saved will occupy several bytes of memory.

- Maximum frequency. It must be several MHz to handle the fastest processors.

- Minimum signal width (important for catching glitches).

- Type and number of triggering events allowed. Important features are pre- and post-trigger delays; these allow the user to display events occurring before or after the trigger event.

- Methods of connecting to the microcomputer. This may require a rather complex interface.

- Number of display channels

- Binary, hexadecimal or mnemonic displays

- Display formats

- Signal hold time requirements

- Probe capacitance

- Single or dual thresholds

All of these factors are important in comparing different logic and microprocessor analyzers, since these instruments are new and unstandardized. A tremendous variety of products is already available and this variety will become even greater in the future.

Logic analyzers, of course, are necessary only for systems with complex timing. Simple applications with low-speed peripherals have few hardware problems that a designer cannot handle with a standard oscilloscope.

DEBUGGING WITH CHECKLISTS

No one can hope to check an entire program by hand; however, certain trouble spots can be checked. **You can use systematic hand checking to find a large number of errors without resorting to any debugging tools.**

The question is where to place the effort. The answer is on points that can be handled with either a yes-no answer or a simple arithmetic calculation. Do not do complex arithmetic, follow all status flags, or try every conceivable case. Limit your hand checking to matters that can be settled easily. Leave the complex problems to be solved with the aid of debugging tools. But proceed systematically; build your checklist, and make sure that the program performs all basic operations correctly.

The first step is to compare the flowchart or other program documentation with the actual code. Make sure that everything which appears in one also appears in the other. A simple checklist will do the job. It is easy to omit an entire branch or a processing section.

Next concentrate on the program loops. Make sure that all registers and memory locations used inside the loops are initialized correctly. This is a common source of errors; once again, a simple checklist will suffice.

Now look at each conditional branch. Select a sample case that should produce a branch and one that should not; try both of them. Is the branch correct or reversed? If the branch involves checking whether a number is above or below a threshold, try the equality case. Does the correct branch occur? Make sure that your choice is consistent with the problem definition.

Look at the loops as a whole. Try the first and last iterations by hand; these are often troublesome special cases. What happens if the number of iterations is zero; e.g., there is no data or the table has no elements? Does the program fall through correctly? Programs will often perform one iteration unnecessarily, or, even worse, decrement counters past zero before checking them.

Check off everything down to the last statement. Don't assume (hopefully) that the first error is the only one in the program. Hand checking will allow you to get the maximum benefit from debugging runs, since you will get rid of many simple errors ahead of time.

Hand Checking Questions

Here is a quick review of the hand checking questions:

1. Does the program include everything that was designed into it (and vice versa for documentation purposes)?

2. Are all registers and memory locations initialized before they are used inside loops?

3. Are all conditional branches logically correct?

4. Do all loops start and end properly?

5. Are equality cases handled correctly?

6. Are trivial cases handled correctly?

Common Errors

Of course, despite all these precautions (or if you skip over some of them), often programs still don't work. You must find remaining mistakes. The hand checklist provides a starting place if you didn't use it earlier. Some of the errors that you may not have eliminated are:

- **Failure to initialize variables such as counters, pointers, sums, indexes, etc.** Do not assume that the registers, memory locations, or flags necessarily contain zero before they are used.

- **Misusing a conditional jump.** Be particularly careful to use the simple jump conditions (MI, PL, Z, NZ) after testing a value, and the comparison jump conditions (LT, LE, GT, GE, etc.) after comparing two values or after arithmetic operations.

- **Updating counters, pointers, and indexes in the wrong place or not at all.** Be sure that there are no paths through a loop that either skip or repeat the updating instructions.

- **Failure to fall through correctly in trivial cases** such as no data present in a buffer, no tests to be run, or no entries in a transaction. Do not assume that such cases will never occur unless the program specifically eliminates them.

Other problems to watch for are:

- **Reversing the order of operands.** Remember that the first operand is the destination. Consult the instruction description for more complex instructions. Remember: The operation is load destination from source.

- **Changing condition flags before using them.** Remember that INC and DEC affect all the condition code flags except Carry. When incrementing through memory, INC R1 may have to be replaced by LDA R1,1(R1) in order to preserve the condition codes. Note also that many byte instructions set the Parity flag, which is also the Overflow flag.

- **Confusing the condition flags on auto-increment and auto-decrement instructions.** Remember that instructions such as CPI and LDDRB use the Zero flag for condition met and the Overflow flag for the counter going to zero.

- **Confusing data and addresses.** Remember that LD R2, #START loads R2 with the address START, while LD R2,START loads R2 with the contents of memory location START. Similarly, if R3 contains 6000, LD R2,R3 results in R2 containing 6000, while LD R2,@R3 results in R2 containing the contents of location 6000.

- **Confusing numbers and characters.** Remember that the ASCII and EBCDIC representations of digits differ from the digits themselves. For example, ASCII 7 is 37_{16}, whereas hex 07_{16} is the ASCII Bell character.

- **Confusing binary and decimal numbers.** Remember that the BCD representation of a number differs from its binary representation. For example, BCD 36, when treated as a simple hexadecimal constant, is equivalent to 54 decimal (try it).

- **Confusing signed and unsigned numbers.** Remember especially that addresses are always unsigned. After comparing two addresses, use the "unsigned" conditions (ULT, UGT, etc). Characters and BCD numbers are also unsigned.

- **Reversing the order in compares.** Remember that CP R0,R1 sets the condition codes as if R1 were subtracted from R0. Following the instruction with JR LT,LABEL0 means jump to LABEL0 if R0 is less than R1. Remember: The test is for destination:condition:source.

- **Accidentally reinitializing a register or memory location.** Make sure that no Jump instructions transfer control back to initialization statements.

- **Ignoring the effects of subroutines and macros.** Remember that calls to subroutines or invocations of macros change flags, registers, and memory locations. Be sure of all changes made by subroutines or macros. Note that it is very important to document these changes so that you do not have to go through the entire listing to find them.

- **Using shift and rotate instructions incorrectly.** Remember the precise effects of the numerous Z8000 shift and rotate instructions.

- **Counting the length of an array incorrectly.** If the first and last byte addresses for an array are given, then the number of bytes is often computed one byte too few. For example, addresses 6300 through 6304 specify five bytes, not four. Remember: The array length is End − Start + 1.

- **Confusing 8-, 16- and 32-bit quantities.** Addresses are 16 bits long if nonsegmented, 32 bits if segmented. MULTL and DIVL use 64-bit quantities. Byte instructions deal with 8-bit quantities. The stack accommodates only 16- and 32-bit values.

- **Confusing high- and low-order register parts.** RH1 is the high-order 8 bits of R1; RL1 is the low-order byte. R0 is the high-order 16 bits of RR0; R1 is the low-order word. That is, RH0 is the high-order byte of RR0, RL0 is the next byte, RH1 is the third byte, and RL1 is the low-order byte of RR0.

- **Confusing most significant and least significant parts of memory locations.** In general, the most significant part of a value has the lowest address. If memory locations 6000 through 6003 contain a long value, the most significant 8 bits are in location 6000 and the least significant in location 6003.

- **Confusing the bit positions in bit instructions.** The BIT, SET and RES instructions use bit 0 as the least significant bit, bit 7 as the most significant bit in a byte, and bit 15 as the most significant bit in a word.

- **Confusing the stack and the stack pointer.** The contents of the stack are always accessed with indirect, or base addressing. LD R15,R0 changes the stack pointer, while LD @R15,R0 changes the value on top of the stack.

- **Forgetting to transfer control past sections of the program that should not be executed in particular situations.** Remember that the computer will proceed sequentially through program memory unless specifically ordered not to do so.

- **Advancing a pointer or index register incorrectly.** When a register contains the address of an item in a list of word values, 2 must be added to it to address the next value. An index into a table of words must similarly be advanced by 2.

- **Restoring registers in the wrong order.** If the order in which they were saved was:

```
PUSH      @R15,R2
PUSH      @R15,R1
PUSH      @R15,R0
```

the order of restoration should be:

```
POP       R0,@R15
POP       R1,@R15
POP       R2,@R15
```

Remember: Restore registers in sequence opposite to the order in which they were pushed.

- **Pushing and popping a different number of values from a stack.** If a program or subroutine pops too many or too few values from the stack, severe errors can (and usually do) occur. When a subroutine tries to return to its caller, a data item can be used instead of the return address, causing transfer to a totally unexpected location.

- **Using memory locations lower than the stack pointer.** Accessing locations relative to, but lower than, the stack pointer can cause unpredictable results. If an interrupt occurs, the contents of the locations could change.

DEBUGGING INTERRUPT-DRIVEN PROGRAMS

Interrupt-driven programs are particularly difficult to debug, since errors may occur randomly. If, for example, the program enables the interrupts a few instructions too early, an error will occur only if an interrupt is received while the program is executing those few instructions. **In fact you can usually assume that randomly occurring errors are caused by the interrupt system.**[2] **Typical errors in interrupt-driven programs are:**

- **Forgetting to reenable interrupts after accepting one and servicing it.** The processor disables interrupts automatically on accepting an interrupt. Be sure that no possible sequences fail to reenable the interrupt system. Remember that, in addition to reenabling interrupts in the CPU, the program often has to perform some action to cause the interrupting signal to be reset. If this is not done, it will appear as if the interrupting device is constantly requesting service.

- **Forgetting to save and restore registers.**

- **Enabling interrupts before establishing all the necessary conditions such** as priority, flags, program status pointer, counters, etc. A checklist can aid here.

- **Forgetting that the interrupts leave the old program counter and Status register in the stack whether you use them or not.**

- **Popping the interrupt identifier off the stack before executing the IRET instruction.** IRET pops and discards the top word of the stack.

- **Not disabling the interrupt during multi-word transfers or instruction sequences.** Watch particularly for situations where the interrupt service routine may use the same memory locations that the program is using.

- **Ignoring the possibility that the interrupt routine may get reentered.**

Hopefully, these lists will at least give you some ideas about where to look for errors. Unfortunately, even the most systematic debugging can still leave some truly puzzling problems, particularly when interrupts are involved.[3]

If nested interrupts are allowed, then interrupt service routines must be reentrant. A routine can be executing in response to one interrupt, but in mid-execution it can itself be interrupted, then reexecuted to service the new interrupt. If this routine changes the contents of locations other than CPU registers and the stack, then you could be in big trouble. We discuss reentrant subroutines in Chapter 10.

PROGRAM EXAMPLES

15-1. Decimal to Seven-Segment Conversion

The program converts a decimal number in memory location 6000 to a seven-segment code in memory location 6001. It stores the code for a blank display if memory location 6000 does not contain a decimal number.

A flowchart of the initial program is shown in Figure 15-4.

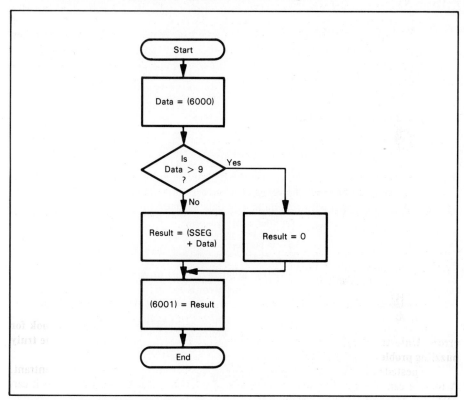

Figure 15-4. Flowchart of Decimal to Seven-Segment Conversion

Program 15-1a:

```
internal
    pgm_15_1a procedure
    entry
        $abs    IBASE

        LDB     RL2,%6000
        CPB     RL2,9               ! Is value between 0 and 9? !
        JR      ULE,DONE            ! No, error !
        LDB     RL0,SSEG(RL2)       ! Get pattern from table !
        LDB     %6000,RL0           ! Return result !
DONE:   HALT

    end     pgm_15_1a

SSEG    ARRAY [10 BYTE] := [%3F %06 %5B %4F %66
                           %6D %7D %07 %7D %6F]
```

The first time the program is assembled, we find an error. The statement LDB RL0,SSEG(RL2) generates an invalid instruction error. After looking at it carefully, we realize that indexed addressing mode requires a word register. So we replace RL2 with R2 and assemble again, this time with no errors.

But Program 15-1a has logic errors. For example, if the data is 7, 7 is less than 9, so we exit. But 7 is valid. We confused the sense of the compare. We really want JR UGT,DONE.

Program 15-1b:

```
internal
      pgm_15_1b procedure
      entry
            $abs      IBASE

            CLRB      RL0               ! Return 0 if error !
            LDB       RL2,%6000
            CPB       RL2,9             ! Is value between 0 and 9? !
            JR        UGT,DONE          ! No, error !
            LDB       RL0,SSEG(R2)      ! Get pattern from table !
            LDB       %6000,RL0         ! Return result !
DONE:       HALT

      end       pgm_15_1b

SSEG      ARRAY [10 BYTE] := [%3F %06 %5B %4F %66
                              %6D %7D %07 %7D %6F]
```

Program 15-1b has been hand checked successfully. Since the program is simple, the next stage is to try it with real data. The data selected for the trials is:

> 0   (The smallest number)
> 9   (The large number)
> 10   (A boundary case)
> $6B_{16}$ (A randomly selected case)

The first trial finds zero in location 6000. When the program completes execution, we find that location 6001 is unchanged. This error is easily found; the result is stored in 6000 instead of 6001.

After this correction is made, the program is run again. This time we find C2 in location 6001. Since there is no C2 in the table, a close look at the instruction that accesses the table shows us that the high byte of R2 has never been initialized. This is corrected by inserting a CLRB RH2 instruction.

The revised version is shown in program 15-1c.

Program 15-1c:

```
internal
      pgm_15_1c procedure
      entry
            $abs      IBASE

            CLRB      RL0               ! Return 0 if error !
            CLRB      RH2               ! Keep high byte 0 !
            LDB       RL2,%6000
            CPB       RL2,9             ! Is value between 0 and 9? !
            JR        UGT,DONE          ! No, error !
            LDB       RL0,SSEG(R2)      ! Get pattern from table !
            LDB       %6001,RL0         ! Return result !
DONE:       HALT

      end       pgm_15_1c

SSEG      ARRAY [10 BYTE] := [%3F %06 %5B %4F %66
                              %6D %7D %07 %7D %6F]
```

The results now appear as follows:

Data	Result
0	3F
9	6F
10	B2
6B	B2

The program has not detected 10 and 6B as errors. Since we already know the jump is correct, we take a closer look at the compare; we are comparing the contents of RL2 with location 9, instead of immediate data 9. We also note that location 9 contains 45_{16}. Had location 9 happened to contain the value 9, this problem might not have shown up until much later.

The 82 generated for 6B is puzzling. 6B is greater than 45, so it should have produced an error, even if 10 did not. What happened? When an invalid value was used, nothing was stored in memory location 6001.

The label DONE should be moved one statement further up.

Since the program is simple, it could be tested for all the decimal digits. The results are:

Data	Result
0	3F
1	06
2	5B
3	4F
4	6G
5	6D
6	7D
7	07
8	7D
9	6F

Note that the result for number 8 is wrong: it should be 7F. Since everything else is correct, the error is almost surely in the table. In fact, entry 8 in the table has been miscopied.

The final version is shown in program 15-1d.

Program 15-1d:

```
        internal
        pgm_15_1d procedure
        entry
            $abs        IBASE

            CLRB        RL0             ! Return 0 if error !
            CLRB        RH2             ! Keep high byte 0 !
            LDB         RL2,%6000
            CPB         RL2,#9          ! Is value between 0 and 9? !
            JR          UGT,DONE        ! No, error !
            LDB         RL0,SSEG(R2)    ! Get pattern from table !
    DONE:   LDB         %6001,RL0       ! Return result !
            HALT

        end         pgm_15_1d

    SSEG    ARRAY [10 BYTE] := [%3F %06 %5B %4F %66
                                %6D %7D %07 %7F %6F]
```

The errors encountered in this program are typical of the ones that Z8000 assembly language programmers should anticipate. They include:

- Failing to initialize registers or memory locations

- Inverting the logic on conditional branches and compares

- Confusing immediate and direct addressing, i.e., data and addresses

- Incorrectly converting a byte value to a word

- Branching to the wrong place so that one path through the program is incorrect

- Copying lists of numbers (or instructions) incorrectly.

Note that straightforward instructions and simple addressing modes seldom cause any problems.

The comparison condition codes (LT, GT, ULT, etc.) when used after a TEST are a particularly annoying source of errors in Z8000 assembly language programs. Confusing signed and unsigned binary data also causes many problems.

15-2. Sort into Decreasing Order

The program sorts an array of unsigned 8-bit binary numbers into decreasing order. The array begins in memory location 6001; its length is in memory location 6000.

Program 15-2a:

```
internal
     pgm_15_2a procedure
     entry
          $abs    IBASE

          CLR     R0              ! Clear interchange flag before pass !
          CLRB    RH1             ! Length in low half of R1 !
          LDB     RL1,%6000
          LDA     R2,%6001        ! Pointer to data !
PASS:     LDB     RL3,@R2         ! Array element !
          INC     R2              ! Point to next !
          CPB     RL3,@R2         ! Is it less than next element? !
          JR      GE,STEP         ! No, no interchange necessary !
          LDB     @R2,RL3         ! Yes, interchange !
          INC     R2
STEP:     DJNZ    R1,PASS
          DEC     R0              ! Was there an interchange? !
          JR      Z,PASS          ! Yes, go through it again !
          HALT

     end     pgm_15_2a
```

A flowchart of the initial program is shown in Figure 15-5.

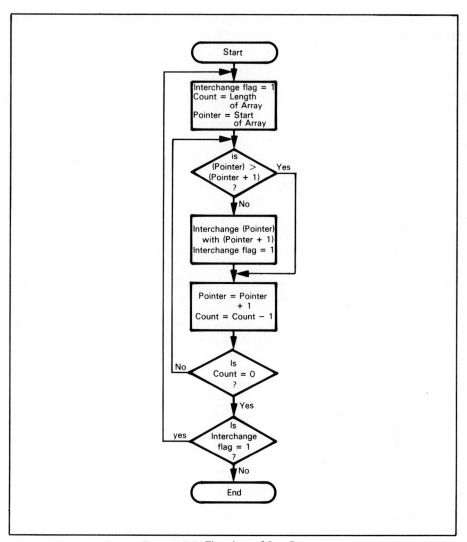

Figure 15-5. Flowchart of Sort Program

The hand check shows that all the blocks in the flowchart have been implemented in the program and that all the registers have been initialized. The conditional branches must be examined carefully. The instruction JR GE,STEP causes a branch if the current value is greater than or equal to the next value. Note that the equality case must not result in an interchange, since this will cause an endless loop with the two equal elements being switched back and forth.

Try an example:

$$
\begin{array}{rcl}
(6000) & = & 30 \\
(6002) & = & 37
\end{array}
$$

CPB RL3,@R2 results in the calculation of 30 minus 37. The Carry flag is set and the sign bit is set. The overflow bit is clear. The following jump is not taken, so an interchange occurs. If the operands are equal, no interchange occurs. What about boundary conditions:

$$
\begin{array}{rcl}
(6001) & = & FF \\
(6002) & = & 00
\end{array}
$$

This results in the calculation of FF minus 00. The Carry flag is clear, the sign bit is set and the overflow bit is clear. So the jump is not taken. But FF is larger than 00, and should have caused an interchange. The problem is that the data is unsigned.

We should have used JR UGE,STEP. Checking all the cases shows this produces the desired result.

What about JR Z,PASS, which appears at the end of the program? If there are any elements out of order, the interchange flag will be one, so the branch is correct.

Now let us hand check the first iteration of the program. The initialization results in the following values:

$$
\begin{array}{rcl}
R0 & = & 0 \\
R1 & = & COUNT \\
R2 & = & 6001
\end{array}
$$

The effects of the loop instructions are:

```
PASS:    LDB     RL3,@R2      ! RL3 = (6001) !
         INC     R2           ! R2 = 6002 !
         CPB     RL3,@R2      ! (6001) - (6002) !
         JR      UGE,STEP
         LDB     @R2,RL3      ! (6002) = (6001) !
         INC     R2           ! R2 = 6003 !
STEP:    DJNZ    R1,PASS      ! R1 = COUNT - 1 !
```

Note that we have already checked the conditional jump instructions. Clearly the logic is incorrect. If the first two numbers are out of order, the results after the first iteration should be:

$$
\begin{array}{rcl}
(6001) & = & OLD\ (6002) \\
(6002) & = & OLD\ (6001) \\
R2 & = & 6002 \\
R1 & = & COUNT - 1
\end{array}
$$

Instead they are:

$$
\begin{array}{rcl}
(6001) & = & Unchanged \\
(6002) & = & OLD\ (6001) \\
R2 & = & 6003 \\
R1 & = & COUNT - 1
\end{array}
$$

The error in R2 is easy to correct. The second INC R2 is unnecessary and should be omitted. The interchange involves a little more care. The EXB instruction handles this operation well:

```
EXB     RL3,@R2        ! RL3 = (6002); (6002) = (6001) !
LDB     -1(R2),RL3     ! (6001) = old (6002) !
```

All of these changes require a new copy of the program, shown in program 15-2b.

Program 15-2b:

```
internal
        pgm_15_2b procedure
        entry
            $abs    IBASE

            CLR     R0              ! Clear interchange flag before pass !
            CLRB    RH1             ! Get length in low half of R1 !
            LDB     RL1,%6000
            LDA     R2,%6001        ! Pointer to data !
PASS:       LDB     RL3,@R2         ! Get array element !
            INC     R2              ! Point to next !
            CPB     RL3,@R2         ! Is it less than next element? !
            JR      UGE,STEP        ! No, no interchange necessary !
            EXB     RL3,@R2         ! Yes, interchange !
            LDB     -1(R2),RL3
STEP:       DJNZ    R1,PASS
            DEC     R0              ! Was there an interchange? !
            JR      Z,PASS          ! Yes, go through it again !
            HALT

        end     pgm_15_2b
```

How about the last iteration? Suppose there are three elements:

```
(6000) = 03
(6001) = 02
(6002) = 04
(6003) = 06
```

Each time through the program increments R2, so at the start of the third iteration we have:

R2 = 6001 + 2 = 6003

The effects of the loop instructions are:

```
LDB     RL3,@R2        ! RL3 = (6003) !
INC     R2             ! R2 = 6004 !
CPB     RL3,@R2        ! (6003) - (6004) !
```

This is incorrect; the program has tried to move beyond the end of the data. The previous iteration should, in fact, have been the last one, since the number of pairs is one less than the number of elements. The correction is to reduce the number of iterations by one; this can be accomplished by placing DEC R1 after LDB RL1,%6000.

How about the trivial cases? What happens if the array contains no elements at all? The answer is that the program does not work correctly and may change all of memory improperly and without any warning (try it). What happens if the array contains only one element? The corrections to handle the trivial cases are simple but essential; the cost is only a few bytes of memory to avoid problems that could be very difficult to solve later.

The new version is shown in program 15-2c.

Program 15-2c:

```
        internal
            pgm_15_2c procedure
            entry
                $abs    IBASE

                CLR     R0              ! Clear interchange flag before pass !
                CLRB    RH1             ! Length in low half of R1 !
                LDB     RL1,%6000
                DEC     R1              ! One less pair than elements !
                JR      LE,DONE         ! Catch 0 or 1 element cases !
                LDA     R2,%6001        ! Pointer to data !
    PASS:       LDB     RL3,@R2         ! Array element !
                INC     R2              ! Point to next !
                CPB     RL3,@R2         ! Is it less than next element? !
                JR      UGE,STEP        ! No, no interchange necessary !
                EXB     RL3,@R2         ! Yes, interchange !
                LDB     -1(R2),RL3
    STEP:       DJNZ    R1,PASS
                DEC     R0              ! Was there an interchange? !
                JR      Z,PASS          ! Yes, go through it again !
    DONE:       HALT

            end     pgm_15_2c
```

Now it is time to check the program on the computer or on the simulator. Here is a simple set of data:

$$
\begin{aligned}
(6000) &= 02 \\
(6001) &= 00 \\
(6002) &= 01
\end{aligned}
$$

This set consists of two elements in the wrong order. The program should take two passes. The first pass should rearrange the elements, producing:

$$
\begin{aligned}
(6001) &= 01 \\
(6002) &= 00 \\
R0 &= 0001
\end{aligned}
$$

The second pass should find all elements in order and produce:

$$
R0 = 0000
$$

This program is rather long for single stepping; we will use breakpoints instead. Each breakpoint will halt the computer and print the contents of all the registers. Four breakpoints will be placed as follows:

1. After LDA R2,%6001 to check the initialization.

2. After CPB RL3, @R2 to check the comparison.

3. After LDB −1(R2),RL3 (i.e., just before the label STEP) to check the interchange.

4. After DEC R0 to check the completion of a pass through the array.

The contents of the registers after the first breakpoint were:

$$
\begin{aligned}
R0 &= 0000 \\
R1 &= 0001 \\
R2 &= 6001
\end{aligned}
$$

These are all correct, so the program is performing the initialization correctly in this case.

The results at the second breakpoint were:

R0	=	0000
R1	=	0001
R2	=	6002
R3	=	00
Carry	=	1

These results are also correct. The results at the third breakpoint were:

R0	=	0000
R1	=	0001
R2	=	6002
RL3	=	01

Checking memory showed:

(6001)	=	01
(6002)	=	00

The results at the fourth breakpoint were:

R0	=	FFFF
R1	=	0000
R2	=	6002
RL3	=	01

Here, R0 does not contain the correct value — it should have been set to one to indicate that an interchange had occurred. In fact, a look at the program shows that no instruction ever changes R0 to mark the interchange. The correction is to place the instruction LDK R0,#1 after JR GE,STEP.

At this point in the debugging process you would load R0 with the correct value and continue. The second iteration of the second breakpoint gives:

R0	=	0000
R1	=	0001
R2	=	6003
RL3	=	02
Carry	=	1

Clearly the program has proceeded incorrectly without reinitializing the registers (particularly R2). The conditional jump that depends on the interchange flag should transfer control all the way back to the start of the program, not to the label PASS.

The final version is shown in program 15-2d.

Program 15-2d:

```
internal
    pgm_15_2d procedure
    entry
        $abs     IBASE

SORT:   CLR      R0            ! Clear interchange flag before pass !
        CLRB     RH1           ! Length in low half of R1 !
        LDB      RL1,%6000
        DEC      R1            ! One less pair than elements !
        JR       LE,DONE       ! Catch 0 or 1 element cases !
        LDA      R2,%6001      ! Pointer to data !
PASS:   LDB      RL3,@R2       ! Array element !
        INC      R2            ! Point to next !
        CPB      RL3,@R2       ! Is it less than next element? !
        JR       UGE,STEP      ! No, no interchange necessary !
        LDK      R0,#1         ! Yes, set interchange flag !
        EXB      RL3,@R2       ! Interchange data !
        LDB      -1(R2),RL3
STEP:   DJNZ     R1,PASS
        DEC      R0            ! Was there an interchange? !
        JR       Z,SORT        ! Yes, go through it again !
DONE:   HALT

    end      pgm_15_2d
```

We cannot check all the possible input values for this program. Other simple sets of data for debugging purposes are:

1. Two equal elements

$$
\begin{array}{lcl}
(6000) & = & 02 \\
(6001) & = & 00 \\
(6002) & = & 00
\end{array}
$$

2. Two elements already in decreasing order

$$
\begin{array}{lcl}
(6000) & = & 02 \\
(6001) & = & 05 \\
(6002) & = & 00
\end{array}
$$

3. Data with the high (sign) bit set:

$$
\begin{array}{lcl}
(6000) & = & 03 \\
(6001) & = & 05 \\
(6002) & = & 83 \\
(6003) & = & 00
\end{array}
$$

TESTING

Program testing is closely related to program debugging. Some of the test cases should be the same as the test data used for debugging. These include:

· Trivial cases such as no data or a single element

· Special cases that for some reason cause the program to execute in special ways

· Simple examples that exercise particular parts of the program

In the case of the decimal to seven-segment conversion program (Example 15-1), these cases cover all the possible situations. The test data consists of:

· The numbers 0 through 9

· The boundary cases 10 and FF

· The random case 6B

The program does not distinguish any other cases. **Here debugging and testing are virtually the same.**

In the sort program (Example 15-2), the problem is more difficult. The number of elements could range from 0 to 255, and each of the elements could lie anywhere in that range. The number of possible cases is therefore enormous. Furthermore, the program is moderately complex. How do we select test data that will give us a degree of confidence in that program? **Here testing requires some design decisions.** The testing problem is particularly difficult if the program depends on sequences of real-time data. How do we select the data, generate it, and present it to the microcomputer in a realistic manner?

TESTING AIDS

Most of the tools mentioned earlier for debugging are helpful in testing also. Logic or microprocessor analyzers can help check the hardware; simulators can help check the software. Other tools can also be of assistance, e.g.,

- **I/O simulations** that can simulate a variety of devices from a single input and a single output device

- **In-circuit emulators** that allow you to attach the prototype to a development system or control panel and test it

- **ROM simulators** that have the flexibility of a RAM but the timing of the particular ROM or PROM that will be used in the final system

- **Real-time operating systems** that can provide inputs or interrupts at specific times (or perhaps randomly) and mask the occurrence of outputs. Real-time breakpoints and traces may also be included

- **Emulations** (often on microprogrammable computers) that may provide real-time execution speed and programmable I/O[4]

- **Interfaces** that allow another computer to control the I/O system and test the microcomputer program

- **Testing programs** that check each branch in a program for logical errors

- **Test generation programs** that can generate random data or other distributions.

Formal testing theorems exist, but they are usually applicable only to very short programs.

You must be careful that the test equipment does not invalidate the test by modifying the environment. Often, test equipment may buffer, latch, or condition input and output signals. The actual system may not do this, and may therefore behave quite differently.

Furthermore, extra software in the test environment may use some of the memory space or part of the interrupt system. It may also provide error recovery and other features that will not exist in the final system. A software test bed must be just as realistic as a hardware test bed, since software failure can be just as critical as hardware failure.

Emulations and simulations are, of course, never precise. They are usually adequate for checking logic, but can seldom help test the interface or the timing. On the other hand, real-time test equipment does not provide much of an overview of the program logic and may affect the interfacing and timing.

SELECTING TEST DATA

Very few real programs can be checked for all cases. The designer must choose a sample set that in some sense describes the entire range of possibilities. Testing should, of course, be part of the total development procedure. Top-down design and structured programming provide for testing as part of the design. This is called structured testing.[5] Each module within a structured program should be checked separately. **Testing, as well as design, should be modular, structured, and top-down.**

Special Cases

But that leaves the question of selecting test data for a module. The designer must first list all special cases that a program recognizes. These may include:

- Trivial cases

- Equality cases

- Special situations

- Boundary conditions

The test data should include all of these.

Classes of Data

You must next identify each class of data that statements within the program may distinguish. These may include:

- Positive or negative numbers

- Numbers above or below a particular threshold

- Data that does or does not include a particular sequence or character

- Data that is or is not present at a particular time

If the modules are short, the total number of classes should still be small even though each division is multiplicative; i.e., two two-way divisions result in four data classes. **You must now separate the classes according to whether the program produces a different result for each entry in the class (as in a table) or produces the same result for each entry (such as a warning that a parameter is above a threshold).** In the discrete case, one may include each element if the total number is small or a sample if the number is large. The sample should include all boundary cases and several cases selected randomly. Random number tables are available in books, and random number generators are part of most computer facilities. Remember that these sources may produce the same "random" numbers each time they are used, unless you exercise care to prevent this. **You must be careful of distinctions that may not be obvious. For example, an 8-bit unsigned number greater than 127 can be treated as negative; you must consider this when using the Jump instructions that depend on the Sign bit. You must also watch for instructions that do not affect flags and overflow in signed arithmetic.**

Example: Testing a Sort Program

The special cases that a sort program must deal with are obvious:

- No elements in the array
- One element, magnitude may be selected randomly

The other special case to be considered is one in which elements are equal.

There may be some problem here with signs and data length. Note that the array itself must contain fewer than 256 elements. We could check the effects of sign by picking half the regular test cases with numbers of elements between 128 and 255 and half between 0 and 127. All magnitudes should be chosen randomly, thus avoiding unconscious bias as much as possible.

Example: Testing an Arithmetic Program

Suppose we are testing a 64-bit addition program (see Chapter 8 for an example program). Here we will presume that a prior validity check has ensured that the number has the right length. Since the program makes no other distinctions, test data should be selected randomly. Here a random number table or random number generator will prove ideal; the range of the random numbers is 0 to 255 for each byte in each number.

TESTING PRECAUTIONS

The designer can simplify the testing stage by designing programs sensibly. You should use the following rules:

1. Try to eliminate trivial cases as early as possible without introducing unnecessary distinctions.

2. Minimize the number of special cases. Each special case means additional testing and debugging time.

3. Consider performing validity or error checks on the data prior to processing.

4. Be careful of inadvertent and unnecessary distinctions, particularly in handling signed numbers or using operations that refer to signed numbers.

5. Check boundary cases by hand. These are often a source of errors. Be sure that the problem definition specifies what is to happen in these cases.

6. Make the program as general as reasonably possible. Each distinction and separate routine increases the required testing.

7. Divide the program and design the modules so that the testing can proceed in steps in conjunction with the other stages of software development.[6]

CONCLUSIONS

Debugging and testing are the stepchildren of the software development process. Most projects leave far too little time for them and most textbooks neglect them. But designers and managers often find that these stages are the most expensive and time consuming. Progress may be very difficult to measure or produce. Debugging and testing microprocessor software is particularly difficult because the powerful hardware and software tools that can be used on larger computers are seldom available for microcomputers.

The designer should plan debugging and testing carefully. We recommend the following procedure:

1. Try to write programs that can easily be debugged and tested. Modular programming, structured programming, and top-down design are useful techniques.

2. Prepare a debugging and testing plan as part of the program design. Decide early what data you must generate and what equipment you will need.

3. Debug and test each module as part of the top-down design process.

4. Debug each module's logic systematically. Use checklists, breakpoints, and the single-step mode. If the program logic is complex, consider using the software simulator.

5. Check each module's timing systematically if this is a problem. An oscilloscope can solve many problems if you plan the test properly. If the timing is complex, consider using a logic or microprocessor analyzer.

6. Be sure that the test data is a representative sample. Watch for any classes of data that the program may distinguish. Include all special and trivial cases.

7. If the program handles each element differently or the number of cases is large, select the test data randomly.[7]

8. Record all test data and results as part of the documentation. If problems occur, you will not have to repeat test cases that have already been checked. When you make changes you will want to use the test data again.

REFERENCES

1. For more information about logic analyzers, see:

   N. Andreiv, "Special Report: Troubleshooting Instruments," *EDN*, October 5, 1978, pp. 89-99.

   R. L. Down, "Understanding Logic Analyzers," *Computer Design*, June 1977, pp. 188-91.

   R. Gasperini, "A Guide to Digital Troubleshooting Aids," *Instruments and Control Systems*, February 1978, pp. 39-42.

   R. Lorentzen, Troubleshooting Microprocessors with a Logic Analyzer System," *Computer Design*, March 1979, pp. 160-64.

   M. Marshall, "What to Look for in Logic Timing Analyzers," *Electronics*, March 29, 1979, pp. 109-14.

   K. Pines, "What Do Logic Analyzers Do?" *Digital Design*, September 1977, pp. 55-72.

   I. Spector, "Logic Analysis by Telephone," *EDN*, March 20, 1979, pp. 139-42.

2. W. J. Weller, *Assembly Level Programming for Small Computers*, Lexington Books, Lexington, MA, 1975, Chapter 23.

3. R. L. Baldridge, "Interrupts Add Power, Complexity to Microcomputer System Design," *EDN*, August 5, 1977, pp. 67-73.

4. H. R. Burris, "Time-Scaled Emulations of the 8080 Microprocessor," *Proceedings of the 1977 National Computer Conference*, pp. 937-46.

5. D. A. Walsh, "Structured Testing," *Datamation*, July 1977, pp. 111-18.

   P. F. Barbuto, Jr. and J. Geller, "Tools for Top-Down Testing," *Datamation*, October 1978, pp. 178-82.

6. R. A. DeMillo et al., "Hints on Test Data Selection: Help for the Practicing Programmer," *Computer*, April 1978, pp. 34-41.

   W. F. Dalton, "Design Microcomputer Software," *Electronics*, January 19, 1978, pp. 97-101.

7. T. G. Lewis, *Distribution Sampling for Computer Simulation*, Lexington Books, Lexington, MA, 1975.

   R. A. Mueller et al., "A Random Number Generator for Microprocessors," *Simulation*, April 1977, pp. 123-27.

   The following reference provides many useful techniques for software debugging and testing:

   Glenford J. Meyers, *The Art of Software Testing*, John Wiley and Sons, New York, 1979.

16

Documentation and Redesign

DOCUMENTATION

A working program is not the only requirement of software development. Adequate documentation is also an important part of any software product. Not only does documentation help the designer in the testing and debugging stages, it is also essential for laer use and extension of the program. A poorly documented program will be difficult to maintain, use, or extend.

Documentation must be prepared as the program is designed. It must be kept current as the design changes. Documentation which is put off is likely to be incomplete, incorrect, or never done at all.

SELF-DOCUMENTING PROGRAMS

Although no program is ever completely self-documenting, some of the rules that we mentioned earlier can help. These **include:**

- Use clear, simple structure with as few transfers of control (jumps) as possible

- Use meaningful names and labels

- Use names for I/O devices, parameters, numerical factors, etc.

- Emphasize simplicity rather than minor savings in memory usage, execution time, or typing

For example, the following program sends a string of characters to a teletypewriter:

```
internal
      pgm_16_1 procedure
      entry
              LDA       R2,%6001
              LDB       RH0,%6000
      X:      INB       RL0,%FF1F
              BITB      RL0,#2
              JR        Z,X
              LDB       RL0,@R2
              INC       R2
              OUTB      %FF1B,RL0
              DBJNZ     RH0,X
              RET

      end       pgm_16_1
```

Even without comments we can improve the program as follows:

```
constant
      TTY_CTL      := %FF1F
      TTY_READY    := 2
      TTY_DATA     := %FF1B
      BUF_SIZE     := 80

internal
      $abs      %6000
      MSG_LEN BYTE
      MSG_BUF ARRAY [BUF_SIZE BYTE]

internal
      TTYOUT    procedure
      entry

              LDA       R2,MSG_BUF
              LDB       RH0,MSG_LEN
      TTWAIT: INB       RL0,TTY_CTL
              BITB      RL0,#TTY_READY
              JR        Z,TTWAIT
              LDB       RL0,@R2
              INC       R2
              OUTB      TTY_DATA,RL0
              DBJNZ     RH0,TTWAIT
              RET

      end       TTYOUT
```

Surely this program is easier to understand than the earlier version. Even without further documentation, you could probably guess at the function of the program and the meanings of most of the variables. **Other documentation techniques cannot substitute for self-documentation.**

Choosing Useful Names

Some further notes on choosing names:

1. **Use the obvious name** when it is available, like TTY or CRT for output devices, START or RESET for addresses, DELAY or SORT for subroutines, COUNT or LENGTH for data.

2. **Avoid acronyms** like S16BA for SORT 16-BIT ARRAY. These seldom mean anything to anybody.

3. **Use full words** or close to full words when possible, like DONE, PRINT, SEND, etc. However, don't carry this too far. Avoid overlong names like END_OF_BASIC_SYMBOL_TABLE.

4. **Keep the names** as **distinct** as possible.

COMMENTS

The most obvious form of additional documentation is the comment. However, few programs (even those used as examples in books) have effective comments. You should consider the following guidelines for good comments.

1. **Don't repeat the meaning of the instruction code.** Rather, explain the purpose of the instruction in the program. Comments like

    ```
    DEC     R2              ! R2 = R2 - 1 !
    ```

    add nothing to documentation. Rather, use

    ```
    DEC     R2              ! Decrease line number !
    ```

    Remember that you know what the operation codes mean and anyone else can look them up in the manual. **The important point is to explain what task the program is performing.**
    Because this book is an introductory text for the Z8000 processor, the program examples in other chapters sometimes fail to follow the rule above.

2. **Make the comments as clear as possible.** Do not use abbreviations or acronyms unless they are well-known (like ASCII, SIO, or UART) or standard (like no for number, ms for millisecond, etc.). Avoid comments like

    ```
    DEC     R2              ! LN = LN - 1 !
    ```

    or

    ```
    DEC     R2              ! DEC LN BY 1 !
    ```

    The extra typing simply is not all that expensive.

3. **Comment every important or obscure point.** Be particularly careful to mark operations that may not have obvious functions, such as

    ```
    RES     R7,#9           ! Turn tape reader bit off !
    ```

    or

    ```
    LDA     R4,GRAY_TBL     ! Convert to Gray code using !
                            ! table                      !
    ```

Clearly, I/O operations often require extensive comments. If you're not exactly sure of what an instruction does, or if you have to think about it, add a clarifying comment. The comment will save you time later and will be helpful in documentation.

4. **Don't comment the obvious.** A comment on each line simply makes it difficult to find the important points. Standard sequences like

```
LDB      RL0,@R2
INC      R2
```

need not be marked unless you're doing something special. One comment will often suffice for several lines, as in

```
CLR      R0              ! Start 64 bit sum at 0 !
CLR      R1
CLR      R2
CLR      R3

LD       R0,SUM0         ! Add SUM1 to SUM0 with !
                         ! carry                 !
LD       R1,SUM1
ADC      R0,R1
LD       SUM0,R0
```

5. **Comments that continue over several lines should be clearly marked as continuations:**

```
ADD      R2,R2           ! Multiply by ten using ... !
LD       R3,R2           ! ... 2x ...                 !
SLA      R2,#2           ! ... plus 8x ...            !
ADD      R2,R3           ! ... equals 10x             !
```

6. **Place comments on the lines to which they refer, or at the start of a sequence.**

7. **Keep your comments up-to-date.** If you change the program, change the comments.

8. **Use standard forms and terms** in commenting. Don't worry about repetitiveness. Varied names for the same things are confusing, even if the variations are just COUNT and COUNTER, START and BEGIN, DISPLAY and LEDS, or PANEL and SWITCHES.

   Why be inconsistent? The variations may seem obvious to you now, but may not be clear later; others will get confused from the very beginning.

9. **Make comments brief if they are mingled with instructions.** Put complete explanations in header comments and other documentation. Otherwise, the program gets lost in the comments and you may have a hard time even finding it.

10. **Keep improving your comments.** If you come to one that you cannot read or understand, take the time to change it. If you find that the listing is getting crowded, add some blank lines. The comments won't improve by themselves; in fact, they will just become worse as you leave the task behind and forget exactly what you did.

11. **Before every major section, subsection, or subroutine, insert a number of comments describing the functions of the code that follows.** Care should be taken to describe all inputs, outputs, and side effects, as well as the algorithm employed.

12. **It is good practice when modifying working programs to use comments to indicate the date, author, and type of modification made.**

Remember, comments are important. Good ones will save you time and effort. Put some work into comments and try to make them as effective as possible.

COMMENTING EXAMPLES

1. Multiple-Precision Addition

The basic program is:

```
        internal
           pgm_16_2 procedure
           entry

                LD        R2,%6000
                TEST      R2
                JR        Z,DONE
                ADD       R2,R2
                LDA       R3,%6002
                ADD       R3,R2
                LDA       R4,%6402
                ADD       R4,R2
                RESFLG    C
     ADD_NXT:DEC         R3,#2
                DEC       R4,#2
                LD        R0,@R3
                LD        R1,@R4
                ADC       R0,R1
                LD        @R3,R0
                DEC       R2,#2
                JR        GT,ADD_NXT
     DONE:    RET

           end      pgm_16_2
```

First, comment the important points. These are typically initializations, data fetches, and processing operations. Don't bother with standard sequences like updating pointers and counters. Remember that names are clearer than numbers, so use them freely.

The new version of the program is:

```
!*
 * Multiple precision addition
 *
 * This program performs multi-word binary addition
 *
 * Inputs:  Location 6000: Length of numbers (in words)
 *          Locations 6002 to 6002 + (2 * Length): First number,
 *                most significant word in 6002
 *          Locations 6402 to 6402 + (2 * Length): Second number
 *
 * Outputs: Locations 6002 to 6002 + (2 * Length): Sum
 *!
internal
      $abs      %6000
      LENGTH    WORD
      DEST      ARRAY [10 WORD]
      $abs      %6402
      SOURCE    ARRAY [10 WORD]

internal
      LONG_SUM procedure
      entry

          LD        R2,LENGTH        ! Count = Length of numbers in words !
          TEST      R2
          JR        Z,DONE
          ADD       R2,R2            ! Point past least significant word... !
          LDA       R3,DEST
          ADD       R3,R2            ! ...of each string !
          LDA       R4,SOURCE
          ADD       R4,R2
          RESFLG    C
ADD_NXT:  DEC       R3,#2
          DEC       R4,#2
          LD        R0,@R3           ! Next word from destination string !
          LD        R1,@R4           ! Next word from source string !
          ADC       R0,R1
          LD        @R3,R0           ! Store result in destination !
          DEC       R2,#2
          JR        GT,ADD_NXT       ! Continue until all words are added !
DONE:     RET
      end       LONG_SUM
```

Second, look for any instructions that might not have obvious functions and mark them. In this program, use of the Carry flag may be confusing.

Third, ask yourself whether the comments tell you what you would need to know if you wanted to use the program, e.g.:

1. Where is the program entered? Are there alternative entry points?

2. What parameters are necessary? How and in what form must they be supplied?

3. What operations does the program perform?

4. From where does it get the data?

5. Where does it store the results?

6. What special cases does it consider?

7. What does the program do about errors?

8. How does it exit?

Some of the questions may not be relevant to a particular program and some of the answers may be obvious. Make sure that you won't have to sit down and dissect the program to figure out what the answers are. Remember also that too much explanation is just dead wood that you will have to clear out of the way. Is there anything that you would add to or subtract from this listing? If so, go ahead — you are the one who has to feel that the commenting is adequate and reasonable.

```
!*
 * Multiple precision addition
 *
 * This program performs multi-word binary addition
 *
 * Inputs:   Location 6000: Length of numbers (in words)
 *           Locations 6002 to 6002 + (2 * Length): First number,
 *                  most significant word in 6002
 *           Locations 6402 to 6402 + (2 * Length): Second number
 *
 * Outputs: Locations 6002 to 6002 + (2 * Length): Sum
 *
 * Sample call:
 *
 *       LD        %6000,#nwords
 *       (strings start at 6002 and 6402)
 *       CALL      LONG_SUM
 *       (result starts at 6002)
 *!
internal
    $abs      %6000
    LENGTH    WORD                     ! Length of numbers in words !
    DEST      ARRAY [10 WORD]          ! First number, starting with MSBs !
    $abs      %6402
    SOURCE    ARRAY [10 WORD]          ! Second number !

internal
    LONG_SUM procedure                 ! Entry point LONG_SUM !
    entry

              LD    R2,LENGTH          ! Count = Length of numbers in words !
              TEST  R2
              JR    Z,DONE
              ADD   R2,R2              ! Point past least significant word... !
              LDA   R3,DEST
              ADD   R3,R2              ! ...of each string !
              LDA   R4,SOURCE
              ADD   R4,R2
              RESFLG C                 ! Clear carry for first add !
ADD_NXT:DEC   R3,#2                    ! Note carry not changed by LD or DEC !
        DEC   R4,#2
        LD    R0,@R3                   ! Next word from destination string !
        LD    R1,@R4                   ! Next word from source string !
        ADC   R0,R1
        LD    @R3,R0                   ! Store result in destination !
        DEC   R2,#2
        JR    GT,ADD_NXT               ! Continue until all words are added !
DONE:   RET

        end   LONG_SUM
```

2. Teletypewriter Output

The basic program is:

```
RDYWAIT:INB     RH0,%FF1F
        BITB    RH0,#2
        JR      Z,RDYWAIT
        OUTB    %FF1B,RL0
        RET
```

Commenting the important points and adding names gives:

```
!*
 * Teletypewriter output subroutine
 *
 * This program prints the contents of Register RL0 to the
 *   teletypewriter.
 *
 * Inputs:  Character to be transmitted in RL0
 * Output:  None
 *
 * The contents of RH0 are lost
 *!
constant
        TTY_DATA    := %FF1B       ! SIO data port !
        TTY_CTL     := %FF1F       ! SIO control port !
        TTY_READY   := 2           ! Bit 2 in TTY_CTL is ready !

global
        TTY_OUT_CH procedure
        entry

RDYWAIT:INB     RH0,TTY_CTL        ! Get status byte !
        BITB    RH0,#TTY_READY     ! Is ready bit set? !
        JR      Z,RDYWAIT          ! No, loop until ready !
        OUTB    TTY_DATA,RL0       ! Ready, send character !
        RET

        end     TTY_OUT_CH
```

Note how easily we could change this program so that it transfers a whole string of data, starting at the address in register R1 and ending with an "03" character (ASCII ETX). Try making the changes before looking at the listing.

```
!*
  *  String output to teletypewriter
  *
  *  This program transmits a string of characters to a teletypewriter.
  *     Transmission ceases when an ASCII ETX (03 hex) is encountered.
  *
  *  Input:   R1 contains the address of the first character in the string
  *
  *  Outputs: R1 points past the ETX character
  *
  *  Sample call:
  *        LDA       R1,string
  *        CALL      TTY_OUT
  *!
constant
      ETX          := %03
      TTY_DATA     := %FF1B        ! SIO data port !
      TTY_CTL      := %FF1F        ! SIO control port !
      TTY_READY    := 2           ! Bit 2 in TTY_CTL is ready !

global
      TTY_OUT procedure
      entry

             PUSH   @R15,R0
NXTCH:       LDB    RL0,@R1
             INC    R1
             CPB    RL0,#ETX       ! End of string? !
             JR     EQ,DONE
NREADY:      INB    RH0,TTY_CTL    ! Get status of teletypewriter !
             BITB   RH0,#TTY_READY ! Is device ready? !
             JR     Z,NREADY       ! No, keep looping !
             OUTB   TTY_DATA,RL0   ! Send character !
             JR     NXTCH
DONE:        POP    R0,@R15
             RET

      end     TTY_OUT
```

Good comments can make it easy for you to change a program to meet new requirements. For example, try changing the last program so that it:

- Starts each message with ASCII STX (02_{16}) followed by a three-digit identification code stored in memory locations IDCODE through IDCODE+2

- Transmits 40 characters, starting with the one located at the address in Register R1.

- Ends each message with two consecutive ASCII ETXs (03_{16})

FLOWCHARTS AS DOCUMENTATION

We have already described the use of flowcharts as a design tool in Chapter 14. Flowcharts are also useful in documentation, particularly if:

- They are not so detailed as to be unreadable

- Their decision points are clearly explained and marked

- They include all branches at the relevant level of detail

- They correspond to the actual program listings

Flowcharts are helpful if they give you an overall picture of the program. They are not helpful if they are just as difficult to read as an ordinary listing.

STRUCTURED PROGRAMS AS DOCUMENTATION

A structured program can serve as documentation for an assembly language program if:

- You describe the purpose of each section in the comments

- You make it clear which statements are included in each conditional or loop structure by using indentation and ending markers

- You make the total structure as simple as possible

- You use a consistent, well-defined language

The structured program can help you to check the logic or improve it. Furthermore, since the structured program is machine-independent, it can also aid you in implementing the same task on another computer.

MEMORY MAPS

A memory map is simply a list of all the memory assignments in a program. The map allows you to determine the amount of memory needed, the locations of data or subroutines, and the parts of memory not allocated. The map is a handy reference for finding storage locations and entry points and for dividing memory between different routines or programmers. The map will also give you easy access to data and subroutines if you need them in later extensions or in maintenance. Sometimes a graphical map is more helpful than a listing.

A typical map would be:

	Address	Routine	Purpose
Program Memory	4600-47FE 4800-4840 4842-487A 487C-4A04 4A06-4C2A	INTERRUPT BREAKPOINT DELAY DISPLAY MAIN	Interrupt Service Routine for Keyboard Service Routine for Break Instruction Delay Program Display Control Program Main Program
Data Memory	6000 6002 6100-614F 6150-619F 61A0-61AF 7E00-7FFE	NKEYS KPTR KBFR DBFR TEMP STACK	Number of Keys Keyboard Buffer Pointer Keyboard Buffer Display Buffer Temporary Storage RAM Stack

Note that odd addresses are used only for byte values; word and long word values and instructions must have even addresses.

PARAMETER AND DEFINITION LISTS

Parameter and definition lists at the start of the program and at the start of each subroutine make it much easier to understand and change the program. The following rules can help:

1. **Separate memory locations, I/O units, parameters, definitions, and memory system constants.**

2. **Arrange lists alphabetically when possible,** with a description of each entry.

3. **Describe each parameter that might change and include it in the lists.** Such parameters may include timing constants, inputs or codes corresponding to particular keys or functions, control or masking patterns, starting or ending characters, thresholds, etc.

4. **List the memory system constants separately.** These constants will include Reset and interrupt service addresses, the starting address of the program, data areas, stack areas, etc.

5. **Give each port used by an I/O device a name,** even though devices may share ports in the current system. The separation will make expansion or reconfiguration much simpler.

A typical list of definitions will be:

```
!*
 * Memory system constants
 *!
constant
     INTERRUPT     := %4600          ! Interrupt entry point !
     RAMSTART      := %4460          ! Start of data storage area !
     RESET         := %4800          ! Reset address !
     STACK_BASE    := %8000          ! Top address in stack !
!*
 * I/O units
 *!
     RETI_CTC      := %FF29          ! Reset port address !
     TTY_CTL       := %FF1F          ! SIO control port !
     TTY_DATA      := %FF1B          ! SIO data port !
!*
 * I/O control
 *!
     ETX           := %03            ! End of transmission character !
     STX           := %02            ! Start transmission character !
     TTY_READY     := 2              ! Bit 2 in TTY_CTL is ready !
!*
 * Data storage
 *!
constant
     BUF_SIZE      := 80
     TMP_SIZE      := 14

internal
     $abs    %6000
     BUF_PTR     WORD                ! Buffer pointer !
     NKEYS       BYTE                ! Number of keys !
     TTY_BUF     ARRAY [BUF_SIZE BYTE]    ! Data buffer !
     TEMP        ARRAY [TMP_SIZE BYTE]    ! Temporary storage !
!*
 * Parameters
 *!
constant
     MS_COUNT      := %C7            ! Count for 1 MS delay !
     RETRIES       := 4             ! Retry count on error !
!*
 * Definitions
 *!
constant
     FALSE         := %0000          ! False value !
     PARITY_BIT    := 7              ! Bit 7 is parity bit !
     PARITY_MASK   := %7F            ! Mask to strip off parity bit !
     TRUE          := %FFFF          ! True return value !
```

LIBRARY ROUTINES

Standard documentation of subroutines will allow you to build up a library of useful programs. The idea is to make these programs easily accessible. A standard format will allow you or anyone else to see at a glance what the program does. The best procedure is to make up a standard form and use it consistently. Save these programs in a well-organized manner (for example, according to processor, language, and type of program), and you will soon have a useful set. But **remember that without organization and proper documentation, using the library may be more difficult than rewriting the program from scratch.** To debug a system you must understand all the effects that a subroutine might have.

Information that you will need in the standard form includes:

- Purpose of the program

- Processor used

- Language used

- Parameters required and how they are passed to the subroutine

- Results produced and how they are returned to the calling program

- Registers affected, if any

- Flags affected

- Number of bytes of memory used

- Number of clock cycles required. This number may be an average or a typical figure, or it may vary widely. A formula may be given. Actual execution time will, of course, depend on the processor clock rate and the memory cycle time.

- A typical example

- Error handling

- Special cases

- Documented program listing

If the program is complex, the standard library form should also include a general flowchart or a structured outline of the program. As we have mentioned before, a library program is most likely to be useful if it performs a single distinct function in a reasonably general manner.

With the Z8000, the way you use registers is very important. If subroutines use registers inconsistently, the library will not be very useful.

For example, we could decide that R0 through R3 can be used for input parameters. R0 is used to return the result, and R1 through R15 are guaranteed unchanged. Exceptions are allowed, but should be well-documented.

LIBRARY EXAMPLES

1. Sum of Data

Purpose: The subroutine SUM16 computes the sum of a list of unsigned 16-bit values.

Language: Non-segmented Z8000 PLZ/ASM assembler.

Initial Conditions: The address of the first word in the list is in R1; the length of the list (in words) is in R0.

Final Conditions: The sum is in R0; R1 points past the end of the list. No other registers registers are affected.

Requirements:

        Memory -   10 words
        Time   -   50 + 22n cycles, for length n

Typical Case: (all data in hexadecimal)

        Start: R1   = 6000
                  R0   = 0004
               (6000)   = 05A8
               (6002)   = 1AD8
               (6004)   = 51EF
               (6006)   = 4EF0
        End: R0   = C15F
                  R1   = 6008

Error Handling: The program ignores all carries. The carry bit reflects only the last operation.

Listing:

```
    !   *
        *  Sum of 16 bit data
        *
        *         Call:
        *                    LDA      R1,LIST
        *                    LD       R0,#LENGTH
        *                    CALL     SUM16
        *                    LD       SUM,R0
        *  !
        global
          SUM16 procedure
          entry
                             PUSH     @R15,R2        ! Save R2            !
                             LD       R2,R0          ! R2 will be counter !
                             CLR      R0             ! Sum                !
                             TEST     R2             ! Count = 0?         !
                             JR       Z,DONE
                 ADD16:      ADD      R0,@R1
                             INC      R1,#2
                             DJNZ     R2,ADD16
                 DONE:       POP      R2,@R15        ! Restore            !
                             RET

                 end         SUM16
```

2. Decimal to Seven-Segment Conversion

Purpose: The subroutine D2SEVEN converts a decimal number to a seven-segment display code.

Language: Non-segmented Z8000 PLZ/ASM assembler.

Initial Conditions: Data in Register RL0.

Final Conditions: Seven-segment code in RH0.

No other registers are changed, including data in RL0.

Requirements:

Memory - 14 words, including the 5-word seven-segment code table.
Time - 52 cycles.

Typical Case: (data in hexadecimal)

Start: RL0 = 05

End: RH0 = 6D

Error Handling: Program returns zero in RL0 if the data is not a decimal digit.

Listing:

```
! *
 * D2SEVEN converts one decimal digit to one byte of seven-segment display
 * code
 *
 *      Call:
 *                  LDB     RL0,decimal
 *                  CALL    D2SEVEN
 *                  TESTB   RH0
 *                  JR      Z,ERROR
 *                  LDB     code_7,RH0
 * !

global
    D2SEVEN procedure
    entry
                    CLRB    RH0                 ! Result and high byte of index !
                    CPB     RL0,#10             ! Valid decimal?                !
                    JR      UGE,DONE
                    EX      R0,R1               ! Save R1                       !
                    LDB     RH1,SSEG(R1)        ! Convert                       !
                    EX      R0,R1               ! Restore R1                    !
          DONE:     RET

              end D2SEVEN

  internal
      SSEG ARRAY 10 BYTE  := [%3F,%06,%5B,%4F,%66,
                              %6D,%7D,%07,%7F,%6F]
```

Note that R0 cannot be used as a base or index register on the Z8000, so we use R1. The EX (exchange) instruction is more convenient than PUSH, LD and POP R1.

3. Binary to ASCII Hexadecimal Conversion

Purpose: The subroutine B2HEX converts a 16-bit unigned value to four ASCII hex digits.

Language: Non-segmented Z8000 PLZ/ASM assembler.

Initial Conditions: Value in R0, beginning of string in R1.

Final Conditions: The 4-byte string replaces contents of locations addressed by R1; R1 points past end of string. R1 is the only register to change

Requirements:

        Memory -   19 words
        Time   -   335 cycles

Typical Case:

        R0   = 89AB
        R1   = 6000
        (6000) = 38 = '8'
        (6001) = 39 = '9'
        (6002) = 41 = 'A'
        (6003) = 42 = 'B'

Error Handling: No errors are possible.

Listing:

```
! *
* B2HEX converts a 16 bit unsigned value to 4
* ASCII hex characters
*
*       CALL:
*               LD      R0,value
*               LDA     R1,string
*               CALL    B2HEX
*               (Result in string  0  - string  3 )
* !

global
   B2HEX procedure
   entry
                PUSHL   @R15,RR2          ! Save R3 and R2           !
                LDK     R3,#4             ! 4 digits                 !
HEXLP:          LDB     RL2,RL0
                ANDB    RL2,#%0F          ! Low 4 bits in RL2        !
                CPB     RL2,#10           ! 0-9 or A-F?              !
                JR      ULT,ADDZ
                ADDB    RL2,#'A'-'9'-1    ! Gap between 9 and A       !
ADDZ:           ADDB    RL2,#'0'          ! Convert to ASCII          !
                LDB     @R1,RL2           ! Store next digit          !
                INC     R1
                RRC     R0,#2
                RRC     R0,#2             ! Next digit to low nibble !
                DJNZ    R3,HEXLP
                POPL    RR2,@R15
                RET

        end     B2HEX
```

TOTAL DOCUMENTATION

Complete documentation of microprocessor software will include all or most of the elements that we have mentioned. So, **the total documentation package may involve:**

- **General flowcharts**
- **A written description of the program**
- **A list of all parameters and definitions**
- **A memory map**
- **A documented listing of the program**
- **A description of the test plan and test results**

The documentation may also include:

- **Programmers' flowcharts**
- **Data flowcharts**
- **Structured programs**

The documentation procedures outlined above are the minimal acceptable set of documents for non-production software. Production software demands even greater documentation efforts. The following documents should also be produced:

- Program Logic Manual
- User's Guide
- Maintenance Manual

The program logic manual expands on the written explanation produced with the software. It should be written for a technically competent individual who may not possess the detailed knowledge assumed in the written explanation in the software. The program logic manual should explain the system's design goals, the algorithms used, and what tradeoffs were necessary.

It should then explain in great detail what data structures were employed and how they are manipulated. It should provide a step-by-step guide to the operations of the program. Finally, it should contain any special tables or graphs that help explain the program. Code conversion charts, state diagrams, translation matrices, and flowcharts should be included.

The user's guide is probably the most important and most overlooked piece of documentation. No matter how well a system is designed, it is useless if no one can take advantage of its features. The user's guide should introduce the system to all users, sophisticated and unsophisticated. It should then provide detailed explanations of system features and their use. Frequent examples will help to clarify the points in the text. Step-by-step directions should be provided (and tested!). Programmers with detailed knowledge of a system often take shortcuts that the general reader cannot follow. The writing of the user's guide should begin early in the program definition stage. It often makes sense to write a user's guide before doing anything else. The guide will, of course, need to be changed as the system design develops.

Further discussion of the writing of user's guides is beyond the scope of this book. However, remember that you can never spend too much effort in preparing a user's guide, since it will be the most frequently referenced system document.

The maintenance manual is designed for the programmer who has to modify the system. It should outline step-by-step procedures for those reconfigurations designed into the system. In addition, it should describe any provisions built into the program for future expansion.

Documentation should not be taken lightly or postponed until the end of the software development. Proper documentation, combined with proper programming practices, is not only an important part of the final product but can also make development simpler, faster, and more productive. The designer should make consistent and thorough documentation part of every stage of software development.

REDESIGN

Sometimes the designer may have to squeeze the last microsecond of speed or the last byte of extra memory out of a program. As larger single-chip memories have become available, the memory problem has become less serious. The time problem, of course, is serious only if the application is time-critical; in many applications the microprocessor spends most of its time waiting for external devices, and program speed is not a major factor.

Squeezing the last bit of performance out of a program is seldom as important as some writers would have you believe. In the first place, the practice is expensive for the following reasons:

1. It requires extra programmer time, which is often the single largest cost in software development.
2. It sacrifices structure and simplicity with a resulting increase in debugging and testing time.
3. The programs require extra documentation.
4. The resulting programs will be difficult to extend, maintain, or re-use.

In the second place, the lower per-unit cost and higher performance may not really be important. Will the lower cost and higher performance really sell more units? Or would you do better with more user-oriented features? **The only applications that would seem to justify the extra effort and time are very high-volume, low-cost and low-performance applications where the cost of an extra memory chip will far outweigh the cost of the extra software development.** For other applications, you will find that you are playing an expensive game for no reason.

However, if you must redesign a program to make it more efficient, the following hints will help. First, determine how much more performance or how much less memory usage is necessary. If the required improvement is 25% or less, you may be able to achieve it by reorganizing the program. If it is more than 25%, you may have made a basic design error; you will need to consider drastic changes in hardware or software. We will deal first with reorganization and later with drastic changes.

REORGANIZING TO USE LESS MEMORY

The following procedures will reduce memory usage for Z8000 assembly language programs:

1. **Replace repetitious in-line code with subroutines.** Be sure, however, that the Call, Return, Push, and Pop instructions do not offset most of the gain. Note that this replacement usually results in slower programs because of the time spent in transferring control back and forth.

2. **Load data into registers whenever possible.** Register pointers use less memory than direct and indexed addresses, unless the setup offsets the gain. For the same reason, when accessing word lists, try to use the Push and Pop instructions.

3. **Use the stack when possible.** The stack pointer is automatically updated after each use so that no explicit updating instructions are necessary.

4. **Eliminate Jump instructions.** Try to reorganize the program instead.

5. **Use leftover results from previous sections of the program.**

6. **Use INC or DEC to set or reset flag bits.**

7. **Use INC and DEC instead of ADD and SUB whenever possible.**

8. **Watch for special short forms of instructions,** such as LDK and LDB Rx, #data.

9. **Use relative jumps rather than jumps with direct addressing.**

10. **Use the CALR instead of CALL when possible.**

11. **Use algorithms rather than tables** to calculate arithmetic or logical expressions and to perform code conversions. Note that this replacement may result in slower programs.

12. **Reduce the size of mathematical tables by interpolating** between entries. Here again, we are saving memory at the cost of execution time.

13. **Inspect complex tables for redundant information.** Large tables are often the most rewarding place to start looking for wasted memory space.

14. **Two separate parts of the program might be able to share a data area,** such as an I/O buffer, especially when neither depends on the contents of the other.

15. **Use of the several auto-increment and auto-decrement instructions can save updating instructions** (CPI, LDDR, etc.).

Saving Execution Time

Although some methods of saving memory also save time, you can generally save an appreciable amount of time only by concentrating on frequently executed loops. Completely eliminating an instruction that is executed only once can save at most a few microseconds. But a savings in a loop that is executed frequently will be multiplied many times over.

So, if you must reduce execution time, proceed as follows:

1. **Determine how frequently each program loop is executed.** You can do this by hand, by using the software simulator, or by temporarily adding extra instructions to count iterations.

2. **Examine the loops in the order of execution frequency,** starting with the most frequently used loop. Continue through the list until you achieve the required reduction.

3. **First, see if there are any operations that can be moved outside the loop,** i.e., repetitive calculations, data that can be stored in a register or on the stack, special cases or errors that can be handled elsewhere, etc. Note that this will require extra initialization and memory, but will save time.

4. **Try to eliminate Jump statements.** These are very time-consuming.

5. **Use the stack for temporary data storage.**

6. **Use any of the hints mentioned in saving memory if they also decrease execution time.** However, the shorter Z8000 instructions often execute more slowly than their explicit counterparts. DJNZ, CLR and the shift instructions are particularly slow.

7. **Do not even look at instructions that are executed only once.** Any changes that you make in such instructions only invite errors for no appreciable gain.

8. **Avoid indexed and indirect addressing whenever possible** because they take extra time.

9. **Use tables rather than algorithms;** make the tables handle as much of the tasks as possible, even if many entries must be repeated.

10. **Use the special repeating instructions whenever possible** (LDIR, CPSIR, etc.).

MAJOR REORGANIZATION

If you need more than a 25% increase in speed or decrease in memory usage, do not try reorganizing the code. Your chances of getting that much of an improvement are small unless you call in an outside expert. You are generally better off making a major change.

Better Algorithms

The most obvious change is a better algorithm. Particularly if you are doing sorts, searches, or mathematical calculations, you may be able to find a faster or shorter method in the literature. Libraries of algorithms are available in some journals and from professional groups. See, for example, the references at the end of this chapter.

More hardware can replace some of the software. Counters, shift registers, arithmetic units, hardware multipliers, and other fast add-ons can save both time and memory. Calculators, UARTs, keyboards, encoders, and other slower add-ons may save memory even though they operate slowly. Compatible parallel and serial interfaces, and other devices specially designed for use with the Z8000, may save time by taking some of the burden off the CPU.

Other Major Changes

Other changes that may help include:

1. **A CPU with a longer word will be faster** if you are handling multi-word data. Such a CPU may use less total memory. 16-bit processors, for example, use memory more efficiently than 8-bit processors, since more of their instructions are one word long.

2. **Versions of the CPU may exist that operate at higher clock rates.** But remember that you will need faster memory and I/O ports, and you will have to adjust any delay loops.

3. **Two CPUs may be able to do the job in parallel or separately** if you can divide the job and solve the communications problem.

4. **A specially microprogrammed processor may be able to execute the same program much faster.** The cost, however, will be much higher even if you use an off-the-shelf emulation.

5. **You can make tradeoffs between time and memory.** Lookup tables and function ROMs will be faster than algorithms, but will occupy more memory.

This kind of problem, in which a large improvement is necessary, usually results from lack of adequate planning in the definition and design stages. In the problem definition stage you should determine which processor and methods will be adequate to handle the problem. If you misjudge, the cost later will be high. A cheap solution may result in an unwarranted expenditure of expensive development time. Do not try to just get by; the best solution is usually to do the proper design and chalk a failure up to experience. **If you have followed such methods as flowcharting, modular programming, structured programming, top-down design, and proper documentation, you will be able to salvage a lot of your effort even if you have to make a major change.**

REFERENCES

1. "Collected Algorithms from ACM." ACM, Inc., P. O. Box 12105, Church Street Station, New York 10249.

2. T. C. Chen, "Automatic Computation of Exponentials, Logarithms, Ratios, and Square Roots," *IBM Journal of Research and Development*, Volume 18, pp. 380-88, July 1972.

3. H. Schmid, *Decimal Computation*, Wiley-Interscience, New York, 1974.

4. D. E. Knuth, *The Art of Computer Programming, Volume 1: Fundamental Algorithms*, Second Edition, Addison-Wesley, Reading, Mass., 1973.

5. D. E. Knuth, *The Art of Computer Programming, Volume 2: Seminumerical Algorithms*, Addison-Wesley, Reading, Mass., 1969.

6. D. E. Knuth, *The Art of Computer Programming, Volume 3: Sorting and Searching*, Addison-Wesley, Reading, Mass., 1973.

7. B. Carnahan et al., *Applied Numerical Methods*, Wiley, New York, 1969.

8. A. M. Despain, "Fourier Transform Computers Using CORDIC Iterations," *IEEE Transactions on Computers*, October 1974, pp. 993-1001.

9. Y. L. Luke, *Algorithms for the Computation of Mathematical Functions*, Academic Press, New York, 1977.

10. K. Hwang, *Computer Arithmetic*, Wiley, New York, 1978.

11. New methods for performing arithmetic operations on computers are often discussed in the triennial Symposium on Computer Arithmetic. The Proceedings (starting with 1969) are available from the IEEE Computer Society, 5855 Naples Plaza, Long Beach, CA 90803.

12. A. D. Edgar and S. C. Lee, "FOCUS Microcomputer Number System," *Communications of the ACM*, March 1979, pp. 166-177.

17

Sample Projects

PROJECT 1: A DIGITAL STOPWATCH

Purpose. This project creates a digital stopwatch. The operator enters two digits (minutes and tenths of minutes) with a calculator-like keyboard and then presses the GO key. The system counts down the remaining time on two seven-segment LED displays (see Chapter 11 for a description of unencoded keyboards and LED displays).

Hardware. The project uses one input port and one output port (one Z80 PIO Parallel Input/Output Device), two seven-segment displays, a 12-key keyboard, a 7404 inverter, and either a 7400 NAND gate or a 7408 AND gate, depending on the polarity of the seven-segment displays. The displays may require drivers, inverters, and resistors, depending on their polarity and configuration.

The hardware is organized as shown in Figure 17-1. Output lines 0, 1, and 2 are used to scan the keyboard. Input lines 0, 1, 2, and 3 are used to determine whether any keys have been pressed. Output lines 0, 1, 2, and 3 are used to send BCD digits to the seven-segment decoder/drivers. Output line 4 is used to activate the LED displays (if line 4 is '1', the displays are lit). Line 4 will be '0' when lines 0, 1, and 2 are being used to scan the keyboard. Output line 5 is used to select the left or right display; output line 5 is '1' if the left display is being used, '0' if the right display is being used. Thus, the common line on the left display should be active if line 4 is '1' and line 5 is '1', while the common line on the right display should be active if line 4 is '1' and line 5 is '0'. Output line 6 controls the right-hand decimal point on the left display.

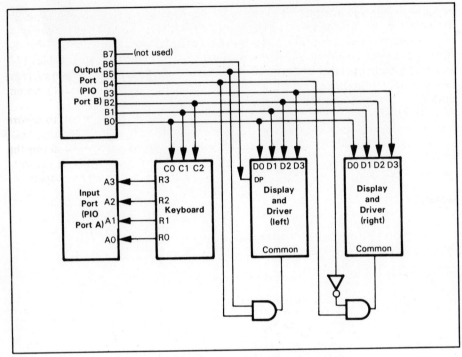

Figure 17-1. Digital Stopwatch I/O Configuration

Table 17-1. Input Connections for Stopwatch Keyboard

Output Bit	Keys Connected
0	'0', '2', '3', '4'
1	'1', '8', '9', 'GO'
2	'5', '6', '7'. '.'

Table 17-2. Output Connections for Stopwatch Keyboard

Input Bit	Keys Connected
0	'3', '5', '8'
1	'2', '6', '9'
2	'0', '1', '7'
3	'4', '.', 'GO'

Keyboard Connections. The keyboard is a simple calculator keyboard, generally available for 50¢. It consists of 12 unencoded key-switches arranged in four rows of three columns each. Since the wiring of the keyboard does not coincide with the observed rows and columns, the program uses a table to identify the keys. Tables 17-1 and 17-2 contain the input and output connections for the keyboard. The decimal point key is present for operator convenience and for future expansion; the current program does not actually use the key.

In an actual application, the keyboard would require pullup resistors to ensure that the inputs are actually read as logic '1's when the keys were not being pressed. Also, current-limiting resistors or diodes are needed on the output port to avoid damaging the drivers if two outputs drive against each other. This could occur if two keys in the same row were pressed at the same time, thus connecting two different column outputs.

General Program Flowchart:

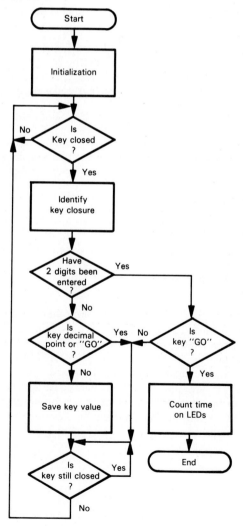

Display Connections. The displays are seven-segment displays with their own integral decoders. A typical example would be the Texas Instruments TIL309 device, which has an internal TTL MSI chip with latch, decoder, and driver. Clearly, standard seven-segment displays would be cheaper but would require some additional software (the seven-segment conversion routine shown in Chapter 7). Data is entered into the display as a single binary coded decimal digit; the digits are represented as shown in Table 11-4. The decimal point is a single LED that is turned on when the decimal point input is a logic '1'. You can find more information about displays in References 11 and 12 at the end of this chapter.

Program Description

The program is modular and uses several subroutines. The program stresses clarity and generality rather than efficiency; it does not utilize the full capabilities of the Z8000 processor. Each section of the listing will now be described in detail.

1. Introductory Comments

The introductory comments fully describe the program; these comments are a reference so that other programmers can easily apply, extend, and understand the program. Standard formats, indentations and spacings make the program easier to read.

2. Definitions

All definitions are placed at the start of the program so that they can be checked and changed easily. Each symbol is placed in a list alphabetically with other variables of the same type; comments describe the meaning of each symbol. The categories are:

    a.   Memory system constants that may vary from system to system depending on the memory space allocated to different programs or types of memories

    b.   Temporary storage used for variables

    c.   I/O (PIO) port addresses

    d.   Parameter and constant definitions

Memory system constants are placed in the definitions so that the user may relocate the program, temporary storage, and memory stack without making any other changes. The memory constants can be changed to accommodate other programs, or to coincide with a particular system's allocation of ROM and RAM addresses.

Temporary storage is allocated by means of ARRAY declarations. A $ABS pseudo-operation places the temporary storage locations in a particular part of memory. When temporary storage locations must be initialized, it is done by instructions in the program, rather than by assembler directives. Thus the program could eventually be placed in ROM or PROM and the system could be operated from power-on reset without reloading.

Each port address occupied by a PIO is named so that the addresses can easily be changed to handle varied configurations. Names also distinguish control registers from data registers.

Definitions clarify the meaning of certain constants and allow parameters to be changed easily. Each definition is given in the form which describes the content most clearly (binary, hex, octal, ASCII, or decimal). Parameters (such as debounce time) are placed here so that they can be varied with system needs.

3. Initialization

Memory locations 0002 and 0004 are the reset locations for the Z8002 microprocessor; they contain initial values for the Flag and Control Word, and for the program counter. The new program counter value is the starting address for the initialization program. Thus the initialization program is executed whenever the Z8002 microprocessor is reset.

Initialization consists of these four steps:

a. Initialize the stack pointer

b. Configure the PIO control registers

c. Initialize the counter which records the number of digit keys depressed; writing 0 into the counter initializes it

d. Select the beginning of the digit key storage space as the location into which the code for the next depressed key will be written. Address variable KEYAD holds this address.

4. Look for Key Closure

Flowchart:

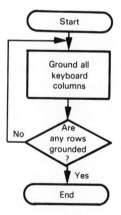

A key closure is identified by grounding all the keyboard columns, and then checking whether any rows are grounded. The program does not assume that unused input bits are high; all bits not attached to the keyboard are masked out using a logical AND instruction.

5. Debounce Key

Key closures are debounced in software. This is done by generating a 2 ms delay after a key closure has been detected. 2 ms is usually long enough for a clean contact to be made. The delay is created using subroutine DELAY. This subroutine creates a standard 1 ms delay by loading an initial constant into Register R1, then decrementing R1 register contents. The initial constant MSCNT is specified as a parameter, since this value will depend on the microprocessor clock speed. Thus if the clock speed varies, you simply redefine MSCNT. Subroutine DELAY requires the length of the delay to be passed as a parameter via RL0. The parameter specifies the length of the delay as a number of ms.

6. Identify Key Closure

The particular key closed is identified by grounding one column at a time and looking for a closure. Once a closure is found, the key column is known. The key row can be determined by shifting the input.

Table KTAB holds key codes in memory. Codes are ordered by rows within columns. That is to say, codes for keys in the first column appear first, followed by codes for keys in the second column, etc. Within each column the code for the key in the first row appears first, followed by the code for the key in the second row, etc. The index to Table KTAB is incremented by NROWS to advance from one column to the next. NROWS equals the number of keys in each row. The index to KTAB is incremented by 1 to select the next row within a column.

If a key closure cannot be identified the error code constant, ECODE, is returned.

Flowchart:

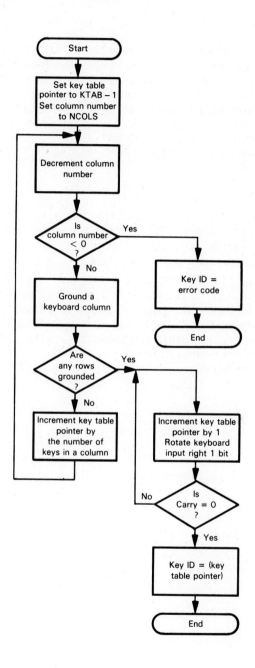

7. Key Identification

When the program identifies a valid digit key, the key code is saved in key array; the key array index and the key counter are both incremented. The program must then wait for the key closure to end before attempting to read another key, otherwise it may reread the same key.

After the program has received the expected number of keystrokes, it looks only for the "Go" key, ignoring all other keys.

The key identification program, as written, is rather simple. It ignores two keys that are pressed at approximately the same time; the program will only identify the first depressed key that it finds.

8. Set Up Display Output

Bits 4, 5, and 6 encode control signals for the display. Bit 4 must be set to 1 to indicate that the digit is to be displayed. Bit 5 determines whether the digit will be output to the most significant digit display or the least significant digit display. Bit 6 is set to 1 in order to turn on the decimal point display.

9. Pulse the LED Displays

Each display is turned on for 2 ms. This process is repeated 1500 times in order to generate a 6-second total display time. Pulses are frequent enough to make the display appear continuously lit to the human eye.

10. Decrement Display Count

Flowchart:

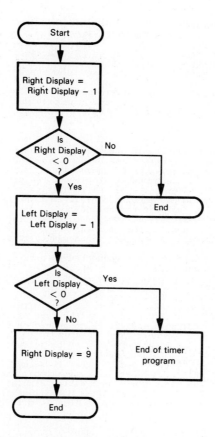

The value of the least significant digit is reduced by one. If the digit becomes negative, a borrow must then be obtained from the most significant digit. If the borrow from the most significant digit causes that digit to decrement past zero, the countdown is finished. Otherwise, the program sets the value of the least significant digit to 9 and continues.

Comments describe sections of the program and individual statements. Comments explain what the program is doing, not what specific instruction codes do. Spacing and identation have been used to improve readability.

Program TIMER:

```
TIMER    module

!*
 *  Program name:     TIMER
 *  Date:             10/24/78, 04/03/80
 *  Programmers:      Lance A. Leventhal, Adam Osborne, Chuck Collins
 *  Program Memory:   0112 bytes (274 decimal)
 *  Data Memory:      0003 bytes
 *  I/O Devices:      1 Input Port, 1 Output Port (1 Z80 PIO)
 *
 *  This program is a software timer which accepts inputs from a
 *    calculator-like keyboard, then provides a stopwatch countdown
 *    on two 7-segment LED displays, in minutes and tenth minutes.
 *
 *  KEYBOARD
 *
 *  A 12-key keyboard is assumed
 *  3 column connections are outputs from the processor so that a
 *    column of keys can be grounded
 *  Four row connections are inputs to the processor so that
 *    completed circuits can be identified
 *  The keyboard is debounced by waiting for two milliseconds after
 *    a key closure is recognized
 *  A new key closure is identified by waiting for the old one to
 *    end since no strobe is used
 *  The keyboard columns are connected to bits 0, 1 and 2 of the
 *    PIO B port
 *  The keyboard rows are connected to bits 0, 1, 2 and 3 of the
 *    PIO A port
 *
 *  DISPLAYS
 *
 *  Two 7-segment LED displays are used with separate decoders
 *    (7447 or 7448 depending on the type of display)
 *  The decoder data inputs are connected to bits 0, 1, 2 and 3
 *    of the PIO B port
 *  Bit 4 of the PIO B port is used to activate the LED displays
 *    (Bit 4 is 1 to send data to LEDs)
 *  Bit 5 of the PIO B port is used to select which LED is being
 *    used (Bit 5 is 1 if the leading (most significant) display
 *    is being used, 0 if the trailing display)
 *  Bit 6 of the PIO B port is used to light the decimal point
 *    LED on the leading display (Bit 6 is 1 if it is to be lit)
 *
 *  METHOD
 *
 *  Step 1 - Initialization
 *    The stack pointer is initialized. The number of digit keys
 *    pressed is set to 0, and the address into which the next
 *    digit key identification will be placed is initialized to
 *    the first address in the digit key array.
 *  Step 2 - Look for key closure
 *    All keyboard columns are grounded and the keyboard rows are
 *    examined until a closed circuit is found
 *  Step 3 - Debounce key closure
 *    A wait of 2 ms is introduced to eliminate key bounce
 *  Step 4 - Identify key closure
 *    The key closure is identified by grounding single keyboard
 *    columns and determining the row and column of the key
 *    closure. A table is used to encode the keys according to
 *    row and column number. In the key table, the digits are
 *    identified by their values. The decimal point key is 10
 *    and the "GO" key is 11. After two digits have been entered,
 *    the program waits for the "GO" key and then jumps to Step
 *    6.
 *  Step 5 - Save key closure
 *    Digit key closures are saved in the digit key array until
 *    two digits have been identified. Decimal points, further
 *    digits and closures of the "GO" key before two digits have
 *    been identified are ignored
 *  Step 6 - Count down timer interval on LEDs
```

```
     *    A countdown is performed on the LEDs with the leading digit
     *    representing the remaining number of minutes and the
     *    trailing digit representing the remaining number of tenths
     *    of minutes
     *!


  !*
   * Memory system constants
   *!
  constant
          PMEM    := %4600           ! Program starting address !
          LASTM   := %8000           ! Starting stack address !
          TEMP    := %4000           ! Start of data storage !


  !*
   * I/O units and PIO addresses
   *!
  constant
          PIOADATA := %00E1          ! Port A data: KB (keyboard) input !
          PIOACTRL := PIOADATA + 4   ! Port A control !
          PIOBDATA := PIOADATA + 2   ! Port B data: KB & display output !
          PIOBCTRL := PIOBDATA + 4   ! Port B control !
  !*
   * Bit position assignments in PIO port B
   *!
          DECPT   := %(2)01000000    ! Display decimal point (bit 6) !
          LEDON   := %(2)00010000    ! Send output to LED (bit 4) !
          LEDSL   := %(2)00100000    ! Select leading digit (bit 5) !


  !*
   * Definitions
   *!
  constant
          DECKEY  := 10              ! Decimal point key code !
          ECODE   := %FF             ! Key not found error code !
          GOKEY   := 11              ! "GO" key code !
          MSCNT   := 399             ! Count to give 1 msec delay !
          MAXKEYS := 2               ! Maximum number of key closures !
          NCOLS   := 3               ! Number of columns in KB !
          NROWS   := 4               ! Number of rows in KB !
          OPEN    := %0F             ! Input from KB when no key closed !
          TPULSE  := 2               ! Number of msec per digit display !
          TWAIT   := 2               ! Number of msec to debounce keys !


  !*
   * Reset location points to program entry point
   *!
  internal
          $abs    2
0002 0000  FCWRD   word := 0          ! Initial FCW value !
0004 4600  PCINIT  word := BEGIN      ! Program entry point !


  !*
   * Data temporary storage
   *!
  internal
          $abs    TEMP
4000      KEYNO   array [2 byte]     ! Digit key array holds 2 key values !
4002      NKEYS   byte               ! No. of digit key codes received !


  !*
   * Program entry point
   *!
  internal
      MAIN procedure
      entry
          $abs    PMEM


  !*
   * Start with initializations
   *!
```

```
4600 760F   BEGIN:   LDA    R15,LASTM          ! Set up stack pointer !
4602 8000
4604 2100            LD     R0,#%4F0F
4606 4F0F
4608 3A06            OUTB   PIOACTRL,RH0       ! Configure PIO port A input !
460A 00E5
460C 3A86            OUTB   PIOBCTRL,RL0       ! Port B output !
460E 00E7
4610 4D08            CLR    NKEYS              ! Initially 0 keys depressed !
4612 4002

            !*
            * Scan KB for closures
            *!
4614 5F00   START:   CALL   SCANC              ! Wait for key closures !
4616 4686
4618 C802            LDB    RL0,#TWAIT         ! Debounce time in msecs !
461A 5F00            CALL   DELAY              ! Delay for debounce !
461C 46BA

            !*
            * Identify the depressed key and act on it
            *!
461E 5F00            CALL   IDKEY              ! Get key ID in RL0 !
4620 46CA
4622 0A08            CPB    RL0,#ECODE         ! Key or error? !
4624 FFFF
4626 E6F6            JR     EQ,START           ! Error, wait for another closure !
4628 6101            LD     R1,NKEYS           ! Get number of keys in R1 !
462A 4002
462C 0B01            CP     R1,#MAXKEYS        ! Already received all keys? !
462E 0002
4630 E60A            JR     EQ,KEYF            ! Yes, wait for GO key !
4632 0A08            CPB    RL0,#10            ! A valid digit? !
4634 0A0A
4636 E104            JR     LT,WAITK           ! No, ignore it !
4638 6E18            LDB    KEYNO(R1),RL0      ! Store in next slot !
463A 4000
463C 6900            INC    NKEYS
463E 4002
            !*
            * Wait for current key closure to end
            *!
4640 5F00   WAITK:   CALL   SCANO              ! Wait for key to be released !
4642 46A0
4644 E8E7            JR     START

            !*
            * Look for GO key if enough digits found
            *!
4646 0A08   KEYF:    CPB    RL0,#GOKEY         ! Is it the GO key? !
4648 0B0B
464A EEFA            JR     NE,WAITK           ! No, ignore it !

            !*
            * Put digits into registers for display
            *!
464C 6003            LDB    RH3,KEYNO          ! Count digits down in R3 !
464E 4000
4650 600B            LDB    RL3,KEYNO+1
4652 4001
4654 A031   HILED:   LDB    RH1,RH3            ! Get high order digit !
4656 0401            ORB    RH1,#DECPT+LEDSL+LEDON  ! Set control bits ...!
4658 7070                                      ! ...to turn on decimal point, ...!
                                               ! ...select high digit... !
                                               ! ...and light display !
465A A0B9   LOWLED:  LDB    RL1,RL3            ! Get low order digit !
465C 0409            ORB    RL1,#LEDON         ! Set "light" control bit !
465E 1010

            !*
            * Pulse the LED display
            *!
```

```
4660 2102            LD      R2,#1500         ! Set counter for 6 seconds !
4662 05DC
4664 3A16   LEDISP:  OUTB    PIOBDATA,RH1     ! Output high order digit !
4666 00E3
4668 C802            LDB     RL0,#TPULSE      ! Inter-digit delay count !
466A 5F00            CALL    DELAY
466C 46BA
466E 3A96            OUTB    PIOBDATA,RL1     ! Output low order digit !
4670 00E3
4672 C802            LDB     RL0,#TPULSE      ! Inter-digit delay count !
4674 5F00            CALL    DELAY
4676 46BA
4678 F28B            DJNZ    R2,LEDISP        ! Repeat for 6 secs (1/10 min) !

            !*
            * Decrement count on LED display
            *!
467A AAB0            DECB    RL3              ! Decrement tenths digit !
467C EDEE            JR      PL,LOWLED        ! If > 0, continue !
467E AA30            DECB    RH3              ! Decrement seconds digit !
4680 E5BF            JR      MI,BEGIN         ! If < 0, wait for next input !
4682 CB09            LDB     RL3,#9
4684 E8E7            JR      HILED            ! Display again !

4686        end     MAIN
            !*
            * Subroutine SCANC scans the KB waiting for a closure.
            * All keyboard inputs are grounded.
            *!
            internal
4686            SCANC procedure
                entry

4686 93F0            PUSH    @R15,R0
4688 8C88   WSCANC:  CLRB    RL0
468A 3A86            OUTB    PIOBDATA,RL0     ! Ground all KB columns !
468C 00E3
468E 3A04            INB     RH0,PIOADATA     ! Read rows !
4690 00E1
4692 0600            ANDB    RH0,#OPEN        ! Ignore unused inputs !
4694 0F0F
4696 0A00            CPB     RH0,#OPEN        ! Any keys closed? !
4698 0F0F
469A E6F6            JR      EQ,WSCANC        ! No, wait until a closure !
469C 97F0            POP     R0,@R15
469E 9E08            RET

46A0        end     SCANC


            !*
            * Subroutine SCANO scans the KB waiting for closure to end
            * so next closure can be found
            *!
            internal
46A0            SCANO procedure
                entry

46A0 93F0            PUSH    @R15,R0
46A2 8C88   WSCANO:  CLRB    RL0
46A4 3A86            OUTB    PIOBDATA,RL0     ! Ground all KB columns !
46A6 00E3
46A8 3A84            INB     RL0,PIOADATA     ! Read KB rows !
46AA 00E1
46AC 0608            ANDB    RL0,#OPEN        ! Ignore unused inputs !
46AE 0F0F
46B0 0A08            CPB     RL0,#OPEN        ! Any keys still closed? !
46B2 0F0F
46B4 EEF6            JR      NE,WSCANO        ! Yes, continue scanning !
46B6 97F0            POP     R0,@R15
46B8 9E08            RET

46BA        end     SCANO
```

```
            !*
            * Subroutine DELAY creates an "n" millisecond delay. "n"
            * is the value in register RL0 when DELAY is called
            *!
            internal
46BA            DELAY procedure
                entry

46BA 93F1           PUSH    @R15,R1         ! R1 is used as a counter !
46BC 2101   DELOOP: LD      R1,#MSCNT       ! MSCNT is clock speed dependent !
46BE 018F
46C0 AB10   MSEC:   DEC     R1              ! Loop for 1 msec !
46C2 EEFE           JR      NZ,MSEC
46C4 F805           DBJNZ   RL0,DELOOP      ! RL0 specifies number of msecs !
46C6 97F1           POP     R1,@R15
46C8 9E08           RET

46CA            end     DELAY


            !*
            * Subroutine IDKEY determines the row and column number of the
            * key closure and identifies the key by using a table. Digit
            * value is returned in RL0.
            *!
            internal
46CA            IDKEY procedure
                entry

46CA 91F2           PUSHL   @R15,RR2        ! Routine needs R2 & R3 !
46CC 2102           LD      R2,#NCOLS       ! Number of columns to scan !
46CE 0003
46D0 7603           LDA     R3,KTAB-1       ! Set translate table pointer !
46D2 4705
            !*
            * Scan columns looking for closure
            *!
46D4 AB20   FCOL:   DEC     R2              ! Next column number !
46D6 E515           JR      MI,IDERR        ! No closure found, error !
46D8 C8FF           LDB     RL0,#%FF        ! Get grounding pattern !
46DA 2202           RESB    RL0,R2          ! Put 0 in one column's bit !
46DC 0800
46DE 3A86           OUTB    PIOBDATA,RL0    ! Ground 1 column !
46E0 00E3
46E2 3A84           INB     RL0,PIOADATA    ! Read the row outputs !
46E4 00E1
46E6 0608           ANDB    RL0,#OPEN       ! Ignore unused inputs !
46E8 0F0F
46EA 0A08           CPB     RL0,#OPEN       ! Any keys in the column closed? !
46EC 0F0F
46EE EE03           JR      NE,FROW         ! Yes, determine closed row !
46F0 0103           ADD     R3,#NROWS       ! No, try next column !
46F2 0004
46F4 E8EF           JR      FCOL
            !*
            * Detect closed row
            *!
46F6 A930   FROW:   INC     R3              ! Identify next row !
46F8 B28C           RRCB    RL0             ! Next row grounded? !
46FA E7FD           JR      C,FROW          ! No, keep looking !
            !*
            * Return key in RL0
            *!
46FC 2038           LDB     RL0,@R3
46FE 95F2   IDRET:  POPL    RR2,@R15
4700 9E08           RET

            !*
            * If error, return error code
            *!
4702 C8FF   IDERR:  LDB     RL0,#ECODE
4704 E8FC           JR      IDRET

4706            end     IDKEY
```

```
           !*
            * Keyboard translate table
            *
            * Keyboard codes are arranged with column as the primary
            * index and row as the secondary index. The columns are
            * arranged in reverse order since we ground column 2 first
            *!
           internal
              KTAB array [* byte] := [
4706 05 06          5  6  7  DECKEY         ! Col 2 rows 0 1 2 3 !
4708 07 0A
470A 08 09          8  9  1  GOKEY          ! Col 1 !
470C 01 0B
470E 03 02          3  2  0  4              ! Col 0 !
4710 00 04
                   ]

           end    TIMER
```

PROJECT 2: A DIGITAL THERMOMETER

Purpose. This project creates a digital thermometer which shows the temperature in degrees Celsius on two seven-segment displays.

Hardware. The project uses one input port and one output port, two seven-segment displays, a 74LS04 inverter, a 74LS00 NAND gate or a 74LS08 AND gate depending on the polarity of the displays, an Analog Devices AD7570J 8-bit monolithic A/D converter, an LM311 comparator, and various peripheral drivers, resistors, and capacitors as required by the displays and the converter. (See Chapter 11 and Hnatek, Reference 1, at the end of this chapter for discussions of A/D converters.)

Figure 17-2 illustrates hardware organization. Output line 7 from PIO Port B is used to send a Start Conversion signal to the A/D converter. Input lines 0 through 7 are attached directly to the eight digital data lines from the converter. Output lines 0 through 3 are used to send BCD digits to the seven-segment decoder/drivers. Output line 4 activates the displays and output line 5 selects the left or right display (line 5 is '1' for the left display).

The analog part of the hardware is shown in Figure 17-3. The thermistor simply provides a resistance that depends on temperature. Figure 17-4 is a plot of the resistance and Figure 17-5 shows the range of current values over which the resistance is linear. The conversion to degrees Celsius in the program is performed with a calibration table. The two potentiometers can be adjusted to scale the data properly. A clock for the A/D converter is generated from an RC network. The values are $R7 = 33\,k\Omega$ and $C1 = 1000$ pF, so that the clock frequency is about 75 kHz. At this frequency, the maximum conversion time for eight bits is about 100 microseconds. A much longer delay is allowed for conversion so that no check for the end of conversion is necessary. The 8-bit version of the converter requires the following special connections. The eight data lines are DB2 through DB9 (DB1 is always high during conversion and DB0 low). The Short Cycle 8-bit input (pin 26, SC8) is tied low so that only an 8-bit conversion is performed. In the present case, High Byte Enable (pin 20, HBEN) and Low Byte Enable (pin 21, LBEN) were both tied high so that the data outputs were always enabled.

The A/D converter uses the successive approximation method to perform a conversion. The ADC's data register is connected to the inputs of an internal D/A converter whose output (available at OUT1 and OUT2) is compared to the analog input. When a conversion is initiated, the ADC logic sets the data register to all zeros with the exception of the most significant bit (MSB), which is set to 1. If the analog input is less than the resulting internally generated analog value, then the MSB is reset to 0; otherwise it remains a 1. The next most significant bit is then set to 1 and the process repeated until all eight bits have been "tested" in this way. After the eighth cycle, the value in the register is the value which most closely corresponds to the analog input.

This method is fast, but it requires that the input be stable during the conversion process. Rapidly changing or noisy inputs would require additional signal conditioning. The references at the end of this chapter describe more accurate methods for handling analog I/O.

General Program Flowchart:

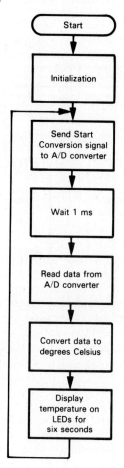

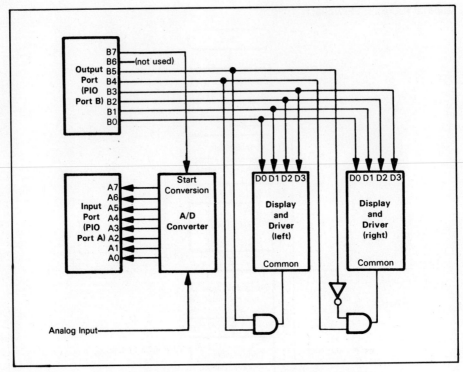

Figure 17-2. I/O Configuration for a Digital Thermometer

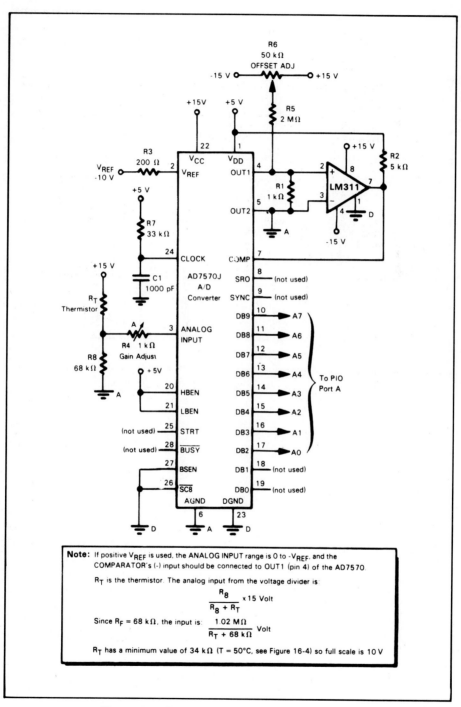

Figure 17-3. Digital Thermometer Analog Hardware

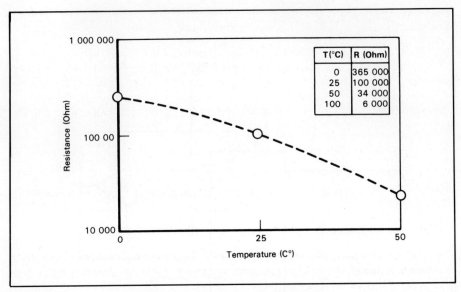

Figure 17-4. Thermistor Characteristics
(Fenwal GA51J1 Bead)

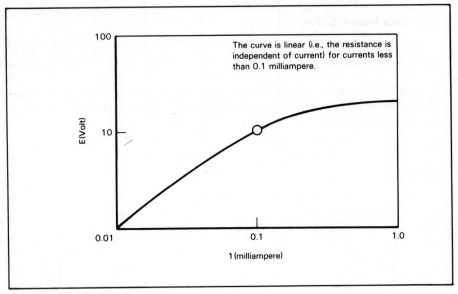

Figure 17-5. Typical E-I Curve for Thermistor (25°C)

Program Description

1. Initialization

Locations 0002 and 0004 are the Z8002 RESET locations. Location 0002 contains the initial Flag and Control Word value. Location 0004 contains the RESET program entry address; this is the address of the first instruction executed in the RESET program. The RESET program initializes the system; to do this it configures the Z80 PIO appropriately and loads the stack beginning address into Register R15.

2. Send START CONVERSION Signal to A/D Converter

The CPU pulses the START CONVERSION line by first placing a '1' on line 7 of PIO Port B and then placing a '0' on that line. Each input from the converter requires a starting pulse.

3. Wait 1 ms for Conversion

A delay of 1 ms after the START CONVERSION pulse guarantees a completed conversion. Actually, the converter needs a maximum of 100 microseconds for an 8-bit conversion. We could reduce the delay by checking the $\overline{BUSY}$ signal from the converter. $\overline{BUSY}$ is either a '1' (conversion complete) or '0' (conversion in progress) if the BUSY ENABLE line is 1. In the present case there is no reason to speed up the conversion process. Interrupts could be used with $\overline{BUSY}$ tied to the PIO STROBE line.

4. Read Data from A/D Converter

Data is read with a single input operation. The Analog Devices AD7570J has an Enable input and tristate outputs so that it could be tied directly to the microprocessor data bus.

The 7570 converter is, of course, underutilized in this particular application, particularly since we are interfacing it to the Z8000 processor through a PIO. A simpler 8-bit A/D converter such as the National 5357 device would do the job.

5. Convert Data to Degrees Celsius

Flowchart:

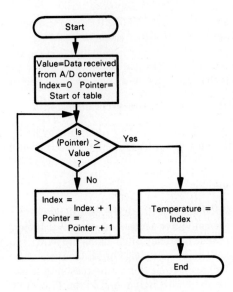

The conversion uses a table that contains the largest input value corresponding to a given temperature. The program searches the table, looking for a value greater than or equal to the value received from the converter. The first such value it finds corresponds to the required temperature. For example, if the tenth entry is the first value larger than or equal to the data, the temperature is 10 degrees. This search method is inefficient, but adequate for the present application.

The table could be derived by calibration or by a mathematical approximation. The calibration method is simple, since the thermometer must be calibrated anyway. The table occupies one memory byte for each temperature value to be displayed.

To calibrate the thermometer you must first adjust the potentiometers to produce the proper overall range; then determine the converter output values corresponding to each temperature.

6. Prepare Data for Display

Flowchart:

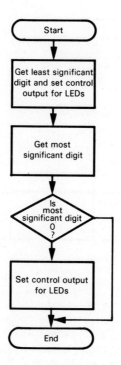

The least significant digit is masked off. We set the bit that turns on the displays. The result is saved.

If the most significant digit is a leading zero, it is blanked (i.e., the displays show "blank 7" rather than "07" for 7°C). This simply involves not setting the bit that turns on the displays if the digit is zero.

7. Display Temperature for Six Seconds

Flowchart:

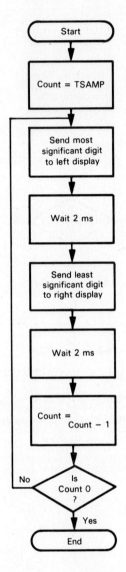

Each display is pulsed often enough so that it appears to be lit continuously. If TPULSE were made longer (say 50 ms), the displays would appear to flash on and off.

Program THERMOMETER:

```
THERMOMETER module

!*
 * Program Name:    THERMOMETER
 * Date:            10/20/78, 04/07/80
 * Programmers:     Lance A. Leventhal, Adam Osborne, Chuck Collins
 * Program Memory:  00D4 bytes (212 decimal)
 * Data Memory:     None
 * I/O devices:     1 input port, 1 output port (1 Z80 PIO)
 *
 * This program is a digital thermometer. It accepts inputs from
 *   an A/D converter attatched to a thermistor. It converts the
 *   input to degrees Celsius and displays the results on two
 *   seven-segment LED displays.
 *
 * A/D CONVERTER
 *
 * The A/D converter is an Analog Devices 7570J Monolithic
 *   converter which produces an 8-bit output
 * The conversion process is started by a pulse on the start
 *   conversion line (bit 7 of PIO port B)
 * The conversion is completed in 50 microseconds and the digital
 *   data is latched
 *
 * DISPLAYS
 *
 * Two seven-segment LED displays are used with separate
 *   decoders (7447 or 7448 depending on the type of display)
 * The decoder data inputs are connected to bits 0, 1, 2 and
 *   3 of PIO port B
 * Bit 4 of PIO port B is used to activate the LED displays
 *   (bit 4 is 1 to send data to LEDs)
 * Bit 5 of PIO port B is used to select which LED is being
 *   used (bit 5 is 1 if the leading display is being used, 0
 *   if the trailing display is being used)
 *
 * METHOD
 *
 * Step 1 - Initialization
 *   The stack pointer is initialized and the PIO ports are
 *   configured
 * Step 2 - Pulse start conversion line
 *   The A/D converter's start conversion line (bit 7 of PIO
 *   port B) is pulsed
 * Step 3 - Wait for A/D output to settle
 *   A wait of 1 millisecond allows for completion of the
 *   conversion
 * Step 4 - Read A/D value, convert
 *   A table is used for conversion to degrees Celsius. It
 *   contains the maximum input value for each temperature
 *   reading
 * Step 5 - Display temperature
 *   The temperature is displayed on the LEDs for six seconds
 *   before another conversion is performed
 *!


!*
 * DEFINITIONS
 *
 * Memory System Constants
 *!
constant
    PGM      := %4600          ! Program memory !
    LASTM    := %8000          ! Stack origin !

!*
 * I/O units and PIO addresses
 *!
constant
    PIOADATA := %00E1          ! Port A data: converter input !
    PIOACTRL := PIOADATA + 4   ! Port A control !
```

```
                        PIOBDATA := PIOADATA + 2    ! Port B data: display output !
                        PIOBCTRL := PIOBDATA + 4    ! Port B control !

             !*
             * PIO bit assignments
             *!
             constant
                    LEDON_BIT    := 4                ! Bit 4 port B send data to LEDs !
                    LEDON_MASK   := %(2)00010000     ! Binary value for bit 4 !
                    LEDSL_BIT    := 5                ! Bit 5 port B select high digit !
                    LEDSL_MASK   := %(2)00100000     ! Binary value for bit 4 !
                    STCON_BIT    := 7                ! Bit 7 port B start conversion !
                    STCON_MASK   := %(2)10000000

             !*
             * Timing constants
             *!
             constant
                    MSCNT    := 399           ! Count needed for 1 msec delay !
                    TPULSE   := 2             ! 2 msec display pulse length !
                    TSAMP    := 1500          ! Number of times display is pulsed !
                                              ! in 1 sampling period. The sampling !
                                              ! period length becomes !
                                              ! 2 * TPULSE * TSAMP msec !
                                              ! since each of the two displays !
                                              ! is pulsed for TPULSE msec !


             !*
             * Reset location for Z8002
             *!
             internal
                    $abs    2
0002 0000           RESFCW  WORD := 0         ! Initial FCW value !
0004 4600           RESPC   WORD := BEGIN     ! Program entry point !


             !*
             * THERMOMETER program entry
             *!
             global
                    MAIN procedure
                    entry
                        $abs    PGM

4600 760F    BEGIN:  LDA     R15,LASTM         ! Initialize stack pointer !
4602 8000
4604 2100            LD      R0,#%4F0F
4606 4F0F
4608 3A06            OUTB    PIOACTRL,RH0      ! Configure PIO A input !
460A 00E5
460C 3A86            OUTB    PIOBCTRL,RL0      ! Configure PIO B output !
460E 00E7

             !*
             * Send a pulse on the start conversion line
             *!
4610 C880    START:  LDB     RL0,#STCON_MASK
4612 3A86            OUTB    PIOBDATA,RL0      ! Send start conversion high... !
4614 00E3
4616 8C88            CLRB    RL0
4618 3A86            OUTB    PIOBDATA,RL0      ! ...then low !
461A 00E3

             !*
             * Allow 1 msec delay for conversion, then read data
             *!
461C C801            LDB     RL0,#1            ! Number of msec to delay !
461E 5F00            CALL    DELAY
4620 465A
4622 3A84            INB     RL0,PIOADATA
4624 00E1

             !*
             * Convert A/D data to two BCD digits
             *!
```

```
4626  5F00              CALL    CONVR                  ! Two BCD digits returned in RL0 !
4628  466A
462A  A082              LDB     RH2,RL0
462C  A08A              LDB     RL2,RL0                ! RH2 & RL2 will hold digits !
462E  060A              ANDB    RL2,#%0F               ! Isolate less significant digit !
4630  0F0F
4632  A4A4              SETB    RL2,#LEDON_BIT         ! Set send data bit !
4634  B221              SRLB    RH2,#4                 ! Isolate most significant digit !
4636  FFFC
4638  E602              JR      Z,PULSE                ! Don't turn display on if 0 !
463A  0402              ORB     RH2,#LEDON_MASK+LEDSL_MASK  ! Set control bits !
463C  3030

                   !*
                    * Pulse the LED displays
                    *!
463E  2101  PULSE:  LD      R1,#TSAMP              ! Get pulse counter !
4640  05DC
4642  3A26  DSPLY:  OUTB    PIOBDATA,RH2           ! Output most significant digit !
4644  00E3
4646  C802          LDB     RL0,#2
4648  5F00          CALL    DELAY                  ! Delay 2 msec !
464A  465A
464C  3AA6          OUTB    PIOBDATA,RL2           ! Output least significant digit !
464E  00E3
4650  C802          LDB     RL0,#2
4652  5F00          CALL    DELAY
4654  465A
4656  F18B          DJNZ    R1,DSPLY               ! Decrement pulse counter !
4658  E8DB          JR      START                  ! When R1 = 0, sample temperature !

465A              end     MAIN

                   !*
                    * Subroutine DELAY comes from the previous example. It is now
                    * part of our subroutine library. Its code must be included in
                    * this program, too
                    *
                    * Subroutine DELAY creates an "n" millisecond delay. "n"
                    * is the value in register RL0 when DELAY is called
                    *!
                   internal
                         DELAY procedure
                         entry

465A  93F1          PUSH    @R15,R1                ! R1 is used as a counter !
465C  2101  DELOOP: LD      R1,#MSCNT              ! MSCNT is clock speed dependent !
465E  018F
4660  AB10  MSEC:   DEC     R1                     ! Loop for 1 msec !
4662  EEFE          JR      NZ,MSEC
4664  F805          DBJNZ   RL0,DELOOP             ! RL0 specifies number of msecs !
4666  97F1          POP     R1,@R15
4668  9E08          RET

466A              end     DELAY

                   !*
                    * Subroutine CONVR converts input from A/D converter to degrees
                    * Celsius by using a table. Input data is in RL0. The 2 BCD
                    * digit result is returned in RL0
                    *!
                   internal
                         CONVR procedure
                         entry

466A  91F2          PUSHL   @R15,RR2               ! Save 2 regs !
466C  7602          LDA     R2,DEGTB               ! R2 addresses conversion table !
466E  469E
4670  2123          LD      R3,@R2                 ! Length of table !
4672  A921          INC     R2,#2                  ! Point to actual first entry !
4674  BA24          CPIRB   RL0,@R2,R3,ULT         ! Find first larger entry !
4676  0387
4678  6100          LD      R0,DEGTB               ! Get length of table !
467A  469E
```

```
467C 8330              SUB     R0,R3           ! Number of entries skipped... !
467E AB00              DEC     R0              ! ...is degrees Celsius !
               !*
               * Temperature (in R0) is less than 99. Convert binary value to
               * decimal, assuming no carry
               *!
4680 A080              LDB     RH0,RL0
4682 8C88              CLRB    RL0             ! RL0 will hold decimal value !
4684 0200      HODEC:  SUBB    RH0,#%0A        ! Continually subtract 0A ...!
4686 0A0A
4688 E503              JR      MI,LODEC        ! ...until it goes negative !
468A 0008              ADDB    RL0,#%10        ! Count high order decimal digit !
468C 1010
468E E8FA              JR      HODEC
4690 0000      LODEC:  ADDB    RH0,#%0A        ! Add that last 0A back in !
4692 0A0A
4694 0600              ANDB    RH0,#%0F        ! Isolate low order 4 bits !
4696 0F0F
4698 8408              ORB     RL0,RH0         ! Merge with high order digit !
469A 95F2              POPL    RR2,@R15
469C 9E08              RET

469E           end     CONVR
```

```
               !*
               * A/D values to Celsius table, DEGTB, is obtained by calibrating
               * against a known reference. Each entry in DEGTB contains the
               * largest input value corresponding to a Celsius temperature.
               * Temperatures begin at 0 and increase by 1 degree per entry.
               * Thus an entry of 58 or less corresponds to 0 degrees Celsius.
               * Values between 59 and 61 correspond to 1 degree Celsius, etc.
               *!
               internal
469E 0033          DEGTB   word := DEGEND - DEGVALS    ! Length of table !
46A0               DEGVALS array [* BYTE] := [
                       58   61   63   66   69   ! 00 - 04 degrees Celsius !
                       71   74   77   80   84   ! 05 - 09 !
                       87   90   93   97  101   ! 10 - 14 !
                      104  108  112  116  120   ! 15 - 19 !
                      124  128  132  136  141   ! 20 - 24 !
                      145  149  154  158  163   ! 25 - 29 !
                      167  172  177  181  186   ! 30 - 34 !
                      191  195  200  204  209   ! 35 - 39 !
                      214  218  223  227  232   ! 40 - 44 !
                      236  241  245  249  253   ! 45 - 49 !
                      255 ]                     ! 50 !

46D3               DEGEND:

               end     THERMOMETER
```

REFERENCES

1. E. R. Hnatek, *A User's Handbook of D/A and A/D Converters*, Wiley, New York, 1976.

   A method that uses far less memory is described in T.A. Seim, "Numerical Interpolation for Microprocessor-Based Systems," *Computer Design*, February 1978, pp. 111-16.

2. D. H. Sheingold, ed., *Analog-Digital Conversion Notes*, Analog Devices, Inc., P.O. Box 796, Norwood, MA 02062, 1977.

3. D. P. Burton and A. L. Dexter, *Microprocessor Systems Handbook*, Analog Devices, Inc., P.O. Box 796, Norwood, MA 02062, 1977.

4. J. B. Peatman, *Microcomputer-based Design,* McGraw-Hill, New York, 1977.

5. F. Molinari et al., "Shopping for the Right Analog I/O Board," *Electronic Design*, October 11, 1978, pp. 283-43.

6. Auslander, D. M. et al., "Direct Digital Process Control: Practice and Algorithms for Microprocessor Applications," *Proceedings of the IEEE*, February 1978, pp. 199-208.

7. R. J. Bibbero, *Microprocessors in Instruments and Control*, Wiley, New York, 1977.

8. A. Mrozowski, "Analog Output Chips Shrink A-D Conversion Software," *Electronics*, June 23, 1977, pp. 130-33.

9. P. R. Rony et al., "Microcomputer Interfacing: Sample and Hold Devices," *Computer Design*, December 1977, pp. 106-08.

10. P. H. Garrett, *Analog Systems for Microprocessors and Minicomptuers*, Reston Publishing Co., Reston, VA, 1978.

11. *The Optoelectronics Data Book*, Texas Instruments, Inc., P. O. Box 5012, Dallas, TX, 1978.

12. *The Optoelectronic Designer's Catalog*, Hewlett-Packard, Inc., 1820 Embarcadero Road, Palo Alto, CA 94303, 1978.

Index

Z8000 Instructions

About the Authors

Lance A. Leventhal is a partner in Emulative Systems Company, Inc., a San Diego based consulting firm specializing in microprocessors and microprogramming. He is a national lecturer on microprocessors for the IEEE, the author of five books and over forty articles on microprocessors, and a regular contributor to such publications as Simulation, Digital Design, and Kilobaud.

Dr. Leventhal has authored four previous books in this series and has just completed work on **6809 Assembly Language Programming**. He received a B.A. degree from Washington University in St. Louis, and M.S. and Ph.D. degrees from the University of California at San Diego.

Dr. Adam Osborne, President and General Manager of OSBORNE/McGraw-Hill, has worked to produce a growing library of microcomputer books and software. He authored the well-known four volume series, **An Introduction to Microcomputers**, and co-authored titles in the **Programming for Logic Design** series. In 1979 Dr. Osborne explained the microcomputer revolution to the layman in **Running Wild — The Next Industrial Revolution**. Most recently, he authored **The 8089 I/O Processor**, the first book in the new Osborne Handbook Series.

He is an international speaker and consultant for such organizations as the IEEE, IBM, and Sony, and the author of two monthly columns, "From the Fountainhead" and "The Micro Merchant." Dr. Osborne received his B.S. degree from the University of Birmingham, England and his Ph.D. in Chemical Engineering from the University of Delaware.

Chuck Collins is a Senior Software Engineer with the Microcomputer Systems Division of Zilog, the primary source for the Z8000 microprocessor. He works in the Machine Languages Group and maintains the Z8000 PLA/ASM Structured Assembler. Previously, Mr. Collins worked for Logicon-Intercomp and Datalogics, Inc., developing operating systems software. He received his Bachelor of Science degree in Math and Computer Science from the University of Illinois.